THE HISTORY OF THE ROYAL SCOTS FUSILIERS

THE HISTORY OF
THE ROYAL SCOTS FUSILIERS
(1678–1918)

BY
JOHN BUCHAN

WITH A PREFACE BY
H.R.H. THE PRINCE OF WALES
COLONEL-IN-CHIEF

The Naval & Military Press Ltd

in association with

The Imperial War Museum
Department of Printed Books

BY THE SAME AUTHOR

A HISTORY OF THE GREAT WAR.
In Four Volumes. With Maps and Plans. Each
25s. net.   [*Third Impression.*

THE HISTORY OF THE SOUTH AFRICAN
FORCES IN FRANCE.   15s. net.
                              [*Third Impression.*

FRANCIS AND RIVERSDALE GREN-
FELL: A MEMOIR. 15s. net. [*Third Impression.*

LORD MINTO: A MEMOIR.   21s. net.
                              [*Fourth Impression.*

THE NORTHERN MUSE: AN ANTHOLOGY
OF SCOTS VERNACULAR POETRY.   10s. 6d. net.
                              [*Sixth Thousand.*

(With Sir HENRY NEWBOLT)
DAYS TO REMEMBER: THE BRITISH
EMPIRE IN THE GREAT WAR.   1s. 9d. net.
                              [*Seventh Thousand.*

THOMAS NELSON AND SONS, LTD.
LONDON, EDINBURGH, AND NEW YORK

Published jointly by
The Naval & Military Press Ltd
Unit 10 Ridgewood Industrial Park,
Uckfield, East Sussex,
TN22 5QE England
Tel: +44 (0) 1825 749494
Fax: +44 (0) 1825 765701
www.naval-military-press.com

and

The Imperial War Museum, London
Department of Printed Books
www.iwm.org.uk

In reprinting in facsimile from the original, any imperfections are inevitably reproduced and the quality may fall short of modern type and cartographic standards.

Printed and bound by Antony Rowe Ltd, Eastbourne

H.R.H. THE PRINCE OF WALES, COLONEL-IN-CHIEF
(From a photograph by Vandyk, London)

First impression September 1925

Printed and bound by Antony Rowe Ltd, Eastbourne

PREFACE

THIS history has been compiled when the 250th anniversary of the birth of the Royal Scots Fusiliers is only three years distant. It tells vividly of the great and glorious heritage handed down by a regiment which has served thirteen sovereigns, and has enhanced its worth to the British Empire in each succeeding reign.

It is a regiment which has ever upheld the great traditions of British courage and loyalty. Its story will appeal to all who revere the great deeds by which that Empire was won and held, and will inspire all who now endeavour to follow in the footsteps of those who served their King and Country in time past.

The whole work of compiling and publishing this book has been undertaken by John Buchan (who has old family connections with the regiment) as a memorial to his brother, who fought and died gallantly in the Great War while serving in the Royal Scots Fusiliers. The thanks of all connected with the Royal Scots Fusiliers are due to John Buchan for his great and inspiring work.

Edward P
Col- in Chief - R. S. F.

AUTHOR'S NOTE

THE obligations of a writer of regimental history must be innumerable, and I would confess most gratefully how heavily I have leaned on the assistance of the officers of the Royal Scots Fusiliers. One or two debts call for specific acknowledgment. The Rev. Thomas Scott, who was a chaplain in the regiment from 1889 to 1910, has for the past three years given up most of his time to helping me. He has pursued inquiries which were impossible for me in the press of other duties; he has visited English and Scottish libraries on my behalf to consult authorities; and his devoted co-operation has made this book largely his own. I cannot put it lower than that. To Major F. T. V. Dunne I am indebted for his invaluable summaries of the diaries of the various battalions in the Great War. Lieutenant-Colonel F. G. Jackson has permitted me the use of the manuscript journals of old Scots Fusiliers in his possession; and Lieutenant-Colonel A. H. Abercrombie has placed at my disposal his unrivalled knowledge of regimental history. Finally, I have to thank Air Chief-Marshal Sir Hugh Trenchard, the colonel of the regiment, for his good counsel, and Major-General Sir W. D. Smith, Major-General J. H. W. Pollard, Brigadier-General R. K. Walsh, Lieutenant-Colonels A. M. H. Forbes, A. G. Baird-Smith, D. M. Wilkie, H. C. Maitland-Mackgill-Crichton, F. E. Buchanan, J. R. Turner, J. E. Utterson-Kelso, Major Yuille, and Major W. Kerr Kelso for revising my later chapters in the light of their special knowledge.

In the matter of illustrations I am much indebted to Lieutenant-Colonel A. C. Adair. Lieutenant-Colonel A. G. Baird Smith has most kindly prepared the coloured illustrations of uniforms at different periods. I have to thank the Earl of Caithness for permission to reproduce the picture of Major-General Thomas Buchan which hangs at Auchmacoy.

In my notes I have endeavoured to acknowledge my debts to the various printed sources of information. One I must specially name. In common with every writer of military history, I have owed much to my friend, the Hon. J. W. Fortescue, whose classic *History*

AUTHOR'S NOTE

of the British Army is the greatest historical enterprise of our day, and I have further to thank Mr. Fortescue for his kindness in answering my private queries.

Every history of a regiment should possess a nominal roll of the officers who have served in it since its creation. I would fain have included this, but the imperfect character of the old records made anything approaching a complete roll impossible.

J. B.

ELSFIELD MANOR, OXFORD,
June 1925.

CONTENTS

CHAPTER I.—THE EARL OF MAR'S REGIMENT

Scotland in the seventeenth century—The Duke of Lauderdale—The Highland host—The formation of Mar's Regiment—Drumclog and Bothwell Brig—Claverhouse—Thomas Buchan—The Highland Watch—The Revolution of 1688 1

CHAPTER II.—FIGHTING IN FLANDERS

The British soldier at the close of the seventeenth century—The regiment's first foreign campaign—Steenkirk—Landen—The regiment returns to Scotland 23

CHAPTER III.—THE WARS OF MARLBOROUGH

The War of the Spanish Succession—Marlborough and Boufflers—The campaign of Blenheim—Marlborough and Villeroy—Ramillies—The North British Fusiliers—Oudenarde—The siege of Lille—The campaign of Malplaquet—The campaign of 1711—The Royal North British Fusiliers 41

CHAPTER IV.—SHERIFFMUIR, DETTINGEN, AND FONTENOY

The influence of Marlborough—The regiment in Scotland—The rebellion of 1715—Sheriffmuir—The condition of the soldier—Sir Andrew Agnew of Lochnaw—Dettingen—Fontenoy 73

CHAPTER V.—THE "'FORTY-FIVE"

The meaning of Jacobitism—The rebellion of 1745—The defence of Blair Castle—Culloden 97

CHAPTER VI.—FROM LAUFFELD TO SARATOGA

Lauffeld—The Royal Warrant of 1751—Gibraltar—Belleisle—Service in Canada—Changes in the British army—The American revolution—General Burgoyne—The Saratoga campaign—The surrender . . 110

x   CONTENTS

CHAPTER VII.—THE REVOLUTION WARS

The reconstruction of the regiment—Service in Nova Scotia—The French Revolution—Service in the West Indies—Martinique—Guadaloupe—Return to Scotland—Service in Ireland—The Dublin riots . . 128

CHAPTER VIII.—THE WAR WITH NAPOLEON

The 2nd Battalion formed—The 1st Battalion in Sicily—Sir Frederick Adam—The expedition to Egypt—The Ischia expedition—The defence of Messina—Service in the Spanish Peninsula—The entry into Genoa—The 2nd Battalion in Ireland—The attack on Bergen-op-Zoom—The 2nd Battalion disbanded—The 1st Battalion in America—Bladensburg—The capture of Washington—The failure at Baltimore—The Louisiana campaign—New Orleans . . . 147

CHAPTER IX.—THE LONG PEACE

The condition of the British army—The regiment in Paris—Service in the West Indies—Colin Campbell—The Scots Fusiliers in Portugal—Service in Australia—Service in India—George Deare—The outbreak of the Crimean War. 179

CHAPTER X.—THE CRIMEA

Arrival at Varna—The landing in the Crimea—The Battle of the Alma—Balaclava—Inkerman—Frederick Haines—The siege of Sebastopol—The bombardment of Kinburn. 197

CHAPTER XI.—THE FIRST BATTALION TO THE EVE OF THE GREAT WAR

Malta—Sir John Pennefather's tribute—Service in the West Indies—Ramsay Stuart—Service in India—The Royal Scots Fusiliers—Home service—The Tirah campaign—South Africa, 1910–1914 . . 221

CHAPTER XII.—THE SECOND BATTALION: ZULULAND—THE TRANSVAAL—BURMA

The 2nd Battalion at home and in India—The Zulu War—Ulundi—The war with Sikukuni—The first Transvaal war—The defence of Potchefstroom—The defence of Pretoria—The defence of Rustenburg—The Burma war 235

CONTENTS xi

CHAPTER XIII.—THE SECOND BATTALION—THE SOUTH AFRICAN WAR

Nature of the campaign—Colenso—Spion Kop—Vaal Kranz—The crossing of the Tugela—Pieter's Hill—The relief of Ladysmith—The relief of Mafeking—Potchefstroom revisited—Frederikstad—The last year of the war 253

CHAPTER XIV.—THE GREAT WAR—1914

Causes of the War—Recruiting in Scotland—The 1st Battalion at Mons—The retreat—Le Cateau—The First Battle of the Marne—The Aisne—The race to the sea—The First Battle of Ypres—The 2nd Battalion destroyed—The attack of the Prussian Guard—The first winter in the trenches 281

CHAPTER XV.—THE GREAT WAR—1915

The spring in Flanders—Neuve Chapelle—Festubert—The Second Battle of Ypres—The Battle of Loos—The Gallipoli campaign—The battle of 12th July—The summer and autumn at Helles—The evacuation of Gallipoli—The beginning of the Salonika campaign . 312

CHAPTER XVI.—THE GREAT WAR—1916

The spring training—Fighting in the Ypres and Hohenzollern sections—Mr. Winston Churchill—The opening of the Battle of the Somme—Capture of Montauban—The attack of 14th July—The attack on Guillemont—The advance of 15th September—The capture of Martinpuich—Winter on the Somme—The Scots Fusiliers in Egypt—Stand at Bir-el-Dueidar—Romani—The Palestine frontier reached—Salonika in 1916 341

CHAPTER XVII.—THE GREAT WAR—1917

Haig's plans for 1917—The plans modified—The Battle of Arras—The Third Battle of Ypres—Salonika in 1917—First Battle of Gaza—Second Battle of Gaza—The summer in Palestine—Allenby's plan—The fall of Beersheba—The advance on Jerusalem 371

CHAPTER XVIII.—THE GREAT WAR—1918

Germany's final strategy—Her new tactics—The position of the British front in March 1918—The attack of 21st March—The retreat to the

CONTENTS

Avre—The fighting at Arras—The Battle of the Lys—The fight for Kemmel—The six Scots Fusilier battalions—The capture of Meteren—The advance to victory—The capture of the Drocourt-Quéant line—The fighting at Mœuvres—The Canal du Nord—The fall of the Hindenburg Line—The defeat of Bulgaria—The last movements in the West—The Armistice 410

CHAPTER XIX.—CONCLUSION

Summary of the work of the Scots Fusiliers in the Great War—Distinguished officers—A typical British regiment—The Scottish Lowland soldier—The Scots qualities in war—The Fusilier type—Regimental tradition 451

APPENDICES

I. SUCCESSION OF COLONELS, LIEUTENANT-COLONELS, AND OFFICERS-COMMANDING 463

II. REGIMENTAL VERSE 471

III. REGIMENTAL MUSIC 479

INDEX 485

ILLUSTRATIONS

H.R.H. the Prince of Wales, Colonel-in-Chief . *Frontispiece*
(*From a photograph by Vandyk, London*)

Charles, fifth Earl of Mar . . . . . *facing page* 6
(*From a portrait by Scougal, in the possession of the Earl of Mar and Kellie, K.T.*)

Major-General Thomas Buchan . . . . „ „ 20
(*From a portrait in the possession of the Earl of Caithness at Auchmacoy House*)

Sir Andrew Agnew . . . . . . „ „ 82
(*From a portrait in the possession of Sir Andrew Agnew, Bart., at Lochnaw Castle*)

Sir Frederick Adam . . . . . . „ „ 156
(*From a crayon drawing by G. F. Watts, R.A., in the possession of Mrs. Frederick Adam*)

Field-Marshal Lord Clyde . . . . „ „ 202
(*From a portrait by Sir F. Grant, P.R.A., in the possession of the Guards' Club*)

Lieut.-General Sir de Lacy Evans . . . „ „ 216
(*From a portrait by Fenton, in the Mess of the 1st Battalion*)

Colours of the 1st Battalion . . . . „ „ 220
(*From a painting by Mrs. Coulson, Ayr*)

Field-Marshal Sir Frederick Haines . . . „ „ 228
(*From a portrait by the Hon. John Collier, in the possession of the United Service Club*)

Air Chief-Marshal Sir Hugh Trenchard, Bart. „ „ 452
(*From a photograph by Maull & Fox, 187 Piccadilly, W.*)

Colours of the 2nd Battalion . . . . „ „ 456
(*From a painting by Mrs. Coulson, Ayr*)

Uniforms at Various Dates . . . . „ „ 470

MAPS

		PAGE
1. Battle of Blenheim		51
2. Battle of Ramillies		59
3. Battle of Oudenarde		63
4. Battle of Malplaquet		68
5. Battle of Sheriffmuir		77
6. Battle of Dettingen		88
7. Battle of Fontenoy		93
8. Battle of Culloden		107
9. Battle of Lauffeld		112
10. Saratoga	facing page	124
11. Campaign in West Indies		136
12. Campaign in Sicily		150
13. The Attack on Bergen-op-Zoom	facing page	164
14. Bladensburg		169
15. New Orleans	facing page	176
16. Sebastopol		204
17. Battle of Inkerman		209
18. The Tirah Campaign		231
19. The Transvaal Campaign		245
20. The Advance across the Tugela		262
21. The Advance on Pretoria		273
22. Frederikstad		276
23. The First Battle of Ypres	facing page	300
24. The Battle of Neuve Chapelle	,, ,,	314
25. The Battle of Loos	,, ,,	324

MAPS

26. The Gallipoli Peninsula	facing page	332
27. The Battle of the Somme.	,, ,,	352
28. Crossing of the Sinai Desert		366
29. Battle of Arras	facing page	376
30. The Third Battle of Ypres	,, ,,	384
31. The Advance on Jerusalem	,, ,,	400
32. The Retreat from the Somme.	,, ,,	420
33. The Battle of the Lys	,, ,,	424
34. The Advance on the Hindenburg Line	,, ,,	436
35. The Victory in the West	,, ,,	446
36. The Allies on the Rhine	,, ,,	448

THE HISTORY OF THE ROYAL SCOTS FUSILIERS

CHAPTER I

THE EARL OF MAR'S REGIMENT

Scotland in the seventeenth century—The Duke of Lauderdale—
The Highland Host—The formation of Mar's Regiment—
Drumclog and Bothwell Brig—Claverhouse—Thomas Buchan
—The Highland Watch—The Revolution of 1688.

THE second half of the seventeenth century was *1678* the crucible from which emerged in their modern form the main institutions of our country. It saw the rise of parliamentary government, the establishment of the House of Commons in its financial prerogatives, the limitation of monarchical power, and the dawn of a Cabinet system; it saw vital developments in the constitution of the Churches of England and Scotland; it saw the beginning of the effective union of the two nations of Great Britain; and, not least, it saw the formation of a regular and standing army. For this last the foundations had been laid in that work of genius, the New Model, for Cromwell gave to his country, between the years 1646 and 1658, the finest military force in the world. Much of his great work was undone at the Restoration, but not all; for the fact that it was the New Model under Monk which had brought back the King, involved in some degree its perpetuation. The two troops of Life Guards—the King's and the Duke of York's—formed the nucleus of the First and Second Regiments of Life Guards; the Blues were

1678 in existence in the shape of Lord Oxford's regiment of horse; the First Regiment of Foot Guards (now the Grenadier Guards) was raised in 1661, representing the Cavaliers; while Monk's Foot Guards (now the Coldstream Guards) represented the survivors of the New Model. Douglas's Regiment, successor of the famous Scots Brigade of Gustavus Adolphus, returned from France in 1662, to take its place at the head of the line as the Royal Regiment, later the Royal Scots; in 1661 Lord Peterborough recruited forces of horse and foot, largely from troops then at Dunkirk, to form a garrison at Tangier, and the consequence was the First Dragoons (the Royals), and the Second or Queen's Regiment of Foot, now the Queen's Royal Regiment (West Surrey). In 1665, when war broke out with Holland, the English troops in the Dutch service returned home and formed the Third Regiment of the line, known from its facings as the Buffs. The regular army of Britain was now in being.

But it is with Scotland that we are concerned, and with Scotland in the year 1678. At that date the only regular forces north of the Tweed were one troop of the Scottish Life Guards, under the Marquis of Atholl (raised in 1661 and disbanded in 1746), and a regiment of Foot Guards (the ancestors of the Third, or Scots Guards) who had been engaged at Rullion Green. Bodies of horse had been raised spasmodically as the service required, and a national militia, representing the old territorial defence force of the land, had been authorized by an Act of 1663, with an establishment of 20,000 foot and 2,000 horse. The force was embodied in 1668, and its blue coats were seen at Bothwell Brig.[1] But the main defensive strength of the country was still to be found in the feudal levies, which could be summoned to arms at the call of a

[1] " The Lowdien-Mallisha they
  Came with their Coats of Blew;
  Five hundred men from London came
  Claid in a reddish hew."
LAING's *Fugitive Scottish Poetry, principally of the XVIIth Century* (Edinburgh: 1823–5).

Lowland nobleman or Highland chief, and consisted largely of his kinsmen, clansmen, or vassals. In every Scottish shire there were men accustomed to the use of weapons: old soldiers who had fought on the Continent of Europe, or the "Laird's Jock" and his kind, who had no special trade, and lived at the beck and call of the head of their house. In the Highlands forces drawn from this class were the only police, for troops of the small standing army could scarcely be spared for such remote service. George Monk, who understood mountain campaigning, had brought Cromwell's peace north of the Highland line, but when the strife of Royalists and Parliamentarians was ended, that vexed region was still in turmoil. Ancestral feuds still lingered—between Campbell and Maclean, Clan Donald and Clan Chattan—and there was much brigandage, levying of blackmail, and cattle-driving, so that in 1667 a commission under the Great Seal was issued to John, Earl of Atholl, empowering him to raise and keep an armed guard "to watch upon the braes." Such was the origin of the Highland Watch, from which the Black Watch descends—independent companies raised and commanded by territorial magnates, and paid by the State, to perform tasks for which regular troops could not be spared, and were, indeed, but indifferently fitted.[1]

In 1678 the Duke of Lauderdale was the ruler of Scotland. This is not the place to write the tale of the troubled years after the Restoration, when the Government of Charles II., which had no special ecclesiastical bias, drifted by a series of blunders into the morass of religious persecution. Unhappily, the extreme left of Presbyterianism was identified with certain theocratic claims inconsistent with civil government—the tyranny against which Montrose had warred —and as a barrier against these claims the Government attempted to erect a moderate Episcopacy. But almost every step in its policy was a tactical error, and presently the string of tests and oaths and indulgences

[1] *A Military History of Perthshire*, page 28, etc.

1678 stirred up among plain men in the Lowlands the same passionate assertion of freedom as had taken their ancestors to Bannockburn. Charles and Middleton and Lauderdale might have isolated the wilder anarchic elements with the approval of all honest citizens; instead, they drove honest citizens into a reluctant defiance of the law. Lauderdale, who had been a Covenanter, and had by this time no preference for any Church, set a single aim before him—to make the King's power absolute, and to crush with a harsh hand any impulse to revolt; and he had the justification that the tenets of the extreme sectaries meant the end of all government. The character of this singular man may be read in Burnet and Clarendon, and it looks out of his eyes in the canvas of Cornelius Janssen. Gross, florid, always gobbling and spluttering, for his tongue was too big for his mouth; scandalous in his life, even judged by Caroline standards; an admirable scholar, theologian, orientalist, and bibliophile; a wit, who at last became so prolix and disgusting as to sicken even the King; a shrewd, bold intriguer, owning no scruples or loyalties; an able administrator, who prostituted every talent to one sinister purpose—he is the most formidable, and, on the whole, the basest figure in those dark years. But his policy was never in doubt. He was resolved to extirpate once and for ever the anarchy of extreme Presbyterianism, and he schemed to bring things to a head in an open rebellion. Such a result would enable him to get troops from Ireland to assist the small Scottish forces in its suppression, and would form a cogent argument for the maintenance of a larger standing army in England.[1]

He had still another string to his bow. He proposed to call for levies from the nobles north of the Forth, who had bodies of armed men at call in the shape of "independent companies." The Highlanders cared nothing for the Covenanting cause, and would

[1] This view is confirmed by the authority given to the Scottish Commander-in-Chief, Sir George Munro, in 1677 (*Warrant Book*, Car. II., III., No. 35), and by the arrangements made with Lord Granard in Ireland (*Lauderdale Papers*, III., page 90). It was the opinion also of Burnet and Wodrow.

THE HIGHLAND HOST

not be unwilling to make a jaunt to the Lowlands if there were good hopes of booty. He proposed to introduce a "bond" under which heritors and masters would be responsible for the good behaviour of all residents on their land, and this, he believed, would either ensure the observance of the law, or, as he hoped, provoke the revolt which he desired. The gentry of the west country—Hamiltons, Cochranes, Montgomerys, Kennedys, and Dalrymples—were bitterly opposed to the step, but they were powerless to prevent it. By the end of October 1677 Lauderdale had sent word to the northern nobles : the rendezvous was Stirling, and the time of assembly the first month of the new year. The leaders were to be the Marquis of Atholl and the Earls of Perth, Caithness,[1] Moray, and Mar, and in December the Earl of Linlithgow was appointed to command the whole force. There were some 6,000 Highlanders—2,000 with Atholl, 1,500 with Caithness, 500 with Perth, 200 with Moray, and 700 with Mar, besides the Angus militia ; there was a body of 600 horse ; and in addition the regular foot was marched to the west, and a considerable contingent of militia from Stirling and the Lothians.[2] The men were armed with matchlocks and daggers, they had with them four field-pieces, and, says Wodrow, "vast numbers of spades, shovels, mattocks, as if they had been to have attacked great fortifications."[3]

The news of the coming of the Highland host inspired terror in the west. But the reality proved something of a fiasco. They marched by Glasgow into the shires of Lanark and Ayr, occupying the little burghs, and living at free quarters among the disaffected gentry and peasantry. There was a great deal of robbery, but there is no record of atrocities, and by the end of February the Highland leaders were clamouring to be permitted to go home. They had shown themselves as humane and reasonable as their business allowed, especially

---
[1] This earldom was held at the time by Campbell of Glenorchy, who is represented to-day by the family of Breadalbane.
[2] Law, *Memorialls*, page 136.
[3] *Sufferings of the Church of Scotland*, II., page 389.

Atholl and Perth.[1] The arms seized were sent to Dumbarton Castle, and by the end of March the clansmen were trooping north again, laden with cottage plenishing, much of which, however, they were forced by the students and apprentices of Glasgow to surrender at the bridge of Clyde. The Highland host passed like a sudden flood in a stream, changing in no wise the tangled politics of Scotland, but leaving to the people of the west another angry memory, and to the world a futile and fantastic tale. But it had one consequence of importance, since it led directly to the birth of the Scots Fusiliers—a paradox, indeed, that the regiment specially identified with the western Lowlands should have had its origin in an incursion of Highland marauders.

Charles Erskine, fifth Earl of Mar, had, ten years before, succeeded his father.[2] He was a young man in the late twenties, a member of the Scottish Privy Council, but holding for the most part aloof from politics, though staunch for the King. His interests seem to have lain chiefly in soldiering, and at the time he was colonel of the Stirling and Clackmannan militia, and claimed as an hereditary office the Keepership of Stirling Castle.[3] Of all the northern lords he was best fitted to raise a regiment, for he had his foot both in Highlands and Lowlands, and could recruit in the Carse of Stirling and along the shores of Forth, as well as on the Braes of Mar. In July 1678 the Convention of Estates voted a sum of 1,800,000 pounds Scots, to be raised within five years, for the suppression of lawlessness, and on 23rd September the first step was taken under the grant to increase the forces of the Crown— in addition to the raising of various troops of horse

[1] Wodrow, *op. cit.*, II., page 423.
[2] See Balfour Paul's *The Scots Peerage*, V., page 626, etc.
[3] His claim must have been allowed at the mustering of the Highland host, for Mar was then entrusted with the strengthening of the castle. See Hamilton's letter to Queensberry of October 27, 1677, *Hist. MSS. Commission*, Report XV., App. VIII., page 229. But the claim seems to have been questioned later, for I find in the Mar and Kellie Papers (*Hist. MSS. Commission*, 1904, page 214) a memorial by Sir John Cunningham, dated 1683, setting forth its historical grounds. The claim, it will be remembered, was dramatically asserted in 1578 by John, the second Earl, when he took possession of the person of the young King James.

CHARLES, FIFTH EARL OF MAR
(From a portrait by Scougal, in the possession of the Earl of Mar and Kellie, K.T.)

MAR'S REGIMENT 7

and dragoons—by the issue of a commission to Lord 1678
Mar as colonel of a new foot regiment. History has
little to tell us of the first colonel, or what part he
played in the recruiting other than that of lending his
name. He stood by the Stuarts, and died in 1689,
and, judging by his bequests to his son, must have been
poor even when judged by the modest standard of the
Scots nobility. That son was to fill a more conspicuous position in the public eye, for he was the John,
Earl of Mar, who married a sister of Lady Mary Wortley
Montagu, and led the futile Jacobite rising of 1715.
His younger brother, James, was a judge on the Scots
Bench, the Lord Grange whose incarceration of his
shrewish wife on the remote isle of St. Kilda was for
long the scandal of two capitals.

Lord Mar's commission is dated 23rd September,
and on 26th November an order was issued to the
keeper of His Majesty's magazine in Edinburgh Castle
to deliver over to the colonel "548 English musketts,
also many stand of bandeliers, with 272 picks." The
earliest extant list of the Scots establishment is of that
year, and gives "the Foot Regiment commanded by
the Earle of Marre" as follows :—

	£	s.	d. (sterling)
Colonell, as Colonell, per diem . . .	0	12	12
Lieutenant-Colonell, as such . . .	0	7	0
Major, as Major	0	5	0
Quarter Master	0	4	0
Chyrurgeon and Mate	0	5	0
Marshall	0	2	0
Eight Companies of Foote belonging to that Regiment and to each company thereof.			
Captaine, as such	0	8	0
Lieutenant	0	4	0
Ensigne	0	3	0
Two sergeants, each 1s. 6d. . . .	0	3	0
Three Corporalls, each 1s. . . .	0	3	0
Two Drummers, each 1s.	0	2	0
One hundred souldiers, each 5s. (Scots) .	2	1	8 [1]

[1] The Quarter Master seems also to have performed the duties of
Paymaster. The Marshall had to take offenders into custody, see that camp-
followers and victuallers kept to the rear during marches, and regulate prices.
See *Compleat Body of the Art Military*, 1650.

8 THE ROYAL SCOTS FUSILIERS

1678 The new regiment was thus equipped with officers, weapons, and some reasonable expectation of pay.[1] To describe in detail the organization of a military unit in the seventeenth century would be out of place in this story. But certain questions arise about the misty beginnings of our regiment. Whence were the men recruited? There were Highlanders among them from the Braes of Mar, and men from the Aberdeenshire lowlands, and, judging by the names, recruits from the northern shores of Forth, where the Erskines were powerful. The bulk were probably Lowlanders, those bannock-fed peasants who were inured to toil and hard living, the same breed as supplied the Covenant levies, of whom Sir James Turner said that " he never saw lustier fellows or better marchers." The majority of the Scottish people was committed to neither extreme in politics, and there was enough of bitter poverty to force young men into the King's uniform. The officers were cadets from the local gentry, the senior men being selected from those who had seen service in other regiments like the Royal Scots, or in one of the Scots brigades abroad. Among the commissioned names on the rolls for the first dozen years there are comparatively few Highland patronymics—only an occasional Mackenzie, Fraser, and Menzies. But the regiment cast a wide net among the Lowland families, both north and south of the Forth. There are Bruces, Balfours, Stirlings, Ogilvies, Buchans, Erskines; there are Dalyells, Douglasses, Straitons, a Murray of Philiphaugh; and from Tweedside a Burnet of Barns and a Veitch of Dawyck.[2]

How were they clad? To begin with, I have no doubt, in coats and breeches of " hodden grey," the coarse country cloth, cheap, easy to obtain, and inconspicuous on a hillside where it might be necessary

---

[1] The suitability of its name was noted by a contemporary versifier, Alexander Pennecuik of Romanno, the historian of Tweeddale.
" And those commanded by the Earl of Mar
Are sons of Mars, swift thunderbolts of war."
Works (ed. 1815), page 341.
[2] An ancestor, on the female side, of Field-Marshal Earl Haig.

EQUIPMENT

to move with caution. The captain was responsible for the supply of uniforms, and Scotland at the time offered no facilities for fancy dress. Scarlet for long had been the King's colour, but it had not yet extended to the whole line, and Cromwell's troops in Ireland stuck to the grey breeches, though their coats were of "Venice-red."[1] The new regiment was soon known popularly as the "Earl of Mar's Grey-breeks," and up to 1683 at any rate, and probably till after the Revolution, grey was the ordinary dress of the private and non-commissioned officer, though drummers were given purple coats.[2] Their head-dress would be the hat of felt or some imitation, which had superseded the old morion and buff cap.

There is also doubt about the exact equipment. Britain has always been noted for her conservatism in the matter of weapons: the arquebus struggled for generations with the long-bow, the pike with the bill, the flintlock with the matchlock, the bayonet with the pike. By 1678 the fusil, or flintlock, had largely replaced the old matchlock, being a lighter, surer, and handier weapon. The Covenanters at Drumclog had fusils,[3] and as early as 1668 we find Lord Atholl complaining of his instructions to arm the Perthshire militia with matchlocks, on the ground that his men were "altogether unacquainted with the use of any other gunnes but fyrelocks and wherewith they are weill provydid."[4] A French regiment was armed entirely with the fusil in 1671, and by 1678 it had become

---
[1] Fortescue, *Hist. of British Army*, I., page 237. It may be noted that the Scots Guards, whose uniform in 1686 was red coats and white breeches, are shown as wearing grey breeches in the pictures of the battle of Bothwell Brig preserved at Dalmeny and Dalkeith.
[2] Grose, *Military Antiquities*, I., page 329. See also Clifford Walton, *Hist. of British Army*, 1660–1700, II., page 363. It has been suggested that the use of the name "grey-breeks" implies that some part of the dress was not grey, and it has also been asked why, if most of the troops wore grey, the Mar Regiment was specially singled out for the name of "grey-breeks." I am inclined to think the "grey-breeks" had become a generic term for any soldier among the Scots peasantry, on the analogy of the later "red-coat." The 90th Perthshire Light Infantry (now the Second Battalion of the Scottish Rifles), when raised by Lord Lynedoch in 1794, was known as the "Perthshire Grey-breeks," which seems to point to a traditional use of the word.
[3] Claverhouse to Lord Linlithgow. (Napier, *Mem. of Dundee*, II., page 222.)
[4] *Priv. Council Reg.*, June 4, 1668.

1678 the custom of the British army to arm certain special troops in a regiment thus, their principal duty being the protection of the field-pieces. It is not clear at what date Mar's became exclusively fusilier—probably at the great re-arming of 1685—but I have little doubt that in 1678 the common weapon was the matchlock, those " English musketts " which we have seen issued from Edinburgh Castle. Nor can I find any evidence for the claim that they possessed a grenadier company from the start. According to John Evelyn each British regiment had a grenadier company added to it in 1678, and it has been alleged that the Scots Guards and Mar's (then in embryo) had theirs a year before. But the only evidence is the royal instruction to the Scots Treasury on March 21, 1677, empowering one John Slezer to choose twenty men out of the Scots Guards and the garrisons of Edinburgh, Stirling, and Dumbarton to instruct troops in the use of grenades. The training may have begun, and in December of that year the Treasury certainly provided large stocks of grenades, but the grenadier companies were not instituted till 1682. We are to conceive, I think, of Mar's Regiment at the start as carrying the old matchlock, though a certain proportion—probably the regulation one-third—still had the pike. The colonel, lieutenant-colonel, and the captains carried pikes eleven feet long, the lieutenants partisans, and the ensigns half-pikes.[1] Cartridges had been introduced by Gustavus Adolphus, but the device was apparently not yet adopted in the north. The men carried their bullets in a leather bag, and their powder was in the wooden tubes, called *bandeliers*, attached to their shoulder belts—an improvement upon the ancient practice of the British army, which, in the sixteenth century, carried it loose in its pockets.[2]

The first lieutenant-colonel, according to the

---

[1] See instructions of Linlithgow to Mar, *Hist. MSS. Com.*, 1904, page 210. These instructions would seem to prove that it was not a fusilier regiment at the start, for fusilier officers carried fusils, and not half-pikes or spontoons.

[2] Fortescue, I., page 137. See page 77 *infra*.

THE COVENANTERS

Warrant Books, was William, third Earl of Dalhousie.[1] The major was Andrew White of Markle, an old officer of the Douglas Regiment. The first order for quartering is dated November 22, 1678, when Lord Linlithgow directed that five companies should be stationed at Musselburgh, Fisherrow, and Newbigging, and three at Dalkeith. At this time the infantry was little used in the struggles with the Covenanters, that task being left to dragoons, but was employed to provide garrisons for the larger towns, and, judging from the Treasury accounts, to supply detachments for the preservation of order in the Highlands, when lawlessness in those parts increased beyond permissible limits. Both of these duties fell upon the Mar Regiment, and its officers were also occasionally detailed for special service. For example, we find Major Andrew White sent from Lanark in March of the following year in command of a party of dragoons to disperse an armed conventicle near Lesmahagow.[2]

That year, 1679, was to be one of storm. On 2nd May a band of the wilder Covenanters, including Balfour of Kinloch (called " Burley ") and Hackstoun of Rathillet, murdered Archbishop Sharp on Magus Moor, near St. Andrews. The challenge to the Government was violent and unequivocal. The assassins hurried across Scotland by way of Dunblane, and on 29th May burned a number of Government Acts at the cross of Rutherglen. John Graham of Claverhouse, a cadet of the Montrose family, had, after some years of distinguished service abroad under the Prince of Orange, been given a troop of the Royal Horse Guards in the preceding November. From his headquarters at Dumfries he was ordered to deal with the Rutherglen defiance, and on Sunday, 1st June, came upon the rebels at a place called Drumclog, in the Strathaven district. There he found a considerable force of foot

---

[1] He was the hero of the couplet quoted by Pope (*Art of Sinking*, xi.):
  " And thou, Dalhousie, the great god of war,
    Lieutenant-colonel to the Earl of Mar."
[2] *Lauderdale Papers*, III., pages 162–163.

1679 and horse drawn up in a strong position, and, being outnumbered, sent off a message to Lord Ross in Glasgow for reinforcements. But battle was joined, he was beaten before supports could arrive, and by nine o'clock that night his defeated remnant was clattering into the streets of Glasgow. Recruits poured in to swell the Covenanters' army, and Ross, after barricading the streets and beating off one attack, fell back on Stirling, where he was joined by Linlithgow and his Edinburgh troops. Meantime the enemy had occupied Glasgow with 6,000 men.

The Government was seriously alarmed. The militia was called out, the young Duke of Monmouth was appointed Commander-in-Chief in Scotland, and troops were promised from England. Meantime the victorious Covenanters had split up into sects, and were quarrelling so violently about the principles of theology and politics that, had they been left alone, they might well have exterminated each other. On 18th July Monmouth was in Edinburgh, and on the 22nd he reached Bothwell Brig, where the Clyde flows deep and swift between precipitous banks. He had no English foot with him, but he may have had four or five troops of English dragoons; for the rest he had a considerable force of Scottish horse, the Foot Guards, and the militia. His artillery consisted of four pieces, served by one gunner and three unwilling amateurs from Leith. Altogether he may have brought to the field 2,500 men.

The Covenanters had at least double that number, and held a strong position at the old bridge; but they were hopelessly disunited, and their leader, Robert Hamilton, was little better than a madman. After some futile parleying, Monmouth ordered a frontal attack, and the Scots Guards, under Linlithgow's son, advanced on the bridge. Rathillet, who fought with a halter round his neck, resisted stoutly, but he soon ran short of ammunition; the passage was lost, and the Covenanting horse left their foot to the mercy of the Royal cavalry. After that it was a mere massacre and rounding-up of fugitives, and the fury of the

Royalists was not abated by the sight of a huge gibbet which Hamilton had erected to deal with them in the event of the victory which he assumed. Bothwell Brig was a battle from which neither side had much credit. Mar's Regiment was not engaged as a whole in the battle, and I doubt if any troops from it were in action. The quartering orders of February 1679 [1] show that it was distributed by companies, and it is probable that one at least of these companies was stationed at Glasgow or Lanark. Major White took part in the defence of Glasgow, and is mentioned by Wodrow as, along with Claverhouse, urging Monmouth, after the battle, to lay waste the Westlands and burn the little burghs.[2] It is alleged by Blackader[3] that the prisoners lay all night in the field in the charge of Mar's Regiment, " some of whose officers were very barbarous to them, and would not suffer the servant-women who came to give them water to drink in their vehement drouth . . . but despitefully broke the vessels." It seems likely that a company or two of the regiment may have been in Glasgow, and may have been used as reserves, to whom the care of prisoners would naturally be entrusted. Had they been engaged in the actual fighting, it is certain that there would have been some reference to them in the contemporary records of so much-canvassed an affair; but for such reference I have searched in vain.[4]

After Bothwell Brig began that harrying of the western and south-western shires of Scotland, which has lived in the popular memory as the " Killing Time," a season when the best of the Lowland peasantry were driven by the perversities of the Government into an unnatural alliance with wild revolutionaries and shady political intriguers. The policy was bad; and even had it been good, irregular levies, led often by rascally

[1] *Priv. Coun. Reg.*, Third Series, VI., page 124.
[2] *Op. cit.*, III., page 71.
[3] *Memoirs*, page 226.
[4] The contrary view is held, but without evidence adduced, by Dalton (*Scots Army*, 1660–1688, page 115, *n.*) and by Cannon (*Historical Record of Twenty-First Foot*, page 2), from which the other regimental historians, like Clark and Groves, have copied the statement.

14 THE ROYAL SCOTS FUSILIERS

1679-82 captains, were not the best executants. Ruffians like Lag and Bonshaw have tarnished the fame of the wiser and humaner leaders, who often complained bitterly of the orders they had to enforce. Monmouth fell upon dark days, and was succeeded as Commander-in-Chief in Scotland in November 1679 by Thomas Dalyell of Binns, a warrior of eighty, who had fought in a dozen foreign campaigns, had escaped from the Tower in 1652, and had won a kind of lurid fame for his stern discipline and his ferocious beard. Both beard and sternness have been exaggerated. The former he only adopted late in life, when it was too much trouble to shave, and not, as the common story went, as a solemn memento of the execution of Charles I.—the ancient warrior was no connoisseur of sentiment. The latter seems to have been tempered with a rough geniality; he protested against the use of torture; and that he was loved by his friends is shown by the beautiful elegiac verses on his death.[1] But the dominant figure was Claverhouse, as to whose character men will in all ages differ. One thing is certain: he had no taste for barbarities for their own sake, and would have punished only the ringleaders and let the dupes alone. "I am as sorry," he wrote, "to see a man die, even a Whig, as any of themselves. But when one man dies justly for his own faults, and may save a hundred to fall in the like, I have no scruples." Of the company seen round that grim tavern-board in Hell in *Wandering Willie's Tale* we may surrender "the fierce Middleton and the dissolute Rothes and the crafty Lauderdale," as well as Earlshall and Bonshaw, but I have compunction about "Dalzell, with a bald head and a beard to his girdle," and Claverhouse, sad and proud, with his hand hiding the wound made by the silver bullet.

It is with Claverhouse that, for the next eight years, our regiment is chiefly associated. From 1679 to 1682 it seems to have been for the most part in the Westlands, for we find records of courts martial at Irvine, when a deserter was shot, and at Kilmarnock, where

[1] They may be found in Dalton, *op. cit.*, pages 65, 66.

THE REGIMENT IN 1682

one James Davidson had his tongue bored through with a hot iron for blasphemy—the statutory punishment. In 1681 two new companies were added, to whom was entrusted the arduous duty of "uplifting the cess and taxation" in the Highlands.[1] The Camerons, as we know from Fountainhall, were giving trouble about that time, offering "deforcement and violence" to the King's troops, and the Lords of the Council fined Lochiel himself, and ordered certain of his clan to be deprived of their swords, pistols, and dirks—an order about the fulfilment of which I take leave to doubt. In 1682 regulations were issued as to military precedence in Scotland, and it was laid down that the colonel of the Foot Guards should be the first foot colonel, and the regiment the first foot regiment, and that in the field horse should have the precedence of infantry.[2] In that year the Mar regimental rolls begin with a complete return of officers and men, showing ten companies distributed among the towns of Glasgow, Ayr, Stirling, Leith, Dumfries, and Lanark. Each company had three commissioned officers, two sergeants, three corporals, and two drummers. There were three pipers on the rolls, but they appear in the ranks as "sentinells," and not apart, like the drummers. Nearly three-quarters of the names are Lowland. Two changes of note took place in that year. In July a company of grenadiers, under Captain William Garioch, was added to the regiment—sixty men, paid at the rate of 5d. a day. These grenadiers were armed with fusils, and this is the first actual record of that weapon in the regimental history.[3] In the autumn Lord Dalhousie died, and the regiment in December got a new lieutenant-colonel.

---

[1] These new companies were to replace two companies of the Highland Watch which had been disbanded. One was under Captain Kenneth Mackenzie of Suddie, and was known as "Suddie's Independent Company"; the other was under Captain Alexander Cairnes. The Mar and Kellie Papers contain letters from Suddie to Mar, which show that he was perpetually short of ammunition.
[2] Mar and Kellie Papers, *Hist. MSS. Com.*, 1904, page 211.
[3] Andrew Ross, *Old Scottish Regimental Colours*, page 13. Dalton, *op. cit.*, page 115.

16   THE ROYAL SCOTS FUSILIERS

1682 This was Thomas Buchan, a third son of the ancient Aberdeenshire house of Auchmacoy. He had been trained in France in the Douglas Regiment, and reached the rank of captain in 1671.[1] He was one of six officers specified in the Privy Council warrant of that year as authorized to recruit in Scotland. We next hear of him as lieutenant-colonel of Hugh Mackay's Regiment in the Scots Brigade in Holland. Some time after 1680 he returned to Scotland, and in 1682 was lieutenant-colonel of Mar's. He was to be its principal figure during the next six years, and at the Revolution was Brigadier-General of the Foot north of the Tweed. In a drawing preserved at Windsor Castle of the colours of the regiment when under his command, what seems to be the Buchan sunflower is charged on the cross of St. Andrew. The flight of James II. saw the end of his military career in the British army, for he adhered to the Stuarts, served in Ireland under James in 1689, and next year came to Scotland as major-general and Jacobite Commander-in-Chief. But on May 1, 1690, Sir Thomas Livingstone surprised and routed him in the haughs of Cromdale, and thereafter he was a wanderer, commanding a Highland band in Aberdeenshire, making abortive schemes to seize Inverness, and finally taking refuge with Glengarry in Lochaber. When the chiefs made their submission in 1692 Buchan went to France, but he was back in 1707 at Inverlochy, and for some years was a busy Jacobite plotter. He was not, I think, in the rebellion of 1715, for if he had been he would have held a high command. In 1721 he died.[2]

The duties of the regiment for three years were the not very glorious ones of furnishing garrisons for Low-

[1] Commission dated May 15, 1671, preserved at Auchmacoy. He was never in the Scots Life Guards, as Cannon says, or in any other cavalry regiment.

[2] A number of his kinsmen followed him into the regiment, including his nephews James and George, the sons of the laird of Auchmacoy; while his brother John, who took the other side in politics, succeeded to the command of Cunningham's Regiment in 1691, and, judging from a letter in the Leven and Melville Papers, fought on the Whig side at Killiecrankie. The career of Thomas Buchan is treated fully in a MS. history of the family of Buchan by James, 16th Earl of Caithness.

land towns, and detachments to scour the western and south-western moorlands for conventicles and recalcitrant Covenanters. The rolls show one company in Stirling, and the rest at Glasgow, Ayr, and Dumfries; and the troops at the last two places must have led an arduous life, for they were hurried off at all hours of the day and night in pursuit of an evasive enemy. The lieutenant-colonel spent most of the time in the west, and became one of Claverhouse's chief assistants, though, curiously enough, he seems not to have shared in his leader's popular odium, for I can find no reference to him in the immense comminatory literature of the Covenant. In 1684 he had five companies at Ayr, and it was in June of that year that he was left in charge of the pursuit in the Lesmahagow and Cairntable districts, while Claverhouse was wedding Lady Jean Cochrane at Paisley. Buchan, hot on the trail of a party of rebels led by a "lusty dark fellow with one eye and a velvet cap," fell into an ambuscade, and this brought Claverhouse back post-haste from his nuptials. That summer was hot and very dry, and there must have been some weary men among the five companies. "We were at the head of Douglas," Claverhouse wrote. "We were round and over Cairntable. We were at Greenock-head, Cummer-head, and through all the moors, mosses, hills, glens, woods, and spread in small parties, and ranged as if we had been at hunting, and down to Blackwood, but could hear nothing of those rogues. So, the troops being extremely harassed with marching so much in grounds never trod on before, I have sent them with Colonel Buchan to rest at Dalmellington." [1]

On February 6, 1685, Charles II. died, and the succession to the throne of a Catholic King in James II. brought to a head both the discontents at home and the plots of exiles abroad. The Duke of Monmouth was to land in England, and Argyll, Polwarth, Sir John Cochrane, and other Scots in Holland, were to

[1] Claverhouse to the Archbishop of St. Andrews. (Napier, *Mem. of Dundee*, II., page 403.)

1685 raise the standard of revolt north of Tweed. Both ventures were doomed from the start; but Argyll's was pre-eminently hopeless, for the stricter Covenanters looked on him with suspicion as responsible for the death of Donald Cargill, and the chief of Diarmaid could not even count upon his own clan. He landed in Orkney, as Montrose had once done, and moved south, to learn that the Campbell cadets would not rise, that Atholl was commanding for the Government in his own castle of Inveraray, and that Peden the Prophet was bidding the wilder sectaries to stand aside from an uncovenanted enterprise. He had acute differences of opinion with his Lowland colleagues, and after some skirmishing on the shores of the Clyde estuary, set out with a motley following for Glasgow, only to find the way barred. The leaders crossed the Clyde into Renfrewshire, and Argyll was captured at Inchinnan ford by two servants of Sir John Shaw of Greenock, and on the 30th June laid his head on the block in Edinburgh. The affair at no time gave the Government serious anxiety, but, none the less, every precaution was taken. The militia was called out, a force of regulars was assembled under the Earl of Dumbarton, the new Scottish Commander-in-Chief—that Lord George Douglas who had commanded and given his name to the Royal Scots, and who is commemorated in their regimental march of "Dumbarton's Drums." But there was to be no fighting, except for some brushes with the militia, and a skirmish at Muirdyke between Sir John Cochrane and a troop of dragoons. There are orders extant from Dumbarton to Mar: on 30th May, to provide powder and to send men to co-operate with the Ayrshire gentry at Largs in watching the coast, and on 1st June bidding him march from Beith to Ayr by way of Kilwinning with his own regiment and two companies of the Foot Guards.

Argyll's rising led to the revision and enlargement of the forces in Scotland. In that year, 1685, there was a general re-arming of troops, and it was then in all probability that fusils were distributed to the whole of

SERVICE IN THE HIGHLANDS

Mar's Regiment, so that they became in the full sense Fusiliers.[1] Two new companies of infantry were raised, and one, under Captain Walter Maxwell, was given to Mar. A change was also made in that side of the regiment's duties which concerned the policing of the Highlands. We have seen that the companies of Cairnes and Mackenzie of Suddie were detailed for that task in 1682; now Suddie was given a special commission [2] and posted at Inverness, where for three years he enforced the peace with a strong hand.[3] On August 4, 1688, however, he was ordered to aid the Mackintoshes against the Macdonalds of Keppoch, and in the fight which ensued, the last of the great Highland clan battles, the Macdonalds were victorious, and Suddie and most of his company were left dead on the field.[4] In the orders for the quartering of the regiment in the winter of 1685 we find the twelve companies thus disposed: six at Ayr, three at Glasgow, two at Paisley, and one—Suddie's—at Inverness. In June the King, after Argyll was a prisoner, proposed to transfer certain Scots troops to England, including five companies of Mar's, but the Scottish Privy Council remonstrated so solemnly that the project was abandoned.

For two years there is little to record. The fires of the Covenant were beginning to burn low, and more and more the extreme sectaries became an intractable remnant which was at war with all civil society. Scotland had grown weary of strife, and men's eyes were turning to England, where the King was moving blindly to disaster. In 1686 the regiment was reduced by ten men out of each company, and the pay of the private soldier was raised by one shilling Scots per

---

[1] The Royal Fusiliers (the 7th of the Line) came into existence in the same year. Though the Royal Scots Fusiliers is the older military unit, it probably dates its existence *as a fusilier regiment* from the same year as its English counterpart.
[2] *Priv. Coun. Reg.*, October 21, 1685.
[3] His duties covered a wide field. For example, in October 1685 we find him with detachments at Abertarf, at Balquhidder, and Kincardine O'Neil. (Mar and Kellie Papers, *Hist. MSS. Com.*, 1904, page 217.)
[4] *Military History of Perthshire*, pages 38, 39.

1686-88 day. In that year Lord Mar was deprived of his colonelcy,[1] having fallen out of favour with the King on account of his opposition to the Bill for the relief of Catholics, and was succeeded by Thomas Buchan. In June 1688 two new companies were added, bringing the number up to fourteen, and for the first time the pay-roll made provision for a drum-major.

Already the King was growing anxious, for he was aware of what was going on across the Channel, and on 5th April he wrote to the Scottish Privy Council, ordering to London eight companies of the Foot Guards, and Dumbarton's Regiment, "the Battalion of Foot under the command of Colonel Thomas Buchan now here to be carried thither"[2] (*i.e.*, to Leith). A month later Sir John Lauder of Fountainhall noted: "Buchan's soldiers arryve at Leith from London."[3] There is no mention in the regiment's records of its being in England in that year, or of its return; but it is certain that when the First Battalion of the Royal Scots was moved in August 1686 from Hounslow to Portsmouth, it was relieved by troops of Buchan's. The only conclusion I can suggest is that the ten men withdrawn from each company by the warrant of March 24, 1686, were sent to England. It is clear, at any rate, that by the early summer of 1688 the whole regiment was in Scotland.

On Monday, 5th November, William of Orange landed at Torbay; on the 19th, James, with what troops he could command, marched to Salisbury to meet him; on the 24th the great soldier who was afterwards to be Duke of Marlborough deserted the Royal cause, and the Royal army began to crumble; on 18th December James left Whitehall never to return, while William's army lay in the London suburbs. Thus simply and expeditiously was achieved the most successful revolution known to history. On 24th September James had ordered the Scottish Commander-

[1] See the letters in the Mar and Kellie Papers, pages 217-219.
[2] *Warrant Book*, Scotland, Vol. XII.
[3] *Historical Notices*, page 966.

MAJOR-GENERAL THOMAS BUCHAN
(From a portrait in the possession of the Earl of Caithness at Auchmacoy House)

THE REVOLUTION OF 1688

in-Chief—James Douglas, brother of the second Earl of Queensberry—to march all regular troops to the Lothians and the Borders, and three days later came a further summons to bring the whole Scots army into England. Apart from cavalry, that army consisted of the six companies of the Foot Guards left in Scotland, and of Buchan's Regiment.[1] On 11th October the army was at Penrith, and by the end of the month it had reached London, where Buchan's men were quartered in Spitalfields and the Tower Hamlets. On 12th November Claverhouse was created Viscount Dundee, and one of James's last acts before his flight was to appoint him his commander in Scotland, since Douglas—a good soldier who was afterwards to win fame in William's service at Limerick, but a man of a jealous and irascible temper—had already turned his eyes to the rising sun.

The soldiers from the north were not inclined to fight in James's losing cause. The Scots Guards, who in London had declared that they would never take arms against a Protestant prince, went over to William at Maidenhead. Buchan's Regiment, sick of their westland forays, and representing the attitude of the rank-and-file in Scotland, followed suit, and were sent into camp at Witney in Oxfordshire. Only the Royal Scots, whose service had been mainly foreign, did not share in the popular feeling, and three months later, when Schomberg was appointed their colonel, revolted and set out for Scotland—an incident which led to the passing of the first Mutiny Act. But if the men for the most part welcomed the change of dynasty, many of the officers followed the example of Dundee and Dumbarton rather than of

---

[1] Dalton (*op. cit.*, page 82) says it was fourteen companies strong. But the Highland company, stationed at Inverness, must have remained behind, for we have seen that in August, under Suddie, it had been almost annihilated by Keppoch. On 15th August Mar was informed (probably as Governor of Stirling Castle) that Captain Charles Straiton had been sent to take order with the Macdonalds (Mar and Kellie Papers, page 220), which would imply an immediate reconstruction of the Highland company. This Charles Straiton seems to have come from the Foot Guards (*Warrant Book*, Scotland, Vol. IX.). The Straitons already in Buchan's Regiment were John and Alexander.

1689 Douglas. Mar, the former colonel of our regiment, stood for James during the few remaining months of his life, and Buchan took the path which was to lead to defeat and wandering and exile. By a commission dated March 1, 1689, William conferred the colonelcy upon Colonel Francis Fergus O'Farrell.

CHAPTER II

FIGHTING IN FLANDERS

The British soldier at the close of the seventeenth century—The regiment's first foreign campaign—Steenkirk—Landen—The regiment returns to Scotland.

WE have seen our regiment as part of the Scots establishment, learning its trade in garrison duty and moorland wars. It is now to be caught up into the great movement of Europe, and to form part of the British line in the ancient cockpit of Flanders and France. For a moment we may pause to glance at the manner of life of a Scots soldier two centuries ago.

1689

We are to conceive of the officers as members of good Lowland houses, with now and then a Highlander, and the men as drawn mainly from the shires of Aberdeen, Angus, Stirling, Ayr, and Renfrew—youths from the plough-tail, unprosperous artisans, ne'er-do-weels who could no longer pay their scores at the ale-house, lads whom a brawl or a girl's eyes had driven from their homes. There was not much in the emoluments to tempt gentleman or cottar. Commissions were bought after the French fashion. The officer found his pay diminished by a preposterous number of taxes and charges before it reached his pocket; and even the reduced sum was commonly in arrears. There were several ways in which he could recoup himself. The pay of a private in the line was roughly 8d. a day, or £12, 13s. 4d. in the year. Of this, £3, 0s. 10d., called the "gross off-reckonings," was subject to a deduction of five per cent. for the Paymaster-General,

1689 and of one day's pay for Chelsea Hospital, reducing it to £2, 8s. This sum was handed to the colonel for the clothing and equipment of the regiment, including sword, bayonet, and cartridge-box—a purpose for which it was manifestly insufficient, so that an honest colonel was bound to be out of pocket. The colonel worked through contractors, from whom he took commissions, and who in turn had their own profit to earn, so that the equipment of the men was apt to be in a parlous state. In theory the balance of the private's £12, 13s. 4d.—£9, 2s. 6d., or 6d. a day—was regarded as his subsistence allowance, and inviolable; but in practice it was also at the mercy of the colonel. This miserable system, or something like it, was to endure throughout some of Britain's most famous campaigns. Officers were plundered by the Treasury and the Paymaster, and saddled with duties for which they had no adequate funds : they recompensed themselves by plundering or neglecting their men, and by the old device of false muster-rolls. It is small wonder that at one end of the scale Paymasters-General made fortunes, and at the other the unhappy private starved and went in rags.

The regiment that spent the Christmas of 1688 in Oxfordshire must have had some of that " vileness of port " which the historian observed in the Scots troops at the battle of Pinkie. It had still in all likelihood its grey coats and breeks, though in two years' time it was to blossom, like the rest of the British infantry, into scarlet. It had its drummers in their purple coats, and its three pipers who served in the ranks. It had its grenadier company, the tallest men on the rolls, and the whole regiment had abandoned the old hat and adopted the conical cap, so as to be able to sling their fusils comfortably over both shoulders. Greatcoats, called " surtouts," had probably now been issued ; the men had stockings and shoes, and loose breeches with cloth bows adorning the gaiter bands. The officers and sergeants wore sashes over the shoulder. The appearance can scarcely have been smart, except perhaps in the grenadier company, who had their coats 1689 ornamented with loops and embroidered button-holes. The weapon for all by this time we may take to have been the fusil. The pike, which Sir James Turner called the " prince of weapons," had disappeared save for the half-pike, or spontoon, carried by officers throughout the Line in regiments not fusilier, except in the grenadier companies. Grenadier officers carried the fusil, sergeants the halberd. I take it that bayonets were issued before the regiment left for the Continent. That arm had had a curious history. Invented in 1640 in its " plug " form, a double-edged knife with three inches of wooden haft to be thrust into the musket-barrel, it was issued to the Tangier Regiment in 1673, withdrawn, and again in 1683 issued to the Foot Guards. At the Revolution it was extended to the whole of the infantry. But presently its form changed. For on July 27, 1689, at Killiecrankie, Hugh Mackay, with five battalions of foot and two of horse, suffered defeat at the hands of Dundee and the clans. Mackay noticed that his men had not time to force their plug-bayonets into the muzzles of the guns, and so were taken at a disadvantage by the Highland charge. He therefore blended the pike and the musket, as the French had done some years before, by introducing the screw-bayonet, and thus enabled his men to fire with bayonets fixed.[1]

With these details we can make a picture of the regiment when, in March 1689, it paraded at Gravesend and embarked for the Low Countries. It was well up to strength, but it had no depot, or second battalion, or other means of getting drafts. The men looked forward with little enthusiasm to foreign service, for, like Leezie Lindsay, they knew nothing of the land they were going to or the lad they were going with. William, facing war in Scotland, in Ireland, and on the Con-

[1] It has been occasionally asserted (*e.g.*, by Stewart of Garth and Hill Burton) that the Scots Fusiliers fought at Killiecrankie, when, as a matter of fact, they were on the Continent. The confusion is due to the presence of " 200 choice fuseliers of the whole army " under Colonel Lauder. See the " Short Relation " in Mackay's *Memoirs*.

26   THE ROYAL SCOTS FUSILIERS

1689 tinent, was sending four battalions of Guards and six of the Line under Lord Marlborough to assist Holland in the war which had been declared against her by France. The Scots Fusiliers did not mutiny, but they embarked with glum faces and angry mutterings. They had never heard of Lord Marlborough, or of their new colonel. Buchan had ridden the mosses with them, and was one of their own folk, but now they were commanded by a stranger who was not a Scot.[1] It was an inauspicious beginning for an exile which was to give the regiment some of the most glorious pages in its annals.

The campaign in the Low Countries was part of the long-drawn war to restrain the ambition of Louis XIV. of France. The immediate purpose was the defence of the Spanish Netherlands, and to this end King William was the head of an ill-assorted confederation—Britain, Spain, Holland, the Empire, Denmark, and various German principalities. Of the Continental allies, all were selfish and laggard, and most were inefficient. William was an able soldier by the book, but in the conduct of a campaign he was apt to flag and blunder. He could stage a battle, but not a series of actions; and though he had a considerable talent for strategy, he was without an instinct for tactics. His great personal courage and his steady resolution were never questioned; but otherwise he lacked most of the gifts of a commander, notably that of inspiring personal loyalty in masses of men. His character as a British general has been not unfairly summed up by Mr. Fortescue. "Stern, hard, and cold, William had little feeling for England and Englishmen, except in so far as they ministered to that hostility for France which was his ruling passion. Probably he felt more kindly towards the English soldier than towards any other Englishmen. The iron nature melted at the sight of the shattered battalions at Steenkirk, and, if

---

[1] I can find no record of the family of O'Farrell. In 1743 a certain Richard O'Farrell, who may have been a kinsman, commanded the Twenty-second Regiment.

we are to believe Burnet, the cold heart warmed sufficiently towards the red-coats to prompt him to relieve the starving men, so shamefully neglected by Parliament, out of his own pocket. But, on the whole, it may be said that no commander was ever so well served by British troops, nor requited that service, whatever his good intent, so unworthily and so ill."[1]

1689

To a somewhat motley host, led by generals for the most part of small ability, under a commander-in-chief of notable limitations and harassed by rivalries and conflicting interests, Louis opposed the strongest, best-equipped, and most experienced army then in existence. He had in Luxemburg a general of the first rank—the greatest produced by the famous house of Montmorency, a brilliant second in Boufflers, and a great war minister in Louvois. Moreover, he had by far the best strategic position. Between the Meuse and Dunkirk he held a chain of posts in Spanish Flanders—Dinant, Philippeville, Maubeuge, Condé, Valenciennes, Cambrai, Douai, and so to Menin and Aire; while between the sea and the Scheldt lay a series of fortified towns. He had thus his frontier covered and a garrison on every river, so that he was able at any time to anticipate the Allies in taking the field, and to play that game of raiding and living on his enemy's lands and picking up their fortresses which drove his opponents to desperation and often to folly. In the campaign we have to consider, the one man who was more than a match for Luxemburg was never more than half in William's confidence, and for some years, and with good reason, out of it altogether. The days were to come when Marlborough turned every apparent asset of France to her disadvantage.

The terrain was that quadrilateral, a hundred miles by fifty, defined by the mouth of the Scheldt, Maestricht, Namur, and Dunkirk, which deserves to rank as the main battleground of British arms. Extend it a little to the west, and it embraces many of the major British actions in the Great War. Its nature is best understood

[1] I., page 395.

by remembering that it is a land of rivers flowing generally east and north—the Meuse and its tributary the Sambre; the Demer; the Scheldt, with its tributaries the Scarpe, the Haine, and the Lys; and in between a host of lesser streams like the two Geetes, the Mehaigne, the Dyle, the Senne, and the Dender. On all these streams water transport was possible, and on the banks stood the fortresses. The strategy of each campaign was therefore determined by the network of rivers.

O'Farrell's Regiment arrived in Flanders in the spring of 1689. William that year had too much to do at home to take the field in Europe, so that the Allied army was commanded by the Prince of Waldeck. That general reported ill of the British contingent: clothing and arms were defective; the men were listless, unruly, and sickly, and their toes stuck out of their shoes; their officers were discontented by irregularities of pay. Things were better when the Earl of Marlborough arrived. But the campaign of 1689 was of little note, except for the action of 15th August at Walcourt in the Namur area, where O'Farrell's men were engaged, and Marlborough gave Marshal d'Humières and the army of France the first taste of his quality. Presently the regiment went into winter quarters; and in the following summer, while William was still engaged in Ireland, took the field again. But before it could join the Allies at Brussels the Prince of Waldeck had engaged the French without British troops and had been soundly beaten. Thereafter operations languished, and for the rest of the year the Allies were on the defensive.

These two seasons of unsatisfactory campaigning had lowered the strength of the regiment, and it was very necessary to get drafts. O'Farrell's was one of the three units which were looked upon as having a special right to recruit in Scotland, and two warrants for the purpose are to be found in the Privy Council records for 1690. But the men did not come in readily, and in January 1691, when William was preparing for a great Continental campaign, Brigadier-General George Ramsay, who commanded the Scots troops under orders for Flanders, proposed that the various prisons should be visited, and such prisoners as should, in presence of a magistrate, declare their willingness to enter His Majesty's service, be handed over to the military authorities.[1] Captain Francis Scott of O'Farrell's, a brother of the Earl of Tarras, was authorized to represent his regiment in this gaol-delivery.

William's first summer was not successful. Luxemburg placed 10,000 men on the Lys to hold the Allies in the west, and sent a corps to the Moselle to threaten Cleves, which was the territory of the Elector of Brandenburg, thereby making it certain that the Prussian contingent would not appear at the rendezvous. William was waiting at Brussels for his army, when news came that Boufflers was in movement. The French Marshal swooped from Maubeuge on the fortress of Mons, and took it on 10th April after a poor defence, thereby piercing the Allies' frontier line between the Scheldt and the Sambre. William crossed the Sambre, and might have recovered the place, for he had taken Luxemburg by surprise, had he not given his enemy time to recover by one of those meaningless delays which we find in all his campaigns. He was forced to fall back on Brussels, whence he presently returned to England. The only other incident of that summer was a cavalry action at Leuse, when the Allies were decisively beaten, and the reputation of the French cavalry swelled into a legend. The British troops were, except for the Life Guards at Leuse, never in action. O'Farrell's spent the spring at Halle in Brabant, in company with the Second Battalion of the Royal Scots, and for the rest of the year lay near Brussels, brigaded, under Brigadier-General Ramsay, with the two battalions of the Royal Scots, the Angus Regiment (the 26th, or Cameronians), and the regiments of Mackay and Ramsay from the old Scots

---

[1] *Priv. Coun. Reg.*, January 1, 1691.

Brigade in the Dutch service. We shall hear more of Ramsay and his Scots Brigade.[1]

Early in 1692, after unexpectedly securing the assent of the House of Commons to an army of 63,000 men, William crossed the North Sea. This time he was without Marlborough, who had been detected in flagrant treason, and the coming campaign was to be the test of his unaided talent. Twenty-three thousand British troops were now in the Low Countries. Meantime the French had not been idle. They had collected a huge siege-train, under Vauban, on the Scheldt and the Meuse; Joyeuse, with a corps, held the Prussians in check on the Moselle; while Boufflers, with 18,000 men, was on the Meuse at Dinant, and Luxemburg, with 115,000 men, lay behind the river Haine. On 20th May, near Mons, Louis reviewed the most magnificent force that had ever crossed the borders of France —eight miles of glittering troops, led by the princes of the blood, with Racine in attendance to chronicle their victories.

Louis loved above all things a siege, and Namur was at hand, the key alike of the Meuse and the Sambre. By 26th May he was west and north of the town, and Boufflers marching up from Dinant completed the investment. When the news arrived, William was at Brussels trying to whip up the Allied contingents, and by that time relief was out of the question, for Luxemburg barred the only route to the fortress. Moreover, heavy rains swelled the rivers, and thus formed an additional obstacle. On 5th June, Namur fell after a feeble defence, and Louis returned in triumph to Paris, where his exploit was celebrated by medals and flamboyant odes.

[1] It should be noted that Scots troops played a part altogether disproportionate to the size of their nation in the campaign which ended in 1697 with the Treaty of Ryswick. In 1691, there were serving in Flanders seven English infantry battalions (including Huguenot regiments in British pay) and eight Scots (including the Scots Brigade in Holland); in 1692, fourteen English and eleven Scots; in 1693, fourteen English and thirteen Scots; in 1694, twenty-three English and fifteen Scots; in 1695, twenty-five English and fifteen Scots; in 1696, twenty English and fifteen Scots; in 1697, twenty-five English and fifteen Scots.—Andrew Ross, *The Lowland Scots Regiments*, page 307.

STEENKIRK

The campaign was now a duel between William and Luxemburg, that little harsh-featured hunchback who, except for John Churchill, was the greatest of living soldiers. Luxemburg, in order to draw off the Allies from Namur, marched northwards, as if to threaten Brussels. William followed, and on 2nd August both had crossed the river Senne. William lay west of the river at Hal, Luxemburg four miles south of him between Steenkirk and Enghien, while Boufflers was some seven miles in Luxemburg's rear. The French Marshal desired, not a battle, but a strong position from which he could securely watch the enemy, and he believed that he had found it. His right flank rested on the Senne, and along his front ran a ravine, with beyond it a wilderness of rough gullies, thickly clothed with woods. He was convinced that in such a position no enemy could take him unawares.

But in William's camp was a certain adventurer, Millevoix by name, a spy of France, and, as luck would have it, his character was detected. Here was a chance to outwit the enemy. With a pistol at his head the spy was forced to write a letter to Luxemburg telling him that the Allies meant to send out a strong foraging party next morning, with a force of infantry to protect it. But let not the Marshal concern himself; there was no question of an Allied attack. In the dusk before the next dawn, 3rd August, the "foraging party" set out—first a strong body of pioneers to clear a road through the thicket; then the striking force under the Duke of Würtemberg, containing the Royal Scots and O'Farrell's Regiment, and presently, a little in the rear, the whole Allied army in two columns. No drum or trumpet sounded, and the French patrols, who saw the movement and reported it to Luxemburg, were met with the reply that it was only a foraging party. Then came the news that Allied cavalry were advancing to the Senne. Only foragers, said the French Marshal, and went to sleep again.

Meantime Würtemberg's striking force was struggling through the hot undergrowth till it reached the woods in front of Steenkirk, while the rest of the army halted in an open space some way to the rear. The plan was to attack the French right, which was held by cavalry, with only one infantry brigade, Bourbonnois, in position. About eleven o'clock Luxemburg, from a hill on his right, saw the scarlet of the British Guards in the woods beneath him, and realized his peril. He was a man whose lethargic, self-indulgent nature required an instant crisis to bring out its greatness. In a few minutes he had sent off a summons to Boufflers, and had set Bourbonnois in order of battle. Most of his guns had been left behind at Mons, and it would take time to get up the infantry from the centre and left. If the Allies could only attack at once they had an easy task. But for an hour and a half it remained an artillery duel, for Würtemberg was left unsupported owing to the error of putting the horse before the infantry in defiles where there was no room for both to pass. Eventually six battalions were disentangled from the cavalry, and half an hour after midday Würtemberg sounded the assault.

That assault was a splendid but most costly feat of arms. The Royal Scots and O'Farrell's were on the left centre, where they had to cross the ravine and face a strong hedge with the French behind it. Sir Robert Douglas of Glenbervie, the Royal Scots colonel, led his countrymen through the palisade and swept the enemy before him. On his right the young Lord Angus, the heir of the house of Douglas and not yet of age, was slain at the head of his Cameronians. Hugh Mackay—he of Killiecrankie—who had warned his General that the attack would be a shambles, and had replied " God's will be done " when he was ordered to advance, fell among the first. Yet the French were in retreat, almost in flight. Bourbonnois, Chartres, Orleans, famous regiments all, had given way ; there was a great breach in the front line. Given supports, in an hour Würtemberg would be in possession of Luxemburg's camp.

But there were no supports. The Dutch General,

COUNT SOLMES

Count Solmes, whether from jealousy, error of judgment, or mere native stupidity, refused to send a man from the mass of infantry congested together a mile and a half to the rear. Instead he sent cavalry, which was useless.[1] The twelve Allied battalions—all British except for two of Danes—had broken through or paralysed five French lines of foot and two of horse,[2] but they could do no more. The French and Swiss Guards, led by young princes like Philip of Chartres, Armand of Conti, and Louis of Bourbon, forced them back by sheer weight of numbers. A Royal Scots colour was taken; Sir Robert Douglas rushed through a hedge and recovered it, and flung it to his men before he fell dead. Junior British officers had taken the matter out of Solmes's hands, and reinforcements were coming up, under cover of which Würtemberg's weary troops could retire. They were needed, for Boufflers had now joined Luxemburg. Twenty-four hours after it had marched out, William's army regained its camp, having fought what may perhaps be regarded as, up to that date, the bloodiest battle in which infantry were ever engaged. The losses on both sides were approximately the same; but it may be noted as a proof of the difficulty which the French had in making their men stand against the British attack, that they lost not less than 620 officers killed and wounded. The battle was for the Allies a magnificent chance flung away by the incompetence of Solmes and his staff—a plan, says Mr. Fortescue, "admirably designed and abominably executed." But for the British soldier it was a triumph of gallantry and fortitude.

Luxemburg had had enough of fighting for that season, and O'Farrell's was presently in winter quarters at Ghent. It had distinguished itself at Steenkirk, where it had had Major Keith and six other officers killed, besides many non-commissioned officers and men. Some weeks before the battle, its colonel,

---
[1] For the English opinion of Solmes the reader may consult *Tristram Shandy*, Book V., chapter XXI.
[2] Fifty-three battalions of infantry and seven regiments of dragoons.

1693 O'Farrell, had been taken prisoner by the enemy while on his way to a conference with the Duke of Würtemberg, but had been released on paying the customary ransom. In 1693 the spring was late and the winter rains protracted, and it was not till the middle of May that Louis appeared in Flanders with 120,000 men. He hoped for another siege—Liége, or even Brussels—but he found that William was in better time this season, and that these places would not fall as readily as Namur. Wherefore, having no love of field actions, he returned to Versailles, leaving Luxemburg to conduct what campaign he pleased.

The two old antagonists looked at each other on the Senne for the better part of June. On 6th July Luxemburg moved in the direction of the Meuse and took Huy, while his opponent tried in vain to divert him by sending Würtemberg against the lines of the Scheldt and Lys. William, alarmed for Liége, left his fortified camp at Park, and appeared on the Geete. His army, which had been reduced, partly by Würtemburg's detachment and partly by reinforcements sent to the Meuse garrisons, took up its ground in the triangle between the Little Geete and the Landen brook, which joins it at the village of Leuw. The front ran from Neerlanden, on the Landen stream, to Neerwinden, a distance of four miles, and lay on a slight rise above the dead-flat levels. The disadvantages of the position were that it involved a long front, a hinterland too circumscribed to permit of the action of cavalry, and an unfordable river in the rear. If the defence were once pierced, the place might prove a death-trap. William thought otherwise, for the action of Leuse in 1691 had put him in awe of the French cavalry, and he congratulated himself on having found a position inaccessible to those dreaded horsemen. He strengthened the ground with entrenchments and palisades, and awaited battle. The danger-point was his right around the village of Laer, and there he posted the Scots Brigade under General Ramsay—O'Farrell's, Leven's (the 25th or King's Own Scottish Borderers),

Munro's (the 26th or Cameronians), Mackay's and Lauder's, with the Buffs and the 4th in support. Between Laer and Neerwinden were the Brandenburgers. The latter place was held by the Hanoverians, the Dutch, and two battalions of the British Guards; to the left of it there were more Guards battalions, the 7th Fusiliers, and a battalion of Royal Scots, whose other battalion was at Neerlanden.

Luxemburg, who had ordered the attack just after sunrise, was amazed at the strength of the new Allied defence. He flung six battalions, backed by cavalry, against the Scots at Laer, and seven brigades in three columns against Neerwinden. There ensued some hours of desperate hand-to-hand fighting, and two attacks were repulsed with heavy slaughter, though the defenders lost a third of their strength. Once again Luxemburg sent in his infantry, this time the flower of the household troops led by the young dukes, and again they were beaten back by the stubborn valour of the Guards and the Scots. But the ammunition failed, and presently Neerwinden was lost. This meant that the right wing at Laer was isolated, and Ramsay, who had fought a superb battle, was driven out of the village. The redoubtable French horse were now through the defences, and there was nothing for it but retreat. William, who throughout the day had shown the utmost coolness and gallantry, charged with six British cavalry regiments to cover the retirement of the infantry. Tolmash, commanding the Allied left, managed to fall back in good order, but on the right there was dire confusion and heavy losses of men and material. Ramsay's brigade withdrew fighting to the Geete, struggled over the stream, and joined the main retreat, which moved by the bridge of Neerhespen in the direction of Tirlemont.

Such was the battle of Landen, in which the nineteen British battalions present lost 135 officers. O'Farrell's, considering its position in the battle, came off lightly, for it had only six officer casualties. Solmes, the evil genius of Steenkirk, was killed, as was Sarsfield on

1694-95 the other side, and Berwick and Ormonde were taken prisoners. Corporal Trim, as readers of Sterne will remember, was left wounded on the field. It was a clear victory for Luxemburg; but the Allies were not disgraced, for they opposed only 50,000 men to the French 80,000. William managed his difficult retreat with great skill. "In the battle," Louis confessed, "the Duke of Luxemburg behaved like Condé, and since the battle the Prince of Orange has behaved like Turenne." Three weeks later William reviewed, near Brussels, a larger army than he had commanded on the morning of Landen. But the honours of the season's campaign were with the French, for Charleroi fell, and with it the whole line of the Sambre.

O'Farrell's spent the winter at Bruges, and the summer of 1694 in long marches throughout Brabant and Flanders—manœuvring in which William was hopelessly out-generalled by Luxemburg. British troops were not in action, save for the disastrous expedition to Brest, which was the death of the gallant Tolmash. That year a board of general officers was appointed to determine the order of precedence among the different corps in the army. The principle adopted was that Scots and Irish regiments should rank from the date of their first arrival in England, or from the time when they were first placed on the English establishment. O'Farrell's, though it had been raised in 1678, and therefore from its date of origin might have ranked as Fourth of the Line, had first entered England for general service in 1688, and so became the Twenty-First Regiment of Foot. Numerical titles were not in general use till the reign of George II., but for the sake of simplicity I will adopt them henceforth in this narrative, up to the period when they were replaced by territorial names.

The Twenty-First was at Deinse, on the Lys, in the winter of 1694-95, and, when the spring campaign began, remained as garrison of that place, which had become one of the chief supply depots. The great Luxemburg had died in January 1695. Since the

CAPTURE OF NAMUR

French had now extended their fortified lines from Namur to the sea, a considerable part of their forces would be absorbed in garrison duties; the chance had therefore come for William to recover Namur. Leaving Vaudemont with an army in Flanders to watch the new French Commander-in-Chief, Marshal Villeroy, he marched on the city and forced Boufflers inside the gates. For the strength of that fortress, its scarps and counter-scarps, its bastions and ravelins, the study of which was the life-work of Captain Tobias Shandy, and for the fine tale of its capture, let the reader have recourse to Macaulay: unfortunately it does not belong to our chronicle. For the Twenty-First, though for a short time part of Vaudemont's covering army, was soon back at Deinse, of which place O'Farrell, now a brigadier-general, was governor. It had received in May a new lieutenant-colonel in the person of John Dalyell of Binns, the third son of old General Thomas. The fortifications of Deinse were poor, and when, on 21st July, Villeroy's army, having taken Dixmude, appeared before its gates, O'Farrell surrendered the town without firing a shot. The attacking force was commanded by the Marquis de Feuquières, whose *Memoirs* are among the best military writings of the period. The regiment became prisoners of war, and was set free after Namur fell, as one of the conditions of the return of Marshal Boufflers. For its surrender O'Farrell was formally held responsible, tried by court-martial in the autumn, and cashiered, the colonelcy of the Twenty-First being conferred, on 13th November, on the Hon. Robert Mackay.

Mackay was the third son of the second Lord Reay, and a nephew of Hugh Mackay of Scourie, who opposed Dundee. Originally an officer in the Scots Brigade in Holland, he had accompanied William to England, had commanded the grenadier company in his uncle's regiment, and had been severely wounded at Killiecrankie. He was then promoted lieutenant-colonel, and given command of a new regiment of two battalions, one of which was at the siege of Namur, while the other remained in Scotland. When he received the colonelcy of the Twenty-First he took out with him to Flanders a large draft from his old regiment. He was not fated to see much further service. The Twenty-First was at Bruges for the winter, and in the summer of 1696 took part in a campaign which was merely a manœuvring for position with a view to an early peace, for France was very weary of war. Some time during the autumn Mackay came home, worn-out with wounds and hard service, and died in December at his family seat of Tongue. His successor, whose commission was dated January 1, 1697, was Lieutenant-Colonel Archibald Row.

Row, who was to lead the regiment to one of the greatest of its triumphs, though a young man as compared with his predecessor, had already a varied experience of war. We find him a year before the Revolution an ensign in the Royal Scots, and in December 1688 he became a captain in the 16th Foot (now the Bedfordshire Regiment), being promoted major in 1692. With the 16th he served at Steenkirk, Landen, and the siege of Namur. There were no serious operations during 1697, and in September of that year the Treaty of Ryswick was signed, and the war was over. The Twenty-First returned to Scotland in November, and the colonel and the officers began the long and weary process of trying to extract from the Government arrears of pay. Once more the soldier became the sport of the politician, and in 1698 the Mutiny Act was not renewed—which, says Mr. Fortescue, " placed England for three years at the mercy of France "—and wholesale reductions were made in the army. The infantry left in Scotland were the Foot Guards, the Twenty-First, Colyear's, and the 25th.[1]

For the next few years there is little to record.

---

[1] Andrew Ross, *Old Scottish Regimental Colours*, pages 34, 35. Mr. Fortescue (*op. cit.*, I., page 390), adds, " the 26th, George Hamilton's, and Strathnaver's "; but the first was at the time on the Dutch establishment, the second (the Royal Scots) was in England or Ireland, and the third appears to have remained in the Low Countries.

Now that the regiment was at home it had less difficulty in finding recruits, and was soon brought up to strength. In the last year of William's life, when his unpopularity was great and the idea of a new war on the Continent singularly unenticing, it was found necessary to enlist for foreign service by drastic means, and the Scots regiments in Flanders were brought up to strength by forced drafts from units like the Twenty-First left at home.[1] In the same year the old Highland company was revived. Immediately after the Revolution the policing of the Highlands was done chiefly by the 26th and the Argyll Regiment,[2] and then by independent companies attached to various regiments at home. As a regiment left for foreign service its Highland company was transferred to some other unit then in Scotland. By a commission of June 28, 1701, Captain Alexander Campbell of Fonab, formerly of the Argyll Regiment, and Captain William Grant of Tullibardine's Regiment, were appointed to special companies " for the security of the Highlands and adjacent countries," that of Campbell to be attached to Ferguson's Regiment, and that of Grant to the Twenty-First. Since these companies were to be always on the road, and since the conditions of service were hard, they were given full pay instead of the half-pay then usual with troops at home. The captains, however, had to provide clothing for their men, " who by reason of their special service will need the same more frequently," and do not seem to have had any extra allowance for the purpose. Captain Grant's company, which the muster roll shows to have been composed mainly of Highlanders, was entrusted with the oversight of Badenoch and Kintail.

At the close of 1701 the war clouds were drawing down again over Western Europe, and in March 1702 William died. The War of the Spanish Succession

---

[1] *Priv. Coun. Reg.*, Scotland, February 24, 1701.
[2] The regiment mainly responsible for the Massacre of Glencoe. It should be noted—in spite of legends to the contrary—that the Twenty-First was never near Glencoe.

1702 was about to begin under a new sovereign and a new commander—the greatest in the history of British arms. The Twenty-First, when it received its orders for Holland, had on its rolls a colonel, lieutenant-colonel, major, aid-major, and ten companies, including the grenadiers, but excluding the Highland company, each with captain, lieutenant, ensign, two sergeants, two corporals, and a drum. The fusilier was now what we know from contemporary drawings—with his high conical cap, his red coat and blue facings, his blue breeches, his many-buttoned gaiters. Most of the men were recruited from the Scottish Lowlands, and especially the south-western shires; and though the bulk were new recruits, there was still a substantial remnant of old soldiers who had fought at Landen and Steenkirk, and a few even who had tramped the Galloway moorlands with Buchan. The regiment already had a history and a tradition, for it had proved its manhood against the most illustrious troops in the world. It was now to win ampler laurels on more fateful fields.

CHAPTER III

THE WARS OF MARLBOROUGH

The War of the Spanish Succession—Marlborough and Boufflers—The campaign of Blenheim—Marlborough and Villeroy—Ramillies—The North British Fusiliers—Oudenarde—The siege of Lille—The campaign of Malplaquet—The campaign of 1711—The Royal North British Fusiliers.

I

IN November 1700 died Charles II., King of Spain, leaving a will wherein Philip, Duke of Anjou, grandson of the King of France, was named heir to his throne. When, after a short delay, Louis, in the famous sentence from the balcony at Versailles, accepted the bequest, the balance of power in Europe, secured by the laborious Partition Treaties of 1698 and 1700, was fatally changed. War became inevitable, but at first the alliance against France was purposeless and ill-compacted. Only the Emperor in Austria took action, and it needed the march of Louis into Flanders and a wholesale capture of Dutch garrisons to waken the lethargy of Holland. Britain was too busy with parliamentary quarrels to take much interest, but when the States-General appealed to her for the quota which, under treaty, she was bound to furnish, she ordered twelve battalions to be sent to the Low Countries from Ireland under John, Earl of Marlborough, now restored to favour. In September 1701, when, on the death of James II., Louis recognized his son as King of England, the spirit of the people awoke. A new Parliament agreed that Britain

1701

should furnish 40,000 men, 18,000 of whom were to be British, and in a wild hurry the neglected army was brought up to war strength. But the new campaign was not to be fought by William, for on March 8, 1702, he died, and Anne reigned in his stead.

The situation was changed since the last war. Now Spanish Flanders was on the side of France, and Louis's frontier was virtually that of Dutch Brabant, while he held the line of the Meuse as far as Maestricht. The area of operations had therefore been shifted farther east. The main French army, under Boufflers, lay on the Meuse, and the Allies, under Athlone (that Ginkell who had commanded in 1691 in Ireland), for Marlborough was engaged in tedious diplomacy with the Dutch, lay around Nimeguen on the lower Rhine. The campaign of 1702 was indeterminate and inglorious. When Marlborough at last took the field in June he was hampered by preposterous Dutch commissioners and Dutch generals in whom petty jealousies took the place of any understanding of the art of war. " We had all the advantage," wrote Row of the Twenty-First, " that a tired, disorderly, and inferior army could give to good troupes, but the States were against fighting." Nevertheless Marlborough outmanœuvred Boufflers, and would, without doubt, have beaten him decisively but for the recalcitrance of his colleagues at critical moments. The season ended with the capture of Liége and all the lower Meuse by the Allies. But elsewhere things had gone ill, for the Elector of Bavaria had declared for France, Villars had defeated Prince Louis of Baden on the upper Rhine, Tallard had possessed himself of the fortresses of the Moselle, and the Emperor, with Hungary in revolt behind him, feared for Vienna, since Villars's opening of the Black Forest passes made a road for France to the Danube. The Twenty-First crossed the Channel that summer, but did not form part of the field army, acting for most of the time as the garrison of Breda.

The year 1703 was a repetition of its predecessor.

MARLBOROUGH AND EUGENE

The plan of France was to win back the lower Meuse fortresses and threaten Holland with her main army under Boufflers and Villeroy, while Tallard held Prince Louis of Baden on the upper Rhine, and Villars pushed through the Black Forest, joined hands with the Elector of Bavaria, and combined with the advance of Savoy through the Tyrol in a movement on Vienna. The last part of the scheme failed owing to the withdrawal of Savoy from the French alliance; but Villars defeated the Imperial troops at Hochstadt, and France was strongly established on the upper Danube. Marlborough, now a Duke, desired as a counter-move a vigorous invasion of Flanders; but his Dutch colleagues preferred sieges, and he was compelled to start the campaign with the taking of Bonn. He then began operations for the capture of Antwerp, but the blunders of the Dutch generals ruined the plan, and the season showed no further results except the taking of Huy and Limburg. In these petty sieges the Twenty-First, now brigaded under the Earl of Derby along with the 2nd Royal Scots, the 10th, the 16th, and the 26th (Cameronians), played a considerable part, and at Limburg it was employed to make the chief assault. Marlborough returned to England sick at heart, and resolved to resign the command. But a month or two at home restored him to a better temper, and he began to devise a new and audacious plan for the coming year. Moreover, he found in the Imperial service a general who not only held his views, but was competent to share in their execution.[1]

This was Prince Eugene, a cadet of the house of Savoy, now a man of forty, whose health in youth had been so delicate that he had been destined for the Church. He had won the great victory of Zenta over the Turks eight years before, and had recently met the French with success in Italy. All his life, like William III., he was inspired by a hatred of the French power;

[1] There seems to be no warrant for crediting Eugene, rather than Marlborough, with the first inception of the plan. The possibility of a march to the Danube was obvious to any bold mind, and the merit lay less in the idea than in the way it was put into execution.

1704 and when, later, he was offered high command by the French King, he replied that indeed he hoped to re-enter France, but as an invader. In him Marlborough found quick comprehension, an unfailing loyalty, and an enduring friendship. The plan was to leave the Low Countries to the Dutch, slip across Europe, destroy the French armies on the Danube, and free Vienna once for all from their menace. The States-General and the English House of Commons would alike take fright if the thing were put to them crudely, so infinite secrecy and circumspection must be used. Marlborough managed to secure the raising in England of one new regiment of dragoons and seven new battalions of foot, by means of which many a luckless fellow escaped the hangman's cart, and, crossing to Holland in mid-winter, he wrung supplies out of the timid States-General. He breathed no word of his main scheme, talking only of operations on the Moselle, and in April 1704 he left England on his great adventure.

To understand what followed, it is necessary to recall the geography of central Europe and be clear as to the disposition of the opposing forces in the spring of that year. The upper Rhine is separated from the upper Danube by the woody uplands of the Black Forest. An Allied army, once through the forest passes, would be at a great distance from its base, and liable to have its supplies interrupted, except in so far as it could draw upon the German depots of Nuremberg and Nordlingen. It must defeat the enemy, or find itself in a predicament. Therefore the first requirement was speed. The second was secrecy, for if the plan were known or guessed, it would be easy for the French to bar the road. For this Marlborough had one advantage, in that, in those days, when news travelled slowly, his route was such that it would be hard for the enemy to realize his destination till he was within reasonable distance of his goal. Marching up the Rhine valley, he would be assumed to be making for the Moselle till he had passed Coblentz, and for Alsace till he had passed the Neckar. Villeroy, with

THE MARCH UP THE RHINE 45

the main French army, lay in Flanders, watching the lower Rhine. Tallard, with his army, was in Alsace, watching the upper Rhine, while the Comte de Coignies, with 10,000 men, was on the Moselle. The Elector of Bavaria and a French contingent under Marsin held the whole of the upper Danube from Ulm eastward. On the Allied side the Dutch, and for the moment Marlborough, were in the north, on the Meuse and on the Rhine. On the upper Rhine, watching Tallard, was Prince Eugene with a considerable force. In upper Germany, with posts in the Black Forest, was Prince Louis of Baden. That is to say, the main weight of the Allies was on the lower Rhine; it was Marlborough's task to shift it to the Danube.

In the last week of April the British troops began to cross the Meuse, and by the middle of May 16,000 had collected at Bedbourg. In that force we are concerned principally with Row's brigade, which, under the colonel of the Twenty-First, embraced the 10th (now the Lincolnshire Regiment), the 3rd (Buffs), the 23rd (Royal Welch Fusiliers), the 24th (South Wales Borderers), and the Twenty-First. Not a soul knew where the English commander was going, and the States-General and the English ministers were in no better case. Only Eugene knew, and the Emperor and Prince Louis of Baden perhaps by this time suspected. On the 23rd Marlborough was at Bonn, still talking about the Moselle; but when he passed Coblentz it was plain that the Comte de Coignies would not be troubled. Presently he was at Cassel, and was making arrangements for bridging the Rhine at Philipsburg. Clearly, thought Tallard, he is making for Alsace, and sent for reinforcements. Tallard had just managed with considerable skill, by a dash through the Black Forest, to pass a contingent to Marsin and the Elector of Bavaria. On the last day of May Marlborough crossed the Main, and pushing on at high speed over abominable roads was, on 3rd June, beyond the Neckar. That settled the question. Marlborough was making for the Danube, and was now nearer than Tallard to the Elector of

1704

1704 Bavaria. Villeroy came down from the north to consult, and the two sent off an urgent request for orders to Louis in Paris. Marlborough waited for two days for his troops to concentrate, and then struck across the bend of the Neckar, and on 10th June was at Mondelheim, where, for the first time, he met Eugene face to face. The latter was amazed at the fine condition of the British cavalry after their long march. Thither came Prince Louis of Baden, a difficult colleague, who insisted on dividing the command with Marlborough, each taking it on alternate days. Eugene was left on the Rhine, and Marlborough, like Montrose before Inverlochy, disappeared into the hills. His van crossed the pass of Geislingen in a deluge of rain, and made contact with Prince Louis's force in the neighbourhood of Ulm. The Elector of Bavaria retired down the Danube, and presently Charles Churchill arrived with the rest of the Allied infantry, having overcome the difficulties of country and weather through the excellent arrangements made in advance by Marlborough, and having paid for every pennyworth requisitioned—a thing new to the history of German war.

The situation now was that the Elector of Bavaria and Marsin were lying to the south of the Danube, Marlborough and Baden to the north, while the main armies of France were no nearer than the Rhine. Marlborough's purpose was to enter Bavaria and force the Elector out of the alliance with France, and to do this he must first take Donauwörth—the key of the country, for it would give him the crossing of the Danube and also of the Lech flowing from the south. He had ninety-six battalions of foot, two hundred and two squadrons, and forty-eight guns—nearly 70,000 men; while the enemy on the south bank numbered at the most 45,000. So, disregarding the Elector, he marched on Donauwörth, and on 1st July was encamped to the west of the town. The place was not strongly fortified, but above it to the north-east rose the low, broad, flat-topped height of the Schellenberg, steep on the river side, but sloping gradually to the north-west. The Elector, foreseeing his intention, had sent Count d'Arco to hold the hill with 2,500 horse and 10,000 foot.

Next day was Marlborough's turn for command, and at early dawn he marched out with a picked force of 6,000 foot and thirty-five squadrons of horse for the assault. It was essential to carry the Schellenberg before further enemy troops could come up. But the infantry travelled slowly along the vile roads, and it was midday before the van of the picked troops arrived. About the same time a letter was put into his hand from Eugene, informing him that Villeroy and Tallard were sending strong reinforcements to the Danube, and this intelligence decided him to attack forthwith. He selected sixteen battalions from the special force—five of them British [1]—and hurled them against the northern face, while eight battalions were detailed in support, and eight more held in reserve. The advance was not made till six in the evening, and was in truth a desperate expedient, for he could not expect to carry strong works with such a force, and can only have hoped to draw the defence to the northern face and thereby open a road elsewhere for the rest of his army. That was what happened. The attack, pressed with splendid resolution, failed to break the defence, but it drew the whole garrison to it, and left the west face unguarded. The depleted infantry held the ground they had won, and the cavalry were moved up into the front line to support them. Presently came the rest of his army, which climbed the west face and took the French and Bavarians in flank. The Scots Greys, who had been fighting on foot, remounted and charged the rout, till the whole of D'Arco's contingent was in flight. Not a fourth part escaped to join the Elector. The Allies lost in one hour and a half 1,400 killed and 3,800 wounded, and the British lost a third of their troops

1704

---

[1] Mr. Fortescue states that these were the 1st Guards, two battalions of the Royal Scots, the 23rd, and possibly the 37th (Hampshires)—(*op. cit.*, I., page 426, *n.*).

1704 engaged. At the end of the day, of the seventeen officers of the 1st Guards, twelve were casualties. The Twenty-First, which does not seem to have been in the main attack, had several men killed, and Captain Kygoe and Lieutenants Johnston and Campbell wounded.

Donauwörth had fallen, and the gate of Bavaria lay open. The Elector destroyed the Lech bridges and entrenched himself at Augsburg, while Marlborough crossed first the Danube and then the Lech, and entered Bavaria by the north-western gate. The Elector was beginning to waver in his allegiance to Louis, and the English General endeavoured to force his decision by ravaging his country. The crops were destroyed in the fields, one hundred and twenty villages were burned, and the land was laid waste up to the walls of Munich. Munich, indeed, would have fallen had Marlborough possessed a siege train. He was preparing for the siege of Ingolstadt, which would give him the whole length of the Danube from Ulm to Passau, when news came that Tallard was marching from the Rhine to aid the distraught Elector, with an army which would place the superiority in numbers with the enemy.

Tallard had not the speed of his great antagonist. On the day of the Schellenberg action he took counsel with Villeroy and began to cross the Rhine. On 4th July he started the passage of the southern half of the Black Forest, and on the 16th in the orthodox fashion began the siege of Villingen, the principal fortress between him and the Danube. There he received an urgent letter from Marsin, telling him of the fall of Donauwörth, and warning him that unless reinforcements came speedily the Elector would change sides. On the 21st arrived a second and more urgent appeal, which told the story of the ravaging of Bavaria. The French Marshal hesitated no longer; next day he raised the siege of Villingen, and hurriedly made his way across the hills. The route was ill-provisioned, men and horses alike suffered from sickness and poor feeding, but on the 29th Tallard was in sight of Ulm, and on 4th August he joined Marsin and the Elector at Augsburg. He believed that now he could confront Marlborough with an army stronger in numbers and far stronger in guns.

But he had not reckoned with Prince Eugene. The latter's place was on the Rhine, where he had French forces to hold in check, since Villeroy had moved down from the north. He resolved to throw his weight into the scale of the great contest now impending on the Danube, but, in order to minimize the risk, to deceive the enemy before him up to the last possible moment. He pretended that he was detaching a few battalions to cover Würtemberg, and then marched slowly down the Neckar as if bound for the Rhine. Suddenly, at Tubingen, he turned east, vanished from Villeroy's ken, and, two days after Tallard had arrived at Augsburg, appeared at Hochstadt on the Danube with 15,000 men. The situation had now changed enormously in the Allies' favour. The arrival of Eugene enabled Marlborough to get rid of the incubus of Prince Louis of Baden by sending him off to the siege of Ingolstadt, and it gave him the aid of a military talent which, after his own, was the best in Europe.

Marlborough was now east of the Lech, Tallard and the Elector were at Augsburg, and Eugene north of the Danube. It was clearly the business of the French to get the Allies out of Bavaria by cutting their lines of supply, which ran from Nuremberg by Nordlingen. If Marlborough crossed the Danube and joined Eugene, the way was open for the French into Bavaria; if Eugene marched south to join him, the French could cut off the supplies. Tallard began to move northwards towards the Danube, and Marlborough followed him up the east bank of the Lech. The English General had decided that he must join Eugene on the northern shore of the Danube. On the 10th the Franco-Bavarian army crossed that river, while Eugene moved eastward, where 3,000 of Marlborough's cavalry joined him. On the 11th the Allied infantry were crossing in two columns, one at Merxheim, and the other at

1704 Donauwörth by way of the Lech bridge at Rhain. Late that evening, after twenty-four hours' marching, the whole army lay north of the river, its left resting on the village of Munster, which had been occupied by Row's brigade. Next day the artillery arrived, and the junction with Eugene was complete.

The opposing armies now lay five miles apart. It was not Tallard's wish to fight a battle. He had at least equal numbers and a strong position, and he hoped, by blocking the road up the Danube, to force the Allies to retreat upon Nordlingen as their northern base. He did not believe that Marlborough would dare to attack, for, unless the result was a decisive victory, the Duke would be left in a precarious situation. The English General was perfectly aware of the critical nature of such an attempt. " I know the difficulties," he told his colleagues, " but a battle is absolutely necessary, and I rely on the discipline of my troops."

When Marlborough and Eugene surveyed the landscape from the church tower of Tapfheim they saw a scene but little different from what meets the traveller's eye to-day. To the north lay a line of low wooded hills; three miles to the south flowed the Danube with patches of swamp and undergrowth along its banks. Between was a plain only a few feet above the river level, cut by three little marshy streams running south from the uplands. The land was mostly under crops which had now been reaped, though labourers were still busy with the aftermath of the hay. Among the fields rose an occasional church spire, with cottages and gardens clustered round it—chiefly near the river and just above flood-water mark. It was open country, without cover, and therefore with no chance of surprise. In that hot August weather both armies lay clear and bare to each other's view.

The Franco-Bavarian camp was on the west bank of the brook called the Nebel. Half-way between the hills and the river stood the hamlet of Oberglauheim, looking across to Unterglauheim on the east bank.

BLENHEIM

On the left, a little withdrawn from the stream, stood another hamlet, Lutzingen, close to the wooded hills. To the south above the Danube and the Nebel mouth was the larger village of Blenheim. Tallard on the right had his headquarters at Blenheim, Marsin in the centre at Oberglauheim, and the Elector on the left at Lutzingen; Tallard had thirty-six battalions of foot and forty-four squadrons of horse, while Marsin and the Elector had between them forty-two battalions

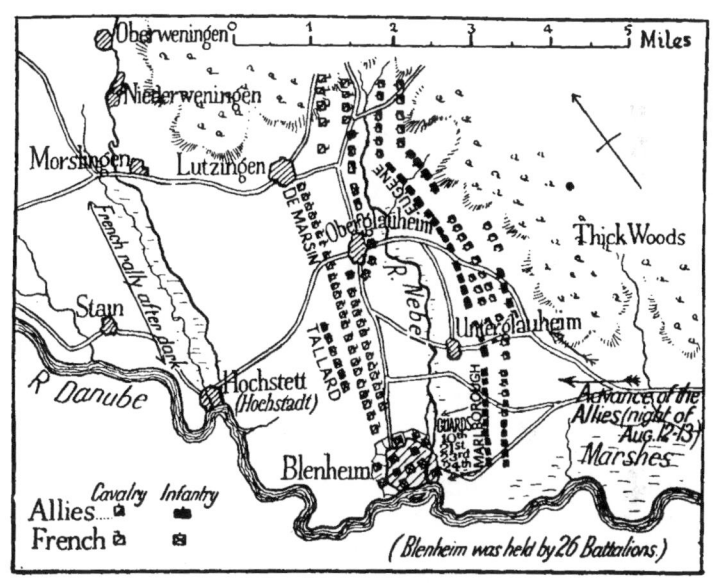

1704

BATTLE OF BLENHEIM

and eighty-three squadrons.[1] The ordering of the line was curious. The fashion of the day was to have the infantry in the centre and the cavalry on the wings; but the Franco-Bavarian command was treated as two armies with cavalry on the wings of each, so that the centre on this occasion was a solid mass of cavalry. The position was very strong; the hills on one side and the river on the other side made a turning movement

---

[1] These are the figures from the French records. Mr. Fortescue (I., page 434) gives forty-six battalions and one hundred and eight squadrons.

almost impossible, and if Blenheim, the key-point, held, a frontal attack seemed doomed to failure. Therefore Tallard put into Blenheim nine battalions of foot, and later sixteen battalions and four regiments of dragoons, while he held in immediate reserve some 10,000 men. This left him with only nine battalions to support his cavalry on the two-mile front between Blenheim and Oberglauheim.

The early morning of Wednesday, 13th August, was thick with a fog which rolled up from the river and the marshy brooks, and cloaked the stubble. The Allies broke camp about two a.m., and by five o'clock Tallard was aware of their movement, but believed that it was the beginning of a retreat to Nordlingen. At seven a.m., when the sun was well up and the fog was lifting, they were within a mile of the enemy position and in plain view. The village of Unterglauheim was soon in flames, and presently the ninety French and Bavarian guns opened along the front. The Allied columns began their deployment, but, since the right had much farther to go and had difficulties in the skirts of the hills, this was not completed before noon. Meantime pioneers were repairing or preparing the bridges of the Nebel. The chaplains read prayers at the head of the regiments, and Marlborough, splendid in his red coat and the Garter, rode through the length of the position in full view of the assembled troops. When completed, the Allied front ran thus: on the left, against Blenheim, were six lines of infantry under Lord Cutts—first Row's brigade, then Hessians, then Ferguson's brigade;[1] then Hanoverians, and two reserve lines. On Cutts's right were two lines of infantry (one British) with two lines of cavalry between, and beyond the Allied main army.

There is no record of the Duke's original plan.

[1] Row's brigade—3rd, 10th, 21st, 23rd, 24th. Ferguson's brigade—2nd Royal Scots, 15th, 26th, 37th. Hamilton's brigade—1st Foot Guards, 1st Royal Scots, 8th, 16th, 20th. This was the order of battle, but in the actual attack on Blenheim, the Guards took the place of the Buffs in Row's brigade. The distribution of battalions given above is that quoted by Mr. Fortescue from Dumont's *Histoire Militaire*, but other accounts vary. See Atkinson, *Marlborough and the Rise of the British Army*, page 247.

CUTTS'S ADVANCE

Whether he hoped to carry Blenheim village, or intended by his attack merely to draw off troops for its defence and so weaken the enemy centre, must remain in the realm of speculation. About one o'clock he gave Cutts the order to advance, and the "Salamander" moved forward to what were to be the fieriest hours of his torrid life. The assault was more hopeless by far than the frontal attack on the Schellenberg six weeks before. The four guns posted outside the village poured a stream of grape on the troops crossing the brook. Once on the other side the men halted and re-formed, the Hessians being left in reserve, while Row's brigade advanced. The five battalions, 1st Guards, 10th, Twenty-First, 23rd, and 24th, with unfaltering step, crossed the hundred and fifty yards of meadow which separated them from the palisade. It was one of the great feats of human discipline in the world's history. Deliberately, steadily, they moved, with orders to reserve their fire; when thirty paces from the enemy, a volley crashed out and one man in three fell, but the line did not waver. At last they were at the palisade; Row struck it with his sword; the English muskets spoke, and the men tore at the planks with their hands in the effort to make a gap. Again the French volleyed, and a third of the remnant of the brigade was down. Row fell mortally wounded, and in their attempt to carry him off, Lieutenant-Colonel Dalyell and Major Campbell of the Twenty-First were killed—such a death as old Thomas of Binns would have wished for his son.

The Twenty-First, maddened by the loss of their field officers, attacked again with fury, seeking for an entrance among the palings and barricades. But the fire of the white-coats inside added every second to the red swathes on the ground, until the moment came when flesh and blood could no longer endure. The brigade halted, wavered, and began to retire. Tallard unloosed three squadrons of Gens d'Armes on the left, who swept down on the retreat and captured the colours of the Twenty-First. But the Hessians left in reserve checked the horse and recovered the colours. The doom of the Gens d'Armes was at hand. Cutts begged for cavalry to protect his flanks, and General Lumley sent five British squadrons across the Nebel, who charged the French horse and put the scarlet-clad sabreurs to flight.

Cutts now sent in the remaining two-thirds of his force. Over the brook and across the ground swept by grape-shot went the British—Ferguson's brigade with what was left of Row's—till they had won the outskirts of the village. But there they were fast held, for Tallard had nearly doubled the garrison, and once again the attack ebbed. Marlborough realized that that splendid infantry could do no more. He resolved to turn the assault into a holding attack, and gave orders that the survivors should take cover and keep up a feint of attack. Meantime he took the Hanoverians, the only brigade of Cutts's left intact, and turned his attention to his centre.

This centre—the main army—was now for the most part across the Nebel. That crossing was the chance for Tallard, had he known it. He had guns, he had infantry to spare in Blenheim, he had Silly's cavalry in reserve; one concentrated effort might have broken the Allied centre before it could deploy beyond the stream. But the chance was seized too half-heartedly for success. The British cavalry on the left, being under the guns of Blenheim, were in peculiar difficulties, and they had scarcely crossed when they were charged by the French horse. The fire of the British infantry checked that attack; but the position was critical, and for a moment, while Marlborough was getting over his Danish and Hanoverian squadrons, it looked almost as if the battle leaned to the French. The Prince of Holstein-Beck had attacked the brigade of Irish exiles in Oberglauheim, and the Prince of Holstein-Beck had failed and was dead.

It was now well on in the afternoon, and the Allied centre was across the Nebel. Marlborough formed his cavalry in two lines for the final attack, with the

THE VICTORY

foot to the left rear, while Tallard brought forward to 1704 the first line the nine battalions of infantry in his centre. Word came that Eugene was holding his own, but no more, for he was not yet fully beyond the stream, since the Elector had made his stand on the very edge of the water. The daylight was fast dying, and the time had come for a great stroke if victory were to be won. The French foot stood bravely, but the weight of the Allied horse was too much for them. Marsin could send no reinforcements, the infantry massed in Blenheim were too distant—thus far had Cutts's hopeless battle served the main issue—and the French cavalry could not abide the Allied charge. The centre broke, and through the gap rode the Duke's cavalry in pursuit. The battle of Blenheim had been won.

Marsin and the Elector were compelled to retreat, with Eugene at their heels. The twenty-seven battalions of foot and four regiments of dragoons in Blenheim village were cut off, for Charles Churchill was now at their rear. An attempt to break out was checked by the Scots Greys, and late in the evening the flower of the army of France made unconditional surrender. The Duke, borrowing a leaf from a commissary's notebook, scribbled a letter to his wife, which is among the most dramatic reports on record. " I have not time to say more, but to beg you will give my duty to the Queen, and let her know her army has had a glorious victory. Monsieur Tallard and two other generals are in my coach, and I am following the rest." The Elector and Marsin were in incontinent flight for the Rhine.

The Franco-Bavarian losses were some 12,000 killed, as many wounded, 11,000 prisoners, about one hundred guns of different kinds, and the whole *impedimenta* of the French camp. The Allies had 4,500 killed and 7,500 wounded, of whom the British casualties amounted to over 2,000. It is notable that the troops who had borne the brunt of the Schellenberg attack were again in action, and again had desperate losses— a proof of unshakable *moral*. The Twenty-First suffered

1704-5 heavily for its share in Row's heroic venture. Row himself was dead, and Dalyell and Major Campbell; of captains, the two Straitons; of lieutenants, Vandergracht, Hill, Campbell, and Trevallion; while Captains Crauford and Fairlee, and Lieutenants Dunbar, J. Douglas, Elliot, Ogilvy, Maxwell, Stuart, Primrose, and Gordon had been wounded. Altogether there were 23 officer casualties.[1] Of the losses among non-commissioned officers and men there is no record.

Blenheim was a decisive battle, for it shattered all the far-flung intrigues of Louis and broke the legend of the invincibility of France. It forced the Bourbons upon the defensive, and patched up the rickety structure of the Empire. It revealed to the world the shining talents of Marlborough, and restored to the British people their ancient pride. " Welcome to England, sir," said a Nottingham butcher to Tallard, as he was being ceremoniously escorted to the castle. " We hope to see your master here next year."

II

The Twenty-First was chosen, along with four other shattered battalions, to escort the French and Bavarian prisoners on the three weeks' journey down the Rhine, under the command of Brigadier-General Ferguson. Meantime, as successor to the gallant Row, it was given a new colonel in John, Viscount Mordaunt, the eldest son of that eccentric genius, Charles, Earl of Peterborough. Mordaunt, a young man of twenty-three, had led the 1st Guards in the attack on the Schellenberg, and, fighting with the same famous regiment, had lost his left arm at Blenheim. The Twenty-First went into winter quarters in Holland, and received sufficient recruits[2] from Scotland to bring it up to strength for the next year's campaign.

For 1705 Marlborough had prepared a plan on

[1] Blenheim roll in Dalton's *Army Lists and Commission Registers*.
[2] According to the Blenheim roll it had mustered in that action 36 officers and 593 men.

THE DUTCH

the largest scale, for he hoped to advance on the Moselle and carry the war into Lorraine. But what he proposed his Allies disposed, for none of them appeared in time, and after waiting a month at Treves, he was compelled to hurry back to the Meuse to deal with Villeroy, who had taken Huy and invested Liége. On his approach the French commander fell back inside the lines which he had fortified from the Meuse near Namur, along the Mehaigne, the two Geetes, and the Demer to Aerschot, and thence by Lierre to Antwerp. The Duke resolved to force these lines at the place where they were most difficult and therefore least likely to be strongly held, close to the old battle-ground of Landen. He recaptured Huy, and then pushed Overkirk with the Dutch army up to the edge of the right of the French position. Villeroy concentrated troops at the threatened point, which was what his opponent had looked for. Marlborough recalled the besieging force from Huy, made it up to 8,000 men, and sent it off from the right wing, Overkirk's troops silently following. By dawn on 17th July his men found themselves on the field of Landen, close to the Geete, and in the morning mist they forced that river, broke the French reinforcements which arrived, and captured a vital part of the enemy's line. The Twenty-First, who had been with the Duke on the Moselle, played an important part in this surprise attack.

Villeroy fell back upon Louvain, and Marlborough was prevented from exploiting his success by the nervousness of his Dutch colleagues. This same timidity and jealousy crippled all the later operations of the summer. It spoiled his plans for forcing the Dyle at the very moment of success; it did the same thing on the Yssche. But it eventually became so patent both to the English and Dutch Governments, that the worst offenders were deprived of their commands. "Jealousy, timidity, ignorance, treachery, and flat imbecility," says Mr. Fortescue, "seem to have been the motives that inspired these men, whose conduct has never been reprobated according to its demerits."

1705

1706 The Duke spent the late months of 1705 visiting the courts of Austria and Germany in the endeavour to put energy and common sense into his difficult Allies. He was back in England in January 1706, struggling to make up his deficiency in supplies. When he visited The Hague in April he hoped to be allowed to lead a force to aid Eugene in Italy. But the incompetence of Prince Louis of Baden, and the sudden activity of Villars, so alarmed the States-General that, much against his will, he was compelled to remain in Flanders.

The season of 1706 opened with Villeroy snugly ensconced behind the Dyle. But the French General thought he saw a chance for an offensive, for he heard that Marlborough was having trouble with his Danish troops, and had not yet received the Prussian and Hanoverian contingents. Accordingly he marched out to Tirlemont on the Great Geete, and presently crossed the stream. It was precisely what the Duke had hoped for. He marched towards the head of the Geete, intending to camp at the village of Ramillies, and at ten a.m., on 23rd May, when the mist had cleared, he saw the French army before him. The place is a tableland, the highest point is Brabant, with the Mehaigne on the south, the Great Geete to the west, and the infant stream of the Little Geete flowing north among swamps. Villeroy was surprised at the sight of Marlborough, whom he had not expected till the morrow, but he was not averse to a battle, for he knew the ground. He took up position with his right on the Mehaigne, the four villages of Tavières, Ramillies, Offus, and Autréglise along his front, and his left and left centre protected by the marshes of the Little Geete. His front, four miles long, was disposed in two lines. His left was infantry backed by cavalry, his centre infantry, and his right mainly cavalry, with the famous Maison du Roi in the first line. The fault of the position was that of Tallard's at Blenheim, the component parts being unrelated; the villages were too far apart, and the French left paid for its security by an incapacity to attack. Marlborough resolved to turn his opponent's right.

To prevent that right being reinforced he began 1706 about one o'clock by an attack on the left. Villeroy, seeing the British scarlet which he knew too well, diverted to that wing battalions from his right and centre. Orkney, with the British, managed to cross the Little Geete with a dozen battalions, and attacked Offus, when he was ordered, much to his disgust, to withdraw, since the supporting horse were needed for

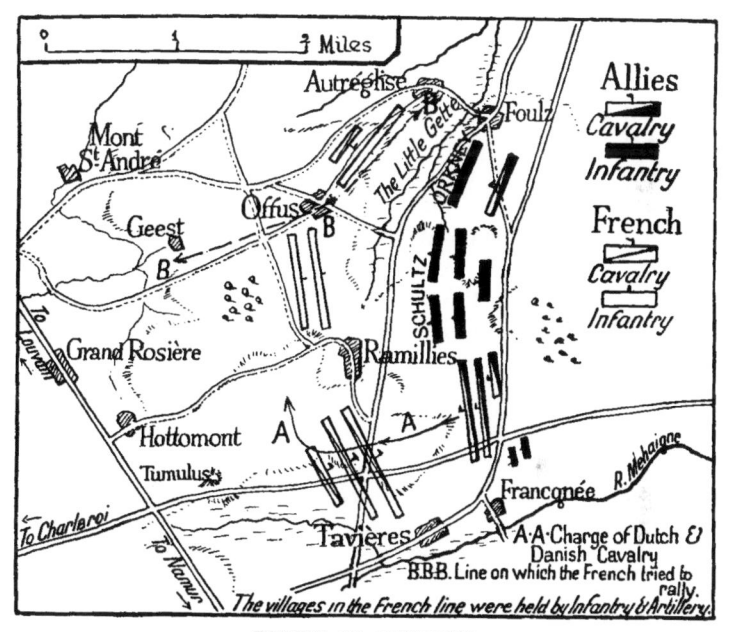

BATTLE OF RAMILLIES

the main attack. He had, however, done his work in compelling Villeroy to alter his dispositions. Meanwhile the Dutch on the Allied left had stormed Tavières, and the main advance of the Allied infantry under Schultz upon Ramillies had developed, which was supported about 2.30 p.m. by the attack of the Allied horse. The first French cavalry line was driven in; a gallant charge by the Maison du Roi restored the line for a little, but Marlborough himself rallied his horse (he was all but captured), while the Danish

1706 squadrons on the left lent their aid. Orkney's men, drawn up east of the Little Geete, immobilized Villeroy's left, and enabled Marlborough to bring his horse from that wing to the support of his centre and left. Meanwhile Schultz, with whom were the Buffs and the Twenty-First, was gaining ground in the savage struggle for Ramillies village. Between the hours of four and five, when the Duke of Argyll brought up the Scots battalions in the Dutch service, the issue there was decided. The Buffs and the Twenty-First drove three French battalions into the marshes, and the famous Picardie Regiment met its doom when the Twenty-First forced it out of Ramillies into the arms of Borthwick's battalion of the Scots Brigade.[1] The cavalry on the Allied left had worked their way round the French right, and at five o'clock Orkney began to cross the Little Geete, while Schultz turned north against Offus and Autréglise. The battle of Ramillies was won, and it only remained for the cavalry to complete the rout. Lord John Hay and his Scots Greys led the van, and charged at a gallop two battalions of the Regiment du Roi, killing or capturing them all. In no battle of the campaign was more deadly toll taken of the flower of the French horse and foot.[2]

[1] One "John Scot, Souldier," composed in verse a diary of the doings of the Scots Brigade. Here is how he writes of Ramillies:—
"A regiment of French was called Picardie,
Whom our Scots Fizanires had beat out,
From the center of our armie could not win away,
They were forced throu hedges thereabout," etc.
Papers Illustrating the History of the Scots Brigade (Dutch Service),
ed. by James Ferguson, Vol. II.
The Scots Brigade in Holland had its origin in the sixteenth century, when the States-General appealed to Scotland for help against Spain, and 2,600 men were raised for the service. Regiments from it landed with William of Orange, and were present at Killiecrankie. It fought at Steenkirk and Landen, was present at all the great battles of Marlborough except Blenheim, and won great fame for its performance at Bergen-op-Zoom in July 1747. Up till 1782 it wore the British red and beat the Scots march, and when this was altered in that year its officers resigned and came home, and in 1794 raised the Scots Brigade or 94th Foot (later the 2nd Battalion of the Connaught Rangers).

[2] Mr. Fortescue (*op. cit.*, I., pages 470-474) makes Orkney's attack merely a demonstration, and places the Twenty-First with him on the Allied right. My version follows the account of Mr. C. F. Atkinson (*Marlborough and the Rise of the British Army*, 1921), who uses authorities, in the shape of Lord Orkney's letters and those of Colonel Cranstoun of the Cameronians, which were not available when Mr. Fortescue wrote.

THE PURSUIT

Villeroy's army was more than defeated—it was 1706 utterly broken. It fled helplessly westward, beyond Judoigne and towards Louvain, and then on, under Lord Orkney's pressure, across the Dyle. The British cavalry, being for the most part quite fresh, all night relentlessly urged the pursuit. Nor was Marlborough himself far behind. Within four days he was across the Senne, while the demoralized enemy fell back on Ghent. No victory was ever more assiduously followed up. Brussels, Malines, Alost at once surrendered, followed by Ghent and Bruges, and presently by Antwerp. Within a fortnight the armies of Louis were back on their own frontier. In the battle itself the French casualties were some 15,000, and their losses in prisoners alone were more than the total Allied losses. Villars was recalled from the Rhine, and had Prince Louis of Baden possessed any real capacity, he might have worked his will on that river. The rest of the summer's campaign was as brilliant as the start. Ostend was taken; Menin surrendered to British battalions, who there recaptured four of the guns lost at Landen. Every fortress in Flanders and Brabant fell, and Vendôme, who had now succeeded Villeroy, was anxiously watching the Sambre, lest the Duke should thrust by that route into France. The campaign was one of the swiftest and most wholly successful on record; in one month Marlborough had conquered from the Meuse to the sea, and had forced France to a defensive on her own doorstep. Small wonder that, as Mr. Fortescue relates, he "made urgent request for fresh stores of champagne."

In June, just after Ramillies, the Twenty-First got a new colonel, Lord Mordaunt exchanging places with the colonel of the 28th (the 1st Battalion of the Gloucestershire Regiment). The new commander was Sampson de Lalo, a French Huguenot who had been forced by the revocation of the Edict of Nantes to leave his native land, and had fought his way upward from subordinate commands, earning "great favour and esteem in the British army." After Dalyell's death at

62   THE ROYAL SCOTS FUSILIERS

1707-8 Blenheim the regiment was under Lieutenant-Colonel Lindsay, but he seems in 1706 to have given place to Lieutenant-Colonel Walter Sharp, who first appears as an ensign of Buchan's in 1688.

The year 1707 opened badly with Berwick's defeat of the British in the Peninsula at Almanza. The Emperor had made a secret arrangement with France, which allowed the French garrisons in Italy to be withdrawn, with the result that Marlborough in Flanders was faced with a considerably superior force. All he could do was to cover his conquests in Brabant and Flanders—the Dutch deputies and the rain effectually prevented his schemes for the surprise of Vendôme coming to fruition. It was an empty year, but it was of some importance for the British army, for the Treaty of Union was signed between England and Scotland. The Scots regiments were now called North British, and the Twenty-First became officially the North British Fusiliers.[1] In 1708 all regiments took the field under the Union Jack, in which the cross of St. Andrew was combined with the cross of St. George.

In the early spring of the year came the alarm of a Jacobite invasion from France, and Marlborough, who had received early warning, hurried ten battalions to Ostend to watch the coast, one of which is said by Sir Walter Scott to have been the Twenty-First. In April he met Eugene at The Hague, and agreed with him that he would command on the Moselle and be ready to bring his army by forced marches to Flanders, should the need arise. France had concentrated nearly all her strength in Flanders, and Vendôme, with the heir to the French throne and the Old Pretender on his staff, disposed of nearly 100,000 men as against the Allies' 80,000. The campaign opened with manœuvring on both sides in the neighbourhood of the field of Waterloo. Early in June, Bruges and Ghent opened

---

[1] Officially; but the title was never popular, and the regiment seems to have been generally known as the Scotch (or Scots) Fusiliers. At the same time the 7th (Royal Fusiliers) became the South British Fusiliers (Grose's *Military Antiquities*), a title which it seems to have dropped at once.

their gates to Vendôme, and the Allies thereby lost
the keys to the navigation of the Scheldt and the Lys.
Marlborough marched straight after his antagonists,
being joined by Eugene at Brussels, for it was clear
that Vendôme was aiming at Oudenarde, which controlled the Scheldt. By a brilliant march, though he
had a longer distance to cover, he arrived there first,
and placed himself between the French and their own
frontier. It was now his business to force an action.

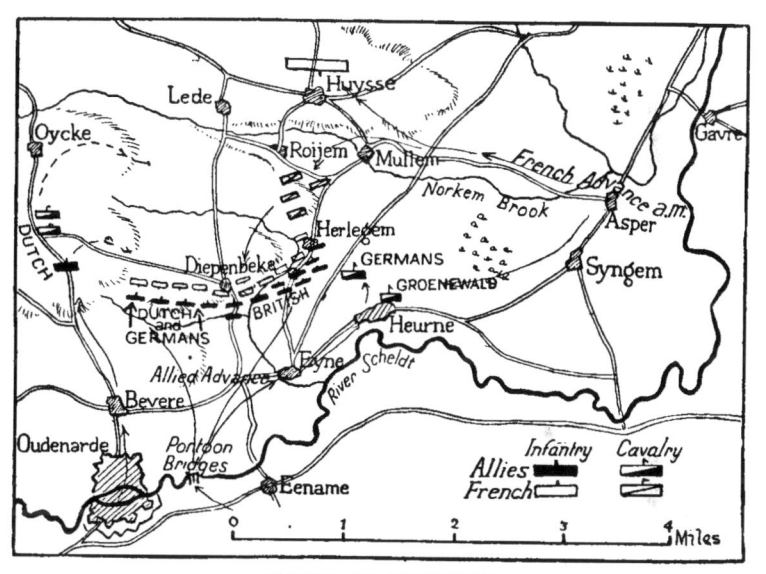

BATTLE OF OUDENARDE

On the morning of 11th July he began the passage of
the Scheldt, and the French, believing that they had
found a strong position, were willing to give battle on
a line behind the Norken stream, which flowed roughly
parallel to the main river. But by four o'clock in the
afternoon the Allies were not yet in order of battle, so
the Duke of Burgundy, who was Vendôme's superior,
pushed his right and centre across the Norken, where
Cadogan's advanced troops held the village of Groenewald.

The action began with the attack on Groenewald,

1708 where Cadogan was presently reinforced by twenty battalions under John, Duke of Argyll. Marlborough kept sending up reserves, with the result that the battle was extended farther to the left, and became a series of separate duels in a much-enclosed ground. Eugene, with eighteen battalions, now took charge of the right, and the see-saw engagement continued, in which at one moment the French front line was pierced and at the next the Allies were repulsed by the charge of the Maison du Roi. Meanwhile Marlborough on the left, with the Dutch and Hanoverian infantry, was pressing slowly on, till Overkirk, with twenty Dutch and Danish battalions, managed to outflank the French right and roll it up. The French left, beyond the Norken, now moved forward under Vendôme's personal leadership, but it was too late. By nine o'clock the battle was won, and in the darkness the Allies sounded the "Cease fire," while the French streamed off towards Ghent. The Twenty-First was among the troops employed to watch the enemy left, and had little more than a musketry duel.

Oudenarde was one of the most curious battles ever fought, and of all Marlborough's triumphs it was the one in which he took the greatest risks. There was no order of battle. His men were very weary, for they had covered fifty miles over bad roads in sixty hours. He crossed the Scheldt in the face of the enemy, who might have defeated him in detail. He gambled upon the quarrels and incompetence of the French commanders and his own superb judgment on a battlefield. The enemy lost 9,000 prisoners and 6,000 killed and wounded; the Allies lost some 3,000, of which the British share was only a little over 200. Though an impromptu battle, it came very near being a decisive victory, and Marlborough always declared that another hour of daylight would have enabled him to end the war.

By 15th July the Allied army was encamped inside the French frontier along the Lys, between Menin and Comines. But the position was not comfortable, for

SIEGE OF LILLE

the French still held Bruges and Ghent, and so could 1708
close the Scheldt and the Lys to Allied supplies. Marlborough proposed to march straight into France, but even Eugene condemned the plan as too bold, unless the great fortress of Lille were first captured. Marlborough began by getting his siege train safely over the seventy-four miles from Brussels without the loss of a wagon, though both Vendôme and Berwick lay within striking distance. These two commanders had between them 94,000 men. Marlborough and Eugene, with only 84,000 men, had to hold them at bay, and at the same time take a city, a masterpiece of Vauban's skill in fortification, defended by a garrison of 15,000 under old Marshal Boufflers, one of the most gallant and skilled of French generals. Yet the bold course succeeded. When the road from Brussels was barred, convoys arrived safely from Ostend. Eugene directed the siege. The Twenty-First [1] was in the attack on the approaches, and in the assault on the counterscarp it had 13 men killed, and 3 officers, 4 sergeants, and 66 rank and file wounded. But the end came on 9th December, when Boufflers marched out with the honours of war, 5,000 of the garrison having perished, and 14,000 of the attackers. Before the close of the year Ghent and Bruges had been taken, the Scheldt and Lys re-opened, and France reduced by famine and defeat to the last desperation. Louis attempted to make peace; and peace there would have been had Marlborough had the chief voice, for he saw that the Allies had won all for which they had embarked on the strife. But he was overruled from home; impossible conditions were laid down, and the war continued.

[1] The other British battalions engaged were the 16th, 18th, 23rd, and 24th. There is a letter extant from a subaltern of the Twenty-First, one William Nodding, which says: " These outworks are so large and numerous that whatever way we make our approaches, notwithstanding of all our boyous, blinds, and angles, we are always flanked and our men very often kild both with small and cannon shot at the very bottom of the trench. The enemy having a very strong garrison and defends vigorously hitherto have disputed inch by inch." Quoted by Atkinson, *op. cit.*, pages 355, 356.

III

1709 France was now pinned down to the defensive, a despairing effort to prevent the invasion of her soil and a march upon her capital. Villars was given the command of all the troops she could gather, and his first step was to fortify the famous lines from the Lys to the Scarpe at Douai, known as the lines of La Bassée. He held three fortified towns east of these lines—Ypres, Tournai, and Mons; but the Allied possession of Lille, which gave them a salient between Ypres and Tournai, made his hold on these two latter precarious. It is probable that Marlborough's first plan was for a direct assault upon the La Bassée lines, but their careful reconnoitring by Cadogan convinced him that they would not easily be pierced. So on June 26, 1709, he marched suddenly on Tournai, the garrison of which had been depleted by Villars for the defence of his lines. The trenches were opened on 7th July, and in three weeks the city surrendered. The citadel did not capitulate till 3rd September, after five weeks of underground fighting, which Mr. Fortescue has called "the most desperate enterprise yet undertaken by the Allied troops."

But Tournai was not Marlborough's main objective. Before the citadel had fallen, he had made his plans and set part of his army in motion. He would invest Mons, and with his main force break through on the extreme right of the French position, and march into France by the ancient gate of the Sambre. Lord Orkney, with the grenadiers of the army and twenty squadrons of horse, marched east on 31st August to St. Ghislain on the Haine. Three days later Cadogan and the Prince of Hessen-Cassel followed. By 6th September the Allied army had invested Mons and was south of the river Haine. The French now came up, and lay to the south-west, across the gap called the Trouée d'Aulmois in the great woods which there muffled the countryside.

THE EVE OF MALPLAQUET

This was on 9th September, and Marlborough 1709 would fain have attacked at once, for he knew of old the prowess of the enemy with the spade. But his Council of War decided otherwise—to wait for the troops from Tournai, and to send a detachment to capture St. Ghislain. The result was a delay of two days, which Villars turned to excellent account. His position lay across the Trouée, with the wood of Sars on his left and the wood of Lanières on his right. In the woods he strengthened the tangled covert with abatis; across the two thousand yards of the gap he built a triple line of entrenchments for one-third of the way and a line of nine redans for the rest. Behind this was another line of earthworks, and defences were erected also in the village of Malplaquet in the rear. It was a strong position, having for its only defects the small wood of Tiry farther up the gap (which might mask the Allies' attack, though it would also split up a general advance), and the fact that the wood of Sars had a long tongue stretching to the north-west which would conceal any operations against the French extreme left. The two opposing forces were approximately equal. Old Boufflers, who arrived to offer his services, put heart into all who saw " his masterful, prominent face, large, direct, humorous in expression, full of command," [1] and to him was entrusted the direction of the French right.

The morning of Wednesday, 11th September, broke in heavy mist, and after prayers had been read at three o'clock the Allied guns moved into position. Marlborough's dispositions were quaint, consisting as they did of two powerful wings and practically no centre. On the extreme right seventeen battalions and six squadrons under General Withers were sent round the wood of Sars to turn the extreme French left. Against the north face of the wood of Sars General Schulemberg had forty battalions, and against the eastern face Count Lottum took twenty-eight battalions. In the centre, Orkney with fifteen British

[1] The phrase is Mr. Belloc's, *Malplaquet*, page 58.

1709 battalions waited to advance against the entrenchments when Schulemberg and Lottum should have cleared the wood on his right. Thirty-one battalions—mainly Dutch, but containing certain Highland regiments in the Dutch service—were directed under the Prince of Orange against the wood of Lanières. The cavalry was in the rear of the foot. Eugene was in command of the forces of Schulemberg and Withers and the supporting horse, Marlborough of the rest.

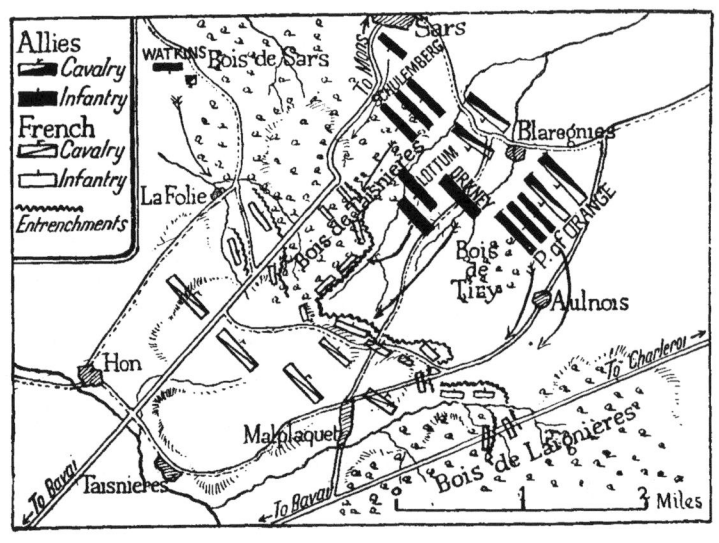

BATTLE OF MALPLAQUET

The French right at Lanières was under d'Artagnan, and included the Bourbonnois and Navarre regiments and the Guards; in the centre was the Irish brigade of Lee and O'Brien, and the Bavarians; the left, in the wood of Sars, included the Picardie and Champagne regiments. Of the cavalry, the Maison du Roi was behind Lanières, the Carabiniers behind Sars, and the Gens d'Armes held the centre.

At half-past seven the mist lifted, and the first guns spoke. Marlborough's plan was to force the wood of Sars as early as possible, while Orange threatened

MALPLAQUET

Lanières. Once Sars were cleared, the left of the French in the gap could be turned, and Orkney would deal with the centre. It was an admirable plan, but he had underrated the strength of the defences in the woods. Both Schulemberg and Lottum found their progress slow and very costly, and Picardie, the first regiment of the French line, sustained its ancient fame. Orkney was obliged to detach two British battalions [1] to Lottum's aid, and Marlborough himself had to take command of the supporting horse. Meantime Orange was in graver straits. He chose to convert what had been meant as a demonstration into a real attack. The Highlanders of the Scots Brigade, under Hepburn and Tullibardine, went to their death among the scrub of Lanières, and Orange led his own Blue Guards with fruitless gallantry against the earthworks which were manned by the Regiment Navarre. Soon the Dutch had lost 6,000 men, and had effected nothing. By noon the Allied right had at last cleared Sars, but Lanières was still intact.

The Duke accordingly revised his plan. He ordered Orkney, reinforced by Dutch drafts from the Allied left, to advance in the centre against the redans and the entrenchments. The French centre had been weakened by the detachment of the Irish brigade to the wood of Sars, where the culminating point of the battle had now been reached. Withers had arrived, and his 18th Regiment (the Royal Irish) met and drove back the French Royal Regiment of Ireland. It was a moment of desperate crisis. Eugene was wounded in the head, Villars in the leg, but neither gallant man would leave the field. Both sides were so exhausted that the Allies, as they emerged from the trees, could scarcely re-form. But Orkney's attack turned the tide. He forced the Bavarians from the earthworks and redans, while Orange on his left renewed his assault. The French infantry centre gave, but behind it stood the unbroken squadrons of the French horse. Then began a wild spell of charge and counter-charge, a " *mêlée* of

---

[1] The 1st Guards and the Royal Scots.

sabres," which resulted, so far as the cavalry was concerned, in something like a drawn battle. But the French front had been driven from its position, and at three o'clock Boufflers and Villars drew off, leaving the Allies in possession of the field.

So ended Malplaquet—a victory, but an indecisive victory, and one of the costliest in the story of war. That woodland fighting, where neither side gave quarter, carried men beyond the limits of mortal endurance. The French lost some 12,000 men, the Allies not less than 20,000 killed and wounded, to which losses the Dutch, out of thirty battalions, contributed 8,000, and the British, out of twenty battalions, 1,900. I cannot discover in what part of the field the Twenty-First fought, but I hazard the conjecture that it was with Orkney, for the reports speak of a fight among earthworks, and Withers's detachment can have had little of that. It lost of officers Captains Monroe, Wemyss, and Farley killed, and Captains Montressor and Lowther wounded. Its colonel, de Lalo, fell with a bullet through his head while leading a brigade. "The action will remain throughout history a standing example of the pitch of excellence to which those highly-trained professional armies of the eighteenth century with their savage discipline, their aristocratic command, their close formations, and their extraordinary reliance upon human daring, could arrive."[1]

Marlborough returned to the siege of Mons, in which the Twenty-First played a part, and received the surrender of the town on 9th October. But the star of the great Duke was now declining. In the campaign of 1710 he took Douai, where the Twenty-First was employed in storming the outworks, and lost heavily in men. The regiment then passed to the siege of Béthune, which capitulated on 28th August, and it was present at the later surrenders of Aire and St. Venant.

---

[1] The best description is in Parker's *Memoirs* (1746). See also Belloc, *Malplaquet*, page 90. In 1914 the 1st Royal Scots Fusiliers, on their way to Mons, crossed the field of Malplaquet, where their colonel halted them and reminded them of the gallant deeds of the regiment in 1709.

THE FALL OF MARLBOROUGH

After Malplaquet, Lord Mordaunt had returned to its colonelcy, but he died of smallpox in April 1710. His successor was Thomas Meredith,[1] who had fought under William III., and received a troop in the 2nd Dragoon Guards. He had raised and commanded the 37th Foot, and had been at Blenheim as adjutant-general to Marlborough. Thereafter his rise was rapid, for he was brigadier-general in 1704, major-general in 1706, and lieutenant-general in 1709. He held the colonelcy for only nine months, when he was succeeded by Charles Boyle, Earl of Orrery, who had commanded with great credit a brigade at Malplaquet, and who had a scholarly and a literary taste then rare in the profession of arms. More important for the regiment than the colonel was the lieutenant-colonel; but beyond the fact that at this time he was a certain William Murray we know nothing.

The winter of 1710 was spent by the regiment at Dendermonde, and in the summer of 1711 it took part in that remarkable performance of Marlborough, the most miraculous, perhaps, of all, when he succeeded in outwitting Villars, and planting himself beyond the Scheldt between the French General and France, and within easy reach of Arras and Cambrai. That tale is not to be told here, but it deserves to be studied as one of the most delectable in military history. The Twenty-First was at the capture of Bouchain on 13th September, where the men fought for days up to their waists in water, as did their successors two hundred years later. With that feat the career of Marlborough came to an end. His enemies were too much for him, and on the last day of the year he was dismissed from all his posts. The Duke of Ormonde succeeded him; but the Duke of Ormonde was there merely as an instrument of the British Ministry to make peace. In July 1712 he was ordered to suspend hostilities and

1710–12

---

[1] Meredith would seem to have received the colonelcy as a sop to Marlborough, whose intimate friend he was, and who had wished him to have Essex's Dragoons. *Cf.* Coxe's *Life*, III., page 21, and Atkinson, *op. cit.*, page 415, *n.*

1712-14 withdraw his troops from Eugene, and at Le Cateau, with bitter shame, the British left their allies—Le Cateau, which was destined to be on a later day the shrine of nobler memories. In the April of next year came the Peace of Utrecht, which formally ended the war by sacrificing almost every object for which the war had been fought. History has long ago recorded its opinion of those in high places who obstructed peace when it could have been made with honour, and in the end closed the war on terms which were as disgraceful as they were impolitic. But the blunders and crimes of others cannot lessen the fame of the greatest of English captains, and the victories of " Corporal John " are among the brightest on the battle-roll of the Twenty-First. The regiment continued during 1713 in Flanders, and some time about that date became a royal regiment, and was known as the Royal North British Fusiliers, a name which it was to bear until the year 1877. On August 23, 1714, after the accession of George I., it landed at Gravesend, having been absent from the shores of Britain for a dozen years.

CHAPTER IV

SHERIFFMUIR, DETTINGEN, AND FONTENOY

The influence of Marlborough—The regiment in Scotland—The rebellion of 1715—Sheriffmuir—The condition of the soldier—Sir Andrew Agnew of Lochnaw—Dettingen—Fontenoy.

THE Peace of Utrecht was followed by the usual thriftless reductions in the British army; 33,000 of all ranks were discharged as soon as the treaty was signed, and by 1714 the British establishment, including colonial garrisons, had sunk below 30,000 men. The Twenty-First, when in that year it returned to Scotland, had no depot, and its first endeavour was to beat up recruits. It had maintained its strength on the Continent because of the system of dividing the year into a campaigning season and winter quarters: during the latter a certain number of officers were sent home to enlist men to fill the gaps. The methods of enlistment were still the old ones—criminals and debtors from the gaols, and bounties for volunteers. A short service system of three years was tried after Almanza; but it worked badly, and by 1711 the recruiting problem had become desperate. Marlborough had done much for the soldiers by seeing that the subsistence money was regularly paid, by cutting down irregular deductions, and by reforming the whole business of clothing; but both men and officers still suffered from flagrant abuses. The men, when they returned from campaigning, found miserable provision in the garrison quarters at home, and the officers were blackmailed by civilian authorities and regimental agents, and put to

1714

heavy personal expenses in the raising of recruits. There was much jobbery in the granting of commissions, children of the tenderest years being sometimes made officers in famous regiments, and steadily advanced in rank while still in the nursery. There is a tale of a visitor in a Scots house asking what the noise upstairs signified, and being told that " it was the Major greetin' ower his parritch." One infant of twelve actually took the field in Flanders, and behaved well till he spoiled his career by killing his man in a duel at the age of sixteen.[1]

In other respects the Twenty-First which came home in 1714 was not greatly different from the regiment which had left in 1702. The pike had been abolished, except for officers, and the musket and socket-bayonet were universal. The drill was much the same as it had been under Gustavus Adolphus, and the savage discipline, which Marlborough had modified in the field, was still employed in its rigid form in Britain. One advantage, however, had been gained. Marlborough had made his personality felt among the troops he led, and had turned some of the roughest material on earth into sober and self-respecting men. Any regiment that fought under him had acquired a standard of soldierly conduct, and had learned the moral value of serving one who could be both trusted and loved. From his wars we may date the great regimental traditions of the British army, and the Twenty-First, as part of his *corps d'élite*, must have had its share of this ennobling influence. One link with " Corporal John " still remains. In connection with his victories the White Horse of Hanover was granted to certain regiments, to be worn on the " drum carriage," the broad shoulder belt to which the side drum was attached. In time the drum carriage was narrowed and the badge was dropped; but the drum-major of the Royal Scots Fusiliers wears the old broad belt and carries the White Horse to this day.

The Twenty-First returned to a land distracted by

[1] Cited by Mr. Fortescue, I., page 579.

THE RISING IN BRAEMAR

Jacobitism and poverty, and its first task was to take 1715 the field against its own countrymen, led by the son of its first colonel. Few enterprises have been more grossly mismanaged than the " 'Fifteen." There were the usual hopes of aid from Charles XII. of Sweden, of money and troops from France, and of widespread agitation in England; but the nemesis which dogged the path of Jacobitism was sleepless, and the undertaking began in a muddle. The Duke of Berwick, natural brother of the Old Pretender and the nephew of Marlborough, had persuaded James that his honour demanded instant action. In July 1715 James received tidings from Ormonde which seemed to show that the moment was opportune, so, without consulting Berwick or Bolingbroke, he sent a message to Mar in London, fixing 10th August for the rising. Presently he had bad news from Mar and Ormonde, and immediately took steps to countermand his first order. But one Allan Cameron, the bearer of the message, was delayed, and Mar, in spite of his fuller knowledge of the situation, decided to act upon James's first hasty message. He had been Secretary for Scotland, and had been at a levée of King George on 1st August. On 26th August he held a great hunting in Braemar, to which all the Jacobite nobles came, and on 6th September he set up the standard. Berwick, who was a fine soldier, was prevented from taking the command by his duties as Marshal of France, and Mar himself was not only a highly incompetent general, but was opposed by the wisest and ablest of living Scotsmen, John, Duke of Argyll and Greenwich, whom we have already met at Oudenarde and Malplaquet.

The details of the campaign are dreary reading. At the start Mar may have had 12,000 men, such an army as Montrose or Dundee never commanded; but after his first recklessness he was incapable of swift action, and dallied at Perth waiting on James and reinforcements. James, hopelessly in the dark as to what was happening, did not appear, and the only assistance came from the north of England, where a small knot of Jacobite gentlemen raised the standard—a mistake, beyond doubt, for it broadened the area of operations beyond what was reasonable for so small a force. Mar, instead of concentrating against Argyll, sent an expedition under Mackintosh of Borlum across the Forth, which seized Leith, ignominiously failed to take Edinburgh, and then marched south to join Forster and Kenmure. The rising now divided itself into a Scottish and an English campaign. Wintoun, Nairne, Mackintosh, and Kenmure were prevailed upon by the Northumbrian Jacobites, Widrington, Forster, and Derwentwater, to cross the Border and attempt to rouse the north of England. It was a fatal blunder, against the wish of the Highlanders and of such men as Wintoun, and it involved the leadership of the incompetent Forster. With bagpipes skirling and drums beating, surely the oddest mixture of Highland and Lowland ever seen, they traversed the northern counties. Marlborough, it is said, was consulted by the English Ministry, and placing his finger at Preston on the map, he said, " You will take them there." He was not mistaken, for Preston proved to Forster, as long before it had proved to Hamilton, the Marathon of the Scottish invasion. The invaders surrendered on 13th November, Derwentwater and Kenmure went to the scaffold, and the ill-timed venture came to a dismal end.

So much for the south. In the north things went no better. Mar lay idly in the Scottish midlands, where he received the unexpected support of Breadalbane, that cynical old gentleman of eighty who had had mysterious dealings with the Highlanders before the Massacre of Glencoe. He still waited for imaginary reinforcements from the north and west, while his force grew thin from desertions, and the scandalous Simon Fraser of Lovat took his clan over to King George and captured Inverness. Mar's command was ill-provided, heterogeneous to the last degree, and ill-led. " The army had little powder, few flints, and no powder-horns, though there were tinkers and gipsies enough

MAR'S ARMY

in the host, whose business was the making of such 1715
utensils. . . . The Highlanders continued to keep their
powder loose in their pockets, where it was ruined if
the weather was wet; while, if a warrior thoughtlessly
put his lighted pipe in his pocket, the results were
damaging and instantaneous. . . . Mar seems to have
regarded powder as a rare product of the soil in certain
favoured regions, not as a commodity which could be
made at Perth or Aberdeen by arts known to men." [1]
At last, on 8th November, Mar set out from Perth at

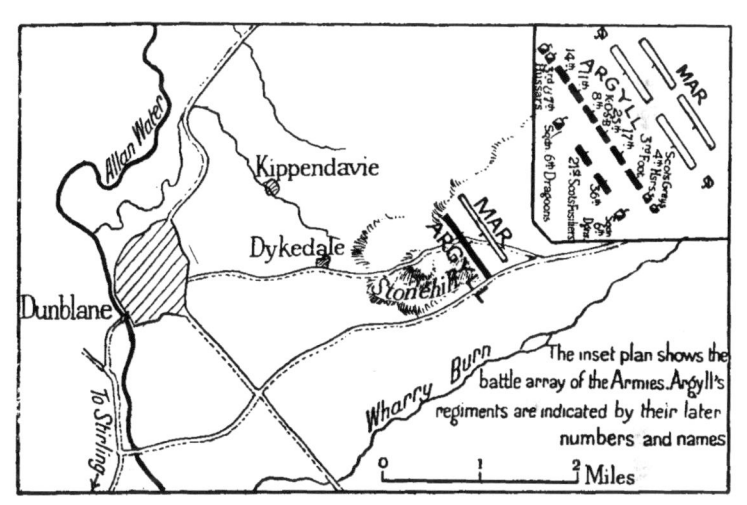

BATTLE OF SHERIFFMUIR

the head of his forces, accompanied by six brass and
five iron cannons, the value of which could only have
been moral, for there was no ammunition. His aim
was the crossing of the Forth on the way to England,
and at Stirling lay Argyll. On the 9th he was at
Auchterarder, where he delayed for two days; on the
12th the main body encamped at Ardoch, while the
Gordons went ahead to seize Dunblane. The total
Jacobite strength was some 6,000 or 7,000 foot, and
seven squadrons of horse.

That day Argyll marched out from Stirling with

[1] Andrew Lang, *History of Scotland*, IV., Chap. IX

2,500 foot and 1,000 cavalry. That night he lay with his left at Dunblane, and his right under the southern slopes of the Sheriffmuir ridge, which lies north of the Wharry burn. Mar spent the night at Kinbuck, in a cramped hollow with the river Allan below it, a dangerous position for 7,000 men. At dawn on Sunday, 13th November, he formed his army in two lines on the moor east of Kinbuck, and then did nothing till eleven a.m., when he held a council of war, at which it was agreed to attack forthwith. Lord Marischal's horse and the regiment of Macdonald of Sleat were sent on to seize the hill where Argyll's cavalry had been seen, and the rest of the army advanced in four columns, echeloned from the right. The dispositions were: on the right, the horse of Huntly and Linlithgow and 2,000 of the western clansmen under Gordon of Achintoul; then the Gordon clan; then the regiments of Seaforth, Huntly, Panmure, Tullibardine,[1] Strathallan, Drummond of Logiealmond, and Robertson of Struan; and on the left, the Perthshire, Angus, and Fife horse. It was bitter frosty weather, and Argyll realized that the bogs he had looked to for protection would now be hard as granite; so he was compelled in a hurry to change ground, a movement which was not complete before the attack began. He had his men in two lines: in the front line from left to right, the 3rd Hussars (two squadrons), the 7th Hussars (two squadrons), the 14th, 11th, 8th, 23rd, 25th, 17th, and 3rd Foot, the 4th Hussars (two squadrons), and the Scots Greys (two squadrons); in the second line, the 6th Dragoons (one squadron), the Twenty-First, the 36th Foot, and another squadron of the 6th Dragoons.

The battle began with the Jacobite army still in some confusion after its march. Its right wing was at once successful. The Western Highlanders, with Glengarry at their head, caught Argyll's left while it was struggling up the hill, still ragged in formation with infantry preceding cavalry, and, charging with the

[1] The successor of the Marquis whom we met in Flanders, and who fell at Malplaquet.

broadsword, drove it back in confusion. The troops that suffered most were the 8th, 11th, and the Twenty-First. But this victory on Mar's right was balanced by the disaster of his left, where the Greys had outflanked and broken their opponents and driven them across the Allan. Rob Roy, who commanded the MacGregors and Macphersons in reserve, might have turned the tide of battle, but that wily outlaw was determined to fight only on the winning side, and he was still not clear which that was. His judgment was right, for the issue was as yet open : the situation was very like that at Marston Moor; but Mar was no Cromwell, and "Red John of the Battles" had no supports. Mar did nothing; and well might Gordon of Glenbucket cry, "Oh, for one hour of Dundee!" Argyll was allowed to draw off in good order towards Dunblane when the dusk gathered, and though Mar remained in possession of the field, he had lost his solitary chance, and the fate of the rising was decreed. The Jacobite casualties were apparently small—some 150 killed and wounded, among the dead being the young Lord Strathmore and the Captain of Clanranald. Argyll lost 477 officers and men, including Lord Forfar, and of these the Twenty-First contributed one captain, two lieutenants, three sergeants, and eighty-five rank-and-file killed, and one captain, one sergeant, and twenty-five rank-and-file wounded—about one-fourth of the whole. In this preposterous moorland fight they paid almost as high a toll as in some of their great Flanders battles.[1]

The Twenty-First was employed in the early months of 1716 in stamping out the embers of the rebellion, and then settled down to a period of home service which was to continue for twenty-five years. It was a quarter of a century, so far as the British army was concerned, of inglorious discomfort. Every year the

[1] A good account of the "'Fifteen" will be found in Lang's *History of Scotland*, IV., Chaps. VIII.–X. By far the best narrative of Sheriffmuir is that of the Duchess of Atholl, *Military History of Perthshire*, pages 274–288, in which will be found a careful examination of contemporary authorities.

Jacobites in the House of Commons brought forward a motion for the reduction of the forces, and " No Standing Army " became the cry of each short-sighted Opposition. The establishment was reduced far below the level of safety, and periodically and hastily enlarged under some threat of foreign war. Except in one or two of the larger towns, there were no barracks capable of accommodating so much as a battalion, and regiments were split up into small detachments, which were billeted among the ale-houses. This was bad for discipline : it led to troops being mixed up with politics, for it was not till 1735 that the Mutiny Act provided for the withdrawal of all soldiers during an election at least two miles from the polling-station ; and it induced perpetual friction between the military and civilian authorities. Inn-keepers detested the billeting imposition, town councils and magistrates were on the look-out to magnify every cause of offence, and the popular reputation of the soldier sank so low that Doctor Johnson could quite naturally, in his talk, bracket Life Guardsmen along with scoundrels and assafœtida as inflictions which a landlord might have patiently to put up with in his hostelry. Moreover, the confusion in the higher administration and the power of the Secretary-at-War to interfere with the authority of commanding officers made the army a plaything of party politics and weakened all proper sense of subordination. The class attracted to the ranks was apt to be dissolute and discontented even if not actually criminal, and the barbarous penalties for desertion and indiscipline, such as picketing,[1] were made a show for the public, and did not increase the reputation of the soldier. The experiment of short service enlistment was abandoned, apparently, Mr. Fortescue thinks, because it was feared that the potential Jacobite forces might be strengthened if men were passed quickly through the ranks of the British army, and the country returned to the old bad plan

[1] It consisted in hanging a man up by one wrist, with no rest for his bare feet except a pointed stake.

SERVICE IN SCOTLAND

of fraudulent bounties and gaol-deliveries. The marvel is that under such a system a disciplined body of men could exist at all in times of peace, and that when war came it so nobly proved its quality; for, let it not be forgotten, the wonderful fighting machine which Marlborough had created was comprehensively and systematically destroyed by his successors.

We are to picture the Twenty-First, between the years 1716 and 1727, as quartered in small detachments up and down the Scottish Lowlands; for, except in Edinburgh, there were no barracks capable of holding even half a battalion. We can see the half-companies billeted in the ale-houses, squabbling with provosts and town-clerks; or furnishing guards to protect the unpopular preventive officers in their watch upon the ways of smugglers; or, when the regiment was united for a short season, route-marching on the muddy Lothian roads, with the grenadiers in their Pope's hats bringing up the rear—such a sight as David Balfour saw on his way to the House of Shaws. In the Scotland of that time, bitterly poor, jealous of England and of all things that pertained to the Government in London, and honeycombed with Jacobitism, it cannot have been a comfortable existence either for officers or men. The old duty of policing the Highlands had gone,[1] for that was now done, first by the Independent Companies who were disbanded in 1717, and after 1725 by General Wade, the road-maker, who raised four companies, wearing the tartan, that were the formal beginnings of the famous Black Watch. In 1716 Lord Orrery was displaced in the colonelcy of the regiment by Lieutenant-General George Macartney, who in 1703 had commanded a newly-raised regiment of foot,[2] which was disbanded

---

[1] It is possible that drafts from the Twenty-First were at this time occasionally used for the nearer Highland garrisons. Inversnaid may have been such a case, for the baptismal register of the parish of Buchanan records that on December 8, 1723, the son was baptized of "Thomas Somervell . . . souldier in the Regiment of Phusioneers." Thomas, on the other hand, may have been a Buchanan native who had left his wife at home.

[2] To this regiment the Earl of Mar's Regiment of the second creation (1702-18) had contributed one hundred men. (Mar and Kellie Papers, pages 23-25).

at the Peace of Utrecht, and had fought both in Flanders and Spain, being taken prisoner at the battle of Almanza. In 1727 Macartney changed to the 9th Horse (now the 6th Dragoon Guards), and was succeeded by Sir James Wood, an old soldier of the Dutch service, who had accompanied the Prince of Orange to England, and had had a brigade in Marlborough's wars. In 1718 William Murray was succeeded as lieutenant-colonel by Edward Wolfe, of an Irish family, who had been captain in Temple's Foot, had served as brigade major with Marlborough, and had been with Wade after the " 'Fifteen." He was to see much service later, and to die as a lieutenant-general at seventy-five. But his chief interest to posterity is that in 1727, in a Kentish manor-house, there was born to him the plain red-haired son who was to win immortal fame by the taking of Quebec.[1] The Twenty-First had a new lieutenant-colonel in 1721, when Wolfe was followed by John, Lord Lesly, who next year succeeded his father as Earl of Rothes.[2] Lesly, who began his military career in the cavalry, became colonel of the 25th (King's Own Scottish Borderers) in 1732 (when one Francis Fleming took his place with the Twenty-First), and had a long and distinguished record of service, being colonel in turn of the Scots Greys and the 3rd Guards, and ending as a lieutenant-general and a Knight of the Thistle.

In 1727 there was an alarm of a war with Spain. Walpole increased the British establishment by 8,000 men, and the Twenty-First was held in readiness to embark for Holland. The danger passed, and in the course of the following year the regiment was placed on the Irish establishment. In 1729 it proceeded to Ireland, and remained there till the autumn of 1739. Of its life in Ireland we know nothing, except that it must have been more comfortable than in Scotland, for

---

[1] Dalton (*English Army Lists*, Vol. VI.) makes Edward Wolfe lieutenant-colonel of the 3rd Guards in 1717 (his commission was countersigned by Joseph Addison), and I conclude that he transferred next year to the Twenty-First.
[2] Balfour Paul's *The Scots Peerage*, VII., page 305.

SIR ANDREW AGNEW
(From a portrait in the possession of Sir Andrew Agnew, Bart., at Lochnaw Castle)

SIR ANDREW AGNEW

barracks had been built there owing to the scarcity of inns and ale-houses! Its colonel, Sir James Wood, died in 1738, and was succeeded by John Campbell of Mamore,[1] who had been aide-de-camp to the Duke of Argyll at Sheriffmuir, and became himself fourth Duke of Argyll in 1761. He came to the regiment from the colonelcy of the 39th (1st Battalion Dorsets), and remained with it for fourteen years, till he became colonel of the Scots Greys. He had a brigade at Dettingen and in the " 'Forty-five," and did not close his long life till 1770. By those whom military history does not interest he may be remembered as the husband of the beautiful and short-lived Miss Bellenden, Gay's " smiling Mary, soft and fair as dawn," whom Horace Walpole reported as " so agreeable that I never heard her mentioned afterwards by one of her contemporaries, who did not prefer her as the most perfect creature they ever knew."

Meantime there was advancing in the regiment one who was destined to be perhaps the best remembered and the best loved figure in its history—Sir Andrew Agnew of Lochnaw, the twelfth and last of the hereditary Sheriffs of Galloway, who was born in 1687, and went to Flanders as a volunteer with the Scots Greys, receiving a cornet's commission in Lord John Hay's troop in May 1705. He won his spurs at Ramillies, and was in the thick of the Greys' charge at Malplaquet. Even in his early twenties he was something of a " character," full of a dry and whimsical humour expressed in the broadest of broad Scots, and of an imperturbability which no crisis could shake. Once when in command of a burial party, a perplexed orderly asked what he was to do with " a heap of folk yonder, that say they are juist wounded." " Bury them a' at once," said Agnew, " for if ye tak their ain word for it they'll no be deid for a hundred years." The man started off to carry out the order, which, it is said, was only rescinded just in time. In 1709 he became a captain in Strathnaver's Regiment, and in 1715

[1] Balfour Paul's *The Scots Peerage*, I., page 383, etc.

exchanged to the Twenty-First, which was his home regiment, for it had long acquired a territorial association with the south-west district of Scotland. He succeeded his father, the fourth baronet, in 1735, and during his regiment's service in Ireland we hear of him returning often on leave to Lochnaw, and engaging vigorously in farming, in which he had more good-will than science. "Sir Andrew was a graund warrior," said an old tenant, "but he didna ken the lee-side o' a rick." In 1738 he attained his majority, and when the regiment returned from Ireland in 1739 he realized his ambition at last, and on November 2, 1739, received the lieutenant-colonelcy of the Twenty-First. He was then fifty-two years old, an enthusiast in his profession, who had seen no fighting since Malplaquet. The next decade was to give him an outlet for thirty years of suppressed military vigour.[1]

The Twenty-First landed at Liverpool in 1739, and marched to Andover in Hampshire. During 1740 it was stationed at various places in the south of England, and during 1741 it was part of the concentration of foot and horse on Lexdon Heath, held in readiness for foreign service. The long era of peace was over, and the war with Spain, caused by the legend of Jenkins's ear, was moving towards the tragic failure at Cartagena, where yellow fever immobilized the contending forces. The Twenty-First was fortunate enough to escape the fate of the Royal Scots, and to be left out of that deadly expedition. But next year came its call to action. The War of the Austrian Succession had begun. France was leagued with Bavaria to defeat the claims of Maria Theresa, and Frederick of Prussia had begun that fishing in troubled waters which was to earn him the title of "The Great." George II., anxious for the safety of Hanover, brought Britain into the conflict. Walpole fell from power, and Carteret induced Parliament to send 16,000 troops

---

[1] Sir Andrew's great-great-grandsons, Major Charles Agnew and Lieut.-Colonel Quentin Agnew, D.S.O., M.V.O., Royal Bodyguard, served in the Royal Scots Fusiliers during the period 1879–99.

to Flanders. John, Earl of Stair, was chosen as the commander, by far the ablest of British soldiers then alive, and perhaps the greatest of the pupils of Marlborough.

His first duties were diplomatic, for the position was sufficiently delicate. Britain was still officially at peace with France, and her troops were supposed to be "auxiliaries" on the side of the Austrian queen, as the French were "auxiliaries" on the side of Bavaria. The French and British ambassadors still consorted as if their nations were in amity. Stair had to induce the Dutch, sunk in lethargy and torn with faction, to take an active part in the coming campaign, and to permit the occupation of Nieuport and Ostend as British bases. Only the success of Frederick at Chotusitz, and the presence of a French army in Westphalia, persuaded Holland to grant the latter concession, but it was clear that no vigorous action could be expected from her. Stair knew that Frederick was the dangerous foe, and believed that he could be detached from the French side, and presently Frederick's alliance was purchased at the cost of Silesia. The old Field-Marshal now saw his game clear before him. With Frederick out of the way, the full strength of Austria could be turned on the French in Bohemia; a threat to the French frontier would bring back Maillebois from Westphalia, and allow the British and the Hanoverians to join hands; that done, with 14,000 Austrians to help, an attack could be made on Dunkirk, and the road opened for a march on Paris.

It was a plan worthy of Marlborough, but Stair was bolder and more far-sighted than the King his master. George suddenly remembered that he was not officially at war with France, and decided to go slowly. He submitted Stair's plan to Wade, who also took alarm. The orders for the Hanoverians to march were unaccountably delayed, and the campaigning season of 1742 passed with nothing done. But Stair did not relax his efforts. The winter was bitter, the hard ground made movement possible, the floods on which

France relied to defend her frontier were frozen, and he prepared to attack the northern fortresses. This time the Austrians objected, for their one object was to get the British into Germany and compel some of the minor German princes to join the Empress's side. Moreover, George was giving his own orders to the Hanoverians, and not informing his Field-Marshal. But at last it was possible to move, and in February 1743 the army began to march eastward. The Twenty-First had been at Ghent in the last months of 1742; in January of the new year it was at Bruges, and in March at Aix-la-Chapelle. It was part of the brigade of John Campbell of Mamore, who was also its colonel.

Stair, now forced to change his plans, proposed to march to the Danube and take the French there in rear. But George, who had not the slightest knowledge of the military art, demurred, and ordered the army to occupy the heights at the junction of the Rhine and the Main—apparently to help his nominee for the Electorate of Mainz, which was then vacant. In May the Allies lay facing south from the Rhine to Aschaffenburg, while Noailles with 70,000 French lay on the upper Rhine near Spires, to keep open the communications with Broglie and Bavaria. Stair prepared to cross the Main, and so threaten Noailles that he could not help Broglie, after which he would cross the Rhine and force the French back into Alsace, leaving the Lorraine and Netherlands frontiers undefended. On 3rd June he crossed the Main. Noailles advanced to meet him, but when he saw his strong position, did not venture to attack. George, from Hanover, sent furious orders to recross the river, and Stair was obliged to comply.

On 19th June George arrived in camp, to the consternation of all, and took over the command. Supplies had become a serious problem, for the French had not been idle, and on 26th June it was decided to retreat to Hanau. The retirement must be by the narrow strip of ground between the wooded Spessart hills and the Main, and Noailles had batteries waiting on the other side of the river to harass the Allied march. Moreover, he sent Count Grammont with 28,000 men to cross farther down and block the road at the village of Dettingen, where was a small boggy glen crossed by a single bridge. Further, he had troops on the Allied rear at Aschaffenburg to cut off the Allied retreat upstream. He had his enemies nearly entrapped, owing to the ineptitude of the royal command.

At four o'clock in the morning of 27th June the Allies were on the move, with the British cavalry in the van, and a strong rear-guard, since it was believed that the main danger lay from behind. About seven o'clock they had passed the hamlet of Klein Ostheim, and the batteries across the Main came into action. Also news arrived of Grammont at Dettingen. George hastened to put his army in order of battle, but there was much confusion with the baggage, and Noailles' guns increased the pandemonium. At last, after a miserable hour, British guns were got up to reply to the batteries, and about midday the troops had somehow or other found their places. On the extreme left were the British—in first line the 33rd, the Twenty-First, the 23rd, 12th, 11th, 8th, and 13th Foot; then an Austrian brigade; then the Blues, Life Guards, 6th Dragoons, and Royals: in the second line, the 20th, 32nd, 37th, 31st, and Buffs; the 7th Dragoon Guards, King's Dragoon Guards, 4th Dragoons, 7th Dragoons, and Scots Greys. Grammont had his infantry in the centre, and on his right, opposite the British foot, the French Maison du Roi.

The French commander now made a blunder which lost him the day. Instead of waiting where he was in his impregnable position behind Dettingen, he advanced and crossed the boggy ravine, thereby getting his forces into disorder. The Allies were moving forward, the 3rd Dragoons extending their left to the river, struggling through marshes and much harassed by Noailles' batteries. They had to halt now and then for breath, while all the while George was brandishing his sword and shouting out excited encouragements,

1743 till his horse bolted and carried him to the rear, whence the valiant little man, still shouting, returned on foot to the front. By this time the French infantry of the Guard were within firing distance and delivered a ragged volley. The British, controlled by Stair's iron discipline, replied with a merciless fire, and then, with a terrible cheer, for which Stair gave the signal by waving his hat, drove the enemy back in complete rout.

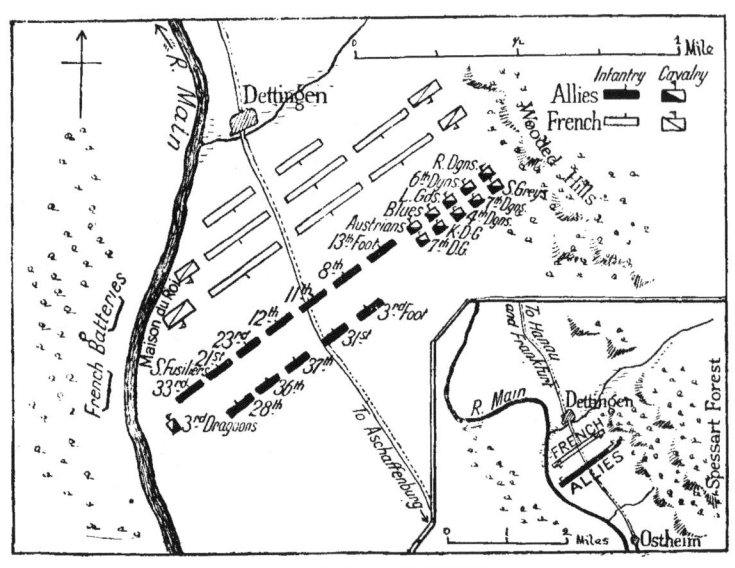

BATTLE OF DETTINGEN

Meantime the Maison du Roi had charged the British left. The 3rd Dragoons closed with them—two squadrons against nine, three ranks against eight—and cut their way through. The foot, notably the 33rd, the Twenty-First, and the 23rd, met the pistols and swords of the French with their deadly platoon-fire, which crashed out as steadily as if on parade. But again, and yet again, the flower of the French Household came on, and the 3rd Dragoons twice again cut their way through them. The 1st and 7th Dragoons came up in support, and the Blues behind them, but

STAND OF THE TWENTY-FIRST

the impetuosity of the Allied charge could not stay the French horse. It was the infantry that stemmed the tide. Down upon the two fusilier battalions, the Twenty-First and the 23rd, came the thundering cavalry, and for a moment broke the line. But the two battalions faced inwards, and the invaders did not return. Let James Wolfe, then a young ensign in Du Roure's, afterwards the 12th Foot, describe what happened. "The Mousquetaires Gris attacked the first line . . . they broke through the Scotch Fusiliers . . . but before they got to the second line out of two hundred there were not forty living, so they wheeled and came back between the first and second lines," where all were slain "except an officer with a standard, and four or five men who broke through the second line, and were taken by some of Hawley's regiment of dragoons. These unhappy men were of the first families in France."

The battle was over. The British horse on the right annihilated the French Black Musketeers, and swung round on the flank of the French foot, who broke and fled. The whole of Grammont's army made for the bridges of the Main, and was suffered to escape by George, who was too thankful for an unexpected deliverance to have any mind for pursuit. The French losses were some 5,000, killed, wounded, and prisoners; the Allies half that number, with the British share 265 killed and 561 wounded. The chief casualties were in the battalions on the left, which, however, in the case of no unit exceeded 100 men. The Twenty-First had Lieutenant Yonge, one sergeant, and 35 rank-and-file killed; Major Colville, Lieutenant Livingstone, one sergeant, two drummers, and 53 rank-and-file wounded —a small loss, indeed, for four hours of severe fighting.

Dettingen is remarkable as the last battle in which an English king in person commanded his troops. It was a singular action, not without its touches of comedy. This came chiefly from the valiant and ridiculous George; from the Duke of Cumberland, who was also run away with by his horse and escaped from the midst

90 THE ROYAL SCOTS FUSILIERS

1743-44 of the French infantry with a bullet in his leg; and not least from the lieutenant-colonel of the Twenty-First. That regiment covered itself with glory,[1] and it was associated with certain whimsical incidents dear to the heart of the British soldier. Sir Andrew Agnew, having his attention called to Grammont's movement by a staff officer, is said to have replied: "Sir, the scoondrels will never have the impudence to attack the Scots Fusiliers." But seeing that a serious engagement was certain, he resolved to steady his men by a homely expedient: he ordered the dinner-call to be sounded, rations were served out, and he himself set-to busily with knife and fork. When a bullet struck a chicken-bone out of his hand he observed, "They're in earnest noo," and the drums beat to quarters. Mounting his charger, he thus encouraged his troops: "My lads, ye see thae loons on yon hill there. If ye dinna kill them, they'll kill you." When the Maison du Roi charged, he bade his men "Dinna fire till ye see the whites o' their een." All through the action he moved about as stolidly as if he had been in his park at Lochnaw. After the battle the King in high good humour thought fit to rally the Sheriff. "So, Sir Andrew," he said, "I hear the cuirassiers rode through your regiment to-day." "Ay, please your Majesty," was the reply, "but they didna gang back again."

After Dettingen Stair resigned—he had no wish for any such further divided commands—and Wade was appointed in his stead. Early in 1744 war was openly declared against France, and the campaigning area was changed to the familiar cockpit of the Austrian Netherlands. The French had a new commander there, that natural son of Augustus the Strong who was to win fame as Marshal Saxe. He was tormented by disease, but France was traditionally at her best under a sick Marshal. The campaign of 1744 moved slowly, for the British recruits were late and there were the usual quarrels with the Dutch and Austrian allies.

[1] For the ballad on the subject see Appendix II.

CUMBERLAND AS COMMANDER-IN-CHIEF 91

In June Saxe marched north between the Scheldt and the Lys, obviously with the intention of cutting off Wade from his base at Nieuport and Ostend. The latter, torn with anxiety for Ghent and Brussels and still short of reinforcements, did nothing, and it was not till 31st July that he crossed the Scheldt. Stair, from his retirement in Galloway, advised that the Allies in turn should threaten the French fortresses; but the Dutch and Austrians proved so dilatory and recalcitrant that Saxe was never brought to action, and at the end of the season the British Field-Marshal resigned in disgust.

In 1745 the Duke of Cumberland, then twenty-five years of age, was appointed Commander-in-Chief, and concentrated his army at Brussels on 2nd May. The Twenty-First had spent the winter in Ghent, and its commander had had frequent leaves of absence home, where he could attend to his farms and plantations, and press the authorities for troops to defend Galloway from a Jacobite landing. Nothing is stranger in the history of the time than the way in which officers were permitted to absent themselves for long periods from the army in the field. Sometimes it was in order to attend to Parliamentary duties or to lobby for promotion. " I thought it hard to refuse them permission," Stair wrote bitterly in 1743, " when they said that their preferment depended on the interest of their friends at Court. They had no notion that it depended on their exertions here."[1] We find Sir Andrew spending most of the winter of 1744–45 at Lochnaw, dealing with the affairs of his sheriffdom, with the result that he was too late for a great battle.

Saxe, on 30th April, invested Tournai, and Cumberland, marching from Soignies, arrived on 9th May within sight of the enemy. The French lay on a gentle slope stretching from the village of Fontenoy, with advanced posts in the broken country at the foot. Cumberland was a mile and a half to the south-eastward, and next day he pushed closer, clearing the

[1] Quoted by Fortescue, II., page 88.

enemy from the copses. Saxe's position was on the crest of the slope, with his right resting on the village of Anthoin and the Scheldt, and his left bent back at right angles to the forest of Barry. It was strong by nature, and had been made stronger by fortification. Three redoubts had been constructed between Anthoin and Fontenoy, and two more—one of them the Redoubt d'Eu—on the edge of the forest of Barry. He had some 56,000 men, against whom the Allies mustered about 50,000. The Allied plan was that the Austrians and Dutch under Königseck and Waldeck should attack the French right and centre, while the British advanced against the French left, which contained the best troops, both horse and foot, between Fontenoy village and the forest of Barry.

At two o'clock on the morning of 11th May the advance began. Brigadier-General Ingoldsby, with the 12th and 13th Foot, the Black Watch,[1] and a Hanoverian battalion, was directed on the extreme right against the Redoubt d'Eu, the Dutch were to be responsible for Fontenoy, while the rest of the British were to march up the thousand yards of slope between these points against the main French position. It was a bold scheme in defiance of the text-books, for it involved an assault upon a re-entrant angle, and should the salients not be carried simultaneously, it might go hard with the attack. The British dispositions, apart from Ingoldsby's detachment, were—in the first line, from left to right, the 19th, 33rd, 25th, 8th, 31st, Twenty-First, and 1st Foot; a battalion of Scots Guards, one of the Coldstream, and one of the 1st Guards: in the second line, the 20th, 34th, 28th, 11th, 32nd, 23rd, and Buffs.

Things went ill from the start. For some reason Ingoldsby misunderstood or disobeyed his instructions, and delayed his attack on the Redoubt d'Eu, while the Dutch and Austrians on the left fell into a panic and

---

[1] Adam Ferguson, afterwards famous as professor and historian, accompanied the Black Watch as chaplain, and fought, unclerical broadsword in hand, at the head of the men.

could not be induced to advance. The British in 1745 perfect order, and with a slow, measured step, moved into the perilous re-entrant, with the salients on each side uncaptured. On that famous march Mr. Fortescue has written a splendid page :—

" Forward tramped the ranks of scarlet, silent and stately as if on parade. Full half a mile of

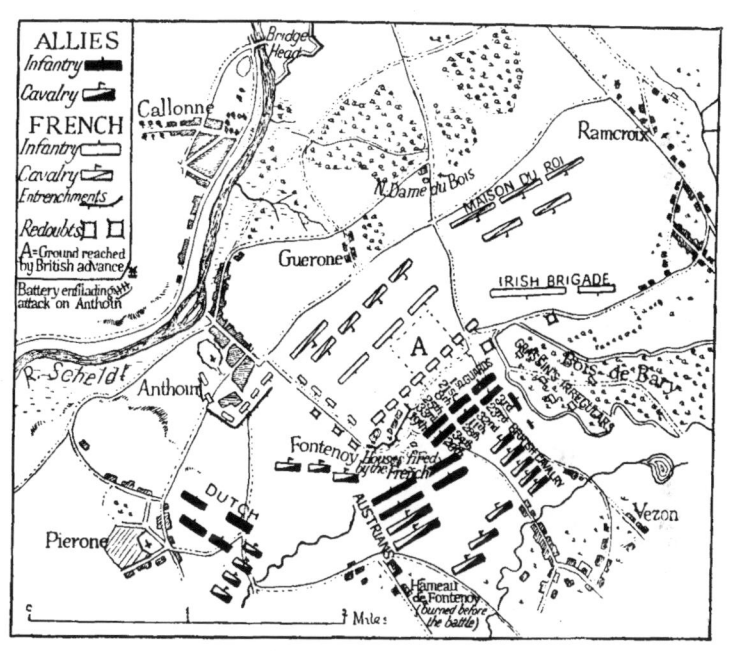

BATTLE OF FONTENOY

ground was to be traversed before they could close with the invisible enemy that awaited them in the entrenchments over the crest of the slope, and the way was marked clearly by the red flashes and puffs of white smoke that leaped from Fontenoy and the Redoubt d'Eu on either flank. The shot plunged fiercely and more fiercely into the serried lines as they advanced into that murderous crossfire, but the gaping ranks were quickly closed, the perfect order was never lost, the stately step was never hurried. . . . Silent and inexorable the scarlet lines strode on. They came abreast of village and redoubt, and the shot which had hitherto swept away files now swept away ranks. Then the first line passed beyond redoubt and village, and the French cannons took it in reverse. The gaps grew wider and more frequent, the front grew narrower as the men closed up, but still the proud battalions advanced, strewing the sward behind them with scarlet, like some mass of red blossom that floats down a lazy stream and sheds its petals as it goes."

The crest was passed, and a hundred yards away the shoulders of the French infantry were seen above the earthworks—the red of the Swiss Guards, the blue of the French Guards, the white of the Regiment du Roi. At fifty yards' distance Lord Charles Hay of the 1st Guards stepped forward and raised his flask to the enemy. " I hope, gentlemen," he cried, " that you are going to wait for us to-day." Then, turning round : " Men of the King's Company," he said, " these are the French Guards, and I hope that you are going to beat them to-day." At thirty yards came the French volley, and then with crash upon crash rang the return volleys of the British, so that 19 officers and 600 men fell at the first discharge. Steadily, evenly, with the officers tapping the men's barrels to keep the fire low, that incomparable British force marched for three hundred yards into the heart of the French camp.

The battle was almost won. But Saxe was no Grammont or Noailles, and, chewing a bullet to ease his dropsical thirst, he took prompt and resolute measures. He sent a message to the French King and the Dauphin to seek safety across the Scheldt; he sent cavalry to repel the attack on Fontenoy, where British troops had come to the help of the incompetent Dutch; from the forest of Barry he charged with his horse the

THE BRITISH ACHIEVEMENT

British right, and he sent in the Household Cavalry to avenge Dettingen. The Maison du Roi was hurled back in utter rout: " It was like charging two flaming fortresses," wrote a French historian, " rather than two columns of infantry." But faster and faster arrived the French reserves, including the hard-bitten Irish brigade of Jacobite exiles, who fought with fury since they could expect no mercy. The odds were too desperate for human endeavour, penned as the British were in a creek between flanking fires. A mere shadow of itself, that heroic foot retreated slowly and proudly as it came, and Fontenoy, instead of a famous victory, was a glorious failure.

It is a tremendous story, one of the finest in the history of war, and Mr. Fortescue's telling of it is not the least of his claims to the gratitude of his countrymen. Never has British infantry risen to greater heights of achievement. " The battalions formed under a cross-fire of artillery, remained halted under the same fire, advanced slowly for half a mile under the same fire, and marched up to within pistol-shot of the French infantry to receive their volley before they discharged a shot. They shattered the French battalions to pieces, repulsed three separate attacks of cavalry, halted under a heavy cannonade, retired for some distance and re-formed under a cross-fire, advanced again with both artillery and musketry playing on front and flanks, made the bravest brigade in the French service recoil, repelled another desperate attack of cavalry, and retired slowly and orderly under a cross-fire almost to the end." [1] Cumberland was not a great general, but he made no heinous mistake, and the principal factor in the failure to achieve victory was the cowardice of the Dutch. The Twenty-First suffered terribly, and its losses were inferior only to those of the 12th and 23rd. It had Lieutenants Campbell, Houston, and Sergeant killed ; Major Charles Colville (who commanded the regiment that day and was later to succeed Sir Andrew Agnew), Captains

[1] Fortescue, II., page 119.

Latan, Oliphant, and Knatchbull, and Lieutenants Maxwell, Colville, Bellenden, McGachan, and Townsend wounded; Captain Andrew Sandilands, Lieutenant Stuart, and Quartermaster Stewart taken prisoner; 11 sergeants and 259 rank-and-file killed, wounded, and prisoners.

Sir Andrew rejoined at Bruges, and found the Twenty-First too weak for anything but garrison work. In these months he seems to have had considerable controversy with his colonel, Campbell of Mamore, who was of an orderly and somewhat finicking temper,[1] and was apt to be sharp with a subordinate who tried to combine the local government of Galloway with fighting the French. The regiment was at first under orders for Ghent, but eventually in July was sent to Ostend. The place was poorly fortified, and was compelled to surrender on 24th August, the garrison marching out with the honours of war. There was much loss of arms and accoutrements, which Mamore had to make good, and he seems to have done his duty promptly and generously. The Twenty-First was then stationed at Mons, when orders came to return home, and on 4th November it arrived in the Thames, passing thence to billets at Aylesbury, Buckingham, and Thame. Four months earlier Prince Charles Edward had landed in Moidart, had won the battle of Prestonpans and occupied Edinburgh, and was now marching south with the clans into the heart of England.

[1] *The Hereditary Sheriffs of Galloway*, II., Chap. XLV.

CHAPTER V

THE " 'FORTY-FIVE "

The meaning of Jacobitism—The rebellion of 1745—The defence of Blair Castle—Culloden

JACOBITISM in Scotland, though its adherents were in a minority, was a plant which found there a congenial soil. The Union had taken the land unawares and left it handicapped. In spite of the fiascos of past risings, the irritation with England, caused by schemes like the Malt Tax and the disarmament of the Highlands, and incidents like the Porteous Mob, was so keenly felt, and the hopelessness of any solution so bitterly realized, that the eyes of even peaceable folk kept turning towards foreign invasion. The old Scotland of blind faiths and impossible loyalties was moribund, but not yet dead, and it had to perish utterly before the new Scotland could be born. Even without Charles Edward it is likely that another Jacobite attempt would have been made, but the existence of a young and ardent prince hurried on the enterprise. He had none of his father's religion and patience, but he had what was more important for an exile—irrepressible gaiety, charm, and courage. His passion for Scotland was the most lasting of his qualities, from the day when at Rome, on one of the Seven Hills, he laid his hand on Hamilton of Bangour's shoulder and asked the poet if he liked the view as much as that from North Berwick Law, to his tragic latter years when he wept at the sound of the bagpipes. The value of invasion is that when a people is prepared for change it gives the necessary impetus. But Scotland was not prepared; in England the Jacobites were no more than a handful; France was less than lukewarm; Charles of Sweden was dead; and there was no hope of European intervention. No Jacobite leader had shown conspicuous talent in the field; there was no statesman to raise and administer funds; there was not even unbroken loyalty in their slender ranks. When Prince Charles sailed in the *Du Tellier* with the " Men of Moidart," it was in truth on a desperate venture.

Yet the invasion shook the Government of Britain to its foundations. There is no room in this narrative for the melancholy twice-told tale of the " 'Forty-five." Cope was an indifferent soldier; his troops were of the worst, and could not stand against the Highland charge. Prestonpans was won, Edinburgh was occupied, and the army crossed the Border to the conquest of England. Marshal Wade may have been right in his view that " England was for the first-comer," and had Charles won a victory in the Midlands disaffection might have spread like wildfire, for the South had little love for Government or dynasty. But the turn at Derby, demanded by Lord George Murray against the Prince's judgment, sounded the doom of the cause. Thereafter the rising changed from a bold stroke of invasion to what Horace Walpole thought the feeblest of things, " a rebellion on the defensive." The clans straggled back over the Border to six months of wandering and starvation, and then to an utter destruction.

The Twenty-First came upon the scene when the retreat from Derby had begun. It was apparently with Cumberland's army when he made an attack on the Jacobite rear-guard at Clifton on 29th December, and was repulsed by Lord George Murray. On that occasion it was not in action, the fighting being confined to dismounted dragoons. It was present at the capture of Carlisle, when Cumberland took prisoner the small garrison which Charles had left behind him.[1]

[1] Mackenzie, *History of Galloway*, II., page 417.

BLAIR CASTLE

Meantime Charles had occupied Glasgow, and having been joined by certain French levies which had landed at Montrose, was marching to the siege of Stirling Castle. The Twenty-First seems to have been used to protect its own Scottish south-west, and was not present at the battle of Falkirk, fought on January 18, 1746, when Hawley, the new Commander-in-Chief in Scotland, won on one flank and was ignominiously beaten on the other—a repetition of Sheriffmuir. The truth is, that for anything but the pick of the British regiments the Highlanders were too strong; a superstitious terror of the clansmen had gone abroad among the English troops, who were for the most part young and little better than militia. Cumberland arrived to take over the command, and on 11th February moved forward to Falkirk. Charles did not await him. He raised the siege of Stirling Castle, and acquiesced in the desire of the chiefs, who were nervous and ill at ease in the south, for a retreat beyond the Grampians. It was a fatal blunder, for it meant famine, the loss of all Lowland support, and leisure for Cumberland to recruit and train his demoralized army.

On 15th February the Twenty-First was at Dunblane, and on the 17th at Perth. There it remained for a little as part of the garrison, and there the bulk of the regiment, under Major the Hon. Charles Colville, marched north with Cumberland to Aberdeen, when they were relieved in Perth by 5,000 Hessians under King George's brother-in-law, Prince Frederick of Hesse. Our story now divides into two channels, for Sir Andrew Agnew on the 17th had been selected for special service to garrison Blair Castle and the neighbourhood, and so cut off Prince Charles from direct communication with the south. Two hundred men of the 27th Foot were dispatched to occupy Castle Menzies, parties of Argyll Highlanders were sent to the lesser country houses, and all the detachments were under Sir Andrew. He himself was established at Blair with 500 men, whom we may assume to have been partly drawn from the Twenty-First.

1746 The tale of the holding of Blair is a spirited piece, which, like all Sir Andrew's doings, is within hailing distance of comedy. He arrived there and found the bed yet warm which Prince Charles had occupied, and the rear-guards of the Jacobites still in sight retreating towards the Badenoch passes. There were two Dukes of Atholl about—Duke William with Prince Charles, and Duke James at Dunkeld, striving to settle the district in King George's interest. But the Atholl men were mostly for the Prince, and every little farm and shieling was a centre of intelligence for the enemy. Sir Andrew's first trouble was with Duke James, who arrived to take possession of his house, a thing the Sheriff would by no means permit, as his orders were to garrison it. The Duke expostulated in vain, and presently left the district in high dudgeon, after a letter of protest, in which he declared that quartering in his house was absurd, since all the rebels had gone to Badenoch. It was fortunate that Sir Andrew adhered strictly to his instructions, for his view of the situation was more accurate than the Duke's. He had much trouble also with the ladies of the neighbourhood. Only Lady Faskally was on the Government side, and at his headquarters at the inn of Blair Sir Andrew had many difficult interviews with ardent female Jacobites. He seems to have shown surprising tact in these matters, for when the wife of Robertson of Lude, a sister of Lord Nairne, was brought to him under arrest, he gave her the best dinner the house could afford, drank her health, and released her with many courtesies.

The garrison at Blair was provisioned from Perth, and as Cumberland thought its communications secure, he allowed no accumulation of military stores. Now was the chance for Lord George Murray, who burned to avenge the overrunning of Atholl, and desired also on strategical grounds to put an end to its occupation as a base in the Jacobite rear. He withdrew the Jacobite post at Dalnaspidal in order to lull the garrison into a false security, and then, on 15th March, moved secretly from Inverness with 700 men of his

SIR ANDREW'S DEFENCE

Atholl regiment, picking up Cluny Macpherson on the way. On the 17th he surprised thirty of the posts held by the Argyll Highlanders, including one commanded by Campbell of Glenure, who happened to be absent, and so survived to be the victim, five years later, of the Appin murder. Sir Andrew was in the castle, which was not attacked, but the inn of Blair was taken, though the officers there succeeded in escaping and fighting their way to the castle. Lord George took 300 prisoners, held all the strath as far as Dunkeld, and sent the fiery cross round the Atholl braes. The Sheriff and his little garrison of 270 were completely surrounded.

Sir Andrew began by a vigorous attempt at a counter-attack. Leaving a small guard in the castle, he marched straight for Lord George's headquarters at the Bridge of Bruar. Here he had a chance of a counter-surprise, for the Jacobites were scattered over the whole countryside. Unfortunately for him the alarm was given in time, and Lord George's men, by extending behind a peat dyke and setting twenty pipers to work, persuaded the Sheriff that he was faced with the whole force. That cautious warrior, having no artillery, accordingly fell back, and on the morning of 18th March the siege of Blair began. Sir Andrew in haste collected all the forage and fuel he could lay his hands on, and then withdrew just in time inside the walls. So close were the Jacobites upon his heels that the picket guard was cut off, but managed to fight its way in, bringing in all the officers' horses except one, which was thrust into a cellar and left there without food or water. The castle was strong enough, but suffered as a defensive position from the number of adjacent enclosures where the enemy could secrete marksmen. The weak point was its wretched provisioning. There was a scarcity of ammunition, inadequate water from the castle well, and for food only a moderate quantity of biscuits and cheese. The daily ration was fixed at a pound of biscuit, a quarter of a pound of cheese, and a quart bottle of water.

1746 Lord George in orthodox fashion summoned the garrison. On a dirty piece of paper he wrote: "Sir Andrew Agnew, baronet, is hereby required to surrender forthwith the castle of Blair, its garrison, military stores, and provisions, into the hands of Lieut.-General Lord George Murray, commanding the forces there of his Royal Highness the Prince Regent. And the said Sir Andrew Agnew shall answer to the contrary at his peril." But now came the question of how to deliver the summons, for none of the prisoners would venture to make trial of Sir Andrew's temper. Molly, the pretty maid of the Blair inn, was requisitioned for the task. She went to the castle, and with tears in her eyes hailed some of the young officers at a window, and besought them to surrender, promising them the best of treatment. One timid lieutenant, "with a constitution impaired by drinking," took the summons from her and carried it to his commander. Sir Andrew, roaring like a bull, promptly kicked him downstairs, and announced that he would shoot through the head any one who brought a similar message. Molly, who had heard the threats, as she was meant to, fled back to the inn.

Lord George thereupon began the bombardment. He had two four-pounders served by French gunners, and the first shot was fired by Sir Andrew's late guest, the lady of Lude. They made poor shooting, for, though trained within a half-musket shot, they frequently missed the castle altogether. Cannon balls could make no impression on the stout walls, so the enemy tried to fire the roof with red-hot shot. These Sir Andrew caused to be picked up with iron ladles and dropped in pails of water. "Is the loon clean daft," he asked, "knocking down his ain brither's house?"

Presently belts were drawn tighter, and the cheese disappeared from the ration bill. All attempts failed to provoke the commander to a sally, and for a weary fortnight the siege went on. Some of the young officers, to pass the time, dressed up a dummy of Sir Andrew, which they placed at one of the tower windows, and on this the best hunters of Atholl and Badenoch wasted their ammunition, till they began to think that the Sheriff must be as invulnerable as had been Claverhouse in the Covenanters' eyes. Soon starvation came very near, and Sir Andrew made an attempt to communicate with Lord Crawford and the Hessian cavalry. By this time the Government troops had recovered Dunkeld, but none were nearer Blair than a couple of miles below Pitlochry, for Killiecrankie was still a name of terror. A gardener called Wilson volunteered to take a message, but he was fired at by Lord George's pickets, and, as a Highlander was seen next day riding his horse, it was assumed that he had been taken prisoner.

Wilson, however, got through, but the relief was not to be due to him. When the 1st of April dawned the position of the garrison was very desperate. They were out of biscuit, almost out of ammunition, and the sole ration was now horse flesh. Only surrender or a wild sally seemed left to them. Suddenly Molly from the inn was seen approaching the castle with a smiling face, and the news that Lord George had drawn off his men. He had been summoned to join the Prince at Inverness for the last act of the drama which was now imminent. Next day, the 2nd, Lord Crawford arrived, the drums of the garrison beat the turn out, and when the trumpets of the relieving force were heard in the avenue, the Sheriff paraded his lean, unwashen troops. "My lord, I am very glad to see ye," said Sir Andrew, "but, by all that's good, ye have been very dilatory, and we can give ye nothing to eat." Crawford, however, had brought ample provisions, and soon in a garden summer-house the Sheriff and his officers were having their fill of mutton and good claret. The delay had not been Crawford's fault. Long before he got Wilson's message he had sent off two Hessian battalions and a regiment of German hussars, but nothing could induce these heroes to attempt Killiecrankie till they heard that Lord George Murray had marched away. The presence of the

1746 foreign troops is one of the incidents which give a touch of farce to the grim tale of the " 'Forty-five." Their only communication with their Jacobite captors, when they were taken prisoner, and with the Atholl inn-keepers when they were at large, was by means of the Latin tongue! Another is the story of the horse which at the beginning of the siege had been thrust into a cellar. It belonged to a certain Captain Wentworth, who went sadly to look for its skeleton. To his amazement he found the beast still alive after seventeen days' abstinence from food and water, but naturally very weak on its legs. It soon recovered, and he sent it to England as a present to his sister.

Sir Andrew received high commendation for his performance at Blair, and, while Cumberland was busy in the north, he was engaged in clearing Atholl, and, with the assistance of Duke James, in mending the castle roof. His temper might be short, but his mind was just and his heart was kindly, and he left a pleasant memory in the countryside. It is still told how, when Cumberland returned south, and approached Blair, the Sheriff caught sight of the royal party from the drawing-room window, and observed that his men were still lounging in groups, and the piper oblivious of his duty. Flinging up the sash, he bellowed in a voice of thunder, " Blaw! blaw! ye scoondrel! Dinna ye see the King's ain bairn?"[1]

We turn now to the main body of the Twenty-First, which about the time when Crawford was relieving the Sheriff, was marching with Cumberland from Aberdeen. The Duke, by a stern and unremitting discipline, had got his forces into good condition, and had taught them to meet the charge of target and claymore by directing the bayonet not against the immediate

[1] The story of the siege of Blair will be found in *The Original and Genuine Narrative of the Remarkable Blockade and Attack of Blair Castle by a subaltern officer of H.M. garrison* (General Melville), 1808; *The Hereditary Sheriffs of Galloway*, II., pages 304–323; and *The Military History of Perthshire*, pages 328–330.

BEFORE CULLODEN

enemy but against the man on the right front, so as to get under the Highland guard. His was not an elevated or attractive character, but his conduct of a winter campaign in wild country, and his success in restoring the *moral* of his men, showed his skill in the business of war. It should be remembered, however, that he had a great superiority of numbers, and that when the two sides drew together for the final battle Prince Charles had exhausted his money, was ill-provisioned, was miserably served with guns, and had a considerable part of his forces absent on a foray in Sutherland. On 12th April (Old Style)[1] Cumberland crossed the Spey and advanced to Nairn, and on the 14th Prince Charles lay twelve miles off at Culloden House. The 15th was the Duke's birthday, and the Government forces rested; an attempt that night by Charles to surprise the enemy in camp failed from the weariness of his men, and it was clear that he must fight where he stood. Between four and five on the morning of the 16th Cumberland marched out from Nairn, and after eight miles on the road had news of the enemy, and formed order of battle.

It was a wild morning, with a gale of snow and sleet blowing from the east. Charles, who had scarcely 5,000 men, drew up his force in two lines, with his left near Culloden House and his right resting on some walls and enclosures not far from the river Nairn. On his right, where Lord George Murray commanded, were the men of Atholl, the Stuarts of Appin, the Camerons, and the Frasers; in the centre, the Mackintoshes, Farquharsons, Macleans, and Chisholms; and on the left, under the Duke of Perth, the Macdonalds of Clanranald and Keppoch and Glengarry, sore hurt because they had not the place of honour on the right. In the second line were the scanty cavalry, Lord Lewis Gordon, and the French troops, with Lord Ogilvy's men in reserve. They had four old, badly served, and ill

---

[1] I have hitherto given dates in the New Style, but the chronology of Culloden is traditionally remembered in the Old Style—*i.e.*, eleven days earlier.

supplied guns, and the whole force was faint from short rations. The Duke's army was at least 10,000 strong, drawn up in three lines, each of the two first consisting of six battalions of infantry and two regiments of dragoons, with four other battalions, the Argyll militia, and various Highland irregulars in the third line. There were ten guns, well served, stationed in pairs between the battalions of the first line. In that line was the Twenty-First, 500 strong, under Major the Hon. Charles Colville.

Cumberland's plan was for a double outflanking. He sent forward Hawley with a body of dragoons and three companies of the Argyll militia to break down the enclosures on which the Jacobite right rested, and while this movement was in progress the Prince's guns opened the battle. Cumberland's cannon replied with a torrent of grape-shot, which was new in Highland experience, for there had been nothing like it at Prestonpans or Falkirk. The Prince had intended to await Cumberland's attack, hoping that the position he had taken up would prevent the use of cavalry, but the grape-shot was more than the clans could endure, and Lord George sought and obtained permission to attack. The Jacobite right and centre swept forward in the teeth of the storm, flinging away their muskets and using the broadsword. " Plied with guns in front and flank," says Mr. Lang, " and by a front and flanking fire of musketry, blinded by smoke and snow, they broke Barrel's regiment,[1] they swept over the foremost guns, and then, enfiladed by Wolfe's, they died on the bayonets of the second line." Few more desperate charges were ever made than by those weary and starving clans ; as an example of one mode of war it was as splendid as the British advance at Fontenoy. It failed because it was outflanked, for the Argyll Highlanders, having broken down the enclosures, opened the way for Hawley and the dragoons, and permitted four guns to be brought into action on that

[1] James Wolfe wrote to his uncle that Barrel's fought "in the most obstinate manner against the Camerons, the best clan in the Highlands."

flank.¹ Meantime on the Prince's left things went ill. 1746 The Macdonalds had been ordered to advance at the same time as Lord George, but having more ground to cover, they could not come to grips with the enemy before Kingston's horse and Pulteney's regiment had turned their left, and the grape was galling their flank.

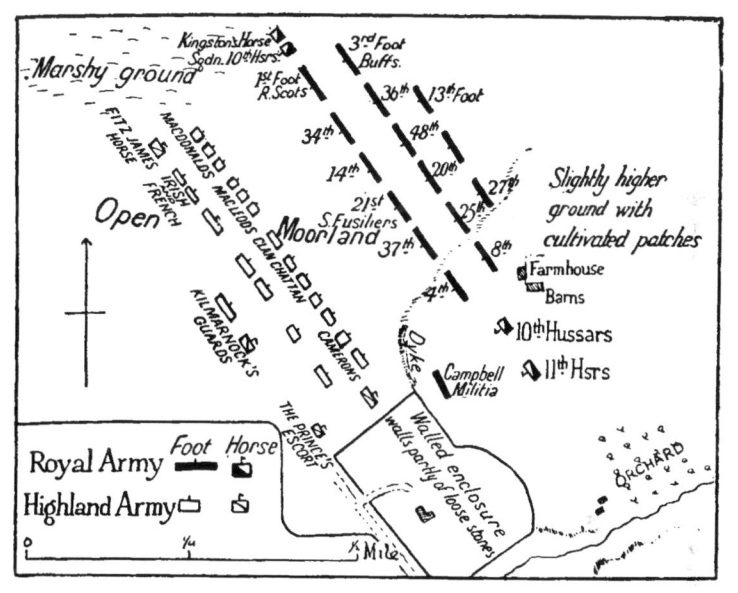

BATTLE OF CULLODEN

There fell Scottos and Keppoch, and, with the leaders gone, the attack languished and broke.²

---

¹ One of the best narratives of the battle is contained in a letter of James Wolfe, who was present as a brevet-major in Barrel's (the 4th Foot) and aide-de-camp to Hawley (Willson's *Life and Letters of Wolfe*, pages 62–66).

² There are still obscurities in the account of Culloden, but Mr. Lang's careful narrative (*History of Scotland*, IV., Chap. XIX.) has cleared up the worst. In particular he has exploded the story of the refusal of the Macdonalds to charge, for which Sir Walter Scott seems to have been chiefly responsible. The author of *The Hereditary Sheriffs of Galloway* attributes the breaking down of the enclosures on the Highland right to the Twenty-First, and assumes that when contemporary chroniclers speak of "Campbells" they mean "Campbell's Regiment." But James Wolfe's letters are conclusive. He speaks of "150 Argyleshires," and would not have been likely to confuse a famous regiment with Highland militia. He always calls the Twenty-First the "Scotch Fusiliers." See also the explicit statements in the various contemporary accounts.

108 THE ROYAL SCOTS FUSILIERS

1746   In ten minutes all was over, and the Prince's army was shattered beyond hope. A thousand of his men died on the field, and 400 prisoners were taken, while the Government losses were not more than 300. Then began that pursuit and that harrying of the Highlands which has left so dark a stain on Cumberland's name.[1] Charles was forced by his attendants to ride south to the hills, and so entered upon that Odyssey in the heather which has made him the last prince of fairy tales. Jacobitism ended in a sharp and utter cataclysm, as a mountain stream falling over a high cliff disappears in spray, and Scottish regiments were no more required to wage war on their own countrymen.

After the battle the Twenty-First was encamped at Inverness, where Sir Andrew Agnew joined it, and in the early summer it moved to Glasgow. There, on 15th August, we take farewell of the Sheriff, who was given the colonelcy of a regiment of marines, and handed over his command to the Hon. Charles Colville,[2] son of the seventh Lord Colville of Culross, who had begun life in the Cameronians, had fought as a youth at Malplaquet, had been wounded at Preston in the "'Fifteen,'" had had a horse shot under him at Dettingen, and had commanded the Twenty-First at Fontenoy and Culloden. A historian of the regiment must part from Sir Andrew Agnew with regret, for he is one of the most memorable figures in its records, and the quick-step, "The rock and the wee pickle tow," is still known as

---

[1] The Twenty-First did not imitate its general. Captain O'Neil, an aide-de-camp of Prince Charles, was saved from barbarous treatment in Benbecula by Captain M'Gachan (who was among the wounded at Fontenoy). See *The Lyon in Mourning*, I., page 374. With the Twenty-First at Culloden was Lord Boyd, the heir of the unfortunate Earl of Kilmarnock, who was with the Prince, and perished later on Tower Hill. The story of Lord Boyd's covering his father's head with his own hat, and of his saving the life of a Jacobite officer named Fraser, may be read in M'Kay's *History of Kilmarnock* (1880), and Brown's *History of the Highlands*, III., page 252. Boyd afterwards succeeded to the Earldom of Erroll through his mother, and was visited by Johnson and Boswell at Slains Castle in 1773. He was six feet four inches in height, and reminded Dr. Johnson of the Homeric Sarpedon. See Croker's notes to *A Tour in the Hebrides*, *The Complete Peerage* by G. E. C., Vol. V., page 100, and Balfour Paul's *The Scots Peerage*, III., page 581.

[2] Balfour Paul's *The Scots Peerage*, II., page 562.

"The Sheriff's March." He was raised to the rank of major-general in 1756, and to that of lieutenant-general in 1759, and lived to the age of eighty-four, dying in the year 1771. The piety of his descendants has preserved many tales of his later years—his stout Whig principles, his staunch Presbyterianism, his kindly despotism over his estates, his quick temper and robustness of speech, as quick and as robust as those of his friend the redoubtable Lord Braxfield, who married his niece. He was a little king in his own countryside, and has left a memory which Galloway will not easily let die. We may take leave of the stalwart old figure with Sir Walter Scott's eulogy—"Famous in Scottish tradition, a soldier of the old military school, severe in discipline, stiff and formal in manner, brave to the last degree, and somewhat of a humourist."[1]

[1] *Tales of a Grandfather.*

CHAPTER VI

FROM LAUFFELD TO SARATOGA

Lauffeld—The Royal Warrant of 1751—Gibraltar—Belleisle—Service in Canada—Changes in the British army—The American revolution—General Burgoyne—The Saratoga campaign—The surrender.

1746-47 DURING the winter of 1746-47 the Twenty-First remained in quarters at Glasgow. The Jacobite war had meant the almost complete evacuation of the Low Countries by British troops, and during the first half of 1746 the French took Brussels, Antwerp, and Ostend, and threatened an invasion of Holland. Ligonier, in July, appeared with his Hessians and a few British battalions, but was unable to induce his colleagues to take the offensive, and Namur fell early in September. On 11th October Saxe forced an action between the Meuse and the Jaar, and only the better quality and discipline of the Allied troops enabled them to retire with small losses.

For the campaign of 1747 the Twenty-First crossed the Channel. The Duke of Cumberland was now the Allied Commander-in-Chief, and the British contingent numbered four regiments of cavalry and fourteen battalions of foot. Operations began in vile weather, and the French succeeded in closing the southern mouth of the Scheldt and thereby hampering the Allied transport. It was Cumberland's aim to force an action, and as Saxe lay between Malines and Louvain, he marched towards him, and on 26th May encamped on the Great Nethe. The French General remained for three weeks secure in his entrenchments, and the news of the approach of the Prince of Clermont with 30,000 men induced Cumberland to move to intercept him. But Saxe was not to be caught napping. He concentrated upon Tongres, marching fifty miles in two days, and when Cumberland arrived he found to his dismay that the enemy had occupied the very position he intended for himself. There was a chance for a second Oudenarde, but Cumberland was not the man to fight that type of battle; so he permitted the rest of the French force to come up, while he himself took the rising ground from the south-east of Bilsen to the Jaar a little south of Maestricht. He was facing nearly due south; the Austrians on the right covered Bilsen, with their flank resting on the Demer; in the centre lay the Dutch; and on the left the British and the Hanoverians occupied the villages of Val and Lauffeld.

At daybreak on 2nd July Saxe, seeing that nothing could be done against the strongly posted Allied right, doubled his left wing in rear of his right in order to overwhelm the Allied left. About nine o'clock the French attacked. The British troops holding Val and Lauffeld were a battalion from each of the 1st and 3rd Guards (before Val), the 3rd, 4th, 13th, 19th, Twenty-First, 23rd, 25th, 32nd, 33rd, 36th, 37th, and 48th Foot, with the Scots Greys, 4th Hussars, 7th Hussars, Inniskillings, and Cumberland's Dragoons on the right of the infantry and linking it up with the Dutch centre. Saxe began by seizing the small hamlets beyond the Allied left, and then directed six infantry brigades and twenty guns against Val, and five brigades and as many guns against Lauffeld. Among the walls and hedges the British and Hanoverians stood firm; but the pressure was severe, and the Austrian right was unable to make any attack in relief. Again Saxe advanced, this time with two fresh brigades, and the Allies were driven to the inner defences. Two more brigades, including the Irish troops who had won fame at Fontenoy, were sent in, and the British at Lauffeld were pressed back to the northern edge of the village.

112 THE ROYAL SCOTS FUSILIERS

1747 Cumberland ordered his whole infantry line to advance, and the French began to give way, though their cavalry was urging on their foot at the sword's point. Victory might have been his, had not some Dutch horse in the centre been seized with panic, and galloped back upon the British, carrying away the Hessians, and coming full upon the two regiments of fusiliers. The 23rd suffered most, for the Twenty-First fired a volley at the Dutchmen, as, sixty-seven years later, the British fired on the retreating Belgians at Waterloo. Nevertheless

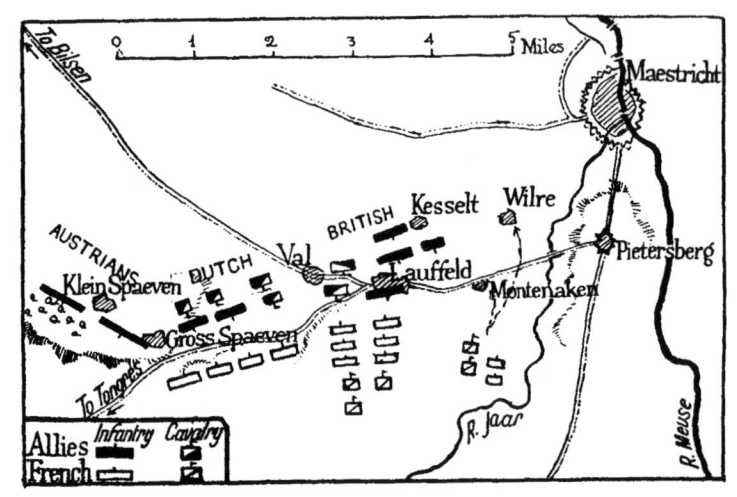

BATTLE OF LAUFFELD

the whole British line was flung into confusion, and before it could be restored Lauffeld village was lost.

There was nothing for it but retreat. The French were massing for a final cataclysmic blow on the Allied left, and the one hope remaining was to save the British foot. Ligonier performed prodigies of valour. He led the Scots Greys, the Inniskillings, and Cumberland's Dragoons, supported by the Twenty-First, in a wild charge against the oncoming masses of French cavalry, and cut his way through them to the infantry beyond, he himself being taken prisoner. So too Cumberland, who all but shared the same fate. The heroic sacrifice

TREATY OF AIX-LA-CHAPELLE 113

had its effect, and the whole Allied front was able to retire in good order.

Such was the battle of Lauffeld, which may be classed as a defeat, but which nevertheless thwarted Saxe's main purpose of cutting off the Allies from Maestricht. The victors were the heavier losers—10,000 casualties as against 6,000; the British losses were close on 2,000, to which the Twenty-First, who had been in the forefront of the action, contributed the surprisingly small total of eight rank-and-file killed, a sergeant and fifteen rank-and-file wounded, and five men missing. The British troops behaved so magnificently that Cumberland declared himself unable to commend any one regiment without doing injustice to the rest. " What splendid infantry! " exclaims the French historian. " Happily for their foes there are not many of them! "

Lauffeld was to all intents the end of the War of the Austrian Succession. In 1748 Cumberland again took the field against a French army more than three times as large. The Austrians were more obstructive than ever, the Dutch more supine, and under such conditions campaigning became a farce. The British people were sick of the business, and Cumberland pressed hard for peace. On 30th April preliminaries were signed, and six months later came the Treaty of Aix-la-Chapelle. The war left the international position formally unchanged. But it had had one effect which was to be of supreme importance for the future of the world: it had perfected the training of the British army which, in the course of the next thirty years, was to create the British Empire.

In that great tale which must be followed among the jungles of India and the forests of North America the Twenty-First had no part. For twenty-three years, with one small break, it was condemned to garrison duty at home and abroad. From the end of 1748 to the early winter of 1751 it was stationed at different places in England, where it conducted itself with such

1748-60 good discipline and propriety that it secured a special commendation from the Duke of Cumberland. In those years, when Clive and Dupleix were fighting their great duel for the prize of India, the only event in the history of our regiment was the issue of a Royal Warrant on July 1, 1751, regulating the colours, standards, and clothing of the British army. These were the directions given for the " Twenty-First Regiment, or Royal North British Fusiliers " :—

" In the centre of their colours, the *Thistle* with the *Circle of St. Andrew*, and the *Crown* over it; and in the three corners of the second, or regimental colours, the *King's Cypher* and *Crown*. On the grenadier caps the *Thistle* as on the colours; the *White Horse*[1] and motto over it, *Nec Aspera terrent*, on the flap. On the drums and bells of arms, the *Thistle* and *Crown* to be painted as on the colours, with the rank of the regiment underneath."

In the winter of 1751 the regiment embarked for Gibraltar, where it remained for nine years—the years which witnessed Braddock's disaster in America, Byng's loss of Minorca, the victory of Plassey, the beginning of Chatham's rule and the Seven Years War, the capture of Louisburg, the fight at Ticonderoga, and James Wolfe's taking of Quebec.[2] Of its life at Gibraltar we possess no record, but it cannot have been pleasant. The defences of the overseas stations at the time were, almost without exception, neglected, and there was small provision for the comfort of the troops. In May 1767, after Minorca had fallen and the situation in the western Mediterranean had become critical, we find the Governor, Lord Tyrawley, complaining bitterly that the Government at home paid no heed to his

---

[1] For the White Horse, see page 74 *supra*.
[2] There was at least one Scots Fusilier with Wolfe. In a letter to Lord George Sackville from Portsmouth, dated February 11, 1758, Wolfe writes: " Adam Livingstone of the Scottish Fusiliers, and Delaine of Kingsley's, are formed by nature for the American War."

requests, and declined even to answer his letters. "The guns mounted on the fortress were too short, the spare carriages were too few, the palisades better fitted for hen-coops than for fortifications."[1] During the Gibraltar years the regiment had a new colonel and lieutenant-colonel. On April 29, 1752, John Campbell of Mamore was transferred to the Scots Greys, and the colonelcy of the Twenty-First was given to William Maule, the first Earl of Panmure.[2] Panmure had begun his soldiering in the Scots Guards, serving with them at Dettingen and Fontenoy, and in 1747 had been colonel of the 25th Foot. In 1756 he was appointed second-in-command at Gibraltar, and he lived till 1782, rising to the rank of general. In April 1758 the Hon. Charles Colville was transferred to the colonelcy of the 69th Foot, and was succeeded as lieutenant-colonel by Edward Maxwell, whom we find in 1748 a captain in the Twenty-First, and who had fought at Dettingen and been wounded at Fontenoy.

It must have been with relief that early in 1760 the regiment received orders for home. In 1756 that coalition against Prussia had been formed which occasioned the Seven Years War, and Britain was engaged on the side of Frederick. Chatham was in power, and under his strong hand the British army had become a formidable weapon, second battalions had been added to fifteen regiments of the line, and two new Highland regiments had been raised, Fraser's and Montgomery's, to which the existing Scottish regiments were required to contribute eighty non-commissioned officers who could speak Gaelic. It does not appear that any were drawn from the Twenty-First, which had by this time lost all its old Highland connections. The true work of the army was to defeat France outside Europe, and the expeditions to the Continent were never more than a grand-scale diversion.

The Twenty-First was not to share in the glory of

[1] Fortescue, II., page 574, quoting from the *Warrant Books*, May 14, 1757.
[2] See Balfour Paul's *The Scots Peerage*, VII., page 23.

1761 Minden, where the French General Contades cried in the anguish of his spirit: " I never thought to see a single line of infantry break through three lines of cavalry ranked in order of battle, and tumble them to pieces." Its part, when it came, was to be in one of those futile sporadic attacks on the coast of France which were the only defects in Chatham's masterly plan. On March 29, 1761, it formed portion of a force under Major-General Hodgson which sailed from Spithead under the convoy of Admiral Keppel for the island of Belleisle in the Bay of Biscay.[1] On 7th April the expedition anchored off the island, and next day a landing was attempted at Port La Maria (sometimes called Port Andro) on the south-eastern side. The coast was one vast fortress, and where the unscalable crags ceased the French had prepared formidable entrenchments. The troops were carried ashore in flat-bottomed boats; but the ground was so steep and the enemy's fire so severe that, though a gallant struggle was made by men climbing on each other's shoulders, the attempt had to be abandoned. Sixty men of the 37th did indeed reach the summit, but they were presently overpowered. The force re-embarked with 500 casualties; the Twenty-First had three sergeants, a drummer, and eight rank-and-file killed, eight rank-and-file wounded, and Lieutenants Innis and Ramage and thirty-five rank-and-file prisoners, most of these last having serious wounds. On the 22nd came the second attempt. Feint attacks were made on La Maria and on Sauzon in the north-west, and a landing was effected at a point between, the grenadiers of the 19th Foot succeeding in seizing and holding a post on the summit of the cliffs. The French garrison retired into the town of Palais, where they had time to strengthen the fortifications, since, owing to the gale, Hodgson could not get his heavy guns ashore. On 2nd May these were at last landed, on the 13th the enemy entrenchments were carried by storm, and

[1] Mr. Fortescue, II., page 530, omits to mention the Twenty-First. The other foot were drawn from 9th, 19th, 30th, 34th, 36th, 67th, 69th, Morgan's, Stuart's, and Grey's regiments.

on 7th June, after a gallant defence, the citadel yielded. At the cost of some 700 losses in killed and wounded, Britain had won an advanced base for the fleet which was blockading France.[1]

After Belleisle the Twenty-First was not again in action for fifteen years. It was quartered in England in the latter part of 1761 and in 1762, and during the two following years in Scotland. In the spring of 1765 it sailed for America, and for five years did garrison duty in Florida. In 1770 it moved to Canada, being stationed for some time at Quebec, returning to England in 1772, where it remained till the spring of 1776. Lord Panmure ceased to be its colonel in 1770, when he went to the Scots Greys, and his successor was the Hon. Alexander Mackay, a son of the third Lord Reay, who had begun life in the King's Own Scottish Borderers, had fought with Loudon's Highlanders in the " 'Forty-five " and been taken prisoner at Prestonpans, and had served afterwards in Flanders and America. In 1780 he became Commander-in-Chief in Scotland. Edward Maxwell was succeeded as lieutenant-colonel in March 1774 (when he became colonel of the 67th) by James Hamilton from the 113th Foot, who was to hold the post for eighteen years, and then, after two years' absence, to return to the Twenty-First as its colonel.

The quarter of a century after Lauffeld saw changes of the first importance in the administration of the British army, and a vast improvement in both the status and the comfort of the troops. The reforms were due principally to two men—one a civilian, and the other a soldier. They were due to Chatham, who encouraged the growth of a new school of officers, who, in Mr. Fortescue's words, " looked upon their men not as marionettes to be dressed and undressed, used up and thrown away, but as human flesh and blood, with good feelings that could be played on, good under-

[1] The British soldier's view of the operation may be gathered from the well-known couplet :—

" At the siege of Belle Isle
We were there a long while."

standings that could be instructed, self-respect that needed only to be cultivated, and high instincts that needed only to be evoked." Wade's road-making in Scotland, when men and officers were brought into closer contact off parade, may have begun the change, for James Wolfe, who was with Wade, was a chief example of the new school. The reforms were due also to Cumberland, who, though a martinet and narrow in a score of ways, was a good administrator, saw to supplies, stopped the old picnicking habits of officers on active service, had a quick eye for a good man, put the Secretary-at-War in his proper place, and established a uniform discipline throughout the army. It was not for nothing that Horace Walpole ranked him with Sir Robert Walpole, Mansfield, Grenville, and Chatham, as one of the five great men he had known.

The method of raising troops was still far from perfect. The short-service system was reintroduced soon after the struggle with France began; but an attempt to establish the principle during peace as well as war was rejected by Parliament in 1750. The system began again with the outbreak of the Seven Years War, and the usual bounties were offered to volunteers. Impressment was also used, for the army as well as for the navy. The Highlands furnished a new reservoir of recruits, and Irish Catholics were again admitted to the ranks—with excellent results at the taking of Quebec. The rudiments of a depot system were introduced with Lord Stair's plan for forming two extra companies of infantry and one extra troop of cavalry for every regiment on active service; but the additional companies were soon combined into separate regiments. The old bad plan of drafting remained the staple expedient during the campaign. The soldier was still shabbily treated by the civil authorities, and the burden of providing any kind of comforts still fell wholly on the officers. But as these officers advanced in professional skill and keenness, they performed their difficult duties with greater conscientiousness. One small change which helped to establish a regiment's

CHANGED METHODS OF WARFARE

identity was the use of numbers instead of the colonel's name, which began about 1753.

In methods of warfare a revolution was beginning, based largely upon the experience of wars outside Europe —a revolution which was not to be completed till nearly half a century had elapsed. The British army had little need to go to school to Frederick the Great : its fire discipline, as Fontenoy, Quebec, and Minden proved, was nearly perfect ; and in matters of general discipline it probably learned less from the example of the Prussians than from the awful warning of the French. The most important change which these years witnessed was perhaps the introduction of light infantry for skirmishing and quick movements; the first instance was the Highlanders, and Wolfe and Amherst carried the practice further in their American wars. For the rest, the soldier had still a life of immense hardship and fatigue. He marched heavily burdened—a grenadier carried more than sixty-three pounds weight on his back ; he had the same cumbrous clothing and head-dress for Canadian snows, Flanders mud, the jungles of Hindustan, and the baking islets of the West Indies ; he was constantly short of supplies ; he was often sick, and rarely well tended ; and if he escaped death from battle or disease abroad, he might find it, when discharged, from starvation at home.

The period following the close of a great war is always a time of crisis for the victor. The land is weary of campaigning, and is inclined to rest on its laurels and think of other things than armies and fleets. There is certain to be a drastic reduction in military and naval establishments, for the problem of defence is believed to be temporarily settled. It is usually, too, a time of faction ; politicians, who have been shouldered out of the public eye by admirals and generals, hasten to assert their importance. After her triumphs over France Britain was in a position of peculiar difficulty. She had won a vast Empire, and had given no thought as to how she was to hold it.

1761-76 Above all, she had not considered what effect the acquisition of her new territories and the removal of the French menace were to have upon her old settlements in the American continent. She had no theory of Empire to guide her, and her traditional colonial practice was not revised in the light of changed conditions. No man in England—not Chatham, not even Burke—had a clear vision of the new problem; they could point out blunders in policy and fallacies in argument, but they had nothing to offer in the way of fruitful construction. Hence the nation drifted before it knew into a quarrel which lost it its oldest American possessions; a loss, it must seem to us to-day, inevitable—and fortunate, too, for the future of the Empire and the world.

We are not concerned here with the details of the quarrel. Now that historians on both sides of the Atlantic can view the facts without prejudice, the faults of both disputants are generally admitted. Formally, America was in the wrong; there was much that was churlish and ungracious in her conduct, as there were many blunders in tact on the part of Britain. But the small minority of determined men who forced through the American Revolution had an instinct behind them far wiser than the crudities of their public arguments. America had outgrown the old colonial system, and, since Britain was not ready with a revised version, the breach must come. Undoubtedly, had King George's Government shown anything like the vigour and foresight which they had displayed in the wars with France, the rebellion could have been stamped out in the first year. But the country detested the war. It slipped into it by degrees; it waged it half-heartedly and, so to speak, with its left hand; and it awoke one morning to find that the task had grown beyond its power, and that if victory were won at a desperate cost it would be less victory over a foreign foe than over the best elements among its own people. The surrender to the logic of facts was the first step in the consolidation of the British Empire.

From a military point of view every stage in Britain's conduct of the campaign was thick with errors. On December 16, 1773, the tea-chests were tumbled into Boston harbour, and the struggle began. On April 19, 1775, the skirmish at Lexington took place, the action at Bunker's Hill followed in June, and in March of the following year, after a dreary winter of blockade, Howe evacuated Boston. Meantime the insurgents had made a bold attempt at an offensive against the new British possession of Canada. In May 1775, Benedict Arnold and Ethan Allen surprised Ticonderoga, the post between Lake George and Lake Champlain, and sailing down the latter lake, seized St. John's on the Richelieu River. General Carleton, who was in command at Montreal, had for his whole defence force two weak British battalions. He succeeded in recovering St. John's; but in August Montgomery with 2,000 men left Ticonderoga to attack Montreal, while Benedict Arnold with 1,500 men marched through the Maine woods against Quebec. Montgomery took St. John's, and forced Carleton to evacuate Montreal, and on 5th November Arnold appeared before Quebec, where in December he was joined by Montgomery. The fortifications were weak and the garrison small; but Captain Allan Maclean beat up local recruits, and when, on the last day of December, the Americans attacked in a snowstorm, they were decisively repulsed. It was a bold adventure; but success was possible only for disciplined troops, and the men of Montgomery and Arnold were to the last degree lawless and insubordinate.

In the spring of 1776 Carleton got reinforcements— the 9th, 20th, Twenty-First, 24th, 34th, 53rd, and 62nd from home, and the 47th from Howe at Halifax. He had already driven Arnold from the Plains of Abraham, and now pursued him to Trois Rivières, and then to Sorel, finally forcing him back to Crown Point, and so out of Canada. Arnold, though his numbers were shrinking daily from sickness, by the end of September had built a flotilla of sixteen vessels, mounting seventy guns, to protect the lakes. He was attacked by Carleton on 11th October, and driven back on Ticonderoga. There for the present Carleton left him, having conducted the operation with something less than the vigour required. Had Arnold been the British commander, not an American would have been permitted to escape.

It was this Canadian diversion which determined the plan of 1777. Already the wiser heads among British soldiers had begun to see the hugeness of the task. Harvey, the Adjutant-General, wrote: "To attempt to conquer it [America] by our land force is as wild an idea as ever controverted common sense." "Unless a settled plan of operations be agreed upon for next spring," he wrote in 1775, "our army will be destroyed by damned driblets." The plan ultimately devised was that of isolating the New England provinces, which were the heart of the rebellion, by advancing forces simultaneously from New York and Canada and occupying the line of the Hudson River. By the close of 1776 both New York and Rhode Island were firmly held as bases, and Canada had been cleared—the "terrible news," it will be remembered, which distressed the patriotic soul of Fox. Lord George Germaine, now Secretary of War, who had been degraded for cowardice at Minden, was working out the details during the winter without consulting Howe, and without arranging for adequate numbers. Burgoyne was to move south from Lake Champlain upon Albany; but no provision was made for Howe's operations in the south to conform, though the junction of the forces of these two generals was the kernel of the whole scheme.

General John Burgoyne, a Member of Parliament and a showy orator as well as a good soldier, assembled his forces on June 20, 1777, at Cumberland Point on Lake Champlain. He had just over 7,000 regulars, including the Twenty-First, which had spent the winter at St. John's; and following the example set by the Americans, he had a contingent of Indians and a small body of Canadian recruits. On 1st July he was before Ticonderoga, and four days later the American garrison withdrew by way of the South River towards Skenesborough. General Simon Fraser, with a brigade of light infantry and grenadiers, pushed on overland in pursuit, and by nine a.m. on the 6th Burgoyne had burst the boom on the South River and was advancing with the rest of his army. Early on the 7th Fraser attacked the Americans in their stockade; but for two hours, being outnumbered by two to one, he made no progress. Before noon, however, the rest of the British approached by water, and the 9th, 20th, and Twenty-First landed, and worked round to the back of the enemy position. The Americans retired, leaving 200 dead, and as many prisoners in British hands. The 9th Foot was now sent on fifteen miles to Fort Anna to intercept the retreat, and being attacked by superior numbers, had a hard fight of it till the Twenty-First came up in support. General Schuyler, who was in command of the Americans, fell back on Fort Edward, barricading the road as he went with felled timber. On the 10th Burgoyne had his whole army at Skenesborough, and was busy clearing the southward trails. He reached Fort Edward on the 30th, having taken twenty days to cover the twenty miles. He was now on the Hudson River, and the first part of his task was completed.

But his difficulties were increasing. Schuyler had fallen back to Stillwater, thirty miles above Albany, and all the country between was creek and tangled forest, admirable ground for the enemy's methods of war. It was no easy business to get his supplies and guns overland to the Hudson, and he had too few men to provide escorts for convoys. The easiest plan, to turn east into New England, was forbidden by his instructions. It had been arranged that Colonel St. Leger should make a diversion to assist him on the Mohawk, a tributary which enters the Hudson on the west bank above Albany. But if he was to get the benefit of St. Leger's movement he must advance

1777 simultaneously. Burgoyne, desperate about his supplies, resolved to capture the magazine of the New England militia at Bennington, thirty miles to the south-east. On 13th August he sent 500 men under Colonel Baum on the expedition; but there was treachery at work, and Baum's little force was destroyed.

Meantime St. Leger was faring ill on the Mohawk. He had trouble with his Indians, became involved in the siege of Fort Stanwix, and Benedict Arnold with 1,200 Massachusetts volunteers was hanging on his rear. Burgoyne saw his position becoming critical; but, since his orders allowed him no latitude, he managed to collect thirty days' provisions, and continued his advance. On 13th September he crossed to the west bank of the Hudson, and encamped in heavy rain for some days at Saratoga. On the 19th he moved towards Stillwater by the riverside road, and found the enemy strongly entrenched on Bemis Heights covering that place. On the preceding day, though he did not know it, the Americans had cut his line of supply and captured his store depot at the head of Lake George. General Horace Gates, who had succeeded Schuyler, had some 14,000 men, and, though himself an indifferent soldier, had Benedict Arnold among his lieutenants. There was an unoccupied hill on the American left which commanded the position, and to this Burgoyne directed his attention. He advanced in three columns —General Riedesel's on the left, General Fraser's on the right, and the centre under his own command. Burgoyne, with the 9th, Twenty-First, 62nd, and 20th from right to left, was soon in position—the total was less than 1,100 men—and when Arnold, who had at last induced Gates to move, tried to turn his right, Fraser's column was there to hold him. Arnold thereupon flung himself upon Burgoyne's centre, which was the weakest part in the British dispositions; but the Twenty-First, 62nd, and 20th held their own, and again and again hurled him back. For four hours their agony lasted, till at last Riedesel's pressure

SARATOGA

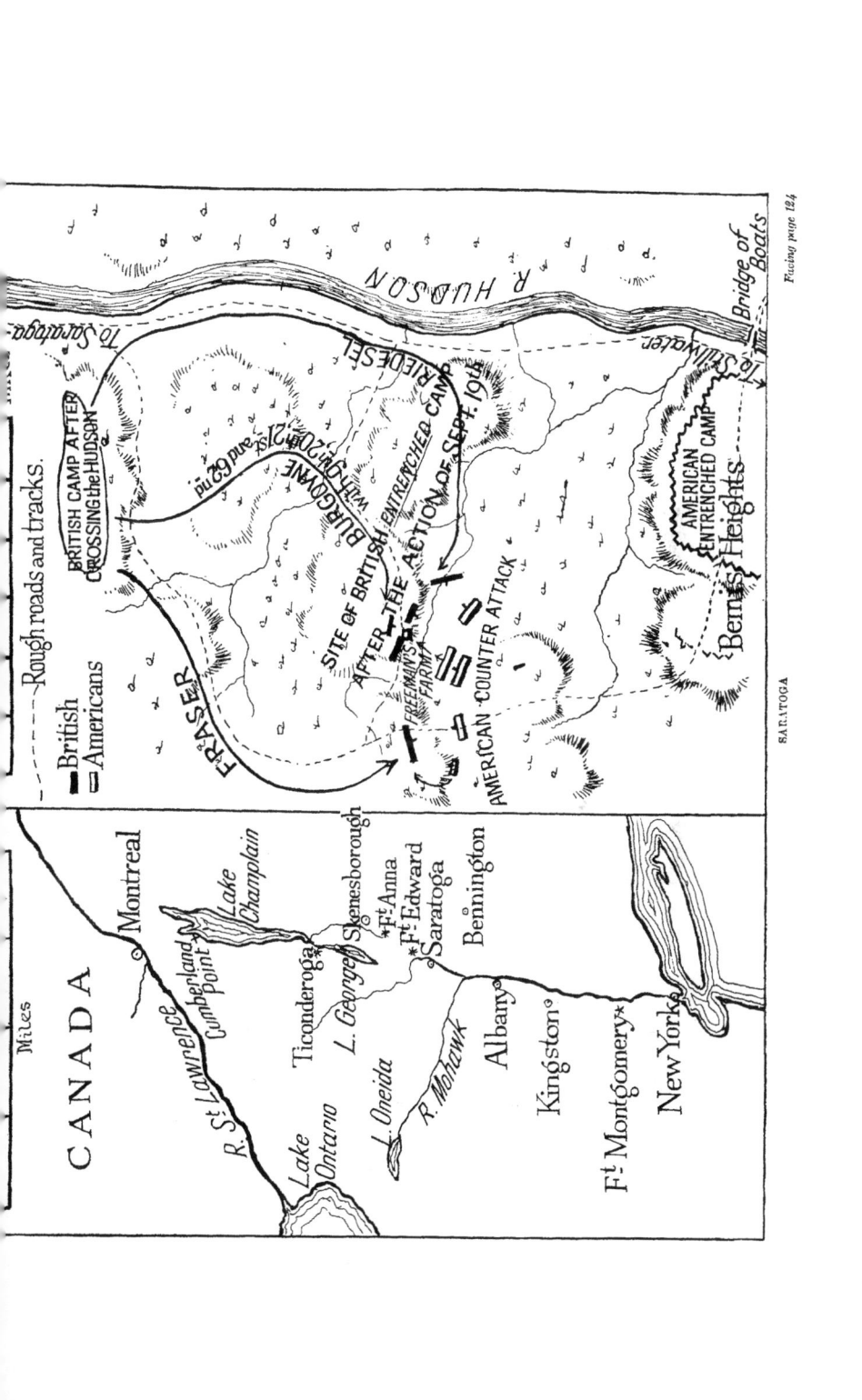

upon his flank forced Arnold to retreat. The British remained masters of the field, and bivouacked that night upon the ground they had won. But they paid a heavy price for victory. Simon Fraser was carried dying into camp, and the Twenty-First, the 62nd, and the 20th had 350 killed and wounded out of a total strength of 800. " Never were troops more hardly tried," Mr. Fortescue writes, " nor met their trial more grandly than these three noble battalions, with the forty-eight artillerymen who worked their four guns by their side."

Over Burgoyne the skies had darkened. The two armies lay facing each other in entrenchments, while the Americans sent expeditions to intercept British supplies and seize the British flotilla on Lake George. General Clinton at New York tried to save the situation and open the navigation of the Hudson from the south. He broke through the boom, taking Forts Clinton and Montgomery, and ascended the river as far as Kingston. But Burgoyne's position was too desperate for relief. Gates's army before him was daily increasing; he might still have retreated to Canada, but he dared not release a portion of the enemy's forces lest Washington might thereby be strengthened against Howe. On 7th October, when Clinton was at Fort Montgomery, Burgoyne made an effort to turn the enemy's left, but a sudden attack of the American General Morgan on his own left upset his plan. The battle that day became for the British a stubborn defensive. No sooner were they back inside their entrenchments than Benedict Arnold delivered a general assault. Burgoyne's right was turned, but with great skill he effected a retirement to a new front on some heights above the river. There next day he offered battle; but the enemy was outflanking his right, and he was forced to retreat upstream to Saratoga, leaving behind him 500 sick and wounded. Rain fell heavily, and his wearied troops, staggering into camp, had not the strength to cut wood and kindle fires, but sank like logs on the wet ground. At dawn on the 9th the Americans were

1777 revealed entrenching themselves on the heights across the river, and barring the road to Canada. Burgoyne trusted that by abandoning his guns and baggage he might cut his way back to Fort Edward, but his scouts brought word that the enemy held every road and ford. He waited a day or two, hoping for a message from Clinton which never came. He was surrounded and his troops were starving, so on 17th October he capitulated, and his 3,500 men laid down their arms to Gates and his 20,000.

Such was the surrender of Saratoga. The terms were that the troops should march out with the honours of war, and be shipped from Boston to England on the understanding that they did not serve again in America during the campaign. The American Generals, Gates, Washington, and the others, behaved with honour and chivalry. Fighting was suspended during Simon Fraser's burial, while the Americans fired a minute-gun in honour of the dead. At the frugal banquet after the surrender, in answer to Burgoyne's toast of General Washington, Gates drank to King George; everything that brave men could do was done to spare the feelings of the conquered. But Congress, then as ninety years later in the American Civil War, showed that baser standards ruled in civilian minds, and evaded every article of the compact. The Twenty-First had Lieutenants Currie, Mackenzie, Robertson, and Turnbull killed, and Captain the Hon. Malcolm Ramsay and Lieutenant Richardson wounded. Save for the officers who were exchanged and the few men who later escaped, the 200 or so who survived at Saratoga vanish into the mist. It was a surrender which dishonoured no man, except Lord George Germaine in his Downing Street cabinet. Burgoyne showed skill, resource, and courage; and for the rank-and-file let Mr. Fortescue speak: " In the whole history of the army I have encountered no grander display of steadfastness and fortitude than the heroic stand of the Twentieth, Twenty-First, and Sixty-Second, with their little handful of gunners, on the 19th of September; and it is surely a marvellous instance of gallantry and discipline that fifteen hundred men should have moved out cheerfully and confidently as they did on the 7th of October, in spite of much hardship and heavy losses, to attack an enemy of five times their number; that when forced back they should have retired with perfect order and coherence; and that, though fighting all day and marching or entrenching all night, they should never have lost heart." [1] The Twenty-First has no cause to blush for the autumn day which saw it, like Antony, " not cowardly " put off its harness.

[1] III., page 243. The story of Saratoga may be read in Fortescue, in *Burgoyne's Orderly Book* (ed. by O'Callaghan, 1860), and in Sir G. O. Trevelyan's *The American Revolution*, Part III., Chap. V.

CHAPTER VII

THE REVOLUTION WARS

The reconstruction of the regiment—Service in Nova Scotia—The French Revolution—Service in the West Indies—Martinique—Guadaloupe—Return to Scotland—Service in Ireland—The Dublin riots.

1777 SARATOGA, as we have seen, was the virtual end of the Twenty-First. The obligation of civilized peoples to observe a treaty even when it goes against their interest—as Britain observed the Convention of Cintra which restored to Napoleon at a critical moment 25,000 picked troops—was disregarded by Congress, and even so warm a partisan of the American cause as Sir G. O. Trevelyan " would give much if those unseemly pages could be expunged from their history." [1] We are able to follow in the diary of Lieutenant Dalgleish, who was afterwards to be lieutenant-colonel of the regiment, the stages in the melancholy progress. The troops marched first to Cambridge, Massachusetts, arriving there on 8th November. There were officers' wives in the party, including Lady Harriet Acland and Madame Riedesel and her children. In New England they were well treated, the country people flocking in to see the show, and much disappointed in the appearance of the unfortunate Lord Napier, a lieutenant in the 31st, who, muddy and dishevelled, did not come up to their notions of a peer. "If that be a lord," said one woman, "I never desire to see any other lord than the Lord Jehovah." A year later they were

[1] *The American Revolution*, Part III., page 225.

JOHN DALGLEISH

on the march for Charlottesville,[1] in Virginia, six hundred miles distant, through deep snow, where on arrival they found neither food nor shelter prepared. Congress was busy meantime in exchanging British officers for American officers of equal rank, which was in flat defiance of the Saratoga terms, and the state governments were competing with each other to seduce the rank-and-file into the Revolutionary army, though Washington from Valley Forge bitterly protested against the shameful practice.[2] A few of the men accepted the offer, more managed to escape to the British army, and the rest, after they were separated from their officers in 1781, disappear from our ken. Dalgleish, while at Charlottesville, rented a house on a plantation, which he called Solitary Hall, and abode there till November 1780, when he was exchanged for a lieutenant of the Connecticut militia. In general the Virginian gentry were hospitable towards the British officers, who, we may assume, unlike the rank-and-file, were treated with some consideration. But Dalgleish was very weary of confinement when he reached New York in December 1780. Two months later he was back in Scotland, whither various other officers had preceded him, and the business of beating up recruits began.[3]

The recruiting area seems to have been at first the Scottish midlands. We find the adjutant at Stirling instructing Dalgleish to raise men in West Fife and along the Forth. A year later the headquarters were moved to Dunbar, and Dalgleish was busy in the

1777-81

[1] Then a shabby little country town, not yet beautified by Thomas Jefferson's noble University of Virginia.
[2] Washington to the President of the Council of Massachusetts, March 17, 1778.
[3] According to *Burgoyne's Orderly Book* the officers of the Twenty-First who surrendered at Saratoga were Brigadier-General James Hamilton; Major George Forster; Captains Neill Maclean, Alexander Baillie, James Lovell, Jasper Farmer, George Petrie, Thomas (Michael) Kirkman, and George Brodie; Lieutenants W. Featherstone, John Hepburn, George Edward Schlagel, William Douglas, Robert Innes, Robert Burnet, John Blackwood, John Dalgleish, and Lord Torphichen; and Surgeon William Pemberton. Of these, all except Maclean and Baillie appear in the Army List for 1779. In the Army List for 1784, the names of Kirkman, Featherstone, Hepburn, Burnet, and Lord Torphichen have dropped out.

neighbourhood of Duns, Kelso, and Jedburgh. By the summer of 1782 the Twenty-First was in shape again, and early in 1783 it was quartered in Edinburgh. Meanwhile the American War had dragged to its ignominious close. On October 19, 1781, Cornwallis had surrendered at Yorktown, and the regiment was placed on the peace establishment. Late in 1783 it marched across Scotland, and embarked at Saltcoats for Dublin, where at the time were six regiments of infantry and one of cavalry, and mess expenses were on a scale to distress Dalgleish's frugal soul. For six years the Twenty-First remained in Ireland, scattered by companies up and down the land—not always in comfortable quarters, for in many places there were no barracks, and the peat-reek was hard on the men's clothes. In June 1785 we find it being reviewed by General Charno in the presence of the Commander-in-Chief, and being complimented as the finest battalion in the country. The regiment was back in Dublin in 1787, where its duties were lightened by the establishment of police guards; and in the beginning of 1789 it received, along with the 20th Foot, orders for Nova Scotia. There was much delay in procuring transports, and it was not till 1st June that it sailed on board the *Actæon*, carrying with it a new pair of silk colours from London. James Hamilton, now a major-general, was still in command of it, but that month, Mackay, the Scottish Commander-in-Chief, having died, it got a new colonel. This was the Hon. James Murray, a younger son of the fourth Lord Elibank, and one of the most famous of living Scottish soldiers. He had fought at Rochefort and Louisburg, and had commanded a brigade under James Wolfe at the taking of Quebec, thereafter acting with distinction as Commander-in-Chief in Canada; and in the beginning of 1782, as Governor of Minorca, had defended Fort St. Philip against the forces of France and Spain. He was now a full general in the army, and had been triumphantly acquitted of the charges brought against him after the Minorca surrender.

The four years which the regiment spent in Nova Scotia were, according to Dalgleish's diary, a time of deadly dullness.[1] It was stranded among great woods in raw townships still in the building, and the men had to set to work and erect quarters and make gardens. Living was dear, the local population was sparse, and the regiment, not altogether to its loss, was forced back upon its own society. Its chief duty seems to have been that of gamekeepers, and we find during the first winter there an expedition, which got badly frost-bitten, sent out to help the authorities to capture a band of moose-poachers in the snowy forests. At Halifax it had better entertainment, for living was cheaper (beef, 4d. a lb.; fowls, 6d. each; trout, 2s. a dozen; and a 22-lb. salmon for 3s.), the band was presented with new instruments, and we hear of a ball given by Governor Wentworth, to which three hundred guests were invited. It was a peaceful interlude for the regiment, when all got to know each other, and had the opportunity of training in reasonable comfort and in a climate which enlarged a man's vigour. Many a soldier of the Twenty-First during the next years must have looked back with regret on the greenery and the cool winds of that northern land.

In March 1793 came a violent transition. The decade since Yorktown had been, on the whole, a time of peace, when the British army could digest certain hardly-learned lessons. The American War had wrought a revolution in tactics and training, though the full consequences were not yet apparent. The old solidity of Fontenoy and Minden was no longer the ideal. The importance of the firearm was realized, and the aim was the greatest possible front of fire; so the depth of the ranks was reduced from three to two, and movements were conducted with greater elasticity and more independence on the part of small units and individuals. There were still soldiers who held firm by the Prussian methods; Sir John Moore had not

---

[1] Sir John Moore, serving there ten years earlier in Hamilton's Regiment, had the same complaint to make.

1793 yet arisen to harmonize what was best in the new and in the old; but, on the whole, the double rank had carried the day. In lesser matters there had been also changes. The cumbrous clothing and headgear of the soldier had been revised in the light of experience in the East Indies. The cocked hat had developed from the old broad hat of the Cavalier to the most absurd creation that ever vexed the head of a fighting man, and was now looped up in back and front—for which see any picture of Napoleon—thereby leaving both the eyes and the back of the neck at the mercy of the sun. Such a head-dress, as well as the old coat and breeches, was preposterous in a torrid sun, so about 1790 a simple round hat and a jacket and trousers were devised for fighting in warm climates, while light infantry were given a cap of black leather. It was all very far from perfection, but it was an advance which enabled the infantryman to face in the next quarter of a century campaigns which, in respect of sheer physical misery, had not been known before in the history of the army.

The French Revolution was an event which had its roots deep in the past, and its consequences overshadowed the century which followed. Like a new chemical added to a mixture, it left no one of the old constituents unaltered. The movement, which may be dated from that July day in 1789 when the Bastille fell, was to involve the whole round earth, and affect the destiny of the remotest lands. Here we are not concerned with the main march of that epic tale, for it was the fate of our regiment to be engaged not in the centre but at the periphery of the struggle. It was a pawn in that strange aberration of Pitt's policy, based upon the notion that France could be beaten outside Europe by destroying her overseas trade. Pitt wanted to bankrupt the enemy, to hasten his financial exhaustion by closing to him the distant seas—a cheap way, it seemed to him, of winning the war, and a sure one, for, though Britain had let her army fall into a great decline, she had still her invincible navy. The error was twofold. He fixed upon the sugar islands of

THE FRENCH REVOLUTION

the West Indies as the vital spot for attack, forgetful of the lesson of English history—of Cromwell's expedition to Hispaniola, of the Cartagena affair—that white troops could not fight a protracted campaign in such climates under the then existing conditions of service. There was also the strategic blunder. He was attacking his enemy in an unvital part, and he was frittering away his strength on divergent operations. In the years 1793–94, when it was his business to scotch the Revolutionary Government of France by striking at its head, he set out on adventures in every quarter of the globe. He took six West Indian islands —strategically as important as the North Pole; he landed in Haiti; he sent a force under the Duke of York to the Netherlands; he held Toulon as long as he could; he seized Corsica; he sent an expedition to La Vendée. The consequence was that he succeeded nowhere, and the Revolutionary Government at the end of that time was stronger than ever. Next year, 1795, when things were going badly on other battle-grounds, he chose to send an expedition to Cape Town, to attack Demerara, and to make a disastrous landing on an island in Quiberon Bay. And so he continued to indulge his passion for outlandish geography, while France grew in strength and the star of Napoleon rose above the horizon.

On April 23, 1793, the Twenty-First [1] embarked at Halifax in four sailing brigs of about 130 tons each, and on 20th May arrived at Bridgetown in the island of Barbados. The 65th Regiment accompanied it, and presently there arrived the 32nd from Gibraltar. General Bruce was in command, and his instructions were to take Martinique. Bruce, who had been promised 2,000 men and found only 1,100, considered his numbers inadequate. But his orders were explicit—the French royalists in the island were said to be very strong— and so on 10th June the force, under Major-General

---

[1] In August 1792 Hamilton became colonel of the 15th Foot, and was succeeded as lieutenant-colonel of the Twenty-First by Colin Graham, who had come from the 16th to the Twenty-First as major in 1789.

1793 Garth, sailed with Admiral Gardner's squadron. It made Martinique on the 12th, and on the 14th the battalion companies of the infantry, under Lieutenant-Colonel Graham of the Twenty-First, were landed at Case de Navire on the south-west coast near Fort Bourbon, in order to occupy the chief royalist area. The rest of the little army, including the flank companies [1] of the Twenty-First, made a landing two days later on the north-west shore, not far from the town of St. Pierre, which was the main objective. Then came a swarm of misfortunes. The weather broke in a downpour of rain; the royalists, who knew the country, and from whom much was expected, marched in two columns to join the British, mistook each other in the darkness of the night, and opened a fire which broke the thigh of their general; thereupon panic set in, the two columns dispersed, and there were no more royalists to be looked for. General Bruce, seeing the hopelessness of his allies, decided to withdraw his troops, and accordingly on the 21st re-embarked, taking with him such of the unhappy royalist families as desired to leave. The Twenty-First was for seven days in camp at La Costa, almost under the guns of Fort Bourbon, in order to cover the embarkation, and Dalgleish's diary is eloquent of the perils of the situation.

After landing the royalists at Dominica and Barbados, the Twenty-First arrived at Antigua, where it was quartered in salubrious barracks some fifteen miles from the capital. There for a little it had peace, for General Bruce had told the Government that, since the republicans were enlisting the black inhabitants by free grants of citizenship, it was useless to attack the French islands except with a considerable force. But disaster was soon to overtake it from a more insidious enemy than the French. Yellow fever broke out in

---

[1] The Fusilier regiments had at one time both grenadier and light companies (there is a painting of a grenadier *circa* 1763), but the custom soon arose of designating them "right flank" and "left flank" companies. The same practice obtained in Light Infantry regiments.

YELLOW FEVER

the islands, and in August Lieutenant Sandby, and in October Major Farmer, died while on visits to Barbados. On 1st November a vessel brought the disease to Antigua, and before the end of the year the regiment had lost nine officers besides Sandby and Farmer—Captains Ward, Offley, and Garforth, Captain-Lieutenant B. Lewis, and Lieutenants Grandby, Knox, C. McGachan, William Neate, and Second Lieutenant Appleby, in addition to 94 rank-and-file, and a number of women and children. Dalgleish, the diarist, now a captain, had the fever, but was fortunate enough to recover. Hitherto Antigua had been supposed to be a health resort, for only one British officer had died there in the past ten years.

It was a forlorn little remnant that began the year 1794, but during January some fifty recruits arrived from home, and drafts to the number of 200 were received from the 32nd, 40th, and 67th Regiments. Meantime the Government was preparing another island campaign on a larger scale than the last. The disastrous expedition to St. Domingo was dispatched, and preparations were made for operations in the Windward group. In these last the Twenty-First was fated to play a notable part. General Sir Charles Grey had sailed for the West Indies with Sir John Jervis in November 1793, with instructions to take Martinique, Guadeloupe, and St. Lucia, and then proceed to St. Domingo, Henry Dundas having previously compromised his chances of success by taking away half his battalions for the La Vendée affair. Grey arrived at Barbados in January 1794, Bruce having returned sick to England. The transports were slow in coming, and many of the troops arrived in bad health; but the flank companies of all the regiments in the Windward Islands had been dispatched to Barbados, and Grey had at his disposal nearly 7,000 men. He resolved to strike first at Martinique, where, in spite of the abilities of the French commander, Rochambeau, he believed that the excessive number of forts must dissipate the strength of the defence.

1794 The Twenty-First at this time was scattered far and wide. On 15th January three companies had been sent to Dominica, two were at St. Kitts, and one at Montserrat, while a detachment of forty men, under Captain Darrah, was at St. John's in Antigua, guarding French prisoners. When Grey set out on 3rd February, he took with him three companies of the regiment, two of which were the flank companies—all the grenadier

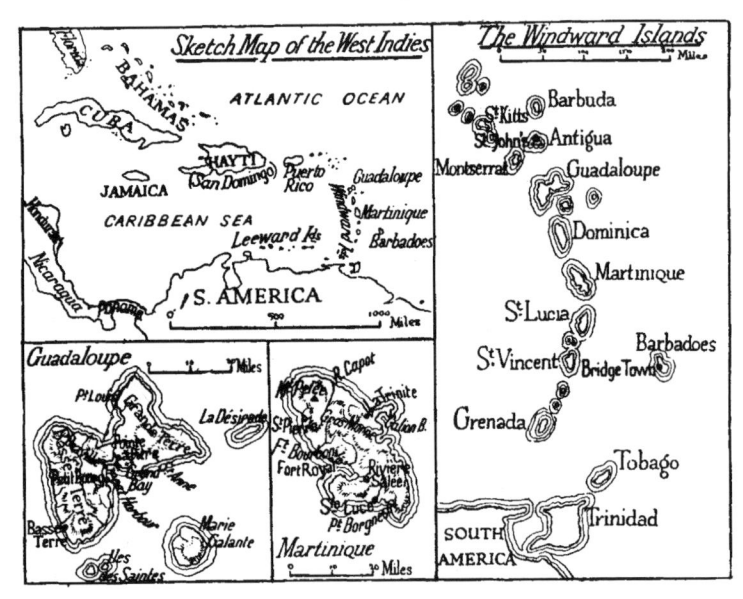

CAMPAIGN IN WEST INDIES

battalions being brigaded together under Colonel Campbell and the light battalions under Colonel Myers. Besides these he had three infantry brigades, under Sir C. Gordon, Thomas Dundas, and John Whyte. Martinique was reached on 5th February.

The attack was arranged in three divisions. Dundas made for the Bay of Galion on the east coast, Gordon for the old landing-place of Case de Navire in Fort Royal Bay, and Grey and Sir John Jervis for the Bay of Marin at the extreme south-eastern point. Grey landed safely that evening, and destroyed the batteries

CAPTURE OF MARTINIQUE

at the Point de Borgnese and Sainte Luce. Next morning, the 6th, he landed his whole division at Trois Rivières to the west of Sainte Luce, and marched overland to Rivière Salée, while Whyte followed the coast and captured the garrisons, among them the formidable post on Pigeon Island. This enabled the British fleet to enter Fort Royal Bay. Meantime from Case de Navire Gordon had mastered the country north and west of Fort Royal, and was encamped within a league of the fortress. Dundas at Galion Bay had fought his way through the fields of sugar-cane, taken the little town of Trinité, and by driving the enemy from the peak called Gros Morne, had virtually cut the island in two. By the 9th Dundas, moving from the north-east, was within three miles of Fort Royal, and on the 14th had joined hands with Grey. That night Dundas returned to Trinité, and dispatched Colonel Campbell with a picked force to make his way north-west to the ridge of Mont Pelée to the north of St. Pierre, while he himself with his grenadiers followed the east coast of the island north to the mouth of the river Capot. There he turned west and climbed through the ravines and forests to the crater of Pelée, doing twenty rough miles within twelve hours in the darkness of a February night. The day of the 16th was occupied in forcing the enemy out of various strongholds, and on the 17th the capital, St. Pierre, fell without resistance into the British hands.

It now remained to reduce Forts Bourbon and Louis, the defences of Fort Royal. Bellegarde, the mulatto general, resisted stoutly, but on 28th February he was forced to surrender. Then came the final attack upon the forts, where Rochambeau stood at bay—an attack delivered in a deluge of rain. The army and the navy worked in perfect co-operation, Fort Royal was carried by the grenadiers and light companies, and at last, on 23rd March, the French garrison surrendered and moved out with all the honours of war. The capture of Martinique was a brilliant achievement, and so skilful was Grey's generalship that the total British casualties did not exceed 350.

1794

1794 Leaving six battalions to hold Martinique, Grey sailed at once for St. Lucia. There he pursued the same tactics of converging attacks, and in twenty-four hours the island was in his hands. Two more battalions were left there as garrison, and after a visit to Martinique, Grey arrived at Guadeloupe on 10th April. Here the problem was more serious. The island is shaped like a short dumb-bell, and the great harbour, which forms the southern side of the handle, was strongly fortified. Early on the 11th Grey landed 1,000 men at Grand Bay on the east shore of the harbour, after the ships had silenced the shore batteries. To the west was the strong Fort Fleur d'Épée, which was impregnable from the seaward side; but behind it lay a second fort, Morne Mascotte, the capture of which would render it untenable. Grey sent a detachment under Edward, Duke of Kent (the father of Queen Victoria), against Morne Mascotte, and with it went the right flank company of the Twenty-First; another force under Dundas was directed against Fleur d'Épée from the west; while a third, under Colonel Symes, cooperated with Dundas along the coast. At five a.m. on the 12th the firing of a gun from Sir John Jervis's flagship gave the signal for the conjoint attack. Soldiers and bluejackets swarmed over the defences before the tropic darkness had gone, and when the daylight came the enemy had fled to Pointe-à-Pitre, and Grande Terre, the northern half of Guadeloupe, was in Grey's hands. In that attack the Twenty-First lost Captain John Macdonald, of the ancient house of Kinlochmoidart, who fell mortally wounded and died on the 15th, and twenty-one men of his right flank company. Macdonald appears on the regimental roll as a second lieutenant in 1790, but in those latitudes promotion came fast. The capture of the rest of the island quickly followed. On the 14th Grey landed at Petit Bourg on the other side of the great harbour, while Dundas landed on the west coast, and the two forces moved upon the town of Basse Terre, which capitulated on the 21st. The campaign proved what could be done by a small army working in unison with a small naval squadron, if every unit were efficient, against enemy numbers which were entangled in too numerous fortresses.

To capture French islands was one thing, but to hold them was another. Sickness and weariness were beginning to take heavy toll of the British, and reinforcements were sorely needed, when the battalion companies of four regiments arrived in May from Ireland. The flank companies of the Twenty-First were returned to Antigua, and Grey was compelled to send a detachment under General Whyte to St. Domingo. Then came yellow fever, which carried off the gallant Thomas Dundas at Guadeloupe, and presently news arrived from Virginia of a French fleet in Hampton Roads. Grey was at St. Kitts on his way home to England when he had word that seven ships and 1,500 troops had reached Guadeloupe from France. He immediately turned back, and at the same time the flank companies of the Twenty-First, which had now been made up to sixty men each, exclusive of officers and drummers, were ordered again to Guadeloupe. The work of April had to be done over again.

Grey found that things had gone ill in his absence. He arrived on 7th June at Guadeloupe to find Pointe-à-Pitre and all its defences in the hands of the enemy, largely owing to the cowardice of the French royalist volunteers; and the black population, inflamed with the doctrines of the republicans, was led by one Victor Hugues, a former colleague of Fouquier-Tinville, and a man in whom brutality was conjoined with resource and vigour. The northern half of the island, Grande Terre, was temporarily lost, so Grey took up his headquarters at Basse Terre in the southern half, while Francis Dundas, at Petit Bourg, kept watch on Pointe-à-Pitre, and the British fleet blockaded the great harbour. On the 19th a landing was effected on Grande Terre, and batteries were thrown up against Fort Fleur d'Épée. By the end of the month the enemy was driven from his Morne Mascotte position, and the way was prepared for the final assault on Pointe-à-Pitre

1794 There was need for a decisive blow at the earliest possible moment, for the British troops were weak with sickness, and mostly shoeless and in rags, since no stores had reached them from England. The rainy season had begun, when a dripping gloom alternated with blazing heat, and as the hurricane season was also due, the fleet would soon be no longer safe at sea. Grey struck his blow on 1st July, when he ordered Symes, now a brigadier, to attack the hill commanding the town. Symes, with his little force of grenadiers and light infantry, among which were the flank companies of the Twenty-First, started off in the darkness; but by some mistake, instead of assaulting the hill, marched on Pointe-à-Pitre itself. There he found himself under a desperate fire from the heights; his men fell into confusion, and at daybreak he was compelled to withdraw after heavy losses. He himself died of his wounds. Of the two companies of the Twenty-First, one third were casualties: Lieutenant Knollis fell, Lieutenants Price and Colepepper were wounded, the former mortally. Grey, convinced that his men were being tried beyond human endurance, withdrew from Grande Terre.

Nothing remained but to isolate the southern half of Guadeloupe from the northern. A fortified quadrilateral was established at Berville on the connecting isthmus—an ill-chosen site, for the ground was swampy and low, and the men died like flies. There Grey left 1,800 men under Colin Graham of the Twenty-First, now a brigadier, and departed for Martinique. The situation in the Windward Islands had become most grave, for the flames of revolution were raging everywhere, and there were not more than thirteen complete British battalions to hold the ground. The Government in London seemed to have forgotten this poor remnant, and no supplies or reinforcements reached them. Then, at the end of July, came orders from home about prize money which compelled both Grey and Jervis to resign their commands—the last step in the bungling of Pitt and Henry Dundas.

THE CAMP OF BERVILLE

Presently the enemy took the offensive in the southern part of Guadeloupe, while in the camp at Berville the British troops were dying at the rate of 300 a month, and scarcely 500 were fit for duty. Hugues, the mulatto, took Petit Bourg, where was the British hospital, and massacred every man in it. By capturing Bacchus Point he cut off communications between Berville and the fleet, and by 30th September he was assaulting Berville itself. The British, weak with sickness, nevertheless beat off the first attack; but Graham was severely wounded, and his second-in-command was killed. Through a desperate week the attacks continued, until on 6th October, provisions being at an end and scarcely a man able to stand, Graham surrendered on condition that the garrison should march out with the honours of war and be at once shipped to England. Let Mr. Fortescue complete the tale. " Thereupon one hundred and twenty-five ghastly figures staggered out of the lines, ' fitter for hospital than to be under arms '—all that remained of what had once been three battalions and twenty-three companies of infantry and two companies of artillery. For a whole year, despite the capitulation, they were detained as prisoners; but they died so rapidly in the weeks that followed the surrender that probably few of them ever saw England again. Yet though the tale of their noble service must remain for ever but half told, the records of the British army contain no grander example of heroism than those of the dying garrison of the Camp of Berville."

There were none of the Twenty-First at Berville except their former lieutenant-colonel, who did not survive his captivity. Thomas Meyrick had succeeded him in the command in September 1794, from the 99th Foot; but he was at the time in England, so Dalgleish, the diarist, took command as senior officer till Meyrick arrived in June of the following year. The companies which had been with Symes retired in July to St. Kitts and the right flank company to Antigua, where were the battalion companies. In both stations fever raged, and in August the regiment was over 800 short of establishment. In June old General Murray had died, and James Hamilton, formerly its lieutenant-colonel, returned from the 15th Foot to the regiment as colonel. For two years the Twenty-First had a miserable life, divided between Antigua, Dominica, and Guadeloupe, taking its full share in the comfortless and futile campaigns, and something more than its share in the prevailing diseases. When the triumphant mulatto, Hugues, moved upon Basse Terre in the late autumn of 1794, three companies of the regiment were with General Prescott in the defence of Fort Matilda. They had been originally ordered to join Graham at Berville, but arrived only to find the place fallen. They took part in the stubborn defence and in the skilful withdrawal on 10th December, and were reduced by casualties to one captain, three lieutenants, six sergeants, and ninety-two rank-and-file. Prescott in his dispatch praised highly their courage and endurance. Guadeloupe was now wholly lost, and Dalgleish at Antigua was busy mounting heavy guns in case of an invasion of that island. In June of next year came the attempt of the revolutionists to stir up rebellion in Dominica, which was held by between 400 and 500 men of the 15th and Twenty-First (respectively under Captains Bathe and Darrah), of whom two in every five were on the sick list. By a swift march across the island the little force surrounded and captured the invaders, and, since the negroes remained loyal to Britain, Dominica was never in serious danger.

In 1796 the most wretched period in the whole history of the regiment came to an end. The Twenty-First had won great honour, but it was worn to a shadow of its former self by three years of abject misery. Everybody was disheartened, not least the officers, for they saw the frequent vacancies filled up by men from other regiments who had not, like them, endured the heat of the day. Dalgleish did not even get his majority till he had been in command for over a year. The last straw came in 1796, when the bulk of the

RETURN TO SCOTLAND

regiment was drafted to other formations, principally the 59th, instead of being sent home as a unit. Dalgleish went to England that summer in a merchantman, and the rest, who were able or permitted to move, followed in transports, one of which was lost at sea with Captain Grant and a party of rank-and-file. In November the remains of the Twenty-First were in home waters, and embarking at Gravesend for Leith. Thus concluded what Mr. Fortescue has called " perhaps the most discreditable campaign in the records of the army "—a campaign fought in a white man's graveyard for no conceivable strategic purpose of the slightest value. Some 80,000 soldiers had been lost to the service, " including forty thousand actually dead, the latter number exceeding the total losses of Wellington's army from death, discharges, desertion, and all causes from the beginning to the end of the Peninsular War. Yet with all this miserable squandering of life France . . . was little the worse, and England even less the better." [1]

At the close of 1796 the Twenty-First was at Perth under the temporary command of Major Dalgleish. On New Year's Day, 1797, it was at Paisley—a total of 119 men—while recruiting parties were busy everywhere in the Scottish Lowlands. Paisley was a pleasant abode and the people hospitable; the men had for barracks an old granary, while the officers were in lodgings in the town or at the Abercorn Inn. Dalgleish, the diarist, was now a lieutenant-colonel, and for a time there seems to have been a divided command, for Meyrick, now on the headquarters staff, still remained senior lieutenant-colonel, while Dalgleish commanded the regiment in Scotland. The first business was refitment, and Meyrick sent down from London by wagon new hats and uniforms, silver lace for the

---

[1] Fortescue, IV., Part I., page 496. The doings of the Twenty-First in the West Indies have found a place in fiction. That prolific romancer, James Grant, himself formerly of the 62nd Regiment, has given in *Oliver Ellis, or the Fusiliers* (1861), a vivid and fairly accurate picture of regimental life in the last decade of the eighteenth century, and of certain episodes in the Martinique and Guadeloupe fighting, including the death of Kinlochmoidart.

coats of the sergeant-major and drum-major, and black cloth for the gaiters; and also, since all the musical instruments had gone down with Captain Grant's ill-fated party in the *Mackerel*, a new set of drums. In the summer the regiment moved to Glasgow, which it found much less pleasant than Paisley, and a few months later to Dundee. In October Dalgleish disposed of his commission, and passed out of the regiment, his place being taken by Lord Evelyn Stuart of the Bute family, a young gentleman of twenty-four, who had been in the 1st Guards.[1]

For three years the regiment occupied various stations in Scotland, slowly increasing its strength. In January 1800 we find it furnishing, at the order of the Commander-in-Chief, a detachment of three officers and thirty-four men " to be instructed in the use of the rifle and the exercise of true light infantry "—an anticipation of the famous Shorncliffe camp which began two years later under Sir John Moore. In June of that year it embarked at Portpatrick for Ireland, where its numbers were presently increased to 800 rank-and-file by volunteers from the Scots Fencible regiments,[2] which had been sent there after the 1798 rebellion. Its first station was Enniskillen, where it remained for two years and soon became 1,000 strong. It was a notably respectable and well-behaved body of men, and the people of Enniskillen took the regiment to their hearts; so much so, that in 1802, when it moved, a number of the inhabitants sent a memorial to the Irish Commander-in-Chief, begging that it might be sent back, and offering to defray the expenses of the return.

At Londonderry its establishment was reduced

---

[1] There is some confusion about the command of the regiment at this time. Meyrick remains in the Army List as senior lieutenant-colonel till 1814. In Appendix II. in Groves's *History of the Twenty-First Regiment*, a certain Andrew Ross appears as junior lieutenant-colonel between September 1, 1795, and November 7, 1797; and there is no mention of Dalgleish, who, we know, was lieutenant-colonel on December 14, 1796. Ross, who came from the 31st Foot, may have been junior lieutenant-colonel up to Dalgleish's appointment.

[2] The Fencibles were regular troops, enlisted for the duration of the war, and for home service only.

THE DUBLIN RIOTS

because of the Peace of Amiens; but next year, when 1803-5 the brittleness of that peace was apparent and the regiment was in Dublin, the establishment was again augmented. These years saw changes in the commands. Hamilton, the colonel, died in 1803, and was succeeded by William Gordon of Fyvie, a son of the second Earl of Aberdeen. Gordon had raised a Highland regiment of his own in 1777, and had been colonel-commandant of the 60th Royal Americans, and colonel successively of the 7th Foot and the 71st Highlanders. Lord Evelyn Stuart ceased to be junior lieutenant-colonel in June 1802, and was succeeded by Lyde Brown, from the 85th Foot.

In 1803 the Twenty-First was involved in one of those sordid Irish affairs which the British soldier has always detested—a fight with a crazy and childish rabble. On 23rd July the men were quartered in Cork Street, Thomas Street, and Coombe Barracks, while the officers were in private lodgings. That evening a mob assembled in the " Liberties," armed with pikes and muskets, and started on a career of outrage. It fell in with the Lord Chief-Justice, Lord Kilwarden, dragged him from his carriage and murdered him, and presently met and murdered Lieutenant-Colonel Lyde Brown of the Twenty-First as he was hurrying from his quarters. The regiment, now under the command of Major Donald Robertson, took a leading part in quelling the insurrection, and during the fighting of that hot July night had twelve men killed and wounded. Its discipline stood it in good stead, and it earned the compliments of the Commander-in-Chief in Ireland, Lieutenant-General the Hon. H. E. Fox, and the official thanks of the City of Dublin. Two of its officers, Lieutenant Stuart Home Douglas, who commanded a flank company, and Second Lieutenant and Adjutant Felix Brady, distinguished themselves especially, and were each presented with a piece of plate by the Corporation.

Donald Robertson succeeded the dead lieutenant-colonel, and gave place in 1804 to John Wilson, who held the post for a year only, being followed in 1805

1805 by Frederick Adam (long afterwards, as a famous soldier, to return to the Twenty-First as colonel), with, as a junior colleague, William Paterson, who had risen steadily in the regiment since he entered it as a lieutenant in 1791. In 1804 it moved from Dublin to Loughrea, and the following year embarked for England. Then for a year it was stationed at various places in the south—Weymouth, and Lewes, and Colchester; and in January 1806 marched to London to take part in Nelson's funeral at St. Paul's, when the people of Britain mourned, as they had never mourned before, for a hero who had captured both their imagination and their heart. The Wars of the Revolution had ended, and the sun of Napoleon was now blazing in the sky. The very shores of England were threatened, and the nation had awakened at last to its peril and its duty. The Twenty-First was to be used no longer in outland wars, but in the main battle-ground of Europe.

CHAPTER VIII

THE WAR WITH NAPOLEON

The 2nd Battalion formed—The 1st Battalion in Sicily—Sir Frederick Adam—The expedition to Egypt—The Ischia expedition—The defence of Messina—Service in the Spanish Peninsula—The entry into Genoa—The 2nd Battalion in Ireland—The attack on Bergen-op-Zoom—The 2nd Battalion disbanded—The 1st Battalion in America—Bladensburg—The capture of Washington—The failure at Baltimore—The Louisiana campaign—New Orleans.

THE renewal of war drove the Government of Britain to fresh efforts towards the recruiting of adequate armies, since Pitt's various Volunteer Acts and the Militia Act of 1802 had proved to the last degree unsatisfactory. On July 6, 1803, an Act was passed known as the Additional Force Act, to raise by ballot a new army of reserves of 50,000 men to serve within the United Kingdom. This levy was to be formed into fifty battalions, which were to act as second battalions to regiments of the line, and the men were to be encouraged by bounties to fill up gaps in the first battalions as occasion arose. Like all Addington's measures, it was half-hearted, for, though meant to increase the regular army, it tended to attract into second battalions men who might have been enlisted for the regular first battalions. Nevertheless, it added considerably to the fighting power of Britain; and, since there was no lack of patriotic feeling in the land, the force was quickly raised. Six thousand was the number fixed for the Scottish contribution, and from the men of Ayr and Renfrew a second battalion for the Twenty-

1806

1806 First was embodied at Ayr, and placed on the establishment on December 25, 1804. For the rest of the war with Napoleon our regiment had therefore two battalions, which between them fought over a great part of the earth's surface. The record may be divided into the service in the Mediterranean of the first battalion, and its subsequent service in America, and the short campaign of the second battalion in the Low Countries.

I

On May 1, 1806, the 1st Twenty-First, under one of its junior lieutenant-colonels, Frederick Adam,[1] embarked at Tilbury for Sicily, and disembarked at Messina on 26th July. For Britain it was not a cheering stage of the war. At Ulm and Austerlitz the year before Napoleon had shattered the armies of Austria, and was now preparing to do the same by Prussia at Jena and Auerstadt; Trafalgar had indeed been won, but Pitt was dead; in Italy a French kingdom had been established, and the iron crown of Lombardy had been placed on the conqueror's head; in the spring of that very year Joseph Bonaparte had entered Naples as king, and its wretched Bourbon monarch had fled to Sicily and British protection. Sicily could not be regarded by the British Government without anxiety. The squalid court of Naples, which held the Sicilian crown, was nothing to them; but if Sicily fell into French hands it would imperil, as Nelson had always urged, British ascendancy in the Mediterranean, and France's hold on Italy was a similar menace. As soon as the scare of invasion had passed, Pitt had prepared plans for an Italian campaign, in conjunction with Austria and Russia; but Austerlitz upset one half of the scheme, and Neapolitan treachery the other.

[1] Adam, who was born in 1781, entered the army in 1795, and served as a volunteer in Sir Ralph Abercrombie's expedition to the Helder. On his return he was given a company in the 9th Foot, and transferred in 1799 to the Coldstream Guards, accompanying the regiment to Egypt. In 1805, at the age of twenty-four, he purchased a lieutenant-colonelcy in the Twenty-First. See the monograph in German by Alfred von Reumont, 1854.

THE SITUATION IN SICILY 149

Naples was evacuated, and the small British force   *1806*
concentrated at Messina for the defence of Sicily.
Presently the garrison, under Sir John Stuart, was
increased to nearly 8,000 men, heavy guns were sent
out, and a squadron under Sir Sidney Smith was detailed for its protection. Joseph Bonaparte at Naples
was in sore straits, with an undisciplined army and
subjects for the most part in rebellion, and the way
seemed open for an effective stroke by a British combined land and sea force. Such a chance was squandered
by the vanity of Stuart and Sidney Smith. A descent on
Calabria did indeed lead to the victory of Maida on July
4, 1806, a battle won by the superiority of the British
soldier's fire. But this success had no fruitful results,
and was soon followed by the surrender of Gaeta, the
mainland fortress which the Prince of Hesse-Philipstadt
had gallantly held for King Ferdinand. The only
redeeming feature in that muddled operation was the
capture of the fortress of Scilla by the British, after
which Sir John Stuart, leaving garrisons there and at
Reggio, returned to Sicily. When the 1st Twenty-First
arrived on 26th July, General Henry Fox, a brother of
the statesman, had taken over the chief command in
the Mediterranean, and with him was Sir John Moore,
who was not likely to tolerate bungling. But the
mischief had been done. Naples, which might have
been made an awkward distraction for Napoleon, was
secure in Joseph Bonaparte's hands, and the whole
French army in Italy was released for active operations.
Presently came Jena and Auerstadt, and the plans of the
British Government had to be revised in furious haste.

The next months were spent by the Queen of Naples
in her customary intrigues, for she was ready to deliver
up Sicily to Napoleon if he would restore her Naples, and
by the British army in weary waiting and small and
futile mainland enterprises. The Twenty-First, as we
learn from the diary of Corporal David Brown, who
had joined from the second battalion, did turns of duty
at Faro Point, Milazzo, and Messina. By the close of
the year the main problem for Britain was how to

1807 create a distraction in favour of Russia. Italy offered one chance, Constantinople another; but, being obsessed by the idea that Napoleon coveted Egypt above all things, we adopted the strange course of sending an expedition to an area where success could have no direct effect upon the main contest. Fox at Palermo was ordered to hold a force of 5,000 men in readiness to proceed to Egypt, the primary object being the capture of Alexandria, and at the same time Admiral Duckworth was dispatched on his famous journey through the Dardanelles.

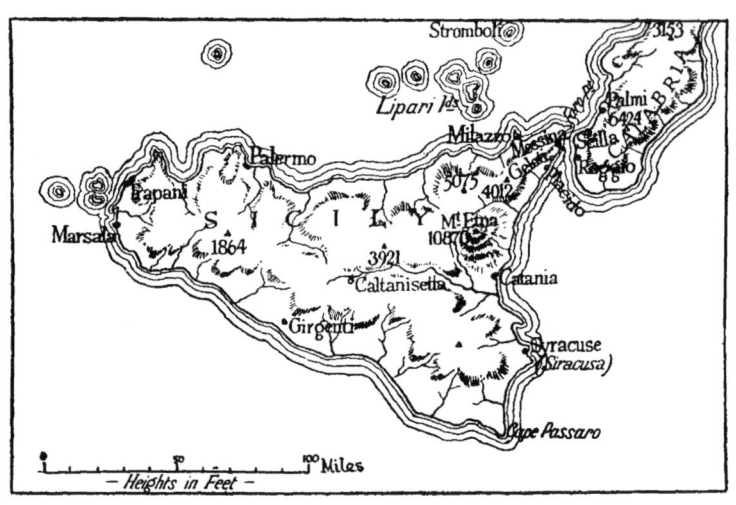

CAMPAIGN IN SICILY

The expeditionary force embarked at Messina on March 7, 1807, 6,000 strong, under Major-General Fraser Mackenzie, with Major-General Wauchope as second in command. Its misfortunes need not be recapitulated. Suffice it to say, that after a luckless voyage Mackenzie did indeed seize Alexandria. But in order to assure the town's food supply he sent 1,600 men against Rosetta, where Wauchope was killed and the British repulsed, with the loss of nearly a third of their strength. Other misfortunes followed, till it was clear that the expedition was about to end in utter disaster.

THE ALEXANDRIA EXPEDITION 151

Fox at once sent two battalions as reinforcements, the Twenty-First and the 62nd, which arrived on 29th May and worked at strengthening the defences of Alexandria. Throughout the hot summer negotiations went on between Mackenzie and that Albanian tobacconist of genius, Mohammed Ali, who behaved honourably and wisely; and, since it became plain to the British Government that Sicily and Alexandria could not be both held, the little army was withdrawn on 19th September, and returned to Messina. The only result of the expedition was a lowering of our prestige throughout the Mediterranean and a bad outbreak of ophthalmia among the troops, which it took months to cure. " I am sorry to say," wrote Corporal Brown, " we had upwards of two hundred men in the regiment blind of both eyes and some blind of one, and those that could see a little on being disembarked were put in the front, and those that could not see took hold of their neighvours' coat-tails until they arrived at the general hospital, which was a shocking thing to see."

1807

In July 1807 Sir John Moore succeeded Fox as Commander-in-Chief in the Mediterranean. He had no illusions about the folly of the Neapolitan Court or the worthlessness of the Neapolitan troops, and he saw that Sicily was in hourly danger of a French attack. He made plans for its defence; but in the autumn he was ordered to repair to Gibraltar with most of the Sicilian force, handing over his command in the island to Major-General Sherbrooke, who had little more at his disposal than the expeditionary force returned from Egypt. Napoleon now began to prepare in earnest for the conquest of Sicily. His first objective was the north-eastern point of Faro, which would give him Messina, and for this purpose it was necessary to take Reggio and the fort of Scilla on the mainland, which were held, the former by a Neapolitan garrison, and the latter by four British companies [1] under Major

---

[1] Mr. Fortescue says " detachments of the 27th, 58th, and 62nd "; Bunbury says " four companies." The fourth was from the Twenty-First, under Captain Norman Pringle.

1808 Robertson of the 35th. Reggio fell on February 2, 1808, through Neapolitan treachery; but the handful of British in Scilla made a gallant defence, holding it till 17th February, and then withdrawing by a rock stairway to the sea, leaving behind them only such of the wounded as could not be moved. Norman Pringle commanded the rear-guard, and was hit. " Our general in command in Sicily," he writes in his diary, " gave us great credit for the gallant defence we had made, but thanks were all we got in those days."

Happily his preoccupation with Corfu prevented Napoleon from following up this success. Castlereagh, who had awakened at last to the peril of Sicily, asked Fox and Moore what force was necessary to hold the island; they replied that in the present embarrassing state of Neapolitan politics 25,000 men were not too many. Sir John Stuart, who was also consulted, thought that 10,000 might suffice, and he accordingly was appointed to the command. He was given a draft of 1,200 men, and a reinforcement of some 5,000 more, drawn principally from the King's German Legion, while Sherbrooke departed to join the army in the Peninsula.

The summer of 1808 was bad for the health of the troops in Sicily. The Twenty-First, which was stationed in Messina and other places, lost more than seventy men from fever in the course of a few days, and habitually had one twelfth of its strength in hospital. Along with the 62nd, it was sent on a cruise along the coast till the late autumn. Meanwhile the prospect was not brightening for Stuart. He was not beloved of his men; the capable Murat had succeeded the incapable Joseph Bonaparte on the throne of Naples; and in October the island of Capri was taken by the French from Sir Hudson Lowe. It was incumbent on Stuart to do something to restore British prestige and reassure the scared Sicilians, and he refused, in spite of the entreaties of Castlereagh and Admiral Collingwood, to send any part of his forces to operate on the east coast of Spain. Early in 1809, when Austria was meditating

ISCHIA AND SCILLA

a campaign in northern Italy, he decided to create a diversion by an attack on the coast of Calabria, where he hoped for assistance from the patriotic insurgents. He was slow to start, however, though his transports were early ready for the sea, and the news in May of Napoleon's entry into Vienna did not hasten his resolution. Finally, in June he thought he saw a chance of gaining an easy success by the occupation of Ischia, an island in the Bay of Naples, though Collingwood pointed out with reason that this would serve no serious military purpose. On 11th June the expedition sailed, some 13,000 men in all, and with it went the Twenty-First.[1] Next day a detachment under Colonel Haviland Smith, including the bulk of the Twenty-First under Lieutenant-Colonel Adam, left the main force and sailed through the straits of Messina for an attack upon the mainland. The Ischia expedition was successful enough, for its task was simple. The flank companies of the Twenty-First were employed in it, and the most brilliant episode was connected with the regiment. Thirty-four of Murat's gunboats, while endeavouring to escape from the British fleet, were attacked by six British gunboats under the command of its senior subaltern, Lieutenant Angus Cameron, which hung on to the enemy till the main British flotilla arrived. Twenty-four gunboats were taken, five were destroyed, and only five, riddled with shot, made good their escape. But the gallant young Cameron was among the British dead.

Less fortunate was the mainland enterprise. The plan was to wait till the French General Partonneaux, alarmed by the threat to Naples, should withdraw his troops northward, and then to besiege the castle of Scilla. The investment duly began, but Haviland Smith was doubtful about the intelligence he had received of the French withdrawal, so he ordered Lieutenant-Colonel Adam to reconnoitre the country northwards to Palmi. A picket of the Twenty-First, under Lieutenant Taylor, was posted a mile out of the town,

1809

[1] Mr. Fortescue omits to mention the regiment in his note on the troops embarked, VII., page 295.

154   THE ROYAL SCOTS FUSILIERS

1809 while three companies were left in barracks in Palmi. On the following night Partonneaux's advanced guard attacked the picket, which, by some blunder of the officer in charge, retreated without firing a shot. The consequence was that the French broke into Palmi unheralded. The three companies put up a gallant fight, but they were hopelessly outnumbered. Captain Hunter and one corporal were killed, and nine men were wounded, while Captains Donald Mackay and William Conran, Lieutenants James McNab and Angus Mackay, four sergeants, two drummers, and seventy-six rank-and-file were made prisoners.[1]

Partonneaux now swept on to the castle of Scilla. But Haviland Smith had due warning, for a handful of the picket of the Twenty-First, under Sergeant Isaac Robertson, had made good their escape. It was impossible for the small British force to remain on the mainland, so the guns were spiked, the men embarked, and the straits recrossed. The rest of the Twenty-First acted as rear-guard, and Lieutenant-Colonel Adam was the last man to go on board, thereby earning the admiration of the enemy General. Sir John Stuart's expedition had been, in Mr. Fortescue's words, no more than a "military parade," and the result was a panic in Messina. Meanwhile Partonneaux, recalled to Naples by Murat, had blown up the castle of Scilla and retired, and the Twenty-First was able to return and carry away the guns which Haviland Smith had been compelled to abandon.

For the rest of the year Stuart did nothing. In October came grave news—that France and Austria had made peace; which meant that the French army in Italy, being free from other menace, could concentrate on the conquest of Sicily. Queen Caroline, half crazy with drugs and debauchery, began to intrigue with Napoleon, and, but for Oswald's successful operation in the Ionian Islands, there was little comfort that winter for the British commander. In the spring

[1] Corporal Brown's account is difficult to follow, for he confuses Palmi and Palermo, with the light-hearted geography of the British soldier.

THE FRENCH CROSS THE STRAITS

of 1810 it was clear that Murat was making extensive preparations, for French columns were moving south into Calabria and conscription was being enforced, while the treachery of the Neapolitan Court had become a crying scandal. The British Government ordered Stuart to send to Wellington in the Peninsula four of his best regiments, including the Twenty-First,[1] and Stuart not unnaturally refused. He had no more than 13,000 men, half of them foreigners, and he could place no reliance upon the mutinous, starved, and undisciplined Sicilian troops.

In July 1810 Murat, with his army of invasion, arrived on the Calabrian shore. The urgent danger improved the feeling in the island, and the Sicilian peasants toiled alongside the British troops at the defence of the straits. Through the heats of July and August the armies stared at each other across the ribbon of sea, and then on the night of 17th September came the attack. General Cavaignac, with 4,000 men, landed on the shore of Sicily, seven miles south of Messina. They were observed by a patrol of the 20th Light Dragoons, and Major-General Campbell, Stuart's adjutant-general, hastened to take charge of the defence. As the dawn broke it was seen that Murat's troops were everywhere embarking on the far shore of the narrows between Scilla and Pezzo. Colonel Adam was engaged with Cavaignac, and the forces under him were the Twenty-First, and the third battalion of the German Legion. Farther south the French were landing between Gelati and San Stefano, and pushing inland to gain position on the heights. Campbell set himself to occupy the passes behind Mili, Colonel Fischer, with a light battalion, moved from Placido on the enemy's flank, while Adam dealt with the main landing. The fire of the last-named drove Cavaignac to his boats, leaving many men behind him, and then Fischer and Adam turned upon an isolated battalion which had occupied a little hill. The flank companies

---

[1] The Twenty-First at the moment was 1,000 strong (Fortescue, VII., page 440).

of the Twenty-First, under Captain McHaffie and Lieutenant Macdonald, rushed the hill, and the enemy, to the number of 850, surrendered. So ended in complete failure the much-advertised invasion of Sicily, a result due in no way to Stuart, but to the energy and speed of his subordinates. He had the generosity to recognize this, for he told Colonel Adam: "I return you and your regiment my sincere thanks for your conduct this morning, for your attack on the enemy and the gallant manner in which you made them surrender. I hope you have satisfaction for your loss in Palmi."

The British Ministers continued to urge the dispatch of four of Stuart's battalions to Wellington; but Stuart, with Murat's siege artillery stored at Scilla and the conviction in his mind that the attack would presently be renewed, declined, to Wellington's indignation, to part with more than one. He was justified in his fears, for so long as the preposterous Neapolitan Court continued to oppress the Sicilians and intrigue with the French, the island was in a parlous state. In 1811 the British Government at last saw the wisdom of the advice which Sir John Moore had offered years before, and resolved to make the British military commander also the chief political agent, so that he might take a hand in reforming the civil administration. Stuart retired in the spring, and was succeeded by Lord William Bentinck, who combined the duties of Commander-in-Chief and Minister at the Court of Palermo. Bentinck was no great soldier, but he was in an infinitely stronger position than his predecessor, and he was able to dictate, when occasion arose, to his treacherous allies. The year 1811 found the Twenty-First doing dreary garrison work on the north shore, strengthened by a large detachment of volunteers from its second battalion at home. Adam, now a colonel in the army, and aide-de-camp to the Prince Regent, went on leave, and Major Ross took his place, while Captain Kidd of the regiment acted as governor of Faro. Adam returned to duty at the close of the

SIR FREDERICK ADAM
(From a crayon drawing by G. F. Watts, R.A., in the possession of Mrs. Frederick Adam)

year, and early in 1812 the Twenty-First was transferred to Palermo. Then came a change in the command, for Adam was appointed assistant-adjutant-general, and relinquished the regiment to Major Ross, who was presently succeeded by Lieutenant-Colonel Paterson from the second battalion. Nothing happened in Palermo, says Corporal Brown, " except that two of our men were killed by the Neapolitan artillery and two other unfortunates were hanged for robbery." In September the Twenty-First was transferred to the Faro coast, where Quartermaster Sutherland was killed by a shot from a British gunboat, which took him for a spy signalling to the enemy, the poor man being then engaged in hunting for a key which he had lost on the road. In November the right flank company, under Captain Norman Pringle, and the left flank and another company were sent to Alicante in the force of Major-General Campbell, to take part in the war in the Peninsula. In February 1813 two companies under Captain Douglas shared in the successful capture of the little island of Ponza in the Gulf of Gaeta, which was intended to form a station for the British fleet.

The year 1813 saw a serious recrudescence of trouble in Sicily. Bentinck was a doctrinaire Whig who believed that the cure for every evil was a parliamentary government on the British model, and who longed, moreover, to play a dazzling part at the head of a war of liberation in Italy. The star of Napoleon was declining, and he believed that the hour had come for a bold stroke, so he made plans for an Italian campaign with Russia by his side. Failing that, he wanted to be in the Peninsula, and at the end of May he sailed for Alicante, leaving General Macfarlane to command in Sicily. In March, owing to the danger in Sicily, the strength of two battalions had been withdrawn from the Sicilian contingent in the Peninsula, and in these battalions were two companies of the Twenty-First. The army at Alicante under Sir John Murray, a general of tried incompetence, which had Colonel Adam among its brigadiers, was making little headway

1813 against Suchet. Bentinck, who arrived on 17th June, found the troops very weary of their commander, and the expedition to Tarragona a distinguished failure. He acted with promptitude, crossed the Ebro on 29th July, and by 18th August had reached Tarragona, with Suchet retreating before him. On 12th September he pushed forward Adam to hold the pass of Ordal on the Barcelona road, and, believing that Suchet was incapable of showing his teeth, he left his main body out of supporting distance. The result was that Adam's post was overwhelmed, Adam was severely wounded, and Bentinck himself was put in serious jeopardy. This was the only fighting in that famous theatre which any part of the Twenty-First was destined to see, for the crisis in Sicily now compelled Bentinck to return thither, and with him went Norman Pringle and his right flank company.

Things had gone much amiss in his absence. The " free constitution " had proved a fiasco, the so-called Sicilian Parliament was petitioning against the British officers, the populace was almost in revolt, and the wretched Queen, who had professed to be sailing for Constantinople, had gone no farther than Zante, where she was plotting as busily as before. Bentinck, who, according to Charles Greville, " committed some grave blunder or other in every situation in which he was placed," had been guilty of consummate folly in bestowing a constitution upon an ignorant people, and instead of citizens had manufactured demagogues. He proclaimed martial law and restored order on his return in October, and presently his imagination was fired by a second communication from Murat, offering an alliance with England. The proud ship of Napoleon's power was beginning to founder, and the rats were leaving it; to Bentinck's excited mind it seemed that he might yet lead a crusade of freedom in Italy and be enshrined in the Pantheon of the Whig liberators. News came of the great defeat at Leipzig, and thereafter Lord William's soul was afire with grandiose schemes. He proposed to occupy Corsica ; then his thoughts turned to the Italian mainland, especially the littoral of the Gulf of Spezia. His scheme was that the Austrians should drive Eugène Beauharnais from the Adige, the Neapolitans move along the south bank of the Po, while he himself should take Genoa and advance towards the Maritime Alps. In all this he took no account of the main army under Wellington, which was slowly and quietly breaking the power of France. Lord William had all the passion of his countrymen for meaningless divergent operations.

In 1813 Charles Furlong, whose diary we possess, had arrived to join the Twenty-First in Sicily. He reported that it was in magnificent condition, 1,200 strong, and that " we are ripe for going to Spain and are half mad at not participating in that magnificent campaign." The chance of the regiment, bored to death by garrison work, was coming, though it was not to share in the honours of the Peninsula. In February 1814 Bentinck embarked his first division of troops, including the Twenty-First, at Palermo, under orders for Leghorn. It reached that port on 10th March, and the transports were sent back for the second division. Bentinck, whose head was now in the clouds, was busy proclaiming a general war against all tyrants, and he left to General Montresor the conduct of the campaign against the French. It was not a lengthy or very glorious enterprise. Marching through historic Italian towns, which ravished the poetic soul of Charles Furlong, the British, on 12th April, drove the French from Nervi, and on the 17th broke the enemy's stand at San Martino and forced him back on Genoa. There the French General capitulated, the garrison marched out with the honours of war, and the Twenty-First, after long years in shabby Sicilian barracks, found itself to its joy in a clean and spacious city, where it was idolized by the populace. About the same time Napoleon was taking leave of the Guard and setting out for Elba. All but the brief epilogue had been written of the greatest drama in modern history.

II

1804-7   We return now to the second battalion, which we have seen embodied at Ayr towards the close of the year 1804. For two years it remained in the county town, and, as the men were mostly from the shires of Ayr and Renfrew, it found the quarters pleasant. Certain of its officers fell in love with and married young ladies of the place—Lieutenant-Colonel Wilson a daughter of Mr. Oswald of Auchencruive, Major Campbell a daughter of Provost Bowie, and Captain McHaffie a daughter of Mr. Rankine of Drumdow. There were few incidents during that peaceful sojourn, except the firing of a *feu-de-joie* in honour of Trafalgar, when the news arrived on a Sunday morning, November 14, 1805; and a great parade, along with the Ayr and Newton Volunteers, on the Low Green, when the regiment was reviewed by the Commander-in-Chief in Scotland, Lord Moira, who had Ayrshire connections owing to his marriage with the Countess of Loudoun. The regiment had for its lieutenant-colonel, William Paterson. Its members were enlisted strictly for home service, but volunteering was encouraged for the first battalion, and there was a steady flow of recruits to Sicily.

In August 1806 the battalion embarked at Portpatrick for Ireland. On 23rd June in the following year, while it was quartered at Armagh, there befell a tragedy which made a great talk at that day. There had been an inspection by General Kerr, and in the mess in the evening there arose a discussion between Major Alexander Campbell, a cadet of the house of Breadalbane,[1] and Captain Boyd, as to the former's way of giving the word of command. Something in Boyd's manner irritated Campbell, who left the mess in a fury, went to his quarters, had tea with his wife (the daughter of the Ayr provost), and returned to the mess in search of Boyd. A challenge was given and

[1] See Balfour Paul's *The Scots Peerage*, II., page 198.

THE FATAL DUEL

accepted. The next thing was the report of a shot, and when his brother officers rushed in, they found Boyd sitting in a chair coughing blood, with a bullet in his lungs, and upbraiding Campbell for having hurried on the duel without the presence of seconds. The two men had fought alone in a room at a distance of seven paces, and Boyd's bullet had just missed Campbell's head. Next day Boyd died, and Campbell fled to Ayr, where he was concealed by his wife's relatives, while a warrant was issued for his arrest on a charge of murder. After this point accounts differ. One alleges that he was arrested in a hiding-place near Greenan Castle; but the better-authenticated story is that he and his wife lived for some months in London under an assumed name, till his conscience forced him to surrender himself. He was tried for murder at the summer assizes at Armagh in 1808, and condemned to death; but a temporary respite was granted by the Lord-Lieutenant, in case of the royal clemency being exercised. The poor wife set off post-haste for London, and saw the King and the Prince of Wales without effect. Campbell was hanged on 24th August, meeting his fate with fortitude and resignation. It is said that the guard on the scaffold, as a token of respect, took off their caps, while the doomed man saluted in turn, and that when the body was brought to Ayr the commander of the troops there sent a fatigue party to receive it and accompany it to the churchyard. It is an inexplicable tale: the slender provocation, the fury which not even an interval of consideration could mitigate, the secret, lonely duel, the bitter awakening, and the scrupulous later behaviour of the guilty man. Some hidden streak of madness seems the fairest explanation of this aberration of a humane and popular officer.

In September 1811 the battalion returned from Belfast to Scotland, where it was stationed for more than two years. During that time it sent its lieutenant-colonel, William Paterson, to Sicily to take Adam's place, and came under the command of Lieutenant-

1813-14 Colonel Robert Henry. Towards the close of 1813 it was at Fort George, when, being now eligible as a unit for foreign service, it received orders to embark for Holland. At this time the armies of the Allies were pressing Napoleon to his doom, and on 15th November the Dutch had risen in insurrection against their French masters. The British Government decided to send out a force of 6,000 men under Sir Thomas Graham (the future Lord Lynedoch) to assist the rebellion and co-operate with Bernadotte's Army of the North. The victor of Barossa, now in his sixty-sixth year and very blind, accepted the command with reluctance, for he had no belief in the strategical wisdom of Ministers. With the earlier operations and the futile attempt upon Antwerp we are not here concerned. The Twenty-First, after a tempestuous journey, arrived in Holland early in January 1814, and joined Sir Thomas Graham shortly before the Antwerp failure. For some weeks it lay at Tholen, suffering much from the damp cold, and heartily sick of its first experience in campaigning. But Graham was not the man to sit long in idleness. He saw that Bergen-op-Zoom was the key to Dutch independence, for only by its capture could the line of French fortifications between Antwerp and Flushing be broken and the path opened for naval co-operation with Britain. It was the bridge-head between Holland and the rest of Europe, and in the past centuries much good Scots blood had been spilled in its assault and defence. At the moment it was held by General Ambert with 2,700 men, which included, it is interesting to note, the 21st Regiment of the French line.

Graham formed the 4,000 men of his attacking force into four columns. On the right the flank companies of the Twenty-First and 37th (200), the fourth battalion of the Royal Scots (600), and the 44th (300), the whole under Colonel Carleton of the 44th, were to move along the Tholen dyke, so as to reach the point where the dyke joined the Scheldt at nine p.m. on 8th March. On the right centre, the Twenty-First (100), the 37th (150), and the second battalion of the 91st (400), under Lieu-

THE ATTACK ON BERGEN-OP-ZOOM

tenant-Colonel Henry of the Twenty-First, were to make 1814 a feint attack from the north on the Steenbergen gate. On the left centre, 1,200 men of the 33rd, 55th, and 69th, under Colonel Morrice of the 69th, were to move from Huibergen against the north-east angle of the ramparts, near the Breda gate. On the extreme left 1,000 men of the Guards Brigade, under Lord Proby, were to attempt an entrance by the Orange bastion, after working round the rear of the entrenched camp on the southern side of the fortress. Major-General George Cooke was in command of the whole. The four columns were to be close under the works at nine that night, and the attack was to begin at half-past ten. It was a sound and ingenious plan, and the enemy within had no inkling of the coming assault.

But from the first the subordinate leaders blundered. Henry delivered his attack at the Steenbergen gate an hour before the agreed time, thereby alarming all the northern front of the fortress. Instead of a feint he made a serious assault, and some 400 of his men effected an entry in scattered parties, while the rear of the column was driven back in disorder by the grape and musketry fire. The garrison was now thoroughly roused, and its attention concentrated on the Steenbergen gate. Carleton, who had with him Major-General Skerrett and Brigadier-General Gore, attacked as soon as he heard the guns opening on Henry, and with difficulty crossed the Zoom at the end of the Tholen dyke. "We got into confusion," wrote an officer of the Twenty-First, "in labouring through this horrible slough, which was like bird-lime about our legs; regiments got intermixed in the darkness, while some stuck fast, and some unlucky wretches got trodden down and smothered in the mud." The columns made too much noise, for their leaders took to shouting, "Remember Badajoz," and when the Water gate was carried, Carleton turned to the left and Skerrett—quite wrongly —to the right, while the Royal Scots were left behind without orders. Carleton, pushing on recklessly along the western and southern ramparts, drove the enemy before him to the Antwerp gate, where he secured the guard-house. He continued almost to the Breda gate, but, as he had been obliged to leave many detachments behind him, he had scarcely 100 men when at last he came across the French in force. He was shot dead, as were most of his following.

Nevertheless, had Morrice been by this time near the Breda gate all might have gone well. But Morrice's column had fallen into an unaccountable panic, which Graham and his staff were labouring to quell, and General Gore could do no more than withdraw Carleton's remnant to the bastion east of the Antwerp gate. Meanwhile Proby's column, with which was General Cooke, had, according to plan, seized the Orange bastion, and was sending out patrols to look for Skerrett at the Steenbergen gate and to get in touch with the British at the Antwerp gate. It was now just after eleven, the bulk of the British force was inside the fortress, and the French retained only six bastions out of sixteen. In spite of many blunders it looked as if the British success was assured. All depended upon the Royal Scots at the Water gate and Morrice's column, now trying to force a way in at the north-east angle. The French behaved with admirable coolness, as soon as they rallied from their first confusion. They attacked and drove back the detachment at the Antwerp gate and the Guards who had gone to its assistance, and Gore was killed. Skerrett, after hard fighting, was routed, and mortally wounded. Cooke, at the Orange bastion, was presently joined by Morrice's troops, and had now some 2,000 men in his command inside the fortress. The moon had risen, and about three o'clock the French made another attack upon Skerrett's remnant, but were repulsed, and they also failed to make any impression upon the British at the Orange bastion. The thing seemed to have reached a complete deadlock.

About half-past three Ambert, seeing the uselessness of small attacks, withdrew all his garrison from the east side of the fortress, divided his forces into three

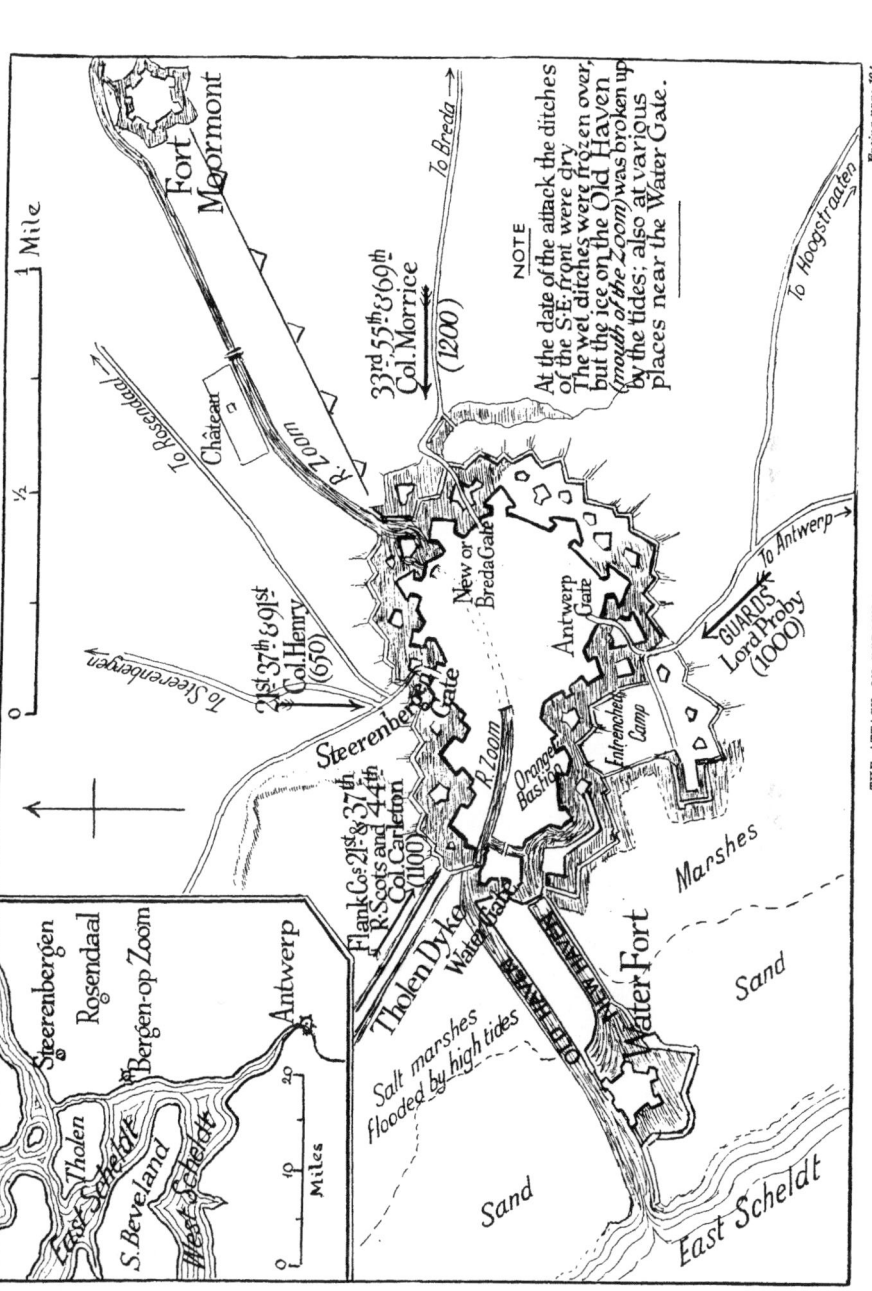

THE ATTACK ON BERGEN-OP-ZOOM

THE FAILURE

columns, and attacked the British in the area between the Water gate and the Antwerp gate. The move was crowned with complete success. The French cleared the northern front and drove the invaders into the water; they forced the Royal Scots from the Water gate, but for some time they encountered a stubborn resistance from the Guards, the 55th, and the 69th around the Orange bastion. Presently, however, when the heavy guns were turned on him from the opposite side of the basin, it became clear to Cooke that he must withdraw. Part of his force managed to retire, but the majority found it impossible, and just before the dawn laid down their arms. Graham, who believed that he had won the place, arrived a little later with reinforcements to take possession, and found, to his bitter chagrin, that he had failed.

Such was the night attack on Bergen-op-Zoom—a strange, wild tale of men fighting blindly in *cul-de-sacs*, suffocating in mud, or drowning in icy water. It was a tragic memory for the officers who fought in it, many of whom broke their swords in bitterness of soul; for over 3,000 men had managed to enter the fortress, and had then been defeated by a garrison of 2,700 indifferent French soldiers. There was nothing wrong in Graham's plan of battle, nor did the troops, though they were for the most part not of the first quality, fail in courage and resolution. The blame must be laid on the errors of the commanders: on Henry, who, being ordered to feint, expended his men in a useless attack; on Skerrett, who unaccountably took a wrong turning; on the colonel of the Royal Scots for his supineness; on Carleton and Gore for their crazy rashness in pushing on too fast and too far. It is pleasant to record that the enemy behaved with rare generosity and chivalry. Bizanet, commanding the troops, had been treated kindly as a prisoner of the British in his youth, and nobly he made return, for he released the captives on the sole condition that, until regularly exchanged, they should not fight against the French in Europe. The defeat cost the British some

1814

400 killed, over 500 wounded, and 1,600 unwounded prisoners. The Twenty-First had Second Lieutenant John Bulteel killed; Lieutenant-Colonel Henry, Captain Nicholas Darrah, Captain Donald Mackenzie,[1] Lieutenants the Hon. Francis Morres and Henry Pigou, and Second Lieutenants John Moody, David Rankine, and Sir William Crosby wounded. Of the casualties in the rank-and-file, which must have been heavy, no record remains.

Bergen-op-Zoom was the one action fought by the second battalion. It remained on the Continent till September, when it returned to Scotland, and on January 13, 1816, the war being over, it was disbanded at Stirling, all men still fit and willing for duty being transferred to the first battalion. Its colours were handed over to the colonel of the Twenty-First, General the Hon. W. Gordon, whose representative, Captain Alexander Henry Gordon of Fyvie, presented them to St. Giles' Cathedral in Edinburgh, where they now rest.[2]

III

For the last stage we take up again the tale of the first battalion.

Through the whole era of the French Revolution and the Napoleonic wars there had been strained relations between Britain and the young republic of the United States. The latter had three principal grievances: the claim of Britain to allegiance over, and consequently to the right of impressing, those of her subjects who had become naturalized American citizens; her claim to search neutral vessels for contraband of war; and her claim to impress for her

[1] Donald Mackenzie, who was the great-uncle of Brigadier-General D. M. Stuart (see page 455), lost a leg. He was reputed at the time to be the strongest man in the British army, and once won a bet for holding out for five minutes two muskets by the muzzles with a third laid across the cocks.

[2] The King's colour is the "Great Union," with the thistle within the circle, and the motto "*Nemo me impune lacessit.*" The regimental colour is of blue silk, and has, in addition to the regimental badge, the royal cypher and crown in the second, third, and fourth corners. Both colours have " XXI. 2nd Bn." in the upper cantons (Groves, *History of the Royal Scottish Fusiliers*, page 25).

THE WAR WITH AMERICA

navy British seamen wherever found. The nascent American mercantile marine was crippled, American sea-borne trade was restricted, and the natural pride of a new state was wounded in its tenderest spot. The British blockade of the Continent of Europe and Napoleon's Milan Decree sharpened the difficulties of America's neutrality. She retorted with futile embargoes and declarations of "non-intercourse," two-edged weapons which cut her hand. The uneasy position continued till, in 1812, Clay and Calhoun forced the unwilling President Madison, about the time of Wellington's victory at Salamanca, into a declaration of war on Britain.

With the naval operations and the campaign on the Canadian frontier we are not concerned. The American frigates played their part brilliantly at sea, but the small Canadian forces under Isaac Brock repelled the land invasion, and by 1814, though the American troops were beginning to win small successes, nothing material had been accomplished. It was a campaign, as Wellington said, highly honourable to British arms. During these two years the great struggle in Europe had been at its most critical stage, but the abdication of Napoleon now released part of the British army, and the veterans of the Peninsula began to cross the Atlantic. The huge strength of the British navy could now be concentrated in American waters, the Chesapeake was occupied, and the war was carried into the American citadel.

The leader of the expedition was Robert Ross, who, in command of the 20th, had played a decisive part in the battle of Maida, had been with Moore in the retreat to Corunna, and in the Peninsula had commanded a brigade with high distinction in Cole's division. He was a soldier of the school of Sir John Moore, a stern disciplinarian and a skilled trainer of troops, and, like his master, was fated to have a career as brief as it was splendid. The 1st Twenty-First, under Colonel Paterson, had reached Gibraltar from Genoa on June 6, 1814, eight years to a day since it had left the Rock for

168 THE ROYAL SCOTS FUSILIERS

1814 Sicily. There it was joined by the 29th and the 62nd; and on the 11th the contingent, under the command of Major-General Gosseling, sailed for Bermuda. At Bermuda the regiment became part of General Ross's expedition (which included also the 4th, 44th, and 85th) for the attack on Washington, while General Gosseling took the 29th and 62nd to Canada. Under the convoy of Admiral Malcolm the troops left Bermuda on 3rd August for Chesapeake Bay, where they met Sir Alexander Cochrane's squadron. On the 19th the disembarkation began on the Maryland coast, at the village of St. Benedict's on the left bank of the Patuxent River, twenty-five miles from its mouth.

The share of the regiment in the subsequent operations can be followed in the diaries of Corporal Brown and Charles Furlong. The force, whose landing was unopposed, was divided into three brigades—the light brigade under Colonel Thornton, comprising the 85th and the flank companies of the 4th, 44th, and Twenty-First; the second brigade under Colonel Brooke—the 4th and 44th; the third brigade under Colonel Paterson—the Twenty-First and a battalion of marines. With 200 gunners and a party of sappers and sailors the total was about 4,500 men. There were no horses, except those belonging to the General and his staff. The first business was to destroy the American flotilla of thirteen armed luggers, under Commodore Barney, which had taken refuge up the Patuxent. Cochrane's seamen ascended the river in boats, while Ross followed by land—a trying march, for the men were soft from being cooped up on board ship, and it rained incessantly. On the 22nd Barney, finding himself hemmed in, blew up his luggers, and his men fell back upon Washington.

Ross was now within sixteen miles of the American capital, and, so far as he could learn, was not opposed by any great force. His lack of cavalry handicapped him, but he gave orders to collect all the horses in the neighbourhood, and managed to mount his artillery drivers. On the evening of 23rd August he began to advance, and next day, without opposition, save from scattered enemy patrols, reached Bladensburg, a village 1814 some five miles from Washington, on the left bank of the eastern branch of the Potomac. There he found the enemy drawn up in a prepared position beyond the river, commanding the wooden bridge which carried the Washington road. The American flank was pro-

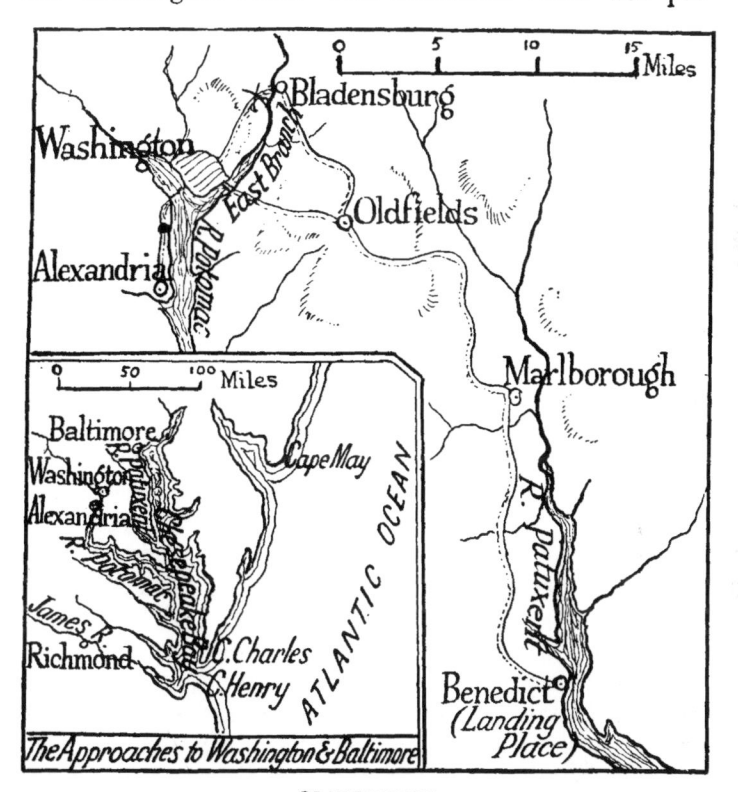

BLADENSBURG

tected by thick woods, and their centre occupied some low hills, while they held as an advanced post a strongly fortified house covering the bridge. Ross had only one 6-pounder and two 3-pounders by way of artillery; while the enemy, under General Winder, had ten guns saved from Barney's flotilla, a force of about 6,000 men, mostly militia, and ample cavalry.

1814 The attack began with the advance of Thornton's light brigade, with which went Furlong, the diarist. "As soon as the enemy," he writes, " perceived the head of our column halt to draw breath for a moment, they set up three cheers, thinking, I dare say, that we were panic-struck with their appearance. We were immediately ordered to advance, which was effected by the 85th and us (the flank companies of the Twenty-First) under a heavy fire from their guns, but with little mischief, as their shots went generally clean over our heads. After passing the river we formed line, and advanced to their centre and left flank. They immediately opened a most destructive fire from all quarters, which we sustained with firmness, and in our turn discharged a volley at them and rushed forward with the greatest impetuosity up the hill. They at first retreated in ordinary time, and loaded and fired frequent volleys at us, but we pressed on so closely that at length they fled precipitately from all quarters. We then poured in our fire, and killed and wounded many. While this was going on in the centre, the 4th and 44th Regiments formed as a reserve. The 4th filed into a thick wood in front of the enemy's right, and advancing steadily on them in line, received a most dreadful discharge of small arms and artillery, but pushed on and put them to a general flight. All was now over with them. We became masters of their guns, and made many prisoners; but our men were so fatigued that an immediate pursuit was impossible. A man in the Twenty-First left flank company took Commander Barney prisoner." Furlong is an accurate narrator, and his account agrees exactly with General Ross's dispatch. At Bladensburg some 1,300 trained men (for Paterson's third brigade was never in action) scattered 6,000 militia and sailors within an hour. The left flank companies of the Twenty-First had two men killed, and Major Robert Renny and Lieutenant James Gracie and eleven men wounded. Most fittingly Bladensburg is inscribed on the regimental colours. There were Peninsula veterans present who maintained that the fire was the hottest they had ever encountered. There was little merit in the generalship, for the British troops were sent into action in dangerous driblets, and the frontal attack of the light brigade was pure bludgeon work and attended by needless losses. But for the rank-and-file it was a signal proof of discipline and courage.

At sunset Ross entered Washington. There was some shooting from the houses, and he had his horse killed under him and his clothes riddled, while there were a number of casualties in the Twenty-First, which led the advance.[1] The British commander had instructions to burn the public buildings in retaliation for the American burning of Newark and York, and that night and the next morning there was a great conflagration. President Madison had prepared a banquet in his house to celebrate the expected victory, and this was eaten by a company of hungry Scots Fusiliers.[2] The House of Congress, the Treasury, the President's residence, the naval and military arsenals, ships in the Potomac and on the stocks—anything that could be labelled public property went up in flames. Furlong was shocked, as well he might be, by the barbarous performance, however justifiable by the laws of war. " Although they were the pride of the Americans, I must confess I felt sorrow when witnessing such magnificent buildings demolished." Private property of every kind was strictly respected. In the process of burning a spark fell into a powder magazine, which cost the incendiaries some twenty or thirty lives, and many others were poisoned by American whisky. On the night of the 25th the British withdrew, and by the 29th were back at St. Benedict's.

Ross's next objective was Baltimore, after the town of Alexandria had been taken by the fleet and a good haul made of American merchantmen. He seems to

---

[1] Furlong says "two killed"; Clark, *Hist. Record of R.S.F.*, says "sixty-eight killed and wounded"—an improbable story.

[2] Mr. Fortescue says it was eaten by Ross and his staff. My story is Corporal Brown's, who had every reason to know, for he helped to eat the dinner.

have had no particular inclination for the enterprise which was forced upon him by Cochrane and the navy in their desire for prize-money. On 11th September the British ships sailed up the Chesapeake to the Patapsco, the river on which Baltimore stands, and on the 12th the troops were landed at North Point and began their advance. Ross had with him the better part of 6,000 men, including sailors and marines, and the enemy troops mustered some 15,000. Driving in outlying pickets, after six miles the British came into a country of thick woods, where they encountered the first serious resistance. The light brigade, which led the advance, scattered the enemy outposts; but the gallant Ross, not the least of "Lord Wellington's men," was killed by a bullet from a sharpshooter. He "only survived to recommend a young and unprovided-for family to the protection of his King and country." Brooke of the light brigade now took command of the force. In a thicket called Godly Wood 5,000 of the enemy, with six guns, held a prepared position defended by breastworks and palisades. The light brigade charged the concealed enemy under a heavy fire—grape, canister, and other things, for the Americans loaded their guns to the muzzle with every kind of oddment. The 44th formed line in their rear; the Twenty-First, now under Major John Whitaker, since Paterson had a brigade, and the marines formed column in reserve, while the 4th moved to turn the enemy left. In a quarter of an hour the action was over, and the enemy scattered, but not without heavy loss to the attack. The left flank companies of the Twenty-First had Lieutenant Gracie and fifteen men killed; Renny, who had been promoted Brevet-Lieutenant-Colonel after Bladensburg, received further wounds; Furlong, the only surviving officer of his company, escaped miraculously with a bullet in his black silk neckcloth; while among the other companies of the regiment Lieutenant Leavach, two sergeants, and seventy-seven men were wounded. Colonel Paterson was specially mentioned in dispatches for the steadiness with which he handled his troops.

BALTIMORE

Next day Brooke resumed his march, and in the evening reached the chain of low hills in front of Baltimore. The American position was immensely strong—a series of palisaded redoubts linked together by breastworks and defended by swamps on its flanks, mounting many pieces of artillery, and manned by some 15,000 men, for there had been a general levy in the city. Brooke prepared to storm it, and in the early darkness advanced to within fifty yards of the outposts. It was a wild night of thunder and rain, and as he waited for dawn news reached him which made him change his purpose. The enemy had blocked the river with sunken ships so that the fleet could not co-operate in the attack. He believed, as every man in his army believed, that he could carry the position, though his numbers were about a fourth of the enemy's, but he realized that it would mean the loss of half his little army. Accordingly, after a council of war had been held, he gave the order to retreat, and his men most unwillingly obeyed. It was a sovereign chance for the Americans to strike a counter-blow; but they remained inert on their hills, contenting themselves with sending out some cavalry, which took prisoners six men of the left flank company of the Twenty-First who acted as rear-guard. On the 15th Brooke was back on the coast.

So ended a creditable little affair, which showed the quality of the British soldier when trained and perfected by long campaigns under the inspiration of good leaders. To him no odds were too tremendous, no tasks too hard. The Twenty-First was now to be part of a project less fortunately conceived. It reached Jamaica with Brooke on 1st November, Furlong having been granted leave and having gone by a different route from the rest, during which he had the felicity to be engaged in a fight with the famous American privateer, the *Saucy Jack*. At Jamaica the Twenty-First received a strong draft from its second battalion commanded by Major Alexander Ross, and presently there arrived from England Major-General Sir John Keane

1814 with an expedition destined for a descent upon the American coast in the neighbourhood of New Orleans. It was a scheme of the same type as Whitelock's attack on Buenos Ayres, convincing on paper, but making no account of the difficulties of the terrain. Its inspiration was naval, and its purpose prize-money. " Prize-money," says Mr. Fortescue, " had for nearly two centuries been the motive for all amphibious operations recommended by the navy, and this of New Orleans was no exception. If any naval officers had shown stronger lust of prize than others, they were the Scots ; and all three of the Admirals engaged in this expedition —excellent men in their own profession—were by a singular coincidence Scotsmen—Cochrane, Cockburn, and Malcolm." [1] Keane had under his command three West India regiments, the 93rd Highlanders, the 95th (Rifle Brigade), a brigade of artillery, and two dismounted squadrons of the 14th Light Dragoons, as well as Brooke's little army.

The expedition sailed at the end of November. In those strange days women accompanied their husbands on active service, and the wife of Major Douglas of the Twenty-First died of fever on board ship. The capture of New Orleans was the main purpose, but since the direct road to the city by way of the Mississippi seemed too hazardous, it was resolved to disembark the troops on the shore of one of the lagoons to the north-east which communicated both with the Mississippi and with the Gulf of Mexico. The plan was known to the enemy, who had several armed vessels on the lagoon, but these were captured by the boats of the British fleet under Commander Lockyer.

It was the only gleam of success in the whole venture. On 8th December the expedition reached Ship Island, near the mouth of Lake Borgne, and for nearly a fortnight bivouacked among the sand and mud of the little coastal inlets. The weather was severe, and men perished from sheer cold. On the 22nd the troops were conveyed in open boats to the mouth of the Bayou

[1] X., page 151.

Bienvenu, where the light brigade, under Colonel Thornton, effected a landing and captured two American pickets. Next day the rear-guard advanced slowly towards the city, and that evening was fiercely attacked by Andrew Jackson, the American commander, with 4,000 men, assisted by guns from the ships in the river. The first attack was beaten off; it was repeated at 10.30 p.m., by which time Thornton had been reinforced by four companies of the Twenty-First and part of the 93rd Highlanders, before whose bayonet charge the enemy broke. Norman Pringle thought the enemy "fine-looking men, but almost totally undisciplined." In that night action the Twenty-First lost Captain Conran (who was stabbed with a carving-knife) and two men killed; one sergeant, two drummers, and eight men wounded; and two men missing.

On the 25th there arrived from England Major-General Sir Edward Pakenham, Wellington's brother-in-law (who took command), and Major-General Gibbs, and a little later Major-General Lambert with the 7th Royal Fusiliers and the 43rd Regiment. Had the attack on the still incomplete American position been made before the 25th the city might have fallen, but the delay gave Jackson time to add to his forces and strengthen the defences of a most defensible piece of country. The British troops slowly crept forward, much galled by fire from the river, against which they were only half protected by the high embankments, and by concealed batteries which they could not silence. Moreover, it was a heavy task to bring up stores and guns from the ships in the gulf eighty miles away. At last, on the afternoon of January 7, 1815, when Lambert had arrived, Pakenham issued orders for a general attack on the following morning.

Andrew Jackson had chosen his position at Chalmette with judgment. It was a mile long, with the river on the right and a cypress swamp on the left, protected throughout with a ditch and breastwork, while the approach to it was enfiladed by a redoubt on the river bank and General Morgan's batteries beyond

1815 the Mississippi. Pakenham hoped to meet this last menace by passing a body of troops across the river, and, in order to allow boats from the fleet to co-operate, he had widened the canal from the head of the Bayou Bienvenu. The dispositions were as follows : Thornton, with the 85th, the 5th West India Regiment, and 600 seamen, was to cross the river during the night of the 7th and take order with Morgan ; Gibbs, with the 4th, the battalion companies of the Twenty-First, and parts of the 44th and the 95th, was to attack the American left ; Keane was to attack the American right and right centre on the left bank in two sections—the flank companies of the 7th, 43rd, 93rd, and Twenty-First, under Renny of the Twenty-First, were to storm the riverside redoubt, while the rest of Keane's brigade, the 93rd and the 1st West India Regiment, filled the gap between Renny and Gibbs. The bulk of the 7th and 43rd, under Lambert, was to form the reserve. It was a complex plan, where everything depended on correct timing, and where the failure of any one part might mean the ruin of the whole.

At daybreak on the 8th the battle began, and from the start everything went ill. Thornton was delayed in crossing the river, though he had no difficulty in capturing Morgan's batteries. When the advance of the main body commenced it was discovered that by some blunder the scaling-ladders and fascines had been left behind, and the redoubt was only stormed by Renny with disastrous losses. The main attack—that of the 4th, Twenty-First, and 44th—reached the ditch under heavy fire, but found it a desperate business to scale the parapet without ladders, though men essayed it by clambering on each other's shoulders. A gallant few, under Lieutenant Leavach of the Twenty-First, did indeed cross the parapet, and found only two American officers and the American left apparently in flight. Unhappily they were not supported, and Leavach[1] was taken prisoner. But the incident shows

---

[1] Leavach, who was born in 1789 (the son of an officer of the Twenty-First), retired in 1822, and died at Millport, in Cumbrae, in 1875, at the age of eighty-six.

NEW ORLEANS

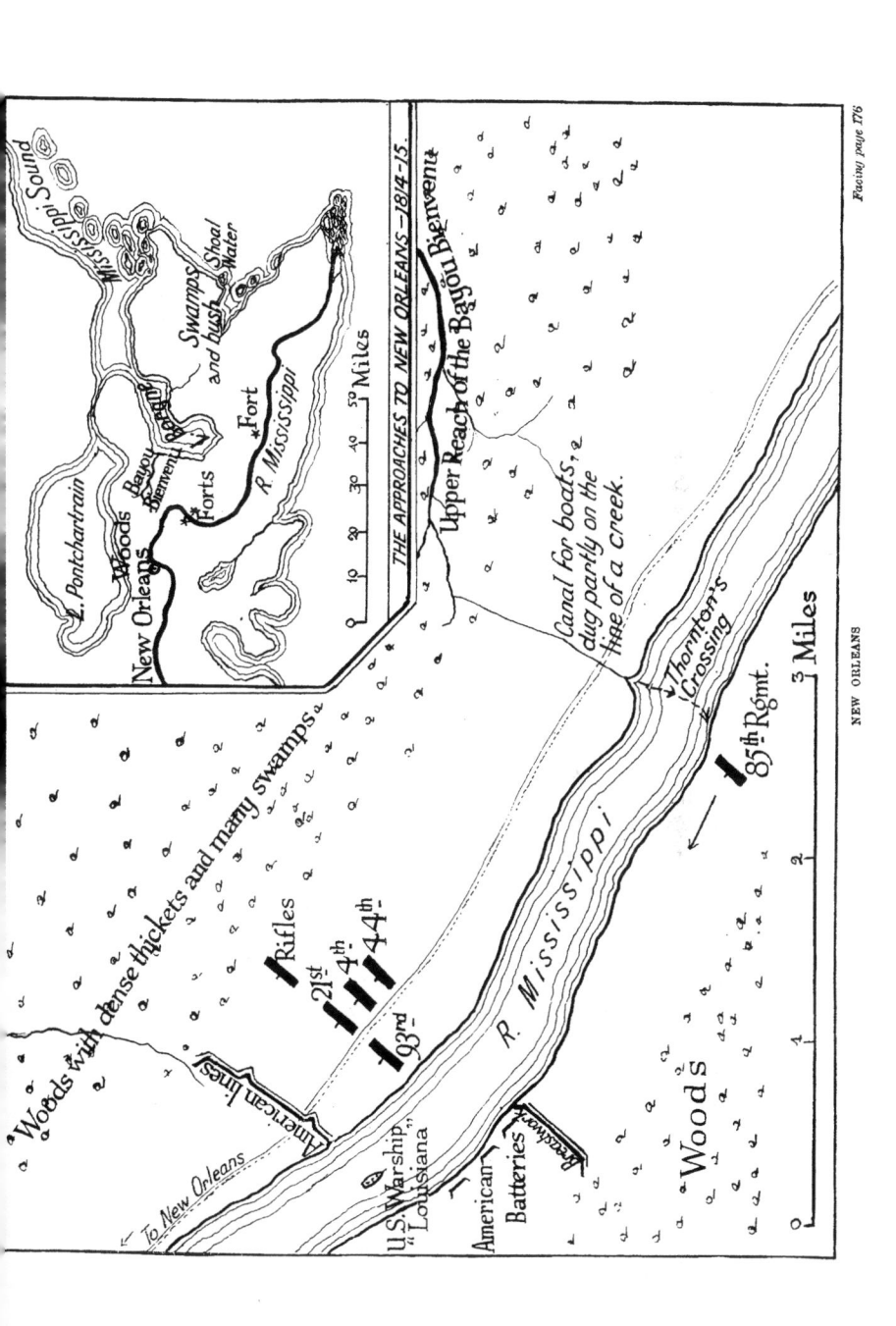

NEW ORLEANS

how narrowly victory was missed. The rest persisted 1815 as long as flesh and blood could endure, and at last were driven back by the American fire, leaving more than half their number dead. Pakenham and Gibbs were killed, and Keane severely wounded. The retreat might have been a rout but for the action of the reserve, the 7th and the 43rd, whose appearance kept the enemy within his lines.

By 8.45 a.m. it was all over. Lambert, who now took command, heard of Thornton's success across the river, and hoped for a moment to hold that position. But he was warned that the captured batteries could not be held by less than 2,000 men, so he resolved to retire. The enemy remained that night in position, and next day fell back to the ground they had formerly occupied. It was a signal disaster, for out of the 6,000 British engaged 2,000 fell. The Twenty-First was among the chief to suffer; of the 800 men who paraded that morning scarcely half were on duty by night. The commanding officer, Major Whitaker, fell, as did Brevet-Lieutenant-Colonel Renny (who closed with a notable exploit a gallant life [1]) and Lieutenant Donald Macdonald, together with two sergeants and sixty-five rank-and-file. Colonel Paterson, Major Alexander Ross, Lieutenant John Waters, and Second Lieutenant Alexander Geddes were wounded, as well as six sergeants and 144 rank-and-file; while among those who were made prisoners were Brevet-Major James McHaffie, Captain Archibald Kidd, Lieutenants James Brady, Ralph Carr, James Stewart, John Leavach, John de Grenier Fonblanque, and Alexander Boswell Armstrong, Second Lieutenant Peter Quin, eight sergeants, two drummers, and 217 rank-and-file. The list tells its own tale; it does not need the tribute of Andrew Jackson to convince us that whoever failed on that day it was not the officers and men of the Twenty-First.

Lambert abandoned hope of New Orleans, and contented himself with operations elsewhere on the coast.

[1] The Americans sent back his watch to the regiment, with compliments on his gallantry.

1815 He took Fort Bowyer, where the Twenty-First, now under Norman Pringle, played its part, and was preparing to attack Mobile when a sloop of war arrived bearing news of the Treaty of Ghent, which had been signed between Britain and America the previous Christmas Eve. The two nations had actually been at peace when the battle of New Orleans was fought. On 15th February General Lambert inspected the Twenty-First and paid its commanding officer high compliments on the appearance of his men. The expedition was now at an end, and after a brief stay in Cuba and Bermuda the regiment sailed for home, and arrived at Portsmouth on 15th June, proceeding next month to Cork.

So ended its services in the Napoleonic wars—services performed not in the main current of the great stream, but in difficult and often inglorious backwaters, so that it cannot claim the glory of those who marched with Wellington from Torrés Vedras to the Pyrenees. But one thing may be claimed: that on no occasion however hard, and against no odds however great, did it fail to add to its ancient repute. If they took part in no battle of the first magnitude, its two battalions had a singular record of diverse campaigning grounds from the day when the revolution in France first released the waters of strife—the fevered swamps and hot sands of the West Indies, mob fighting in Dublin slums, the long, dull days where the Mediterranean narrows between Scylla and Charybdis, the Egyptian desert, a dozen skirmishes on the coast of southern Italy, a brief vision of Catalonia and the fringe of the Peninsula War, entries into proud cities like Genoa and Washington, the Maryland forests, the Louisiana marshes, and the icy winter escalade of Bergen-op-Zoom. *Quæ caret ora cruore nostro ?* [1]

---

[1] In writing this chapter I have had the advantage of the manuscript diaries of Corporal David Brown, Charles Furlong, and Norman Pringle, and of the account of Bergen-op-Zoom by the unnamed officer of the second battalion published in the *United Service Journal* for 1830.

CHAPTER IX

THE LONG PEACE

The condition of the British army—The regiment in Paris—Service in the West Indies—Colin Campbell—The Scots Fusiliers in Portugal—Service in Australia—Service in India—George Deare—The outbreak of the Crimean War.

THE end of every great war is assumed by those who have suffered under it to mean an instant descent upon the earth of the blessings of prosperity and peace. The expectation is invariably belied. The world, tortured and disrupted by years of strife, has to undergo a slow and painful convalescence, during which its sufferings are not less great than in the time of conflict, and lack, moreover, the relief of hope and the stimulus of a great national effort. When after Waterloo an uneasy peace settled upon Europe, it found Britain on the brink of social disorders, and suffering everywhere from the sharp economic dislocation of a time of transition. The embarrassments of agriculture and industry, the destitution of many classes, the nursing fires of revolution may be read of in the histories; here we are concerned only with the condition of the army. And that was in no better plight than civilian society. Peace meant drastic reductions in its establishment, the revival of the old jealousy on the part of the civil Government, and a perpetual cheeseparing in military estimates; and it did not lessen the burden of its duties, though these were now of a duller and flatter kind. The unrest in Britain imposed a perpetual strain upon the home

1815

garrisons. At the beginning of the war Britain had had comparatively few foreign possessions which involved the presence of British soldiers; now she had outposts or territories everywhere throughout the globe, all of which needed military surveillance and defence. The British army, greatly reduced in numbers, had to undertake a multitude of new duties, and the soldier's life was by so much the harder.

There had been many changes in the army, but few which alleviated the soldier's lot. Recruits were still attracted by bounties, which were really advance allowances for kit, which they spent before joining their regiment, with the result that they started in debt, and often found themselves without wages for half a year. Barracks—even those of the Guards in London—were cramped and unhealthy. Wooden cribs, holding four, did duty for beds; wives and children were huddled together with the men; washing and sanitary arrangements scarcely existed.[1] Food at home was poor, ill-cooked, and inadequate; in foreign stations it was merely abominable. Clothing was tight and unsuitable and of poor material. The Peninsular War had, indeed, got rid of the pipe-clayed gaiters; but everything else—cotton shirt, stock, boots, coatee— was of a ridiculous pattern for active service. There was no provision for the soldier's comfort, amusement, or education off duty, though two out of every three recruits were illiterate; games were unknown, except that the Guards in 1815 seem to have played a little football; the men were driven to drink as their only relaxation, and the stuff supplied by the canteens (which were farmed out to civilian contractors) was expensive and vile. Life was bad enough in Britain, but it was far worse on foreign stations, where a soldier was obliged to serve ten years for every five years' service at home. Some of these stations were no

[1] "The mortality among the soldiers in Great Britain was later found to be much higher than that of their peers among the civil population, and that of the Guards in London appallingly higher." See Fortescue, Vol. XI., Chap. I., from which most of the details given above are taken.

CONDITION OF THE SOLDIER

better than cemeteries: in West Africa the annual death-roll ran from seventy-five to eighty in the hundred. The Duke of York [1] had done his best to regulate flogging, and the number of lashes permitted had been greatly reduced, but punishment in the army was still unconscionably severe.

The difficulties of the officers were no less than those of the men. The purchase of a commission was a wild hazard, and in normal cases the return for the investment was ridiculously small. "The taxpayer," says Mr. Fortescue, "had the privilege of grumbling at military expenditure; and the officers had the privilege of discharging a great part of that expenditure out of their own pockets, without indeed earning the slightest gratitude from the taxpayer for their self-sacrifice, but with at least the satisfaction of getting a gamble for their money." Out of his slender earnings an officer had to spend large sums on his uniform, which was constantly varied by the sartorial enthusiasm of the Prince Regent, who, however, made some return by establishing what was known as the "Prince Regent's allowance," which enabled poor men to drink a glass of wine at mess. There was little financial inducement to enter the profession of arms, even in the case of the Guards. "It is not difficult to calculate that a lieutenant-colonel of the Guards who paid £12,000 for his commission, commanded his regiment for twenty years for the magnificent sum of £38, 3s. 9d. as his annual net receipts, and, finally, by great good luck, came in for a colonelcy worth £1,000 a year, might, financially, have done far better for himself." [2] During the long peace, which is the subject of this chapter—a peace broken by many little wars, but by none which involved the whole military strength of the land—there was little attempt at army reform. Reductions in establishment continued, till the duties falling on the

---

[1] This admirable military reformer was in his infancy appointed Bishop of Osnabrück, and Sydney Smith wrote: "It is rumoured that our right reverend father in God has been weaned."
[2] Fortescue, XI., page 41.

remaining units became almost unbearable, and in 1829 four regiments, which had been only four years at home after twenty-four years' service abroad, were under orders for foreign stations. When Lord Howick, afterwards the third Earl Grey, became Secretary-at-War in the Melbourne Cabinet of 1835, some little was indeed done. Flogging was drastically reduced, and the system of good conduct badges and good conduct allowances was brought into being. But, speaking generally, for the first half of the nineteenth century the British soldier, officers and rank-and-file alike, had a life little less hard, comfortless, and burdensome than under the early Georges.

Nevertheless something had been gained. Wellington, by his fire tactics in the Peninsula and by abolishing the custom of depleting regiments of their best men through brigading the grenadiers and light companies of different regiments together, and Sir John Moore by the new spirit he had introduced into training, had created a high and sound tradition of technical skill. The army had won prestige in the eyes not only of its opponents, but of the nation which produced it. Economists might rave in Parliament about its waste and folly, but the ordinary Briton, remembering how, in dark days, it had stood between him and his foes, and the way in which he had thrilled to its achievements, was less disposed to listen. There had gone for good the old severance between the military life and civilian decencies. Moreover, the work begun by Wolfe and perfected by Moore had borne fruit in the new attitude of the officers towards their men. A good commanding officer was faced indeed by immense obstacles, owing to the way in which his battalion was often sprinkled among a dozen different stations, and it was hard to foster the regimental spirit in units which for years never came together. But the Napoleonic wars had created a conscience on the part of the leaders towards the rank-and-file. Regimental medals and badges were given for good service, in the belief that rewards were better than punishments; savings-banks were established; attempts were made to provide books and amusements in out-of-the-way stations as an alternative to drink for the soldier's leisure; and officers, often endowed with the scantiest of private means, provided out of their own pockets extra meals and better food for their men. It was another step in the creation of that wonderful thing, the regimental tradition; and, let it be remembered, the initiative came from the officers themselves, and not from Whitehall.

The Twenty-First had now rest from war for all but forty years. Its service in Sicily, where it was continually split into small detachments, had somewhat impaired its corporate unity and tone, and, though it had given a good account of itself in America, it had not compared for discipline with the veteran regiments from the Peninsula. But the fiery trial of the Louisiana campaign seems to have pulled it together, and it was selected to form part of the Army of Occupation in France after Waterloo. After a short stay in Ireland, when half the regiment was at Cork under Major Quinn, and half at Fermoy under Major McHaffie, it embarked for Ostend on July 5, 1815, and marched by way of Ghent to St. Denis in the vicinity of Paris. It lay in and around the capital for five months under the temporary command of Lieutenant-Colonel Charles William Maxwell, who had behind him a long record of West India fighting. Lieutenant Leavach had recovered from his wounds and rejoined, and he records the interesting fact that the Twenty-First acted as guard when the Allies removed from the Tuileries some of Napoleon's plunder and returned it to the proper owners—notably the much-travelled bronze horses of St. Mark, which, having journeyed from Byzantium to Venice and thence across the Alps with Napoleon, now returned to their perch above the great Piazza. In December the British army left the capital, and the Twenty-First marched to Compiègne, when Maxwell retired on half-pay, and handed over the regiment to Major Quinn. In February 1816 it was

1816-18 at Valenciennes, where Lieutenant-Colonel Henry, from the disbanded second battalion, took command, to be followed in a month's time by John Marvin Nooth from the 7th Foot, who had won the Order of the Bath at Albuera. In October, while at Valenciennes, the Twenty-First took part in a great review of the British army in France by the Duke of Wellington, which deeply impressed the imagination of Corporal Brown. "I have been at several reviews on the plains of St. Denis by the Duke of Wellington, but never experienced such an one as this. We turned out at a quarter before four in the morning, and did not return to camp until eleven o'clock at night." In March 1817, the British Army of Occupation being reduced, the regiment marched to Calais, whence it sailed for England, and reached Harwich on 3rd April. Meanwhile it had received large additions from the disbanded second battalion, and it had got a new colonel, owing to the death of William Gordon of Fyvie. This was James, Lord Forbes,[1] the seventeenth of his line, formerly of the Coldstream Guards, who had been with his regiment through all the Flanders fighting in the last decade of the previous century, and for a short time had been Sir John Stuart's second-in-command in the Mediterranean.

The Twenty-First had now a two-years' spell of home service, being stationed at Harwich, Colchester, Birmingham (where there was an expectation of trouble with the starving artisans), and Brighton, where it was called on to put down a ridiculous Guy Fawkes Day riot, and acted as a guard for the Prince Regent during his indecorous days at the Pavilion. In April 1818 the whole regiment was assembled at Portsmouth, where it remained till the following March, when it embarked for the West Indies. Previous to its departure it was highly praised in a special order by the General commanding the district, Lord Howard of Effingham, who complimented it on its discipline and efficiency: "The regiment is more like one parading for inspection than for embarkation for the West

[1] See Balfour Paul's *The Scots Peerage*, IV., page 66.

THE WEST INDIES

Indies." A year before the officers had been authorized to don a new long coat specially designed by the old Duke of York; and the men, drilled in the rigid manœuvres of the time, and wearing the rigid dress, fulfilled the contemporary military idea of good soldiers. Strange and uncomfortable figures they seem to us, with their skin-tight coatees, their shoulders ornamented with " shells " and " wings," their black leather stocks, their scarlet-striped black trousers, their high-heeled boots, their capacious ammunition pouches, their old Brown Besses, and their bearskin caps with the stiff white hackles. Strange and uncomfortable figures for a tour of service in the hottest lands on earth!

Barbados was reached in April, where, in spite of the heat, the men remained for a year in good health. In 1820, however, two companies were sent, under Brevet-Major Cameron, to Tobago, where a severe fever broke out, of which died four officers—Cameron himself, Colville the surgeon, Lieutenant Lindsay, and Second Lieutenant Walker—and thirty-seven men. About this time Major Leahy joined the regiment by exchange from the 7th Fusiliers. In March 1821 the Twenty-First was moved to British Guiana, three companies sailing under Major Champion for Berbice, and seven companies under Major Leahy for Demerara. Colonel Nooth could not leave Barbados, for he was gravely ill, and in the following August he died. A certain Lieutenant Booth of the regiment, who kept a diary, has recorded the pathetic farewell address which the dying Colonel sent from his deathbed. " Lieutenant-Colonel Nooth for the last time addresses his comrades, brother soldiers, and friends, and in making his adieu regrets he has not a more glorious field in which to say farewell, and that he has not had an opportunity of leading those who have hitherto been his pride and pleasure to command to a field where he must have seen proved the gallantry that best becomes good and loyal subjects. In dying as he does he has no regret, as it is in discharge of a duty which the service required, and all ranks should be willing everywhere and ready in all situations to make the return that is due to a magnanimous and grateful country. He takes leave of his military friends generally—and it is with one regret only—that of not doing it personally with them in the Field of Battle." There is a tablet to Nooth's memory outside the west front of Bath Abbey, erected by the officers and men of the Twenty-First.

A month earlier, on July 8, 1821, another officer of the regiment had died under far other conditions on the shores where the Twenty-First had fought eight years before. Edward Elliker Williams had been a lieutenant in the Twenty-First, but had retired on half-pay in 1818. He and his wife were close friends of Shelley the poet, and made part of the group in Pisa which included Byron and Medwin and Trelawny. On 8th July, Shelley, Williams, and a sailor boy set out from Leghorn in the little schooner, the *Don Juan*, which had been built to Williams's order. The boat was fast but unsafe, and as, in the evening, they steered for Casa Magni across the Gulf of Spezia a squall blotted out the sky. When it had passed, the *Don Juan* had disappeared. The bodies of Williams and Shelley were washed up on the beach, and were burned on a pyre by Trelawny in the ancient Greek fashion. Assuredly no officer of the Twenty-First had ever stranger obsequies in auguster company.

Leahy succeeded Nooth in the command, and for six years the regiment was stationed in British Guiana, St. Vincent, and Grenada, losing on those deadly shores no less than fourteen officers and 400 men. The monotony of its task was relieved by an abortive negro rising in August 1823, in the Mahaica district near Demerara, where a detachment of the Twenty-First had been sent to recuperate. Ample but confused narratives of this affair are contained in the diaries of Corporal Brown and Lieutenant O'Hara Booth. A missionary, the Rev. J. Smith, was believed to have fomented the trouble; but it was proved at his trial by court-martial that he had done his best to curb it. The mischief arose from a notion which the negroes had got into

THE DEMERARA RISING

their heads that the King had sent letters granting them their freedom, which letters had been kept back by the authorities. The insurrection was a feeble and pathetic affair, soon suppressed by Lieutenant Brady, who commanded the detachment at Mahaica, and by the reserves which Colonel Leahy sent up. The chief rebel leaders were hanged out of hand, but Leahy showed a wise moderation in dealing with their half-crazy and bewildered followers. The success of the regiment in this " bush-thwacking " episode earned it the thanks of the King, the Duke of York, and the Governor of the Windward and Leeward Islands, while the Court of Policy of British Guiana voted a gift of five hundred guineas to purchase plate for the mess, two hundred guineas for a sword of honour for Colonel Leahy, and fifty guineas for a sword for Lieutenant Brady.[1] The first gift was expended on a silver centre-piece, which still adorns the mess table of the 1st Battalion.

At St. Vincent nothing happened of note, except that Major Champion, who was a strict disciplinarian and not generally loved, was shot dead by a sentry, who was handed over to the civil power, convicted of murder, and hanged. Booth's diary gives us some insight into the infinite boredom and the petty quarrelling of life in an island station. He was something of a practical joker, and got into trouble, and was court-martialled, for introducing a goat into the room and a large turtle into the bath of Captain Scott, the barrack-master. He occupied his leisure in exploration, during which he was the first to discover in St. Vincent a seam of coal, and in various forms of sport. In British Guiana he went jaguar hunting, and ate a jaguar steak—as good as a veal cutlet to the taste, he reported, but " qualmish " in its after effects. In St. Vincent he performed remarkable pedestrian feats for very small bets—fifty miles in under twelve hours on one occasion; and on another sixty-four miles between 5.30 a.m. on one day and 2.50 a.m. on the

[1] See page 145.

next. During the regiment's term in the West Indies a noted soldier served with it, Colin Campbell, the future Lord Clyde, who came to it in 1818 from the 60th, and left it in 1832 for a staff appointment. Twenty-three years later the Twenty-First met him again in command of the Highland Brigade in the Crimea.[1]

Early in 1827 the regiment embarked for home. That summer it did duty at Windsor, when Corporal Brown left it—and his heart with it—and returned to his native Kilmarnock and a pension of half a crown a week. Next year it was at Portsmouth and Bath (where the memorial was erected to Lieutenant-Colonel Nooth), and in October it crossed to Ireland. During 1829 it was at Fermoy and Mullingar, and in 1830 its headquarters were Kilkenny. In September of the following year it marched to Dublin *en route* for England, and the year 1832 was spent at Chatham. Instructions from the Horse Guards had, in the meantime, again altered its dress. The gorgets worn by officers were abolished, white clothing with the regimental facings was ordered for the band, and the old " regimental pattern lace " used to trim the coats (in the case of the Twenty-First it was white with a blue stripe) was probably now finally changed to plain white worsted. The bearskin cap remained, for it was not till 1840 that the bell-top chaco with its white plume came in.

While the Twenty-First was peacefully pursuing its dull routine at Chatham, a force bearing the name of Scots Fusiliers was engaged in a little war on the old battle-ground of Portugal. A Scottish appellation was no new thing in a foreign army—there had been a Spanish regiment of " Scotch Grenadiers " in the Peninsula; but in this case there is a curious link between the regular and the irregular units. In 1870 Frederick Torrens Lyster became the commanding

---

[1] See General Shadwell's *Life of Colin Campbell, Lord Clyde* (Blackwood). Campbell, like Sir John Moore, was at the High School of Glasgow. He came to the Twenty-First by exchange as captain, and purchased his majority in 1825. As an ensign in the 9th Foot he was with Moore in the retreat to Corunna.

officer of the second battalion of our regiment, having come to it as major six years before from the 11th Foot. Colonel Lyster wore on his breast the unfamiliar Portuguese Order of the Tower and the Sword, for in his youth he had served Dom Pedro and taken part in the defence of Oporto in this very Scots Fusiliers battalion whose story we are now to glance at. Portugal, it will be remembered, was all through the 'twenties in the thick of the strife between Constitutionalists and Absolutists, which was the form taken there by the universal division of Liberals and Tories. Canning had sent out 4,000 British troops, including a brigade of Guards, under Sir William Clinton, but next year Wellington had withdrawn them. Thereupon that most unpleasing character, Dom Miguel, snatched the crown from Maria II., who fled to Brazil; and only in the Azores could her supporters, Saldanha and Palmella, maintain her flag. By 1831 the crimes of Dom Miguel had cried so loud to heaven that his elder brother, Dom Pedro, the Emperor of Brazil, came to Europe to support his niece's cause, and secured the assistance of France and the tacit support of Britain. Palmella raised a loan in England, with which he purchased a small fleet, and irregular levies were recruited in Britain and France. On the details of the campaign we need not linger. Oporto was taken by Dom Pedro, and promptly besieged by Dom Miguel, who had the country on his side, and 80,000 troops as against his brother's 6,000. But the generalship was all with the latter. Charles Napier took Lisbon, Saldanha broke the enemy in the field, and on May 16, 1834, Dom Miguel surrendered, and Maria—the " little urchin queen " of Lord Grey's phrase—was settled on her uneasy throne.

The adventure was a godsend to restless spirits in Britain, and among the " Liberators " was one Charles Shaw, an Ayr man, who, after serving under Wellington in the 52nd, became a rolling stone throughout Europe till the year 1831 and the outbreak of the trouble in Portugal. He started recruiting in Scotland for a foreign legion, his ingenious advertisements asking for

1831-34 "intelligent men as settlers for Brazil and elsewhere wanted by a Trading and Colonial Company." He seems to have got the equivalent of a weak battalion, which, remembering the regiment which had paraded before his boyish eyes at Ayr, he dubbed the Scots Fusiliers, a name to which Dom Pedro's staff presently added the word "Royal." The men were enlisted in the Saltmarket of Glasgow, and were mostly Radical weavers who had got into trouble with the police—"the most knowing fellows," writes Shaw, "I ever encountered." They began by electing a Soviet among themselves, which they called a "Comitee," and disputed about rates of pay with the zest of a trade union secretary. The rate of exchange puzzled them, as it has puzzled many since, and they had dark suspicions that they were being swindled. Shaw and Lyster handled them with humour and tact, but they were a difficult team to drive. The rations were poor and scanty, and their delegates complained that a tablespoonful of rice and a square inch of pork were "no eneuch for a workin' man to leeve on, forbye the fechtin'." They occasionally took the commissariat into their own hands, and stole and ate Shaw's greyhound and terrier, while certain Irish liberators did the same by his pointer. In the field, however, they did not disgrace the famous name they had assumed, and fought stoutly for "Dony Maree" against Dom Miguel, whom they spoke of as "yon damned John Macdowall." [1]

In 1832 the regiment, which was now a model unit in appearance and discipline, was split into detachments, and given the dreary task of escorting batches of convicts to Botany Bay and Van Diemen's Land.[2] This work continued through the following year, and in 1834 the whole regiment was in Australia and Tas-

[1] The curious will find the full story in *The Personal Memoirs and Correspondence of Colonel Charles Shaw*, 2 Vols., London, 1837.
[2] In the Royal Scots Fusiliers the orderly room is traditionally known as the "haul up," and the name is said to date from its convict-escorting service. O'Hara Booth became Governor of Port Arthur Penal Settlement.

mania—the headquarters with two companies at Hobart, and the rest in small parties employed throughout Tasmania, and at Perth, Port Philip, and Swan River, in charge of convict stations and of convict gangs engaged in public works. These police duties were difficult, incessant, and laborious, and brought no honour with them; but it is to the credit of the Twenty-First that its discipline stood the test. For the four years of its service in Australia its conduct was exemplary, and earned it the high commendation of the Government. Lieutenant-Colonel Leahy retired from the army in 1835, and was succeeded by John Charles Hope from the 95th Rifles, who had distinguished himself at the battle of Waterloo. He held the post for two years, when he returned to the command of his old regiment. His place was taken by George Warren Walker, who had been deputy-adjutant-general in Ceylon, and the following year Walker was replaced by George Deare, who had joined the Twenty-First in 1818 from a West India Regiment.

In February 1839 the weary police work came to an end, and the regiment embarked at Hobart for Calcutta to make its first acquaintance with a famous theatre of British arms. The great reforming viceroyalty of Lord William Bentinck was over, and his successor, Lord Auckland, was involved once more in frontier wars. His ill-judged interference in the dynastic affairs of Afghanistan brought about the First Afghan War. In 1839, just after the Twenty-First landed at Calcutta, Afghanistan was in the military occupation of Britain—an occupation which continued for two years, till in the winter of 1841 came the murder of Burnes and Macnaghten, and the British army was compelled to retreat through the snowy passes, till its 4,000 men and 12,000 camp followers perished, and the sole survivor, Dr. Brydon, rode up to the gates of Jalalabad. Next year, after their fashion, the British returned, and Kabul was taken; and then the troops marched back to India, having accomplished nothing, and leaving Dost Mahommed, the originator of all the trouble, secure upon the throne. Lord Ellenborough, who had succeeded Lord Auckland, had a taste for war, and presently came Sir Charles Napier's brilliant victory of Meeanee and the annexation of Sind. In 1844 Ellenborough was replaced by Lord Hardinge, a Peninsula veteran who had lost a hand at Ligny, and the secular quarrel with the Sikh power came to a head. Under Sir Hugh Gough the battles of Moodkee, Ferozeshah, and Sobraon were fought, and the way was prepared for the control of the Punjab. Then in 1848 came Dalhousie, the greatest of India's viceroys, during whose régime the conquest was completed, and the foundations of modern India laid.

In all this the Twenty-First had no part. It spent its first year at Chinsurah, and then in August 1840 moved to Dinapur, where for the first time for eight years the whole regiment was together. In November 1842 it started for Agra, but its destination was changed to Kamptee in the Madras Presidency, where it remained for nearly three years. On the first mutterings of the Sikh war it was hurried off to the North-West Provinces, starting from Kamptee on December 6, 1845, full of hopes of service in the field. But when, after thirty-four days' marching without a halt, it reached Agra on February 7, 1846, to its bitter disappointment it was ordered to occupy the barracks in that city, the neighbouring Raja of Gwalior having threatened trouble, and the Twenty-First being the only British regiment then in the North-West Provinces which was not actually in the field. It was a heavy blow, for the regiment was in superb form—1,100 men of fine physique thoroughly acclimatized. In spite of the long and trying march from Madras only fourteen were in hospital.

The Twenty-First spent a year at Agra, and moved to Cawnpore in February 1847. Here orders arrived for its return to England, and, after the custom of the day, its members were permitted to volunteer to stay on in the country in other units. Induced by liberal bounties, 396 of its best men accepted the offer; and

GEORGE DEARE

when it reached Calcutta at the close of the year, another 86 chose to remain. It was a serious loss to the regiment, for these 482 were naturally the best soldiers in physique, training, and character. While the Twenty-First lay at Calcutta awaiting embarkation, it took part in the official reception of the new Governor-General, Lord Dalhousie—a duty which we may believe it fulfilled with a special goodwill, for Dalhousie came from that part of Scotland where it had first been raised, and many of his family had served with it.

Those nine years in India, though inglorious, were not unfruitful. Owing to having been scattered so long in detachments about Australia it had lost something in discipline and tone, and the new recruits which joined it in India were very raw. When George Deare took command in 1840, he set himself—along with the senior captain, Ainslie, whom we shall meet again in the Crimea—most vigorously to the work of reconstruction. Of his success let Sergeant Clark speak :—

" He began at the beginning—first squad, and then company drill. He was a perfect master of drill, even to its most minute details; he went from squad to squad, or from company to company, directing, correcting, and instructing officers, non-commissioned officers, and men. By the end of the drill season of 1840 the regiment was fairly well drilled, and by the end of the succeeding season it could not be surpassed, perhaps not equalled, by any regiment in the service. . . . He was the *beau ideal* of a commanding officer : about six feet in height, well proportioned, and of such a dignified and soldierly bearing as to inspire respect. His word of command was surprisingly loud, clear, and ringing; he had an eye like an eagle that could detect any unsteadiness or inattention in the ranks, front or rear, from No. 1 to No. 10 company ; and, as he knew the name of almost every man in the regiment, the offender was at once indicated by name. It ought also to be mentioned that he was an excellent horseman, and was always well mounted. As an 'orderly-room colonel' he was unequalled; possessed of clear perception and an unerring judgment, he was quick to discern the false from the true in any matter brought before him; and no judge that ever sat on the bench was ever more free from bias and prejudice in his decisions. He was what is called a 'light punisher' of the crimes that soldiers are ordinarily guilty of, but anything mean, unmanly, or unsoldierlike was visited by him with scathing reproof and well-merited punishment. The men were proud of 'George' (their pet name for him), and they knew that he was proud of them; they believed that their own regiment was the best in the army, and they were not mistaken."[1]

It is a fine portrait of a wise commanding officer, and the justice of Deare's judgment is shown by what happened on St. Patrick's Day in 1840. It had been the custom of the regiment to start celebrations at midnight on St. Patrick's eve with the band playing, and since this led to unnecessary drunkenness the music was forbidden. It is difficult, however, to lay violent hands on a regimental custom, and on this occasion the purpose of the order was frustrated by the pipers and drummers on guard starting a pandemonium on their own account. The outbreak was visited with no more than a reprimand, for the Colonel had an eye to the weakness of human nature. In his work for the regiment he was assisted by very able subordinate officers, such as Ainslie and John Ramsay Stuart, who got his company in 1840. The most distinguished of these subordinates was Charles Richard Sackville, who came as a captain to the Twenty-First from the 15th Foot in 1842, and who was an aide-de-camp and afterwards military secretary to Sir Hugh Gough in the Sutlej campaign, where he obtained a brevet-majority. Sackville, under

[1] *Hist. Record of R.S.F.*, pages 46, 47.

the name of Lord West, we shall hear much of in the future, as of another of Gough's military secretaries, Frederick Paul Haines of the 4th Foot, who was at Moodkee and Ferozeshah, Chillianwallah and Gujerat, was severely wounded, given a company and then a brevet-majority, and joined the Twenty-First on its return to Scotland.

In May 1848 the regiment, after having been absent on foreign service for sixteen years, was back in England. Its first station was Canterbury, where it received 470 recruits to fill the places of the men left behind in India. In July it moved to Edinburgh—travelling for the first time in its history by the railway—and was quartered at the Castle, with detachments at Leith, Berwick, and Glencorse. Deare retired in 1848,[1] to the profound regret of the regiment, and was followed by John Crofton Peddie, of a family whose members had served in the Twenty-First since its earliest days. Next year Peddie exchanged with Thomas Gore Brown of the 41st, who had commanded that regiment in the First Afghan War. Then began some years of constant movement. In April 1850 the Twenty-First went to Glasgow, sending detachments to Paisley and Dumbarton Castle. Next year it went to Newcastle-on-Tyne, with companies at Carlisle, Sunderland, and Tynemouth; and in 1852 to Hull, with companies at Scarborough, Bradford, and Leeds. Edward Thorpe from the 89th Foot had succeeded Gore Brown in 1851, and on his retirement next year the command fell to Frederick George Ainslie. Ainslie, who had been Deare's right-hand man in India, continued Deare's tradition. At Hull there was an experimental issue of one hundred Minié rifles; and in order to encourage marksmanship, Ainslie instituted a system of granting a distinctive badge to the best shots, to be worn on the upper right sleeve of the fatigue jacket—an early anticipation of the modern schools of musketry. In 1853 the regiment moved to Dublin, where it was

---

[1] While in India the regiment had two junior lieutenant-colonels, Richard Tyrrell Robert Pattoun (1843–47), and John Thomas Hill (1847–48).

1853-54 reviewed by Queen Victoria and the Prince Consort, who were visiting Ireland in connection with the Industrial Exhibition. That year died Sir Frederick Adam, who, ten years before, had succeeded Lord Forbes as colonel of the regiment—himself an old officer of the Twenty-First, who had led it in various actions in Sicily and Calabria, and who had commanded later a famous brigade at Waterloo. Adam may well rank as one of the most distinguished sons of the regiment. He was succeeded by Sir de Lacy Evans, who had seen fighting in every corner of the globe, and was soon to command a division in the Crimea. One of his first acts as colonel was to apply successfully for permission to inscribe " Bladensburg " on the regimental colours.[1]

The Twenty-First at this time was in the perfection of condition. Deare's training, continued by Ainslie, had raised it to the highest pitch of efficiency and discipline. It had now been increased to twelve companies, with a total strength of 1,400. In Scotland it earned nothing but praise; in Ireland the Generals commanding the Dublin and Cork districts were loud in their commendation. Said the latter : " That will do, Colonel Ainslie. Close your ranks and march past. I never inspected such a regiment." The Cork correspondent of the *Times* declared that " the equal of the Fusiliers never paraded in Cork barrack square, not even excepting the Guards." It had need of its quality, for the long reign of peace in Europe, celebrated three years before by the Great Exhibition in Hyde Park, was drawing to a close. On March 28, 1854, in the interests of Turkey, Britain and France declared war against Russia, and on 15th August of that year the Twenty-First, under Ainslie's command, sailed from Cork in the *Golden Fleece* for Varna Bay.[2]

---

[1] The letter from the Horse Guards is dated January 7, 1854.
[2] The regiment had been preparing for several months for the field, and the young officers used to go out in parties to bivouac in the Dublin mountains by way of hardening themselves for campaigning.

CHAPTER X

THE CRIMEA

Arrival at Varna—The landing in the Crimea—The battle of the Alma—Balaclava—Inkerman—Frederick Haines—The siege of Sebastopol—The bombardment of Kinburn.

THE first stage of the Crimean War had closed with the retreat of the Russians from the Danube; the second began with the expedition of the Allies against Sebastopol, the base of the Russian Black Sea Fleet, the destruction of which seemed to Britain and France the only security for peace in the Near East. Few enterprises have been undertaken with so little knowledge on the part of the attackers of the nature or magnitude of the problem before them. It was a leap in the dark, where the preparations were rudimentary, and only the vaguest intelligence had been received about the landing ground. The Twenty-First was fortunate in escaping the pestilential weeks at Varna, when cholera decimated both the crews at sea and the troops on land. It had a fair-weather voyage, during which the new recruits from Dublin were licked into shape, and the soul of Frederick Haines was ravished with the beauty of the sunsets and fortified by the reading of Dickens's *Hard Times*, which was then appearing in parts. He tells in his diary the tale of a young officer " who awoke with a feeling that the ship was on fire, and immediately proceeded to inflate his life-preserver, which hung in his berth. Unfortunately, however, his india-rubber leggings hung there also, and of these in his hurry he caught hold and made most

1854

1854 frantic efforts to inflate. Having blown himself fairly out in this fruitless effort, he became sufficiently wide-awake to be conscious of his mistake." On 1st September the *Golden Fleece* anchored off Scutari, and Haines becomes lyrical in his description of the beauty of the Bosphorus. On 3rd September the regiment reached Varna, where there was grimmer business than scenery and sunsets.[1]

The expedition to the Crimea was made up of 26,000 British troops under Lord Raglan, now in his sixty-sixth year, who, as Lord Fitzroy Somerset, had been a dashing leader in the Peninsula, and had lost an arm while serving on Wellington's staff at Waterloo; 32,000 French under Marshal St. Arnaud, who had done brilliant work in Algeria, but was now enfeebled by sickness; and 7,000 Turks under Omar Pasha, the Croat soldier of fortune who had defended the line of the Danube. The Russian Commander-in-Chief was Prince Alexander Menshikov, who had fought against Napoleon in the campaigns of Moscow and Leipzig and the invasion of France. The command, therefore, belonged to the old régime, and so did the equipment. The French and part of the British troops were armed with the new Minié rifle, but the Russians had still the old percussion musket; the field artillery on both sides was still the smooth-bore, muzzle-loading guns of the Napoleonic wars. The British army consisted of five divisions of infantry and two cavalry brigades. The First Division, under H.R.H. the Duke of Cambridge,

[1] The following were the officers of the Twenty-First as far as I can ascertain them : Lieutenant-Colonel F. G. Ainslie ; Major John Ramsay Stuart ; Captains Lord West, Robert Spring, F. P. Haines, Hon. J. L. Browne, T. C. Hobbs, J. A. Vesey Kirkland, J. T. Dalzell, G. N. Boldero, W. J. Legh, Ellis J. Charter; First Lieutenants F. E. N. Tinley (Adjutant), W. Pole Collingwood, H. W. Clerke, E. A. T. Steward, J. Aldridge, H. F. Berkeley Maxe, Crofton Peddie, J. F. de Carteret, A. Templeman, J. C. Sheffield, W. H. Carleton, L. Trelawney Clark, Henry King ; Second Lieutenants Roger Killeen, H. F. E. Hurt, Stanislas G. B. St. Clair, Arthur Greer, Hon. R. R. Best, J. H. Dunne, J. G. Image, Shadwell H. Clerke, C. Bruce Gaskell, R. Stephens, Edward Isaac Haddock. Of these Haines rose to be a field-marshal; West, Boldero, Dalzell, Ramsay Stuart, and Dunne to be general officers ; and Steward and Templeman to command battalions of the regiment. "Billy" Legh retired as captain, and lived to lead Mr. Gladstone at the poll for South Lancashire, and become the first Lord Newton.

included Bentinck's Brigade of Guards and Sir Colin Campbell's brigade of the 42nd, 79th, and 93rd Highlanders. The Second Division, under Sir de Lacy Evans, the colonel of the Twenty-First, had Pennefather's brigade of the 30th, 55th, and 95th Regiments, and Adams's brigade of the 41st, 47th, and 49th. Sir Richard England led the Third Division, which included Sir John Campbell's brigade (1st, 28th, and 38th) and Eyre's brigade (44th, 50th, and 68th). In the Fourth Division, commanded by a Waterloo veteran, Sir George Cathcart, there were at the start the 20th, Twenty-First, and 63rd, and the 1st Rifle Brigade, to be joined later by the 46th and 57th. The Light Division was under Sir George Brown, and was made up of Codrington's brigade (7th, 23rd, and 33rd) and Buller's brigade (19th, 77th, and 88th), together with the 2nd Rifle Brigade. Lord Lucan led the cavalry, with Lord Cardigan commanding the Light Brigade (4th and 13th Light Dragoons, 8th and 11th Hussars, and 17th Lancers), and General Scarlett commanding the Heavy Brigade (4th and 5th Dragoon Guards, Royals, Scots Greys, and Inniskillings).

1854

The start from Varna, owing to heavy weather, was delayed till 7th September, when one hundred and fifty ships of war and transports set sail for the Crimea. It had been decided to land the troops not in a harbour south of Sebastopol, but at a place called the Old Fort, about thirty miles to the north, where a long beach and a chain of lagoons seemed to provide ideal ground for disembarkation. On the 12th the ships were off the coast, and the landing began. There was no opposition from the enemy, but the weather protracted the operation, so that it was not completed till the 18th. Haines in a letter gives the experiences of the regiment :—

"On the 14th September we landed at Kalamita Bay, on a strip of beach between the sea and a putrid lake, without baggage, merely what we could carry on our back, and with three days' provisions. We landed all the infantry that day without opposition. That night was a terrific one. A gale of wind sprang up, with the heaviest rain I was ever exposed to. The British army in the Crimea was indeed a wretched force that night. I managed to keep my kit dry, but got thoroughly drenched myself. A bright day following put us all right again. A great deal of damage was done to the boats and platforms by the storm, and a heavy surf rendered it impossible to proceed with the disembarkation until evening. We remained on the beach till the 19th; a most unhealthy place it turned out. Our men sickened fast, and we lost many from cholera."

General Sir John Hart Dunne,[1] who lived till 1924, then a subaltern in the Twenty-First, has described in some MS. reminiscences the appearance of the officers at the landing. "We were all in full dress, in tight coatees, with gold wings on our shoulders, a broad white leather sword-belt with breast plate, a tight red sash with tassels fixed to one of our buttons. Our greatcoats were folded up, in some cases covering a spare pair of shoes inside, and were strapped on our backs. Over one shoulder we carried a large haversack stuffed with three days' rations of salt pork and biscuit, and over the other shoulder was carried by a hard thick strap one of the wooden water-bottles the same as used in the Peninsula. . . . The infantry soon threw away the abominable Albert shako and wore their round forage caps. Our officers' caps in the Twenty-First, of blue cloth with a red band and big grenade, had a peak in front which was not restful at night. Remember that then we had always to wear our greatcoats, and though we got tents and some blankets when we got round to the south of Sebastopol, we never

[1] Dunne, who was born in 1835, began his career in the 62nd Regiment, and transferred to the Twenty-First in January 1854. In 1856 he transferred to the 99th Regiment, and was in the China campaign of 1860. He reached the rank of major-general in 1881, and retired as a full general in 1902, after fifty years' service. His son served in the Royal Scots Fusiliers in the Great War (see page 353).

had anything to pillow our heads on, and were only too glad to find a big smooth stone to save a crick in the neck."

On the 19th began the southward march, the British, who alone had their cavalry with them, on the dangerous left flank, the French next the sea, and the fleet moving slowly down the coast. Menshikov had so far given no sign. He had his communications open with the Russian interior, and might either meet the intruders by barring one of the river valleys across which lay the road to Sebastopol, or attempt a flank attack on the British. The first day's march was trying; the day was hot, the downs, bright with autumn crocuses, were dry and slippery to the feet, and there was little water. Haines, with his company of the Twenty-First, had the prosaic duty of acting as cattleguard. That evening they came to the first westflowing river, the Bulganak, where the 11th Hussars had a skirmish with a Cossack detachment. Across the stream there was a gentle rise and then a long slope, beyond which rose the bluffs on the south bank of the next river, the Alma. As the Allies bivouacked in the clear, still night by the Bulganak, they saw the fires of the enemy on the Alma hills, and realized that Menshikov had chosen that natural rampart for his stand.

The position was well reconnoitred from the fleet. The western part of the Alma heights was so precipitous that the Russian commander judged it impossible for a large movement of men; moreover, his left wing there was enfiladed by the ships' guns. He had therefore retired his left, and concentrated his strength on his right centre and right, where he was opposed mainly by British troops. Raglan and St. Arnaud agreed that the British and part of the French should attack the main Russian position, while the rest of the French, in echelon from the right, were to cross the river, climb the weakly defended bluffs, and drive in the Russian left. The scheme was in substance a frontal attack, and it is odd that the far better plan was neglected of turning the Russian right and driving the

1854 enemy seaward toward the guns of the fleet. The Allies had the superiority in numbers, and success in this latter plan would not merely have opened the road to Sebastopol, but would have destroyed the Russian army. The explanation of the choice of plan seems to have been the influence which the presence of a fleet exercises on the strategy of land troops dependent on it. The need of the ships' guns to support an attack is apt to become an obsession.

The 20th dawned bright and clear like a morning in June, but it was not till after midday that the Allies moved forward to the actual attack. The cavalry and the Fourth Division were held in reserve to protect the left flank against Cossack threats, and the Twenty-First had but a single casualty. The spectacle of the advance must have been like some ceremonial review. " Out on the extreme left there was the flash and glitter of Lord Lucan's brigades of British cavalry, red and blue and gold in profusion, hussars, lancers, dragoons, and horse artillery. Then, with a swarm of dark green-uniformed riflemen thrown out in front, four red-coated infantry divisions marched, arrayed in two lines, each more than a mile and a half long, with a fifth division in column behind them as a reserve. The men were formed two deep, with field batteries in the intervals between the divisions. The Russians from the heights saw for the first time the famous ' thin red line.' On the left it was formed by the Duke of Cambridge's splendid division, the Brigade of Guards—three battalions of tall, bearskin-capped Grenadiers, Coldstream, and Scots, with Colin Campbell's Highland Brigade on their left, an array of brilliant tartan and nodding plumes." [1] On the right was the French screen of blue-coated Chasseurs, with behind them three divisions in column, each with a Zouave regiment at its head. Beyond was Bosquet's division, making for the bluffs, with the red-fezzed Turkish infantry on their right rear. On the water, near the

[1] Atteridge, *Famous Modern Battles*, page 11. The battle of the Alma was the last in which the British army fought in full dress uniform.

FIELD-MARSHAL LORD CLYDE
(From a portrait by Sir F. Grant, P.R.A., in the possession of the Guards' Club)

shore, were ten French and three British war steamers, a sight which had still for our troops the fascination of novelty; and out at sea, under shortened sail, moved the main fleets of the Allies.

The battle of the Alma need not be described here in detail, for our regiment had no part in it. The flanking movement miscarried, for Bosquet's division and the Turks got so far to the enemy's left that there was nothing for them to turn, and the French attack on the bluffs progressed too slowly to have much effect on the issue of the day. The brunt of the fighting fell on the British, who from the start found themselves badly cramped for space. The main attack was made by de Lacy Evans's Second Division and the Light Division under heavy fire and with heavy losses. The Brigade of Guards and Colin Campbell's Highlanders followed, and in the end Kurghana Hill was carried with a loss of nearly 3,000 men. There was little generalship either in the original plan or in the direction of the action, for Lord Raglan disappeared into the battle. By a curious chance his passion for "thrusting," which had made him a name in the Gloucestershire hunting-field and taken him alone up to the drawbridge at Badajos, carried him into the heart of the enemy's position, and actually played a considerable part in demoralizing the defence. The battle was won long before dusk, but the Russians were allowed to retreat without molestation. The victory was a proof of what our discipline learned in the Peninsula and in India could do against the most formidable of positions. The news of it had to be sent by messenger to Belgrade, which was the nearest telegraph post, and did not reach London till Saturday, the 30th.

Had the Allied generals pressed their advantage, no Russian guns would have escaped, and Sebastopol might have been attacked from the north side. But it was not till the 23rd that the victors left the banks of the Alma; and the day before Menshikov had blocked the harbour of Sebastopol by sinking seven men-of-war at its entrance, thereby leaving the rest of the Russian

1854 fleet free to take part in the defence, and, wisely refusing to shut up his army in the fortress, maintained it at large in the Crimea to await a favourable chance for a blow at the invaders. On the 23rd the Allies were on the banks of the Kacha, and next day they were on the Belbek. That afternoon it was clear to their commanders that the north side of the fortress was impracticable, and that they must find a new sea base

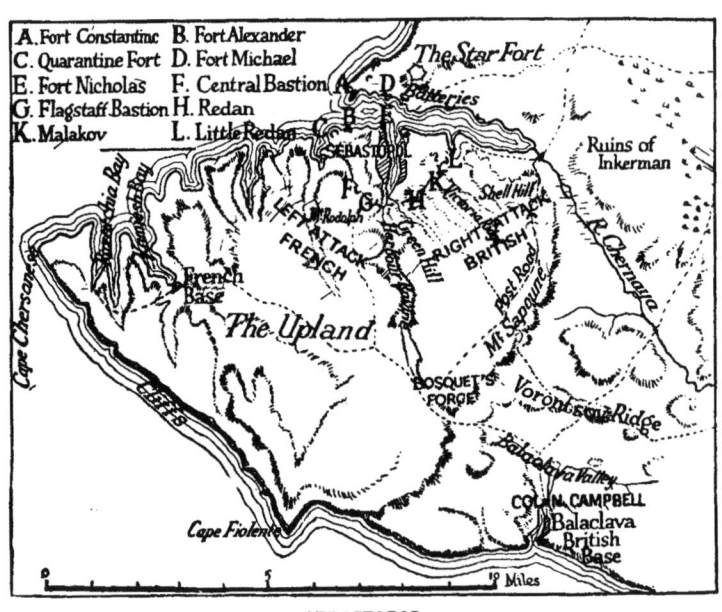

SEBASTOPOL

somewhere to the south. On the 25th St. Arnaud handed over his command to Canrobert, and set out, a dying man, for home. The Allies made a flank march by the river Chernaya to Balaclava, while Menshikov, moving out towards Baksherai, unwittingly crossed their front. By the 27th they had reached the neighbourhood of Balaclava, which became the British base, while the French occupied Kamiesh. They were now on that part of the Chersonese which was to become famous as " The Upland," close upon the south side of Sebastopol, and casting curious eyes at the earthworks which the enemy was throwing up.

The first half of October was spent in digging trenches and bringing up guns, while on the Russian side Todleben was busy completing his great defences. The Twenty-First was in camp on Cathcart's Hill, just below the highest point of the Upland, with a wonderful view over Sebastopol town and harbour. It was vile weather, sickness was rife, and medical comforts did not exist. For ten days, Ramsay Stuart of the Twenty-First reported, there was nothing in the hospital but a little rum. On 15th October he noted that his clothes had only been off twice since the landing. "We sleep on the ground every night. . . . I always sleep in my red coat, with spurs and boots on, and very often the saddle is not off my horse for twenty-four hours. . . . The dirty state of our clothes and persons is something beyond description. Yesterday I managed to get to some water, where I washed my hands and face, two pocket handkerchiefs, and a pair of socks, all with my own hands. I saw Lord West washing a shirt for himself." On 17th October the first attack took place, when the British guns silenced the Malakoff Tower and the Redan; but the French guns failed against the Russian field works, and during the night Todleben was able to repair the damage. By this time a line of Allied works on the Upland protected the siege corps, and the harbour of Balaclava was strongly defended, but the Vorontsov ridge between the two was lightly held. The troops were already very sick of this form of war. "There is none here," wrote Ramsay Stuart, "that would not hail peace with a shout that would make the Crimea ring again."

Presently came news of Menshikov and his field army. On 25th October he struck at the Vorontsov ridge and began the battle of Balaclava. General Liprandi carried the Turkish redoubts at the first attack, but as he advanced he was charged from the flank by Scarlett's Heavy Brigade of British cavalry, and was held and broken by the fire of the 93rd outside

1854 Balaclava.[1] Then came the famous blunder which ended in the charge of the Light Brigade against the enemy field batteries. The Fourth Division was hurried to the field, but the battle was over before it could come into action, and the Twenty-First had no casualties. The enemy was left in possession of the Vorontsov ridge, for Canrobert refused Raglan's suggestion of a counter-stroke. The position was far from comfortable, since the defence of Balaclava was now narrowed to the inner line, and the besiegers had to face the double task of conducting the siege and protecting an extended line of communications against a mobile army. Another stroke by the latter might be anticipated, and we find Haines and Lord West spending the close of October and the first days of November in reconnoitring the difficult country to the east and north-east of the Upland, while the French closed upon the Flagstaff bastion and the British upon the Malakoff.

The blow came on 5th November, and led to one of the most glorious and desperate engagements in British history. To understand the battle of Inkerman, to which Kinglake found it necessary to devote an entire volume, we must examine carefully the terrain. The British line stretched roughly south-east of Sebastopol along the Upland, which on the east falls sharply to the Chernaya valley. Beyond that stream lay the heights of Inkerman, occupied by the Russians, but the Allies applied the name also to the hills occupied by themselves on the west side of the valley. These hills were a series of spurs running down to the upper end of the harbour, and bounded on the south-west by a long hollow called the Careenage Ravine. On the British left was Shell Hill, then came the Inkerman Tusk, then the Fore Ridge with the Sandbag Battery at its northern edge. Between Shell Hill and the Tusk lay Quarry Ravine, through which ran the Post Road from the Chernaya to Balaclava. This Post Road

---

[1] The phrase "thin red line" was first used in describing the stand of the 93rd. The Twenty-First was not in action, but it received the clasp for Balaclava.

demands special attention. After leaving the Quarry Ravine it turned south-east and then south over Home Ridge, a spur set at right angles to Fore Ridge. The camps of the Guards Brigade and the Light Division lay to the south, and nearer Balaclava was the camp of the Fourth Division. At the turn of the Post Road, just north of Home Ridge, a modest breastwork of stone had been built across the path, soon to be famous as the Barrier, while Sandbag Battery, at the north end of Fore Ridge, was an earthwork which had fulfilled its original purpose and had been abandoned. The position was weak at the best, and Sir de Lacy Evans's Second Division, which occupied it, had not strengthened it by serious outworks and entrenchments. Shell Hill could not be held by day, owing to the fire of the Russian ships in the harbour, but even at night the British pickets were not pushed up to its crest.

The result was a startling surprise. The enemy had received large reinforcements, and he had prepared a plan at once bold and crafty. From the Sebastopol garrison a force of 19,000 men, with thirty-eight guns, under General Soimonov, was to march east along the heights and take Shell Hill. There they were to be joined by 16,000 infantry and ninety-six guns under General Paulov, moving from beyond the Chernaya. The united army, now under General Dannenberg, was to attack south, while Prince Gortschakov, who had succeeded Liprandi in the command of the forces on the Vorontsov ridge, was to hold Bosquet's French division in check by a feint attack, and then form the left flank of the main movement.

The November Sunday dawned in mist and sleet, which gave admirable cover for the surprise. In tracing the events of the battle it will be convenient to follow Kinglake's division into stages.[1] Soimonov, moving out from Sebastopol, captured Shell Hill without opposition about six a.m., and Pennefather (who, in the absence of de Lacy Evans from sickness, commanded

[1] In my narrative I have had great assistance from Professor Rait's *Life of Field-Marshal Sir Frederick Haines.* Constable, 1911.

1854 the Second Division) was faced with an ugly problem. The enemy, already 15,000 strong, was threatening his centre and right on Home Ridge and Fore Ridge, while another body of Russians was marching along the Careenage Ravine to attack his left. He might have concentrated upon the defence of Home Ridge, but he chose instead to defend the whole line, sending forward detachments to reinforce the pickets, with the result that the battle became a chain of separate actions. He had now mustered some 3,600 infantry and eighteen guns. Presently Paulov's fresh troops from beyond the Chernaya appeared on Shell Hill, and the enemy was now 25,000 strong. At first numbers ensured success. Three guns of a British battery in the Mikriakov ravine just under Shell Hill were captured, and Soimonov's right was close on the Second Division camp by way of the Careenage Ravine. But the mist, which had helped the surprise, now prevented the enemy from realizing the fragility of the defence. A charge by a handful of British checked the Careenage column; another detachment drove the enemy from the captured Mikriakov guns; while a third cleared the end of Fore Ridge and recovered the Sandbag Battery. By 7.30 a.m. 25,000 Russians had been repulsed by 4,000 British, and Soimonov was dead.

But Dannenberg was now in command of the united force on Shell Hill, and he disposed of 35,000 men and 134 guns—fantastic odds, had they not been concealed by the merciful drizzle. The second stage of the battle, which began at 7.45 a.m., was notable for the attack on Sandbag Battery, which the enemy mistakenly assumed to be a vital point in the British defence. Dannenberg's reinforcements easily cleared Shell Hill, and attacked the Sandbag, where was Adams with his brigade of the Second Division. The Barrier on the Post Road was held, but between it and Fore Ridge there was a gap, so that Adams was attacked on his left as well as on his front. He was driven back and mortally wounded, but the Grenadier Guards, under

THE SANDBAG BATTERY

the Duke of Cambridge, and the Royal Fusiliers re-took 1854
the battery, and for an hour the desperate defence
continued. Six times the position changed hands.
Meantime Bosquet, having realized that Gortschakov's
attack was no more than a feint, sent up two regiments
to the rear of the gap, but there his instructions ceased,
and the supports remained inert. Sir George Cathcart,
with 400 men of the Fourth Division, was hurried to
the gap, but was drawn into the fight at Sandbag. Once

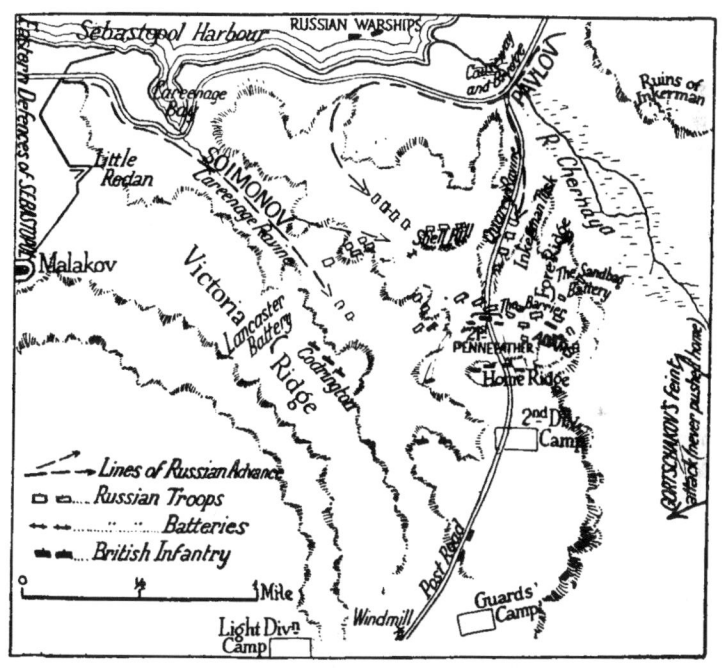

BATTLE OF INKERMAN

again the assailants were routed, but as the British
followed in pursuit, a Russian column entered the gap
and turned the position. Cathcart with fifty men
attacked it, and Cathcart fell, leaving the Duke of
Cambridge with a hundred Grenadiers the only force
in defence. The situation was saved by the advance
of the French, who had at last received their orders.

1854 One thousand of the British defenders lay dead or wounded on that fatal hill.

Meanwhile Pennefather, with the rest of the Second Division, had been holding Home Ridge and the ground about the Barrier. The second stage closed at 8.30 a.m., and the vital centre moved from Sandbag Battery to the inconsiderable breastwork of stone across the Post Road. At this point begins the tale of the great deeds of the Twenty-First.

The Twenty-First had for the most part spent the night in the trenches. When the sound of guns announced the attack, that portion of it which was in camp was turned out, and sixty men went forward. The rest of the regiment, under Colonel Ainslie, followed, and when they reached the cross-roads at the Windmill they were met with an appeal from a distracted officer whose men had run short of ammunition. Ainslie therefore sent 200 men, under Lord West, to the British left, where they were engaged in the defence of Home Ridge along with the 41st Regiment. The remainder, in company with the 63rd, advanced, keeping to the right of the road, where they wheeled into line. The fire from Shell Hill was very heavy, and they were forced to lie down in the wilderness of oak-scrub and rock. Neither of the battalions had any orders, so Ainslie and Colonel Swyney of the 63rd decided to act together.

The right flank of the 63rd was now threatened, and at the same moment came pressure from the front. Ainslie resolved to deal first with the latter menace, and crying " D—n it, we must go in at these fellows first," ordered his men to attack. Weary with night duty, armed only with old-fashioned smooth-bore muskets and with damp powder which led to continual misfires, they responded heroically to the call. " The Russians," wrote Haines, " were driven before us like sheep. It was a weird journey down the hill, with we knew not what before or behind us; the mist was too heavy to allow us to see much in any direction, but away we went, the men evidently caring for none of these things. It was Donnybrook Fair revived. I have never seen troops behave better; my great anxiety was to steady and keep them together, and the thick brush through which we advanced tended much to break our formation." Down the Post Road they went, past the Barrier, till they were only some eighty yards from the trench cut across the road at the entrance to the Quarry Ravine. Here the road ran high above the ravine-bed, and beyond the trench there appeared suddenly through the mist a Russian column, while another column was moving up the hollow below.

Haines, who, though only a captain in the regiment, was a brevet-lieutenant-colonel in the army and found himself the senior officer with the advance, steadied his force and looked round to see what was with him. He had about forty men from both regiments, and three or four officers. He occupied the narrow road with files, and sent a little party as a look-out to the high ground on the left, and another to the right to fire on the column in the hollow. The fire of the Brown Besses, to Haines's amazement, checked the enemy; but the odds were preposterous, and he ran back the three hundred yards to the Barrier to obtain help. There he found Ainslie trying to collect the remnants of the Twenty-First, and these at once marched forward to Quarry Ravine. On the way Ainslie received a mortal wound; he dismounted and struggled on on foot, but soon his strength failed him, and he was borne dying to the rear. Lieutenant Hurt, too, who carried the colours, was fatally wounded. Yet the small force, being protected from the fire from Shell Hill, was able to hold the enemy, and those thin lines for half an hour did deadly execution among the dense masses of the two Russian columns. But their left flank was in constant danger, and when, about nine o'clock, the outpost there gave the warning, Haines was forced to fall back.[1] In perfect order the men retired, and the retreat was

---

[1] Private Patrick McGuire, being isolated from his comrades, was attacked by three Russians. He shot one, bayoneted another, and brought in the third as prisoner

memorable for one gallant exploit. Sergeant Higdon thought he saw Lieutenant Hurt, whose body lay on the road, move slightly, and asked permission to bring him in. He and another sergeant, Rutherford, went out under a heavy fire and brought the officer back, but Hurt died before the next morning.[1]

Haines's task was now to hold the Barrier, for its loss would mean an instant assault upon the British centre on Home Ridge. Besides what remained of the Twenty-First, he had various odds and ends of the 63rd under his command, and stragglers from the Rifle Brigade, the 57th, and the 68th. At the Barrier there was no shelter from the fire of Shell Hill, so he placed a small party of the 68th on his left who, fortunately, had Minié rifles, with orders to fire on the Russian gunners and watch developments. His ammunition was running very low, so, leaving Major Roper of the Rifle Brigade in charge, he set off to find Pennefather. The General assured him of a fresh supply of ammunition, but had no troops to spare as supports except one company of the 77th.

Haines returned to the Barrier about 9.15, as the third stage closed—that stage which, with the exploits of Lord West at the Mikriakov glen and of Haines at Quarry Ravine, had been largely the story of the Twenty-First. He found that the assault had in no way slackened, and that Major Roper was mortally wounded. There was a maddening delay in the supply of ammunition, for the first consignment sent was only for Minié rifles. Meantime the Barrier force was fighting a battle of its own, more or less cut off from the rest of the army. Major Ramsay Stuart, who early in the day had been sent off for supports, was ordered by General Goldie—since Cathcart's death, in charge of the Fourth Division—to gallop to the Second Division camp and bring up the camp guard or any other available troops. Stuart found nothing in that camp, but two miles farther on, in the camp of the

---

[1] Hurt is commonly said to have died on the field, but a letter of Arthur Greer from Malta describes his last hours. He died in camp.

Fourth Division, he managed to collect various details.

Goldie, anxious to see for himself the position at the Barrier, now visited Haines, who took advantage of his presence to go out to the party on his left, who were watching Shell Hill. On his return he found Goldie mortally wounded, and the whole responsibility of the stand resting once more upon himself. But the skies were brightening. The promised company of the 77th arrived, followed soon after by a company of the 49th and a detachment of the Rifle Brigade. Two 18-pounder guns had been ordered up, and these, with the volleys of the Barrier defenders, were able to keep the artillery on Shell Hill in check. By 10 a.m. the fourth stage closed with a slackening of the Shell Hill fire and the arrival of considerable French reinforcements. The latter, under Bosquet, found, in Kinglake's words, "the English thrown forward in advance of Home Ridge exerting the same kind of power and performing the same kind of duty as if they had been the men of the pickets not yet driven in. They combated upon a front which—by help of the Barrier—was riveted fast at its centre, but shifting at all other points."

In the fifth stage, ten to eleven a.m., Bosquet did little good, for he advanced on the Sandbag Battery and got his men on to Inkerman Tusk—a position of no tactical value. Nor did he achieve anything in the sixth stage, between eleven and one o'clock. The British guns ran short of ammunition, the French were defending something which was not threatened, and the true key-point, the Barrier, was left to Haines. He had been slowly augmenting his strength, says Kinglake, " by welcoming or commanding the accession of other troops; and whether the Russians came on by the line of the Post Road to attack him in front, or whether, swarming up from the back of the Quarry Ravine, they strove to turn his right flank, he always found means to repress them, and drive them back into their lair. . . . Our soldiery, whether combating at the Barrier or on its left front, passed gradually and almost unconsciously from the task of defence to the task of attack, for in truth the same kind of acts which before would have been acts of defence had now an aggressive force. To fight for the Barrier in the hours when Dannenberg was an assailant had been to defend the Home Ridge by fighting half a mile in its front. To fight for the Barrier now was, as it were, to hold open by force the gate of the enemy's castle, and grievously embarrass his defence."

While Shell Hill remained in Russian hands the siege of Sebastopol was a hopeless undertaking. Haines, believing that the moment had come for a counter-offensive, went back to Pennefather on Home Ridge, and suggested an attack on Shell Hill from the Barrier. The General declined, and Haines returned to his post. Presently, however, the enemy seemed to weaken, and the arrival of a Zouave contingent increased Haines's strength, so he decided on his own responsibility to advance. He collected all the men armed with the Minié rifle, placed them under Lieutenant Astley of the 49th, and ordered them to advance through the scrub and harass the garrison on Shell Hill, but not to make a definite attack. Lieutenant Acton of the 77th was sent on the same errand, and seeing that the British 18-pounders were having a deadly effect, he moved up the hill, followed by Astley and by reinforcements under Colonel Horsford of the Rifle Brigade. The defence was broken, and at one o'clock Dannenberg gave the order for the Russian retreat. The enemy guns were got away, but Horsford captured eight ammunition wagons; and when Haines and West rode over the ground next day they found, marking the farthest limits of the British advance, the bodies of three men of No. 1 Company of the Twenty-First.[1]

With Dannenberg's retirement from Shell Hill the battle of Inkerman ended. Had Canrobert assented to Lord Raglan's proposal and pressed his retreat, the

---

[1] Kinglake's narrative confuses Haines with Lord West, who was engaged in an entirely different sphere of operations. I have followed Haines's own account.

enemy's field army might have been destroyed; as it 1854
was, the French were supine and ill-directed, as they
had been at every stage of the fight. Inkerman was a
British achievement, and most notably an achievement
of the British rank-and-file and regimental officers.
The Russian plan was good, but it was spoiled at the
only time when it could have attained success by the
restricted area of assembly on Shell Hill and the too
narrow front, which deprived them of the benefit of
their great numerical superiority. The attack was
foiled from first to last by the stubborn resolution and
inborn fighting talents of the British soldier, who in a
dozen separate battles held his ground skilfully and
composedly under desperate fire and the strain of
turned flanks and universal mystification. "Such a
battle," wrote Ramsay Stuart, who was sufficiently
stout-hearted, "may God in all His mercies save me
from for the time He may yet in His great mercy grant
me on this earth."

The Twenty-First may be fairly said to have had
the honours of that fatal and glorious day. They
began the action with 14 officers, 24 non-commissioned
officers, and 375 rank-and-file; of these they had one
in three killed or wounded. The gallant Colonel Ainslie
fell, as did Lieutenant Hurt, and five of the "youngsters" were badly wounded.[1] West and Haines made
for themselves famous names, and Haines indeed, by
the defence of the Barrier and attack on Shell Hill,
contributed more than any other man to the victorious
issue. Like a good soldier he gave the main credit to
his men. "The result to me," he wrote, "is material,
insomuch as we defeated a desperate attack upon our
position, but its moral effect is beyond all calcula-

[1] Captain George Neeld Boldero; Lieutenants Alfred Templeman and Henry King; and Second Lieutenants Roger Killeen and Richard Stephens. Killeen, who was wounded while saving the regimental colours, had risen from the ranks. He retired as a major in 1876. Sergeant James Clark, the historian of the regiment, was in the battle, and, when a man of over seventy, he revisited the Crimea and wrote a spirited account of Inkerman for a local paper in Ayrshire. Clark died in Ayr in January 1917; his son, Corporal David Clark, was killed while serving with the regiment on October 21, 1914. "Inkerman" day is celebrated annually in the 1st Battalion by trooping the colours, and by the "Inkerman Ball."

tion, elevating our infantry both in their own and the enemy's estimation." He himself had no reward except in repute, for both his divisional commanders had fallen, and Pennefather, who belonged to a different division, had some delicacy about referring to him in his report. When the Victoria Cross was instituted, Lord West urged Haines for the honour of the regiment to put in a claim on the ground of his defence of the Barrier. This Haines did, not for himself but for Sergeant Higdon, who had brought in Hurt's body, but the award was not granted. But Kinglake established his fame on a firm foundation, and to-day the defence of the Barrier is recognized as the central fact of the battle. Haines seems to have maintained not only a clear head and a composed mind during the crisis, but to have enjoyed its storm and fury. His letters show that he had an eye for the fantastic incidents of it, like the very fat and very gallant French General who arrived suddenly and whose flow of conversation was cut short by a round shot, and the officer crazy with fever, who had escaped from hospital, and for half an hour babbled by his side in delirium. " It was worth living to have been at Inkerman," he was never tired of repeating, and, when a Field-Marshal, used to say that he would exchange all the other hours of his long life for the six hours spent at the Barrier.[1]

Upon Inkerman followed the winter of 1854–55, when " General Février " proved a more deadly antagonist than Menshikov and Todleben. Tempests, rain, snow, and disease made the Allied lines on the Upland a carnival of misery, and at the end of January Lord Raglan could only muster 12,000 men fit for duty, and the Twenty-First only 180. This is not the place to tell that melancholy tale, redeemed by the patience

[1] There seems to have been some jealousy felt for the reputation gained by Sir Colin Campbell and his Highland Brigade at the Alma. At Inkerman Campbell's brigade, which was not in action, was stationed on the right rear of the Fourth Division camp. When Haines returned to camp, he said to a sergeant : " I am proud to have been with the regiment to-day." " Yes, your Honour," was the reply, " but it won't be two halfpence to us, for there's the Curse of Glencoe on the right." Campbell's service in the Twenty-First seemed to have passed out of the regimental memory.

LIEUT.-GENERAL SIR DE LACY EVANS
(From a portrait by Fenton, in the Mess of the 1st Battalion)

THE SIEGE OF SEBASTOPOL 217

and courage of the sufferers, and the work of the heroic woman who brought a new humanity into war. Ramsay Stuart, who was tormented by rheumatism, and had frequently to retire to a hospital ship, took the gloomiest view. "Twenty-four hours in the trenches under arms with nothing but a greatcoat, and only twenty-four hours off duty—this for a continuance surpasses any hardship I have ever experienced." At first, too, he was far from enthusiastic about the work of Florence Nightingale. "It appears that the whole establishment is one of our English philanthropic absurdities. . . . A military hospital was not the field for their kind intentions. Had they instead sent out a hundred hospital dressers in the shape of young men it would have done some good." Lord West was in command of the Twenty-First during Stuart's absence from sickness, and Haines acted as major. Presently Haines became commandant of Balaclava, where he was a great success, till in January 1855 he was sent home, to be soon gazetted lieutenant-colonel unattached, and appointed assistant-adjutant-general at Aldershot.

Ramsay Stuart returned to duty at the beginning of 1855, and, though much crippled with rheumatism, continued to command the regiment for most of the remainder of the campaign. We need not here recount the slow tale of the siege, while the great fortress grew under the hands of Todleben, and the "White Works" sprang up like magic in the course of a single night. On Easter Sunday a ten days' bombardment began which destroyed the White Works and the Mamelon, but no assault followed, for London and Paris were at variance with the command on the spot. Canrobert resigned, to be succeeded by Pélissier, a good soldier trained in African war, and under the latter the siege operations were pushed forward more vigorously. On 7th June the White Works and the Mamelon were stormed by the French, and the British carried the Quarries close to the Redan; but once again the operations tailed off into ineffectiveness. The great assault on the 18th failed, and ten days later Raglan died,

1855

worn out by futile controversy with his Government at home. But the end was not far off. The Russian counter-attack of 16th August effected nothing. On 8th September the Malakoff was stormed by Bosquet, and next day Sebastopol fell. It was the end of the main operations, though the war dragged on through the winter, till an armistice was signed on February 26, 1856, to be followed on 30th March by the Peace of Paris. So closed a campaign ill conceived and ill guided by the authorities at home, but in the field fought by both sides with a courage and loyalty which have not often been equalled.

The Twenty-First shared to the full in the miseries of the first winter, and in the bitter trench-fighting which a British army was not to experience again for sixty years. The men, on an average, were eleven out of fourteen nights in the trenches, either as working or as covering parties. The regiment had four men killed and seven wounded in the Russian sortie of March 22, 1855; and it furnished a storming party under Lieutenants J. G. Image and S. H. Clarke for the attack on the Quarries on 7th June. In the great assault of 18th June it was heavily engaged, and lost severely. Lord West's words, as they marched off the night before, were long remembered : " Fusiliers, you will have hard work to perform, but I have every confidence in you. I know that you will retain the honour which you gained on the field of Inkerman, and whoever he may be who is spared to come out of this night's work, if we meet in after years, will not be lost sight of by me. Have your hearts in your hands ready to dash them over the parapet and follow them." An advanced party, under Lieutenant R. W. C. Winsloe, repelled an enemy sortie on the night of 15th August. In the great battle of 8th September the regiment was in reserve. On 7th October, along with four other regiments from the Fourth Division, it took part, under Lord West, in the successful bombardment of Kinburn. It was back in the Crimea on 12th November, where it remained to the end of May 1856, when it embarked for Malta.

When the Twenty-First arrived in the Crimea its strength was 33 officers and 974 non-commissioned officers and men, and during its stay there it received reinforcements amounting to 25 officers and 575 other ranks. In the twenty months of its service it lost 623 in dead, wounded, and missing—a moderate casualty list when we remember the fury of some of its engagements and the ravages of disease. Its privations during the first winter were not so great as other troops', owing to the energy of its regimental quartermasters. Yet, from weather, laborious fatigues, sickness, inadequate clothing, and scarcity of food, its sufferings were sufficiently great. Often of a night the men's moustaches became solid lumps of ice, and their whiskers froze to their threadbare blankets. Ramsay Stuart complained that sometimes during the day he was unable to write unless he stood his ink-pot in a cup of boiling water. There is a curious tale of a certain sergeant, Seymour by name,[1] who was reported dead of cholera and struck off the strength, and who returned ultimately to his battalion, where he was believed to be a ghost, and had the utmost difficulty in getting rationed. Ramsay Stuart's letters give a vivid picture of the woes of a commanding officer, whose health prevented him from sharing in much of the fighting, and whose order-loving soul was harassed by the condition of his regiment. He thought little of the new drafts, and complained in December 1855 that the Twenty-First was " little better than a militia regiment, if so good." Gradually he came to a more hopeful view of Miss Nightingale's work, though his distrust of civilians remained. " I hate doctors and all their vile nonsense. The army men are the only honest doctors in the world. And why? Simply because they get nothing for their opinions and advice, and therefore give an honest one." But the gallant and irascible colonel managed to hammer his remnant into shape, for he was an admirable trainer of

---

[1] Seymour was discovered in 1891 selling glass balls in a Glasgow street, and brought up to Maryhill Barracks for an inspection by the Duke of Cambridge.

troops; and when it was reviewed by General Garrett in February 1856, he had nothing to fear from one who had been in the habit of describing it as " rat-catchers and Bashi Bazouks." " Notwithstanding his dislike of us he was obliged to tell the regiment that he was highly pleased to see us in such order, and that he had no idea a regiment could be so soon brought back to something like discipline." When Pennefather inspected it after it arrived in Malta his verdict was the same.

If Blenheim was for the Twenty-First its proudest achievement in attack, Inkerman may be set down as up to that date its greatest record in stubborn defence. Nor was that record surpassed till, in the same autumn weather sixty years later in the mud of Flanders, a day of more fateful issues saw a still more glorious and tragic sacrifice.

These Colours are in Ayr Parish Church, and the brass plate bears the following inscription :—

"Colours of the Royal Scots Fusiliers, carried by the 1st Battalion from 1828 to 1858. Through the Crimean Campaign, including the Battles of ALMA, BALAKLAVA, INKERMAN, siege and fall of SEVASTOPOL, bombardment and capture of KINBOURN. Deposited here in 1883."

(From a painting by Mrs. Coulson, Ayr)

CHAPTER XI

THE FIRST BATTALION TO THE EVE OF THE GREAT WAR

Malta—Sir John Pennefather's tribute—Service in the West Indies—Ramsay Stuart—Service in India—The Royal Scots Fusiliers—Home service—The Tirah campaign—South Africa, 1910–1914.

THE Twenty-First arrived at Malta on June 2, 1856, and there for four years it abode in peace. Once again, as in the Napoleonic wars, the stream of its history forks, for in 1857 it was decided to increase the strength of the British army by the addition of second battalions to all regiments up to and including the 25th. Accordingly, in April 1858, there was formed at Paisley a second battalion of the Scots Fusiliers, the record of which must be left for separate chapters. Here we are concerned with the doings of the 1st Battalion, which, under Lieutenant-Colonel Ramsay Stuart, was busy repairing the damage of the Crimea and regaining its old smartness and tone.

1856–58

The chief episode of those Malta days was the presentation by Lady Pennefather to the battalion of new colours to take the place of those which it had carried since 1828, and which at Inkerman Lieutenant Hurt had died to save.[1] Sir John Pennefather in an eloquent speech sketched the history of the Twenty-First. There were few regiments in Her Majesty's army, he said, which had passed through a more hon-

---

[1] These colours were placed in the Arsenal at Edinburgh when the battalion went to India in 1869. After that they were in the officers' mess at Ayr, and in 1883 were deposited in the Old Church at Ayr. See Clark, *Hist. Record of R.S.F.*, pages 144–47, and illustration facing this page.

ourable career. He re-told the great tale of Inkerman. "On that occasion your cry was for more ammunition; never a selfish word for yourselves, though you had been at work the livelong day without food."

"Young soldiers, think of these things; determine to emulate your elders, and to gain for yourselves the same honourable distinctions they wear on their hearts. These recollections do not pass by us like a summer cloud, to be forgotten; they sink deeply into the mind; and I for one do not envy that man who is not deeply moved by the remembrance of them.

"Ensigns![1] take these colours; they are committed to your charge in the fullest confidence. When next you are engaged, march with them quietly, steadily, firmly, serenely, into the very heart of the enemy; and if you fall in the performance of your honourable office, others will at once take your place and carry on that duty.

"Soldiers! stick to these colours. Move forward steadily, confidently; be silent, watch your officers, obey them. Obedience is discipline, and without discipline a military force is no better than an armed mob. Strike low. And I am perfectly confident that, when again these colours are unfurled in war, they will, like those which have gone before, wave over your heads in victory. And when you next fight, I wish you from the bottom of my heart every success, and pray fervently that God Almighty may bless and prosper the corps wherever it goes."

Forty years were to elapse before the battalion again took part in a campaign. In March 1860 it sailed for Barbados, and two companies were detached to Dem-

[1] Up to 1855 the junior subalterns of Fusilier and Rifle regiments were styled *Second Lieutenants* (save in the 7th Royal Fusiliers, where the lowest rank was that of Lieutenant); then they were *Ensigns* up to 1871, when they became *Sub-Lieutenants*; after 1877 the present rank of *Second Lieutenant* was universally established.

THE WEST INDIES

erara under Major Humphrey Gray, who had commanded the regiment in the expedition, under Lord West, to Kinburn. The four years in the West Indies were the usual record of boredom and ill-health. The chief duties of the Demerara detachment were those of a fire brigade. In 1861 a conflagration destroyed one-fourth of George Town, and the Scots Fusiliers performed such excellent service that they received the official thanks of the Governor. In 1864 there was a second fire, and in blowing up a building to arrest the progress of the flames a newly-joined ensign, Frank Hutton, was killed. At Barbados yellow fever broke out in the autumn of 1862, and the surgeon, Dr. Greer, insisted upon the removal of the battalion into camp at Gun Hill, seven miles from the infected barracks. The arrangements of the commissariat department broke down, but Quartermaster George Graham (who had distinguished himself in this work at Balaclava), though just recovering from fever, made the dispositions himself, and in two days successfully completed the move. Graham was in his way a genius—a type of the resourceful non-commissioned officer who has always been the backbone of the British army. For twenty-seven years he served with the Twenty-First, as his father had done before him, and retired in 1882 with the rank of honorary major. While his men were under canvas, Ramsay Stuart, anxious to find them some occupation, set them to road-making, and to-day the Fusilier Road remains to attest their activity. Otherwise there is little to record in these years, except that in October 1862 Captain Thomas Bruce was sent with No. 7 Company to St. Vincent to suppress a negro rising—a task which he speedily accomplished.

In August 1864 the battalion landed at Portsmouth, where it was inspected by General Lord William Paulet, who declared that " its good name had preceded it, and that it was more like a regiment that had been at home for two years than one just returned from foreign service." A month later it paraded before H.R.H. the Duke of Cambridge, who likewise complimented its commanding officer on its smart appearance and the perfection of its drill. Next year it was at Aldershot, whence it moved to the old Gallowgate Barracks in Glasgow, with detachments at Ayr and Paisley. The Fenian trouble sent it to Ireland in 1866, where it occupied Richmond Barracks in Dublin.[1] There it remained for nearly a year, when it moved to Enniskillen, and earned in that place such general esteem that, on its removal to the Curragh, the inhabitants petitioned for its longer sojourn among them, as they had done sixty-seven years before.

The year 1867 saw the departure of two much-loved officers. Surgeon Greer, who had endeared himself to the regiment in the Crimea, was transferred to the 17th Lancers, and Ramsay Stuart, at a parade on 1st March in Phœnix Park, bade farewell to the corps in which he had served for thirty-five years, and which for fifteen years he had commanded. " Old Ramsay," as he was affectionately called, was one of the last British officers of the ancient régime, an enthusiast for drill, and an exponent of the traditional discipline. He was a most just and kindly commanding officer, whose home was the regiment, and who thought of little beyond its interests. But he was also a "character," with idiosyncrasies of manner and speech which, joined to a portly figure, a jolly face, and a stentorian voice, made him the centre of legend and a purveyor of that occasional comedy which endears a commander to the British soldier. He had much in common with old Sir Andrew Agnew, and, like him, spoke a broad and racy Scots. His usual order to fix bayonets was " Fax pricks." In Sir William Butler's Autobiography [2] there is a picture of him which deserves quotation :—

" Among the old officers of lesser rank the one who gave us youngsters the most unvarying enter-

---

[1] It is interesting to note, in connection with the Irish troubles, that Captain Charles Cunningham Boycott, Lord Erne's agent, who gave a new word to the English language, was an old Scots Fusilier.

[2] Chap. V., page 68. Ramsay Stuart became major-general in 1868, lieutenant-general in 1877, and general in 1880, as well as colonel of the 54th (Dorsets).

tainment was the Colonel of a distinguished Fusilier battalion, a North Briton. . . . A modern dynamite shell, bursting in a brigade, would inevitably have ended the collective life and entire martial capacity of that military unit. This view of the question, however, had not occurred to any of our superiors; and to us subalterns in the ranks these close formations had at least the merit of enabling us to get all the mounted officers of three or four battalions within easy range of our ears and eyes. We knew, in fact, everything that was going on in the brigade. Old Colonel R. S. was our central point of interest. He had a profound contempt and dislike for a staff officer, and in this feeling we were with him to a man.

"An A.D.C., or a Deputy A.D.C., would ride up to the brigade, salute, deliver his orders, wheel his horse round, and gallop away. Colonel R. S., being a very senior officer, was frequently in command of the brigade. He would never move a muscle as the staff officer went through his message. He would then gravely turn to one of the old 'fizzer men,' as they were called (pensioners who had the privilege of hawking ginger beer among the troops), and ask him, 'What did the d— fule say?' 'He said, yer honour, the brigade was to move to the right.' 'Did he? Third brigade, fours left.'

"Or, again, he would on occasion, when he had had words with the messenger of movement, take all the men into his confidence by turning in his saddle, and remarking with a most comical expression of face, 'He'll nae puzzle the Fusiliers, I can tell ye.'

"And, indeed, I am quite sure that nothing which the most conceited young staff officer could do would ever have puzzled that splendid body of men. They would have died to a man with that old Scotsman."

1867-77 Ramsay Stuart's successor was John Thomas Dalzell—a famous name in the Twenty-First, for an earlier John Dalyell had commanded the regiment, and fallen at Blenheim. The new lieutenant-colonel had joined the Twenty-First in 1847, and had distinguished himself with Haines at Inkerman. In February 1869 the battalion sailed for India, travelling by way of Alexandria and Suez, and arriving at Bombay on 22nd March. Its first station was Kurrachee, with two companies at Hyderabad; and while there it lost appallingly from fever—sixteen men, eleven women, and forty-one children in nine months. Early in 1870 it was transferred to Bangalore in Mysore territory, where it recovered its health, and spent two happy years, publishing a regimental magazine, developing much skill in private theatricals, and winning trophies at rifle matches. In 1872 it proceeded to Madras to replace the second battalion, which it now met for the first time. There it remained for three years—years unmarked by incident except that of a camp of exercise at Bangalore in 1874, when the battalion was inspected and complimented by one of its old officers, Sir Frederick Haines, now Commander-in-Chief of the Madras Presidency. In 1875 it moved to Rangoon, where Captain Patterson died while in command of a party which ascended the Irrawaddy. That same year a detachment of 131 men, under Captains T. E. Stuart and W. N. Carey, was sent to Port Blair in the Andaman Islands, to take charge of convicts. There, two years later, a curious fatality occurred. Corporal Henry Collins and four others set off in a boat to fish, in despite of orders which laid down that no boat should be taken out without a crew of thirty men. They found themselves unable to return, and had to land on Havelock Island, where for the rest of the week they were marooned without food. On the seventh day Corporal Collins set out to swim to a steamer, the attention of which they could not attract by their signals, and did not return. Next day the men were rescued.

In 1877 the regiment moved to Secunderabad, and

THE CARDWELL REFORMS

remained there till the autumn of 1881, when it returned to England after thirteen years' Indian service, during which it had lost by death four officers, one bandmaster, one colour-sergeant, nine sergeants, eight corporals, and 137 privates. In January 1878 Lieutenant-Colonel J. T. Dalzell, being appointed to a brigade depot in Scotland, handed over the command to Lieutenant-Colonel Alfred Templeman,[1] who had joined the Twenty-First in 1852. Dalzell was the last officer to hold the post under the old rules, which fixed no limit to the tenure of command. Eight years before, on the death of Sir de Lacy Evans, Sir Frederick William Hamilton had been appointed to the colonelcy. Hamilton had served with the Grenadier Guards in the Crimea, had been military attaché at Berlin, and was now a major-general.

Meantime there had been notable changes in the status of the regiment, for these were the days of the Cardwell reforms, when purchase was abolished, the short-service system instituted, and the whole mechanism of the British army revised. On April 1, 1873, the new localization scheme came into force, and the Twenty-First was allotted to Ayrshire, with the depots of both battalions at Ayr as the 61st Brigade Depot (later known as Regimental District No. 21). In 1873, owing to the exertions of Lieutenant-Colonel Pole Collingwood of the 2nd Battalion, the regiment was given the royal authority to assume the name of the 21st Royal Scots Fusiliers. "Scots," indeed, had always been its popular title, the words "North British" rarely appearing except in official documents and on formal occasions. On July 1, 1881, came the royal warrant by which all the infantry of the line lost their numbers, and our regiment became the 1st and 2nd Battalions Royal Scots Fusiliers. There were other changes which more nearly affected the men. The uniform was altered from the ordinary line tunic to the Highland doublet with tartan trews, the officers' lace to the

---
[1] Major-General Templeman died at the age of over eighty in 1914. There is a tablet to his memory in the old Parish Church of Ayr.

"thistle pattern," and the ordinary sword to the claymore, but the Fusilier busby was still retained. The tartan was the old blue, black, and green Government tartan, which had been issued by General Wade in 1729 to the Independent Highland Companies. It was an evolution from the Campbell tartan, and is still worn to-day by the Argyll and Sutherland Highlanders. Later, the addition of a bluish line created a special Scots Fusiliers tartan.[1] The matter of pipers, too, was put on a proper footing. The Scots Fusiliers had always in the old days had their pipers, but between 1850 and 1870 they seem to have disappeared. In the latter year they were revived, and ten men trained and equipped for the purpose; and in 1876 an establishment of one pipe-major and three pipers was officially authorized for each of the two battalions. Lastly, in November 1882, the question of battle honours was determined. In that year the colours bore "Bladensburg" (authorized in 1854), "Alma," "Inkerman," "Sevastopol," and "South Africa, 1879" (the service of the 2nd Battalion, of which we shall presently hear). The Horse Guards now sanctioned the addition of "Blenheim," "Ramillies," "Oudenarde," "Malplaquet," and "Dettingen."

Fifteen years of home service followed, of which there is little to record. In 1883 Lieutenant-Colonel Templeman retired on half-pay, and was succeeded by Richard William Charles Winsloe, who had been with the 2nd Battalion in the Zulu War. In August of that year he returned to the 2nd Battalion, and George Frederick Gildea, who had led the 2nd Battalion in the Transvaal campaign and had been commandant of Pretoria, came to the 1st. Of Winsloe and Gildea we shall presently hear. On August 25, 1884, the latter retired on halfpay, and was followed by Edward Thomas Bainbridge, who also had served with the 2nd Battalion in South Africa. On July 1, 1887, William Albert Bridge suc-

---

[1] When the Lowland regiments were first consulted about the issue of a tartan the Scots Fusiliers raised strong objections, and the Scots Guards categorically refused. The other Lowland regiments (1st, 25th, and 26th) welcomed the proposal.

FIELD-MARSHAL SIR FREDERICK HAINES
(From a portrait by the Hon. John Collier, in the possession of the United Service Club)

HOME SERVICE

ceeded Bainbridge, to be followed four years later by Edward Charles Browne, another South African veteran.[1] Lieutenant-Colonel Browne retired in July 1895 on half-pay, and J. H. Spurgin took his place. Meantime, in 1890, Sir Frederick Hamilton died, and Sir Frederick Paul Haines, now a field-marshal, became colonel of the regiment which he had led to glory at Inkerman.

The regimental diary gives few details of this period, beyond the places where the battalion was stationed—Aldershot, Portland, Fermoy, Birr, Dublin, Glasgow, Shorncliffe, and Aldershot again—its drafts to the 2nd Battalion, its annual inspections, and the invariably flattering reports, notably that of the Commander-in-Chief, the Duke of Cambridge, at Glasgow, who declared that " such manœuvring was seldom seen nowadays, and that if there was a pattern regiment in the service it was the Royal Scots Fusiliers."[2] One or two incidents break the monotony. In the summer of 1884 the battalion was called on to furnish a detachment, consisting of one officer and thirty-two non-commissioned officers and men, for service with the Mounted Infantry in the Sudan. On 27th August in that year, the detachment, commanded by Lieutenant H. G. Stanuell, embarked for Egypt. It was attached to the Desert Column under Sir Herbert Stewart, took part in the actions of Abu Klea, El Gubat, and Metemneh, and had six casualties. Sergeant M. J. Duggan was twice mentioned in Lord Wolseley's dispatches for gallant conduct. While the battalion was at Glasgow in May 1891, it formed the guard for Queen Victoria at Balmoral, and one of its officers, Lieutenant G. M. Barrett, was drowned while fishing in the Dee. Names afterwards to be well known in the regiment begin to appear in its annals. In 1890 Lieutenant Baird Smith is sent abroad with a draft; in 1891 Lieutenant Donald Stuart, the son of Ramsay Stuart, takes a body to Aldershot for Mounted Infantry training; after the

---
[1] When in command at Glasgow, Lieutenant-Colonel Browne originated "The Regimental Association for the Benefit of Old Soldiers."
[2] September 22, 1891.

inspection of 1892 the Commander-in-Chief made special reference to Sergeant-Major John Smith, who was perhaps at the time the greatest sergeant-major in the army.[1] It is recorded that in March 1893 Lieutenant A. Hull took out a draft to Sialkot—the first mention of Major-General Sir Amyatt Hull, who led the 56th Division in the Great War, and was one of the ablest divisional commanders in France.

In 1895 the battalion received new colours from H.R.H. the Duchess of Connaught, and the following year it sailed for India. At Mian Mir it met the 2nd Battalion, and for eight months occupied various stations in the Punjab. It was now very near to active service, for the mutterings of trouble were beginning in the frontier hills. For sixteen years the Afridis had received from the Government of India a subsidy for guarding the Khyber Pass, which at the time was held by an Afridi regiment in the British service. In July and August 1897 there was a general rising of the tribes, due in part to that wide resurgence of Moslem pride which followed Turkey's easy victory over Greece. The Afridis scuppered the posts of their own countrymen in the Khyber, and attacked the Samana forts near Peshawur, while to the north-east of the pass the Mohmands had risen in the Tochi and Swat valleys. The first business was to deal with the Mohmands, and two brigades of Sir Bindon Blood's division advanced from Malakand, while another division, under Major-General Elles, moved from Peshawur. By October the resistance of these tribes was broken, with the loss of nearly a quarter of the small British expeditionary force. Meantime preparation was being made to deal with the more formidable outbreak of the Afridis, and Sir William Lockhart, commanding the Punjab Army Corps, was assembling the Tirah Expeditionary Force, with the frontier post of Kohat as its base. Between them the Afridis and the Orakzais could bring more than 40,000 men into the field— men armed not with jezails and old muzzle-loaders, but

---

[1] In 1893 he was made Quartermaster of the West Yorkshires.

with Martini-Henrys or stolen Lee-Metfords. The terrain, too, was most intricate and difficult—one of which Wellington's words in the Peninsula were true: " If you make war in that country with a large army, you starve; and if you go into it with a small one, you get beaten."

On 16th August the Royal Scots Fusiliers were ordered to send their headquarters and one wing of the battalion to Kohat. Before Sir William Lockhart could move there was a good deal of confused defensive

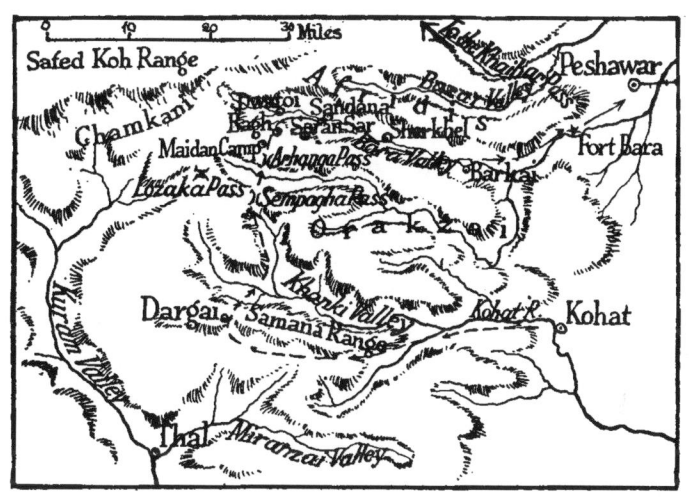

THE TIRAH CAMPAIGN

fighting in the passes. On 27th August two companies of the regiment were engaged as part of Major-General Yeatman-Biggs's force in an action at the Ublan Pass, where Captain Baird Smith and Lieutenant North were seriously wounded. When, on 18th October, Lockhart began to advance, the Scots Fusiliers were not with him, being split up in parties on various duties, and so had no part in the fine action of the Dargai Heights, when the Gordons distinguished themselves. It was not till 11th November, when Westmacott had taken Saran Sar and the expedition was far into the Tirah country, that they were ordered to Maidan to join the main force. Their machine-gun detachment, under Captain de le Bère, was with the Kurram column, and the rest were now attached to the force which Sir William himself took up on the 27th from Bagh to join Gaselee's column (the 2nd Brigade of the First Division) and attend to the Chamkannis, Massizais, Mamuzais, and other septs of the west. Lieutenant-Colonel Spurgin commanded one of the two sections of this force, and the Scots Fusiliers had six casualties. Spurgin was left in command at Dargai, with orders to improve the roads, while Lockhart and Gaselee marched to Hissar to join Hill's column, with which was the Scots Fusiliers machine-gun detachment. The work of taking order with the western tribes was completed early in December, when the various forces returned to Bagh. On the 7th, as part of a scheme for changing the base of operations from Kohat to Peshawur, the Second Division, under Yeatman-Biggs, with which were Lockhart and the Scots Fusiliers, started down the Bara valley to Barkai. There was a good deal of mixed fighting, and many hardships from the winter cold, before a junction was effected with the Peshawur column under General Hammond. This was in effect the end of the Tirah War, and on the last day of December the Fusiliers reached Peshawur and entrained for Sialkot. Their casualties were one man killed and nine wounded, among whom was Captain F. de Sausmarez Shortt. Five men were missing, and one, Colour-Sergeant John Walker, after being wounded and taken prisoner, was released many weeks later by the Afridis, who, contrary to the habits of the frontier tribes, treated him kindly. For this sharp little campaign, in which only the headquarters and four companies were engaged, the regiment gained another honour, "Tirah," for its colours.

For ten years the 1st Battalion abode in India—at Landi Khotal, Peshawur, Cherat, Allahabad, and Bareilly. In 1899 came the South African War, in which the 2nd Battalion played a notable part, but the 1st Battalion had no such break in the monotony of its life.[1] Its records are once again only of drafts and inspections and compliments on its proficiency in signalling, which was an ancient Scots Fusilier tradition. In 1899 Lieutenant-Colonel Spurgin retired, and Major A. H. Abercrombie succeeded to the command, to be followed in July 1903 by H. Hamilton Smythe. Major A. B. H. Northcott succeeded Smythe as commanding officer in 1907. Next year the battalion moved to Rangoon, where it remained till 1910, during which time it seems to have maintained its country's credit as a pillar of the Scots Kirk *in partibus infidelium*. In 1909 His Majesty authorized the addition of another honour to its colours, a belated recognition of one of the regiment's most costly and arduous campaigns—" Martinique, 1794." [2]

In October 1910 it paid its first visit to South Africa, that field of glory of the 2nd Battalion. It was stationed at Roberts' Heights near Pretoria, with a considerable detachment at Harrismith with the Mounted Infantry. Next year Northcott retired, and his place was taken by Major William Douglas Smith. In June 1913 the regiment was engaged in a form of duty, the most unpleasant which can fall to the lot of British soldiers, and one which it had not known since, more than a century before, it had come into conflict with the Dublin mob. That month the miners' strike broke out on the Rand, and since it had all the appearance of an incipient revolution, headquarters and 500 men were ordered to garrison certain mines on 30th June. They were stationed principally at Kleinfontein mine, where the rioters threatened to blow up the power station, and were only repelled by fixed bayonets. On 4th July a further detachment, under Major Forbes, was sent to Johannesburg, where the situation was most critical. It was laborious and anxious work, the men being on watch night after night without relief, and from the bitter cold of the high veld four succumbed

---

[1] It sent 150 picked men to the 2nd Battalion in South Africa.
[2] It was in the reign of King Edward VII. that the Tudor crown was substituted for the Hanoverian on the colours.

1913-14 to pneumonia. The sequel is well known—how the Boer commandos were brought into the city, and dealt with disorder by more summary methods than were possible for British regulars. By 12th July it was all over. But the Fusiliers were kept on at the mines, since there was some fear of native disturbances, and did not return to Pretoria till 3rd August. They received the thanks of the Governor-General and the Union Ministers for " the prompt and expeditious manner in which the troops were made available, and particularly the admirable discipline and behaviour of all ranks employed on this trying duty."

In March 1914 the 1st Battalion returned to England after eighteen years of foreign service. It was the height of the Ulster troubles; but apart from domestic controversy, there was no expectation in the land but of long-continuing peace. The Scots Fusiliers looked forward to a decade of home service. But in five months they were to be swept into a strife which was far to transcend in fury and fatefulness all the battles of their past. We leave them on the eve of the Great War, to consider the doings of the 2nd Battalion during the fifty-six years which had elapsed since its formation.

CHAPTER XII

THE SECOND BATTALION : ZULULAND—THE TRANSVAAL
—BURMA

The 2nd Battalion at home and in India—The Zulu War—Ulundi—
The war with Sikukuni—The first Transvaal war—The defence
of Potchefstroom—The defence of Pretoria—The defence of
Rustenburg—The Burma war.

THE 2nd Battalion, which came into being at Paisley in April 1858, had for its first commanding officer Lieutenant-Colonel Edward Last, who the year before had gone from the 99th to command the 1st West India Regiment. The nucleus was a party of non-commissioned officers and men from the 1st Battalion—an excellent beginning, for they were all trained and experienced soldiers just back from the Crimea. Several officers from the 1st Battalion also joined the new unit on promotion. *1858-63*

For five years the battalion was on duty at home—at Newport in Wales, at Aldershot, at Shorncliffe, at Dublin, and at the Curragh. In 1859 Last was succeeded by Edward de Lancey Lowe from the 32nd Light Infantry, who had commanded that regiment during the Indian Mutiny in defence of the Residency at Lucknow. Three years later this most capable officer exchanged with James Elphinstone Robertson of the first battalion of the 6th, who had distinguished himself in South Africa in the Kaffir War of 1851–53. It was under Colonel Robertson that the battalion sailed from Kingstown for India on July 19, 1863, on its maiden tour of foreign service.

For five years it was stationed at different posts in the Madras Presidency, suffering heavy losses during its stay at Bellary from an epidemic of cholera.[1] In October 1868 it was transferred to Burma, when for three years it was at Rangoon, furnishing convict guards for Port Blair in the Andaman Islands. Colonel Robertson having been appointed adjutant-general at Madras, the command of the regiment devolved upon Edwin Ashley Tucker Steward; and when, in 1870, Steward resigned on account of ill-health, his place was taken by Frederick Torrens Lyster from the 1st Battalion, whom we have already seen serving with Charles Shaw's "Scots Fusiliers" in Portugal. In 1872 the battalion returned to Madras, where presently it was relieved by the 1st Battalion. In May of that year a severe cyclone visited the Madras coast, the vessels in the Roads dragged their anchors, and several ran aground among the boiling surf. The Scots Fusiliers turned out to the work of rescue, and at the hazard of their lives saved many of the crews and passengers of the stranded ships. A massive silver vase, on a square teak plinth made of the wood of the wrecked vessels, which is now in the officers' mess, remains as a testimonial of this service.[2]

The year 1873 saw the battalion back in Scotland, distributed between Stirling Castle, Perth, Dundee, and Hamilton. Next year it was at Aldershot, when Lyster retired, and William Pole Collingwood from the 1st Battalion succeeded. Collingwood seemed to be fated to suffer shipwreck, for he had been in command of the troops on board the *Spartan* when she was wrecked on the Dog Rocks off the African coast on

---

[1] About this time the future Major-General G. F. Gildea (the president of the Band Committee) started the practice of the band playing the evening hymn between the first and last posts. This may have been the revival of an old custom, and something of the kind apparently still prevails in the 10th Hussars and the 12th Lancers, as well as in the Royal Scots Fusiliers. See *Journal of the United Service Institution*, No. 477, Feb. 1925, pages 67, 68.

[2] The inscription runs: "Presented by the Public of Madras to the Officers' Mess H.M.'s 21st Fusiliers, in commemoration of the gallant exertions of the officers, N.C.O.'s, and men of the Regiment in saving the lives of crews and passengers of vessels shipwrecked at the Port of Madras during the cyclone of the 2nd May, 1872."

SOUTH AFRICA

her way home from the Crimea, and had conducted himself with conspicuous gallantry. He was soon to be involved in a similar adventure. From Aldershot the battalion moved to Portsmouth, and in 1877 it was back in Scotland at Fort George and Dundee. Next year it went to Ireland, where it was brought up to full strength by the addition of volunteers and of a large draft of trained men under Major Hazelrigg from the depot at Ayr. In February 1879 it embarked at Queenstown in the *City of Paris* for South Africa.

The Zulu kingdom, now governed by Cetewayo, the nephew of the great Chaka, had long been on doubtful terms with its neighbour Natal and the Boers of the Transvaal; and when, in 1877, Britain annexed the latter country, she fell heir to a tangle of border disputes. The chief Sikukuni, up in his Lydenburg fastnesses, was in arms against the Transvaal, and he was aided and abetted by the Zulu king. The situation was such that, in 1878, the High Commissioner, Sir Bartle Frere, was convinced that there could be no peace unless the Zulu military system, which was a perpetual temptation to brigandage, was remodelled, and a British resident accepted. Cetewayo made no reply to the British ultimatum, and in January 1879 a small British force, under Lord Chelmsford, entered Zululand. The sequel is only too familiar a tale. Cetewayo, who mustered 40,000 warriors, allowed the columns to penetrate well inside the border, and then fell upon the central force at Isandhlwana and destroyed it. The heroic defence of Rorke's Drift followed, the attack became a defence, and Chelmsford withdrew inside the Natal frontier and awaited reinforcements.

The news of Isandhlwana reached England on 11th February, and that very day 10,000 men were ordered to South Africa. Our battalion sighted Table Mountain on the morning of 21st March in wild weather; but while steaming into Simon's Bay, the *City of Paris* refused to answer to her helm, and about eight p.m. ran stern on to the Roman Rock. There are accounts of the incident in a letter written by Major Hazelrigg,

1879 who was in actual command of the troops owing to Colonel Collingwood's ill-health, and in a letter from one of the men to the *Ayr Advertiser*. " It was very dark," says the latter, " it was blowing a gale, and there were 1,100 men on deck. The captain gave his orders with coolness and courage from the bridge, the boats were made ready for lowering, signals of distress were sent up, and all were prepared for the worst. The Scots Fusiliers behaved with admirable coolness; nothing could have been better, the young fellows vieing with their older comrades in their apparent contempt of danger. Happily for all on board, the gale, now increasing and catching the ship on the port side, at the same time as the reversed engines pulled her back, pushed her off the rocks; and putting on full steam, we now went ahead, and passing through forbidden water over sunken rocks, we got into Simon's Bay with no water to speak of in the hold. An episode is worth relating as an illustration of the good behaviour of the men. The instant the ship struck the rocks, the quartermaster at the wheel uttered an exclamation of horror, and crying ' All is lost! ' made a rush to the nearest boat. Two or three young soldiers at once seized the wheel, and did their best to steer the ship until another quartermaster could be got hold of." Captain Fulton of the *City of Paris* wrote to Colonel Collingwood : " Nothing could have surpassed the admirable way your orders were carried out by your officers, the alacrity with which every man obeyed them, and the silence maintained, thereby rendering us the greatest assistance during those few trying moments."

Transferred to H.M.S. *Tamar*, the battalion reached Durban on the last day of March, three days before Chelmsford relieved Eshowe, and the day after Evelyn Wood had beaten off the attack of Cetewayo's main army in northern Zululand—the action in which Redvers Buller won the V.C., and the famous Piet Uys was slain. On 5th April, with pipes playing, the Scots Fusiliers entered Pietermaritzburg, where Captain Willoughby and two companies were ordered to remain behind for

THE ZULU WAR

the defence of the town in case of a Zulu invasion. The headquarters and the remaining six companies reached Ladysmith on the 19th, and, since most of the reinforcements had now arrived, Lord Chelmsford proceeded to reorganize his army. The First Division, under Major-General Crealock, was to advance along the coast; while the Second Division, under Major-General Newdigate, was directed from Rorke's Drift and Kambula direct upon Cetewayo's main kraal at Ulundi. Evelyn Wood's flying column formed an independent command, and acted as a link between the two divisions operating from different bases. Colonel Pole Collingwood was appointed to command the 2nd Brigade (the 24th and part of the 94th Regiments) in Newdigate's division, while Major Hazelrigg took over the Scots Fusiliers, who were in Glynne's 1st Brigade.

On 24th May the battalion joined Newdigate at Landeman's Drift, and four days later advanced to the banks of the Blood River, where further reinforcements brought Newdigate's strength up to 5,700. On 3rd June the division moved forward to the Ityotyosi River, near to the spot where the Prince Imperial of France had been killed the previous Sunday. The river was crossed next day, and after some skirmishing with the enemy an advance was made to Isandhlwana Hill. A fort, called Fort Newdigate, was constructed on the bank of the Nondwene River, where two companies of the Scots Fusiliers with two Gatling guns, a company of Basutos, and a troop of the 1st Dragoon Guards were left as a garrison to protect communications. The next halt was on the Upoku River, where another fort was constructed, and another two Scots Fusiliers companies left behind for its defence.

By 1st July Newdigate and Evelyn Wood had reached the White Umvelosi River, in the very heart of the enemy's country and close to the royal kraal, and the final battle could not long be delayed. The day before, Lieutenant J. H. Scott Douglas of the Scots Fusiliers, who was chief of the telegraph staff of the Second Division, set out, along with Corporal Cottar of

1879 the 17th Lancers, to deliver an important message to Fort Evelyn, twenty miles away. On the return journey they fell into a Zulu ambush, and their bodies, stabbed with many assegais, were found ten days later.

Early on the morning of 4th July Chelmsford, who was now with Newdigate and Wood, led his army, which numbered 4,200 Europeans and 1,000 natives, across the White Umvelosi, and moved upon Ulundi. The Second Division was in a hollow, oblong square, of which the headquarters and two companies of the Scots Fusiliers and two companies of the 94th formed the rear face. The front and flanks were protected by Redvers Buller's horse, while the rear was guarded by the 17th Lancers and the Basutos. The guns moved parallel with the infantry, colours were unfurled for the first time in the campaign, and the bands played a brisk march.

Chelmsford halted his square when he had come within a mile of Ulundi, which lay due east in an amphitheatre, with a bush country to the north, and to the south a range of broken hills. About 8.30 a.m. the white shields of the enemy were first seen flashing in the morning sun. The cavalry sought the shelter of the square, and the infantry closed up, forming fours, with the two front ranks kneeling. The main attack was on the right rear angle of the square, where were the Scots Fusiliers, the 58th, and the 94th. Cetewayo's picked warriors, led by a chief on a white horse, came on with clanging shields in a huge wave, regardless, it seemed, of the hail of rifle bullets or the fire from the 9-pounders. But it never came to the clash of bayonet and assegai. The impis did not get within thirty yards of the infantry, which poured out that terrible and unremitting fire. In twenty minutes the warriors of Cetewayo—between 15,000 and 20,000 had come into action that day—were in headlong flight, with the British horse at their heels, leaving 1,500 of their number dead.

Ulundi ended the Zulu War, and when, on 7th July, Sir Garnet Wolseley arrived to take over the command

THE TRANSVAAL IN 1879

from Lord Chelmsford, the campaign was over, and his task was civil and political rather than military. Cetewayo was captured in August, and the ill-advised partitionment of his country took place, which ended eight years later in a British annexation. Ulundi was an almost bloodless victory for Britain, for our casualties were scarcely a hundred; Major Winsloe and ten men of the Scots Fusiliers were wounded, and the Queen's Colour, carried by Second Lieutenant the Hon. A. Hardinge, had a bullet through it. Newdigate's division was broken up on 10th July, but not before he had complimented the battalion on its "steady valour and coolness under fire." On 5th July Colonel Collingwood, having completed his five years' command, severed, to the regret of all, his connection with a regiment in which he had served for twenty-nine years. His successor was Lieutenant-Colonel George Frederick Gildea, who was at the moment in Scotland, and Major Hazelrigg temporarily commanded the battalion when, on 26th August, it set out for Pretoria.

Our story now leads us into the confusion of Transvaal politics, which the British annexation in 1877 had done nothing to clear. The Boers, under Kruger, were agitating for independence, and the disaster of Isandhlwana had lowered their respect for British troops. Ulundi for a moment checked their hopes, and Sir Garnet Wolseley, who was acting as temporary High Commissioner of the Transvaal as well as of Natal, went north to settle affairs in that uneasy territory. His first duty was to bring about peace, for the war with Sikukuni had been grumbling on ever since 1876, when that chief had ignominiously beaten the Boer commandos. Sikukuni had been hand in glove with Cetewayo, and his punishment was a necessary adjunct to the Zulu campaign.

On 15th September the Scots Fusiliers were at Wakkerstroom, and ten days later reached Standerton, where a company of mounted infantry was formed, consisting of Lieutenants Collings and Lindsell, two sergeants, two corporals, and forty-six men. The battalion next moved to Middelburg, where it joined the 94th, and then, on 20th November, to Fort Webber, where Wolseley's field force was encamped on an affluent of the Olifants River. It was the hot and malarial season of the year, and the country was full of " horse-sickness "; but Wolseley resolved to push on into the Lydenburg hills, for the political situation did not permit of a leisurely campaign. He had with him some 1,400 Europeans and 11,000 natives, and on the 22nd he was within striking distance of Sikukuni's *stad*. An advance force, containing two companies of the Scots Fusiliers, was sent on in the moonlight of the night of the 24th to seize a hill called Water Kopje, and by the night of the 27th the whole army had struggled forward to this point over muddy roads and through the steaming rains. It was a trying march, and the Fusiliers were under arms and without food for twenty-four hours on end.

At two a.m. on the 28th came the final advance. Sikukuni's *stad* lay two miles distant—three great kraals, with a natural citadel which was called the Fighting Kopje, a mass of piled boulders and slabs honeycombed with caverns and surrounded by a fringe of forest. The attack was a converging one; but the main task was that of the central column, under Colonel Murray of the 94th, which consisted of that regiment and six companies of the Scots Fusiliers, and was directed against the Fighting Kopje. By six o'clock the assault on the kraals had begun; by ten they were in flames, and the time had come for Murray's advance. The signal was given by two rockets, and in ten minutes the grey side of the kopje was bright with the scarlet of our troops, while the Fusilier pipers added their skirling to the cries of the native levies. For two hours there was severe hand-to-hand fighting, for the enemy had to be sought in the caves and ravines, but by noon the kopje was won. Yet it was not till the next day that the last remnants of the defence were dislodged from the crevices of the rocks. Sikukuni

DEFEAT OF SIKUKUNI

himself was captured three days later, and the power of the robber chief was finally broken. The Fusiliers had three men killed, and Captains Willoughby and Gordon and sixteen men wounded. At the close of December they marched to Pretoria, a somewhat battered and war-worn body of men. " Two harassing and toilsome campaigns," says Mr. Clark, " during which the battalion marched upwards of one thousand miles, had reduced the men's clothing to a very dilapidated condition. Each man endeavoured as best he could to repair the rents and holes in his apparel; but the material obtainable for patching was most unsuitable, being neither the colour nor texture of the garment itself. Patches of biscuit-bags, blankets, waterproof sheets, may cover deficiencies, but do not add to the splendour of a soldier's uniform. While all were much alike, the general appearance of the Fusiliers did not cause much remark among themselves; but when they marched into Pretoria, the worn-out condition of their clothing, with its many-coloured patches, contrasted grotesquely with the neat, clean uniform of the soldiers in garrison."[1]

For the better part of a year the battalion was quartered at Pretoria. During these months there is little to record, except the great hurricane which, on February 3, 1880, visited the town and flattened tents and huts, leaving the troops exposed to the fury of the weather. Several of the men were hurt, but none seriously. In May Lieutenant-Colonel Gildea arrived from England to take up his command of the battalion, and was also appointed commandant of Pretoria. On 16th July, to the grief of all, Major and Brevet-Lieutenant-Colonel Arthur Hazelrigg, who had led the regiment in Zululand and in the struggle with Sikukuni, and who had served for twenty-five years with the Scots Fusiliers, died of fever. Meantime the clouds were darkening over the country. In the autumn of 1879 Mr. Gladstone had declared, during his Midlothian campaign, that if the possession of the Transvaal was as valuable

[1] *Hist. Record of R.S.F.*, page 80.

1880 as it was valueless, he would repudiate it because it had been obtained by dishonourable methods. In 1880 Mr. Gladstone was at the head of the British Government, and the hopes of the Boers were naturally awakened. Moreover, to add fuel to the fires of their discontent, Sir Owen Lanyon, the administrator of the Transvaal, had begun to enforce the payment of taxes, which the farmers had never granted to their own governments, and were not likely to concede to what now seemed to them a precarious foreign rule. In November came the Bezuidenhout affair, when wagons seized for non-payment of taxes were promptly released by a Boer party. On 13th December a mass meeting at Paardekraal proclaimed the South African Republic. Some days later came the action at Bronkhorst Spruit, where a detachment of the 94th, marching from Lydenburg, was surprised and cut up with every circumstance of treachery. War had broken out, and the British troops in the Transvaal were in the position of garrisons isolated and beleaguered.

The main course of the war does not concern us, with its disasters at Laing's Nek [1] and Majuba, and the speedy surrender, enforced by the home Government, which was to sow dragons' teeth in South Africa. Our business is with a more creditable tale, the doings of the small Transvaal garrison. On 14th November a contingent, containing one company of the Scots Fusiliers, had marched to Potchefstroom to build a fort, while another company went north to Rustenburg behind the line of the Magaliesberg Mountains. When war broke out the regiment was distributed as follows: at Pretoria, the headquarters, A, B, F, and H companies, and a half company of mounted infantry, the officers being Lieutenant-Colonel Gildea, Captains Burr and Dunn, Lieutenant Collings, Second Lieutenants Stanuell,

---

[1] Lieutenant H. J. Lermitte, of the Twenty-First, was with the mounted infantry under Brownlow at Laing's Nek, and took part in the charge up the hill, where his horse was shot under him. Lermitte, a thrifty soul, thus described the charge: "I got up and, seeing no one about, I turned and legged it down the hill. My helmet had fallen off, my sword dropped out of my hand, and I lost my field glasses. It was a dashed expensive day."

Thornycroft, and D'Aeth, Lieutenant and Adjutant Chichester, and Quartermaster Clifford; at Potchefstroom, C and D Companies and the rest of the mounted infantry, with Major and Brevet-Lieutenant-Colonel Winsloe, Captain Falls, Lieutenants Browne and Lind-

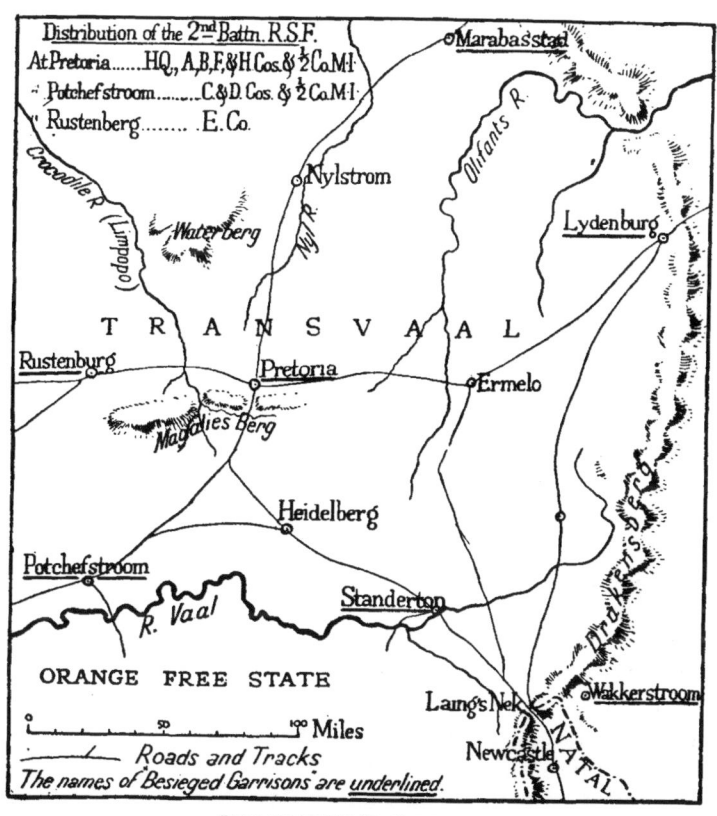

THE TRANSVAAL CAMPAIGN

sell, and Second Lieutenants Lean and Dalrymple-Hay; at Rustenburg, E Company, with Captain Auchinleck and Second Lieutenant Despard. Two drafts from home for the battalion were still down country. Each of these detachments had to fight alone and unaided its own battle.

The first to be in action was the garrison of Potchefstroom. In that delightful little town, the old Transvaal capital, with its tree-lined streets refreshed by the clear waters of the Mooi River, there had been a threatening of trouble as early as 13th November, when a Boer commando had ridden in and seized a wagon impounded by the landrost for arrears of taxes. The fort which the Fusiliers erected was, at the beginning of the siege, defended by a mere shelter trench and a rampart only four and a half feet high, and had in the centre the commissariat stores and the hospital. The fighting began on 15th December, when a commando of 800 Boers entered the town and occupied most of it, the British troops concentrating on the defence of the fort, the gaol, and the landrost's office. On the morning of the 16th the enemy was skilfully placed among the gardens, and could fire from cover on the fort at a range of six hundred yards. An attempt to haul down the British flag at the landrost's office was repulsed with loss. But the situation was impossible, since a force of under 200 men could not hold three separate posts against an army of skilled sharpshooters who were speedily augmented to 1,400. On the 18th the garrison at the landrost's office was compelled to surrender, and in the fighting Captain Falls was killed. Presently it was found necessary to abandon the gaol, the troops evacuating it after dark with the loss of one man killed. By the 20th the whole garrison was in the tiny fort, which had also to shelter the horses and mules, and several women and children.

The first difficulty was water. The well in the fort yielded at the best only ten gallons a day, and though a rainstorm gave temporary relief, it was soon necessary to turn adrift the mules and horses. Happily it was found possible to sink a second well, which was sufficient for the garrison's wants. There was food enough for one month for a field company—a poor provision for 200 men. The defences were feverishly strengthened by sandbags made by the sick and wounded out of tents, so that soon, except for five tents reserved for the hospital, men, women, and children were living in

THE DEFENCE OF POTCHEFSTROOM

the open. The Boers' policy was beleaguerment and starvation. On New Year's Day, 1881, they brought up an old 3-pounder ship's gun, but it was soon silenced by the two British 9-pounders, directed by a young officer, Lieutenant Leslie Rundle, whose name in later years was to be familiar to the enemy. Slowly the investing lines crept nearer till the fort was completely encircled. On 22nd January a trench was opened at a distance of two hundred and twenty yards, and, since it promised to be a perpetual source of annoyance, a party consisting of Lieutenant Dalrymple Hay, a sergeant, and ten men, made a sortie in broad daylight. As they dashed across the open three men fell, but the remaining seven reached the trench, and drove out the enemy, killing or wounding eleven and taking four prisoners. Next day the Boers sent a doctor under a flag of truce to attend to their wounded, and the garrison lent stretchers to convey them into the town. These stretchers were returned laden with fruits and medical comforts—a pleasant fact to record in an implacable struggle.

By February the rations had run very short, and diarrhœa, dysentery, and enteric were weakening the little garrison. On the 10th of that month the enemy made a determined attack, the fire lasting for two days, but the British casualties were few. March opened with no supplies left except mealies and Kaffir corn, and it was clear even to the stout heart of Winsloe that the last limit of endurance was near. On the 19th the food was exhausted, and a flag of truce was sent out, to ask for a parley. Winsloe succeeded in bluffing the Boer commandant, Cronje, with threats of protracted resistance, and on 21st March the garrison was permitted to march out with flags flying, drums beating, and all the honours of war. On the 23rd the survivors left for Natal, which they reached on 2nd May. On the very day of the capitulation Sir Evelyn Wood had made terms with the Boer leaders, and the war had ended. The defence of Potchefstroom was a signal proof of endurance and resolution, for 200 men held out for

1880-81 three months against a force seven times greater, on provisions which were sufficient for one month for half their number, and did not yield until their food was literally exhausted. The Union Jack flown over the fort during the siege was made from the lining of Lieutenant Rundle's cloak, the lining of a sergeant's coat, and a blue serge coat belonging to Lieutenant Lindsell. It was presented in 1912 to the Scots Fusiliers by General Sir Leslie Rundle, whose gunners had had the making of it, and is now in the officers' mess of the 2nd Battalion.

We turn to Lieutenant-Colonel Gildea in Pretoria, who, besides the Fusiliers, had under him two companies of the 94th, a number of volunteers, a detachment of sappers, and two 9-pounders. The first shot was fired on 19th December, and on the 21st, while reconnoitring along the Middelburg road, Gildea found a wounded sergeant of the 94th, and heard from him the news of Bronkhorst Spruit. This sergeant had managed to save the 94th's colours, and these for the rest of the siege were in Gildea's keeping, and were entwined with those of the Fusiliers. Reconnaissances in strength were made on 28th and 29th December, and on January 6, 1881, Gildea led an attack on Swartz Kopje, twelve miles from the town, where the Boers fired from sixty yards range under the white flag—wounding three sergeants and eighteen men, and so enraged the Fusiliers that they stormed the laager and killed, wounded, or took prisoner all its defenders. By the middle of January the enemy had massed around Pretoria, but Gildea on the 16th drove them back to the hills, and Sir Owen Lanyon with his staff defeated a counter-attack on the town during the absence of the troops on the sortie. By February the garrison was limited to the defensive, and on the 12th of that month Gildea was badly wounded. Nevertheless he proved more than a match for the enemy, and during the one hundred and two days of the siege, the place was never in serious danger. It was an arduous time for the Fusiliers, who, with scanty food, had to toil day and night, and not less

PRETORIA AND RUSTENBURG

hard was the lot of the civilians shut up within the fort. There was much sickness, alleviated by the self-denying labours of the Colonel's wife, who received in recognition the Royal Red Cross from Queen Victoria. When peace was signed, and the Transvaal was surrendered to the Boers, the British residents in Pretoria, bitter at their betrayal, seized an occasion when the troops were absent to bury a British flag. It was carried on a coffin through the streets, and over its grave was placed a headstone with the inscription—" In loving memory of the British Flag in the Transvaal, who departed this life on the 2nd August, 1881, in her fifth year. In other climes none knew thee but to love thee. *Resurgam*." When Gildea heard of the burial he ordered the grave to be destroyed and took the flag home with him to Scotland. We shall hear more of this historic piece of bunting.

There remains the tale of the handful of Scots Fusiliers at Rustenburg. There E Company, under Auchinleck, endured extreme privations and desolating sickness from December 27, 1880, to March 30, 1881, shut up in a mud fort only twenty-five yards square. There was never a day on which the Boers did not attack, and in the ninety-three days of the siege there were forty-five days of continuous rain, which did not add to the comfort of men who had no kind of shelter. On 29th January Auchinleck was wounded in the head; on 4th February, in a successful sortie, he was shot through the face, the bullet entering below the nose and coming out at the left eye; yet in spite of this serious wound he led another sortie that night, and got another bullet through his elbow. Before the siege ended he had a fourth wound in the thigh. For his conduct he received a brevet-majority; the Victoria Cross might well seem a more suitable reward for such supreme gallantry.

The 2nd Battalion in Zululand and the Transvaal had most nobly won its spurs, and had contributed new honours to the regimental colours. During the

1881-86 autumn of 1881 it was reunited at Durban, and in December sailed for India. On its arrival at Bombay it was ordered to Secunderabad to relieve the 1st Battalion; and there it remained till the close of 1884, engaged in duties and recreations which may be read of in the pages of its spirited regimental magazine, the *Fusee*. Its next move was to Burma, where trouble threatened with the native kingdom of Upper Burma, then under the rule of King Theebaw. Lower Burma had for long been a British province, and the court at Mandalay was proving itself a difficult neighbour, partly because of the king's inability to control his outlying territories and his revolting cruelties, and partly from his constant interference with the legitimate course of trade. An official protest during 1885 produced an unsatisfactory answer, and in October Britain sent him an ultimatum. Theebaw decided on war, and called on his subjects to drive the enemy into the sea. The British force, under General Sir H. Prendergast, assembled on the confines of Lower Burma on 14th November, and moved in light-draught steamers up the Irrawaddy. The resistance was feeble, and in less than a fortnight after the declaration of war Mandalay had fallen, and Theebaw was a prisoner.

But the hardest part of the campaign remained— the suppression of the armed dacoits who roamed through the forests and terrorized the peaceful inhabitants of the land. A guerrilla war dragged on for several years, and British troops lost heavily from the malarial jungles and the attentions of a mobile and crafty enemy. The Scots Fusiliers, split up into detachments, played a prominent part in this " bushthwacking " warfare. Gildea had retired on half-pay in 1884, and Winsloe was now lieutenant-colonel, with Francis William Hamilton as his junior colleague. The troop of mounted infantry, under Lieutenant Lindsell, did good work with the Mounted Corps, while two companies under Lieutenant-Colonel Hamilton, and two companies under Major Law, operated on the right and

THE BURMA CAMPAIGN

left banks of the Irrawaddy. To Law's column fell the taking of the important town of Toungwingyu, where Auchinleck, the hero of the defence of Rustenburg, was killed. To follow in detail the course of the fighting of these small parties under officers of all ranks is outside the province of this work ; it is sufficient to say that the regiment was commended in dispatches, and that men like Winsloe, and Hardinge, and Browne, who had won note in South Africa, as well as new officers like Major Law and Lieutenants C. P. Scudamore,[1] Quentin Agnew, and Churchill were mentioned for conspicuous merit in this most trying form of service.

At the end of 1886 the Scots Fusiliers returned to Rangoon, and a year later to India, where they were quartered first at Dagshai in Bengal. In that year Frederick George Jackson, who had joined the regiment in 1858, succeeded Winsloe as commanding officer. A long spell of peace now followed a decade of war. In 1890 the battalion was at Peshawur, when James Whitton, who had been in charge of the laager at Laing's Nek, took the place of Jackson. Next year there was hope of a share in the second Black Mountain expedition, but the health of the men was too bad, for what was known as " Peshawur fever " had filled the hospitals. In 1892 the Scots Fusiliers moved to Sialkot, and in 1894 Whitton was replaced by Arthur J. Osborne Pollock, who had been D.A.A.G. of the Belfast district. It is clear from the inspection reports that no battalion in India during these years had reached a higher degree of excellence, especially in signalling, in which it held first place till 1896, when it was just beaten by the 1st Gordons.

In the autumn of 1896 it left India after a spell of seventeen years' foreign service. Its first home station was Chatham, where in 1898 Pollock was succeeded by Edward Elliot Carr, who had at one time been adjutant of the 2nd Volunteer Battalion of the regiment. In

---

[1] Scudamore received the D.S.O. for his transport work in Burma.

1899 September of the next year it moved to Aldershot, and there it was stationed when, in October, the long-expected war broke out between Britain and the Boer republics. On November 23, 1899, twenty years after it had paid its first visit to South Africa, it arrived once again in its old campaigning ground.

CHAPTER XIII

THE SECOND BATTALION—THE SOUTH AFRICAN WAR

Nature of the campaign—Colenso—Spion Kop—Vaal Kranz—The crossing of the Tugela—Pieter's Hill—The relief of Ladysmith—The relief of Mafeking—Potchefstroom revisited—Frederikstad—The last year of the war.

PRESIDENT KRUGER'S ultimatum was presented on October 9, 1899, and two days later a state of war began between Britain and the Dutch republics. The first shot was fired on the 12th on the western frontier of the Transvaal, and presently the main Boer army, under Joubert, was streaming through the passes into Natal. For the coming war Britain had had some months of warning, the Natal garrison had been increased, and Sir George White, a capable officer from India, had been appointed to the command; but the nature of the contest was wholly unforeseen, and the advantage of surprise lay with the enemy. The British army system had ossified into a formal thing, formidable on paper, but inelastic in its mechanism and unready for the field. Experience in small barbarian wars had predisposed both officers and men to methods which were bound to fail against a well-armed and intelligent enemy. The Boers never had more than 40,000 men to dispose of, but their force was a nation-in-arms, admirably fitted for the kind of warfare which is most formidable against a mechanically-trained army. Like the troops of Washington, they had a general on their side who could impose his will upon their opponents—the vast wild country in

1899

which they fought. What they lacked in corporate unity, they made up in individual skill and initiative, and their tactics were designed so as to exploit their merits and counteract their defects. They were brilliant riflemen, skilled in marksmanship and with an instinctive fire-discipline; they had an infallible eye for country, and were masters of all the arts of concealment and surprise. Eschewing solid formations, they were adepts in extending their line so as to use each rifleman to the full, and to secure flanking and enveloping fire; and they had the high mobility necessary in such tactics, and possible only for troops where each man had the resource and intelligence to be on occasion his own general. The Boer system was perfectly logical and complete in itself; and since it was peculiarly adapted to the country in which the war was fought, it was able for a while to hold up and inflict deadly losses upon the might of a great empire.

Let it be added that the configuration of Natal, a British wedge thrust into enemy territory, gave the Boers a notable advantage in the first stage of the campaign. Through the eastern, western, and northern defiles of the Biggarsberg they were able to take in flank and rear any power holding the northern apex of that colony. Sir George White hoped to fight among the broken hills between the Biggarsberg and the Tugela, with Ladysmith in the centre of his operations, but the position had already been compromised. Here it is sufficient to sketch briefly what took place there before the arrival of Sir Redvers Buller and the main British expeditionary force. On 20th October Sir W. Penn Symons fought an action at Talana Hill, near Dundee, in which he drove back Lukas Meyer, but lost his own life. Sir George White sent out General French to clear the line of retreat, and next day came the successful action of Elandslaagte. But the Free Staters were threatening the British left rear, and after a fight at Rietfontein on the 24th, the British forces fell back upon Ladysmith. But before the investment began Sir George White made an attempt to break up the line of the invaders by a general attack, the result being the unsuccessful battle of Lombard's Kop outside the town, while a British column on the left was cut off at Nicholson's Nek by Christian de Wet and forced to surrender. On 2nd November the siege of Ladysmith began; but not before General French had escaped by the last train which ran, and a naval brigade had brought into the town a few naval guns of a range to cope with the heavy artillery which Joubert had placed on the environing hills. The Natal Field Force was now out of action, and had become a beleaguered garrison.

1899

I

The day after Lombard's Kop Sir Redvers Buller, the Commander-in-Chief, arrived at Cape Town. The force which followed him was an army corps in three divisions, and his three divisional generals were Lord Methuen, Sir C. F. Clery, and Sir W. Gatacre. With the first were the Guards Brigade under Sir H. Colville, and the English Brigade under General Hildyard; with Clery were the Highland Brigade under General Wauchope, and the Light Infantry Brigade under General Neville Lyttelton; with Gatacre were the Fusilier Brigade under General Barton, and the Irish Brigade under General Hart. It was a formidable force *in posse*, but it was not yet an effective weapon, for no one of the divisions, and only one of the brigades, had ever worked together as a unit. The staffs had been hastily extemporized, and there was a deplorable lack of mounted infantry. Such an army—apart from the fact that it had as yet no knowledge of the enemy's tactics or the power to meet them—was obviously ill-fitted for the task which confronted it on landing in South Africa. For Buller, who had intended to advance with his total strength against the republics through Cape Colony, found that he must break up his army corps. Political considerations made it desirable as soon as possible to relieve Kimberley, where was Cecil Rhodes; the threat of rebellion in the Cape made

1899 it impossible to leave that province open to invasion on its northern borders; above all, the situation in Natal must be faced. Accordingly Clery was sent off to Durban, with Hildyard's, Barton's, and Lyttelton's brigades; while Methuen, with the Guards and the Highland Brigade, was directed on Kimberley; and Gatacre with the remaining brigades, and French with the bulk of the cavalry division, were to watch the northern line of Cape Colony. Presently things in Natal grew worse, and the approach of Boer commandos to Pietermaritzburg convinced Buller that he must go himself to that front. So, taking the bulk of Hart's brigade from Gatacre, he repaired to Durban, and by the last week of November a full half of the army corps was in Natal—sixteen infantry battalions out of thirty-three, eight batteries of field artillery out of fifteen, and two out of the seven cavalry regiments.

The 2nd Royal Scots Fusiliers, under Lieutenant-Colonel Carr, were part of Barton's 6th or Fusilier Brigade. Arriving at Mooi River on 24th November, they marched to Escourt on the 27th, having been too late for the fighting with the Boer raiding column between the 21st and the 23rd, in which other battalions of their brigade were engaged. On 5th December the enemy was behind the Tugela, and Clery at Frere had four brigades of infantry, a mounted brigade under Lord Dundonald, and a quantity of locally recruited mounted infantry, one unit of which, Thorneycroft's, was raised and commanded by a major of the Scots Fusiliers. The campaign seemed, on the whole, to be going well. Methuen had won the victories of Belmont, Enslin, and Modder River; French and Gatacre were advancing, and the invasion of the Natal lowlands had been checked. Buller had little doubt that before Christmas he would be in Ladysmith, and free to collect his scattered legions for the great march on Bloemfontein and Pretoria. Moreover, reinforcements were being made ready at home, a sixth division was being mobilized, and offers of aid were being accepted from the Colonies.

But in the second week of the month came tidings *1899* of disaster. On 10th December Gatacre, essaying a night attack, was badly beaten at Stormberg. Next day Methuen fought the action of Magersfontein, and was repulsed by Piet Cronje, with losses of nearly 1,000, including the commander of the Highland Brigade. It was incumbent upon Buller to redress the balance and break through the enemy front on the Tugela hills which lay between him and Ladysmith. The bad news from Methuen and Gatacre seems to have decided him to make an attack by which victory, as he thought, could be attained in the shortest time. He had no leisure for elaborate flanking movements when his presence was so urgently demanded in the west.

At the little village of Colenso the railway crossed the Tugela. Viewed from the south the place was an amphitheatre six miles in diameter, with the river flowing in tortuous curves from west to east. Beyond the stream the ground was broken into many kopjes which descended to the water's edge. These little hills were from 500 feet to 1,000 feet high, while behind them peeped the flat summits of Grobelaar's and Onderbroek mountains. To the east, on the right bank of the Tugela where it turned north, stood the bold bastion of Hlangwane hill. The Boers, under Louis Botha, had on the kopjes a position of great natural strength which they had improved by art. They had before them a perfect field of fire; the river was fordable at only a few points; their trenches were cunningly sited, extending to the edge of the stream; they had ample facilities for cross-fire; they occupied Hlangwane on the right bank. To a frontal attack the position was nearly impregnable; the weak point was Hlangwane, the occupation of which involved the splitting up of an already scanty force, and the placing there of a detachment which might well be cut off. Botha rightly insisted on holding it; but he had the utmost difficulty in inducing his burghers to remain there. As it was, he could only occupy it with small forces, and the risks he took are the measure of the contempt in which he

1899 held the enemy. He had read his opponent correctly, and gambled on his choosing a blind frontal attack.

Buller, after his first reconnaissance, proposed to turn the Boer position by a wide flanking march. He had the choice of two alternatives—either to move east by Weenen, cross the Tugela at a drift thirty miles downstream, and make for the railway at Elandslaagte; or to use one of the drifts of the Upper Tugela, seize the heights beyond, and strike at the Harrismith railway, which was the line of communication for the Free Staters. He chose the second, and on 11th December gave orders for an advance westward by Springfield to Potgieter's Drift. But that evening—presumably because of the news from Methuen—he changed his mind and decided on a direct attack on the Colenso position. He believed that with a force of nearly 21,000 men and a great preponderance of artillery he could disregard all the principles of the military art and hack his way through. His plan was simple. The Tugela might be crossed at a bridle drift three miles off on the left, or at Colenso itself. Hart was to cross at the drift and work down the left bank; Hildyard to cross by Colenso bridge; Lyttelton and Barton to be in reserve for speedy reinforcement; while Dundonald, with the mounted troops, was to cover the right flank and take up a position on Hlangwane.

The plan, by universal consent, was in the highest degree crude and dangerous. It assumed that the whole Boer position was confined to the Colenso kopjes. Even if a direct attack on Colenso was justified, the immense importance of Hlangwane was never perceived, though its effective occupation would have made Botha's main position untenable. The historian's criticism is the verdict not only of military science but of common sense :—

> "The plan resolved itself into a frontal attack directed on three separate points of an indifferently reconnoitred position, held in unknown strength by an entrenched enemy, a position sheltered along

the greater part of its front by a broad river believed to be fordable at two or three points only, and resting on its left on a high rocky hill. The two main attacks were to take place across absolutely open ground. There was to be no attempt to save the troops either by getting down to the river under cover of darkness and crossing in the grey light of morning, or by working up to the position by a series of entrenchments. Against any enemy, at any period since the introduction of the rifle, such tactics would have been difficult to justify. After the experience of Modder River, the written report on which battle must already have been in Buller's hands, and after the last revelation of Boer fighting power, they were almost inconceivable. . . . Nor can it be urged that the dangers of the dispersed frontal attack were compensated by the exceptional rewards that would have accompanied success. On the contrary, the army would only have found itself in the pit of the Colenso amphitheatre, cramped in between the Tugela and the heights, and face to face with a series of positions which, as the events of February 23–27, 1900, showed, could only be overcome by moving the main body of the force back across the Tugela again." [1]

The battle opened at half-past five on the morning of 15th December, in the blue windless dawn of a South African summer day. Hart's brigade on the left advanced in quarter-column, with no skirmishers or scouts ahead, and when within two hundred yards of the river was met with a whirlwind blast of fire from front and flank. In forty minutes the gallant Irish had over 400 casualties, and, covered by Lyttelton, were forced unwillingly to retire. Meantime strange things had been happening in the centre. Colonel Long, who commanded the artillery, was a believer in fighting his guns at short range; so, without any orders, he galloped his two field batteries, the 14th

[1] Amery, *The War in South Africa*, II., pages 438, 439.

and the 66th, far ahead of the infantry brigades and the slow-moving naval guns, till he was abreast of Colenso village and within 700 yards of the river. No sooner did he give the order to open fire than every rifle in the Boer trenches was concentrated on his batteries. The gunners stuck heroically to their work, but under that hail of bullets officers and men fell fast, and Long himself was desperately wounded. By seven o'clock nearly all the ammunition was spent, and the men were ordered to retire to the big donga in the rear till fresh supplies could be brought up. There the guns' escort, supplied by Barton, overtook them; in this escort were A, B, E, and F Companies of the Royal Scots Fusiliers under Major W. A. Young, the rest of the battalion remaining at Frere for line of communication duty.

By half-past seven Hart had failed, and Long's guns were standing mute and deserted in the empty plain. Meantime Dundonald was attacking Hlangwane, the most vital position, but one which in this mad battle was treated as a mere side-show. He got some way up the hill, but as he was outmatched in numbers and had practically no artillery support, he presently came to the end of his strength. He applied to Barton for help, but Barton, conceiving himself bound by Buller's orders, refused. The only chance now left was the attack by Hildyard; but Buller had lost heart, and was anxious to withdraw from the conflict as soon as he could extricate Long's guns. Hildyard's instructions were therefore changed; he was ordered not to attack, but to send one battalion across the railway to support the guns and another to occupy Colenso village, and to avoid a close engagement. The advance was skilfully made, and the Queen's and the Devons, moving in open order, reached their objective with comparatively light losses. But a handful of men could not absorb the enemy's attention sufficiently to facilitate the task of moving the guns. Buller, in despair, told his aide-de-camp, Captain Scholefield of the R.H.A., to try and bring some of them out. The latter called

THE GUNS ABANDONED

for volunteers, and Captain Congreve of the Rifle Brigade, Lieutenant the Hon. F. S. Roberts of the 60th Rifles, and Corporal Nurse of the 66th Battery and two limber teams set out on an enterprise the heroism of which did something to redeem the tragic fiasco of the day. Congreve and Roberts were wounded, the latter mortally, but the others succeeded in getting two guns back. A little later Captain Reed of the 7th Battery made another attempt; but had to abandon it after losing seven men out of thirteen, and thirteen horses out of twenty-two.

There is no more to tell. Buller, who had shown throughout the day the most dauntless personal courage, seemed to have come to the end of his resources. Though he had still half a score of fresh battalions and three field batteries, besides the naval artillery, he decided to abandon the guns to the enemy. At eleven a.m. he reached this decision, and recalled Hildyard's battalions and Dundonald; yet it was not till four in the afternoon that the Boers dared to advance to seize the ten guns—nearly half of the British field artillery and more than all that Botha had at Colenso. Next morning Buller asked for an armistice to collect his dead and wounded, and then withdrew to Chieveley and Frere. His nerve had so utterly failed that he heliographed to Sir George White suggesting the surrender of Ladysmith, a recommendation which that commander, to his infinite honour, refused for one moment to accept.

The order to retire did not reach all the troops in and about Colenso and in the donga behind the abandoned guns. The result was that some of the Devons and their colonel, with most of the Irish and Scots Fusiliers in the donga, were captured by the enemy. It had been a melancholy day for our regiment. Eleven non-commissioned officers and men were killed, and twenty-eight wounded, while among the prisoners were Captains Dick and Northey, Lieutenants Christian, Rumbold, and McConaghey, Second Lieutenant Briggs, and thirty-nine non-commissioned officers and men. That

1899 day the first Victoria Cross in the history of the regiment was won by Private C. Ravenhill, who " went

THE ADVANCE ACROSS THE TUGELA

several times under a heavy fire from his sheltered position as one of the escort to the guns to assist the officers and men who were trying to withdraw them, when the detachments serving them had all been wounded or driven from them by infantry fire at close range, and helped to limber up one of the guns that were saved."

The first three weeks of January 1900 were spent by the battalion at Frere. As soon as the result of Colenso was known in Britain the Government took prompt action. Field-Marshal Lord Roberts, now in his sixty-eighth year, accepted the supreme command in South Africa a few hours after hearing of his son's death, and with him went Lord Kitchener as chief of staff. Moreover, the people of Britain and the Empire rose manfully to the crisis, and volunteers and yeomanry contingents were speedily prepared for service. Roberts and Kitchener arrived at Cape Town on 10th January, and set about creating a field army. Ladysmith, Kimberley, and Mafeking still held out, but on the 6th White had to repel a desperate attempt to storm the first town, and fought fiercely contested actions at Cæsar's Camp and Wagon Hill. French in the Colesberg region of Cape Colony was more than holding his own against a superior enemy force led by Delarey and De Wet. Buller's army in Natal had been reinforced by Sir Charles Warren and the Fifth Division, and a great complement of artillery, and it was clear that the forces opposed to him were decreasing, so that by 10th January there were probably not 16,000 Boers in Natal, and certainly not more than 6,000 with Botha and Lukas Meyer on the Tugela.

Buller had resolved to make his next attempt by the Upper Tugela at Potgieter's Drift. But it was not a flank march which he contemplated so much as a march to a flank as a preliminary to a new frontal attack. Secrecy and speed, both essential for a true turning movement, were absent. He proposed to use two divisions—Clery's, containing Hildyard's and Hart's brigades, and Warren's, containing Lyttelton's and Woodgate's; he had also with him corps troops, cavalry, and mounted infantry, so that his total force was over 23,000 men—nearly four times the strength of the enemy. The depots were Springfield and Spearman's Kop. This is not the place to tell at length the tale

1900 of the second effort, blunderingly conceived, miserably directed, but most gallantly essayed. The Scots Fusiliers were not concerned in it; they had become corps troops, and their companies were divided between the two depots. It is sufficient to say that Buller virtually abrogated the command in favour of Warren, and that Warren proved no more competent than his superior. After much delay and many changes of plan the advance began on 16th January. Warren crossed the Tugela at Trichardt's Drift on the 17th and 18th. Dundonald on the latter day, scouting to the north-west, surprised a Boer contingent, and, if supported, could have then and there opened the road to Ladysmith; he was peremptorily ordered back to take part in a general right wheel pivoting on Trichardt's Drift. But Warren was too slow to take the vital hill of Tabanyama, and presently Botha had so extended his line that what had been his flank was now his centre. That centre was the hill called Spion Kop, and if this could be taken and held, the enemy front would be cut in two.

It was taken at three o'clock in the morning of the 24th. It was held all that day, a day of blistering heat, by men who had little food or water, and who were subjected to constant convergent fire and repeated Boer counter-attacks, and by officers who seemed to be cut off from or forgotten by their superiors in the valley below. Warren was supine and obtuse, reinforcements were not sent at all or sent too late, and every hour men were falling by scores, so that by the close of the action the casualty roll was 1,700. The inspirer of the defence was Colonel A. W. Thorneycroft, on special duty from the Scots Fusiliers; he was appointed to the chief command by Warren during the action, and it was he who at eight p.m. the following evening gave the order to retire. It was a tragic decision, for, as we now know, the enemy was at his last gasp and Botha was ready to acknowledge defeat. It was also a formal breach of military discipline; for Thorneycroft had no authority to make this decision. But history will make large allowances for the error of an intrepid man suffering from an overpowering sense of betrayal, muddle, and futile waste of life. " With a sure instinct he had divined Warren's policy for the moment, and stolidly and deliberately he now resolved not to carry it out. . . . It is not as an error of judgment, nor as a collapse under excessive strain, but as an act of deliberate disobedience that Thorneycroft's decision must be judged. And if it is to be excused, it must be excused on the grounds that in practice, if not in theory, sometimes make disobedience excusable. The unquestioning subordination of the private judgment, the self-sacrificing obedience prescribed by the military code of duty, presupposes a certain minimum of intelligent direction on the part of those in supreme command. If that is wanting, the moral foundation of the code is undermined; there comes a point at which the system breaks down, when insubordination becomes excusable, even necessary." [1]

On 27th January Buller began his preparations for a third attempt to clear the road to Ladysmith. Between Spion Kop on the west and the high *massif* of Doornkop on the east lay, on the left bank of the Tugela, the low ridge of Brakfontein, with in front of it the little flat-topped hill of Vaal Kranz. The hill of Swartz Kop, on the right bank of the river, dominated Vaal Kranz; if, under cover of fire from the former, the latter could be seized, it might be possible to break the enemy line at its weakest point, and, avoiding the higher ground, to open an easy road to Ladysmith. At the moment it was a flank attack on the left of Botha's Spion Kop position; but there was always the risk that, if the operation was not rapid and unexpected, the enemy might occupy Doornkop, in which case it would be no more than another frontal attack. The first step was to get heavy artillery on Swartz Kop, so from the 27th onward a road was made up the hill, and the Scots Fusiliers assisted in dragging up the naval guns. At six a.m. on 5th February the bombardment began, and a feint attack was made

[1] Amery, *op. cit.*, III., page 290.

upon Brakfontein. Under its cover the brigades of Hart, Lyttelton, and Hildyard were assembled some miles to the east opposite Vaal Kranz, a pontoon bridge was constructed across the river, and fire was concentrated upon the little hill. About two p.m. the infantry crossed, and by nightfall the position was won; but Buller had hesitated to complete the operation without which Vaal Kranz was worthless, and the vital flanking ground was untaken. The result was that on the morning of the 6th the failure of Spion Kop had been repeated. Lyttelton held Vaal Kranz, but he was under a deadly cross fire, and Buller's great strength in infantry and guns was useless to assist him. That afternoon Hildyard's brigade relieved Lyttelton's, and a little later Buller decided to give up the attempt and try elsewhere. Vaal Kranz had not been so disastrous an enterprise as Spion Kop, but, if possible, it had shown a leadership still more futile. It says much for the stamina of the British troops that, in those days of fumbling and mishandling, they did not utterly lose both nerve and temper.

Meantime the light was breaking in the west. On 11th February Roberts began his great march which was to relieve Kimberley on the 15th, and to lead to Cronje's surrender at Paardeberg on the 29th. Buller, having abandoned Vaal Kranz, had decided to make his fourth attempt to the east of Colenso on the enemy's extreme left. His mind turned at long last to Hlangwane, the hill on the right bank of the Tugela which, as we have seen, commanded the Boer citadel north of Colenso. If this were taken it might be possible to cross the Tugela well to the east and move straight on Bulwana Hill, which was the key of Ladysmith. The Scots Fusiliers, one company of which had been slightly engaged on the 6th at Swartz Kop, returned to Chieveley, and on the 11th rejoined Barton's brigade. On the 14th Dundonald, the Second Division, now under Lyttelton (2nd and 4th Brigades), and Warren's Fifth Division, to which part of the 6th Brigade was attached, occupied Hussar Hill to the south of Hlangwane. The plan now was to feint against the main Boer position on Hlangwane and Green Hill, while the real attack was delivered by a flank move to the right round the Cingolo ridge. On the 17th Dundonald and Lyttelton took Cingolo, which compelled the enemy to extend and throw back his flank. Then, on the 18th, Hildyard carried the Monte Cristo position, which enabled Norcott, in the centre, and Barton, on the left, to attack Green Hill and the connecting ridge. By 2.15 p.m. the Scots and Irish Fusiliers held the top of Green Hill, and the Boers were driven out of positions which they had occupied since December.

Once again supineness settled upon the British commander. Had Buller brought Warren's division into action on his left and simultaneously taken Hlangwane, he might have destroyed the enemy force on the right bank of the Tugela. Even had the pursuit been resolute the Boers might have been heavily punished; but when Barton was anxious to press on he was curtly forbidden, and the enemy retreat was unmolested. Hlangwane, however, was cleared, Barton and Thorneycroft occupied it next day, and by the 20th the British held the whole south bank of the Tugela.

Buller had now a choice of plans before him. He could cross the Tugela under the cover of his guns, either at Colenso or near the Falls (where the Scots Fusiliers had repaired the Boer bridge), or lower down between Monte Cristo and the Eagle's Nest; or, as Barton urged, he could make a wide outflanking movement by way of Cingolo Nek to the mouth of the Klip River, and so to the rear of Bulwana. Strategically the second was the true course, for it might have led to a second Paardeberg, but to Buller considerations of high strategy were not attractive; he desired only to reach Ladysmith, with as little trouble as possible from the enemy. Moreover, he believed that the Boers were beginning to retreat, and that all he had to do was to follow them quickly. Accordingly he decided to cross the river forthwith, and advance by Pieter's Hill and the line of the railway.

Botha, north of the Tugela, saw with alarm his commandos melting away. He would himself have preferred to raise the siege of Ladysmith and withdraw behind the Biggarsberg, as the best means of helping Cronje, but the old President in a long telegram full of Scripture texts forbade any retreat. The Boer position would indeed have been hopeless but for the inertia of the British commander. On the 21st Buller began his crossing of the river by the pontoon bridge just west of Hlangwane—first Warren's division, then Lyttelton's, while Barton's brigade, on the right bank down to the Falls, covered the movement. The result was a blow to Buller's hopes. The leading brigade met with fierce opposition among the small kopjes, and made little progress. Next day, the 22nd, a large army was cooped up in the narrow space between the river and the hills. Wynne's brigade was pushed forward into the middle of the enemy position—as at Spion Kop and Colenso—and was then left to be shot at, and passed a day and a night of danger and loss. On the 23rd a general advance was ordered to continue along the west side of the railway line—the divisions, Lyttelton's on the left and Warren's on the right, in column of brigades. But the opposition was so formidable that soon it became clear that this plan could not be followed. Buller sent Hart's brigade forward to cross the Langerwacht stream and occupy the summit to the west of the railway, which came to be known as Inniskilling Hill, helped by the fire of the Scots Fusiliers from the south side of the Tugela. With the utmost gallantry and devotion the Irish carried the first crest, but the feat was beyond the power of mortal troops. With heavy losses the attack was stayed, and on the 24th the British were once again at a deadlock. Buller had his army scattered in dire confusion in the narrow ground north of the Tugela, and wholly at a standstill. Had Botha been able to counter-attack he might have wellnigh destroyed it.

Slowly the impossibility of the position dawned upon Buller's mind. There was a short armistice on

PIETER'S HILL

the 25th, and that day the guns were moved back across the river and concentrated on the edge of the plateau facing Inniskilling Hill. On the 26th it was decided to attack the high ground where the railway turned north—Inniskilling and Railway Hills on the left, and Pieter's Hill on the right, these positions being allotted respectively to Norcott's, Walter Kitchener's, and Barton's brigades. The three brigades were to cross by a bridge under the north end of Hlangwane, and to attack in echelon—Barton leading off at Pieter's Hill. Once again Buller had recourse to a frontal attack, but it was now an attack on a broad front carried out by large forces, and supported by a great weight of artillery in excellent tactical formation; moreover, it was an attack against an enemy whose *moral* had been grievously weakened, while that of the British was raised as they went into action by news of Cronje's surrender.

Barton's brigade—Scots, Irish, and Dublin Fusiliers—crossed the bridge at 10.30 a.m. on the 27th, turned to the right, and moved in single file along the foot of the slopes, till at noon they were formed for the attack below Pieter's Hill. On the right were the Scots Fusiliers, on the left the Irish Fusiliers, each with three companies in the firing-line, while the Dublins were in support. The attack was to pivot on the left, swing round and occupy the long hill which extended for nearly a mile northwards, while the Scots Fusiliers were also to send companies to the right in case of an attack from the direction of Eagle's Nest. At first all went well, for the fire from south of the Tugela had cleared the slopes. After a steep climb of nearly five hundred feet, the troops reached the crest, and the Irish Fusiliers captured the nearest kopjes, though galled by the fire from Railway Hill on the west. The Scots Fusiliers had farther to go, and as they raced over the plateau they were met with heavy fire from the farther kopjes on the summit, so that their line was compelled to contract, and they failed to envelop the highest kopje at the northern end. Colonel Carr

1900 fell wounded, but by 2.30 p.m. they had gained all the centre of the ridge, and prolonged the line of the Irish Fusiliers for some five hundred yards.

Then began a difficult hour. The Boers on the northern kopje, having been now reinforced, kept up a heavy enfilading fire. Moreover, the British guns seemed to be occupied with Railway and Inniskilling Hills, and the only artillery support for Pieter's came from Monte Cristo. It was clear that the northern kopje must be taken, so Barton's brigade-major, Captain McBean, got together one company of the Scots and three of the Dublins, whom he led to the assault. Over the bullet-swept plateau the little force worked its way; but, after all the officers but one had been wounded, the advance came to a halt in a donga three hundred yards from the kopje. The brigade was bearing single-handed the whole brunt of the action.

But relief was not long in coming. Walter Kitchener's brigade began its advance up Railway Hill a little after three p.m., and the men of Lancashire and Yorkshire within two hours had swept the enemy from that position. At five p.m. Norcott attacked and captured Inniskilling Hill. There remained now only the northern kopje of Pieter's. At six p.m. three companies of the Irish Fusiliers carried its southern end, with a loss of a third of their number, and all their officers killed or wounded. There they dug themselves in, and at midnight found that the enemy had gone. It was the end of the Boer stand on the Tugela. Buller next day from the top of Railway Hill saw the retreat streaming north and west across the plateau, but he made no attempt to interfere. Dundonald with his brigade was feeling his way forward, and in the dusk of that day he forded the Klip River and rode into Ladysmith. Sir George White and his sick and famished garrison, who for 118 days had kept the flag flying, were now re-united with their countrymen. The first message from the town after the relief was received about midnight by the signalling sergeant of the Scots Fusiliers.

The fight at Pieter's Hill was, for our regiment, the

costliest since Inkerman. Barton's brigade had most casualties of the three engaged in the attack, and of these the Scots Fusiliers had nearly half. Among the killed were Captains V. Lewis and H. S. Sykes, Lieutenants Simpson and Onract, and twenty-four non-commissioned officers and men. Colonel Carr, Captains A. Hull and E. E. Blaine, Lieutenant C. H. I. Jackson, Second Lieutenants Metaxa and H. C. Fraser, and sixty non-commissioned officers and men were wounded. In General Buller's dispatch Colonel Carr, Captain Lewis, and Captain Hull were specially mentioned for gallant conduct, and Sergeant-Major J. Steele[1] for saving the life of Colonel Carr under fire. The ten weeks of assault on the Tugela bastion had done much to educate Britain in the principles of modern war, but the lesson had been learned at a high cost. Reputations had been shattered—the reputations of those "who applied to a whole army, and against serious opponents, the same methods that they had been accustomed to apply to small columns in little wars against tactical inferiors." But one reputation had not been impaired—the repute of the British rank-and-file, whether inside or outside Ladysmith, for disciplined valour and patience under the most grievous trials. After Colenso the old President believed that God had given his people a final victory, as when, sixty-one years before, they had routed the hordes of Dingaan. But the great man who commanded the burghers on the Tugela heights thought differently. In the very moment of that triumph Louis Botha realized that the war was lost—when, as he afterwards said, he saw the British soldier, mishandled and misled, advancing stolidly to death with unshaken discipline.

II

With the relief of Ladysmith closed the first stage in the campaign—the stage of the Boer invasion. The

[1] Now Lieutenant-Colonel Steele, in charge of Royal Military Hospital, Dublin.

1900 second, the steady crumbling of the Boer field army and the British occupation of the republics, lasted till the occupation of Koomati Poort in October. While Roberts was moving on Bloemfontein, the Scots Fusiliers, with the rest of the 6th Brigade, were stationed in and around Ladysmith. On 3rd March they took part in the triumphant entry into the town, E Company leading, and Major W. A. Young in command of the battalion; on the 6th they were reviewed by General Barton and thanked for their services; next day Major Scudamore rejoined the battalion from India; and on the 18th the first of the volunteer service companies— three officers and 110 non-commissioned officers and men—arrived from Scotland. It was not till April that orders arrived for a move to Cape Colony—the 5th and 6th Brigades having been formed into the Tenth Division, under the command of Sir Archibald Hunter.

Cape Town was reached on the 18th, and before the end of the month the Scots Fusiliers were in the Kimberley neighbourhood, where they obtained a substantial draft from home. On 1st May Roberts began his march northwards towards the Transvaal, and Methuen's and Hunter's divisions formed the left wing. But Hunter had a subsidiary task to accomplish, which at the time was followed by the world more eagerly than any other part of the campaign. Since 13th October the little garrison of Mafeking, under the cheerful and unwearying leadership of Colonel Baden-Powell, had held out against superior enemy forces. Colonel Plumer was now moving south from Rhodesia to its relief, and Hunter detailed a flying column under Colonel Mahon to operate from the south. The column was some 1,200 strong, composed mainly of irregular horse, but with 100 picked men from the Fusilier battalions, of whom our regiment furnished 24. Corporal W. Hunter of the Scots Fusiliers has left an account of that "hussar-ride," which involved heavy marches against time on short rations, but little serious fighting. On the 17th they entered the little town, where the honest corporal

THE TRANSVAAL ENTERED

was thrilled by the sight of Baden-Powell, who had become to the world a hero of legend. 1900

Meantime the rest of the battalion was moving north with Hunter. On 4th May they were in action at Rooidam, driving the enemy before them along the line of the Vaal. On the 6th they shared in the capture

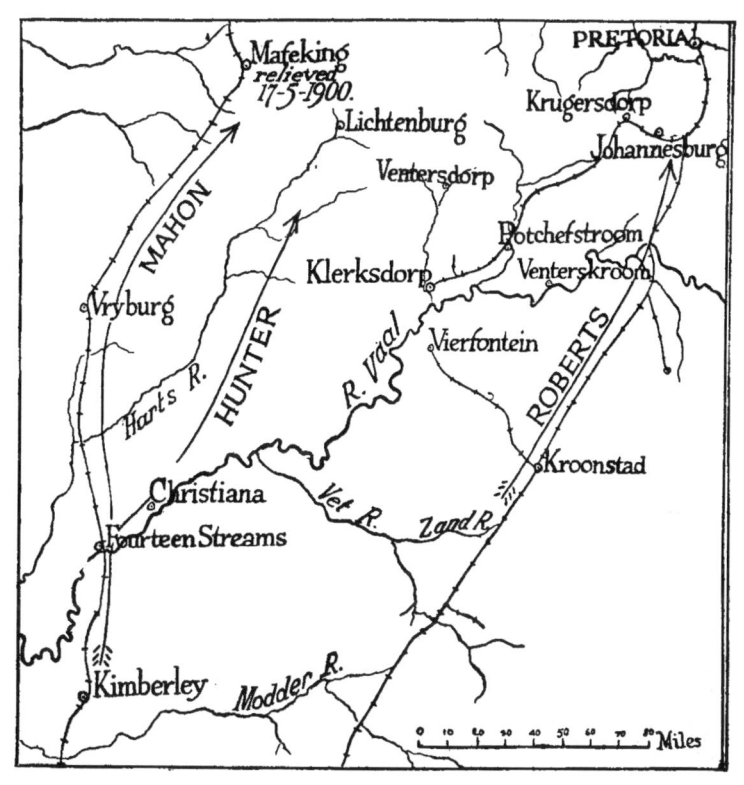

THE ADVANCE ON PRETORIA

of Fourteen Streams, and on the 15th they were the first British regiment to cross the Transvaal border. Next day their pipers played Hunter into Christiana. On the 12th Roberts had occupied Kroonstad, and on the 28th, by proclamation, the Orange Free State was annexed to the British Crown. Two days later, President Kruger fled to Waterval Boven on the eastern

1900 frontier. On the last day of the month Johannesburg fell, and on 5th June Roberts entered Pretoria, freeing some 3,000 British prisoners, among them six officers and 39 non-commissioned officers and men of the Scots Fusiliers who had been captured at Colenso.

The battalion was then at Lichtenburg, and on the 9th a detachment of the Scots Fusiliers, under Lieutenant-Colonel Carr, left that town for Potchefstroom. It will be remembered that in the war of 1881 a British flag had been solemnly buried at Pretoria, but had been dug up by the order of Colonel Gildea, then commanding the 2nd Royal Scots Fusiliers, who took it home with him to England.[1] When the battalion left for South Africa in 1899 his widow sent the flag to Colonel Carr, who saw General Buller on the subject and secured his promise that he would endeavour to have it hoisted at Pretoria. After the surrender of Christiana, General Hunter suggested that the flag, which was carried with the battalion, should be hoisted at Potchefstroom in memory of the Fusiliers' famous defence of that place in the previous war. Accordingly the flag was brought from Lichtenburg with a guard of honour, and on 15th June was hoisted at the old fort amid wild enthusiasm.

By the end of the month the battalion was at Krugersdorp, of which place Colonel Carr was appointed commandant. The fighting now was principally in the eastern Transvaal against Botha and Delarey, and against the ubiquitous De Wet in the western Transvaal and the northern Free State. During July our regiment remained at Krugersdorp, where regimental mounted infantry was raised, under the command of an officer whose name was in after years to become famous, Captain H. M. Trenchard. In August D and E Companies were detached to form part of Methuen's column, and, led by Captain A. C. H. Macgregor, gave a good account of themselves in the action at Venterskroom. The following month the battalion was for four days with Barton's column, but took no part in any operations. That month, September, saw

[1] See page 249.

the end of the second stage of the campaign, for Roberts occupied Koomati Poort, and President Kruger sailed for Europe. The Boer generals had resolved to continue the struggle, but to change its character—to make it a guerilla war, in which their superior mobility would puzzle and paralyse the slower army machine of Britain. Such a policy was certain to import a new bitterness into the contest on both sides, and certain, too, to succeed at the start. When Lord Roberts returned home he left to his successor, Lord Kitchener, a new and as yet unsolved problem of war.

1900

On 25th October the formal annexation of the Transvaal was proclaimed in Pretoria, and in the review Roberts had designated the right of the guard of honour for the Scots Fusiliers and their historic flag. But only a few could be present, for at the moment the battalion was heavily engaged, the flag was with the battalion headquarters, and the railway was cut. We must recount the action of Frederikstad, the principal engagement of our regiment after the conclusion of the Natal campaign.

At the beginning of October Barton was at Krugersdorp, watching the railway line which ran by Potchefstroom to Klerksdorp; Methuen was in Rustenburg, Clements in the Magaliesberg, and Hart at Potchefstroom. Barton had a big area to guard, and it had the disadvantage that it was within easy striking distance of the northern Free State where Christian de Wet and his merry men were active. On 5th October Barton left Krugersdorp with the Scots and the Welch Fusiliers, 500 mounted troops, a field battery, three pom-poms, and a naval gun. He moved slowly southwest along the railway, through the range of low hills known as the Gatsrand. On the 6th at Mulder's Drift there was a brush with a roving commando, when the volunteer company of the Scots Fusiliers acquitted itself well. After that every day brought its skirmish, the bulk of the fighting falling on the Welch Fusiliers and the Scottish Yeomanry. On the 17th the village of Frederikstad was reached, and a halt was

1900 made. Frederikstad stood in a bare valley down which the railway ran beside the Mooi River. It was evident that the enemy was in the neighbourhood in considerable numbers, for foraging parties were frequently attacked, and occasionally cut off.

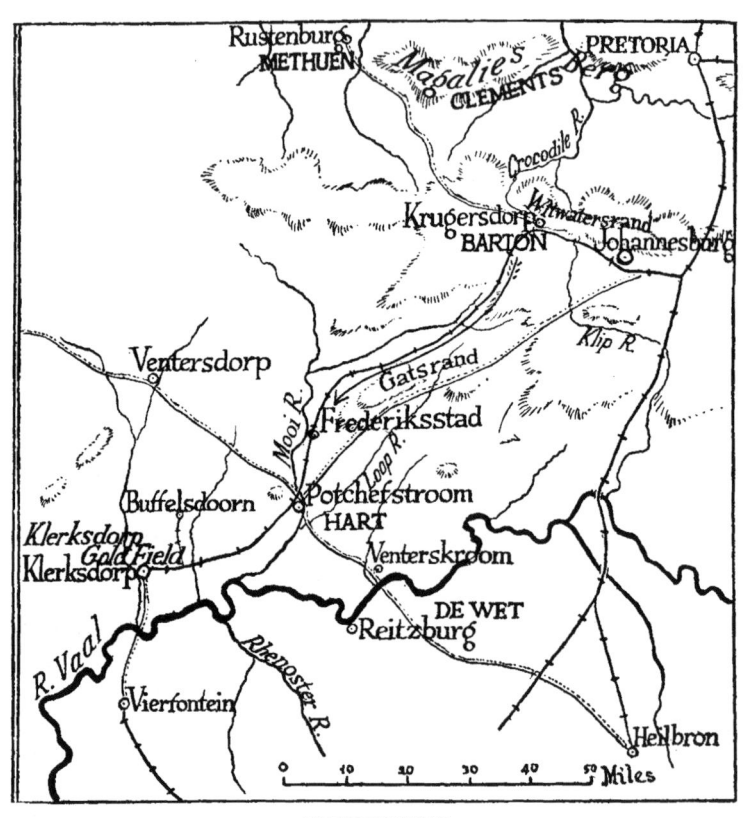

FREDERIKSTAD

On the 19th the scouts reported the advance of a large enemy column from the direction of the Vaal. The glasses showed that they were Boers; and presently it was known that it was Christian de Wet himself, who had been lying quiet for two months in the Free State, and now, with 2,000 men, was on the look-out for an isolated British force to destroy. Barton's seemed to offer the chance he sought, and in a very little while the Boers were dismounted and attacking, covered by the fire of their guns.

The British were taken by surprise, but they had already made light trenches and were able to hold on till darkness, when they could improve their defences. For the next six days the fighting continued, the Boer cordon being drawn closer, while De Wet felt for a weak point on which to deliver his final assault. On the morning of 25th October the Scots Fusiliers held a ridge south of the Mooi, while Barton with the rest of his force lay to the north of the stream. Between the two was the river and the railway line, the latter with adjoining ditches which Boer snipers had managed to occupy. This meant that water could not be fetched from the Mooi for beasts or men except under the attentions of their marksmen. Either Barton must move his position or have the ditches cleared. At noon detachments of the Welch and Scots Fusiliers advanced in open order to attempt the task. A and F Companies of the latter came at once under the enemy fire, and Captain Baillie fell dead. Captain Dick then led them across the mile of open veld under heavy fire, and fell himself, seriously wounded. Nevertheless the ditches were reached, while the Welch Fusiliers closed in from the other side. The Boer snipers did not await the bayonet charge, and they now paid the penalty of their daring, for they had no means of escape except across the open. " A black running mob," wrote an observer, " carrying coats, blankets, boots, rifles, etc., was seen to rise as if from nowhere, and rush as fast as they could, dropping the various things they carried as they ran." Rifles and shrapnel played upon their flight; thirty fell dead, thirty more were wounded, thirty gave themselves up as prisoners—some in their confusion even rushing into the British hospital and surrendering to the doctor.

Barton that day had received reinforcements, and De Wet realized that his bolt was shot. He promptly withdrew in his usual masterly fashion, and recrossed the Vaal—not, however, without suffering from the attentions of Charles Knox and De Lisle. Barton, who had ample mounted troops to harass his retreat, seems to have underrated the blow he had inflicted on the enemy, for instead of pursuing he only strengthened his defences. In the action of Frederikstad the Scots Fusiliers had Captain Baillie, Lieutenant Finch, and eleven non-commissioned officers and men killed, while Captains Dick and Trenchard, Second Lieutenants Bruce and Elliot, and thirty-six non-commissioned officers and men were wounded. On the evening of the 25th Barton issued this order : " The G.O.C. desires to thank the Royal Artillery, the 2nd Royal Scots Fusiliers, and the 1st Royal Welch Fusiliers for the excellent services rendered by them to-day. The gallantry with which the men of the above battalions drove the enemy from their strong positions and followed them up is deserving of the highest praise, and accords with the highest traditions of these distinguished regiments."

III

With Frederikstad the drama of the war closes for our regiment. After that came the first tentative struggles of the British command to cope with the guerilla methods of the enemy ; then, in the spring of 1901, the inauguration of the blockhouse system by Kitchener, and the not very successful device of small punitive columns ; and lastly, with 1902, the systematic " driving " of large areas, which brought about the surrender of the Boer remnant and peace on 31st May of that year. The Scots Fusiliers no longer participated as a unit in any large operations. Odd companies joined this or that column or formed detached posts, while their officers were employed on every kind of special duty. Till the close of 1900 the regiment was in the Frederikstad or Johannesburg areas. For the first five months of 1901 it was at Johannesburg, where Colonel Carr was appointed to the general command of the troops and of the adjacent lines of communication. On June it went east to Nelspruit and the feverish lowlands of the Crocodile valley, where it was split up on line-of-communication work, and where it remained till early in November. The bulk of it then joined Colonel Mackenzie's column at Brugs Spruit, while two companies were stationed at Middelburg. In December it was operating in the Carolina district, and in January 1902 was with General Bruce Hamilton in Ermelo, marching on one occasion thirty-five miles in sixteen hours, and being specially thanked by Lord Kitchener. In March it rejoined Mackenzie's column at Wakkerstroom, and in that difficult eastern country it remained till the proclamation of peace. In September Colonel Carr completed his period of service, and was succeeded by Major W. A. Young. In December, owing mainly to Colonel Carr's efforts, permission was finally granted to the regiment to wear again a white plume on the right side of their Fusilier caps.[1] In February 1903 the Scots Fusiliers returned to England.

The 2nd Battalion had won two new honours for the colours—" Relief of Ladysmith " and " South Africa, 1899–1900." It had played a distinguished part in some of the hardest fighting of the campaign, and it had learned lessons of war which were to stand it in good stead in a sterner conflict. In the three years of war its total casualties were 7 officers and 114 non-commissioned officers and men killed in action or dead of wounds or disease, and 12 officers and 143 non-commissioned officers and men wounded. The volunteer service company, which joined it after the Relief of Ladysmith, served continuously with it till after Frederikstad, and then for seven months was on garrison duty. A further volunteer draft, consisting of one officer and twenty-three non-commissioned officers and men, joined the battalion at Middelburg in March 1902, and continued with it till the end of the war.

Its South African doings have been commemorated by various monuments. A brass tablet in St. Giles'

[1] The plume had been abolished about 1860.

1902-14 Cathedral in Edinburgh was unveiled in March 1908 by Lord Glasgow in memory of the eight officers and 119 men who fell. The fine monument at Ayr, unveiled in November 1902 by Lord Eglinton in the presence of Sir Archibald Hunter, commemorates the fallen in all the campaigns from 1879 to 1902. A tablet was placed, too, in St. Andrew's Church in Pretoria, and the Governor-General, Lord Gladstone, at the unveiling ceremony, said that " to-day, after distinguished services for two centuries, the famous old regiment maintains its high traditions of discipline, gallantry, and devotion to duty." These words were spoken in 1912, and might well be regarded as prophetic. The 2nd Battalion on its return home was, till 1905, at Aldershot, and then at Tidworth, where Lieutenant-Colonel Young was succeeded by Lieutenant-Colonel W. H. Bowes. From 1907 till 1911 it was in Dublin and Londonderry, where, in 1910, Bowes gave place to Lieutenant-Colonel D. M. Stuart, the son of Ramsay Stuart of Crimean days. In the autumn of 1912 the battalion moved to Gosport, and thence, in January 1914, to Gibraltar. In August there broke upon the world the challenge of the Great War.

CHAPTER XIV

THE GREAT WAR—1914

Causes of the War—Recruiting in Scotland—The 1st Battalion at Mons—The retreat—Le Cateau—The First Battle of the Marne—The Aisne—The race to the sea—The First Battle of Ypres—The 2nd Battalion destroyed—The attack of the Prussian Guard—The first winter in the trenches.

I

THE murder of the Archduke Francis Ferdinand and his wife at Serajevo on June 28, 1914, was the spark which fired in Europe the hidden magazines of strife. These magazines had been long accumulating. For twenty years there had been growing a sense of insecurity: all the Great Powers were restless and suspicious; and in one Power—Germany—this *malaise* had advanced to such a pitch that, between ambition and nervousness, she had come to consider seriously the possibility of some bold stroke which would put her beyond the reach of rivalry and menace. If such a stroke were delayed, the growing wealth of Russia and the increasing military strength of France might soon remove the opportunity for ever. The Bosnian murder gave Austria a chance of checking the movement towards unity of the Slav peoples in the Balkans. Germany, for her own reasons, supported Austria's ultimatum; Russia interfered on behalf of Serbia, and mobilized her southern armies. Within three weeks after Serajevo the situation had passed beyond the control of human reason, though every attempt was made

1914

1914 by the statesmen of western Europe, and notably by the British Foreign Secretary, Sir Edward Grey, to limit the quarrel. Germany blocked the way, for she had no desire for a peaceful settlement. She induced Austria to refuse all mediation; and presently, after a peremptory request to the Tsar to demobilize, she declared war upon Russia. Russia and France were allies, and war with France followed naturally within twenty-four hours.

Such is the formal statement of the outbreak of one of the great cataclysms in the history of the world. Behind lay a thousand subtle tendencies and dim causes which this is not the place to analyse. In that feverish month of July 1914 all things were obscure except the momentous fact that war had come, that Germany had been a principal agent in its coming, and that Germany was ready and willing to embark on a campaign of conquest which would submerge the traditional liberties of western Europe, since she fought avowedly for domination. The position of Britain was delicate in the extreme. She had no formal alliance with France, she had barely considered the possibility of a European war, and she was in the highest degree averse from meddling in a quarrel in which she had no direct concern. She might well have hesitated till it was too late to act with effect, or have blundered into some foolish compromise. From such a fate she was saved by Belgium. The German scheme of attack on France was based upon a sudden invasion from the north, and for that a march through Belgium was imperative. The neutrality of Belgium had long before been guaranteed by all the Great Powers; but Germany argued that her necessity must override the law of nations, and demanded a passage. This was heroically refused. The invasion of Belgium accordingly began on Sunday, 2nd August, and the outrage determined the policy of the British Government and the British people.

The main weapon of Britain was her navy, by far the strongest in the world. After that came her wealth and her great manufacturing capacity, by which she could supply the munitions of war required both for her own forces and for those of her allies. If her navy could dominate the seas, then her commerce could go on as before, while that of Germany would cease, and her troops and those of her allies could be moved about the world at her pleasure. " He who commands the sea," Francis Bacon said long ago, " hath great freedom." She had no large military force to throw at once into the conflict, such as the armies of France and Russia. Her small regular army was little more than a garrison for her oversea dominions, and her Territorial force was nominally 300,000 strong and intended for home defence. But Lord Haldane, when Secretary for War, had foreseen the possibility of a Continental struggle, and had prepared plans by which an expeditionary force of about 100,000 men could be placed in a very short time on the Continent of Europe. This force was, for its size, probably the most expert army in the world. It took its place on the left of the French line, and, though small in comparison with the mighty levy of France, it was fated to play a leading part in the first decisive battles.

To many British statesmen, and even to one or two soldiers, it seemed in August 1914 that the war would be as short as it had been sudden. This was not the view of Lord Kitchener, the new Secretary for War, nor was it the view of the British people at large. Instinctively, and quite independent of guidance from the Government, they prepared themselves for a long and desperate struggle. Every item of the regular army, every unit of the Territorials, all the help of the oversea Empire, it was felt would be needed. More, it was realized that, sooner or later, the whole manhood of Britain would be called upon, and that no class or occupation would be exempt from the duty. It was this almost unconscious popular realization of the magnitude of the crisis which enabled Britain to make without complaint the extremest sacrifices, to set the world an example in tenacity, and to produce in four years a land force which fought in a dozen campaigning grounds, which bore the brunt of the final fighting, and

1914 at the close of the war was perhaps the most formidable of all the Allied armies.

For a parallel to August 1914 in Scotland we must go back to the time when old and young were called to man the walls after Flodden. The way of the regulars was plain; so was the duty of the Territorials—those honest fellows who in apathetic years, with small encouragement, had prepared themselves for their country's defence. After them came the natural adventurers, those whom we call "born soldiers," and the scallywags who sought nothing better. Next followed the sober, conscientious men, like Cromwell's New Model army, who had a cause to fight for, and who took a week or two to think things over and make up their minds. Presently that "wind that scatters young men through the world" blew stronger, and thousands were gathered in who had never dreamed at the start that the call was for them, but were moved by those strange, half-conscious impulses that are far deeper than thought. No land had such a record in volunteer recruiting, and it is volunteer recruiting that is the real index to the spirit of a people. Totals under conscription depend on things like number of males, average of bodily health, and so forth, but totals of volunteers depend mainly upon seriousness of purpose and soundness of heart. Nearly half a million men enlisted in Scotland before there was any thought of compulsion.

The Royal Scots Fusiliers, whose doings we are to follow, had at the outbreak of war its two regular battalions, the 1st at Gosport and the 2nd at Gibraltar. It had its 3rd (Militia) Battalion at Ayr. Attached to it were the two Territorial battalions of Regimental District No. 21—the 1st with its headquarters at Kilmarnock, and the 2nd with its headquarters at Ayr.[1]

[1] A note may be added on the Volunteer battalions of the regiment. There was a general muster of the fencibles of Cunningham in August 1715 to resist Mar's rising in the north, and the Kilmarnock men marched to the defence of Glasgow. They afterwards garrisoned the house of Gartartan in Perthshire (see M'Kay's *History of Kilmarnock*). In December 1745 the town of Ayr produced 346 volunteers for a burgh guard, and a company was sent to Glasgow (Paterson's *History of Ayrshire*, Vol. I.). In the Napoleonic wars Kilmarnock raised two volunteer companies. When, towards the close of 1859,

THE NEW BATTALIONS

From these were formed the 4th and 5th Battalions, *1914* who were the earliest, apart from the regulars, to take the field. Meantime the call for the new service army had gone abroad, and units were in process of creation through the sunny autumn months of 1914. To their ranks came the same type of men as had served in the Scots Fusiliers for two hundred years—the miners and industrial workers of Ayr and Renfrew, the farm-labourers and shepherds of Renfrew, Ayr, and Galloway, and youths of all classes and occupations from the cities and burghs of the West of Scotland. The continuity of a regimental type is as marvellous a thing as the prepotence of a regimental tradition, for the men of the new battalions recalled both in appearance and temperament the historic " Fusilier Jock " who had been much the same whether commanded by Mar or Buchan, Marlborough or Stair, Burgoyne or Stuart, Lynedoch or Ross, Raglan or Roberts.

II

The 1st Royal Scots Fusiliers, who had only returned from South Africa in the preceding March, formed part of the 9th Infantry Brigade in the Third Division of the II. Corps. Under the command of Lieutenant-Colonel Douglas Smith, they embarked at Southampton on 13th August. The men were in the highest spirits, but to the colonel's eye the reservists, who numbered over fifty per cent. of the strength, looked a little soft. From Havre they moved to Landrecies, which they

---

the modern Volunteer movement began, Kilmarnock produced the 1st Company Ayrshire Rifle Volunteers. Next year the 1st Administrative Battalion Ayrshire Rifle Volunteers was formed, and this was split up into two in March 1873—the South Ayrshire Corps forming the 1st Administrative Battalion, with headquarters at Ayr, and the North Ayrshire the 2nd, with headquarters at Kilmarnock. In June 1880 the numbers were transposed; the 2nd Battalion became the 1st Ayrshire Rifle Volunteers, and in December 1887 was designated the 1st Volunteer Battalion the Royal Scots Fusiliers, and authorized to wear the uniform of the regiment with volunteer distinctions. In the South African War the battalion was represented by 94 of all ranks. The old 1st Battalion had the same history, becoming in 1887 the 2nd Volunteer Battalion the Royal Scots Fusiliers. Two officers and 62 men from it served in South Africa. See Grierson's *Records of the Scottish Volunteer Force*, 1859-1908 (Blackwood, 1909).

1914
Aug. 17–23

reached on the 17th, and on the 21st the 9th Brigade had its outposts overlooking the old battlefield of Malplaquet, where two of its battalions, the Lincolns and the Royal Scots Fusiliers, had fought under Marlborough two hundred years before. On the 22nd the battalion marched to Ghlin, some two miles north of Jemappes, and was then withdrawn south of the Condé Canal, which was held by the II. Corps. The country consisted of flat, marshy meadows, mining villages, and a network of railway lines. The 9th Brigade held the six miles of the canal bank from the bridge of Nimy to the bridge of Mariette—in order from right to left, the 4th Royal Fusiliers, the 1st Royal Scots Fusiliers, and the 1st Northumberland Fusiliers. Our regiment had the Jemappes section, the scene of Dumouriez' victory over the Austrians when the armies of the Revolution invaded Belgium. That Saturday afternoon Lanrezac, on the British right, was being hard pressed at Charleroi, and the right wing of Kluck's great march was wheeling round in the north to overwhelm the British. But as yet Sir John French knew little of what was happening. Our cavalry had been in touch with the enemy north of the canal, but could not guess at his numbers, and the men of the II. Corps went to sleep in happy ignorance that eight German divisions were marching against the two which were extended thinly in a chain of groups along a front of thirteen miles.

Sunday, the 23rd, opened in mist and rain, which presently cleared to a hot August morning. The bells were ringing in the villages, and the inhabitants were going to church in their best clothes, holiday trains were running into Mons, and in that homely, industrious country war seemed an incredible thing. But as early as six a.m. a German cavalry patrol approached within five hundred yards of our position, and one of them was killed by machine-gun fire from the Scots Fusiliers, and identified as belonging to the 9th Corps. The battalion had outposts north of the canal, and its main position, which had been strengthened with barricades, on the south bank—B and C Companies (Captains

Rose and Innes) on the right, A Company and battalion headquarters in the centre at Jemappes, and D Company (Captain Tullis) on the left. About 10.30 a.m. the German guns opened in earnest, and about eleven the German 9th Corps began its attack on the British Third Division.

The enemy's infantry in great strength advanced from the cover of Ghlin wood, east of Baudour, in a south-easterly direction in dense formation. "Superb target for artillery," wrote Douglas Smith in his diary, "but we had none at the moment." A portion of this force advanced direct on the position held by the Scots Fusiliers; the enemy spread out into attack formation, and, on getting within effective range of our rifles, he continued the advance by alternate rushes of small units. The forward posts north of the canal had been withdrawn, and as the Germans showed themselves they were met with a blast of rifle and machine-gun fire. The enemy checked, took shelter, came on, checked again. He got to within two hundred yards of the bridge west of Jemappes, where the accuracy of the fire of the Scots Fusiliers brought him to a standstill. But two divisions cannot stand for ever against eight, especially when those eight command a far greater strength in artillery. Enemy numbers were crossing the canal east of Obourg and converging upon Mons from north and east, and Major-General Hubert Hamilton ordered his Third Division to begin its retirement to a prepared position to the south, which would link up with the left of Sir Douglas Haig's I. Corps at Harmignies.

At 2.30 the Scots Fusiliers were ordered to fall back through Flenu to Frameries, three miles south of the canal. The retirement was effected without serious difficulty, and with remarkably few casualties. Most of the bridges were blown up behind them by the heroic exertions of the Royal Engineers, and rearguards in the innumerable little houses were able to delay the German advance with rifle and machine-gun fire. Only on the battalion's right was there any mishap. The Jemappes bridge could not be destroyed in time, and the enemy followed too close for comfort, so that all the way to Frameries there was sharp fighting among the slag heaps and cottages. The enemy used his machine guns with great skill, and since the ground was not favourable for the co-operation of artillery, and the Scots Fusiliers were heavily outnumbered, B Company was in serious danger, till the arrival of the supporting companies of the Northumberland Fusiliers allowed it to extricate itself and re-form. There fell two gallant officers of the company, Captains T. A. Rose and John Erskine Young, the story of whose prowess may still be heard from the peasants of Flenu and Jemappes, and some 100 other ranks were killed and wounded.[1]

That night the battalion was billeted in the brewery north of Frameries, and slept in peace. Its first part in the campaign had been most creditably played, for against heavy odds it had completed a dogged and—to the enemy—a costly retirement.[2] But it was mainly a series of merciful chances—Kluck's overestimate of the strength of the British resistance and the absence of Marwitz's cavalry—that enabled French's 70,000 men and 300 guns to check the 160,000 Germans with their 600 guns. For by that Sunday evening the position had become very desperate. At five p.m. Sir John French heard from Joffre of the defeat at Charleroi and the fall of Namur; he learned, too, that Lanrezac's Fifth Army was already a day's march to his rear, that Kluck was attacking with two or three times the force originally estimated, and that he lay alone in face of an enemy more than twice his strength. The only course was to hold on till nightfall, give his men a brief rest, and begin a fighting retreat southward at

---

[1] An interesting letter by an Englishwoman then in Jemappes, describing the stand of the Scots Fusiliers, was published in the *Daily News* of January 10, 1919.

[2] Hauptmann Heubner of the German 20th Regiment witnessed the fight of the Scots Fusiliers at Jemappes, and in his book, *Unter Emmich vor Luttich, unter Kluck vor Paris*, writes: "That they in any case fought bravely and obstinately is proved by the heavy losses that our German troops suffered here."

LE CATEAU

daybreak to a position which he had already selected to retire upon, should a retirement become necessary.

On the 24th the Scots Fusiliers fell back without serious fighting through Frameries to Bermeries, and during the day the Third Division changed places with the Fifth and became the left of the II. Corps. That day had revealed to Sir John French the enemy's intention to drive him into Maubeuge, where he might well have shared the fate of Bazaine in 1870. He decided, therefore, to halt only for the one night in the Jenlain–Maubeuge position, and next day to put the Forest of Mormal behind him. On the 25th, a day of broiling heat, the British II. Corps moved by the west side of the forest in the direction of Le Cateau. All that day there was a running fight, and at nightfall Kluck's advanced troops were in contact with the Third Division. That night the Scots Fusiliers and the rest of the 9th Brigade lay at Inchy. During the day's march A and C Companies, under Major A. M. H. Forbes, which had been the vanguard, were detached under the orders of the divisional commander to form the escort to the divisional ammunition column. This involved their marching in the latter's rear, and, since it was impossible for them to rejoin the battalion that day, they attached themselves to the 19th Brigade, and arrived at Le Cateau at ten p.m. and bivouacked in the central square.

Next day saw the battle of Le Cateau, perhaps the most brilliant and least recognized exploit of the great Retreat. The Third Division—very weary after its labours of the day before—was on the ridge on the left of the Fifth, and the 9th Brigade held the line from Troisvilles westward to Audencourt. It was given just one hour to entrench. The Scots Fusiliers put B Company in the trenches, while D Company remained with the 4th Royal Fusiliers in general reserve; A and C Companies, as we have seen, had been detached. The 9th Brigade had, on the whole, an easy time in the action which began at seven a.m., for it had a good position with a clear field of fire, and the awkward salient on its left at Caudry deflected the enemy's attention. The two detached companies, A and C, had the biggest share in the fight, for they were with the 19th Brigade (which was all Smith-Dorrien had in the way of reserves), and were used to check the flanking movement on the right. The battle had been entered upon by the British commander because he could not help himself; because he saw that if he was to bring off his corps he must first turn and strike. About one p.m. it was clear to him that it was time to leave, for the Fifth Division on his right was in deadly danger, and Kluck's 9th Corps might at any moment arrive. What followed need not be retold in detail. Orders could not reach many of the units, who remained in the trenches, and so protected the retirement of the rest; but under cover of the devoted artillery most of the infantry quietly withdrew from the field. Before the sun set the II. Corps was tramping over the belt of low upland in which the streams of Scheldt and Sambre take their rise, and on the morning of the 27th it halted north of St. Quentin, where the land begins to fall to the Oise. The chief miracle of the Retreat had been accomplished.

The Scots Fusiliers, who had suffered little that day—their casualties were only three wounded—formed the rear-guard of their brigade. The rest of the retreat was hard and anxious marching, but, so far as they were concerned, without harassment from the enemy. On the 27th, after an hour's halt at Villaret, they reached Vermand, where they bivouacked, and, starting again at midnight, were at Ham by the next noon. That day the two halves of the British force, which had been separated at Le Cateau, were reunited. On the 29th the Scots Fusiliers crossed the Aisne, and on the 31st they reached Vauciennes. On 3rd September they crossed the Marne at Meaux, and on the 5th they were at Liverdy, half-way between that river and the Seine. There Captain Boyle arrived with reinforcements, and the battalion took stock, finding that its casualties had been less than it had feared, and that it now mustered some 800 strong. "For the British troops the ten days of the retreat had been like a moving picture seen through a haze of weariness and confusion: blazing days among the coal heaps and grimy villages of Hainault, which reminded our north countrymen of Lancashire and Durham; nights of aching travel on upland roads through the fields of beet and grain; dawns that broke over slow streams and grassy valleys upon eyes blind with lack of sleep; the cool beech woods of Compiègne; the orchards of Ourcq and Marne, now heavy with plum and cherry."

On 6th September the retreating armies turned, and the First Battle of the Marne began, perhaps the greatest, because the most significant, contest of the war. The British army played an important but minor part, for the victory was won by Maunoury on the Ourcq, by Foch in Champagne, and by Castelnau far to the east at Nancy. Smith-Dorrien's II. Corps formed the centre of the British advance, and that night was close on the Grand Morin. Next day the Scots Fusiliers were in touch with the German rear-guards at Orly, and had twenty-four casualties. On the 9th they crossed the Marne at Nanteuil, where their neighbouring battalion, the Lincolns, had a hard fight with a German battery, which they captured. By that evening, though they did not know it, the battle had been won, and the enemy was everywhere in feverish retreat. The 9th Brigade was now the vanguard of its corps, and on the 10th the Scots Fusiliers and the Royal Fusiliers, after much stiff woodland fighting at Vinly and Veuilly la Potière, made a great haul of prisoners. After that for a day or two there were no engagements, and an ugly suspicion dawned on our men that the enemy had escaped. Odd batches of Germans were beaten up in the woods, but there were no signs of a great army. On the 12th the Scots Fusiliers and the Lincolns were ordered to clear Braisne, and found it deserted. They were now looking down the Vesle towards the Aisne valley, with its low wooded bluffs on the farther bank.

1914
Sept. 13–14

From these heights next day they had news of the missing enemy.

Sunday, 13th September, was to see the end of open warfare and the beginning of that stabilization of the battle-line which endured for the better part of four years. The British advanced guards attempted the passage of the Aisne, only to find an enemy most skilfully entrenched and assisted by a mass of heavy artillery. The main German position was on the crest of the plateau north of the stream, at an average distance from it of two miles. A more perfect position could not be found, for it commanded all the crossings of the river and most of the roads on the south bank: even if the Allies crossed, the outjutting spurs gave excellent opportunities for an enfilading fire; moreover, the blindness of the crests made it almost impossible to detect and shell the German trenches, even if the proper guns had been present for that purpose. The British II. Corps, with which we are concerned, attempted the section between Vailly and Missy, and to the Third Division was allotted the Vailly bridge. The 8th Brigade led the crossing at Vailly; but it was late in the afternoon before its first battalions made the passage and pushed their outposts as far as Vauxelles. The 9th Brigade crossed in the darkness, and the position on the morning of the 14th was that the 8th and 9th Brigades were on the north bank, with the 7th Brigade still at Braisne, and the only means of communication a single-plank footway.

On the 14th the general advance began, when the main force was to cross to support its outposts. The chief offensive was the work of Haig's I. Corps, which gave the British an entrenched position on the plateau. The II. Corps had a more intricate and less successful day. Its Third Division had two brigades on the north bank—the 9th on the right, and the 8th on the left—and its orders were to continue the advance. The 8th Brigade climbed slowly up the Jouy spur, while the 9th moved out of Vailly to the spurs north-east of the village, which the Lincolns and the Royal Fusiliers

THE AISNE

secured. There, about 7.30 a.m., the Germans, whose trenches were less than six hundred yards distant, opened a heavy attack, covered by artillery and machine guns. The Northumberland Fusiliers were sent up on the left of the Royal Fusiliers, and the three battalions were ordered to continue their advance. It was very necessary to gain ground here, since, so long as the enemy held the spurs above Vailly, he could burst shells accurately on the pontoon bridge. About nine a.m. came a counter-attack on the 8th Brigade at Jouy, and it was driven back; while the 9th Brigade, fighting its way out of the dripping woods in a thick fog, came into some fields of beet, where it encountered a devastating artillery and machine-gun fire. It attempted to entrench; but its right battalion, the Lincolns, had to retire, and this compelled the whole brigade to fall back. The Scots Fusiliers, the brigade reserve, were ordered up in support, and A and D Companies advanced in aid of the Lincolns, and B and C Companies to reinforce the Northumberland Fusiliers. In the open ground they met the same withering blast of enfilading machine-gun fire, and, after struggling on waist-deep in the muddy roots, were also forced back with heavy losses, their gallant leader, Captain G. C. Briggs, being killed.

The situation was critical, for the 9th Brigade was the extreme right of the II. Corps, and between it and the I. Corps was a gap of nearly two miles. Had the enemy advanced in force he could have cut the British army in two. Colonel Douglas Smith rode back to ask for artillery support, but the British guns could not find the German position, so he collected fifty or sixty men of A and D Companies and sent them up the spur again. Reinforcements, however, were on their way. By one p.m. the 1st Wiltshires of the 7th Brigade had crossed the river, and by 3.30 the Irish Rifles had joined them, both in support of the 9th Brigade. With this accession of strength the brigade was able to maintain its position on the spur, and before nightfall General Hubert Hamilton had his division compactly and safely

1914
Sept. 14

1914
Sept. 15-26

posted on the north shore. It had been a heavy day, for the 9th Brigade had lost between 600 and 700 men, while the casualties of the Scots Fusiliers were 8 killed, 67 wounded, and 90 missing. The 14th saw the only serious action of the battalion during the Aisne battle. On the 15th it was in defensive line behind the Northumberland Fusiliers, working hard at its trenches, while all day German shells rained on Vailly. There were enemy counter-attacks, which were beaten off, and Vailly bridge was made passable for traffic. That day it was clear to General Joffre and Sir John French that it was no longer a question of pursuit, but of a "methodical attack, using every means at our disposal, and consolidating each position in turn as it was gained." The day of deadlock and trench warfare had dawned. For the next week the diary of the Scots Fusiliers had nothing to record except heavy artillery fire and the repulse of small attacks. On the 19th a draft arrived from home; on the evening of the 20th they were withdrawn from the line for two days—the first rest they had received since they left England. General Smith-Dorrien and General Hamilton visited them in their billets, and expressed their admiration of their work in the past week. On the 26th they were back again in the line at Vailly, to the west of the town, with D Company in the Sugar Factory, losing a man or two each day from the steady bombardment of the German 8-in. howitzers. The British army had had its baptism in a new and nerve-racking form of warfare, and had faced it with its traditional fortitude. "The soldiers astonished even those who had trained them by their staunchness, their patience, their indomitable cheerfulness under incessant hardships, and, in spite of a fire which no human being had ever before experienced, by their calm, cool courage at all times. Whether it was the gunner unloading ammunition almost too hot to handle in the midst of blazing wagons; the engineer repairing his bridge under continuous fire; the infantryman patiently enduring heavy shell fire, patrolling no-man's-

THE RACE TO THE SEA

land in the hours of darkness, or, as sniper, lying all night on soaking clay in dripping beet-fields; the transport driver guiding his wagons through bursting shells; or the stretcher-bearer toiling through the dark hours to rescue the wounded—all alike proved themselves worthy soldiers of the King." [1]

1914
Oct. 1-6

On 1st October the French Commander-in-Chief accepted Sir John French's proposal to move the British army to the extreme Allied left. The " race to the sea " had already begun, for since 16th September Joffre had been extending his line to the west, and the Germans had replied by enlarging their right to conform, till by the end of the month the battle front stretched far into Picardy. When, on 2nd October, the Scots Fusiliers moved out of the trenches preparatory to their journey to the north, the British army thought not of defence but of attack, and believed that it was about to turn the enemy's right flank. Antwerp had not yet fallen, and it was hoped to hold the line of the Scheldt from Antwerp to Tournai, continuing southwest by Douai to Arras, and so strike at the enemy communications through Mons and Valenciennes. But by 6th October, when it was clear that Antwerp would fall, this plan was replaced by a second. The Belgian army, covered by Rawlinson's British force, would retire by Bruges and Ghent to the line of the Yser, to protect the Allied left; Lille and La Bassée would be held by the Allies, and the British, pivoting on the latter place, would swing south-eastward, isolate the German army of Antwerp, and threaten the northern communications of the vast German front between Tournai and the Aisne heights. To this scheme the Germans sought to oppose a counter-offensive which would give them Calais and the Channel ports; and to succeed, they must be first through the sally-port between La Bassée and the sea. For both sides it was a race to the salt water. The race was won by the British; but they were too late to win the points

---

[1] *Official History of the Great War:* Vol. I., *Military Operations, France and Belgium,* 1914, page 410.

1914
Oct. 11–16

on which depended their offensive strategy, and in the gap of West Flanders they were to be condemned to fight the most stubborn and critical defensive battle in their records.

In the first weeks of October the northern limit of Maud'huy's French Tenth Army was the highway between Lille and Béthune, with Conneau's French 2nd Cavalry Corps protecting its flanks. On 11th October Smith-Dorrien with the British II. Corps was on the line of the canal between Aire and Béthune. Sir John French's plan at this time was for Smith-Dorrien to make a rapid dash upon La Bassée and Lille; and for that purpose he was directed to move east on the 12th against the line Laventie–Lorgies, to threaten the flank of the Germans in La Bassée and compel them to fall back lest they should be cut off between the British and Maud'huy. " We seem to be well round the German right flank," Douglas Smith noted in his diary, " and ought to be able to roll it up." On the 12th the movement began in thick fog, the Fifth Division on the right, and the Third crossing the canal to deploy on its left. In the latter division the 7th and 8th Brigades were in the firing line, and the 9th in reserve. The enemy, however, was found to be in great strength, and the II. Corps, struggling all day through difficult country, where good gun positions were rare, made little progress. Smith-Dorrien, as a result of that day's experience, resolved to try to isolate La Bassée by wheeling to his right, pivoting on Givenchy, and to get astride the La Bassée–Lille road in the neighbourhood of Fournes.

On the 13th the wheel commenced, but it met with strong resistance. Next day the Third Division lost by shell fire its commander, Major-General Hubert Hamilton—a serious loss to the army, for he was one of the ablest and most beloved of the younger generals. Next day the division avenged its leader's death by a brilliant advance, driving the Germans from hamlet to hamlet, till it had pushed them off the Estaires–La Bassée road. On the 16th it was close on Aubers,

THE FIGHT AT HERLIES

when the Scots Fusiliers moved in support of the Lincolns. On the following day that village was taken, while late in the evening the Lincolns entered part of Herlies. There, however, the advance stopped short. Hitherto the II. Corps had been opposed chiefly by German cavalry and had made progress, but now it was faced with the wall of the new German line, the centre of the VI. Army. On the 18th at Herlies they felt the strength of it.

1914
Oct. 17-18

That day it was the turn of the Scots Fusiliers. The 7th Brigade was directed on Illies, and the 9th on Herlies, the Scots Fusiliers (with the Lincolns in reserve) having for their objective the chateau in the wood south of the latter village, some eleven hundred yards from their position. The terrain over which they had to advance was a dip, with a small farm at the bottom, and all the ground was a maze of ditches. Beyond and north of the wood the land sloped up to the La Bassée road. The Germans were entrenched with machine guns to the south, east, and west of the wood, and on the slopes to the north. The Scots Fusiliers advanced against the centre of the wood, with the 7th Brigade on their right and the Northumberland Fusiliers on their left. The attack was led by A Company under Captain S. F. A. Hurt, with B Company to the left under Captain G. Browne, and the machine guns under Lieutenant Badham between the two; C and D Companies were in reserve, and a battery of field guns supported the assault. The two companies moved forward under a heavy rifle and shell fire till they were within five hundred yards of the wood, when they found that, owing to the inability of the Northumberland Fusiliers to advance, their left was exposed. There Douglas Smith was compelled to halt his men; and there they remained throughout the day, while shells rained upon them and the reserve companies. At 5.15 p.m., just as it was getting dark, orders were received to continue the advance, and C Company, under Captain the Hon. James Boyle, was sent up to support A Company. At 5.30 the Scots Fusiliers were close on the enemy position, and only sixty yards from the wood; but with their flanks in the air they could not maintain themselves, and at six p.m. came the order to retire. Captain Boyle fell as he reached the German trenches, and the companies withdrew in good order to a point some eight hundred yards from the wood. The casualties were heavy. Besides Captain Boyle, Captain S. F. A. Hurt (a grand-nephew of the Hurt who fell at Inkerman), Lieutenant J. G. S. Cozens-Brooke, and Second Lieutenant H. W. F. Barton were killed in the advance, and 20 other ranks, while 4 officers and 100 other ranks were wounded.

On the 19th the battalion was relieved by the Lincolns, and next day Major A. M. H. Forbes took A and B Companies to the support of the Northumberland Fusiliers. On the 21st they were ordered to move back half a mile, and next day Major Forbes was wounded. Smith-Dorrien was now definitely on the defensive on a line pivoting on Givenchy, and then running east in a salient north of the La Bassée–Lille road to the vicinity of Herlies, where it bent westward to Aubers; and his whole energies were devoted to maintaining his ground and blocking the passage to Béthune and the west. Very soon it was clear that the advanced position of the Third Division on his left was untenable, and on the night of the 22nd it was withdrawn. Part of the Lahore Division of the Indian Corps had now come up in support, and for the rest of the month the main fighting was on the left in and around Neuve Chapelle. On the 30th the Scots Fusiliers were transferred to the 8th Brigade, under Brigadier-General W. H. Bowes. On 2nd November there was a fierce assault on the line held by the 2nd Gurkhas, and C Company was ordered up in support. Douglas Smith was placed in command of the Scots Fusiliers and the 59th Indian Infantry for the purpose of counter-attack; but the enemy was too strong, and that night a further retirement was found necessary. Between that day and 7th November, when it was relieved, the work of the battalion, now very weary and depleted, was to hang on in trenches under a deadly pressure of superior enemy numbers and guns. The line of the II. Corps had been slowly forced back till it ran from Givenchy north by Festubert towards Estaires. Happily for the Corps, the German concentration farther north had weakened the attack at the La Bassée port, for it is difficult to believe that a strong enemy thrust would not have forced that gate. On 7th November the Scots Fusiliers returned to the 9th Brigade, and moved northwards to the ill-omened salient of Ypres, where they became part of the reserve of the Seventh Division, and took part in the last stage of a battle in which their 2nd Battalion had already won immortal fame.

III

The 2nd Scots Fusiliers, under Lieutenant-Colonel A. G. Baird Smith, whom the outbreak of war found at Gibraltar, became part of the Seventh Division of British regular troops, which, with the 3rd Cavalry Division, were dispatched early in October, under Major-General Sir Henry Rawlinson, to the relief of Antwerp. But when Rawlinson landed in Flanders he found Antwerp doomed, and there was no other course before him but to retire westward to meet the main British army, now coming north from the Aisne. On 7th October Rawlinson was at Bruges, on the 8th at Ghent; and, forming a rear-guard for the Belgians who were now retreating on the Yser with Beseler's army of Antwerp in pursuit, the Seventh Division, much assisted by its armoured cars, moved through West Flanders till it reached Roulers on the 13th. The 2nd Scots Fusiliers were in the 21st Brigade (Brigadier-General Watts) along with the 2nd Wiltshires, the 2nd Yorkshires, and the 2nd Bedfords. On the 15th the division took up position east of Ypres from Wieltje south-east to the Ypres–Zonnebeke road, with a French detachment on its left, and on its right Byng's 3rd Cavalry Division in touch with Allenby's cavalry to the south. Meantime the four new German corps, which were to form the main strength of Würtemberg's IV. Army, and of which our Headquarters had still no knowledge, were being rushed westward from Brussels, and by the 18th were on the line Roulers-Menin.

On the 17th Sir John French, realizing that La Bassée and Lille were now beyond the power of his II. Corps, decided to advance on Menin in order to use it as a pivot against Courtrai and the line of the Scheldt. Rawlinson was to seize Menin and await the support of Haig's I. Corps, which was due in three days. It was an impossible task, and the nearest the Seventh Division got to Menin was the line Ledeghem–Kezelberg, about three miles from the town. On the 19th it had to fall back to avoid disaster, and entrenched itself on a front of eight miles east of the Gheluvelt crossroads. The section allotted to the 2nd Scots Fusiliers was north of the Menin road, the mile of front between Reutel and Poezelhoek. The position was not a good one. D Company, on the right, was on the low ground about the road from Becelaere, which was in German hands by the 20th, and it had a bad field of fire; B Company, on the left, was five hundred yards farther back up the slope towards the chateau on the spur; C Company was practically isolated on the forward slope towards Becelaere; while A Company was in reserve in the chateau grounds. The Seventh Division was in charge of the whole section from Zonnebeke to Zandvoorde. The Allied offensive had ceased, and the great struggle for Ypres was on the eve of beginning.

On the 20th Haig, with the I. Corps, advanced on a line between Bixschoote and Zonnebeke. On the 21st he had tidings of the strength of the enemy, for in the afternoon he learned that the French on his left had been driven back, and that the Seventh Division on his right was being heavily shelled. He therefore was compelled to halt on the line Bixschoote–Langemarck–St. Julien–Zonnebeke, a line which marked the limit of the last British offensive in the battle. That day Rawlinson had to face an attack of the left wing of

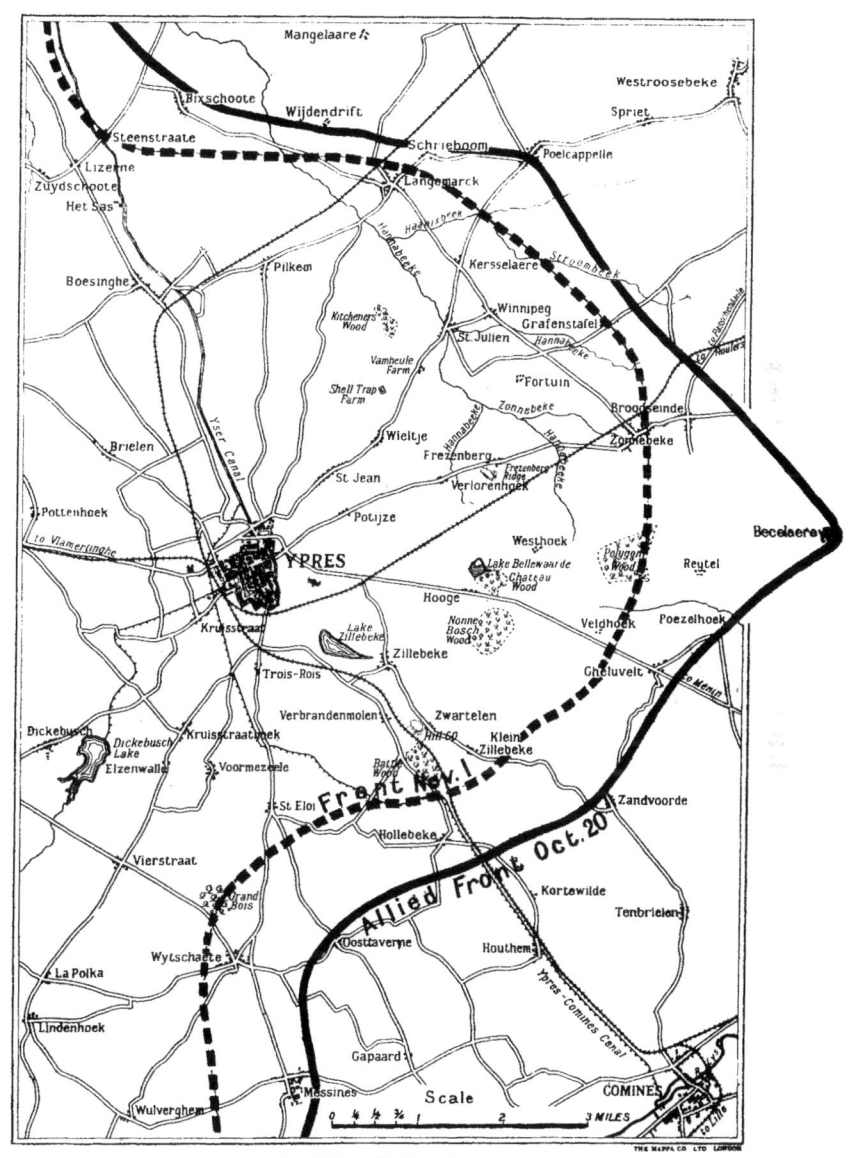

THE FIRST BATTLE OF YPRES

Facing page 300

the German IV. Army. His flank was all but turned by an enemy movement against Zonnebeke, and farther south the Germans succeeded in penetrating the line between the 2nd Yorkshires (Green Howards) and the 2nd Scots Fusiliers. The advance, however, was checked by the stand of a company of the Fusiliers in the enclosure of Polderhoek Chateau. Next day, the 22nd, the gap was filled, but D Company of the latter battalion was forced by machine-gun fire to fall back a little, and C Company on the forward slope was in a most perilous position. In the evening Major Ian Forbes of A Company, with parties from C and D, attacked in order to retake D's position, and cleared the houses in Poezelhoek, but the enemy proved too strong to permit the task to be completed. Captain Frank Fairlie fell; while receiving the surrender of some thirty Germans, he was shot by one of them. That evening the 21st Brigade was in an awkward predicament, for the 22nd Brigade had been retired, and its left was now the apex of a salient. On the 23rd there were further attacks, and a second time the enemy broke through between the Green Howards and the Scots Fusiliers, only to be swept back by the reserve company of the former. Before nightfall came a slight relief, for French troops arrived to take over part of the ground held by the British I. Corps, which was thus enabled to extend to the south, and relieve the hard-pressed Seventh Division of the north end of its line near Zonnebeke.

The failure of the attack of the 22nd, especially the part of it delivered between Bixschoote and Langemarck, seems to have convinced the Germans that they could not break through in that quarter. Accordingly they began in haste to pull out troops wherever they could be spared and to constitute a new army group under von Fabeck, to operate between their IV. and VI. Armies against the Allied front from Ypres to the Lys. This new group was, to start with, about the equivalent in numbers of the British army, and was presently to consist of nine divisions of

1914
Oct. 24

infantry and four of cavalry. Its assembly was to be complete on the 29th, and its attack was fixed for the 30th. Of this menace British Headquarters knew nothing, and their hands were full with the mere holding of their line.

The 24th was a day of crisis at the point of the salient. During the night 40 of the enemy penetrated a gap in the line and were captured by the Scots Fusiliers. Very early in the morning huge German masses from the direction of Becelaere attacked the 2nd Wiltshires and surrounded and captured the bulk of the battalion. The front of the salient had given way, the enemy entered the Polygon Wood, destined to be the scene of much desperate fighting in days to come, and the 2nd Scots Fusiliers found their left flank completely turned. C Company was driven out of its trenches, and reduced to 2 officers and 75 men, and the Germans entered the chateau wood. A message was received from General Capper—" Hold on like hell: the Second Division is coming "—and Baird Smith accordingly faced north with every available rifle in the firing line. The post of danger on the left was thinly held by Lieutenant H. W. V. Stewart, some four hundred yards north of the stream called the Reidelbeck, with his platoon and a few of the Wiltshires whom he had collected. There he remained till reinforcements from the Second Division arrived, and stopped a machine-gun attack by himself, shooting down every member of two teams. The little party continued to take heavy toll of the enemy, and by their courage prevented the left of the battalion being rolled up. In the afternoon an attack on B Company's advanced trenches was repulsed by a bayonet attack led by Lieutenant C. E. G. Mackenzie. With the fall of darkness the assault ebbed away. " Battalion wearied out," is the laconic comment in the diary. Its losses were already more than four hundred.

The enemy did not follow up his achievement in the Polygon Wood; he was waiting for von Fabeck. But that night the 20th Brigade was heavily attacked at

THE KRUSEIK RIDGE

Kruseik, south of the Menin road—a critical point, for if the salient were broken there, the Germans would gain possession of the Zandvoorde ridge. The attack was renewed in force just before the wet, misty dawn of the 25th, and the situation was not saved till after midday by a brilliant counter-attack of the 7th Cavalry Brigade. Orders were issued for an attack by the Seventh and Second Divisions that day, but it failed to materialize.[1] On the 26th it was becoming clear that the line of the Seventh Division was dangerously advanced, and that night General Capper was busy adjusting his brigades. Rawlinson returned to England to supervise the forming of his Eighth Division, and the Seventh Division and the 3rd Cavalry Division were temporarily attached to Haig's I. Corps. At two a.m. on the morning of the 27th the 21st Brigade was relieved, and sent a few miles back to Hooge to rest. The 2nd Scots Fusiliers had been in the trenches since 17th October, and had lost in casualties eight officers and 500 other ranks. They now mustered less than 500 men.

Their period of rest was short indeed. That evening they were ordered back to the line to relieve units holding the key position on the Kruseik ridge, one mile west of the village of that name and two miles south of Gheluvelt. It was a low ridge, affording a fair shelter; but the trenches were poor, and, being taken over by the Scots Fusiliers in the dark, were subsequently under such constant fire that nothing could be done to remedy their defects. Half the battalion—B Company under Major Burgoyne, and A Company under Captain Le Gallais—held the ridge in trenches facing southeast; C Company, under Captain Whigham, prolonged the line to the west, and D Company, under Captain Fleetwood, was in reserve. The battalion had the Green Howards on its left, and on its right the 1st

1914
Oct. 25-27

---

[1] "The principal offensive movement was made by some burying parties of the 2nd Royal Scots Fusiliers, who, being fired on from a house, attacked it, shovels in hand, and captured 20 Germans, including an officer."—*Military Operations, France and Belgium*, 1914, Vol. II., page 238.

1914
Oct. 28-30

Royal Welch Fusiliers of the 22nd Brigade. A stage in the battle had arrived when brigades and even divisions were inextricably intertwined.

The 28th saw little but shelling on the front—a dangerous lull which heralded the storm. It was a sufficiently severe bombardment, and four officers of the Scots Fusiliers, including Major Ian Forbes, were wounded. Very early on the 29th, in a sudden spell of clear weather, the first wave of the German attack broke against the centre of the I. Corps at the point of the salient, the Gheluvelt cross-roads, and all morning the line swayed backwards and forwards. On the Kruseik ridge the pressure was also severe. Burgoyne, by the evening, had under 200 men in his two companies, for his position, sticking out like a bastion, gave the German guns the chance of enfilading fire, and only the fortunate slope of the ground prevented his utter annihilation.

The 30th saw the main German attack. The Duke of Würtemberg, with three reserve corps, pressed against Bixschoote and Langemarck, while von Fabeck flung his weight against the British from Gheluvelt to Messines. Byng's cavalry division was simply blown off the Zandvoorde ridge and forced back to Klein Zillebeke; the First Division was compelled to retire to conform, and the Gheluvelt salient was thereby made so much the sharper. The Kruseik ridge was obviously untenable, and the troops on the right of the Scots Fusiliers were forced back north of Zandvoorde. Burgoyne had now no support except a machine-gun detachment [1] and a few stragglers which he had collected from other units. The tale may be told in the words of Baird Smith, his colonel.

" Burgoyne would have been quite justified, on the night of the 29th, in withdrawing without further orders, but he preferred to remain and send back to me for instructions. Reference to Brigade H.Q. showed that they did not know that any one

Apparently belonging to the 2nd Gordon Highlanders of the 20th Brigade.

THE STAND OF THE 2ND BATTALION

was left on the ridge, but for some reason they did not thereupon order his withdrawal, but told him to hold on. By that time his numbers were dwindling so rapidly that it was a physical impossibility for him to man the position, and the supporting company (D, under Fleetwood) which I sent to him in the course of that evening (the 29th) mustered at the most some thirty men. A Company, under Captain Le Gallais, being in a more sheltered position, had not suffered to the same extent, but its flank was exposed to the enemy in Zandvoorde, and the open ground separating it from the rest of the battalion was swept with fire.

1914
Oct. 30

" The morning of the 30th brought a greatly increased intensity of fire of all arms, so much so that Captain Whigham's C Company, holding a small wood some two or three hundred yards in echelon behind Captain Le Gallais's right flank, was driven out and forced to seek shelter farther back. The Brigadier and the Divisional General, who happened to be close up to the front, agreed to the withdrawal after repeated efforts had been made to maintain the forward line. They also, of course, concurred in the order which I dispatched by runners for Major Burgoyne to withdraw as best he could. But, unfortunately, some of the British artillery, imagining from the general situation that Kruseik ridge had fallen into enemy hands, began at this time a systematic shelling with shrapnel of the back of the ridge. The runners never reached Major Burgoyne, who himself about this time (afternoon of the 30th) was wounded and rendered unconscious. In any case, retirement before dark was impossible; he could not, while daylight lasted, even transmit orders to Captain Le Gallais with any certainty. On recovering consciousness Major Burgoyne took stock of the situation. It was possible to tell by the flashes of gun and rifle fire that the general line had drifted far back, and that he was isolated. Part of a

German regiment had penetrated his trenches, and was separated from his attenuated and exhausted remnant by a traverse or two. The German soldiers showed no disposition to try conclusions; they could not realize how weak their opponents actually were.

"Major Burgoyne, in the absence of orders, had now to decide for himself. Actually at this time I was, with Captain H. W. V. Stewart (acting Adjutant in place of Captain Horn, severely wounded), collecting the remains of Captain Whigham's company (he had been carried off the field) and trying to fill a section of the new line just given to us over a mile farther back. Major Burgoyne, Captain Fleetwood, and Captain Le Gallais agreed that they must retire, the companies to find their way back independently. But Major Burgoyne said that he would take in his retirement the direction of a farmhouse, close to which he had seen my headquarters, for he wanted to be sure that he was not leaving headquarters exposed or ignorant of his movements. Owing to his devotion to duty he, accompanied by Captain Fleetwood and the dozen odd men who were left of his company, walked in the dark night into the middle of a German regiment outside the farm in question. They were all captured. Captain Le Gallais by luck avoided this trap, and eventually, about the middle of the night, rejoined us with some hundred of his men."

The battalion was now the merest remnant—headquarters and a few survivors of Captain Whigham's company, and Le Gallais and his hundred men. On the 31st came the high tide of the First Battle of Ypres. Here we are not concerned with the main crisis of the action—the forcing of the First Division from Gheluvelt, the pouring of the enemy through the gap, and the miracle by which Fitzclarence and the 2nd Worcesters checked the flood, and enabled the gossamer British

THE CRISIS OF FIRST YPRES 307

front to re-form. Our business is with the 2nd Scots Fusiliers south of the Menin road. Early in the morning various fragmentary battalions were thrown in south of the road to make a kind of front, and on the right of two companies of the 1st Loyal North Lancashires was placed Second Lieutenant E. T. O. Boyle with 120 survivors of the Scots Fusiliers. Presently came the break-through on their left, and the flank of the position was turned. The Scots Fusiliers—detachment in the line, reserve, and headquarters—were engulfed in the tide and disappeared. Next day, after the miracle had happened and the flow had been stayed, two officers, Lieutenant Thomson and Second Lieutenant W. E. Clutterbuck, who had been lost in the confusion, found their way to General Watts's headquarters, and learned that they were all that remained of the battalion—they and thirty stragglers. The rest were dead, wounded, or in captivity.

1914
Oct. 31

So ended the most desperate battle in the history of our regiment—a greater defence than Inkerman, a surrender not less honourable than Saratoga. In all that long three weeks' struggle, when the laws of war seemed to be set at defiance, when for ten days one British division defended a front of two miles against two army corps, when 276 Allied battalions held the gate against 402, there was no finer proof of courage and devotion than that given by Burgoyne on the Kruseik ridge and the worn companies behind him. The Seventh Division, as Rawlinson told it, had fought so stoutly that it had made the enemy believe that he had at least four corps against him; but it paid a price for its glory, for at the close of the action out of 400 officers it had 44 left, and out of 12,000 men only 2,336. The losses of the 2nd Royal Scots Fusiliers need not be assessed, for the battalion simply disappeared. But it did not perish in vain, for, as General Capper said, it held for ten days the key of the whole position, and had it given way early on the 30th the whole Allied front might well have crumbled, and Fitzclarence and the Worcesters could not have restored the line. Four

1914
Oct. 31

months later, when the battalion had been reconstructed, their Brigadier, General Watts, thus addressed it:—

"Major Pollard, officers, non-commissioned officers, and men of the Royal Scots Fusiliers,—

"It is only within the last few days that I have learned the true history of the gallant doings of your battalion, on the 31st of October last, and in cases where troops are captured I think that the facts should be known.

"On the 30th[1] of October, in order to cover the right flank of troops on our left, your battalion was ordered to take up a very bad and exposed position on a forward slope, and, sure enough, on the morning of the 31st[2] you were exposed to a very heavy shell fire, followed by an infantry attack by vastly superior numbers. As far as your battalion was concerned all went well, until the troops on your left were driven back, and your left flank exposed.

"The Germans came pouring through, and it soon became obvious that our position was untenable, and we were ordered to take up a position farther back. I tried to telephone to Colonel Baird Smith, but the wire had been cut by shrapnel. I then sent two orderlies with a message to withdraw, but the message was never received. Both orderlies must have been killed or wounded.

"Colonel Baird Smith, gallant soldier that he was, decided—and rightly—to hold his ground, and the Royal Scots Fusiliers fought and fought until the Germans absolutely surrounded and swarmed into the trenches.

"I think it was perfectly splendid. Mind you, it was not a case of 'Hands up' or any nonsense of that sort; it was a fight to a finish. What more do you want? Why, even a German general came to Colonel Baird Smith[3] afterwards and con-

[1] Really the 29th. [2] Really the 30th.
[3] Really to Major Burgoyne. He said, "Your men are warriors."

THE ATTACK OF THE PRUSSIAN GUARD

gratulated him, and said he could not understand how his men had held out so long.

"You may well be proud to belong to such a regiment, and I am proud to have you in my brigade. A regiment with a spirit like that cannot go far wrong, and I feel sure that when next called upon we need, none of us, feel nervous as to the results."

The First Battle of Ypres was not yet over, but the end had come so far as concerned the 2nd Royal Scots Fusiliers. It received drafts which enabled it to be organized into four skeleton companies, and under a succession of commanding officers—Captain R. T. Traill, Captain R. Q. Craufurd, Major A. M. H. Forbes, and Major J. W. Pollard—it continued to hold parts of the line in the area south of Ypres. But in the final stage of the Ypres battle the 1st Battalion played a distinguished part. We have seen that on 8th November the 1st Royal Scots Fusiliers were transferred with other battalions of the II. Corps to Ypres to form a reserve. The Germans had still a shot left in their locker, and von Fabeck having failed, a new group was formed under Linsingen, which included a composite division of the Prussian Guard. This group was to attack on the 11th north of the Ypres–Comines canal, for, as Napoleon used his Guards for the final attack at Waterloo, so the German Emperor used his for the culminating stroke at Ypres. A little after eight a.m. on 11th November the 1st and 4th Brigades of the Prussian Guard were launched on both sides of the Menin road. At first they used their parade march, and our men, rubbing their eyes in the dim light, could scarcely credit the portent. Long before they came to the shock our fire had taken toll of them, but so mighty is discipline that their impact told. The brunt of the attack fell upon the three groups from the II. Corps, organized under Generals M'Cracken, Gleichen, and Shaw, and upon Fitzclarence's 1st (Guards) Brigade, and at several points the enemy pierced our front and won the woods to the west. The

1914
Nov. 8–11

1st Royal Scots Fusiliers, who had been in Shaw's reserve in the wood afterwards called Inverness Copse, were prominent in the counter-attack which drove the Germans back with heavy losses,[1] and the battalion took up a position half a mile east of the chateau of Herenthage. Next morning A Company, which had in it men of the 4th Royal Fusiliers and the 1st Northumberland Fusiliers, attacked a German trench, but failed to take it owing to their extreme fatigue, and the line had to be slightly withdrawn. On the 14th the Germans succeeded in occupying the stables near the chateau, and it was only after repeated bayonet charges that they were ejected. The fighting of these days was costly, for the 8th Brigade entered the Ypres Salient 2,200 strong and marched out 850, while the Scots Fusiliers lost six officers killed, five wounded, and one missing, and had 277 casualties in the rank-and-file. Among the dead were Captain C. J. C. Barrett, the acting C.O., Lieutenants N. W. A. Henderson and G. S. Ness, Second Lieutenant E. L. L. Anderson, and Lieutenant C. J. Lyon, who fell in the fight for the stables. By the middle of the month the enemy had exhausted his strength. Further French reinforcements came up, and the sorely tried British troops were relieved from the trenches which they had held for four stubborn weeks. The weather had changed to high winds and snow blizzards, and in a tempest the First Battle of Ypres died away.

The 1st Battalion, like the 2nd, was now engaged in normal trench warfare, for the most part in the Ypres and Kemmel areas. On 14th November Lieutenant-Colonel Douglas Smith had taken command of the 9th Brigade, after General Shaw had been wounded, and the battalion was temporarily under Major H. P. de la Bère. There was the usual steady casualty list— Captain J. D. Tullis of the 1st Battalion, and Lieutenant A. Ross-Thomson and Second Lieutenant J. A. Chrystie of the 2nd Battalion died in November, and Lieutenant

---

[1] In this action General Shaw was wounded, and Lieutenant-Colonel W. D. Smith took over the group.

K. C. Thomson of the 2nd on the last day of the year. Within five months the regiment had passed through such vicissitudes and perils as few British soldiers of the past had known; it had fought actions of unparalleled magnitude, and was now engaged in learning a new kind of warfare which its old predecessors had once practised under Marlborough. The discomfort of the trenches was alleviated by luxuries unknown in the Crimean winters, and the ennui mitigated by practice with novel weapons of war. But the misery and boredom remained—mud, and water, and cold; and after the fashion of the British soldier, a Scots Fusilier [1] celebrated the amenities of his life in cheerful rhyme :—

*1914
Nov. 14–
Dec. 31*

> " I came to France prepared to shed my blood,
> But not to perish miserably in mud.
> I'm ready to attack with might and main,
> And here I've sat six weeks inside a drain,
> While all that's left of Bill, who took a snooze,
> Is just a bayonet rising from the ooze.—
> You find me out a bit of ground that's dry
> And I'll soon show the savage Alleman why;
> But now I can't advance against the brutes
> With half a ton of France upon my boots ! "

Officers who died in 1914

[The battalion records give an imperfect list of officers who fell. The following roll has been compiled with the assistance of the War Office records.]

Second Lieutenant C. M. ALSTON (25th Oct.); Second Lieutenant E. L. L. ANDERSON (10th Nov.); Captain C. J. C. BARRETT (13th Nov.); Second Lieutenant H. W. F. BARTON (18th Oct.); Captain the Hon. J. BOYLE (18th Oct.); Captain G. C. BRIGGS (14th Sept.); Lieutenant J. G. S. COZENS-BROOKE (18th Oct.); Second Lieutenant J. A. CHRYSTIE (30th Nov.); Captain F. FAIRLIE (23rd Oct.); Lieutenant N. W. A. HENDERSON (10th Nov.); Captain S. F. A. HURT (18th Oct.); Lieutenant N. KENNEDY (22nd Oct.); Second Lieutenant C. J. LYON (13th Nov.); Lieutenant C. G. G. MACKENZIE (25th Oct.); Lieutenant G. S. NESS (10th Nov.); Captain T. A. ROSE (24th Aug.); Lieutenant A. ROSS-THOMSON (30th Nov.); Lieutenant the Hon. R. S. STUART (2nd Nov.); Lieutenant K. C. THOMSON (31st Dec.); Captain J. D. TULLIS (18th Nov.); Captain J. E. YOUNG (24th Aug.).

---

[1] Lieutenant-Colonel A. M. H. Forbes.

CHAPTER XV

THE GREAT WAR—1915

The spring in Flanders—Neuve Chapelle—Festubert—The Second Battle of Ypres—The battle of Loos—The Gallipoli campaign—The battle of 12th July—The summer and autumn at Helles—The evacuation of Gallipoli—The beginning of the Salonika campaign.

I

1915
Jan.–Feb.

THE first months of 1915 were spent by both battalions of our regiment in the comfortless area between Ypres and La Bassée. Both were largely made up of new drafts which had to be trained, and the work was conducted at high pressure in the intervals between their turns of duty in the muddy trenches. The 1st Battalion was still in the 9th Brigade of the Third Division of the II. Corps, but the commanding officers had changed. Sir Charles Fergusson now had the II. Corps, and when he inspected the Scots Fusiliers he reminded them that he was an Ayrshire man and a brother-in-law of the late Captain the Hon. James Boyle; while Major-General Aylmer Haldane had the Third Division. In the middle of February the 9th Brigade was transferred to the Twenty-eighth Division, which with the Twenty-seventh made up Sir Herbert Plumer's new V. Corps, and sent to the trenches south of Ypres, where it had a steady stream of casualties. Major H. P. de la Bère took over the command of the Scots Fusiliers on 25th February, but presently fell sick, and was replaced by Major D. A.

Dick. There we may leave them for the moment, to look at the fortunes of the other battalion.

The 2nd Battalion during the winter months slowly won back the semblance of a regiment. The Seventh Division was presently joined by the Eighth Division, and Rawlinson's IV. Corps was complete. The British force had been organized in two armies, and the IV. Corps, with the Indian Corps and I. Corps, made up the First Army under Sir Douglas Haig. March saw a British army assembled on French and Flemish soil twelve times as large as that which had triumphed under Wellington in the Peninsula, and fifty-five times greater than the force which charged with King Harry at Agincourt. As early as the middle of February it had been decided that an offensive should be undertaken on the British front. The recent success of the French in Champagne seemed to have proved that under certain conditions an attack upon entrenchments must succeed. If a sufficiently powerful artillery fire were concentrated upon a section of a front, parapets and barbed-wire entanglements would be blown to pieces, and if the artillery, lengthening the range, were able to put a barrage of fire between the enemy and his supports, it was believed that the infantry could advance in comparative safety. On this theory the new attack was staged. The section chosen was Neuve Chapelle, where our position to the west of the village was a relic of the unsuccessful advance of the II. Corps in the preceding October. The strategic importance of the place lay in the fact that to the east rose the low ridge of Aubers, the possession of which by the British would threaten the La Bassée–Lille line. The action was intended by Sir John French to be a local enterprise, to prepare the way for the great combined assault of the summer. He had collected a modest reserve of ammunition, and by dint of raking together every spare gun from the whole of his front he hoped to explore the possibilities of the new method of artillery " preparation."

The attack was to be made by the First Army, the

1915
March 9–10

IV. Corps operating on the north and the Indian Corps on the south. The infantry began to assemble on the evening of 9th March, and at 7.30 on the misty morning of the 10th the guns opened, a pandemonium of sound new in the experience of the British army. The bombardment lasted for thirty-five minutes, during which the German trenches crumbled; the gunners lengthened their range, and the houses of the village began to leap into the air. Then the infantry advanced—the Eighth Division on the left and the Meerut Division on the right. The 25th Brigade carried the rubbish heap which had been Neuve Chapelle; but the 23rd Brigade was hung up at the northern corner, where there was still unbroken wire. This check put the whole movement out of gear, communications were cut and messages miscarried, and it was not till 3.30 in the afternoon that the reserves of the IV. Corps, the Seventh Division, could be brought into action.

The 2nd Royal Scots Fusiliers, with the rest of the 21st Brigade, had been in position south-west of Laventie at the opening of the battle, and had moved up to the empty trenches of the 23rd Brigade. They had four companies in the firing line—Major J. W. Pollard with battalion headquarters and A and B Companies on the right, and Major A. M. H. Forbes with C and D Companies on the left. Little progress could be made, for our own guns were causing casualties; and since the 24th Brigade was checked by machine-gun fire from the cross-roads north-east of Pietre village, the right of the 21st was delayed. The line of the Des Layes stream and the Pietre mill was also strongly held by the enemy, and everywhere in the neighbourhood there were positions which our artillery had not yet touched. The Seventh Division had to conform to the Eighth Division on its left, and its advance was necessarily circumscribed. Accordingly, as the grey evening closed in, we devoted ourselves to consolidating the position we had won. Neuve Chapelle was ours; we had advanced a mile and greatly strengthened our line, but a wedge had still to be driven into the enemy's.

THE BATTLE OF NEUVE CHAPELLE

Early on the 11th our guns were directed on the German positions around Pietre; but the enemy had now recovered himself, the asset of surprise had been lost, and our great artillery effort was exhausted. The German counter-attack effected little, but our own threat was now rapidly spending itself. A second effort was made on the 12th, and all that day the Seventh Division struggled round the Des Layes and Pietre Mill. The Scots Fusiliers were maintaining themselves in a forward position against repeated enemy assaults. Just before dawn the salient held by B Company was attacked, and all the officers became casualties. Here it was that Private J. Reid of his own initiative and single-handed brought a machine gun into action at close range and broke the assault of the enemy. At 5.30 a.m. a heavy attack on the battalion front was beaten off when it had come within seventy yards. From 8.30 onwards distressing losses began to be incurred from our own guns, as had happened on the day before. At noon the troops on the left managed to advance a little, and the enemy, retreating before them, came under the fire of the Scots Fusiliers and lost heavily. And so all day the see-saw of the struggle continued. " It was a splendid sight," wrote one of the officers, " to see Ingram [Lieutenant W. W. Ingram, M.O.] running out under a hail of bullets and bringing in one wounded man after another on his back. His mackintosh in ten minutes was covered with blood, and he looked like a butcher."

By the evening of the 12th it was clear that a stalemate had been reached. We could not win to the enemy's position commanding the ridge, and he could not retake Neuve Chapelle. Haig was directed to consolidate the ground won and suspend further operations. On the 13th the weary troops were busy digging themselves into the wet meadows along the Des Layes, but it was no light task to extricate those in the first line. The 1st Grenadier Guards of the 20th Brigade attempted to relieve the Scots Fusiliers at dawn on the 13th, but were compelled to entrench behind them.

1915
March 11-13

1915
March 13-14

An enemy attack came at ten a.m., and all day there was heavy shelling. It was not till the 14th that the Scots Fusiliers left the trenches, having been two days on very short commons owing to the difficulty of getting up supplies. They were moved back to billets in Estaires.

Neuve Chapelle was a severe trial to a battalion which already, five months before, had been all but annihilated, and it met the test with a splendid fortitude. It entered the battle with 25 officers and 666 men, and it emerged with 5 officers [1] and 80 other ranks killed, 10 officers and 162 other ranks wounded, while 50 men were missing, and 3 officers and 37 men went to hospital suffering from exposure. Its divisional commander, General Capper, spoke thus of its achievement: " This battalion got farther forward than any other battalion in the division, and maintained itself in its forward position, doing a great deal of damage to the enemy. Owing to difficulties of ground and its more advanced position, this battalion was without rations for two days, but accepted with a very fine spirit the privations that were thus caused." On 12th April Sir John French addressed them :—

" I want to thank personally every officer, non-commissioned officer, and man for the splendid part you took in the recent operations at Neuve Chapelle. I have not yet had the opportunity of thanking you personally for the magnificent stand which you made near Ypres last autumn, and I am glad to be able to do so now. You had already a great fighting reputation—in fact, you are justified in considering yourselves one of the most distinguished regiments in the army—but the glorious traditions of your regiment have been not only maintained but enhanced by your gallant conduct at that time, and again recently. You have suffered heavily, and I greatly deplore these losses,

[1] Lieutenants A. C. E. Alexander, T. B. Benson, A. C. G. Lonsdale (K.R.R.—attached), R. M. Graham (Essex—attached), and J. L. Moffat.

FESTUBERT

but, believe me, they have not been in vain. You have shown that you can fight and hold on regardless of loss, and I am confident that with your magnificent fighting spirit you will continue to maintain in the future this glorious tradition."

1915
May 9-17

The battalion was restored by drafts to a reasonable strength, so that in May, after two months of ordinary trench service, it numbered 18 officers and 635 other ranks. In that month came the Allied attack designed primarily to relieve the pressure on our Eastern allies, for Mackensen was rolling up the Russian armies in Galicia—the French advance in Artois and the British thrust towards Lille. Once more our objective was the Aubers ridge, while the French were striking towards Lens. On 9th May, while the Scots Fusiliers were in the IV. Corps reserve, the Eighth Division of that corps attacked from Rouges Bancs towards Fromelles on the old battle-ground of Neuve Chapelle; but the artillery preparation was inadequate, and the men came up against unbroken wire and parapets. The next advance was on the morning of Sunday, 16th May, and the ground chosen was that immediately east of Festubert, where the German front showed a pronounced salient. In other wars the battle of Festubert, looking to the casualties and the numbers engaged, would have been a major action, but in this campaign it ranked only as an episode. Our artillery preparation began on the Saturday night, and just after dawn the infantry went forward—the 21st and 22nd Brigades of the Seventh Division, and part of the Second Division and the Indian Corps. On that day the British right, the 22nd Brigade, advanced for more than a mile, reaching a point to the north-west of La Quinque Rue. The Scots Fusiliers were ordered forward in support at eight a.m., and lost 6 killed and 28 wounded in this advance of eight hundred yards into position. Next morning, in a steady rain, they attacked at 9.50 a.m., after having had a number of casualties from our own shells. They reached their objective, when again they were

1915
April 20–23

terribly punished by the British guns, which forced them alternately to retire and advance. That night they were withdrawn, having lost 27 per cent. of their strength. Second Lieutenants R. S. Crawford, R. N. Stuart, A. E. Waller, and R. Hughes fell and 29 other ranks, 2 officers and 137 men were wounded, and there were 15 missing. On the afternoon of 15th June the battalion, along with the 4th Cameron Highlanders, was engaged in a local attack at Givenchy, which failed owing to the inadequacy of our artillery support and the forewarning of the enemy. Three officers fell—Lieutenant J. E. Findlay-Hamilton and Second Lieutenants J. L. L. Sweet and A. A. F. Geddes.

We return to the 1st Battalion, which we left in the Ypres Salient with the Twenty-eighth Division, suffering much from mines and shell fire and mud. On 20th April the division held the front from north-east of Zonnebeke to the Polygon Wood, with the Canadians on its left and the Twenty-seventh Division on its right. On the 17th Hill 60, at the southern re-entrant of the salient, had been taken and held, and on the 20th there began a bombardment of the town of Ypres with heavy shells, which seemed to augur an enemy advance. On the night of the 22nd, in pleasant spring weather, the Germans launched the first gas attack in the campaign, which forced the French behind the canal and made a formidable breach in the Allied line. Then followed the heroic stand of the Canadians, who stopped the breach, the fight of " Geddes's Detachment," the shortening of the British line, and the long-drawn torture of the three weeks' action which we call the Second Battle of Ypres. The front of the Twenty-eighth Division was not the centre of the fiercest fighting, and the 1st Royal Scots Fusiliers were not engaged in any of the greatest episodes. But till the battle died away in early June they had their share of losses. On 22nd April Second Lieutenant Wallner was killed in an attack on their trenches, and next day Second Lieutenant R. W. Sterling, a young officer of notable promise, fell, after holding a length of trench all day with 15 men.

SECOND YPRES

When the battalion was relieved on the 25th, besides these officers it had 41 men killed and 30 wounded. It shared in the gas attack of 5th May, and on the 17th Captain S. B. Stirling-Cookson was killed. On the 26th it took over from the 85th Brigade, and during the month of May it had 1 officer and 10 men killed, and 2 officers and 67 men wounded. Throughout June it was in the trenches at Bellewaarde, and on the 16th took part in an advance, when B Company, under Captain Whigham, and A Company, under Captain Utterson-Kelso, won their objectives, and maintained them till they were relieved. Its casualties in this affair were heavy, for Second Lieutenant G. W. Webster and 36 men fell, 12 officers and 199 other ranks were wounded, and 202 men were missing. In the fight at Hooge in early August the 9th Brigade was in reserve. These were costly weeks for the battalion—weeks of constant bombardment, and fights for a yard or two of trench in the uneasiest section of the British front, and the wastage was scarcely less than in a great battle.

*1915
April 25–
August*

II

In the early summer of 1915 the new divisions raised by Lord Kitchener were beginning to arrive in the field. The 4th and 5th Battalions of the Royal Scots Fusiliers assembled at Stirling, and became part of the Fifty-second Division of Lowland Territorials. We shall see presently their doings at Gallipoli. The first of the Kitchener units, the 6th Battalion, under Lieutenant-Colonel Northey, forming part of the Scottish Ninth Division,[1] arrived in France in the middle of May, and took its turn in the trenches during the summer. In August it suffered a great loss from the death of Major L. Goodeve at the hand of a German sniper. The 7th Battalion, in the Scottish Fifteenth Division, arrived in July, and in August was in the trenches

---

[1] A brilliant account of its training and early days in the field will be found in Ian Hay's (Captain J. H. Beith) *The First Hundred Thousand* (Blackwood, 1915).

1915
Aug.–Sept.

opposite Loos, where its commanding officer, Lieutenant-Colonel A. H. Allenby, was killed by shell fire.[1] Meantime an 8th Battalion had been raised in September 1914 to form part of the Twenty-sixth Division, and a 9th Battalion as a reserve to remain at home.

The four battalions of our regiment in France were now to be drawn together in a great battle. The Allied command in the war, having decided in July to postpone any forward movement till the following spring, changed its mind in August. In the east Germany appeared to be nearing a position where she could neither force a conclusion nor break off the combat, and her difficulties seemed to offer a chance to her opponents. Moreover, the supply of shells for both France and Britain had enormously increased, and there was a clear superiority of the Allied numbers in the West. Neuve Chapelle and the fighting of the summer had taught us that before infantry could advance a section of the enemy's stronghold must be destroyed by bombardment, and that the rent must be broad; otherwise time was given for the local reserves to come up and hold the gap, and the enemy's front hardened like concrete. But if the German position could be broken on a front of, say, twenty miles, there would be no time for the line to re-form, and the assailants, manœuvring in the gap, might cause a general retreat. The new Allied plan, therefore, fell into three stages—the destruction of one or more positions at the first attack; the consolidation of the ground won in such a way as to prepare for the next blow and to leave the enemy no leisure to strengthen his remoter defences; the attack on the final position, and such movements thereafter as fortune might grant.

At the time it seemed a hopeful and convincing scheme, but, as we now know, it was based on a false deduction from Neuve Chapelle and a misreading of the problem before us. We realized in theory that a break-through would be a protracted operation, but we did not guess how protracted it would be. The

[1] In Philosophe, just before going into the trenches; the M.O., Dr. Harris, was also killed.

THE SEPTEMBER OFFENSIVE

conception of a breach in a wall dominated our minds, and we underestimated the strength of the enemy system of defence in depth. Nor did we understand what perfection of staff work was needed for a series of assaults upon successive positions involving new bombardments and a bringing up of fresh reserves. Our preparations were in reality only for a first assault; beyond that they faded into vagueness and improvisation. It is probable, indeed, that even if the full intricacy of the problem had been grasped, the Allies would not have been able to meet it. Months of training were still needed before their troops could become a weapon sufficiently edged and precise to pierce Germany's defence. They could no more have defeated Germany in the West in 1915 than McClellan could have beaten the Confederate armies in 1862.

The attack was staged in three sections—the French in Champagne and in Artois, and the British between Loos and La Bassée. Early in September a general bombardment began along the whole front as a screen for the preparations for attack. Here we are concerned only with the British section, which embraced practically the whole front held by British troops. The main assault was to be delivered by the First Army against the line La Bassée–Haisnes–Hulluch–Loos, and its purpose was the same as that of the French to the south— to isolate the railway junction of Lens and open the road into the plain of the Scheldt. In addition, four attacks were to be undertaken north of the La Bassée Canal—one by the Second Division from Givenchy; one by the Indian Corps from Neuve Chapelle; one by the III. Corps from Bois Grenier; and one by the V. Corps in the south of the Ypres Salient. In this last the 1st Battalion of the Royal Scots Fusiliers participated; the other three—the 2nd, 6th, and 7th— were in the main operations south of La Bassée.

Let us consider first the minor holding battle in the north. It was of high importance, for the whole Ypres region was strongly held by the enemy, and from there, if from anywhere, reinforcements could be sent south.

1915
Sept. 25

The attack was entrusted to Allenby's V. Corps, which for the purpose borrowed the Fourteenth Division from the VI. Corps. The Fourteenth Division was to advance north of the Menin road, the Third Division south of the road, with the 9th Brigade, now restored to that division, on its extreme right. At 3.50 on the morning of 25th September our artillery bombardment started; at 4.20 we exploded a mine north of the road, and a few minutes later the infantry advance began. The Fourteenth Division was attacking towards Bellewaarde Farm, and the Third towards the fortress in the north of Sanctuary Wood. Except in the area of the exploded mine the Germans were not taken by surprise, and when the assault began they hurried up reserves from their front farther south, thereby assisting the Allied purpose. But no forewarning enabled them to support the shock of the British infantry. Bellewaarde Farm and the ridge on which it stood was carried, and south of the Menin road the Third Division advanced for six hundred yards.

The 1st Royal Scots Fusiliers led the attack with A Company. It lost heavily in the first rush, but reached the enemy's position, supported by a detachment of bombers under Second Lieutenant Chisholm, " whose gallant conduct did much to hearten the men." C Company followed in support, and by seven a.m. the position was won and consolidated. But gains in the Ypres Salient were hard to hold. The big guns from the Passchendaele ridge, and from the neighbourhood of Hill 60, came into play against our new front; the Bellewaarde ridge could not be maintained, and long before the evening the British left was driven back to its old line. For the Scots Fusiliers the day was one long bombing combat, and they clung to what they had gained till the troops on their left and right fell back and both their flanks were left in the air. The counter-attack died down in the evening, and shortly after midnight they were relieved. It had been a costly day, for 3 officers—Captain M. K. Pollock, and Second Lieutenants A. E. Chisholm and Y. W. Mercier—were killed and 30 other ranks, 6 officers and 120 other ranks were wounded, and 1 officer and 161 other ranks were missing. Yet it may fairly be said that the threat at Hooge fulfilled its purpose. General Allenby two days later addressed the battalion, and congratulated it on having taken a position which was admittedly one of the strongest in the enemy line. " They had held their own to the very last, and not till the men on their flanks had been forced back had they retired." He assured them that " their inability to hold what they had so gallantly taken did not by any means imply that their splendid efforts had been in vain. They had done what was required of them, and had done it well. . . . They had stuck it through an inferno of machine-gun, bomb, and shell fire in a way that would have been a credit to any regiment." General Haldane, in congratulating the Third Division, specially singled out for mention the 4th Gordons, 2nd Royal Scots, and 1st Royal Scots Fusiliers, and explained the meaning of a " holding battle "—" A victory, such as is possible in parts of the field where superiority of guns and men can be applied, is rarely obtainable by a containing force. The most that such a force can do is to cripple the enemy's freedom of action and prevent him from moving his troops where he pleases. To succeed in doing so is indeed to gain a victory, and this the Third Division, like its namesake at Badajoz, through the gallantry and resolution of all ranks has certainly done."

We turn now to the main battle south of La Bassée. There the German front ran from the rise of Auchy la Bassée over a flattish tract to the Vermelles–Hulluch road ; thence a low swell runs southward, on the west side of which the German lines continued just below the crest till the Béthune–Lens road was reached. Behind the front was a string of mining villages— Haisnes in the north, Cité St. Elie a mile south, Hulluch half a mile farther and a little to the east, Loos in a shallow hollow two miles to the south-west. A mile west of Haisnes stood a slag-heap marked on the map

1915
Sept. 25

1915
Sept. 25

as Fosse 8, commanding all the country to the south. A mile and a quarter west of Cité St. Elie a great redoubt, the Hohenzollern, had been pushed out some five hundred yards in front of the German line, connected with the main front by two trenches known to our men as " Big Willie " and " Little Willie," and also with the defences of Fosse 8. Behind Loos the ground sloped up to Hill 70, and then fell away eastwards to the hamlet of Cité St. Auguste, which was virtually a suburb of Lens. The German reserve position was roughly just west of Loos and through the Quarries half-way between their line and Cité St. Elie. The final position, so far as it had been located, ran from west of Cité St. Auguste northwards behind the string of fortified mining villages.

The British I. Corps, under Sir Hubert Gough, lay from Givenchy to the Vermelles–Hulluch road, with opposite Fosse 8 the Ninth Division, under Major-General George Thesiger, and on the right, facing Cité St. Elie, the Seventh Division under General Capper. To the south lay Rawlinson's IV. Corps—the First Division facing Hulluch, the Fifteenth Division, under General McCracken, facing Loos, and the Forty-seventh Division forming the extreme British right. By midnight on the 24th the great bombardment drew to a head. Every gun on the front was speaking, and speaking without rest. During the small hours of the morning, in the pandemonium of din, the masses behind the front were beginning to percolate into the labyrinth of narrow ways that led to the first line. Dawn struggled through the gloom, and the morning of Saturday, the 25th, opened in a drizzle. Suddenly the guns ceased, and the instant quiet smote on the ear and brain with a shock like icy water. The gunners were shifting range and lengthening their fuses, and at 6.30 a.m. the first of our infantry went over the parapet.

The objective of the Ninth Division was Fosse 8 and the Hohenzollern, and it attacked with the 28th Brigade on its left and the 26th Brigade on its right. The former, being enfiladed from the rise at Auchy la

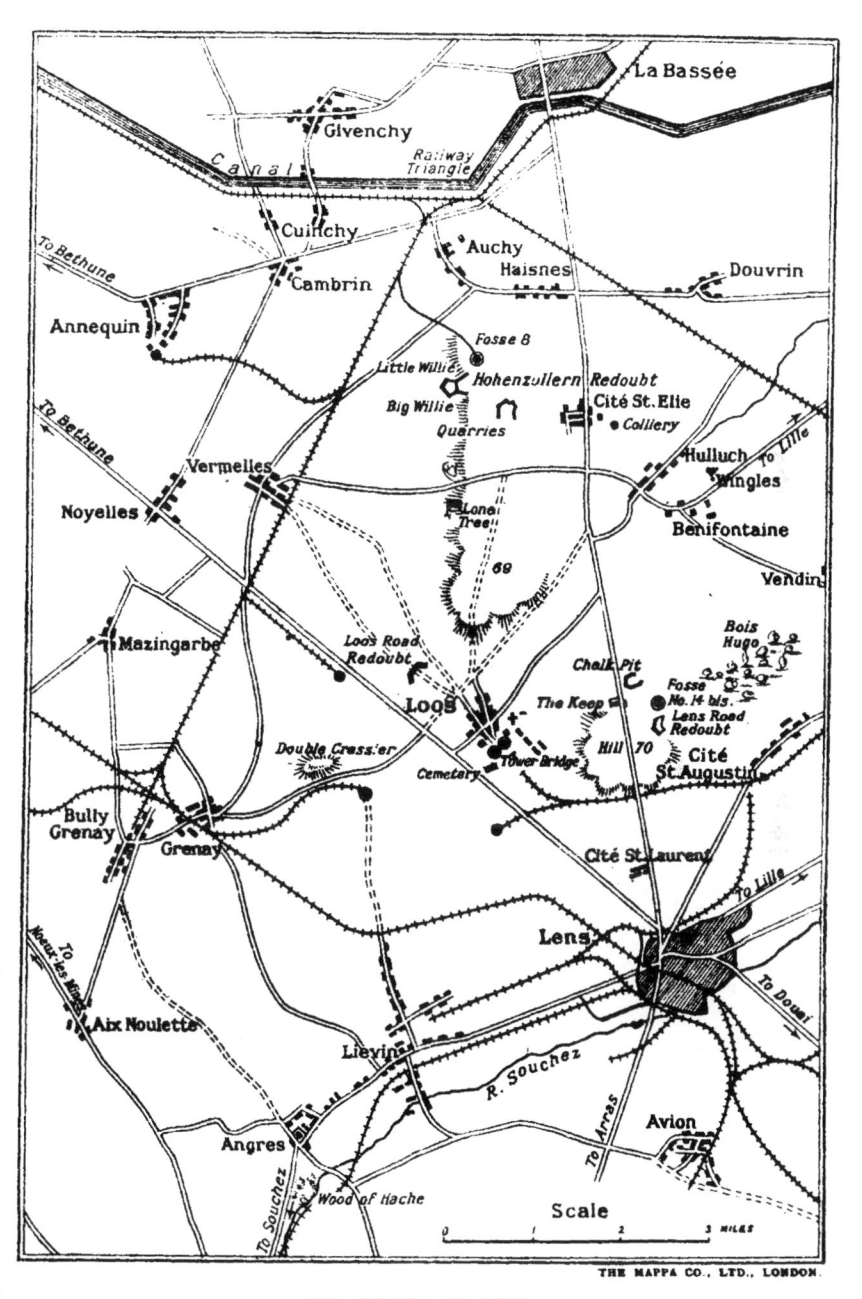

THE BATTLE OF LOOS

Facing page 324

Bassée, had desperate fighting. It pushed beyond the Vermelles–La Bassée railway, and took the first line of German trenches; but the position was too precarious to hold, and slowly during the day it was driven back. Meanwhile the 26th Brigade, composed wholly of kilted battalions, had succeeded better with the Hohenzollern. The redoubt was taken, but not without heavy losses, and Fosse 8 was also captured after a violent struggle. The brigade had to advance over bare, shell-swept ground, the machine guns from the Fosse played on it unceasingly, and, owing to the hold-up of the advance on its left, its flank was in the air. Yet by eight a.m. its leading troops were close on Haisnes, and British soldiers were actually in the village. The 27th Brigade, in which were the 6th Royal Scots Fusiliers, under Lieutenant-Colonel Northey, was now brought forward, to clear the maze of trenches and cottages east of Fosse 8; but it was eleven a.m. before it could reach the advanced front, and by that time the chance of the capture of Haisnes had gone. By midday the Ninth Division had to its credit a remarkable achievement, for it had carried the British front forward in a broad salient and captured all the chief works of the enemy. But its gains were precarious; for the vital Fosse 8 was cleared, but not occupied in strength, since the reserves were scanty, and all the land between it and Haisnes was filled with isolated forts and trench-sections still held by the enemy's machine guns.

On the right of the Ninth the Seventh Division had made good progress. With no Fosse 8 or Hohenzollern to hold it up it swept forward across the first German position. It reached the western side of the famous Quarries, where a sector of the German line, strongly fortified, held up that part of the advance. The 21st Brigade, in which were the 2nd Royal Scots Fusiliers (now under Captain A. H. Connell, Colonel Pollard having been given the command of the 2nd Brigade), was in reserve during the day, and did not share in the main action. The 22nd Brigade, on the left, reached Haisnes by ten a.m., while the right brigade swept towards Cité St. Elie and Hulluch. The extreme ground won, however, could not be maintained. The hold on Haisnes slackened, and by noon the line of the Seventh Division ran from the western end of Cité St. Elie and the west side of the Quarries, and so north to the right of the Ninth Division east of the Hohenzollern. That night Captain Connell, with two companies of the Royal Scots Fusiliers, occupied trenches near the Quarries.

But it was farther south, in the section of Rawlinson's IV. Corps, that the advance reached its height. Its left, the First Division, had varying fortunes. The 1st Brigade on the left held a straight course, swept forward for a mile and three-quarters, and early in the forenoon was in the outskirts of Hulluch. But the 2nd Brigade on its right was held up for long by the German position at Lone Tree, and could not advance till the afternoon, when the hour was too late to enable it to exploit the successes to the left and right. It is with the Fifteenth Division on the right that we must concern ourselves—that brilliant advance which resulted in the capture of Loos and, for a moment, the shaking of the whole German northern front. The direct attack on Loos was made by the 44th Brigade, while on the left the 46th Brigade fetched a circuit and came in on the north side of the village; the 45th Brigade, in which were the 7th Royal Scots Fusiliers (Lieutenant-Colonel Henning), was held in divisional reserve. A gas attack—the first made by Britain and not too successful—was delivered about ten minutes to six. At 6.30 the 44th Brigade went over the parapet, and at twenty minutes to eight, one hour and ten minutes after they had left their trenches, the Highlanders were swinging through the streets of Loos, while the 46th Brigade was closing in from the north. By nine o'clock all resistance was at an end, and Loos was in our hands.

The orders of the division were not only to take Loos, but to occupy Hill 70, the rising ground to the east, and, if circumstances were favourable, to advance still farther. The Highlanders streamed up the slope and took the crest; they streamed onward down the eastern side—now only a few hundreds strong—losing direction as they went, so that, instead of making for Cité St. Auguste, they swung south-east towards Cité St. Laurent, the fortified northern suburb of Lens. The attack had now passed beyond the legitimate operations of war, for it formed a mad salient with no supports south or north. The crest of Hill 70 was manned as well as possible by the remnants of the 44th and 46th Brigades, and an attempt was made to recall the lost advance. It was a forlorn hope, and all down the slopes towards Lens lay the tartans, like driftweed on a shore.[1]

Meantime the reserve brigade, the 45th, had left the old front line at nine a.m., and had reached Loos with few losses. Two companies of the 7th Royal Scots Fusiliers,[2] under Major W. L. Campbell, dug themselves in on the west side of Hill 70. Presently the rest of the battalion arrived, and was temporarily put under the general commanding the 44th Brigade. They occupied an advanced position on Hill 70, and shortly after midnight repelled a German attack. The Fifteenth Division had all but exhausted its strength, and looked anxiously for the reserves which should have been there to support it. But on the 25th no reserves were available, and for nearly three days it had to hold its ground with little help from outside. The new Twenty-first Division did indeed arrive in the evening, when the drizzle of the day was clearing in a stormy sunset, but it was too raw to endure the fiery trial to which it was subjected, and when, in the early hours of Sunday, the 26th, the enemy counter-attacked, it was driven in. The result was to place our whole position on Hill 70 in the utmost jeopardy. The Guards Division was eight miles away, and there was nothing for

---

[1] With the forlorn hope went the Lewis gunners of the 7th Royal Scots Fusiliers, few of whom returned. Major Skipwith fell in this part of the action.

[2] Those two companies, through some misunderstanding, had followed the 44th Brigade into Loos. There they placed themselves under the orders of the O.C. 7th Camerons, of the 44th Brigade, and did excellent work. See *History of 7th Camerons*, by Sandilands and Macleod (1922).

it but to bring back the 44th and 46th Brigades, which had been relieved, to hold the reserve trenches, and to use the 45th Brigade for a counter-attack to regain the lost ground. This attack was gallantly delivered, but owing to the fatigue of the men and the mixture of units it could not succeed. Here Sergeant G. J. Willstrop displayed notable gallantry, for, after all the officers of his company had been killed or wounded, he took command and held the men steady. Till the evening the Scots stuck to their ground, till the 6th Cavalry Brigade came up to support them. They then fell back towards Loos, the 7th Royal Scots Fusiliers being the last to leave the slopes of Hill 70. It was not till Monday, the 27th, that the Guards Division took over the Loos front and the Fifteenth Division could be withdrawn. Its losses were heavy—over 6,000 for the two days' fight. The 7th Royal Scots Fusiliers lost in killed 7 officers—Major F. P. Skipwith, Captains F. G. Burr and E. G. J. Moyna, Lieutenant F. T. Hay, and Second Lieutenants G. S. Shearer, J. E. Watson, and R. T. Stewart—and 63 men, 12 officers and 246 men wounded, and 1 officer and 80 men missing.

The exploits of the Fifteenth Division at Loos earned it a reputation second to none in the British command. A year ago its men had followed civilian trades, and now they ranked in courage and discipline and every military virtue with the veterans of our army. The farthest rush of the Highland Brigade was no doubt a blunder, a magnificent but a barren feat of courage. And yet that madness contained the seeds of future success. It had in it the rudiments of "infiltration," the tactics by which storm troops found weak places in a front and filtered through. Behind them there was now no tactical plan, no certainty of supports; there was no prophetic eye among us to see what was implied in their achievement, and we set it down as a glorious failure. Three years later, when we had learned what the enemy could teach us, the same method was applied by a master hand to break in turn each of the German defences.

RESULTS OF LOOS

The battle of Loos, which began so well, ebbed away in enemy counter-strokes and isolated defensive actions, till, at the end of September, we counted our gains. Everywhere the German first line had been carried, and in many places we had broken into the second. The Seventh Division, whose general, Sir Thompson Capper, fell, still held a line west of the Quarries after many counter-attacks, in the course of which the 2nd Royal Scots Fusiliers lost their commanding officer, Captain A. H. Connell. His place was taken temporarily by Captain R. V. G. Horn, and presently by Major R. K. Walsh. Lieutenants J. L. Stirling, J. W. Bush, and A. V. Young also fell, and 41 other ranks, while 3 officers and 178 men were wounded, and 25 men missing. The Ninth Division lost General Thesiger, and was forced from Fosse 8 after a most gallant defence, though it still held the Hohenzollern. The 6th Royal Scots Fusiliers, whose fighting was in and around the trench called Fosse Alley, had 9 officers killed or died of wounds—Captains G. Robertson, J. Brodie, G. G. de B. Purves, J. Roxburgh, and H. H. Eales White, Lieutenant Viscount Stuart, and Second Lieutenants E. R. Hutt, M. T. Allan, and O. O. Staples—and 34 other ranks; Lieutenant-Colonel Northey, 7 officers, and 24 other ranks were wounded; and 228 men were wounded and missing.[1] In October they were moved to the Ypres Salient, where, during the winter, they learned something of the delight of watery trenches

1915 Sept.–Oct.

---

[1] In Colonel Northey's diary there is a vivid account of his experiences after he was wounded. "I stumbled on through communication trenches, hopping as best I could, for what seemed an interminable distance, the trenches being deep in mud and choked with dead or wounded men. I was eventually helped into a German dug-out by a stretcher-bearer, who tied up my leg. I then imagine I must have fainted, probably because I had lost a lot of blood, and came to, finding myself being pulled out by two of the stretcher-bearers, with a terrific din going on all round. This was the Germans counter-attacking, and I found I was between the German and British lines. I slowly and very painfully made my way along the German trenches towards our own lines— fighting going on all round—and very much afraid of being collared by the enemy. At one point a stretcher was obtained, and the two stretcher-bearers tried to carry me over the open, but just as I was being lifted a shell came, a splinter of which blew one unfortunate stretcher-bearer's brains all over me. The other stretcher-bearer then carried me away over the open on his back, under a very heavy fire, some hundred and fifty yards, until we reached a trench in our original front line. Very soon after this I got another stretcher,

1915
April 25

and crumbling parapets, with which the 1st Battalion was only too familiar.

III

The scene changes to the shores of the Ægean. At the close of 1914 the British Government, greatly exercised by the apparent deadlock in the West, had directed its mind to the possibility of turning the enemy's flank elsewhere, and after much discussion it was resolved to attempt to open the Dardanelles and strike at Constantinople—an operation in which it was believed that the sea power of Britain might play a decisive part. The instinct was sound, the scheme had strategically many merits, but the difficulties of the project were imperfectly realized ; and an enterprise, which might have produced superb results had it been conducted with adequate strength, did not succeed because it was too weakly supported. The land attack was launched too late, and the Allied force, though by August it had grown to a great army, failed to live up to the homely but pregnant summary of the art of war of the American Confederate general, " to git there first with most men." Krithia could have been won in May had the reinforcements of the late summer been present. But as the days passed the Turkish defence was strengthened ; soon Krithia did not involve Achi Baba, nor Achi Baba the Pasha Dagh, and what had originally been the key-points of the citadel were presently no more than outworks ; and the failure in August at Suvla Bay was the inevitable consequence of the earlier missing of the tide of fortune.

Our story is not concerned with the attempt in March to force the Straits by ships alone, or with Sir Ian Hamilton's landing on the Gallipoli Peninsula on that "loud Sabbath," 25th April, one of the greatest feats of arms in Britain's record. Nor does it touch the

and after many and varied vicissitudes I arrived at Bart's, where there was a dressing station. When I arrived there I found that the stretcher-bearer who had carried me had disappeared, and I have never been able to find out anything about him since."

fierce fighting of May at Krithia and Sari Bair. In May the Forty-second East Lancashire (Territorial) Division arrived to relieve the Twenty-ninth Division in the line, and in the middle of June Sir Ian Hamilton received a reinforcement which had been promised two months before—the Fifty-second (Scottish Lowland Territorial) Division, under Major-General G. G. A. Egerton. In the 155th Brigade, commanded by Brigadier-General J. F. Erskine, were the 4th Royal Scots Fusiliers, under Lieutenant-Colonel J. R. Balfour, and the 5th Royal Scots Fusiliers, under Lieutenant-Colonel J. B. Pollok-McCall. Each battalion numbered roughly 900 men.

1915
May 21–
July 12

On 21st May the brigade embarked at Liverpool in the *Mauretania*, and landed at Gallipoli on 6th June, being the first troops of the division to reach the scene of action. They were heavily shelled in their first rest camp,[1] and the two Scots Fusilier battalions were at once put into the line to relieve units of the Twenty-ninth Division, which had been sorely tried in the battle of 4th June. On 11th June the 4th Royal Scots Fusiliers lost Captain A. Logan from shell fire, and both battalions had many casualties before they were withdrawn. In that narrow and congested corner of land a rest camp was very little of a rest, and the 155th Brigade had an uneasy period of waiting, while on the 21st the French attacked and recaptured Haricot Redoubt, and on the 28th the 156th Brigade of their own division, moving on the British left, took the famous Gully Ravine, losing its commander, Brigadier-General W. Scott-Moncrieff, and 48 officers. This success brought our left wing considerably less than a mile from Krithia, and prepared the way for the final frontal attack upon that position—the Turkish front between Kereves Dere and Achi Baba nullah. The day fixed was 12th July, and the operation was to be in two parts—an attack at 7.35 a.m. by the French on the right and the 155th Brigade in the centre,

[1] On the first day the M.O. of the 4th Royal Scots Fusiliers, Major J. Craik Taylor, was mortally wounded—the first officer of the division to fall.

and an attack at 4.50 p.m. by the 157th Brigade on the left.

1915 July 12

The attack of the 155th Brigade was to be delivered in four waves, with a frontage of some five hundred yards. The first wave consisted of two and a half companies of the 4th K.O.S.B., and two platoons of the 4th Royal Scots Fusiliers; the second wave of a company and a half of the 4th K.O.S.B., and two platoons of the 4th Royal Scots Fusiliers; the third wave of two companies of the 5th K.O.S.B., and two platoons of the 4th Royal Scots Fusiliers; and the fourth wave of one company of the 5th K.O.S.B., and two platoons of the 4th Royal Scots Fusiliers. The 4th Royal Scots Fusiliers had also to supply a special company to keep touch with the French on the right, and touch was never lost during the battle. The 5th Royal Scots Fusiliers were in brigade reserve.

At 3.45 p.m. on the 11th the bombardment began, and was resumed at 4.30 a.m. on the 12th, the Turks replying with vigour. At 7.30 to the minute the Borderers and the Fusiliers left their trenches. "Unless one has seen it," wrote an officer, "there is no imagination that can picture a belt of land some four hundred yards wide converted into a seething hell of destruction. Rifle and machine-gun bullets rip up the earth, ping past the ear, or whing off the loose stones; shrapnel bursts overhead and the leaden bullets strike the ground with a vicious thud; the earth is rent into yawning chasms, while planks, sandbags, clods, and great rugged chunks of steel hurtle through the air. The noise is an indescribable, nerve-racking, continuous, deafening roar, while drifting clouds of smoke only allow an intermittent view of the damnable inferno." The 4th Royal Scots Fusiliers began to lose men from the start. They could not move fast, being heavily laden, and the slope of the land was such that they were almost at once out of view of the men behind. Moreover, they had to make a most difficult wheel over ground which was a labyrinth of broken trenches. Two Turkish fire-trenches lay before them, and as wave followed wave these were

THE GALLIPOLI PENINSULA

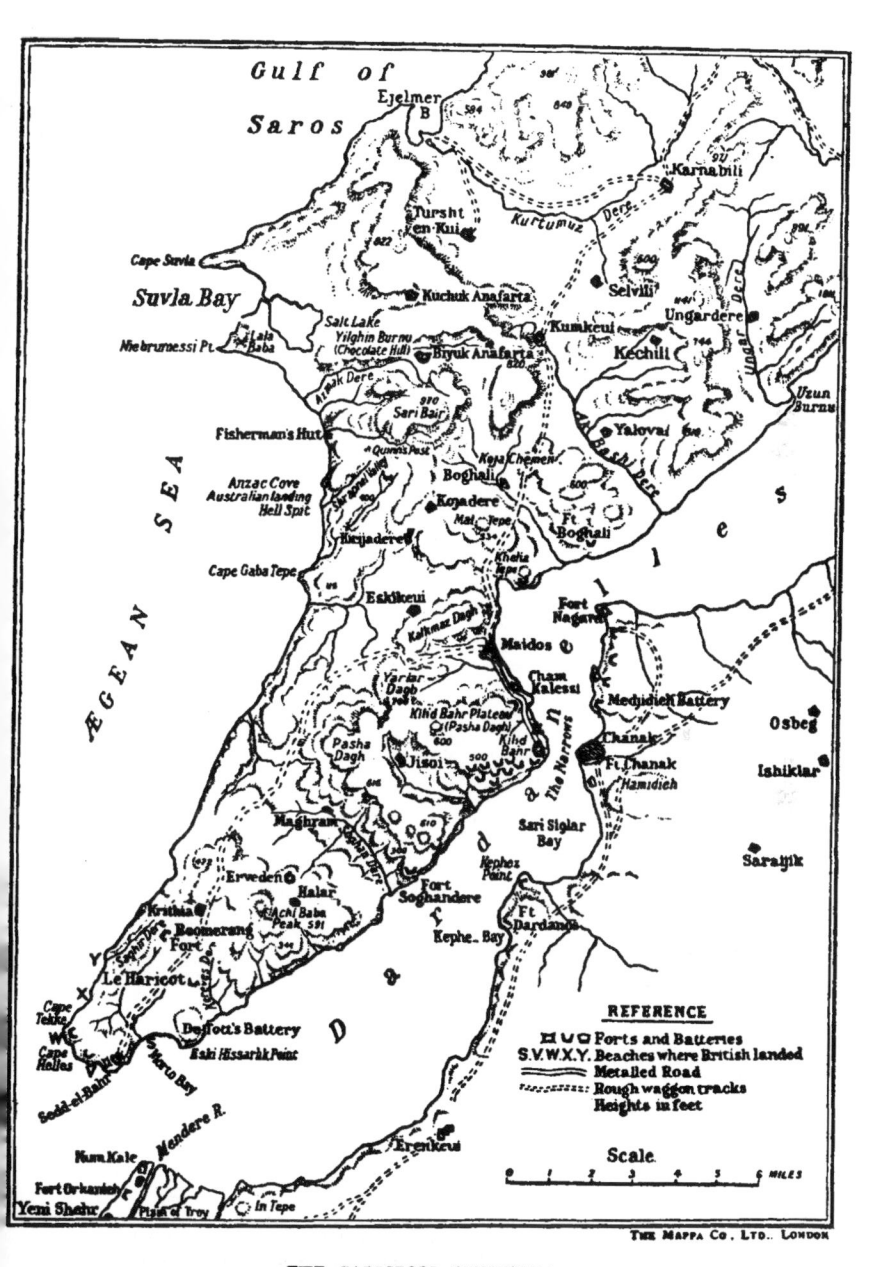

taken; but of the thirteen Fusilier officers who took part in the attack all but one, Captain H. R. Young, became casualties. The remnant was too weak to attempt the main enemy fire-trench beyond, so Captain Young (who was in command of the company that was in liaison with the French) got the survivors together and consolidated what had been won. " The 4th Royal Scots Fusiliers machine-gun officer was among the fallen, but Sergeant T. Murphy brought his guns over the open under a heavy fire, and took up a position whence he materially assisted in covering the consolidation and in repelling counter-attacks." [1]

Meantime the 4th K.O.S.B. were gallantly faring forward, until they came within the zone of our own artillery fire, and it was necessary to call a halt. They had actually penetrated the enemy front, but few of that band of heroes returned. Then the 5th K.O.S.B. advanced, and to support them General Erskine sent in the only reserves he possessed—two companies of the 5th Royal Scots Fusiliers. With their assistance the captured trenches were made good and communication trenches dug. In the afternoon the 157th Brigade on the left progressed well, though with heavy losses, and at the same time the 4th Royal Scots Fusiliers on the right attacked and captured a further trench. The day had been on the whole successful, for the 157th Brigade had made a gap some six hundred and fifty yards wide in the main Turkish trench system, and the 155th Brigade and the French had driven back the enemy to his last fire-line west of the Kereves Dere. Between the latter and the summit of Achi Baba there were only some scattered earthworks, and had we been able to send in fresh troops before nightfall the defence might have crumbled. As it was, we could do no more than repel counter-attacks and hold what we had gained, and an attempt by the Royal Naval Division next day to improve these gains did not succeed. The battle won ground, but it did not alter the stalemate, and it compelled Sir Ian Hamilton to revise his strategy. The

[1] Lieutenant-Colonel Thompson's *The Fifty-second Division* (1923), page 91.

1915
July 12–
Aug. 13

day had gone when a frontal attack on the Turkish fortress could succeed.

The losses of the Fifty-second Division had been such that for the Scottish Lowlands it was a second Flodden. In large areas between Tweed and Forth scarcely a household but mourned a son. On 3rd July the division numbered 10,900 of all ranks; by the 13th it had lost over 4,800 in killed and wounded. The 4th Royal Scots Fusiliers had 6 officers killed—Major W. Stewart, Captain A. Kenneth, Lieutenants J. Barnett, H. G. Kyle, and G. Sturrock, and Second Lieutenant M. B. W. McColl—and 118 other ranks; and 6 officers and 148 other ranks wounded. The 5th Royal Scots Fusiliers suffered scarcely less heavily in the task of support. There fell Captain S. A. Cunningham, and Second Lieutenants R. F. Ferguson, J. G. Hamilton-Grierson, T. Jackson, J. Maxwell, and W. H. Mill, and 69 other ranks; while 1 officer and 139 other ranks were wounded.

The battle of 12th July was the chief of the Gallipoli actions between the landing and the battle which began on 8th August, and it was the one great fight of the Fifty-second Division in that campaign. The Lowlanders were destined for the rest of their stay on the peninsula to the weary task of manning the trenches, and they had only a small part in the holding battle of 8th August in the Cape Helles section. On 13th August, while the guns were roaring at Anzac and Suvla, there was a bombing attack by the Turks on one of the trenches at the Vineyard, which was repulsed by the Scots Fusiliers under Captain J. Howard Johnstone. There the first Victoria Cross of the division was won by Private D. Ross Lauder of the 4th Royal Scots Fusiliers. Lauder, who, like every one else, had had little practice in bombing, threw one which struck the top of the trench and lobbed back inside. " He at once put his foot on it and shouted to the rest to clear. The bomb burst a moment afterwards, blowing off the fore part of his foot completely, and shattering the whole of his lower leg so that he lost it. He undoubt-

THE SUMMER IN GALLIPOLI

edly saved half a dozen comrades from death or wounds."[1] There were various changes in the commands. Lieutenant-Colonel Pollok-McCall took over the 155th Brigade, and was succeeded by Major J. Russell; Russell was killed twelve days later, when Captain J. B. Cook took command of the 5th Royal Scots Fusiliers. Lieutenant-Colonel J. R. Balfour, of the 4th Battalion, was invalided in August, and succeeded by Captain Harold Thompson.

The summer in Gallipoli would have been a wearing experience for the most seasoned troops, and its discomforts were the greater for men who, a year ago, had for the most part lived sedentary and sheltered lives. If there is such a thing as a sub-conscious regimental memory, it might well have been awakened, for the Scots Fusiliers were undergoing some of the miseries which their predecessors had suffered more than a century before on hot West Indian islets; but in this case there were other enemies besides sun and disease. The whole of the position was honeycombed with trenches and dug-outs like a colony of sand martens in the bank of a river. There was no shade from nature, for the copses were only scrub. The sun beat down pitilessly on the acres of rock and gravel, and was reflected from the blue waters around. The men were very close together, and the whole earth soon became tainted in spite of every care. Sunstroke cases were few, for the sun of Gallipoli is not the sun of India; but fevers and dysentery began to take their toll. The scarcity of water, the difficult journeys for the sick down communication trenches and cliff roads, and the long voyage before hospital was reached intensified the discomfort. And everywhere fell a plague of flies. Men who had fought in South Africa remembered the curse of the fly on the veld, but the South African scourge was feeble compared to the clouds which hung over that baked peninsula. There was little movement or chance of movement. The troops had to sit still in their stifling trenches, and every acre of that butt-end

[1] *The Fifty-second Division*, page 135.

1915
Oct.-Dec.

of Gallipoli was searched by the enemy's fire. Under such conditions—inaction, grave losses, grave discomforts—it was a marvel that men maintained so high a spirit and so steady a cheerfulness. In October the sick and wounded of the division in hospital, or still on the strength, reached a weekly average of nearly 3,000.

In October there came the cooler winds of autumn and a change of policy. Sir Ian Hamilton returned to England, and Sir Charles Monro took over the Mediterranean Expeditionary Force. Lord Kitchener visited Gallipoli, and reported in favour of evacuating the peninsula; and on 7th December the British Government decided to abandon the positions at Suvla and Anzac, but to retain those at Cape Helles. The tale of that miraculous departure does not belong to this narrative; but while the evacuation was in progress the troops at Helles had to do their utmost to distract the enemy. The two Scots Fusilier battalions had spent their time in the line mainly in small bombing enterprises around Krithia nullah, in which much personal gallantry was shown. While on 19th December Suvla and Anzac were being emptied of men, the 157th Brigade attempted a surprise attack, with the assistance of the 5th Royal Scots Fusiliers under Lieutenant-Colonel A. H. Leggett, while the rest of the 155th Brigade gave covering fire. The operation was successful, and served its purpose. But presently arrived the Turkish guns from Anzac and Suvla, and Helles became an unhealthy area, for every day saw an enemy bombardment. The British replied with a vigorous offensive. Two mines were run out under a Turkish machine-gun nest, and their explosion at one p.m. on the 29th was followed by an attack of the 5th Royal Scots Fusiliers, supported by four grenade teams from the 4th Royal Scots Fusiliers and the 4th and 5th King's Own Scottish Borderers. The Scots Fusiliers ran for the craters and occupied the ruined trenches, killing or taking prisoner the garrison. One party of fifteen Fusiliers rounded up twenty-six Turks, who

THE EVACUATION OF HELLES

turned out to be members of the Constantinople Fire Brigade! The ground won was held in spite of the enemy bombardment, and on the last day of the year the 155th Brigade was relieved. The 5th Royal Scots Fusiliers had Lieutenants A. N. Mitchell and W. J. M'Naughton and Second Lieutenants S. S. Anderson and J. C. Austin killed, and 24 other ranks, and the wounded brought their casualties up to 86; while the 4th Royal Scots Fusiliers lost 30 killed and wounded.

On 27th December the British Cabinet decided on the evacuation of Helles, and next day General Birdwood issued the orders. The Turks now outnumbered the British more than three times, and it seemed an impossible undertaking to bring away 35,000 troops and over a hundred guns under the eye of a powerful enemy. Towards the close of the month, in the first quarter of the new moon, guns and supplies and supernumerary troops were brought down to the beaches and quickly embarked. As at Suvla and Anzac, two nights were allotted to the final evacuation—those of 7th and 8th January. New positions covering the landing places were prepared, and an embarkation zone was created under the general now commanding the Fifty-second Division, Major-General the Hon. H. A. Lawrence, who, having begun the war as a brigade-major of Yeomanry, was to end it as Haig's Chief-of-Staff. There was no time to be lost, for all must be finished before the moon reached the full and while the fair weather lasted. On 7th January it looked as if a general action might have to be fought by way of farewell, but the Turkish attack died away. The weather changed on the afternoon of the 8th, and made embarkation difficult, though it covered our departure. By 3.30 on the morning of 9th January the last troops were on board, and by a series of incalculable chances the impossible had been achieved. The whole of the 155th Brigade [1]—now reduced to about 1,200—had left the peninsula before the final day. The historian of the Fifty-second Division has described a dramatic episode.

[1] Except the 4th Royal Scots Fusiliers, who embarked on the final night.

" Before the chaplain left, the Presbyterians of the division held a celebration of the Lord's Supper in a dug-out of winter quarters, which presented a scene worthy of some modern Rembrandt. . . . The celebration took place at night. On a rough table of packing-case wood stood a few candles in bottles, and a small Communion service. The dim light revealed some of the stern, resigned faces of the men crowded around under the low corrugated iron roof. Others could barely be seen in the dark shadows, as they leant against the walls of sandbags and clay. Two or three officers acted as elders. For those remaining on the peninsula it was likely to be their last act of assembled worship. Every one felt that the beautiful and comforting words which told of the world's greatest sacrifice, quietly spoken and punctuated by shell-bursts near and far, were peculiarly appropriate." [1]

As the 4th and 5th Battalions of our regiment were preparing to leave the battle-fields on which they had fought so well, another battalion was arriving in the Ægean. This was the 8th Royal Scots Fusiliers, which, under Lieutenant-Colonel H. V. Bunbury, embarked at Folkestone on 20th September to join the 77th Brigade of the Twenty-sixth Division. Its first service was with the XII. Corps of Sir Charles Monro's Third Army, which at that time had taken over from the French a sector on the Somme. During October it was in the trenches opposite Mametz; but in November, when the situation in Serbia became desperate, the Twenty-sixth Division was hurried off to Marseilles. It arrived at Salonika in the beginning of December, and, under Lieutenant-Colonel F. E. Buchanan, became part of the Allied force with General Sarrail, which was engaged in retreating slowly from Lake Doiran and entrenching the Salonika position.

The end of the year 1915 saw seven battalions of the Scots Fusiliers in the field—two on the eve of sailing from Gallipoli for Egypt; one on the grassy flats by

[1] *The Fifty-second Division*, page 220.

THE CLOSE OF 1915

the Vardar; and four, after an autumn of great battles, holding a variety of ugly places between Ypres and Loos. That winter in France and Flanders was not easier than the last, but the troops in the muddy trenches had a different outlook. They were learning the ways of the new campaigning, and under Haig they were being trained for a great and fateful enterprise.

Officers who died in 1915.

Captain W. W. ADAM (14th Dec.); Lieutenant A. C. E. ALEXANDER (11th March); Lieutenant M. T. ALLAN (26th Sept.); Lieutenant-Colonel A. H. ALLENBY (7th Aug.); Second Lieutenant S. S. ANDERSON (30th Dec.); Second Lieutenant J. C. AUSTIN (29th Dec.); Second Lieutenant J. BARNETT (12th July); Captain A. M. M. BELL (28th April); Lieutenant T. B. BENSON (13th March); Second Lieutenant E. C. BLACK (22nd Nov.); Captain J. BRODIE (26th Sept.); Second Lieutenant R. J. G. S. BROWN (22nd May); Second Lieutenant R. B. BUCHANAN (20th June); Captain F. G. BURR (25th Sept.); Second Lieutenant J. W. BUSH (25th Sept.); Second Lieutenant A. E. CHISHOLM (25th Sept.); Major A. H. CONNELL (28th Sept.); Second Lieutenant R. S. CRAWFORD (17th May); Lieutenant H. A. CRUICKSHANK (28th Sept.); Captain S. A. CUNNINGHAM (12th July); Second Lieutenant J. E. H. CURRIE (11th Sept.); Captain H. H. EALES WHITE (26th Sept.); Lieutenant R. F. FERGUSON (12th July); Lieutenant J. E. FINDLAY-HAMILTON (16th June); Captain H. C. FRASER (5th Aug.); Second Lieutenant C. GALLIE (22nd Aug.); Second Lieutenant A. A. F. GEDDES (16th June); Major L. GOODEVE (26th Aug.); Lieutenant R. M. GRAHAM [Essex Regiment—attached] (12th March); Captain H. R. HADDON (12th July); Second Lieutenant J. G. HAMILTON GRIERSON (12th July); Lieutenant F. T. HAY (26th Sept.); Second Lieutenant D. A. HEGGIE (3rd Aug.); Second Lieutenant R. HUGHES (17th May); Second Lieutenant E. R. HUTT (25th Sept.); Lieutenant T. JACKSON (12th July); Captain N. JAMIESON (13th Aug.); Captain A. KENNETH (12th July); Second Lieutenant L. A. KER (4th April); Second Lieutenant H. G. KYLE (12th July); Lieutenant W. A. LAIRD (18th Sept.); Lieutenant M. H. LEWIS (20th June); Second Lieutenant R. H. LOCKHART (11th Nov.); Captain A. LOGAN (11th June); Lieutenant A. C. G. LONSDALE [K.R.R.—attached] (10th March); Second Lieutenant M. B. W. M'COLL (12th July); Lieutenant W. J. M'NAUGHTON (31st Dec.); Honorary Major and Quartermaster J. MASSON (1st May); Second Lieutenant J. MAXWELL (12th July); Second Lieutenant Y. W. MERCIER (25th Sept.); Second Lieutenant W. H. MILL (12th July); Second Lieutenant J. A. MILLAR (25th Sept.); Lieutenant A. N. MITCHELL (30th Dec.); Second Lieutenant J. L. MOFFAT (11th March); Captain E. G. J.

MOYNA (26th Sept.); Second Lieutenant G. PATERSON (21st Jan.); Lieutenant C. W. PECK (29th Sept.); Captain M. K. POLLOCK (25th Sept.); Captain G. G. DE B. PURVES (8th Nov.); Captain G. ROBERTSON (25th Sept.); Second Lieutenant A. E. ROBINSON (16th June); Captain J. ROXBURGH (26th Sept.); Major J. RUSSELL (26th Aug.); Second Lieutenant G. S. SHEARER (26th Sept.); Major F. P. SKIPWITH (26th Sept.); Second Lieutenant O. O. STAPLES (25th Sept.); Lieutenant R. W. STERLING (24th April); Second Lieutenant R. T. STEWART (27th Sept.); Major W. STEWART (12th July); Second Lieutenant J. L. STIRLING (28th Sept.); Captain S. B. STIRLING-COOKSON (17th May); Captain R. W. S. STIVEN (15th Sept.); Lieutenant Viscount STUART (25th Sept.); Second Lieutenant R. N. STUART (17th May); Lieutenant G. STURROCK (12th July); Second Lieutenant J. L. L. SWEET (16th June); Second Lieutenant S. J. K. THOMSON (12th Oct.); Captain T. VIVERS (27th Oct.); Second Lieutenant J. R. WALLACE (23rd April); Second Lieutenant A. E. WALLER (17th May); Lieutenant WALLNER (22nd May); Second Lieutenant J. E. WATSON (26th Sept.); Second Lieutenant S. J. WATSON (28th Nov.); Second Lieutenant G. W. WEBSTER (15th June); Lieutenant A. V. YOUNG (25th Sept.).

CHAPTER XVI

THE GREAT WAR—1916

The spring training—Fighting in the Ypres and Hohenzollern sections—Mr. Winston Churchill—The opening of the battle of the Somme—Capture of Montauban—The attack of 14th July—The attack on Guillemont—The advance of 15th September—The capture of Martinpuich—Winter on the Somme—The Scots Fusiliers in Egypt—Stand at Bir-el-Dueidar—Romani—The Palestine frontier reached—Salonika in 1916.

THE story of the British army in the year 1916 on the Western front falls naturally into two parts. There were six months of waiting and training, diversified by minor actions in the Ypres Salient and the Loos area, while the great German offensive, which was launched at Verdun on 21st February, slowly drifted into failure. During that long-drawn and memorable battle it was the task of Britain to hold the entire front from the North Sea to the river Somme. It was a heavy duty—weary months of desultory trench-fighting with no combined movement, no great offensive purpose, to quicken the spirit. It was a costly duty, for the average daily loss was 500, which gives in six months a total of 90,000 men. The British army was neither attacking nor seriously on the defence, and those indeterminate weeks were for officers and men among the hardest to bear in the whole campaign. Meantime the new Commander-in-Chief, Sir Douglas Haig, was busy with the task for which he was qualified above almost all living soldiers—the training of troops. He had now received the balance of the New Army divisions from home as well as various units released

1916

from Gallipoli, and to produce the homogeneity which is necessary in a field force much thought and time had to be given to training. The British armies in France and Flanders during the first half of 1916 were one vast school of instruction. The second stage opened on the first day of July with the battle of the Somme, which occupied the remaining months of the year. There, for the first time, with ample munitions and adequate numbers, the Allies embarked upon a carefully-devised strategic plan which had a reasonable hope of success.

I

The hardest fighting of our regiment during the first stage fell to the lot of the 1st Battalion in the 9th Brigade of the Third Division. During the last month of 1915 it had held part of the front in the Ypres Salient; the beginning of 1916 was occupied with training behind the line. On 7th March Brigadier-General Douglas Smith took command of the Twentieth Division, and Brigadier-General Potter succeeded to the 9th Brigade. Fighting had been going on in different parts of the Salient since 8th February, and on the 14th the hillock which we called the Bluff, on the north bank of the Ypres–Comines canal, was carried by the enemy. On 2nd March the Third Division, wearing for the first time the new steel helmets, retook it. At the end of the month the British again attacked. The Ypres Salient now represented a shallow semicircle, running from Boesinghe in the north to St. Eloi in the south. At the latter point a small German salient had encroached on our line, to the depth of about one hundred yards on a front of six hundred. It was resolved to get rid of this and straighten the front, the area of action being roughly defined by the cross-roads south of the village of St. Eloi, where the Messines and Warneton roads branched off.

The attack was to be delivered by the 1st Northumberland Fusiliers and the 4th Royal Fusiliers of the 9th Brigade, while the 1st Royal Scots Fusiliers

ST. ELOI

were to act in close support of the latter, and to supply four working parties to aid them in establishing the ground won. On 25th March the battalion entered the trenches. At 4.15 on the morning of the 27th several large mines were exploded within the salient, with a shock so colossal that it was felt in villages far behind the battle-ground. Four minutes later the Royal Fusiliers and the Northumberland Fusiliers were racing across the open to the German trenches. Inside the salient there was nothing but death and destruction, but machine guns were busy on the flanks, and the left of the attack did not quite reach its objective, so that a way was left for the Germans to occupy one of the mine craters. The next few days were spent in repelling counter-attacks and endeavouring to oust the enemy from the crater which he held. It was not a satisfactory position, as the Second Canadian Division found to its cost when, in the beginning of April, it relieved the Third. The water-logged soil had been churned into glutinous mire by the shelling and the mine explosions, the communication trenches had been obliterated, and there was a very general doubt as to where exactly was the British front line and where the German. The Royal Scots Fusiliers in support suffered heavily from the enemy's artillery fire, and when next day they were relieved by the 8th East Yorks, they had lost 3 officers—Captain G. E. O. F. Lambart, Captain W. R. Houston, and Second Lieutenant W. Hay—and 27 other ranks killed; while 4 officers, including Lieutenant-Colonel McConaghey, and 74 men were wounded, and 23 men missing. One of the working parties under Second Lieutenant W. B. McArthur had a notable success, for it killed 7 Germans, and took 45 prisoners.

During the first days of April working parties of Royal Scots Fusiliers were still in the line, and further losses were incurred, including Captain John Nichol. On 7th April the battalion, now under the command of Captain A. H. Thomson, was transferred to the 8th Brigade. For a few days it was in reserve at La Clytte, and Major A. M. H. Forbes took over the command.

1916
March 25–
April 17

1916
March–June

During May and June there was little to record, save trench raids and small gas attacks, but the wastage in that uneasy area was continuous and severe. Meantime strong drafts were arriving, largely from the 1st K.O.S.B. in Egypt, and various officers joined from the now disbanded 6th Battalion. On 1st July the whole brigade left the Ypres area, and on the 5th arrived at Vaux on the Somme.

The 2nd Battalion of our regiment left the Hohenzollern sector in November 1915, and on 15th December was transferred from the Seventh Division to the 90th Brigade of the Thirtieth. The beginning of 1916 saw it at Suzanne in the Somme area, where, with intervals for training behind the front, it remained during the first half of 1916. In March it was attached to the Fourth Army Infantry School for demonstration purposes. The commandant of the school wrote to Colonel Walsh that the "success of the course was in large measure due to the cheerful spirit which all your officers, non-commissioned officers, and men displayed when asked to carry out demonstrations, or any other work. I am sure they must have been heartily sick of it." About the middle of June the battalion moved into the Montauban area, the section allotted to the Thirtieth Division in the coming battle; it had practised the attack in the back areas, and it now carried out the normal duties of a battalion in the line, while the British and French guns spoke without ceasing night and day.

The 6th Battalion, in the 27th Brigade of the Ninth Division, spent the first three months of 1916 in the Ploegsteert section of the front. Few incidents marked these months, the last of its existence as a separate unit, but it served under a most distinguished commander. Mr. Winston Churchill had ceased to be First Lord of the Admiralty on the reconstruction of the Ministry in the early summer of 1915, and his energy of mind could not long be content with the nominal duties of the Chancellor of the Duchy of Lancaster. A soldier by profession, and a profound student of the military art, he went to France in the early winter of 1915, and at the close of the year was put in command of the 6th Royal Scots Fusiliers. The advent of so famous and so controversial a figure was awaited with a certain trepidation, but a week's experience of Colonel Churchill sufficed to convince doubters, and when the 6th Battalion was united with the 7th one of the chief matters of regret to its officers and men was that they must lose their commanding officer. Major A. D. Gibb, who served with him, has written thus of his brief tenure of office.

" I speak with all possible affection of him as the friend of his officers. This was most strikingly demonstrated in the last days of his command, when he was anxious to find employment—congenial employment—for those who were to be thrown out into the cold when the battalions amalgamated. He took endless trouble; he borrowed motor cars and scoured France, interviewing Generals and staff officers great and small, in his efforts to do something to help those who had served under him. . . . No man was ever kinder to his subordinates, and no commanding officer I have ever known was half so kind. . . .

" The early months of 1916 are by far my most treasured war memory. It was my happiest time, and it was my most interesting time. For work in intimate association with Winston Churchill was the last experience in the world any of us expected —our course did not lie that way. At first the prospect frightened us, but those feelings did not survive the first week. We came to realize—to realize at first hand—his tremendous ability. He came to be looked on as really a possession of our own, and one of which we were intensely proud. And much more, he became our friend. He is a man who apparently is always to have enemies. He made none in his old regiment, but left behind him there men who will always be his loyal par-

1916 tisans and admirers, and who are proud of having served under the leadership of one who is beyond question a great man." [1]

The amalgamation of the two battalions—due to the difficulty in keeping so many Scots battalions up to strength—took place in May, when the combined unit became the 6th/7th Royal Scots Fusiliers. The 7th Battalion had continued in the Loos area ever since the battle of the previous September.[2] Lieutenant-Colonel Henning gave place in April to Captain I. V. Paton, who was presently succeeded by Major A. C. H. Smith from the Scottish Rifles. On 11th May, in the evening, there was a German attack at the Hohenzollern on the 13th Royal Scots of the 45th Brigade, who held the centre of the divisional line, at the ugly corner called the "Kink," an attack which won a depth of four hundred yards. Half an hour later Major Smith, with the Royal Scots Fusiliers, counter-attacked, but failed to make ground. At 1.25 on the morning of the 12th the Fusiliers, under Captain Paton, again attacked, but were caught by cross-fire from the enemy machine guns. There was nothing for it but to consolidate a new position. In this action Captain R. R. M'Queen and Second Lieutenant J. J. Scandrett fell.

When the battalions were amalgamated the first commanding officer was Lieutenant-Colonel J. Scott of the Argyll and Sutherland Highlanders. He was succeeded on 25th June by Major E. I. D. Gordon, who had been an officer of the regiment in the South African War.

---

[1] *With Winston Churchill at the Front*, by Captain X. (1924.)
[2] During this period the battalion lost Second Lieutenants E. C. Black and R. H. Lockhart. In this area throughout the winter of 1915–16 the trials of the Fifteenth Division were very severe. The Hohenzollern sector, in particular, could perhaps be best described as an open battlefield when taken over in October 1915 by the 45th Brigade, of which the 7th Royal Scots Fusiliers formed part. The trenches were dominated by Fosse 8 and the Hohenzollern Redoubt. Communications through the old British trench system, across the previous no-man's-land, to the old German trenches now held by our men, were lengthy as well as exposed, so that reliefs and the tasks of carrying-parties were both perilous and exhausting. The mine warfare, combined with the heavy hostile artillery and trench mortar fire, took its toll. The strain on battalions can perhaps be best understood when it is realized that during two of these months in the trenches the Fifteenth Division suffered 3,000 casualties.

July saw further fighting at the Hohenzollern, and on the 22nd of the month the whole Fifteenth Division began to move south to the battlefield of the Somme.

*1916
June 24–
July 1*

II

No man who was then in Picardy will ever forget the month before the battle of the Somme opened—the broken summer weather, the quiet of the front line, the activity of the British hinterland where every road was thronged with guns and transport, the strange, breathless sense of expectation. On 24th June, in grey, cloudy weather with flying scuds of rain, the main bombardment opened. A week followed of drizzle and fog, and then on the last afternoon of June the skies cleared. That night the orders went out. The great attack was to be delivered next morning three hours after dawn.

The purpose of the battle of the Somme needs a word of explanation. The enemy at the moment was suffering from a lack of immediate reserves and the weakened *moral* due to his failure at Verdun and the doings of Brussilov in Galicia. He dared not resort to the expedient of shortening his line, and trusted to the great natural and artificial strength of his position in the West to repel the Allies, whatever weight of men and guns they might bring against him. In no part of the Western front were these positions stronger than between Arras and the Somme, where he held in the main the higher ground, and had in the rear many fortified woods and villages which could be linked into reserve lines.

The Allies had learned the lesson of the unsuccessful offensive of 1915 and the long ordeal of Verdun. They no longer dreamed of breaking the enemy's front by a sudden stroke, for they realized the depth of his fortified zone. The new plan was that of attrition on a colossal scale. Their method was that of " limited objectives," with new troops and a new bombardment for each phase, and they had certain tactical devices

1916
June 24–
July 1

in reserve which they hoped to apply with good effect at the right moment. To quote what I have written elsewhere, the scheme might be presented by the metaphor of a sea-dyke of stone in a flat country where all stone must be imported. " The waters crumble the wall in one section, and the free reserves of stone are used to strengthen that part. But the crumbling goes on, and to fill the breach stones are brought from other sections of the dyke. Some day there must come an hour when the sea will wash through the old breach, and a great length of the weakened dyke will follow in the cataclysm." This method presupposed a war on two fronts. When Russia fell out of line the situation was utterly changed, and the plan became futile against an enemy with a large new reservoir of recruitment. But at the time of its inception, it was a sound, though expensive, plan, and, *ceteris paribus*, would have given the Allies victory before the end of 1917. Even as things turned out, in spite of the unlooked-for *débâcle* in the East, the battle of the Somme struck a blow at the heart of Germany's strength from which she never wholly recovered.

A strategy of intense attrition demands a battle, and a battle requires certain definite objectives. Our aim was to crumble the enemy's defences on the Bapaume ridge so completely that he could not find an alternate position of equal strength, and would be slowly forced into open warfare. The British front of attack was from Gommecourt in the north to Maricourt in the south, whence the French carried the battle across the Somme to a point opposite the village of Fay. It was Sir Douglas Haig's intention to make his main attack between the Ancre and Maricourt, and it is clear from his dispatches that he regarded the movement of his left wing as a subsidiary operation. The left wing indeed faced the strongest German defences, where the enemy was forewarned, for he expected the attack between Arras and Albert. The effort of the British left on the first day failed, and thereafter the battle became a stubborn frontal assault up the slopes

CAPTURE OF MONTAUBAN

from the west between the Ancre and the Somme. When, after six months, the enemy admitted defeat and fell back, he yielded less to any strategical brilliance in our plan than to the incomparable valour and tenacity of the Allied troops.

1916 July 1

On the first day of the battle the British centre and right consisted of Lieutenant-General Sir T. L. N. Morland's X. Corps—Thirty-sixth and Thirty-second Divisions; Lieutenant-General Sir W. P. Pulteney's III. Corps—Eighth and Thirty-fourth Divisions; Lieutenant-General Horne's XV. Corps—Twenty-first and Seventh Divisions; and Lieutenant-General Congreve's XIII. Corps—Eighteenth and Thirtieth Divisions. The 2nd Battalion of our regiment was the first to enter the battle, for it was with the Thirtieth Division on the extreme British right: a memorable position, since there could be seen a sight hitherto unwitnessed in the campaign—the advance in line of the troops of Britain and France. For beyond us on the right moved the French XX. Corps—the corps which had held the Grand Couronné of Nancy during the feverish days of the first Marne battle, and which, by its counter-attack at Douaumont on that snowy 26th February, had turned the tide at Verdun.

The Thirtieth Division attacked from the hollow north of the Albert–Péronne road, where stood the hamlet of Carnoy. Its objective, Montauban, lay on the crest of the ridge in front, now, like most Somme valleys, a few broken walls set among splintered trees. The brick-fields on the right were expected to be the scene of a fierce struggle, but to our surprise they had been so shattered by our guns that they were easily taken. The Montauban attack was perhaps the most satisfactory of the episodes of 1st July. The artillery had done their work to perfection, and the 6th Bavarian Regiment opposed to us lost 3,000 out of a total strength of 3,500. The Thirtieth Division attacked with the 21st and 90th Brigades, and in the latter the assault was delivered by the 16th and 17th Manchesters, with the 2nd Royal Scots Fusiliers under Lieutenant-Colonel

R. K. Walsh in support. Montauban fell early in the day to the Scots Fusiliers and the Manchesters, and Colonel Walsh was made officer commanding the village. Owing to the brigade headquarters being so far back, he had practically commanded the brigade during the operations. The battalion took 20 officers into action, and its fighting strength in men was 743. The day brought it a total of 170 casualties. Two officers—Lieutenant J. W. Towers-Clarke and Second Lieutenant J. L. H. Grierson—were killed, and 18 men; 6 officers and 94 other ranks were wounded; and 58 were missing. General Balfourier, commanding the French XX. Corps, and General Nourrisson, commanding the French Thirty-ninth Division, sent messages expressing their " admiration of the British troops, their neighbours, whose bravery and discipline under heavy and continuous fire were beyond praise."

That night and until the 3rd, when the battalion was relieved, there was heavy enemy shelling from the adjacent copses. The next step was to clear the woods of Trônes and Bernafay. The latter was occupied on the 4th, and on the 8th began the struggle for the former. During the next five days Trônes Wood was the hottest corner in the British southern section, since its peculiar situation gave every chance to the defence. There was only one covered approach to it from the west—by way of the trench called Trônes Alley, while the southern part was commanded by the Maltzhorn ridge, and the northern by the German position at Longueval. Around the wood to north and east the enemy's second line lay in a half moon, so that he could concentrate upon it a converging artillery fire, and could feed his own garrison in the place with reserves at his pleasure. Lastly, the denseness of the covert, cut only by the railway clearing and the German communication trenches, made organized movement impossible. It was not till our pressure elsewhere diverted the German artillery fire that the wood as a whole could be won. Slowly and stubbornly we pushed our way northwards from our point of lodgment in the southern end. On

BAZENTIN-LE-GRAND

the 9th the Royal Scots Fusiliers were engaged in an attack on Maltzhorn Farm, where C Company took many prisoners and two machine guns, and lost its gallant young commanding officer, Captain P. W. T. Macgregor-Whitton. The battalion was relieved on the 11th, and returned to Maricourt, where it learned that the Thirtieth Division had been transferred to the II. Corps. Meantime Trônes Wood had become a Tom Tiddler's ground, which neither antagonist could fully claim or use.

The result of 1st July was that the German first line was won almost everywhere from the Ancre southward. The next step was for the British to attack the German second position, which ran from Pozières through the two Bazentins and Longueval to Guillemont. The capture of Contalmaison on the 13th allowed Sir Douglas Haig to begin the second stage. It was a bold venture, for the four-mile front of attack involved in some parts an advance of nearly a mile before the enemy's line was reached. Indeed, the difficulties before the British were so great that more than one distinguished French officer doubted the possibility of success. "The decision," wrote Sir Douglas Haig, "to attempt a night attack of this magnitude with an army, the bulk of which had been raised since the beginning of the war, was perhaps the highest tribute that could be paid to the quality of our troops." Moreover, every village in the German second line had its adjacent or enfolding wood—Bazentin-le-Petit, Bazentin-le-Grand, and at Longueval the big wood of Delville—while a mile or so behind the enemy position High Wood hung dark upon the sky-line.

The attack was launched in the cloudy dawn of 14th July, and the result of the day was that we carried all our objectives from Bazentin-le-Petit to Longueval— a front of over three miles—and at one moment all but penetrated the enemy third position at High Wood. Here we are concerned only with the left division, the Third, of Congreve's XIII. Corps, whose objective was

1916
July 9–14

**1916
July 14** Bazentin-le-Grand, and which contained in its 8th Brigade the 1st Royal Scots Fusiliers, under Lieutenant-Colonel A. M. H. Forbes. The battalion had arrived at Carnoy on the 5th, and its officers had gone over the ground at Montauban won by the 2nd Battalion. On the 7th, during the march to Bronfoy Farm, it had passed close to that battalion, and had been convoyed for a little way by its pipers. Its strength was 20 officers and 706 men. On the 13th it moved to the quarry in the hollow north of Montauban. At 1.45 on the morning of the 14th it moved forward to the sunken road about a hundred and fifty yards south of the German front line, deployed, fixed bayonets, and waited for the hour of assault.

At 3.20 a.m. the British guns opened an intensive bombardment, but for some reason or other the objective of the 8th Brigade was little touched. The assaulting battalions were the 7th Royal Shropshire Light Infantry and the 8th East Yorks, with the 1st Royal Scots Fusiliers in support. The first line of German wire was found to be cut in a few places, but the second line not at all. The result was that, while at 7.15 the village of Bazentin-le-Grand fell to the 9th Brigade, the 8th Brigade on its right was held up. Here the Scots Fusiliers had some 60 killed, including 5 officers. The assaulting battalions were obliged to return to the sunken road, and there, about ten a.m., a report was received that a small party of mixed Scots Fusiliers and East Yorks had succeeded in entering the enemy front farther to the right and was in urgent need of support. At the same time a message came that the 2nd Royal Scots had sent a detachment round by Bazentin-le-Grand village to bomb eastward. Colonel Forbes accordingly ordered Second Lieutenants Tinley and Smith to take two platoons and join the first-mentioned party and bomb westward. The converging bombing attack was brilliantly carried out, and soon after midday this stubborn knuckle of enemy front was in our hands, with over 350 prisoners and eight machine guns.

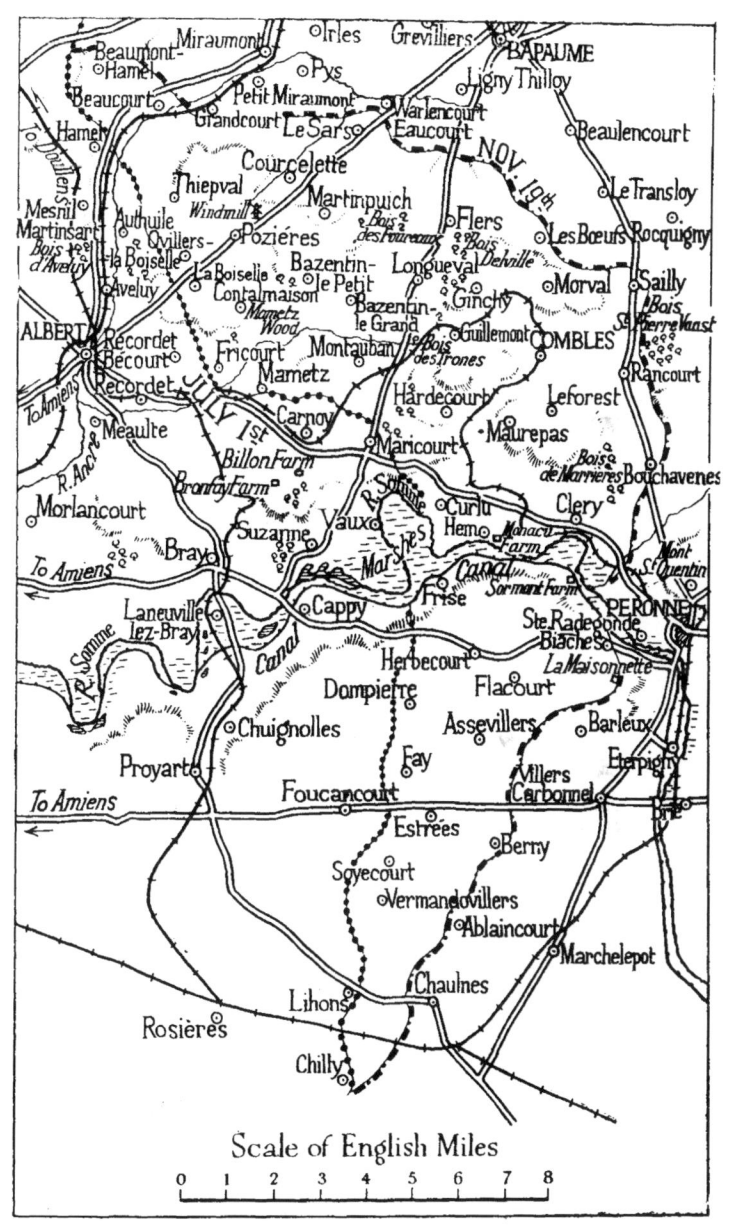

THE BATTLE OF THE SOMME

During the afternoon the new line was established, with Captain F. T. Dunne as second in command of the Fusiliers. On the 19th the battalion was relieved; but during the operations Second Lieutenant J. Tinley, the gallant officer in command of B Company, was unhappily killed. Meanwhile to the south, in Delville Wood, up till the 20th the South African Brigade was winning fame in its heroic battle. On that day the 1st Royal Scots Fusiliers were detached for the defence of Longueval village, and had to endure a severe bombardment till the 25th, when they were relieved and marched back to Meaulte.

The attack of the Third Division on 14th July was a notable performance. The two attacking brigades were each composed of two battalions of the New Army and two of the old regulars, and the four new battalions were in the first wave. The work was completed a little after midday, the apportioned part of the German second line was taken, and 662 unwounded men, 36 officers (including a regimental commander), 4 howitzers, 4 field guns, and 14 machine guns were captured. Of the part played by the 1st Royal Scots Fusiliers let their Brigadier speak. "It was largely due to their prompt and determined action in entering and bombing down the enemy trench with a small party that the brigade was able to accomplish its task after having been stopped by the wire." In that fatal check their chief casualties were incurred. Between the 7th and the 25th July 6 officers—Lieutenants Andrew Sturrock and R. S. Smylie, Second Lieutenants James Tinley, G. H. Swan, J. K. Scott, and James Fleming—and 93 men were killed, 6 officers and 209 men were wounded, and 56 were missing.

The enemy second line having been won from Pozières to Delville Wood, the next main objectives became Pozières and Guillemont—the first because it was part of the crest of the Thiepval plateau, the second because its capture was necessary before we could align our advance with that of the French. Guillemont presented an ugly problem. The approach to it from

1916
July 19–31

Trônes Wood lay over perfectly bare and open country, while the enemy had excellent observation from Leuze Wood in its rear; the quarry west of the village had been made into a strong redoubt; the ground to the south of it between Maltzhorn and Falfemont Farm was broken by a three-pronged ravine with Angle Wood in the centre, which the Germans held in strength, and which made it hard to form a defensive flank or link up with the French advance. Moreover, the weather did not favour us. The third week of July was rain and fog. The last week of that month, and the first fortnight of August, saw blazing summer heat, which in that dusty land told severely on men wearing heavy steel helmets and carrying a load of equipment. There was little wind, a heat haze lay low on the uplands, and this meant poor visibility at a time when air reconnaissance was most vital. On 19th July the first attempt on Guillemont was made from Trônes Wood—an attack by the Eighteenth Division, which did not succeed. On the 23rd it was the turn of the Thirtieth Division, whose 21st Brigade attacked, but failed, owing to the strength of the enemy machine guns. Then on the last day of the month came an assault from the north-west and west, while the French were moving against Maurepas—an assault in which the 2nd Royal Scots Fusiliers were to repeat both in glory and losses their record at First Ypres.

The attack of the Thirtieth Division was delivered by the 89th and 90th Brigades, and in the latter the assaulting battalions were the 18th Manchesters and the 2nd Royal Scots Fusiliers.[1] The Fusiliers assembled just east of Trônes Wood—an indifferent jumping-off ground—with D Company in trenches north of the Guillemont–Trônes Wood road, A and B Companies south of the road, and C Company in an improvised trench near to D. The frontage of the battalion was about two hundred and sixty yards. The attack was delivered at 4.45 a.m. on 31st July in heavy fog, and almost from the first things went wrong. The

[1] The actual attack was also carried out by the 16th and 17th Manchesters.

THE 2ND BATTALION AT GUILLEMONT

Manchesters were late in starting. Colonel Walsh[1] was to move forward in support, with the Fusiliers battalion headquarters and two companies of the 16th Manchesters; but the two companies never appeared, and communication with the first wave very soon became impossible. Meantime the Scots Fusiliers made straight for their objective; but the advance on both their flanks halted, and presently they were a lone spearhead without supports. There was a heavy enemy barrage on the east front of Trônes Wood, and the Guillemont road was swept by machine guns. It would appear that D Company of the Fusiliers and about one-third of A Company reached the east side of Guillemont village, and that B and C Companies were on the western face. The officer commanding D Company, Lieutenant Murray, forced his way back to headquarters about noon to explain that without immediate support the battalion would be cut off. He himself had been right through the village. But there were no adequate reserves available, and soon nothing could move and live on the ground between Guillemont and Trônes Wood. Everywhere, except in the Scots Fusiliers sector, the attack had failed, and the battalion had to pay the price of its lonely glory. Colonel Walsh could do nothing except hold the trenches east of Trônes Wood till he was relieved on the early morning of 1st August.

The 2nd Royal Scots Fusiliers went into action with 20 officers and 750 men. Of these, 3 officers and 40 other ranks, chiefly headquarters staff, remained with Colonel Walsh at the close of the day, and later nearly 100 others dribbled back through another brigade. The rest of the battalion was dead, wounded, or in captivity. The total casualties were 633. Nine officers fell—Captain C. N. J. Kennedy, Lieutenants W. L. Harris, W. S. Lomax, and G. H. W. Blackman, Second Lieutenants A. V. Morrison, R. H. Ashton, H. L. Atkins, G. B. Duncan, and D. P. Irving—and 15 other

---

[1] Again, as at Montauban, Colonel Walsh was in practical command of the 90th Brigade, and this was the reason why his headquarters could not advance with the battalion.

1916
August 1

ranks; 8 officers and 618 men were wounded or missing. It was a disaster which was as splendid as a victory, for the battalion had done the task entrusted to it and suffered not for its faults but for its prowess. Major-General Shea, of the Thirtieth Division, wired to Walsh that day: "I cannot tell you how grieved I am for the loss of your splendid battalion, and, above all, for those left in Guillemont; but they did grandly, and all that men could do." And in his report on the operation he wrote: "It is evident that the Scots Fusiliers fought in a manner which was in keeping with the high tradition and unblemished record of that fine regiment." Sir Henry Rawlinson, commanding the Fourth Army, in his order of 1st August, spoke thus of the attempt on Guillemont: "Though they were not successful in retaining the possession of Guillemont after they had so gallantly captured the greater part of the village, I am satisfied that they did all that was possible." The scanty remnant of the battalion moved north on 11th August to Béthune, where for two months, while it was renewing its strength, it remained in a comparatively peaceful sector of the front.

We leave the 2nd Battalion of our regiment at Béthune and the 1st in the Loos sector—whither it moved in the middle of August—while we turn to the third stage of the battle of the Somme and the appearance on the field of battle of the 6th/7th Battalion in the Fifteenth Division. The advance of 1st July had carried the first enemy position on a broad front; but the failure of the attack north of the Ancre had made the breach eight miles less than the original plan. The advance of 14th July gave us the second enemy position on a still narrower front—from Bazentin-le-Petit to Longueval. The danger now was that any further movement in the same direction might result in the formation of a sharp and precarious salient; so Haig had to broaden the breach by striking out on the left and right, against Pozières and the high ground at Mouquet Farm and on the other flank against Guillemont and

GERMAN SECOND POSITION TAKEN

Ginchy, while in the centre there must be a steady advance against the intermediate line which the Germans had constructed between their old second and third positions.

The Fifteenth Division, under General McCracken, took over on 8th August the left sector of the III. Corps from the Twenty-third Division. On 10th August orders were issued for an attack, in conjunction with the Thirty-fourth Division, on the German switch line south of Martinpuich. The assault was to be delivered by three battalions—the 12th Highland Light Infantry on the right, the 6th/7th Royal Scots Fusiliers in the centre, and the 6th Camerons on the left. Prior to the action there was a heavy bombardment of the enemy trenches, and on the morning of the 11th a smart piece of patrol work was done by a party of Scots Fusiliers, under Second Lieutenant Fairley, who took four prisoners. At 10.32 p.m. on the 12th the attack was delivered. It failed on the right, owing to the ill success of the Thirty-fourth Division, but the centre and left in two minutes won nearly all their objectives, largely because of the excellence of our artillery barrage. The Fusiliers, owing to the check to the H.L.I., had their right flank exposed, but they were able to hold and consolidate their portion of the switch line. The casualties incurred were 12 officers and 141 other ranks, and of these Second Lieutenants R. Warnock, R. B. Strang, and T. Hutcheon were killed.

The next three weeks were filled with small actions necessary to improve the position of the division in view of the great general attack now in contemplation. On 3rd September Guillemont at last was taken, and Ginchy followed on the 9th. The British had now made good the whole of the old German second position, and were everywhere on the crest of the uplands and facing the enemy third line. At the outset of the battle this third position had been only in embryo, but before the assault of 14th July it had been for the most part completed, and by the beginning of September it had been elaborately fortified and a fourth position prepared behind it. The third line was based on a string of fortified villages which lay on the reverse slope of the main ridge—Courcelette, Martinpuich, Flers, Lesbœufs, and Morval. Behind it was an intermediate line, with Le Sars, Eaucourt l'Abbaye, and Gueudecourt as strong points in it. Farther back lay the newly-made fourth line, just west of the Bapaume–Péronne road, covering the villages of Sailly-Saillisel and Le Transloy. This was the line protecting Bapaume, and at the moment the final German prepared position. The fighting during July and August had greatly weakened the enemy's forces. All his most famous units had appeared—the pick of the Bavarians, the 5th Brandenburgers, and every division of the Guard and Guard Reserve Corps. The time was now ripe for a new attack which should accelerate the enemy's decline and give the British a new orientation. Haig's immediate aim was to break through the German third line; but his ultimate objective was a thrust north-eastward across the upper Ancre, so as to get behind the great slab of unbroken enemy positions from Thiepval northward. The moment was propitious for such a blow. The French on the British right had won conspicuous successes; Brussilov was still pinning down the Austro-German forces on the eastern front; Sarrail had just launched an offensive in the Balkans; Rumania had entered the war, and was pouring troops into Transylvania; and recent changes in the German High Command had, for the time being, slightly dislocated the machine.

In the battle staged for 15th September the front extended from a point south-east of Thiepval to Ginchy, and the force to be employed was the whole of Rawlinson's Fourth Army and the right corps of the Fifth. The section allotted to the Fifteenth Division was Martinpuich, and its final objective was at first defined as the southern portion of that village. These orders were, however, extended on 14th September, and, as at Loos, the assaulting battalions, should the first attempt be successful, were instructed to push on. The division was to attack with two brigades—on the right the 45th, with from right to left the 11th Argyll and Sutherland Highlanders and the 13th Royal Scots in first line, and the 6th/7th Royal Scots Fusiliers and the 6th Camerons in support; on the left the 46th Brigade, with the 10th Scottish Rifles, the 7th/8th K.O.S.B., and the 10th/11th H.L.I. in the first line, and the 12th H.L.I. in support.

The morning of 15th September was perfect autumn weather, with a light mist filling the hollows and shrouding the slopes. The attack was launched at 6.20 a.m. with complete and startling success, the chief casualties being incurred through the troops pressing too close upon our own barrage. Shortly after 7 a.m. the final objective was gained. The new tanks were of little assistance to the division, but the troops did not need assistance. At 9.30 a.m. a patrol of the Scottish Rifles entered Martinpuich and returned to report that the enemy was retiring. At noon the 45th and 46th Brigades were ordered to move forward and occupy the village. This final advance began at three p.m., and was completed in an hour, the British line being established north of the village and west of the Martinpuich–Eaucourt l'Abbaye road. That evening the Royal Scots Fusiliers—temporarily under Major T. Smith, Colonel Gordon having gone to hospital—took the place of the Camerons in the first line, and three days later the whole brigade was relieved. Such was the capture of Martinpuich—a perfectly conceived and perfectly executed operation carried through at the minimum of cost. Sir Henry Rawlinson telegraphed to General McCracken : " Please convey to my old friends of the Fifteenth Division my congratulations on their splendid performance. . . . To have captured Martinpuich after having been a month in the line is a very fine performance, and I greatly appreciate their gallantry and vigorous fighting spirit."

On that day of 15th September Haig advanced his line to an average depth of a mile on a front of six. Only on his right, where the Guards were faced with an impossible task, was there any serious check. On

1916
Sept. 15

1916
Sept. 25–26

25th September he struck again between Combles and Martinpuich, and for the second time advanced the same distance on the same length of front, taking Morval, Lesbœufs, and Gueudecourt; while next day Sir Hubert Gough's Fifth Army carried Thiepval and the whole of the crest. That evening the Allied fortunes in the West had never looked brighter, for the enemy was now back in his fourth line, and had lost all the advantage of the higher ground. If heaven granted a fine autumn there was good hope that a farther advance might drive him from the Bapaume ridge, and crumble his whole front between Arras and Péronne.

It was not to be. The guns were scarcely silent after the attack of 26th September when the weather broke, and October was one succession of tempestuous gales and drenching rains. Now appeared—to quote from what I have written elsewhere—the supreme difficulty of trench warfare. " For three months the Allies had been slowly advancing, blasting their way forward with their guns before each infantry attack, and the result was that the fifty square miles of old battle-ground which lay behind their front lines had been tortured out of recognition. The little country roads had been wholly destroyed, and, since they had never had much of a bottom, the road-menders had nothing to build upon. New roads were hard to make, for the chalky soil had been so churned up by shelling that it had lost all cohesion. The consequence was that there were now two no-man's-lands—one between the front lines, and one between the old enemy front and the front we had won. The second was the bigger problem, for across it must be brought the supplies of a great army. It was a war of motor transport, and we were doing what our grandfathers had pronounced impossible—running the equivalent of steam engines not on prepared tracks but on highroads, running them day and night in endless relays. The problem was difficult enough in fine weather, but when the rain came it turned the whole land into a morass. Every road became a watercourse, and in the holes was mud as deep

BATTLE OF 13TH NOVEMBER

as a man's thighs. The army must be fed, troops must be relieved, guns must be supplied—so there could be no slackening of the traffic. Off the roads the ground was one vast bog, dug-outs crumbled in, and communication trenches ceased to be. Behind the British front lay six miles of sponge varied by mud torrents."

Into this miserable warfare the three battalions of our regiment made periodical incursions. The 6th/7th was, perhaps, in the worst area—that of Le Sars—in October, and again in December in a line facing the famous Butte de Warlencourt, where the front was no more than a string of shell holes linked up by shallow trenches. The 2nd Battalion returned from the north in October, and suffered some days of heavy shelling in the Flers section. On 12th October it took part in a local attack, which found the enemy well prepared, and failed to reach the first objective. The casualties were 9 officers and 261 other ranks, and Lieutenant J. R. D. McEwan and Second Lieutenants J. S. Allan and T. H. Boyle were killed. After that the Thirtieth Division was transferred to the Third Army in the Arras section. The 1st Battalion also came back in October from Loos with the Third Division, and took its place in the front opposite Serre—the sector which had proved impregnable on the first day of the Somme battle. There it remained for most of the winter, and had a share in the battle of 13th November when Gough attacked between Serre and the Ancre. The assault of the British left wing on Serre failed, as it had failed on 1st July, for that stronghold, being too far removed from the effect of our flanking fire from the Thiepval ridge, presented all the difficulties which had baffled us at the first attempt. The battalion attacked with A and B Companies at 5.45 a.m., but owing to the fog and the mud touch was lost with the troops on the flanks; and after penetrating to the enemy second line, where it found the wire uncut, it was compelled, along with the rest of the 8th Brigade, to withdraw and re-form in its original line, while its kinsmen of the Fifty-first Division were storming through Beaumont Hamel. It had 201 casualties,

1916
Oct.–Dec.

1916
Feb. 5

and among the officers Lieutenant H. C. Shutt, and Second Lieutenants J. M. Kerr, N. H. Grieve, H. G. Gillies, and T. M. Johnston fell.

The November battle of the Ancre was the concluding stage of the Somme operations, and the winter weather now fell like a curtain on the drama. The Somme had fulfilled the Allied purpose in taxing to the uttermost the German war machine. Haig's sober summary was the barest truth: "The enemy's power has not yet been broken, nor is it yet possible to form an estimate of the time the war may last before the objects for which the Allies are fighting have been attained. But the Somme battle has placed beyond doubt the ability of the Allies to gain these objects." To this may be joined Ludendorff's confession during those winter months: "We could not contemplate an offensive ourselves, having to keep our reserves available for defence. . . . If the war lasted our defeat seemed inevitable."[1]

III

The army released by the evacuation of the Gallipoli peninsula moved by way of Lemnos to Alexandria, training being revived at Mudros in days of bitter wind and rain. With it went the Fifty-second Division, which included the 4th and 5th Royal Scots Fusiliers. The two battalions arrived in Egypt on February 5, 1916.

It was clear that Turkey, once she was free from menace in the Dardanelles, would use her strength in an offensive against the British in Egypt or in Mesopotamia, or in both. The beaver-like activity of German engineers on the Bagdad and Syrian railways, and the accumulation of stores at various points from Alexandretta to Beersheba, presaged, in particular, another effort against the Suez Canal. The original frontier between Turkey and Egypt ran from Rafa, east of El Arish, to the Gulf of Akaba; but on the outbreak of

[1] *My War Memories* (English translation), I., page 307.

BIR EL DUEIDAR

1916
Feb. 29–
April 23

war Sinai had been abandoned, and the line of Egypt's defence was the west bank of the Canal. But if the Canal was to be kept free for traffic the enemy must be held beyond range of it, and accordingly the G.O.C. in Egypt—General Sir John Maxwell—decided to push his lines seven or eight miles out into the eastern desert. East of the Canal lies the level plain of Tina, stretching to the great Katia oases on the ancient coast road from Palestine. When Sir Archibald Murray took over the command from Sir John Maxwell he decided that the Katia oases must be held, and began to construct a railway thither from Kantara—the first stage of a line which was presently to bridge the desert.

The Fifty-second Division was entrusted with the northern sector of the new front, and on 29th February the 155th Brigade, in which were the two Scots Fusilier battalions, was pushed five or six miles out from Kantara into the plain of Tina, while the remaining brigade was busied on the Kantara defences. By 21st April the railway had reached the ancient Pelusium, and, in General Murray's opinion, now offered a base for a serious movement to hold the whole district. This was also the view of the Turks, and they resolved to cut the line by a surprise attack after overwhelming the outpost garrisons.

Between Kantara and Pelusium the railway made a bend to the north-east, and covering the bend and the junction of two caravan tracks was the small entrenched post of Bir el Dueidar. On 22nd April it was held by Captain F. Roberts of the 5th Royal Scots Fusiliers with a company of his battalion and details of Yeomanry and the Bikanir Camel Corps, while the remainder of the 155th Brigade, temporarily under the command of Lieutenant-Colonel A. H. Leggett of the 5th Royal Scots Fusiliers, occupied a line of posts some miles to the west. That night Captain Roberts was under the belief that there was no hostile force within seventy miles; but the little garrison encamped among the palm trees of the oasis left nothing to chance. Dawn on the 23rd broke in fog, and at 5.17 a.m. a

1916
April 23

lookout observed a number of men not thirty yards distant. It was a Turkish force, 1,000 strong, with one gun, who had come by the southern caravan route. They attempted to rush the camp, but were checked by rifles and Lewis-gun fire. Presently the action became general, and the tiny garrison was subjected to heavy fire from the east and south-east. After about two hours it was plain that the enemy was trying to work round the south flank, but Corporal J. Hill and six men of the Scots Fusiliers kept up so steady and accurate a fire on that side that the movement was checked. The fight from seven a.m. onward was at a range of less than two hundred yards, the enemy outnumbered the British by at least eight to one, and the mist which still hung about gave him excellent cover.

Relief, however, was on the way, for at six a.m. Captain Roberts had telephoned to Colonel Leggett, and a party of 250 men from the 4th Royal Scots Fusiliers, under Major Harold Thompson, with two Lewis guns, marched seven miles in two hours, and reached Dueidar about nine a.m. The supporting force occupied a redoubt from which they could bring flanking fire to bear on the enemy. At one p.m. Major Thompson counter-attacked with the whole of his strength. Lieutenant Sutherland of the 4th Battalion charged alone a body of thirteen Turks, and after bayoneting one received the surrender of the others. The enemy now broke, and the Fusiliers pursued for a mile and a half, taking nineteen more prisoners. Half an hour later Lieutenant-Colonel Leggett arrived with the rest of the 4th Battalion and a contingent of the Australian Light Horse.

The Turkish raid had been successful in cutting up the posts at Oghratina and Katia, but it had shipwrecked on the stubborn little garrison at Dueidar, which was the key-point of the railway. The British casualties were fifty-four, of which the 5th Royal Scots Fusiliers had twenty-four, and the 4th had thirteen, including Lieutenant C. S. Brindley killed.

In June came the revolt in the Hedjaz of the Grand

Sherif of Mecca, which delayed for a little the intended Turkish attack upon Egypt. The trans-Sinai railway was slowly creeping eastward, and Sir Archibald Murray was planning an advance on El Arish for the autumn. On 3rd and 4th June the 155th Brigade, in weather which was never less than 108° F. in the shade, and occasionally reached 125° F., was moved by train to the rail-head at Romani,[1] twenty-three miles east of the Canal. There a position was fortified, running inland from the coast for six miles, a pipe line was laid to convey water from Kantara, and the railway was soon carried as far as Er Rabat, one of the northern Katia oases. For several weeks nothing was seen of the enemy, and then suddenly, on the evening of 19th July, our aeroplanes reported that 9,000 Turks were less than twenty miles distant, and that other enemy forces were coming up behind them. The Turkish army, which included many German officers, was under the command of the German General Kress von Kressenstein, and numbered some 18,000 men. It was elaborately equipped with light mountain batteries and a great supply of water tanks carried on camels. It hoped, by timing its attack for the hottest season of the Egyptian summer, to get the benefit of surprise.

Sir Archibald Murray, thus forewarned, resolved to invite attack. The two divisions at Romani were the Fifty-second and the Australian and New Zealand Mounted, and his plan was to leave the British right flank apparently exposed so that the enemy might become entangled in the difficult country to the south, where he could be attacked in flank by troops from Pelusium and Dueidar. Through the last days of July the British worked hard on the Romani position, while the enemy in turn built ten miles of entrenched posts, so that it seemed doubtful whether he meant to attack or force us to attack him by barring our road. But on 3rd August it became clear that he was about to

1916
June 3–Aug. 3

---

[1] One company of the 4th Royal Scots Fusiliers, under Captain J. Hamilton, was left behind, and marched later to Romani. This company, therefore, did the whole distance from Kantara to Jaffa in Palestine on foot, over the worst walking country on earth.

1916
August 3

conform to Murray's plan, for he moved forward to the eastern edge of the Katia oases. The 155th Brigade—4th Royal Scots Fusiliers under Lieutenant-Colonel H. Thompson, 5th Royal Scots Fusiliers under Lieutenant-

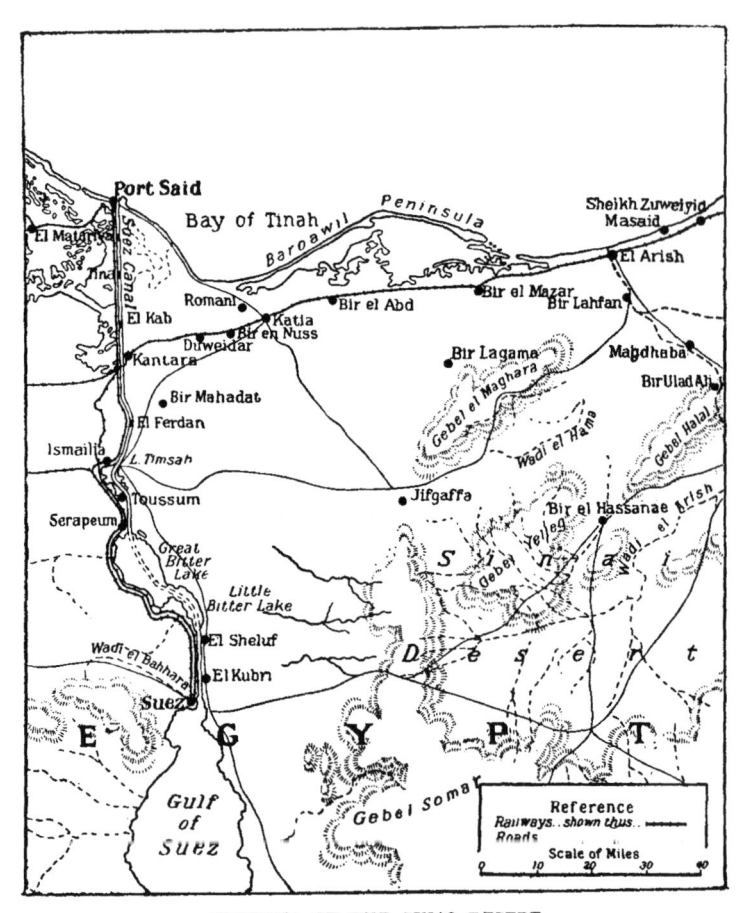

CROSSING OF THE SINAI DESERT

Colonel A. H. Leggett, and 4th King's Own Scottish Borderers—occupied the centre of the Romani position, while General Chauvel's Australian and New Zealand Horse were on the right flank, the left flank being protected by British monitors in the Bay of Tina.

The attack opened at midnight on 3rd August, and the fighting lasted throughout the 4th. It went wholly according to plan. The Lowland infantry in the Romani redoubts stood firm, while the cavalry on the right slowly withdrew, entangling the enemy in a maze of sand dunes. The Turkish advance reached its limit at 12.30 p.m. on the 4th. Thereafter the British reserves arrived—the Warwickshire and Gloucestershire Yeomanry and a brigade from the Forty-second Division; about five p.m. the whole British force advanced to the counter-attack, and before dusk fell the enemy line was hopelessly broken. The defeat was soon changed to a rout. From daybreak on the 5th our cavalry were harrying the Turkish retreat and sweeping up prisoners and guns. On a wide front, too, with mounted troops on their flanks, our infantry pressed on through the blazing heat. By the 7th the fleeing enemy was nineteen miles east of the battlefield. On the 9th he attempted a stand, but was driven on by our cavalry. Then, and not till then, we called a halt and counted our spoils. We had taken some 4,000 prisoners, including fifty officers, and the wounded and dead were estimated at not less than 5,000; so that half the total force of the invaders had been accounted for. The casualties of the Fifty-second Division were well under 200. The 4th Royal Scots Fusiliers had five men wounded, the 5th had one officer and four men wounded and eight men killed. The action of Romani was one of the most successful and decisive in the campaign, for it drove the Turks from Egypt and the Canal, and put them finally on the defensive.

September was largely spent in training for the great advance, which began on 12th October. It was a kind of warfare much the same as the old Sudan campaigns. Before each move large quantities of supplies had to be collected at an advanced base. An action might then be necessary to clear the front, and after it came a pause while the railway was carried forward and a new reserve of supplies accumulated. The task was harder than in the Sudan, for there was

1916
Aug. 3–Oct. 12

1916–17
Oct. 12–Jan. 9
no river to give water. In that thirsty land, after the Katia oases were left behind, water there was none, and supplies had to be brought by rail in tank-trucks till a pipe line could be laid. The work entailed was very great, but the organization of camel transport gradually bridged the gap between the rail-head and the front. The men in the French and Flanders trenches were inclined to look upon the Egyptian campaign as the longed-for war of movement. Movement there was, but it was for the present less the movement of cavalry riding for an objective than the slow progress of engineers daily completing a small section of line in the sun-baked sand.

The Fifty-second Division led the advance with an attendant screen of horsemen. On 23rd December the 155th Brigade reached El Arish, but the enemy did not await us there. The Turkish garrison had fallen back upon Magdhaba, where that day it was destroyed by a flying column under Chauvel. On January 9, 1917, the Desert Column drove the enemy from his last refuge at Rafa. The result was the clearing of Sinai of all formed bodies of Turkish troops. Operations in the interior and the south, conducted by small columns of cavalry and camelry, had kept pace with the greater movement in the north. The British army was now beyond the desert, on the edge of habitable country. The next objective was the Gaza–Beersheba line—the gateway to Palestine.

IV

It remains to chronicle the doings during the year 1916 of the other battalions of the regiment. At home there was the 9th Reserve Battalion, which acted as a feeding unit for the troops in the field. A 1st Garrison Battalion was raised in 1916, which presently went to India, and in the same year the 10th (Works) Battalion was recruited, which became ultimately part of the Labour Corps. The 8th Battalion, in the 77th Brigade of the Twenty-sixth Division, arrived, as we saw, at Salonika at the close of 1915. The year 1916 saw no serious engagement in that terrain. In May the Bulgarians seized the forts of Rupel and Dragotin, the keys of the Struma valley, thereby precipitating the political crisis in Greece, and in August Sarrail undertook an offensive in connection with the situation in Rumania, which gave the French Doiran station and Doldjeli, and the British (78th Brigade) Horseshoe Hill immediately to the west. This was followed immediately by a Bulgarian counter-stroke, when Todorov, with the left wing, drove the Greeks from Kavala. Towards the end of that month the British, under General Milne, took over practically the whole front east of the river Vardar, and by various local activities immobilized Todorov, while the Allied left wing prepared for its attack on Monastir. This latter offensive occupied the autumn, and Monastir fell on 19th November. In that year of toilsome inaction the 8th Royal Scots Fusiliers, under Lieutenant-Colonel Buchanan, had little to record. During the first months the battalion was at work on the defences of Salonika. In March it moved to the Derbend Pass, and in June and July it was in the Hirsova area in support of the French. In the August fighting it was for a short time in the trenches east of Doldjeli village, where it was much shelled, and suffered its first field casualties. On 21st September it was engaged in a raid, when a patrol of sixty men, under Captain Macphail, entered the enemy line, was surrounded, and retired with difficulty, having one man killed, one missing, and an officer and four men wounded. In October and November the battalion was in and out of the Horseshoe sector, which was much shelled, and a number of raids were carried out by the units of the 77th Brigade, in which the Scots Fusiliers had their share. For the rest the time was occupied with tours in the trenches and patrol duties, with no stimulus of either attack or defence, but with all the hardships of weather and disease. If the life of a soldier is " months of acute boredom punctuated by moments of acute fear," the 8th Battalion had its full share of the major ingredient.

Officers who died in 1916

Second Lieutenant M. L. ADAMSON (1st July); Second Lieutenant J. S. ALLAN (12th Oct.); Second Lieutenant W. J. ANGUS [attached 1st S.R.] (29th Oct.); Second Lieutenant R. H. ASHTON (30th July); Second Lieutenant H. L. ATKINS (3rd July); Lieutenant G. H. W. BLACKMAN (30th July); Second Lieutenant T. H. BOYLE (12th Oct.); Second Lieutenant C. S. BRINDLEY (23rd April); Captain C. W. BROWN (1st May); Second Lieutenant W. F. H. CLARK (23rd Feb.); Second Lieutenant R. C. COLQUHOUN [attached 4th S.R.] (3rd July); Second Lieutenant G. B. DUNCAN (30th July); Second Lieutenant JAMES FLEMING (18th July); Captain G. B. FOULKES (12th Aug.); Second Lieutenant H. G. GILLIES (13th Nov.); Second Lieutenant V. GODFREY (1st July); Second Lieutenant J. L. H. GRIERSON (1st July); Second Lieutenant N. H. GRIEVE (13th Nov.); Second Lieutenant A. P. HAGGO (18th Aug.); Lieutenant W. L. HARRIS (30th July); Second Lieutenant W. HAY (27th March); Captain W. R. HOUSTON (27th March); Second Lieutenant T. HUTCHEON (12th Aug.); Second Lieutenant D. P. IRVING (30th July); Second Lieutenant T. M. JOHNSTON (13th Nov.); Captain C. N. J. KENNEDY (30th July); Second Lieutenant R. KENNEDY (10th July); Second Lieutenant D. KERR (12th Aug.); Second Lieutenant J. M. KERR (13th Nov.); Second Lieutenant W. G. KING (7th July); Second Lieutenant W. M. B. LAING (21st June); Captain G. E. O. F. LAMBART (27th March); Lieutenant W. S. LOMAX (30th July); Second Lieutenant G. H. M'ALISTER [5th Battalion and M.G.C.] (24th Aug.); Lieutenant J. R. D. M'EWAN (12th Oct.); Captain P. W. T. MACGREGOR-WHITTON (9th July); Second Lieutenant A. L. MACKAY (31st Oct.); Captain R. R. M'QUEEN (15th May); Second Lieutenant A. V. MORRISON (30th July); Second Lieutenant J. MUDIE [attached 1st R.S.] (30th Sept.); Second Lieutenant T. W. R. NEILL (3rd July); Second Lieutenant R. D. NEILL (26th Oct.); Captain J. NICHOL (5th April); Second Lieutenant W. NICOLSON (13th Aug.); Lieutenant G. C. O. PATON (20th June); Second Lieutenant L. C. POWELL (31st May); Second Lieutenant W. N. RUSSELL (26th Aug.); Second Lieutenant J. J. SCANDRETT (15th May); Second Lieutenant J. K. SCOTT (14th July); Lieutenant H. C. SHUTT (13th Nov.); Second Lieutenant W. SMALL (30th July); Lieutenant R. S. SMYLIE (14th July); Second Lieutenant R. I. B. SPENCER (14th July); Second Lieutenant R. B. STRANG (12th Aug.); Lieutenant A. STURROCK (14th July); Second Lieutenant G. H. SWAN (14th July); Lieutenant F. G. SYMONS (22nd May); Second Lieutenant J. TINLEY (20th July); Lieutenant J. W. TOWERS-CLARKE (1st July); Captain W. TULLIS [Adjutant, 20th Northumberland Fusiliers (Tyneside Scottish)] (1st July); Second Lieutenant R. WARNOCK (12th Aug.); Second Lieutenant D. C. WOODSIDE (26th Feb.); Second Lieutenant W. N. YOUNG (9th Sept.).

CHAPTER XVII

THE GREAT WAR—1917

Haig's plans for 1917—The plans modified—The Battle of Arras—
The Third Battle of Ypres—Salonika in 1917—First Battle of
Gaza—Second Battle of Gaza—The summer in Palestine—
Allenby's plan—The fall of Beersheba—The advance on Jerusalem.

IN November 1916 a conference of representatives of all the Allied Powers was held at French General Headquarters, and a plan was made for the campaign of the following year. In 1917 Sir Douglas Haig desired to undertake a great offensive in Flanders, with the view of clearing the Belgian coast, for in that area he believed that success would give the highest strategic rewards. But before this movement began it was necessary to reap the fruits of the battle of the Somme. In November the enemy was penned in an awkward salient between the valleys of the Ancre and the Scarpe. The British Commander-in-Chief proposed early in the spring to attack this salient simultaneously on two sides—the Fifth Army moving on the Ancre front, and the Third Army attacking from the northwest about Arras. At the same time the First Army was to carry the Vimy Ridge, the possession of which was necessary to secure the left flank of our operations farther south. So soon as these operations were completed the Flanders campaign would begin with an assault upon the Messines ridge, to be followed by an attack eastward from the Ypres Salient. The reasons for Sir Douglas Haig's plan are clear. He was fully

1917

aware of the new great German position which had been preparing during the winter, and which we knew as the Hindenburg or Siegfried Line, and he did not think it good policy to make a frontal assault on it. He knew that the battle of the Somme had seriously weakened the enemy, and he regarded it as a mathematical certainty that the tactics of the Somme, if persisted in during 1917, and supported by a reasonable pressure from the Russian front, would give the Allies victory before the close of that year. He wished, therefore, to stage a second battle of the Somme type— to stage it in an area where its strategic results would be most fruitful, and to begin it sufficiently early in the season to allow a decision to be reached before the close of the good weather.

In December this plan had to be wholly recast. The civilian governments of both France and Britain chose to regard the Somme as a failure, and, ignorant of the mercies vouchsafed to them, declined to reap the fruits of an indisputable success. Haig was ordered to take over a larger front, and before the end of February 1917 the British right was as far south as a point opposite the town of Roye. Close contact with the enemy was lost while Haig was busied with this task, and the retreat of the Germans in February and March destroyed the salient which he had proposed to attack. There now remained nothing of the preliminary movement as originally planned, except the carrying of the Vimy Ridge. But a fresh scheme had been proposed by the French and accepted by the British Government. Under the new French Commander-in-Chief, Nivelle, an ambitious operation was conceived on the heights of the Aisne, which, it was trusted, would open the way to Laon. In this action the old method of limited objectives was to be relinquished; and Nivelle hoped, by means of his new tactics and by an unexampled concentration of troops, to break through the enemy lines on a broad front and restore the war of movement. This attack was fixed for the middle of April. It would operate against the southern pivot of the Hindenburg zone, and it was arranged that Haig should use his forces against the northern pillar east of Arras, and should strike a week before.

The position was, therefore, that the Arras battle, which Haig had regarded as only a preparation for the main campaign of the season in Flanders, became the principal task of the British army during the first half of 1917. That battle, in turn, was considered as subsidiary to the greater effort of the French in the south. It was admittedly an attack in a region where, except for some extraordinary piece of fortune, great strategic results could scarcely be obtained. The British success depended upon what the French could do on the Aisne. If Nivelle failed, then they, too, must fail in the larger strategic sense, however valuable might be their local gains. If, however, Nivelle succeeded, the pressure from Arras in the north would beyond doubt greatly contribute to the enemy's discomfiture. The danger of the whole scheme was that the issue might be indeterminate, and the fighting at Arras so long protracted, without any decisive success, that the chances of the more vital Flanders offensive later in the summer would be imperilled. This was precisely what happened. Nivelle offered a brilliant gamble; but in accepting it in December 1916 the French and British Governments rejected a sober and certain victory. The French *débâcle* of May, the horrors of Third Ypres, Caporetto, the final downfall of Russia, and the crisis of March 1918, may be regarded as implicit in that fateful decision.

I

The three battalions of our regiment—the 1st in the Third Division, the 2nd in the Thirtieth, and the 6th/7th in the Fifteenth—found themselves in March 1917 in various parts of the Arras area. The last-mentioned had its headquarters at Duisans, just west of Arras itself, and on 22nd March furnished a raiding party of two platoons from B Company under Captain W. S. Smith, which assaulted the enemy trenches south

1917
April 7-9 of the Cambrai road and lost its leader. Again, on 7th April, when it had taken up its battle position, it conducted a successful raid, when Second Lieutenant D. Scott was killed. The 2nd Battalion was engaged in February in following up the German retreat in the Mercatel area, and early in April it was in position between Mercatel and Henin, parallel to the Arras–Bapaume road, where its patrols were busy feeling the enemy front.

A word must be said of the nature of the new German position, and especially of the Hindenburg Line. At the hamlet of Tilloy-lez-Mofflaines, on the Arras–Cambrai road, this line branched off from the old front. The enemy position from the northern pivot of the Hindenburg Line to Lens was very strong, consisting of three main systems, each constructed on the familiar pattern of four parallel lines of trenches studded with redoubts, and linked up by numerous switches. The whole defensive belt was from two to five miles deep. But the German High Command were not content with it. They had designed an independent line running from Drocourt, south-east of Lens, to the Hindenburg Line at Quéant as an alternative in case of an assault on the Arras salient. Towards the close of March this position, which was to become famous as the Drocourt–Quéant Switch, was not completed. The country through which the German position ran was peculiarly suited to their purpose. It represented the breakdown of the Picardy wolds into the flats of the Scheldt, the last foothills of the uplands of northern France—an ideal terrain for a defensive battle.

Sir Douglas Haig had, therefore, a formidable programme before him. The immediate key of the area was Vimy Ridge, the capture of which was necessary to protect the flank of any advance farther south. It was clear that no strategic result could be obtained unless the Drocourt–Quéant Switch was breached, and that meant an advance of well over six miles. But this position was still in the making; and if the fates were kind and the first three German systems could

THE ARRAS TERRAIN

be carried at a rush, there was good hope that the Drocourt–Quéant line would never be manned, and that the drive of the British, assisted presently by the great French attack on the Aisne, might bring them to Douai and Cambrai. It was a hope, but no more. A result so far-reaching demanded a combination of fortunate chances, which had not as yet been vouchsafed to us in any battle of the campaign.

1917
April 7–9

The city of Arras, situated less than a mile inside the British lines, was, like Ypres, the neck of a bottle, and through it and its environs went most of the transport for the new battlefield. For two years it had been a place of comparative peace, and, though badly shelled in the first year of war, was still a habitable though a desolated city. But up to April 1917 it had the air of a tomb. It was like a city stricken with plague—whole, yet untenanted. In April Arras awoke to an amazing change. Its streets and lanes were once more full of life, and the Roman arch of the Baudimont Gate saw an endless procession of troops and transport. A city makes a difficult base for a great attack, and, to minimize this danger, the British generals had recourse to a bold plan. They resolved to assemble part of their armies underground. Like many old French towns, Arras had huge ancient sewers; a map of them was found, and the underground labyrinth was explored and enlarged. Moreover, the town had grown over the quarries from which the older part of it had been built, and these also were discovered. The result was that a second city was created below the first, where three divisions could be assembled in perfect security.

The British front of attack was slightly over twelve miles long, from Givenchy-en-Gohelle in the north to just short of Croisilles in the south. On the left was the right corps of Sir Henry Horne's First Army—the Canadian Corps under Sir Julian Byng, with one British brigade, directed against the Vimy Ridge. On their right lay Sir Edward Allenby's Third Army. Its northern corps, next to the Canadians, was the XVII.; the central corps was Sir Aylmer Haldane's VI., with in line the Fifteenth, Twelfth, and Third Divisions, and the Thirty-seventh in support. On the right of the battle front was Sir Thomas Snow's VII. Corps, with the Fourteenth, Fifty-sixth, and Thirtieth Divisions in line, and the Twenty-first forming a pivot on the right. It is interesting to note how largely Scottish was the army of assault. Thirty-eight Scots battalions were destined to go over the parapets—a larger number than the British at Waterloo, and many times the force that Bruce commanded at Bannockburn.

The central area, allotted to the VI. Corps, was, perhaps, after the Vimy Ridge, the most difficult and critical on the battle-ground. Four stages were marked out in its objectives, each defined by a particular portion of the enemy defence. The Black line was his front and support trenches; the Blue line was his second trench system, some nine hundred yards farther east, and included such strong points as Observation Hill; the Brown, nearly a thousand yards farther on, was his third system, which included Feuchy and Battery Valley; while the Green line, the final objective, contained the vital villages of Monchy-le-Preux and Guémappe.

Zero hour was 5.30 on the morning of 9th April. At four a.m. a drizzle had begun, which changed presently to drifts of thin snow. It was bitterly cold and scarcely half light, and the troops waiting for the signal saw only a dark mist flecked with snowflakes. But at the appointed moment the British guns broke into such a fire as had not yet been seen on any battle-ground on earth. It was the first hour of the Somme repeated, but tenfold more awful. As our men went over the parapets they felt as if they were under the protection of some supernatural power, for the heaven above them was one canopy of shrieking steel. There were now no enemy front trenches; there were no second-line trenches—only a hummocky waste of craters and broken wire, over which our barrage crept relentlessly.

For the capture of the Black and the Blue lines the Fifteenth Division used the 45th Brigade on the left

BATTLE OF ARRAS

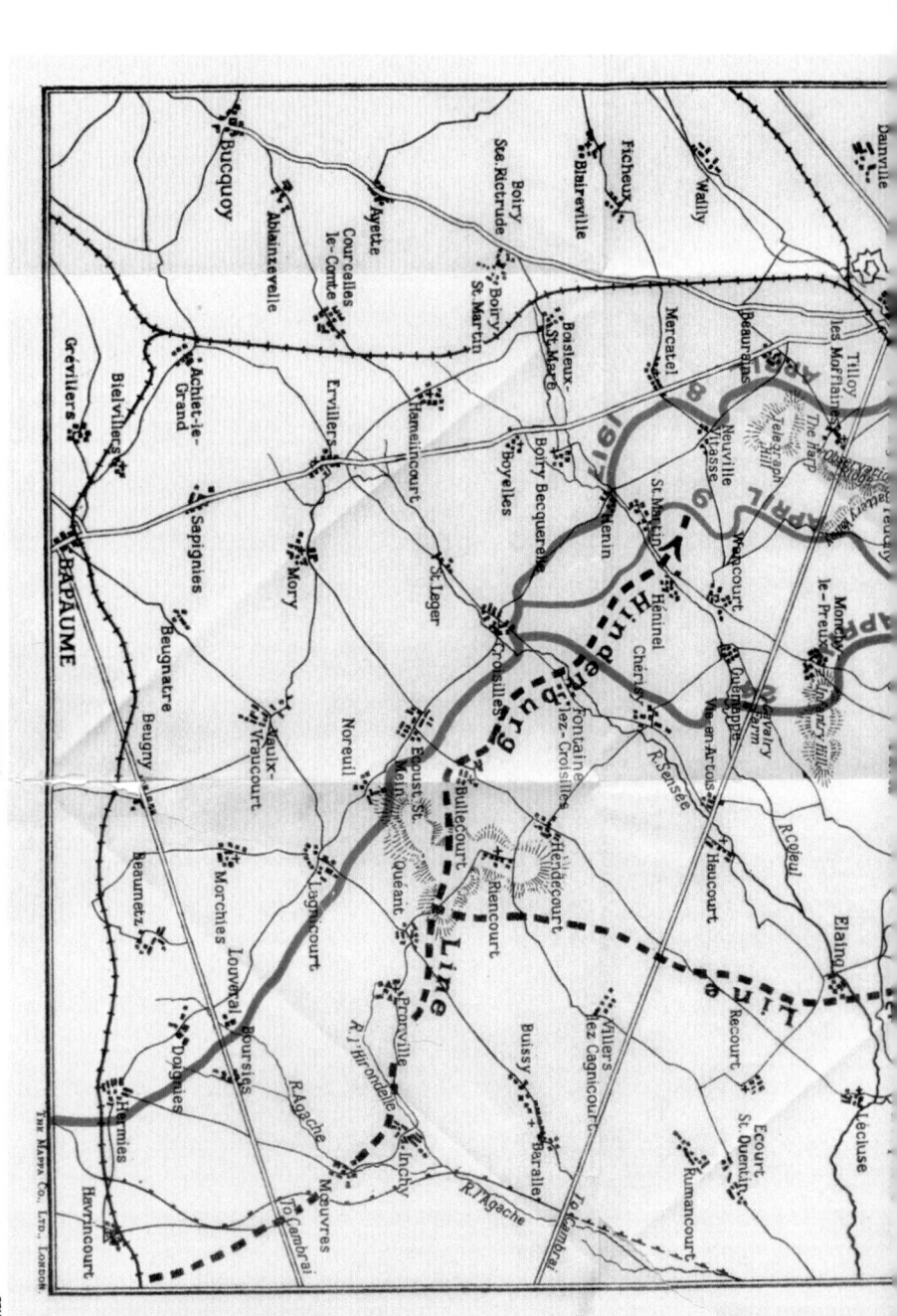

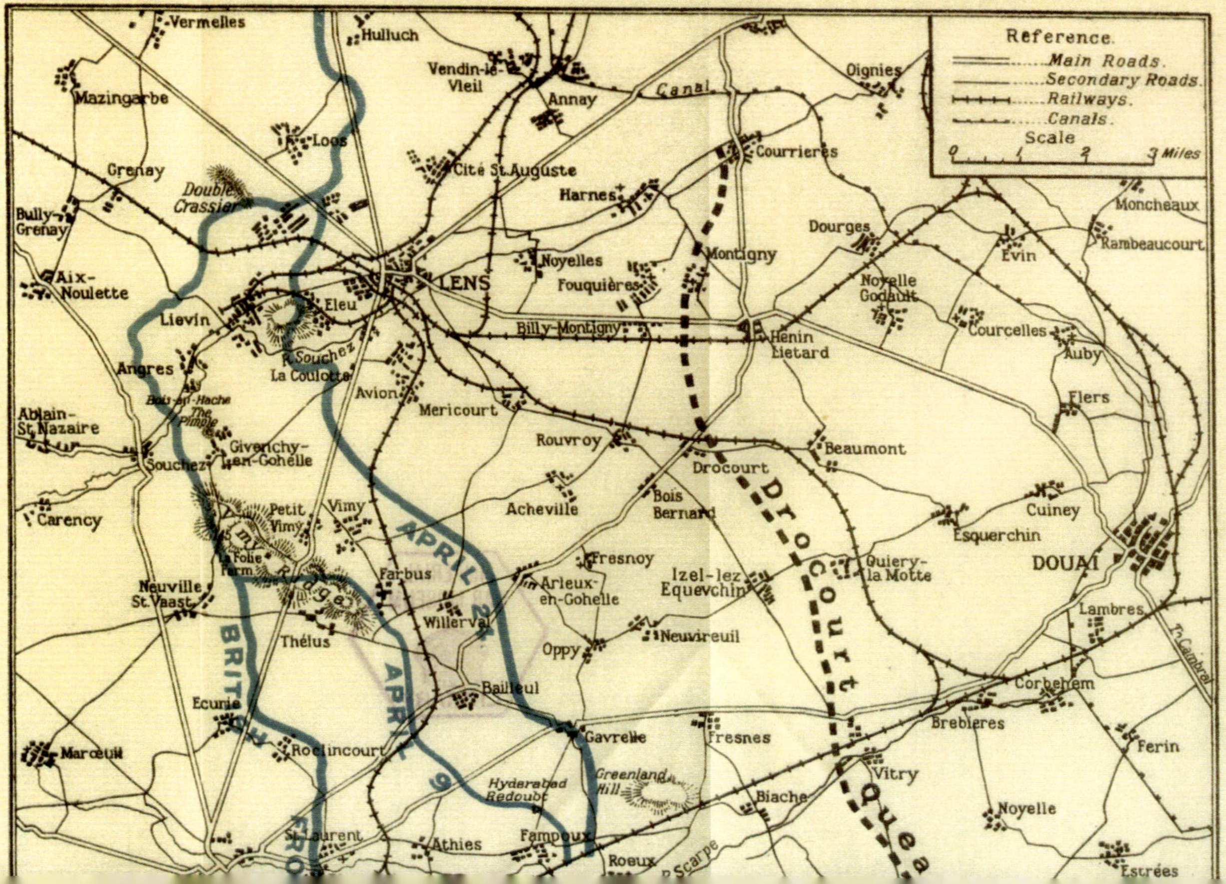
Reference.
Main Roads.
Secondary Roads.
Railways.
Canals.
Scale
0 1 2 3 Miles
Vermelles
Hulluch
Vendin-le-Vieil
Mazingarbe
Annay
Canal
Oignies
Loos
Courrières
Grenay
Cité St. Auguste
Double Crassier
Harnes
Bully-Grenay
Dourges
Moncheaux
Rambeaucourt
Montigny
Evin
Noyelles
Aix-Noulette
LENS
Fouquières
Noyelle Godault
Eleu
Lievin
Billy-Montigny
Courcelles
Henin Lietard
Auby
R. Souchez
Angres
La Coulotte
Avion
Mericourt
Bois-en-Hache
The Pimple
Flers
Ablain-St. Nazaire
Givenchy-en-Gohelle
Souchez
Rouvroy
Beaumont
Drocourt
Petit Vimy
Vimy
Acheville
Bois Bernard
Carency
Cuiney
Esquerchin
Drocourt
La Folie Farm
Fresnoy
Izel-lez Equevchin
Quiery-la Motte
DOUAI
Farbus
Arleux-en-Gohelle
Neuville St. Vaast
Willerval
APRIL 24
Lambres
Neuvireuil
BRITISH
Thélus
Oppy
APRIL 9
Bailleul
Corbehem
Ecurie
Gavrelle
Fresnes
Brebières
Marœuil
Roclincourt
Ferin
Hyderabad Redoubt
Greenland Hill
Vitry
Biache
Noyelle
St. Laurent
Athies
Fampoux
Roeux
R. Scarpe
Estrées
To Cambrai

and the 44th on the right, keeping the 46th for the Brown line. The 45th Brigade attacked with the 6th/7th Royal Scots Fusiliers (Lieutenant-Colonel E. I. D. Gordon) on the right, and the 11th Argyll and Sutherland Highlanders on the left, with the 6th Camerons and the 13th Royal Scots in reserve. The Scots Fusiliers reached the Black line at 5.55 a.m., and the whole position was in our hands by 6.30. The enemy had meantime opened a heavy barrage, and the commander of B Company, Lieutenant Alastair Buchan,[1] fell mortally wounded. Blangy, on the left, proved a serious obstacle, and two companies of the 13th Royal Scots were detailed for its capture. Beyond the Black line lay a still more intricate fortress, the Railway Triangle, a nest of machine guns. Here the artillery of the Ninth Division beyond the river rendered great assistance with flanking fire, and by 12.40 p.m. the 45th Brigade, with the help of a tank, had taken the place, and the whole of the Blue line was won. It was now the turn of the 46th Brigade, which at two p.m. advanced on the Brown line. There was stiff fighting in Battery Valley and at Feuchy Redoubt, but in a little the German third position was taken. At 6.30 p.m. the Thirty-seventh Division passed through the Fifteenth for its assault upon the ultimate Green line, and to support it the 45th Brigade moved up the Scots Fusiliers from the Railway Triangle and the 13th Royal Scots from Blangy to Feuchy and Feuchy Redoubt. The Fifteenth Division had taken and consolidated all its objectives.

Meantime farther south the Third Division had also won a brilliant success. The 8th Brigade, containing the 1st Royal Scots Fusiliers (Lieutenant-Colonel L. L. Wheatley), was in reserve, and had to endure heavy shelling in its assembly trenches. It was not till 1.50 p.m. that it moved forward, after Tilloy-lez-Mouffiaines and the great fortress called the Harp had been taken. The Fusiliers were now on the left of the brigade, and

[1] "A most charming and gallant young officer," Mr. Winston Churchill wrote—"simple, conscientious, and much liked by his comrades."

1917
April 9–10

had established touch with the Twelfth Division, but their advance about 3.15 p.m. was held up by machine-gun fire. The Brown line was attacked at seven p.m., but the assault failed, and the enterprise had to be postponed to the morrow. The casualties that day were mostly from artillery fire, and among the dead were four officers—Lieutenant A. H. P. Murray and Second Lieutenants G. Fairley, W. B. McArthur, and H. D. Buik. The Thirtieth Division, with the 2nd Royal Scots Fusiliers, was on the southern fringe of the great battle. At two p.m. on 9th April the battalion took up position to the south of Mercatel and waited on orders, while news of success came down hourly from the north.

The result of the first day of Arras was that all the enemy's front positions had gone, and his final position —short of the Drocourt–Quéant line—had been breached on a front of two and a half miles. Unfortunately the weather became his ally. It changed to intense cold and wet, and over the sodden earth it took long to bring up our guns. He held us up with machine guns in pockets of the ground, which prevented the use of our cavalry, and there was no chance of a dramatic *coup de grâce*. Little remained but a slow and methodical progress. Our remarkable gains, won at little cost the first day, could only be increased by small daily additions, for the elaborate preliminaries of Arras could not be improvised, and the infantry must wait on the advance of the guns.

On the 10th came the attack on Monchy-le-Preux and the Green line, which had proved impracticable the previous day. The Thirty-seventh Division attempted it without success, and, as no advance was possible till Monchy fell, the Fifteenth Division remained inactive. The Third Division had still to take the Brown line, and for this purpose the 8th Brigade attacked at noon with all four battalions, the 1st Royal Scots Fusiliers being on the left centre. The result was that the German third position in this area was won with few casualties. That day the Thirtieth Division did not move, and next day it was transferred to corps reserve.

The 11th saw the final attack on Monchy in a heavy storm of snow. The assault was delivered by the Fifteenth and Thirty-seventh Divisions, the objective of the latter being Monchy village, and of the former a line from Boiry-Nôtre-Dame to the Scarpe two miles east of Monchy. The Fifteenth Division had two brigades in action—the 46th on the right and the 45th on the left—and the latter had in first line the 6th Camerons on the right and the 6th/7th Royal Scots Fusiliers on the left, with the 13th Royal Scots in support, and the 11th Argyll and Sutherland Highlanders in reserve. The attack was launched at five a.m., and presently the 45th Brigade came under heavy machine-gun fire from Monchy. This fire caused it to swing round to its right to meet it, with the result that the Camerons advanced with the 46th Brigade against the north side of Monchy, while the Scots Fusiliers lost touch with their right-hand neighbours and were held up on the north-eastern spur of Orange Hill. Monchy fell during the day to the Thirty-seventh Division and details of the Fifteenth, assisted by detachments of cavalry; but the British losses were severe, for the place was on a little hill approached on four sides by sunken roads lined with machine guns. Scattered men of the Scots Fusiliers were at the taking of the village, and Second Lieutenant W. McIndoe collected from different battalions about 100 Lewis gunners and riflemen, and established a line of posts outside the south-east end. By this time the Fifteenth Division was exhausted, and during the night it was relieved by the Seventeenth and marched back to Arras. The casualties—just over 300—of the Scots Fusiliers were moderate, considering the nature of the fighting. Between 9th and 11th April, three officers were killed—Captain Thomas Watson, Lieutenant Alastair Buchan, and Second Lieutenant J. W. Whitelaw—and twenty-six men.

The Third Division was in action on 13th April, but the 8th Brigade was not engaged; and that evening the 1st Royal Scots Fusiliers returned to Arras, where

1917
April 11–13

1917
April 13–23

they remained till the 27th, when they took over the Monchy defences. Meantime Major N. M'D. Teacher had assumed command of the battalion. The 2nd Royal Scots Fusiliers were out of the line till 19th April, when they returned to occupy a portion of the Hindenburg Line on the south side of the Cojeul River.

The first stage of the battle of Arras concluded on 11th April, and thereafter for more than a week our front was improved only by small local movements, while the enemy showed vigour in his counter-attacks. On the 16th came Nivelle's great adventure on the Aisne, and it was incumbent on Haig to press his advance so as to divert the German strength. So far as the British armies were concerned, the main task was finished, and their duty now was subsidiary—to distract the enemy from Nivelle rather than to win their own special objectives. Accordingly at dawn on the 23rd Haig attacked on an eight-mile front on both banks of the Scarpe against the line Gavrelle–Rœux–Guémappe–Fontaine-lez-Croisilles.

The capture of Guémappe was essential to the establishment of the Monchy position, and the task was entrusted to the Fifteenth Division. The first objective, the Blue line, included Guémappe village and the enemy trenches north to the Cojeul; the second, the Red line, the German support trenches; and the third, the Green line, a front east of Vis-en-Artois and Boiry-Nôtre-Dame. The 44th Brigade advanced on the right, the 45th on the left; and the attacking battalions of the latter were the 11th Argyll and Sutherland Highlanders and the 13th Royal Scots, the 6th/7th Royal Scots Fusiliers being in support. By 9.30 a.m. the 44th Brigade had won Guémappe, but the 45th Brigade had been held up by the enemy's barrage. At 7.15 a.m. three companies of the Scots Fusiliers were sent forward in support, and C Company, gallantly led by Lieutenant J. Carman, took String Trench, and thereby ensured our hold on the line between Guémappe and the Cojeul. Furious German counter-attacks followed, and a see-saw battle for the Blue line continued

CLOSE OF THE BATTLE OF ARRAS

till the division was relieved on the 28th, after it had incurred some 3,000 casualties. The Scots Fusiliers had 23 men killed, 4 officers[1] and 99 other ranks wounded, and 26 men missing—their small losses being due to the fact that throughout the battle they were in support. This action was one of the most desperate fought during the battle, for the enemy was in strength and fully prepared, and, though some of his troops made but a poor resistance, the 3rd Bavarian Corps lived up to its old renown.

On the 23rd, too, the 2nd Royal Scots Fusiliers were engaged with the rest of the Thirtieth Division in an attack on the high ground overlooking Chérisy in the Sensée valley. The battalion advanced at 4.45 a.m. on a two-company front, and was immediately caught and checked by a terrific machine-gun barrage. At six a.m. the enemy counter-attacked, but was held; at six p.m. the 21st Brigade attempted to repeat the morning's attack, but it too suffered disaster; at nine p.m. the survivors of the Scots Fusiliers were withdrawn to reserve positions. The day depleted the battalion by more than one-half. The commanding officer—Lieut.-Colonel M. E. McConaghey—fell, and with him Second Lieutenants J. Spears, J. McLeod, T. Leishman, H. F. Smith, and J. C. Cameron, and 55 other ranks; 4 officers and 195 men were wounded; 4 officers and 209 men missing. On 26th April Major W. L. Campbell took over command.

The close of April marked the end of the battle of Arras as originally planned. It was an action complete in itself—that is to say, it attained completely its immediate objective; but owing to events outside the control of the British Command, it did not produce the strategical effect upon the Western front as a whole which was its ultimate design. But before the fighting closed our regiment was to be further engaged, for the Third Division was in the attack of 3rd May on the twelve-mile front from Arleux to Bullecourt. That

---

[1] Second Lieutenants T. S. Campbell, R. S. Pooley, E. A. Sinclair, and D. Trench.

1917
May 3

attack failed wholly in the centre, though it succeeded on the flanks. The area of the 8th Brigade was south-east of Monchy, and from the start it found that its own barrage was inadequate and the enemy lines strongly manned, while there was a continuous German fire from Infantry Hill. All the officers but one of the attacking companies fell in the first stage, and the battalion's withdrawal was only achieved with the utmost difficulty. The day brought to the 1st Royal Scots Fusiliers 296 casualties. Six officers were killed—Lieutenants M. Merson, A. T. Newbigging, H. R. Petter, Angus Henderson, and Second Lieutenants E. P. Oatts and J. B. Kincaid, and 27 men; 3 officers and 212 men were wounded; 2 officers and 57 men were missing. Arras exacted a high price from the regiment; but, strangely enough, the battalion which saw most fighting —the 6th/7th—escaped most lightly.

II

When, on the last day of July, Sir Douglas Haig launched his long-contemplated attack in the Ypres Salient, the nature of the war had dramatically changed. The great plan conceived for 1917, of which the Somme had been the logical preliminary, had proved impossible. This was not wholly due to the failure of the ambitious offensive of April on the Aisne and the stalemate at Arras. The principal cause was the defection of Russia, for, by the failure of one great partner, the old military cohesion of the Allies had gone. The beleaguering forces which had sat for three years round the German citadel were weakening on the East. The war on two fronts which had been Germany's chief handicap was changing to a war on a single front. Whatever successes the Allies might win during the remainder of 1917, it was now certain that there could be no decisive blow, for the Teutonic League, just when it was beginning to crumble, had been given a new lease of life. Up till then the campaign had been fought on data which were familiar and calculable. The material and human strength of

MESSINES

each belligerent was known, and the *moral* of each was confidently assessed. But with the Russian Revolution new factors had suddenly appeared out of the void, and what had seemed solid ground became sand and quagmire.

1917 June 12

Haig, as we have seen, was compelled to protract the fighting in the Arras area so long as the French on the Aisne required his help; but by the end of May he was free to turn his attention to the place which, since the previous November, had been his chief preoccupation—the offensive against the enemy in Flanders, with the aim of clearing the Belgian coast and turning the northern flank of the whole German defence system in the West. It was a scheme which, if successful, promised the most far-reaching results; but time was of the essence of the business, for each week's delay meant the aggrandizement of the enemy. Haig's first business was to clear his flanks, and on 7th June, by one of the most perfect operations in the campaign, he won the Messines–Wytschaete ridge at a single bound. His next step was the advance east of Ypres. The famous Salient had, during three years, been gradually contracted, till the enemy front was little more than two miles from the town. The Germans held all the half-moon of little hills to the east, which meant that any preparation for attack would be conducted under their watchful eyes. They were alive to the importance of the position, and the wary general who now commanded their IV. Army was not likely to be taken by surprise. This was Sixt von Armin, who on the Somme had proved himself one of the most original and resourceful of the enemy's tacticians.

The battle of Messines was over by 12th June, but for various reasons it was not till late in July that the date of the main advance could be fixed. It was now more than ever a race against time, for the precarious weather of autumn was approaching, and unless the advance proceeded strictly according to time-table it ran the gravest risk of failure. The high ground east of the Salient must be won in a fortnight to enable us to move against the enemy bases in West Flanders and clear the coast-line. The nature of the countryside made any offensive a gamble with the weather, for the Salient was, next to Verdun, the most tortured of the Western battlefields. Constant shelling of the low ground west of the ridge had blocked or diverted the streams and the natural drainage, and turned it into a sodden wilderness. Weather such as had been experienced on the Somme would make of it a morass where tanks were useless and transport could scarcely move, and troops would be exposed to the last degree of misery.

Von Armin, having learned the lesson of his defeat at Messines, had prepared his defences. The nature of the ground did not permit of a second Hindenburg Line, since deep dug-outs and concreted trenches were impossible because of the water-logged soil. He was compelled to find new tactics, and his solution was the "pill-box." These were small concrete forts, sited among the ruins of a farm or in some derelict piece of woodland, often raised only a yard or two above the ground level and bristling with machine guns. They were echeloned in depth with great skill, and, in the wiring, alleys were left so that an unwary advance would be entrapped among them and exposed to enfilading fire. Their small size made them a difficult mark for heavy guns, and, since they were protected by concrete at least three feet thick, they were impregnable to the ordinary field-artillery barrage. The enemy's plan was to hold his first line—which was often a mere string of shell craters—with few men, who would fall back before an assault. He had his guns well behind, so that they should not be captured in the first rush, and would be available for a barrage if his opponents became entangled in the "pill-box" zone. Any attack would be permitted to make some advance, but if the German plan worked well, that advance would be short-lived and it would be dearly paid for. Instead of the cast-iron front of the Hindenburg Line, the Flanders line would be highly elastic,

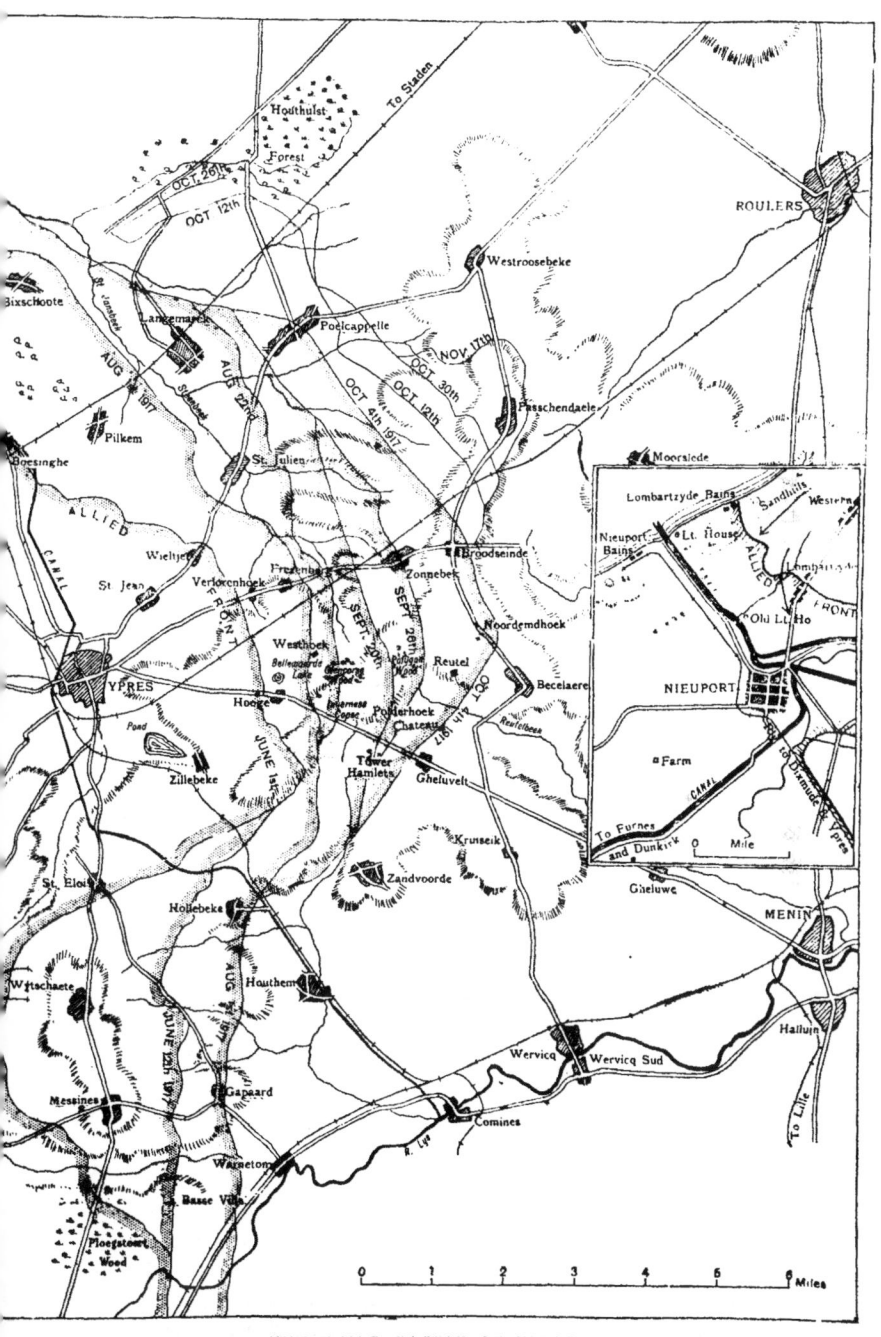

THE THIRD BATTLE OF YPRES

BEGINNING OF THIRD YPRES

but it would spring back into position after pressure with a deadly rebound.

1917
July 31

The British "preparation" for the battle lasted during the greater part of July, and every corner of the enemy area was drenched with our fire. The front of attack was fifteen miles long, but the main effort was planned for the seven and a half miles between Boesinghe and the Zillebeke–Zandvoorde road. On the north Sir Hubert Gough's Fifth Army disposed four corps of assault : from left to right, the XIV., with the Guards and the Thirty-eighth Division ; the XVIII., with the Fifty-first and Thirty-ninth Divisions ; the XIX., with the Fifty-fifth and Fifteenth Divisions ; and the II., with the Eighth, Eighteenth, Thirtieth, and Twenty-fourth Divisions. On the south, to Sir Herbert Plumer's Second Army, was entrusted a subsidiary action with strictly limited objectives. In this narrative we are concerned only with the sections of the Fifteenth and Thirtieth Divisions, where fought respectively the 6th/7th and the 2nd Battalions of our regiment.

The front of the Fifteenth Division ran from the Potijze road to the Roulers railway, immediately facing the Frezenberg ridge. For the purpose of the attack the composition of the brigades was somewhat altered, and a "mixed" 46th Brigade was given the left of the assault, and a "mixed" 44th Brigade the right. The first objective was the enemy's front and support lines ; the second, his second position ; and the third, the defensive system fifteen hundred yards farther east. When the first two objectives had been carried, the 45th Brigade was to pass through and attack the third. The problem of assembling troops was a most intricate one, but it was successfully solved, and at 3.50 a.m. on 31st July, on a grey, misty morning, the battle began.

The whole of the German front position fell at once. By ten a.m. Frezenberg had been taken, the 44th and 46th Brigades seemed to have carried their second objective, and the time had come for the advance of the 45th Brigade against the third. The 6th/7th Royal Scots Fusiliers moved on the right, and the 6th Camerons on the left, with the 11th Argyll and Sutherland Highlanders and the 13th Royal Scots in support. At 10.18 a.m. the advance began, but almost at once it became evident that the enemy second position, which we knew as the Black line, had not been wholly made good. The Scots Fusiliers were checked by machine-gun fire from it, and had many losses. Moreover, the attack of the brigade of the Eighth Division immediately on their right had halted, and directly they passed the old enemy second position they were exposed to enemy fire from their right rear. How far the battalion advanced is not clear, but it seems to have reached the wire in front of Bremen Redoubt, by which time most of its officers had become casualties. At 11.30 a.m. the position of the 45th Brigade was that the Camerons on the left were established in the third objective, while the Scots Fusiliers on the right had one company east of Potsdam, not in touch with the two just west of Bremen Redoubt, while the fourth company was well behind and just south of the Ypres–Zonnebeke road. The Argyll and Sutherland Highlanders in support had dug in on a line four hundred yards west of Potsdam, and were attempting to form a defensive flank along the railway.

At two p.m. came the first enemy counter-attack. The Camerons, finding the brigade on their left retreating, were compelled to fall back from the German third position. With the help of the Royal Scots the pressure was relieved about 5.30 p.m., and a front was formed which was virtually the Black line, the old German second position. On the right this front was in sore confusion. The total rifle strength of the Scots Fusiliers was now less than 150, and what could be collected of the battalion was brought back to the German first position, preparatory to an attack on Beek House, a point in the Black line still held by the enemy. The Argylls had formed a defensive flank on the right, and the isolated company of the Fusiliers under Captain Jape, which had been east of Potsdam, now retired to strengthen their left. About midnight the 45th Brigade

STIRLING CASTLE

was relieved as far as possible by the 44th and the 46th.

Meantime the right of the Fifth Army along the Menin road was making slow and difficult progress. The 90th Brigade of the Thirtieth Division had for its first objective the German front running from Stirling Castle—the strong point which dominated Ypres south of the highway—to Clapham Junction, and for its second (the Black line) a line running in front of Herenthage Chateau to the north edge of Glencorse Wood—ground over which our regiment had fought in the First Battle of Ypres. The brigade attacked on a two-battalion front, and to the 16th and 18th Manchesters was allotted the first objective, while the 2nd Royal Scots Fusiliers, under Lieutenant-Colonel W. L. Campbell, and the 17th Manchesters were to push through them against the Black line. The first attack was successful, and Stirling Castle fell, but before the shell-shattered patches called Glencorse and Inverness Woods the enemy had massed strongly, for they were the key of his position. The 90th Brigade clung to the foothold which it had won on the ridge, but could go no farther, though it beat off the German counter-attack in the afternoon. The Scots Fusiliers had 4 officers—Captain J. B. Orr, Second Lieutenants D. H. Kennedy, J. R. D. Smith, and W. Lindsay—killed, and 16 men; 6 officers and 151 other ranks wounded; and 31 missing. Next day the battalion was relieved.

On 1st August the Fifteenth Division made an effort to adjust its uneasy line. There remained a gap near Beek House, which the enemy aeroplanes noted, and that afternoon there came a resolute German attack astride the Ypres–Roulers railway—an attack which all but re-won the crest of the Frezenberg ridge. That part of the 45th Brigade which had been relieved was called up, and the Scots Fusiliers were ordered to send one company, under Captain Jape, to support the Royal Scots, while the remainder, along with the Argylls, were to attack and to clear up the situation in the Black line. The objective of the Fusiliers was Beek House.

1917
July 31–Aug. 1

1917
Aug. 1–Sept. 1

This was not taken, and they had to dig themselves in for the night as best they could. There they remained during the following day, and were relieved in the evening. During the three days' action the Fifteenth Division advanced its line some two thousand yards, and took and securely consolidated the Frezenberg ridge at a cost of 3,581 casualties. The 6th/7th Scots Fusiliers had 2 officers—Lieutenant W. L. Blackwood and Second Lieutenant E. B. Sykes—killed, and 43 other ranks; 10 officers and 205 other ranks wounded; and 28 men missing. According to plan, the second day of the battle should have seen a second blow with cumulative force. But the weather had joined the enemy. From midday on 1st August for four days and four nights, without intermission, fell the rain. The misery of our troops, huddled in their improvised lines or strung out in shell holes, cannot be pictured in words; nor can the disappointment of the High Command. After months of thought and weeks of laborious preparation, just when a brilliant start had been made, they saw their hopes dashed to the ground. An offensive was still possible; but it could not be the offensive planned, for the time-schedule was fatally dislocated.

The Third Battle of Ypres did not end till 10th November, for it was wholly necessary to engross the enemy's attention while Pétain was nursing the armies of France back to health. It was the costliest battle fought up to date by the British army, but our regiment was not called upon to share greatly in the sacrifice. The Fifteenth Division, indeed, returned to the line on 17th August, and on the 22nd the 44th and 45th Brigades delivered a small attack against Beek House and Potsdam Redoubt—an attack which did not succeed. On this occasion the 6th/7th Royal Scots Fusiliers were in support, and suffered over 200 casualties from the heavy artillery fire. On 1st September the division moved south to the quiet section of Arras. The commander of the Fifth Army, in his farewell telegram, asked, " Will ye no' come back again ? "

and the feeling of the division about that ill-omened battlefield is shown by the laconic comment in one battalion's diary: "No b—y fear." The Thirtieth Division remained in the Ypres area, where, in October, Captain J. E. Utterson-Kelso took command of the 2nd Royal Scots Fusiliers, but it was not again seriously engaged.

But before the Battle of Third Ypres closed, the 1st Battalion was engaged in a costly action. On 15th May the Third Division was transferred to the XVIII. Corps; on 29th May it returned to the VI. Corps; and on 27th June it was moved to the IV. Corps, and held a sector of the British front nearly due east of Bapaume. On 19th September it was transferred to the V. Corps, and brought to the centre of the Ypres front opposite Zonnebeke, where it shared in the great attack of 26th September—the 8th Brigade attacking with the 2nd Royal Scots and 8th East Yorks in the front line, and the 1st Royal Scots Fusiliers and the 7th Shropshire Light Infantry in support, while the 76th Brigade advanced on the right. Zero hour was 5.50 a.m. The Royal Scots reached their goal with ease, and at 7.30 the Scots Fusiliers passed through them to the farther objective. Now, however, they were faced with an impassable swamp, and as they were compelled to circumvent it by going to left and right they lost time and the protection of our barrage. As they re-formed on the far side German machine guns opened on them from Hill 40, near Zonnebeke station. At this point Lieutenant-Colonel Teacher, who from his great height was a conspicuous mark, was fatally wounded, and only six officers were left with the battalion. Orders were sent from the brigade to continue the attack at 6.30 p.m., but it was impossible to get these orders to the front line in time. Later in the evening an enemy attack was repulsed, and the Fusiliers, notably the two right companies under Captain Orr, maintained virtually all the ground they had won on the slopes of Hill 40. On the evening of the 27th the battalion was relieved. The two days' fighting brought it 437 casualties; 8

1917 Nov. 20 — officers—Lieutenant-Colonel N. M. Teacher, Lieutenant George Swales, Second Lieutenants William Cochrane, T. R. Currer, J. H. McCracken, E. L. Wood, Norman Kennedy, W. R. Brown—were killed or died of wounds, and 53 other ranks; 8 officers and 317 other ranks were wounded; and 67 men were missing.

The Third Division took part in a subsidiary attack on the extreme left at Bullecourt during the first day, 20th November, of the battle of Cambrai, but the 8th Brigade was not engaged. Next day D Company of the 1st Royal Scots Fusiliers carried out a raid on the enemy line to obtain identification. For the rest of the year the battalion remained in that sector, retiring on relief from the line to Favreuil or Ervillers. The three battalions of our regiment on the Western front had not been brought together in one single main action since Arras, but the time was drawing nigh when all were to be swept into an immense and protracted defensive battle.

III

The Allied front at Salonika lay unchanged for many months after the capture of Monastir. The British army, under General Milne, faced the Bulgarian II. Army from the Vardar to the Struma, on the line of the lakes Doiran, Butkova, and Tahinos, a distance of some ninety miles. It was a long front for the forces at General Milne's disposal. Moreover, many of the troops had been in line without relief for over a year, and the exceptionally wet and stormy winter did not make his task simpler. At the end of February, General Sarrail informed his commanders that he proposed to attack in the last week of April, as part of the great combined movement of all the Allies. It was not easy during a boisterous March to secure the positions preliminary to a great attack, especially in the Doiran sector, where the main objective was the ridge between the lakes and the Vardar. But by the end of March one thousand yards had been

THE DOIRAN BATTLE

won on a front of three thousand, and we were ready to advance against the strong enemy salient in front of Doiran town.

*1917
April 24–
May 24*

On 24th April, at 9.45 p.m., the British, after a long bombardment, attacked the Doiran fortress, but only the left wing succeeded in winning ground, the Jumeaux Ravine proving a death-trap to the units attacking nearer Lake Doiran. The 8th Royal Scots Fusiliers in the 77th Brigade were not engaged in this action, with the exception of those who were attached as carriers to the 7th Wiltshires of the 79th Brigade. In this connection notice may be taken of the gallant action of Private J. Padley of the 8th Battalion, who, when volunteers were asked for, single-handed rescued Captain Waylen of the Wiltshires, who had been left badly wounded in the enemy trenches. On 8th May General Milne was instructed to make a second attempt, and now he confined himself to the sections between the lake and the sugar-loaf hill called the Petit Couronné, a bastion in the enemy first line, on which no impression had been made in April. On this occasion the 77th Brigade was employed, and the Scots Fusiliers, under Lieutenant-Colonel F. E. Buchanan, were used by companies in support. In the brigade sector the attack failed, and by the following morning the troops were back at their starting-point. On the 24th Sarrail ordered all operations to cease—operations which seemed to have been undertaken without any coherent plan. The British had done their best to carry out orders which were probably the most aimless and unconsidered of any given in the campaign. The problem before Milne was now the advent of the summer heats, with the grave risk of dysentery and malaria among the marshy hollows. To lessen this danger he abandoned his forward position on his right and right centre, and without interference from the enemy withdrew his troops to the foot-hills on the right bank of the Struma and to the south of the Butkova valley. The Salonika front returned to its normal condition of trench bickering. Later in 1917 the 8th Battalion had as neighbours in the line the

French Foreign Legion. No-man's-land at this point was wide, and the diligence of the battalion in preventing any ownership of it by the enemy was the occasion of a complaint by the Legion that the Scots nightly sought to meet the enemy while they were forbidden to move.

Things were very different on the skirts of Palestine. The fall of Rafa on 9th January had brought Sir Archibald Murray to the eastern border of Egypt. The desert railway was being pushed along the coast to form a British line of communication similar to that which the enemy possessed in his military railway from Beersheba. At first it was thought that the Turks would make their next stand close to the frontier, but on 5th March our aircraft reported that the enemy was falling back. A vigorous pursuit was impossible, for the rail-head was still too far in the rear, and Kress von Kressenstein, unhindered, took up ground on the line from Gaza to Tel el Sheria and Beersheba, this last point being strongly entrenched to protect his left.

Murray was now in an area which, for twenty-six hundred years, had been a cockpit of war—the most ancient and famous of all campaigning grounds. It was clear that he must fight a pitched battle before he could advance. He had now left the Sinai desert for the stony hills of Judah, which lie between the Dead Sea and the Mediterranean, and rise in the north-east corner to the noble mass of Hebron. In front of the enemy's position ran in a broad curve from south-east to north-west the dry watercourse called the Wadi Ghuzze. It was desirable to engage him as soon as possible, lest he should fall back upon more favourable lines farther north. Our rail-head was still far behind, for it only reached Rafa in the beginning of March; and if a blow was to be struck soon, it would be necessary, in the words of the official dispatch, to push forward the British forces "to their full radius of action into a country bare of all supplies and almost devoid of water." There were two possible plans. One was to

FIRST BATTLE OF GAZA

strike at Beersheba, and so reach the Central Palestine railway; but the drawback of such a course was that it would have brought the British line of communication from Rafa parallel to the enemy's front. The other, and apparently the safer, plan was to move up the coast with Gaza as the objective, aiming at the Turkish right flank. Such an advance would have its left protected by the sea, it would be better supplied with water, and the railway following it would be easier to build along the levels of the Philistian plain than among the rocks and ridges of the Judæan hills. Sir Archibald Murray accordingly decided upon the latter course. On 20th March Sir Charles Dobell, commanding the Eastern Force, moved his headquarters from El Arish to Rafa, and Sir Philip Chetwode, commanding the Desert Column, joined him there. Chetwode's cavalry were now at the little village of Deir el Belah, south-west of the Wadi Ghuzze, and the Fifty-second and Fifty-fourth Infantry Divisions and the Camel Corps were disposed on its right south of the watercourse. By the evening of the 25th all was in train for the coming battle.

About this time a new battalion of our regiment had come into being. On 4th January the Ayrshire Yeomanry and the Lanarkshire Yeomanry, who had previously served in the Gallipoli campaign, were amalgamated to form the 12th (Ayr and Lanark Yeomanry) Battalion of the Royal Scots Fusiliers, under Lieutenant-Colonel J. D. Boswell, and strengthened with drafts from the 3rd Reserve Battalion at home. The dismounted brigade to which it belonged became the 229th Infantry Brigade, and formed part of the Seventy-fourth Division, which was mainly composed of yeomanry units.[1] In March Lieutenant-Colonel Lord Dunglass succeeded to the battalion command.

The tale of the First Battle of Gaza, fought on 26th March, in which the Royal Scots Fusiliers were not engaged, may be briefly summarized. The cavalry of the Desert Column, though delayed by a thick fog

[1] The division was familiarly known as the "Broken Spurs."

from the sea, flung a cordon east and north of Gaza, while the Fifty-third Division, attacking in front, took the ridge of Ali Muntar, and by 4.30 in the afternoon was closing in on Gaza from the south, while the Australasian horsemen were in the eastern streets, and the Fifty-fourth Division held the Sheikh Abbas ridge on the right rear. But there was a gap of two and a half miles between the two infantry divisions, and darkness fell before the task was completed. The sea fog had done its work, the Turkish reserves from Beersheba were given time to arrive, the long day had exhausted both infantry and cavalry, and in war a task unfinished is often a task not begun. Dobell had still the Fifty-second Division in hand, but to fling it in in the darkness seemed to him a gambler's throw, and he decided to withdraw. By the evening of the following day the British troops were back across the Wadi Ghuzze, and the first assault on Gaza had signally failed.

Three weeks intervened between the first and second battles of Gaza. The position on 17th April was very different from what it had been on 26th March. Then the long, straggling line of posts towards Beersheba had been held by two Turkish divisions; now we had five infantry divisions against us, at least a division of cavalry, and twice the number of heavy batteries. The inner defences of the town—the Ali Muntar ridge—had been enormously strengthened, there was a strong line of outer defences from the sea to Sheikh Abbas, while on the eastern flank a new trench system had been constructed from Gaza south-east to the Atawineh ridge. There was no longer any possibility of surprise; there was no chance, owing to the flank defences, for an encircling cavalry movement; the only tactics were those of a frontal attack, undertaken without superior numbers and with all the disadvantages of lengthy communications. The British plan involved two stages: the first designed to carry the outer defences from the sea to Sheikh Abbas; the second to break through the Ali Muntar position and take Gaza.

For the first stage the Fifty-third Division was to stand north of the Wadi Ghuzze and carry out strong reconnaissances along the coast. On its right the Fifty-second Division was to advance against the ridge running south-westward from Ali Muntar, which contained the formidable defences known as the Warren, the Labyrinth, Green Hill, Middlesex Hill, Outpost Hill, and Lees Hill. Farther east the Fifty-fourth Division was to attack the line Mansura–Sheikh Abbas, its right flank being protected by a mounted division. The Seventy-fourth Division was in general reserve.

The attack began at dawn on 17th April, under a sky which promised a day of burning sun. The first stage was a brilliant success. The whole of the outer defence line—Sheikh Abbas and Mansura—was taken with few casualties by seven a.m., by the Fifty-second and Fifty-fourth Divisions. During the 18th the ground won was secured, and preparations were completed for the final effort on the 19th. This was a far graver business. On the left the Fifty-third Division was to attack towards Gaza along the coast, carrying Sheikh-Ajlin and Samson's Ridge; the Fifty-second Division in the centre was to take Ali Muntar, moving along the El Sire ridge; while on the right the Fifty-fourth Division was to swing round and capture the hills behind Gaza. The key-point of the problem was the part entrusted to the Fifty-second Division, for it meant the carrying of a series of hillocks along the El Sire crest before the final battlements of Ali Muntar were reached.

At 7.30 a.m. on the 19th, after the enemy front had been bombarded for two hours with high-explosive and gas shells, two brigades of the Fifty-second Division, the 155th and the 156th, advanced to the attack. In the 155th Brigade the 4th Royal Scots Fusiliers (Lieutenant-Colonel H. Thompson) were on the right, and the 5th King's Own Scottish Borderers on the left, while the 5th Royal Scots Fusiliers (Major J. B. Cook) followed in support. The first points on the ridge, Queen's Hill and Lees Hill, were taken by 8.15 a.m., by the 4th Royal

1917
April 19

Scots Fusiliers. Middlesex Hill followed at 11 a.m., but two hundred yards from Outpost Hill came a storm of machine-gun and shrapnel fire. Here the commanding officer, Lieutenant-Colonel Thompson, fell mortally wounded, as did his second in command, Major H. R. Young. " The battalion was now scattered over a fire-swept area ; for a time no one knew who was left to take command, and the advance was stayed." Meantime the 5th Royal Scots Fusiliers, whose business was consolidation, were doing their best to assist with covering fire. The Divisional Cyclist Company, which was attached to them, under Captain T. H. Glendinning, was west of Outpost Hill assisting the 5th K.O.S.B. in their attack on the Turkish lunettes on the summit. There Captain Glendinning was killed.

The rest of the day saw desperate fighting for Outpost Hill, a struggle to which it was hard to send reinforcements, since on that sharp ridge the attack must be on a narrow front. Again and again did the Fusiliers and Borderers rush the summit lunette, and again and again they were driven out of it. But after noon it was carried.

" Shortly before midday the 4th K.O.S.B. were ordered to capture this earthwork, and Major W. T. Forrest, the Scottish International Rugby player, went forward with two companies, another following in support. He made his way to the nullah whither the remnants of the Borderers and the Fusiliers had been driven. Units were mixed up, and he found the gallant Lieutenant W. D. Kennedy, 5th Royal Scots Fusiliers, busy reorganizing them. This work Major Forrest carried on, coolly walking about on the edge of the nullah. Despite all they had been through, the Borderers and Fusiliers were ready for another assault. When all was ready, Major Forrest—the ' Wattie Forrest ' of the football field—led his men forward for the last time. This charge of men from almost every unit in the 155th Brigade was a most inspiring sight. Under

OUTPOST HILL

a murderous fire, which struck down many, they rushed up the hill. About fifty Turks saw them coming, leaped from a ravine and bolted away into the cactus hedges on the western slope. Major Forrest was mortally wounded as he entered the works." [1]

1917
April 19

The little garrison on Outpost Hill was soon in a hopeless predicament. It was cut off from communications; of the runners sent back only one got through. Lieutenant J. Logan, of the 4th Royal Scots Fusiliers, tried to get a telephone into the lunette, found the wire too short, set out to get more wire, and was never heard of again. Enemy assaults from the cactus hedges on the slopes were driven back, but only with heavy loss to our men. Meantime things had gone little better elsewhere in the field. The Fifty-third Division had taken its first objective on the left; but the Fifty-fourth Division on the right was unable to get near Ali Muntar, owing to its left flank being in the air. As the sun set there were only seventy left of the garrison on Outpost Hill, while the Turks were working round its flanks. There was nothing for it but to slip away, and this was done in the first hour of darkness. Middlesex Hill had also to be relinquished, and the last Scots Fusilier left that point at 10.15 p.m. A line of defence was prepared covering Lees Hill. Sir Archibald Murray would have renewed the attack on Ali Muntar on the following day, but Dobell and Chetwode protested, and Murray allowed himself to be convinced.

In that disastrous Second Battle of Gaza the Fifty-second and Fifty-fourth Divisions lost some 7,000 men. The 155th Brigade had 1,026 casualties, nearly half its strength, and most were incurred in and around the unhallowed lunette on Outpost Hill. The 4th Royal Scots Fusiliers had 5 officers—Lieutenant-Colonel H. Thompson, Major H. R. Young, Lieutenant J. W. Roxburgh, Second Lieutenants W. W. D. Donaldson and

[1] Lieutenant-Colonel Thompson's *The Fifty-second Division*, page 324.

1917
April 19

A. S. D. Clark—killed, and 25 men; 11 officers and 200 men wounded; while Lieutenant J. Logan and 20 men were missing. The 5th Royal Scots Fusiliers had 5 officers—Captains John Lees and W. S. Pirie, Lieutenant W. D. Kennedy, Second Lieutenants R. P. Mackenzie and J. H. Ross—killed, 6 officers and 140 men wounded, and 14 men missing. Major Paton, from the 5th Royal Scots Fusiliers, took over the command of the 4th Battalion. Of the prowess of the Scots Fusiliers on that grim day let the commanding officer of the 5th Battalion speak : " It is with the greatest pride that I record the magnificent conduct of officers and men in their repeated efforts to achieve the impossible. Men without officers were always ready to put themselves at the disposal of any officer who would lead them forward again, and, once having a foothold, did not give ground except once when withdrawn to be reorganized. I consider that the fact that all Lewis guns were brought back, and all equipment except such as was on men who became casualties in the open, reflects the highest credit upon the discipline of all ranks."

In spite of the check at Gaza the foundation had been laid for future success. The road had been made once and for all across the desert, and it was only a matter of months till troops and guns and supplies could travel by it for a new concentration. In such a land a settled war of positions was not inevitable, and the little branch line creeping eastward from Rafa was the fingerpost pointing to a more deadly offensive. In the end of June Sir Edmund Allenby, who had formerly commanded the Third Army in France, succeeded Sir Archibald Murray in Palestine, and his force was presently increased to seven infantry and three mounted divisions. He resolved to turn the Gaza position from the east by first capturing Beersheba, and then operating against the open enemy left flank.

The summer months were spent in preparation, and in raids along the front. The Turks replied in kind, and in one of their counter-attacks at Umbrella Hill, some five hundred yards north of the British position on Samson's Hill, the 5th Royal Scots Fusiliers performed a notable exploit. A post was raided by the enemy on the morning of 5th June, and Second Lieutenant J. M. Craig took out a rescue party who performed their work under heavy fire, their leader returning again and again to bring in wounded men. For his conduct on this day Second Lieutenant Craig received the Victoria Cross. Within a week the same battalion had its revenge, for it had a share in the successful raid on the Turkish work called Sea Post.

Meantime Allenby's arrangements progressed, and by the middle of October the details of the plan were complete. He proposed to attack Beersheba with Chetwode's XX. Corps, which contained the Tenth, Fifty-third, Sixtieth, and Seventy-fourth Infantry Divisions, while the mounted troops, which formed the Desert Mounted Corps under Lieutenant-General Sir Henry Chauvel, made a wide circuit to cover the town from the east and the north, and get astride the main road to Hebron. A containing attack was meanwhile to be made at Gaza by Sir Edward Bulfin's XXI. Corps—Fifty-second, Fifty-fourth, and Seventy-fifth Divisions —to pin down the enemy's reserves to that quarter. This was to be followed by an attack against the Turkish left at Hareira, to roll up the enemy front from east to west, and let the cavalry through to ride for the wells at Huj and for Junction Station. Beyond that the campaign was on the knees of the gods.

Of the watercourses descending from the hills east of Beersheba the most notable is the Wadi Saba, and south of it, towards the El Auja railway, lies Hill 1070. On 31st October the Sixtieth and Seventy-fourth Divisions (the 12th Royal Scots Fusiliers were not engaged) carried Hill 1070, and attacked the south and south-east defences between the Khalesa road and the Wadi Saba, while the Imperial Camel Corps and part of the Fifty-third Division made a holding attack farther north. By one p.m., with few casualties, the whole position had fallen, and the cavalry, who had made a circuit of thirty miles, had the high ground east

1917
June 5–Oct. 31

of the town. The latter then seized the key hill, Tel es Saba, while an Australian brigade got astride the Hebron road. Before evening Beersheba was securely in our hands.

Two days later, on 2nd November, began the second stage, the frontal attack on Gaza, which place had been under continuous bombardment since 27th October. This was intended as a subsidiary operation to attract the Turkish reserves, and the line of attack was that which had been entrusted to the Fifty-third Division in the Second Battle of Gaza—a six-thousand yards front from Sheikh Hasan on the sea to the ridge which we called Umbrella Hill. It was an ambitious objective, for there was a long space between our front lines and those of the enemy, and the sand dunes of the coast made heavy going. The attack was to be made by the Fifty-fourth Division, strengthened by the 156th Brigade of the Fifty-second Division, and to these latter troops was entrusted the preliminary capture of Umbrella Hill on the night of 1st November. The operations of 2nd November were wholly successful; almost all the objectives were won: so far from the enemy being able to reinforce his left flank, one of his reserve divisions had to be sent to Gaza, and the capture of Sheikh Hasan gave us a position outflanking the town on the west.

All was now ready for the major operation in the east, but water and transport difficulties compelled Allenby at first to move slowly. The XX. Corps and the cavalry felt their way into the hills north-east and north of Beersheba, wheeling north-eastward against the Sheria–Hareira line. By the night of 5th November the troops of assault were in position—the Sixtieth, Tenth, and Seventy-fourth Divisions on the left directed against Kauwukah, while the cavalry on the right moved against Sheria, with the Fifty-third Division on the extreme right flank. The assault was delivered at dawn on the 6th, and by midday most of the objectives had been won. Kauwukah and Rushdi were taken, and Hareira entered; by the evening Yeomanry

THE ADVANCE ON JERUSALEM

Facing page 400

FALL OF GAZA

were in Sheria Station, and the Fifty-third Division had carried Tel el Khuweilfeh. Long before the dark fell the cavalry had ridden northward, with orders to occupy Huj and Jemmamah. In this day's action the 12th Royal Scots Fusiliers were engaged, and bivouacked that night two miles south of Sheria Station. In the fighting they had four officers killed—Captain L. G. Fawcett, Lieutenants W. Jackson and H. J. Weir, and Second Lieutenant A. H. Dunlop.

That night an attack had been ordered by the XXI. Corps on Gaza—the Seventy-fifth Division against Outpost and Middlesex Hills—to be continued next morning by the Fifty-fourth. But there was to be no resistance. Gaza fell, not to assault, but to the far-sighted and methodical strategy of rolling up the enemy front from the east, and the Turks were in general retreat. The position, in the words of the official dispatch, was that " operations had reached the stage of a direct pursuit by as many troops as could be supplied so far in advance of rail-head." The problem, in fact, had become one of transport rather than of manœuvre. It was a sufficiently hard problem, for the supply of water and provisions was scanty, but speed was urgent if we were to reap the fruits of our victory. The Turkish VIII. Army was in full retreat north along the Philistian plain. If Allenby could reach in good time Junction Station, where the Jerusalem line left the main railway to Damascus, he would cut off the Jerusalem garrison from the rest of the enemy forces. The Turkish VII. Army, which had been driven back towards Hebron, hung on the flanks of our advance, but it was too weak to be capable of serious mischief. We were moving far from rail-head, we had a slender force for so great an undertaking, and our problem of supply grew more acute with every mile of advance. But we had a supreme advantage in the demoralization of the enemy.

Of the two divisions with which we are concerned, one was engaged in the van of the pursuit, and the other remained for a fortnight in the vicinity of Gaza

1917 on the line of communication. On the 7th the Fifty-
Nov. 7-13 second Division began its march up the coast on the extreme left, and seized the high ground on the right bank of the Wadi Hesi. Next day the Turks were attacked on Sausage Ridge by the 155th Brigade, the 4th Royal Scots Fusiliers under Lieutenant-Colonel R. G. Maclaine and the 5th Royal Scots Fusiliers under Lieutenant-Colonel J. B. Cook joining the brigade at 10.30 a.m. after an exhausting march of five miles through soft sand. In the attack the 4th Battalion formed the brigade centre and the 5th Battalion the left wing. The place was stoutly contested, and on the glacis of the ridge the assaulting troops had many losses. Lieutenant-Colonel Cook showed great initiative in altering the direction of his battalion at a critical moment, and later in defeating a counter-attack on the brigade flank. Meantime the ridge was forced from the south by the 157th Brigade, and by the early morning of the 9th was in our possession. The 5th Royal Scots Fusiliers had 100 casualties, and the 4th had 76, among the latter being Captain L. L. McKeevor, R.A.M.C.

The pressure farther east was now assisting the pursuit. On the 9th the Fifty-second Division occupied Ascalon, the ruins of that city which had been the last conquest of Richard Cœur-de-Lion, and which in the great days of the Khalifs had been called " the Bride of Syria " for the fairness of its palaces and gardens. On the 10th our line ran from Hamameh, four miles north of Ascalon, to the bend of the Central Palestine railway north-east of El Feluja. It was now clear that the enemy resistance was stiffening, and that the dash for Junction Station would not be unresisted. The weather was very hot, with the scorching *khamsin* blowing from the inland deserts; our troops were thirty-four miles from their rail-head; and the numerous wadis and the sandy roads made marching arduous for men who in the past fortnight had fought many battles. Still we crept on, our left on the coast moving fastest, for there the roads were better, until, on the morning of 13th November, we were prepared to strike

CAPTURE OF JUNCTION STATION

for Junction Station. The eastward turn had begun, the Fifty-second Division being thrown well forward, and the Seventy-fifth wheeling on its right. The orientation of the opposing fronts was now changing from that of west to east to that of north to south.

1917 Nov. 13-14

The Turks, covering the railway, held the ridge north-east of El Mughar and Katrah, the ancient Cedron —a strong position which, if we delayed, might become a second Gaza. The attack was entrusted to the Fifty-second Division, which had all three of its brigades in action, the main movement being that of the 155th. The 4th and 5th Royal Scots Fusiliers carried Katrah about 4.45 p.m. after a long and arduous fight among the sunken roads and cactus hedges. One incident demands quotation. " Captain H. E. Sutherland, 4th Royal Scots Fusiliers, led the fourth company of his battalion in another attempt to outflank the Turks from the south. He was determined to make a proper detour, and led the way a considerable distance ahead of his men. With him were a Lewis gunner with a single drum of ammunition, and a grenadier with only two bombs. Sutherland moved rapidly over the ridge, and struck the end of a trench filled with Turks which marked the end of their support line. The Lewis gunner emptied his only drum into them, the grenadier threw his two bombs, and nine Turkish officers, with sixty-four other ranks, surrendered to these three Fusiliers."[1] Meantime the K.O.S.B. had taken El Mughar, and the whole position was ours. General Kress von Kressenstein left Katrah only half an hour before the Scots Fusiliers entered it, but they took in that place over 400 prisoners. The 4th Royal Scots Fusiliers had 1 officer—Second Lieutenant G. W. McQuaker —and 19 other ranks killed, and 5 officers and 61 men wounded; the 5th had 15 men killed and 2 officers and 64 men wounded—a small price for a success so decisive. Next day Junction Station was in our hands.

Jerusalem was now directly threatened, and Turks and Germans alike made frantic efforts to save it.

[1] *The Fifty-second Division*, pages 421, 422.

1917
Nov. 16–19

Enver came from Constantinople, and departed after haranguing his defeated generals. Falkenhayn came from Aleppo, found he could do nothing, and returned to Nablus (Shechem) to watch events. Allenby continued to advance with his XXI. Corps on a broad front, pivoting on his right. On the 16th, after defeating a Turkish rear-guard at the ancient Gezer, he occupied Jaffa (Joppa) without opposition. He had come to a bold decision. His original plan had been to wait till the improvement of his communications enabled him to collect all his forces before turning east into the Judæan hills. He now resolved to attack at once with what he had got, and take the tide at its flood. But before he could advance on the capital there must be a short delay for reorganization. The troops, who had marched seventy miles in nine days, must be rested, supplies must be got forward, and the position must be made secure. The west side of the Judæan uplands consists of steep bare spurs divided by narrow valleys, and many invaders coming from the coast had found destruction in those difficult passes. For our advance we had, besides the railway, a single highway—that which runs from Jaffa to Jerusalem. To safeguard the flank of that advance and to secure our hold upon the coastal plain, as well as to isolate the city, it was necessary to get astride the one good road which traverses the hills from south to north—the road from Jerusalem to Nablus. The advance upon the Holy City could not, therefore, be by the directest route, more especially as the British commander was anxious to avoid any fighting in its immediate vicinity. He wished to conquer it, as he had conquered Gaza, by blows struck at a distance.

The stage in the campaign which followed was one of slow and hard-won progress in a most intricate country. On the 19th the Fifty-second Division began to move east from Ramleh and Ludd into the foothills. It was on the British left, with the Seventy-fifth Division on its right; the latter was directed on Kuryat el Enab (Kirjath Jearim), while the former was to advance in support through Berfilya to Beit Dukka, just south of the Ajalon valley, where of old Joshua won his unorthodox victory. After some resistance in the narrow defile at Saris, Kuryat el Enab and Beit Dukka were taken on the 20th. The spearhead of the advance was now the Seventy-fifth Division, and on the 21st it reached the ridge called Nebi Samwil (the ancient Mizpah), where stood the tomb of Samuel the Prophet. The place was under three miles from the Nablus road and five from Jerusalem, and was the farthest point reached by King Richard in January 1192.

Here in the driving mist and rain the enemy suddenly developed a new power of resistance. On the 22nd he counter-attacked violently at Nebi Samwil against the Seventy-fifth Division and forced back the Yeomanry at Beitunia. The 156th Brigade of the Fifty-second Division was sent forward to relieve the Seventy-fifth, and presently the whole division was engaged on the ridge. On the 24th the Fifty-second attempted to seize El Jib, which the Seventy-fifth had failed to take, and threw itself across the Nablus road, but with no better success. The attack was made at noon by the 155th and 156th Brigades, the 5th Royal Scots Fusiliers being on the right of its brigade, with the 4th Battalion (now under Lieutenant-Colonel N. G. Stewart-Richardson) in reserve. They reached a point some four hundred yards from El Jib, and there fell the gallant and beloved commander of the 5th Battalion, Lieutenant-Colonel Cook. The division was ordered to discontinue the attack, though the men were eager to go on. Nebi Samwil itself had been taken; but it was still impossible to advance along the ridge, and for the better part of a fortnight Allenby held his hand in that quarter. The Sixtieth Division relieved, and the Fifty-second, now less than the strength of a brigade, began to move back into the Beth-horon region.

But withdrawal from Nebi Samwil did not mean rest for the division. From 25th November onwards the enemy began a series of attacks against the British left wing on the coast, and presently these spread to the

1917
Nov. 28–Dec. 1

left flank of the advance in the Judæan hills. This flank was held at the time by Yeomanry, who had a four-mile front from Beit Dukka to Beit ur el Tahta (Lower Beth-horon). On the left of the Yeomanry there was a gap between them and the next division. On the 28th the Turks endeavoured to force this gap, and were only just prevented by the 155th Brigade, which came up in time. The first intimation which the brigade had of the enemy was when its transport was caught in the open by machine-gun fire. "We made for a spur of a hill across a hundred yards of open," wrote Major Yuille, the quartermaster of the 4th Royal Scots Fusiliers. "Heaven only knows how we got across that with only one camel struck. . . . We got in behind the spur and the camels perched like sea-gulls among the rocks, and there we had to sit the whole day absolutely marooned by machine-gun fire, with bullets pinging against the rocks." The 155th Brigade had a long day of confused fighting, the two Scots Fusilier battalions (Major R. W. Paton now commanding the 5th) endeavouring to get round the Turkish right flank and attack Suffa. In the evening a new defensive line was established north-east of El Burj, and the gap was closed. There was more fighting on the 29th, and late that evening an Australian Light Horse brigade relieved the 155th, except for the 4th Royal Scots Fusiliers, who remained at El Burj. The last Turkish assault took place on 1st December, when the Australians at El Burj were attacked by a fresh enemy force, and, having no grenades, were almost driven from the ridge. A Company of the 4th Royal Scots Fusiliers was hurried forward, and Second Lieutenant S. H. P. Boughey, with a small party of grenadiers, pushed ahead. The Fusiliers took the Turks in flank, completely routed them, and drove them down the hill.[1] The heroic leader far out-

---

[1] The Fusiliers were furious at losing their sleep, and one, as he threw bomb after bomb, was heard thus to address the enemy: "They mairched us a hunner miles (Tak' that, ye —— !), and we've been in five fechts. (Anither yin, ye —— !) And they said we were relieved. (Tak' that, ye —— !) And we're oot o' our beds anither nicht. (Swalla that, ye —— !)."—*The Fifty-second Division*, page 471.

FALL OF JERUSALEM

stripped his men, and received the surrender of a batch of 25 Turks. A few minutes later he fell, shot through the head, receiving posthumously the Victoria Cross for his gallantry. In all, 6 officers and 166 Turks were taken prisoners, and over 100 Turkish dead were found beside the British trenches.

On 2nd December the 155th Brigade reached Ramleh, and on the 5th it marched out to take over the lines north of Jaffa, with the 156th Brigade between it and the sea. There, when it became necessary to strengthen our position on the coast, the Fifty-second Division, on the evening of 20th December, crossed the unfordable river Auja with negligible losses, and the 5th Royal Scots Fusiliers carried the whole Hadrah position on the north bank—the last, and not the least brilliant, of the division's exploits on the soil of Palestine.

Meantime Allenby had attained his purpose. On 4th December he began to bring up the XX. Corps from Hebron, and the Seventy-fourth Division, which had been at Gaza, was by 30th November in place on the left of the Sixtieth Division in the direct assault on Jerusalem. About dawn on 8th December we attacked towards the Nablus road, and by noon the Sixtieth Division had advanced over two miles, while the Seventy-fourth Division had carried the Beit Iksa spur. The 12th Royal Scots Fusiliers were one of the attacking battalions of the 229th Brigade, and after a climb of a thousand feet carried their objective with few losses. The advance halted that night about a mile and a half from Jerusalem on the west, while the Fifty-third Division from the south entered Bethlehem.

The doom of the city was now sealed. Sunday, 9th December, was the festival of the Hanukah, which commemorated the capture of the Temple by Judas Maccabæus. Long before dawn hustled detachments of Turkish soldiers began to pour in at the Jaffa Gate, while an outgoing stream flowed eastward across the Valley of Jehoshaphat. The British, coming from the west, found the enemy in flight, and while the Sixtieth

1917
Dec. 2–20

1917
Dec. 9–11
and Seventy-fourth Divisions were moving to a line across the Nablus road north of the city, the Fifty-third Division on the south cut the main road to Jericho. Jerusalem was isolated, and shortly after sunrise the mayor sent out a parlementaire with the governor's letter of surrender. The last Turkish soldiers straggled out of St. Stephen's Gate, and long before noon British patrols were in the city.

On Tuesday, the 11th, Allenby entered on foot by the Jaffa Gate, which the Arabs call "The Friend." No conqueror had ever entered it with greater prestige. For centuries there had been current an Arab prophecy concerning a deliverer from the West, and in 1898 the people of Palestine had asked if the Kaiser were indeed the man. They were told that the true saviour would bear the name of a Prophet of God, and would enter the city on foot, and would not appear till the Nile flowed into Palestine. To the peasants of Judæa the prophecy now seemed to be fulfilled, for the name of the English general was in Arabic El Nebi, the "Prophet," and his men had come into the land bringing with them the waters of Egypt.

Officers who died in 1917

Lieutenant W. G. AUSTIN (23rd Aug.); Second Lieutenant J. L. BAMFORD (20th Aug.); Lieutenant W. L. BLACKWOOD (31st July); Second Lieutenant S. H. P. BOUGHEY (4th Dec.); Second Lieutenant W. R. BROWN (30th Sept.); Lieutenant A. E. BUCHAN (9th April); Second Lieutenant H. D. BUIK (9th April); Second Lieutenant J. C. CAMERON (23rd April); Second Lieutenant T. S. CAMPBELL (23rd April); Second Lieutenant A. S. D. CLARK (22nd April); Second Lieutenant W. COCHRANE (26th Sept.); Lieutenant-Colonel J. B. COOK (24th Nov.); Captain W. D. COOPER (13th Aug.); Captain J. J. CROALL (4th Oct.); Second Lieutenant T. R. CURRER (26th Sept.); Second Lieutenant G. P. DAVIDSON (3rd May); Second Lieutenant W. W. D. DONALDSON (19th April); Second Lieutenant A. H. DUNLOP (6th Nov.); Lieutenant E. H. EWEN (1st May); Lieutenant G. FAIRLEY (9th April); Captain L. G. F. E. FAWCETT (6th Nov.); Captain J. C. FISHER (6th May); Captain J. GARDNER (27th Sept.); Captain T. H. GLENDINNING (17th April); Second Lieutenant A. C. M. GORDON (1st March); Second Lieutenant H. C. GRAHAM (9th June); Second Lieutenant E. B. GREENHOUS

OFFICERS WHO DIED IN 1917

(26th Aug.); Lieutenant A. HENDERSON (3rd May); Second Lieutenant H. T. A. HONEYMAN (10th Dec.); Second Lieutenant W. L. INGLIS (2nd Oct.); Lieutenant W. JACKSON (8th Nov.); Second Lieutenant A. J. JOHNSTONE (5th April); Second Lieutenant S. JOHNSTON (8th March); Second Lieutenant D. H. KENNEDY (31st July); Lieutenant H. T. KENNEDY (6th June); Second Lieutenant N. KENNEDY (31st Oct.); Lieutenant W. D. KENNEDY (19th April); Second Lieutenant J. B. KINCAID (3rd May); Captain J. LEES (19th April); Second Lieutenant T. LEISHMAN (23rd April); Second Lieutenant A. D. LENNOX (18th Oct.); Second Lieutenant W. LINDSAY (31st July); Captain W. LOFTUS (25th April); Second Lieutenant J. LOGAN (19th April); Second Lieutenant W. B. M'ARTHUR (9th April); Lieutenant-Colonel M. E. M'CONAGHEY (23rd April); Second Lieutenant J. H. M'CRACKEN (26th Sept.); Second Lieutenant W. M'GHEE (9th April); Second Lieutenant R. P. MACKENZIE (19th April); Lieutenant G. L. MACKIE (27th Dec.); Second Lieutenant J. M'LEOD (25th April); Captain J. C. M'MILLAN (6th Feb.); Second Lieutenant G. W. M'QUAKER (13th Nov.); Second Lieutenant E. B. MARKUS (5th April); Second Lieutenant F. R. MARTIN (29th June); Lieutenant R. MAYBERRY (15th Nov.); Lieutenant M. MERSON (3rd May); Second Lieutenant I. M. MILNE (31st Aug.); Second Lieutenant S. J. MOORE (18th March); Lieutenant A. H. P. MURRAY (9th April); Second Lieutenant A. T. NEWBIGGING (3rd May); Second Lieutenant E. P. OATTS (3rd May); Captain J. B. ORR (31st July); Captain W. E. PAULL (31st July); Second Lieutenant H. R. PETTER (3rd May); Captain W. S. PIRIE (19th April); Second Lieutenant R. S. POOLEY (23rd April); Second Lieutenant W. ROBERTSON (3rd May); Second Lieutenant A. C. ROSS (6th Dec.); Second Lieutenant J. H. ROSS (19th April); Lieutenant J. W. ROXBURGH (19th April); Second Lieutenant D. SCOTT (7th April); Second Lieutenant H. L. SCOTT (6th June); Second Lieutenant E. A. SINCLAIR (23rd April); Second Lieutenant H. F. SMITH (23rd April); Second Lieutenant J. R. D. SMITH (31st July); Second Lieutenant R. SMITH (15th Dec.); Major T. SMITH (23rd Jan.); Captain W. S. SMITH (23rd March); Second Lieutenant J. SPEARS (23rd April); Second Lieutenant T. STEEN (1st March); Lieutenant T. K. STEVENSON (28th Jan.); Lieutenant H. E. STEWART (19th Nov.); Second Lieutenant A. STIVEN (24th Jan.); Captain G. SWALES (26th Sept.); Second Lieutenant E. B. SYKES (31st July); Second Lieutenant W. B. TAIT (15th Dec.); Lieutenant-Colonel N. M. TEACHER (26th Sept.); Lieutenant-Colonel H. THOMPSON (22nd April); Second Lieutenant D. TRENCH (23rd April); Captain T. WATSON (11th April); Lieutenant H. J. WEIR (9th Nov.); Second Lieutenant M. WHITE (13th April); Second Lieutenant J. W. WHITELAW (11th April); Second Lieutenant J. G. WILSON (15th Feb.); Second Lieutenant E. L. WOOD (26th Sept.); Captain A. WYLLIE (18th April); Major H. R. YOUNG (21st April).

1917

CHAPTER XVIII

THE GREAT WAR—1918

Germany's final strategy—Her new tactics—The position of the British front in March 1918—The attack of 21st March—The retreat to the Avre—The fighting at Arras—The battle of the Lys—The fight for Kemmel—The six Scots Fusilier battalions—The capture of Meteren—The advance to victory—The capture of the Drocourt-Quéant line—The fighting at Mœuvres—The Canal du Nord—The fall of the Hindenburg Line—The defeat of Bulgaria—The last movements in the West—The Armistice.

I

1918
Jan.-March

DURING the summer months of 1917 the German armies on the Eastern front did not advance, though the way seemed plain before them. But they were not idle. The German High Command had seen the opportunity afforded by the downfall of Russia, and believed that long before America took the field in strength they could deal a fatal blow to the Allies in the West. They prepared most patiently for this final stroke, and turned the whole of the Eastern front into one vast training camp, where picked divisions were practised in open fighting; for their scheme demanded a high perfection of discipline and individual prowess. The history of the war had, so far, been the history of new tactical methods devised to break the strength of entrenched defences. The Allies had tried repeatedly from Neuve Chapelle onward, each time changing their plans; and at last at the Somme they seemed to have found a method which, though slow and laborious in its working, was decisive in its results. But the defection of Russia put an end to the hopes of this plan, and once again our theory of war was recast. But while Byng at Cambrai was feeling his way towards new tactics, Germany had already decided upon her scheme. She saw that surprise was essential, and that therefore a laboured artillery " preparation " was out of the question. She realized, too, that in order to get the full cumulative effect of the blow, division must follow division to strike while the iron was hot. If these two things—surprise, and an endless chain of troops of assault—could be found, then it might be possible to win final victory within the narrow limits of time still permitted to her. A breach here and a breach there meant only a restricted advance, behind which the enemy front grew solid, as concrete hardens with exposure. She therefore aimed not at a breakthrough in the older sense, but at a general crumbling.

Germany's plan was based upon the highly specialized training of certain units, and was a logical conclusion from her use of " storm troops." The first point was the absence of any preliminary massing near the point of attack. Men were brought up by night marches just before zero hour, and secrecy was thus obtained for the assembling. Again, there was no long bombardment to alarm the enemy; the guns opened only at the moment when the infantry advanced, the enemy's back areas being confused by a deluge of gas shells. The assault was made by picked troops in open order—or rather in small clusters—carrying light trench mortars and many machine guns, with the field batteries close behind them in support. The actual mode of attack, which the French called " infiltration," may be likened to a hand, of which the finger tips are shod with steel, and which is pushed into a yielding substance. The picked troops at the finger ends made gaps through which others passed, till each section of the defence found itself outflanked and encircled. A system of flares and rockets enabled the following troops to learn where the picked troops had made the breach, and the artillery came close behind the infantry. The men had unlimited objectives, and carried iron rations for several days. When one division had reached the end of its strength another took its place, so that the advance resembled a continuous game of leap-frog.

The method was the opposite of the old German mass attack, which had been a succession of hammer-blows on one section of front. It was strictly the filtering of a great army into a hostile position, so that each part of the position was turned, and the whole front was first dislocated and then crumbled. This might be achieved by inferior numbers; but a local superiority was aimed at, so as to ensure a complete victory by pushing far behind into unprotected areas. Advance was to be measured out not by metres but by miles, and in every case was to proceed far enough to capture the enemy's artillery positions. Obviously the effect would be cumulative, the momentum of the attack would grow, and, if it was not checked in the battle-zone, it would be far harder to check in the hinterland. It was no case of an isolated stroke, but of a creeping sickness which might demoralize a hundred miles of front. The German Command was confident, for they saw their way presently to a numerical superiority in the West, and they had devised tactics which must come with deadly effect upon an enemy prepared to meet only the old methods. But their plan demanded immediate success. A protracted battle would destroy the picked troops, and without them the new tactics were futile.

The first experiment was made early in September 1917, when von Hutier captured Riga. But the true test came in October, when Otto von Below, with the German VI. Army, broke through the Italian front at Caporetto and drove Cadorna behind the Piave. After that there could be no question of the value of Germany's plan. One other test, and her certainty was complete. On 20th November Byng struck at Cambrai, achieving by means of his tanks a genuine surprise. Ten days later came the German counterstroke—in two parts. The attack on the British left

THE POSITION OF THE ALLIES

at Bourlon, carried out in the old fashion, signally failed. The attack on the British right between Masnières and Vendhuile, following the new fashion, as signally succeeded. But the Allied Staffs had not yet grasped the full meaning of the new method. Caporetto was explained by a breakdown in Italian *moral*, and Cambrai by defective local intelligence. Neither explanation was sound, and four months later the armies of France and Britain read the true lesson in letters of fire.

Ever since the close of 1917 the Allied Command in the West had been conscious that the situation had altered. The Germans were able now to resume the offensive at will, and the next phase of the campaign must see the Allies on their defence. Haig and Pétain were aware that large reinforcements could be brought from the East, which would give the enemy a superiority in numbers until such time as the Americans arrived to redress the balance. Nevertheless, the general temper of the armies of France and Britain was one of confidence. At the moment they believed that they would have to face a small numerical preponderance; but they had faced greater odds at First Ypres and Verdun and had held their ground. Let the enemy attack and break his head against their iron barriers. He would only be the weaker when the time came for their final advance.

But the wiser minds among both soldiers and civilians were uneasy. They believed that the German Staff would make a desperate effort to secure a decision while they still held their opponents at a disadvantage. The German defence had been conducted in a long-prepared fortified zone; the battles of 1917 had given us a new line, in parts only a month or two old. How, it was asked, would we fare against a resolute assault? Worst of all, we were deplorably short of men. Haig had not received during 1917 the minimum levies for which he had asked, and had been compelled to put into the line-of-battle men imperfectly trained, and to strain good divisions to breaking-point. There were

*1918
Jan.–March*

1918
Jan.-March

other drawbacks which bore specially hard upon the British. Up to January 1918 their right wing had been Sir Julian Byng's Third Army. Before the middle of the month the Third Army was moved a little farther north, and the place on its right was taken by Sir Hubert Gough's Fifth Army from the Ypres area, which replaced the French in front of St. Quentin. About the 20th the Fifth Army extended its right as far south as Barisis, beyond the Oise, thus making itself responsible for a line of seventy-two thousand yards, or nearly forty-one miles.

For this new duty Haig had not received proportionate reinforcements. He now held one hundred and thirty miles of line, and these the most critical in the West, with approximately the same numbers as he had possessed two years before, when his front was only eighty miles long and Russia was still in the field. He dared not weaken his northern and central sections, where, in the case of an attack, he had but little room to manœuvre. So he was compelled to leave the Fifth Army on his right in a condition of dangerous weakness. Gough on his forty-mile front had no more than eleven divisions in line, and three infantry and two cavalry divisions in reserve. His three right divisions were holding thirty thousand yards—an average of one bayonet to the yard, while the German average was four.

There was the further handicap that the Germans from their position inside the great salient in the West could concentrate with ease a force of attack, and until the actual assault was made the Allied Command would not know on which side of the salient the blow would fall. For the enemy dispositions would threaten the French in Champagne as much as the British at St. Quentin.[1] There was still no centralized command, though the Versailles Council provided something in the matter of a unified staff. Hence it would not be easy to arrange for co-operation with Pétain, or for

---

[1] Haig had begun to work on the supposition of an attack in the Péronne area as early as November 1917, and some weeks before the attack the British Staff had divined the exact area.

THE BRITISH DISPOSITIONS

French support, till the battle had developed, for the French commander would not unreasonably desire to keep his reserves at the point where they could be used with equal facility for St. Quentin or Champagne. Yet it was to French support that Gough must look in the first instance, since the available British reserves had been allotted to Byng, and it would take time to bring troops from Plumer and Horne in the north.

The British Command attempted to atone for their weakness in numbers by devising defences of exceptional strength. In front, along the ground held by Byng and Gough, lay a " forward zone " organized in two sections—a line of outposts to give the alarm and fall back, and a well-wired line of resistance. In both were a number of skilfully-placed redoubts, armed with machine guns, and so arranged that any enemy advance would come under cross-fire. The spaces between the redoubts were to be protected by a barrage of field guns and corps heavy guns. The line of resistance and the redoubts were intended to hold out till the last, and to receive no support from the rear, except for such counter-attacks as might be necessary. The purpose of this " forward zone " was to break up an advancing enemy, and the principle of its organization was " blobs " rather than a continuous line.

Behind the " forward zone," at a distance of from half a mile to three miles or more, came the " battle zone," arranged on the same plan, except that it had no outposts. It was a defence in depth, elaborately wired, and studded with strong points. A mile or two in its rear lay the third and final defensive zone, which in March 1918 was little more than a sketch. The theory of the system was that the " battle zone " would be impregnable against an attack thus weakened. Consequently the alternative positions in the rear— the third zone and the Péronne bridgehead—were not serious defences. Considering the small number of men available, it was not possible in the time to provide any further safeguards. On the " battle zone " rested the hope of resistance of the Third and Fifth Armies.

1918 Jan.–March

If it failed to hold, the situation would be grave indeed, for there were no prepared defences to fall back upon and no immediate chance of reserves.

During February there had been drastic changes in the British forces. Divisions were reduced from a thirteen to a ten battalion basis, and this meant that one battalion must disappear from each brigade. The 6th/7th Royal Scots Fusiliers accordingly left the Fifteenth Division, to their profound regret, and under Major H. P. Hart became the Pioneer Battalion of the Fifty-ninth Division in the Mory area. Their former commanding officer, Lieutenant-Colonel E. I. D. Gordon, went to the 1st Battalion, which was with the Third Division in the section south of Arras. The 2nd Royal Scots Fusiliers, under Lieutenant-Colonel Utterson-Kelso, remained in the 90th Brigade of the Thirtieth Division, and in March they were holding a section of the ground just west of St. Quentin. The British dispositions on the eve of battle were, from the Arras–Douai road to near Gouzeaucourt, Byng's Third Army, containing from left to right the XVII., VI., IV., and V. Corps; from Gouzeaucourt to the Oise Gough's Fifth Army, containing the VII., XIX., XVIII., and III. Corps. Byng, on his forty thousand yards of front, had in line ten divisions—the Fifteenth, the Third, the Guards, the Thirty-fourth, the Fifty-ninth, the Sixth, the Fifty-first, the Seventeenth, the Sixty-third, and the Second; and in reserve the Fourth, the Fifty-sixth, the Forty-seventh, the Fortieth, and the Nineteenth. Gough, on his seventy-two thousand yards, had eleven divisions in line—the Ninth, the Twenty-first, the Sixteenth, the Sixty-sixth, the Twenty-fourth, the Sixty-first, the Thirtieth, the Thirty-sixth, the Fourteenth, the Eighteenth, and the Fifty-eighth, with in reserve the Thirty-ninth, the Fiftieth, and the Twentieth Infantry Divisions, and the First and Second Cavalry Divisions.

The first weeks of March saw the bright, dry weather of a Picardy spring. As early as the 14th our aircraft reported a big concentration well back in the enemy's

THE EVE OF BATTLE

hinterland, and the Third and Fifth Armies were apprised of an approaching battle. The troops on our front waited with composure on the future. No one either in Britain or France realized how much Germany was prepared to stake on this, her last blow, or the immense asset which her new tactics gave her. Many raids undertaken during those days established the arrival in the line of fresh enemy divisions, but they gave us no notion of the real German strength. One fact, however, we learned from them—that Thursday, 21st March, was the day appointed for the attack. The last eight days were curiously quiet on the British front. On Tuesday, the 19th, the weather broke in a drizzle, but it cleared next day, with the result that a thick mist was drawn out of the ground and muffled all the folds of the downs. That day was spent in an eerie calm, like the hush that precedes a storm. When the sun set, the men in the front trenches were looking into heavy fog which grew thicker as darkness fell. There was no sign of any enemy movement, scarcely even a casual shell or the sputter of outpost fire.

About two a.m. on the morning of the 21st word was passed along our lines to expect an assault. The "forward zone" was always held fully manned, but at 4.30 the order went out to man the "battle zone." Still the same uncanny silence continued, and the same clinging fog, under cover of which the Germans were methodically pushing up troops into line, till by dawn on the fifty odd miles of ground between Croisilles and the Oise they had thirty-seven divisions within three thousand yards of our outposts. Then, precisely at a quarter to five, the whole weight of their many thousand guns was released on the British forward and battle zones, headquarters, communications, and artillery posts, the back areas especially being drenched with gas, which hung like a pall in the moist and heavy air. Under the cover of the mist the vanguards of the enemy were everywhere cutting the wire and filtering through the British outposts. Germany had flung the dice for victory.

1918
March 19–21

II

1918
March 21

It was a perfect occasion for the new German tactics. In the thick weather the enemy was beyond the place where the cross-fire of machine guns might have checked him long before the redoubts were aware of his coming, and the men in the outpost line, beaten to the ground by the bombardment and struggling under clouds of gas, were soon in desperate case. Presently the Germans were in our forward zone, and there the line of resistance did all that man could do; garrisons and redoubts till far on in the day held out gallantly, and messages continued to be received from many up to a late hour, till that silence came which meant destruction. The troops in the battle zone could only wait with anxious hearts through those mad hours of fog till the shock of the assault should reach them.

Before eleven a.m. tidings came that the enemy was through our forward zone on the extreme right opposite La Fère, where it had been vainly hoped that the Oise marshes gave security. At noon came a graver message. The Germans were in Ronssoy—inside the battle zone, and threatening to break through down the valley of the Omignon. Here we are concerned principally with Gough's right centre, where the Thirtieth Division lay around Roupy and Savy. There the forward zone did not fall till the evening, and heavy toll was taken of the advancing enemy. Farther north, in the Third Army area, the pressure was less deadly. The Fifty-ninth Division was holding the front St. Leger–Bullecourt, with one brigade in line and two in support. By midday the Germans had broken through the position, and the 6th/7th Royal Scots Fusiliers, with their colonel wounded, were compelled to make a new line out of some partly-prepared trenches at Vraucourt. On Byng's left the Third Division on the left bank of the Sensée had lost no ground, and the 1st Royal Scots Fusiliers, in support at Heninel, had suffered nothing but heavy shelling. It had been an

THE FIRST SHOCK

amazing day. Against nineteen British divisions in line the enemy had hurled thirty-seven divisions in a first wave, and, before the dark came, not less than sixty-four German divisions had taken part in the battle —a number considerably exceeding the total strength of the British army in France. The forward zone had gone, except some parts in the area of the Ninth Division, but the battle zone still held, though at Essigny and Ronssoy and Noreuil it had worn perilously thin. It behoved us to rearrange our front, so Byng retired from the Flesquières salient, and Gough withdrew his right corps behind the Crozat Canal.

The fog thickened in the night, and at the dawn of the 22nd it was as dense as on the previous morning. At the first light the German masses began to press heavily on the whole battle-ground. That day Byng, for the most part, held his ground, though the Third Division was compelled to retire its right flank to a front facing south-east. In the Fifty-ninth Division, the 6th/7th Royal Scots Fusiliers in the evening fell back from Vraucourt to the third position, losing in the day's fighting Captain W. R. Hutchison and Second Lieutenants W. T. Gooding and A. Sherriff. But the critical struggle was on the front of the Fifth Army. By midday the enemy had forced the gate of the Omignon, and the whole of Gough's centre was out of the battle zone. The Thirtieth Division, on a front of over ten thousand yards, for some hours resisted the assault between the Cologne and the Omignon. The 2nd Royal Scots Fusiliers made repeated counter-attacks under Second Lieutenant J. Blair and Second Lieutenant J. Murray, during which Captain W. C. Mair was killed by a sniper. But in the evening the division found its flank turned, because of the gap which had opened up south of the Omignon. Through this breach the Germans poured, and broke our third zone around Vaux and Beauvois. There was no course left to Gough but to order a retreat to a bridgehead position east of the Somme. As twilight fell the 2nd Royal Scots Fusiliers were making their way in small

1918
March 21-22

1918
March 23–24

parties and in good order through Ham and Verlaines. Lieutenant E. H. Smith with his platoon did not receive the withdrawal order, and remained in position till dark, when, steering a compass course, he brought his men to Ham through the enemy outposts.

Throughout the thick night the divisions of the Fifth Army, now in the last stage of fatigue, retreated under constant enemy pressure. Gough had decided that he must fall back behind the Somme, and all Saturday, the 23rd, the XVIII. Corps swung its right flank towards that river, fighting delaying actions. It was open warfare with a vengeance, and often it seemed that the whole British line had lost cohesion, and had been jolted into a score of isolated detachments. That morning there was trouble at Ham, which the Germans had entered, and where, owing to the incomplete destruction of a bridge, they succeeded in crossing the Somme, though they were temporarily held on the farther bank. North of Ham by nightfall the enemy had passed the river. Meanwhile, farther north, the situation had become very grave. The VII. Corps, late in the afternoon, was forced west of Péronne to the old Somme front held by us before the German retirement in March 1917. Its extreme weakness made its line crack into fissures, which the Germans searched for and widened, so that at nightfall it was still slowly giving ground. It was the beginning of that attempt to divide the Third and Fifth Armies which presently became the immediate strategic objective of the enemy.

Here we are not concerned with the whole of the great drama which led to the appointment of Foch as Generalissimo, and which ended on 4th April with the failure of the German plan. The retreat of the Thirtieth Division, under heavy pressure, was more orderly than that of most of its fellows. On a wide front it had to fight incessant rear-guard actions, which on the whole succeeded in their purpose. After the 23rd it passed under the general command of Fayolle. On the 24th the 2nd Royal Scots Fusiliers and the 2nd Bedfords

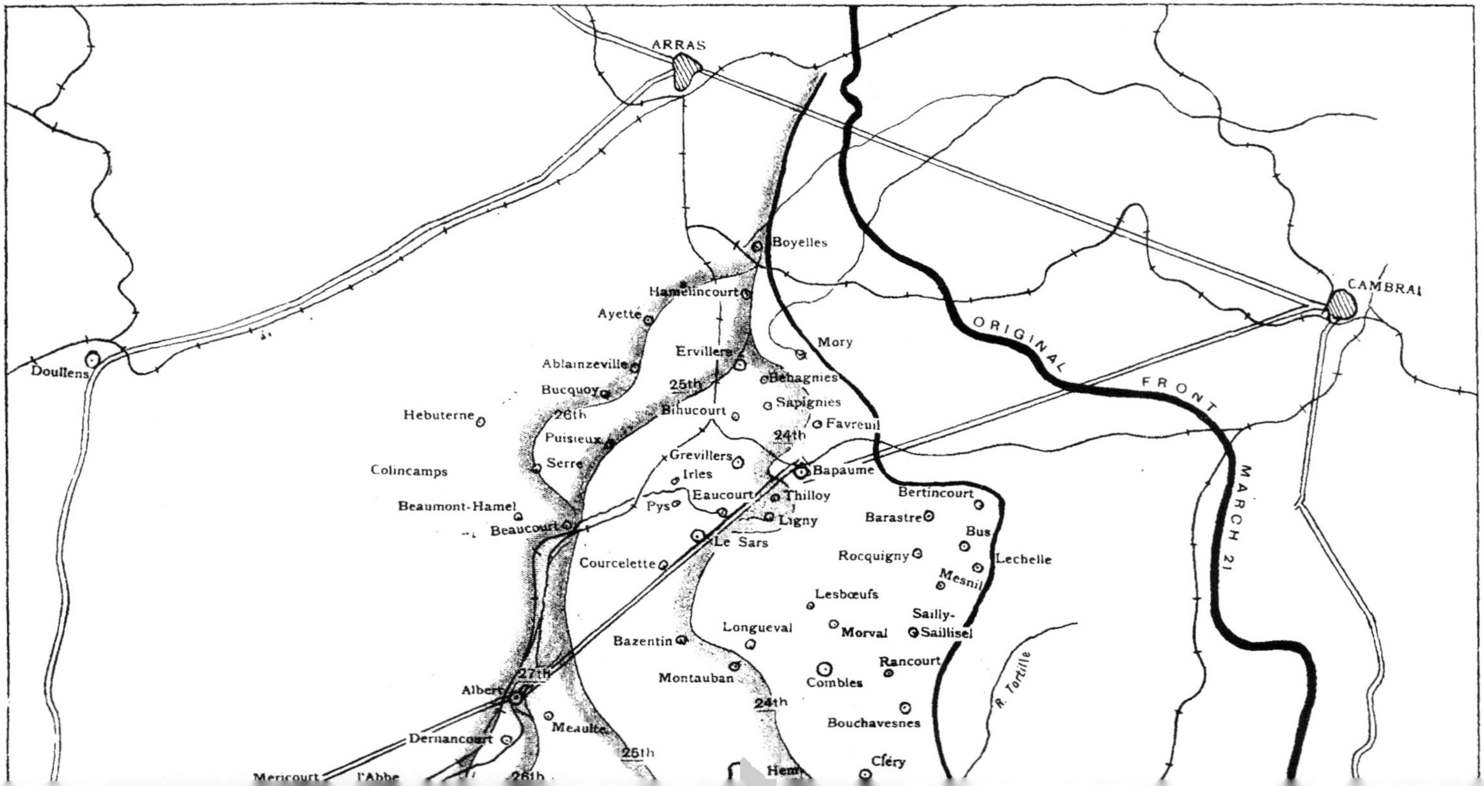
ARRAS
CAMBRAI
ORIGINAL FRONT MARCH 21
Doullens
Boyelles
Hamelincourt
Ayette
Mory
Ervillers
Ablainzeville
Behagnies
Bucquoy
25th
Sapignies
Hebuterne
26th
Bihucourt
Favreuil
Puisieux
24th
Grevillers
Colincamps
Serre
Irles
Bapaume
Eaucourt
Thilloy
Bertincourt
Beaumont-Hamel
Pys
Ligny
Barastre
Beaucourt
Le Sars
Bus
Courcelette
Rocquigny
Lechelle
Mesnil
Lesbœufs
Sailly-
Saillisel
Longueval
Morval
Bazentin
R. Tortille
Rancourt
Montauban
Combles
27th
Albert
24th
Bouchavesnes
Meaulte
Dernancourt
25th
Cléry
Mericourt
l'Abbe
26th
Hem

THE RETREAT FROM THE SOMME

fought a delaying action, and on the 25th the same battalions made a stout resistance on the line of the Libermont Canal, where Captain R. H. Thomas was unfortunately killed by one of our own shells. The chief peril was now in the British centre, for the VII. Corps was six miles farther back than the corps on its right, and had been put under Byng's command, while the Third Army was retreating on the Ancre line. On the XVIII. Corps front the French were pushing up supports, but all day on the 25th and 26th the Thirtieth Division was moving back from the Libermont Canal to the neighbourhood of Le Quesnoy. On the night of the 26th it was at Bouchoir and Arvillers, where next day the Royal Scots Fusiliers held up a strong enemy attack west of the Arvillers–La Folie road. On the 28th the French had not yet arrived, and the division stood firm till the afternoon, though its centre was pierced and its right flank turned. The Royal Scots Fusiliers were not relieved till dusk, when they had to withdraw through an encircling enemy. That day saw the end of the stand of the Fifth Army. What was left of it was now back in the old Amiens defences on the Avre and the Luce, and the divisions which had suffered most were relieved. On the night of the 28th the Scots Fusiliers moved back to billets in Rouvrel, and proceeded to the Abbeville area to refit. On 7th April they were ordered to join the Fortieth Division.

On 24th March the 6th/7th Royal Scots Fusiliers in the Fifty-ninth Division were relieved from the line. Under severe shell fire and constant enemy attacks they had stuck to an improvised position.[1] The 1st Royal Scots Fusiliers in the Third Division were engaged that day on the Henin–Neuville Vitasse road in repelling the German attack in the Cojeul valley. The enemy did not win a yard, and incurred heavy losses from our machine-gun fire. For the next few days

---

[1] Major-General Romer, at a special parade of the remnants of the Fifty-ninth Division, declared that "undoubtedly the stubborn defence put up on those two critical days by the 6th/7th Royal Scots Fusiliers relieved a very difficult situation."

1918
March 25–
April 9

the Third Division had to face the fringe of the attack upon Byng's centre, and had to fall back to conform with the big withdrawal farther south. On the 25th the Scots Fusiliers were ordered to side-step westwards, so that their right now rested on the Arras–Bapaume road. Between seven and eight on the morning of the 28th Otto von Below delivered the assault originally staged for the 23rd, and hurled his weight on Arras. The attack was a signal failure, for though much of our forward zone was carried, the battle zone remained untouched, and before evening we were able by counter-attacks to push out a new outpost line in front of it. The 1st Royal Scots Fusiliers had a difficult day, for the supply of grenades gave out early; their first line was carried, and the survivors made their way to the Welsh Guards on their right. The casualties of the battalion were 364, and among the officers Captain C. M. Hadden was killed.

By 4th April the first bout was ended. The enemy had won a qualified success. The Allied front was for the moment re-established, but it was deplorably weakened; the gate of Amiens was shut, but the next blow might open it; the German Command had not realized their full conception, but they had still the power to win if they had the skill. But one thing was already clear—the splendour of the British performance. The fight had begun with an attack by sixty-four German divisions on thirty-two British; by the end of March seventy-three German divisions had engaged thirty-seven British; by 9th April the total British force in action had grown to forty-six divisions of infantry and three of cavalry, and against these more than eighty German divisions had been launched. The disparity was really far greater, for, owing to the German power of local concentration, in many parts of the field the odds had been three or four to one. Again and again a complete disaster was miraculously averted. Scratch forces, composed largely of non-combatants, held up storm-troops; cavalry did work that no cavalry had ever done before in the history of war; gunners broke every law of the text-books. The retreat was in flat defiance of all precedent and rule, and it succeeded only because of the stubborn valour of the British soldier.

*1918
April 8*

Brought to a standstill on the Somme, the enemy cast about for a diversion, for he could not permit the battle to decline into a stalemate and forfeit the initiative. His main purpose was the same, but he sought to achieve it by another method. He would attack the British elsewhere on some part of the front where they were notoriously weak, and compel Foch to use up his reserves in its defence. Then, when the Allied "mass of manœuvre" had shrunk, he would strike again at the weakened door of Amiens. According to the enemy plan the operation was meant to be a strictly subsidiary one, designed to prepare the way for his main attack farther south. He proposed to allot only nine divisions for the initial stroke, and to choose a battle-ground where even a moderate force might obtain surprising results.

This battle-ground was the area on both sides of the river Lys, between the La Bassée Canal and the Wytschaete ridge. The German Staff were aware that it had already been thinned to supply ten divisions for the contest in the south, and that at the moment it was weakly held, mainly by troops exhausted in the Somme battle. Haig, as we know from his dispatches, had drawn especially upon this sector, since a retreat there would not imperil the whole front so gravely as would the loss of ground between La Bassée and Arras. Nevertheless, it was a very real danger-point. The enemy had the great city of Lille to screen his assembly. Certain key-points of communication, like Béthune and Hazebrouck, lay at no great distance behind the British front. The British communications were poor, and the German all but perfect. Any advance threatened the Channel ports, and might be expected to cause acute uneasiness at British Headquarters. Reinforcements would be demanded from Foch, and the place was far enough from the Amiens battle-ground to put

1918
April 8

a heavy strain upon the Allied power of reinforcement. The enemy's aim was by a short, sharp thrust to confuse the Allied plans and absorb their reserves. If he could break through at once between La Bassée and Armentières and capture Béthune, he could swing north-westward and take Hazebrouck and the hills beyond Bailleul, and so compel a general retirement west of Dunkirk and the floods of the river Aa. But to succeed he must have a broad front. He must take Béthune at once and the Messines ridge soon after, for, if the British pillars of the gate at Givenchy and Messines should stand, his advance would be squeezed into narrows where even a weak and tired force might hold it.

On 8th April the British dispositions in the Lys area were, from left to right, the IX. and the XV. Corps, with seven divisions in line—the Ninth, the Nineteenth, the Twenty-fifth, the Thirty-fourth, the Fortieth, the Second Portuguese, and the Fifty-fifth. After a prolonged bombardment with gas shells the Germans, under von Quast, attacked at seven a.m. on the 9th, and at the first thrust broke the Portuguese. The right flank of the Fortieth Division was consequently exposed, and the enemy streamed through the gap. By 10.15 a.m. the Germans were more than a mile in the rear of the right battalion of the Fortieth Division, and that division was gradually forced back to a line facing south from Bois Grenier to the Lys at Fleurbaix. The Fifty-fifth Division, on the right of the Portuguese, had also its flank turned, and was compelled to form a defensive flank facing north between Festubert and Le Touret. The enemy had thus created a new salient, on the north side of which the Fortieth Division had a feverish day. The 2nd Royal Scots Fusiliers had been joined with the 10th/11th H.L.I. and the 14th H.L.I. to form the 120th (Scottish) Brigade, and in the action were on the brigade left. By noon the Germans had reached the Lys below Estaires, thus separating the Fortieth Division from the Fiftieth Division, which had been rushed up to fill the gap. The right of the

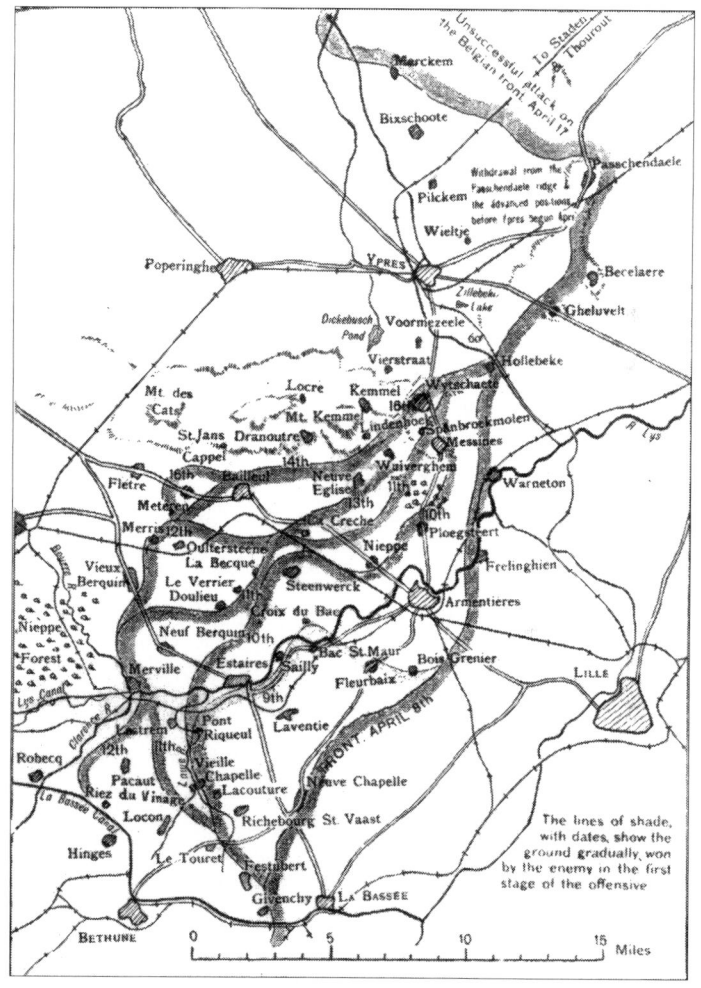

THE BATTLE OF THE LYS

Fortieth was therefore compelled to withdraw across the Lys at Bac St. Maur. The 120th Brigade, after crossing, held the bridge against repeated enemy attacks, Sergeant Baxter of the Scots Fusiliers working a Lewis gun long after the rest of his team had become casualties. Nevertheless the Germans won the crossing in the dusk, and we were compelled to a further retirement. It had been a mad and tangled day, but in spite of his success the enemy had failed at the vital point, for the Fifty-fifth Division still stood like a rock at Béthune and Givenchy.

1918
April 8–12

Next day the Germans forced the Fiftieth Division from Estaires, and, east of the town, so enlarged their bridgehead that they were able to press the left of the Fortieth Division beyond Steenwerck—an advance of nearly four miles. They were broadening their salient by striking northward. That day, too, a second German army, von Armin's, entered the battle, attacking north of the Lys between Frelinghien and Hill 60. By noon it had carried Ploegsteert village and most of Messines, though it was checked by the Ninth Division on the Wytschaete ridge. That evening we were forced to evacuate Armentières.

The 11th saw a fierce pressure by von Quast and von Armin on the whole front. The Fifty-fifth Division still stood firm at Givenchy, but the line of the Lawe stream was lost, the Thirtieth Division was driven west of Merville, and the Fortieth well north of Steenwerck. Every battalion of the last division was engaged, and when troops of the Twenty-ninth Division came up in support, only three officers and twenty men of the Scots Fusiliers could be collected on the new line. It was a repetition of the retreat from St. Quentin three weeks before, for units had become hopelessly entangled. That evening the Scots Fusiliers—what was left of them —were on the line Le Verrier–Doulieu on the left of the 120th Brigade, and were being rejoined by stragglers. Next day, the 12th, the remnant of the Fortieth Division was relieved by the Thirty-first, and withdrew to Strazeele. The casualties had been chiefly wounded and missing, and only one officer, Second Lieutenant John Boyd, fell. Of the performance of the Scots Fusiliers the commander of the Fortieth Division may speak. Major-General John Ponsonby wrote to Lieutenant-Colonel Utterson-Kelso : " Although your battalion has been only a short time under my command I cannot allow them to leave my division without expressing my sincere admiration for the very gallant manner in which, in spite of being greatly outnumbered, they withstood the German attack in the last battle. The 2nd Royal Scots Fusiliers have maintained the highest traditions of their regiment, and from all sides their courage and determination under trying circumstances were repeatedly brought to my notice. I can only express my deep regret at losing your battalion, and I hope that you will convey to the officers, non-commissioned officers, and men my sincere congratulations on their gallant behaviour."

As the 2nd Royal Scots Fusiliers left the battle the 1st Battalion entered it. Among the British reinforcements which were arriving on the 11th was the Third Division, which took up position on the right of the Fifty-first Division, just north of the La Bassée Canal. Early on the 12th the left centre of the Fifty-first had been broken near Pacaut due south of Merville, but the advent of the Third and Sixty-first Divisions steadied the front between Locon and the Clarence River. The Scots Fusiliers had a difficult task in preventing the enemy working round their flanks, orders were delayed or received in imperfect form, and in the evening a slight retirement was necessary. On the 13th there was only shelling, and on the 14th the battalion was relieved, after suffering 323 casualties. Four officers were killed or died of wounds—Second Lieutenants W. R. B. Wolstencroft, J. F. Logan, Hugh Lambroughton, and W. A. How.

The fight of the 12th had let the enemy through south-west of Bailleul, and Merris and Outtersteene fell. On the 13th this avenue towards Hazebrouck was closed by the stalwart defence of the Twenty-ninth and Thirty-first Divisions and the 4th Guards Brigade, supported later in the day by the First Australian Division. Though the British front was now partially stabilized, the situation was still full of anxiety. The enemy had driven a great wedge into our line, which threatened two vital centres of communication—Béthune in the south and Hazebrouck in the northwest—and he was on the edge, too, of the line of uplands from Mont des Cats to Kemmel, which commanded all the northern plain towards the Channel. On the 11th Haig had issued his famous order of the day : " With our backs to the wall, and believing in the justice of our cause, each one of us must fight to an end." Bailleul fell on the 14th, and on the 16th the defence of the Wytschaete ridge at last crumbled. On the 17th came von Armin's great effort in the Ypres Salient, which failed; and on the 18th von Quast delivered a fierce attack between Merville and Givenchy, which was repulsed with heavy slaughter. That day saw the end of the first and principal phase of the battle, and for nearly a week there was no further assault. No battalion of our regiment had been in action since the 14th, though the 1st Royal Scots Fusiliers in line northeast of Le Hamel suffered, between the 18th and the 22nd, considerable losses from shell fire.

Meantime the 6th/7th Battalion, the Pioneers of the Fifty-ninth Division, had arrived at Reninghelst on 15th April, when two companies were sent to the 176th Brigade and two to the 177th Brigade to assist in occupying the " Army Line " behind Bailleul. Next day that battalion concentrated at Locre, and on the 17th one hundred men, under Second Lieutenant J. V. Macdonald, were placed at the disposal of the 100th Brigade for the counter-attack. In this action Lieutenant Macdonald fell, and on the 19th the Fifty-ninth Division was relieved by the French. During their period of work as Pioneer Battalion the 6th/7th Royal Scots Fusiliers appear to have had a variety of arduous duties. They were " nobody's child," and from time to time

1918
April 13–22

1918
April 25

were attached to different formations, besides acting directly under the orders of divisional headquarters. In the view of men who had served since Loos the two last actions, at Vraucourt and at Locre, were among the severest they had ever faced. On 5th May, at St. Omer, they were reduced to a battalion training cadre, 13 officers and 678 other ranks being sent to "M" Scottish Base Depot at Calais. During May they were at various points on the front, and in June returned to Britain with the Sixteenth Division, to be absorbed into the 17th Scottish Rifles. Thus passed out of the history of the war a unit which, at Loos, on the Somme, at Arras, and at Third Ypres, had shown a prowess not excelled by any battalion of our regiment.

In the last phase of the battle of the Lys the 2nd Royal Scots Fusiliers were alone engaged. They had by this time left the Fortieth Division, and had joined the South African Brigade of the Ninth Division—a brigade which also comprised the 9th Scottish Rifles and that South African Composite Battalion which was all that remained of the famous original South African Brigade, which at Delville Wood, at Marrières Wood, and on the Wytschaete ridge had thrice sacrificed itself, and each time to the salvation of the British front. If the enemy could seize Kemmel Hill, he would broaden his comfortless salient and win direct observation over the northern plain. In front of Kemmel was the junction of the British and the French lines, which he regarded as the weakest spot on our front. Accordingly, on 25th April, he opened his last and greatest attack on Kemmel.

The attack came at five a.m., delivered by nine German divisions, five of which were fresh. The enemy purpose was to capture Kemmel by a direct assault on the French, and by a simultaneous attack to turn the flank of the British right south of Wytschaete. At first he seemed likely to succeed. He took Kemmel hill and village, and by midday forced the right of the Ninth Division back to Vierstraat. That evening the

British front ran from Hill 60 in the north by Voormezeele and Ridge Wood to the hamlet of La Clytte on the Poperinghe–Kemmel road, where it linked up with the French. Next day General Tanner, commanding the South African Brigade, took over the section held by the 20th Brigade. He had the 9th Scottish Rifles in line, and the 2nd Royal Scots Fusiliers in support, and late in the afternoon the first-named were relieved by the Fusiliers, who now held the front from Vierstraat to the south end of Ridge Wood. There for two days the battalion suffered heavy shelling and many losses.

1918
April 25-29

The final attack came on the 29th at five a.m. in a dense mist—five German divisions against the British Twenty-fifth, Forty-ninth (with which for the moment were the 2nd Royal Scots Fusiliers), and Twenty-sixth Divisions. It never became an infantry action, for our barrage and machine-gun fire took terrible toll. Says the historian of the Ninth Division : " All three battalions of the brigade, though continually harassed by artillery fire, inflicted enormous casualties on the enemy. . . . Rarely has heavier fire heralded an attack. On that day the Royal Scots Fusiliers signally distinguished themselves. They were employed in front of and behind the Cheapside line, and suffered horribly from the bombardment ; but of their eight Lewis guns which were out in front of their position, only one was knocked out, so that when the enemy's infantry advanced they were immediately checked, and their own barrage came down on the top of them. First a few rose up and bolted, and then the remainder fled in panic, whereupon the Royal Scots Fusiliers fairly took toll of them with their rifles and Lewis guns. The enemy's attack was utterly defeated. That date marks the failure of the enemy's design in Flanders." [1] In the evening the Scots Fusiliers, who had had considerable losses from the German bombardment—6 officers and 140 men were casualties, including Second Lieutenant W. Riddell killed—were relieved by the South African Composite

[1] Ewing's *The Ninth Division*, Chapter XIII.

Battalion, and six days later the Ninth Division moved out of the line. It was the close of the battle of the Lys—for the enemy a tactical success, but a strategic failure. He had achieved no one of his principal aims, and in the struggle he had weakened his chance of a future offensive by squandering some of his best reserves. By the end of April he had employed in that one northern area thirty-five fresh divisions and nine which had been already in action. These troops were the cream of his army and could not be replaced.

III

The summer months of 1918 were, for the northern part of the British line, a time of comparative quiet. The main tides of war had flowed southward, and before May was out came the German thrust on the Aisne, which drove the French back upon the Marne, and in seventy-two hours advanced the enemy front by more than thirty miles. In the southern area the enemy tactics of April were repeated, and presently he pressed forward on his right, and carried the Lassigny Hills. Then, after a delay of six weeks, came the last attack on the Marne, which was to open the way to Paris, and with it Ludendorff's final and irretrievable failure. But in the early summer that consummation could not have been foreseen, and the months of May, June, and July were an anxious season for the Allied command. When Foch became Generalissimo his first problem was to create reserves, and his second to use just enough of these to hold the enemy. While the American armies were growing in numbers and efficiency, he had to be ready, with still scanty resources, to face at any moment a new assault on any one of the four sections of his long line. But his defence was not stagnant—it was as vigilant and aggressive as any attack; and there were two facts in the situation which might well have seemed to him of happy augury. He had devised an answer to the new German tactics, and formed his own scheme against the day of *revanche*. Again, the German Command were clearly fumbling. The Lys had seen the decadence of their original plan, and the later adventures were blind and irrelevant hammer-blows. Germany, with waning strength, was being forced to stake all on a last throw; if that failed, she might soon be helpless before the waxing might of the Allies.

In April three battalions of our regiment had been engaged on the Western front. In May the 6th/7th Royal Scots Fusiliers disappeared, but four others arrived in the field, since it had become necessary to bring to the main campaign every infantry unit that could be spared from home defence or from the Eastern battle-grounds. The 11th Royal Scots Fusiliers, under Lieutenant-Colonel R. P. Maclachlan, left Dover on 5th May with a strength of 29 officers and 1,071 men. This was a garrison battalion, and at first it would appear that the *personnel* was below the " A " medical class. It became part of the 178th Brigade in the Fifty-ninth Division—the division in which the 6th/7th Battalion had, till recently, been Pioneers. It was at first employed behind the line, and in June had the misfortune to suffer from a severe epidemic of fever. In July it took its part in regular trench duties in the Givenchy sector. The 12th Royal Scots Fusiliers, in the 229th Brigade of the Seventy-fourth Division, after much strenuous work in Palestine in the first months of 1918, embarked, under Lieutenant-Colonel W. T. R. Houldsworth, at Alexandria on 30th April, and on arrival in France became part of the 94th Brigade in the Thirty-first Division. In June and July they were in the Bailleul area, operating under the orders of the 92nd Brigade, and for the most part engaged in patrol duties. The Fifty-second Division arrived at Marseilles from Palestine on 17th April, and in May and June it was in the Vimy area. There the 155th Brigade was reconstituted on a three-battalion basis, and now included the 4th Royal Scots Fusiliers (Lieutenant-Colonel B. Cruddas), the 5th Royal Scots Fusiliers (Lieutenant-Colonel D. M. Murray Lyon), and the 4th K.O.S.B. At the end of July it was in the line in the Oppy section in front of Arras.

1918
June 24–
July 19

The 1st Royal Scots Fusiliers remained with the Third Division till August in the neighbourhood of Hinges and Locon, and earned high praise for their trench discipline from the brigade and division commanders. On 22nd July Lieutenant-Colonel E. I. D. Gordon gave up the battalion command, and was succeeded by Major G. Bisset. Colonel Gordon, first with the 6th/7th Battalion and then with the 1st, had had nearly three years of unremitting field duty, which included the battles of the Somme, Arras, Third Ypres, the retreat from St. Quentin, and the Lys. The 2nd Royal Scots Fusiliers were with the Ninth Division in the vicinity of Kemmel. In July, therefore, six battalions of our regiment were in the British armies north of the Scarpe. All these units were now approximating to a common type, and were losing their old regular, new army, Territorial, or Yeomanry character. All, save the 11th, had had a varied experience of battle, and were veterans of the new warfare. The units from the East were already familiar with open actions, and were thus well prepared for the final stage of the campaign which the autumn was to bring.

During the summer months only the 2nd Royal Scots Fusiliers were seriously engaged. Up till the end of May a repetition of the German assault on Kemmel was daily expected. The position of our front in that section was far from comfortable, for it was overlooked by the Germans in Meteren, and in June it was resolved to make an effort to improve it. On the 24th we made an advance of some four hundred yards, the attack being delivered by the 1st Australian Brigade and the South Africans, with the co-operation of one company of the Scots Fusiliers. In July it was decided to attempt the capture of Meteren, the date ultimately fixed being 19th July. The operations had been most carefully rehearsed by the two brigades selected for the task—the South African and the 26th. The first was on the right, and its attacking units were the South African Composite Battalion and the 2nd Royal Scots Fusiliers. At 7.55 a.m. on the 19th the troops of assault left their trenches in artillery formation, and under cover of a smoke and high-explosive barrage rapidly overran the enemy's front-line posts and prevented the use of his machine guns. The main attack, admirably led by the section commanders, bore down all resistance, and both battalions reached their objectives by the appointed time. On the extreme left a pocket of Germans in a trench behind a wired hedge gave some trouble, but they were ousted by the Scots Fusiliers. Everything went well on the right, and by the afternoon the position in Meteren and on the ridge had been established, and one of the most awkward corners of the British front made secure. The Germans had been completely taken by surprise, and no counter-attack developed; they had expected only a gas discharge, and were wholly unprepared to meet the rush of our infantry. The Scots Fusiliers were relieved on the 22nd. At the close of August the South African Composite Battalion left the Ninth Division, and the 2nd Royal Scots Fusiliers became part of the 28th Brigade.

IV

On the day before the capture of Meteren, Foch, on the Marne, had delivered the great counter-stroke which decided the issue of the campaign. When on that July morning the troops of Mangin breasted the Montagne de Paris, they had, without knowing it, won the Second Battle of the Marne, and with it the war. Germany's offensive had been given the *coup de grâce*, the initiative had been wrested from her, and she was forced back in confusion on her defences. By the end of July the accession of American troops had given the Allies a decisive superiority both in men and material over anything which the enemy could compass. But the final blow could not yet be struck. It was the business of Foch to keep the battle " nourished," and at the same time to economize his forces till the moment came for the grand climax. He had to wear down the enemy methodically by attrition on

1918
Aug. 8–21

limited fronts, ringing the changes over the whole battle-ground. The possession of ample reserves and of such a weapon as his light tanks enabled him to " mount " a new action rapidly in any sector. After each blow he must stay his hand as soon as serious resistance developed, and attack instantly in another place. The enemy would therefore be subjected to a constant series of surprises. Before his reserves could be brought up he would have lost heavily in ground and men ; his " mass of manœuvre " would be needed to fill up the gaps in his front, and by swift stages that " mass of manœuvre " would diminish. From 8th August to 26th September it was Foch's task to crumble the enemy front, destroy the last of his reserves, force him behind all his prepared defences, and make ready for the final battle which would give victory.

The tale of that great achievement can here only be sketched. The record of battalions moves for the most part in the mist ; their story is of tactical successes, which may play only a minute part in the major purpose. Rarely indeed do they appear, like the 2nd Worcesters at First Ypres, in the very centre of the stage, when the work of a small unit becomes the key to the strategical fortunes of an army. The initial step was Haig's advance on 8th August, east of Amiens, followed by Humbert on the 9th, and Mangin on the 18th. The first action—in Ludendorff's phrase, " the black day of the German army in the history of the war "— drove the enemy beyond reach of Amiens and the Paris railway, and freed the British communications in the same way as the French had already freed theirs on the Marne. The British were now in the old battle area of the Somme, a wilderness which gave unrivalled opportunities for defence. Haig decided to outflank it from the north, and on the 21st Byng struck with his Third Army.

It was a thick morning when Byng advanced at 4.55 a.m., the weather of 8th August and of 21st March ; all the great blows of the last stage of the campaign seem to have been struck in fog. The front was the nine miles between Moyenneville and Beaucourt, and the attack was delivered by the IV. and VI. Corps, in the latter of which were three battalions of our regiment—the 1st in the Third Division, and the 4th and the 5th in the Fifty-second Division. The 1st Royal Scots Fusiliers came first into action. The Third Division was one of the three whose duty it was to pass through the troops of attack and complete their work. By the evening we had advanced between two and three miles to where the enemy made a stand along the Albert–Arras railway. On that day the Scots Fusiliers lost Second Lieutenant R. L. McMutrie. Next day Rawlinson's Fourth Army had a like success between Albert and the Somme, the town of Albert and the village of Meaulte being recovered. On the 23rd both Byng and Rawlinson struck again on the whole thirty-three miles of line between Lihons in the south and Mercatel in the north. On Byng's extreme left was the Fifty-second Division, whose 156th Brigade attacked through the Fifty-ninth Division south of Mercatel, won all its objectives, and came close to the ruins of Henin-sur-Cojeul. Beyond lay Henin Hill, with the Hindenburg Line behind its crest, and on the 24th the 156th and 157th Brigades took Henin village, and would probably have taken the hill had they not run into their own barrage. The 155th Brigade, with the two Scots Fusilier battalions, was that day in reserve.

1918
Aug. 21–26

On the 26th came the great attack by Horne's First Army astride the Scarpe—the beginning of the last of the battles of Arras. Sir Arthur Currie, with the Canadian Corps and the Fifty-first Division, advanced on a five-mile front, taking Wancourt and the old storm centres of Monchy and Guémappe, and, next day, Rœux and Gavrelle. Byng's left, the Fifty-second and Fifty-sixth Divisions, co-operated, and to the 155th Brigade of the former was entrusted the capture of the Hindenburg Line on Henin Hill; it was then to await the Canadians, and fight its way down the Hindenburg Line to the south-east. The attack was delivered at

1918
Aug. 26-30

three a.m., with the 5th Royal Scots Fusiliers on the right and the 4th Royal Scots Fusiliers on the left, and by five a.m. they had broken into the Hindenburg Line and secured their objectives. For some hours the brigade had both its flanks exposed. Presently, however, the Canadians carried Monchy-le-Preux and the Wancourt ridge, and the two Scots Fusilier battalions were able to swing round to the south-east, and followed the 5th K.O.S.B. in the capture of Henin Hill. The situation was awkward, for on the right Croisilles still held out against the Fifty-sixth Division. Next day, the 27th, the 157th Brigade attacked the remainder of Henin Hill, and the 155th Brigade attempted to turn the enemy position at Croisilles. Croisilles fell at last in the evening. The day was one of the hardest in the experience of the Fifty-second Division. It was fighting on two fronts, facing east and facing south-west, and before it was relieved in the early hours of the 28th, had lost half its numbers. That day it withdrew to the Mercatel area for three days' rest to reorganize. The 5th Royal Scots Fusiliers had Captain G. C. Millar, Lieutenant T. W. Gudgeon, and Second Lieutenants T. R. M. Taylor and S. B. Hurst killed.

On 29th August the German Command saw the Bapaume ridge all but lost, and Horne, on the Scarpe, threatening to turn the whole Hindenburg front. They still hoped, however, to make an intermediate stand, so that they might withdraw in good order to the main Hindenburg system when the weather broke. In that great fortified position, seven miles deep, they believed they could stand fast for the winter. But on the 30th, Horne, moving along the Arras–Cambrai road, was in close touch with the famous Drocourt–Quéant Switch, which had been constructed to link up the Hindenburg Line proper with the old German front south of Lens, after the battle of Arras had destroyed the northern pivot. Next day the Australians carried the defences of Péronne, which meant that the intermediate position had been lost to the enemy. His only hope now was to hold Byng on the Canal du Nord, while north and

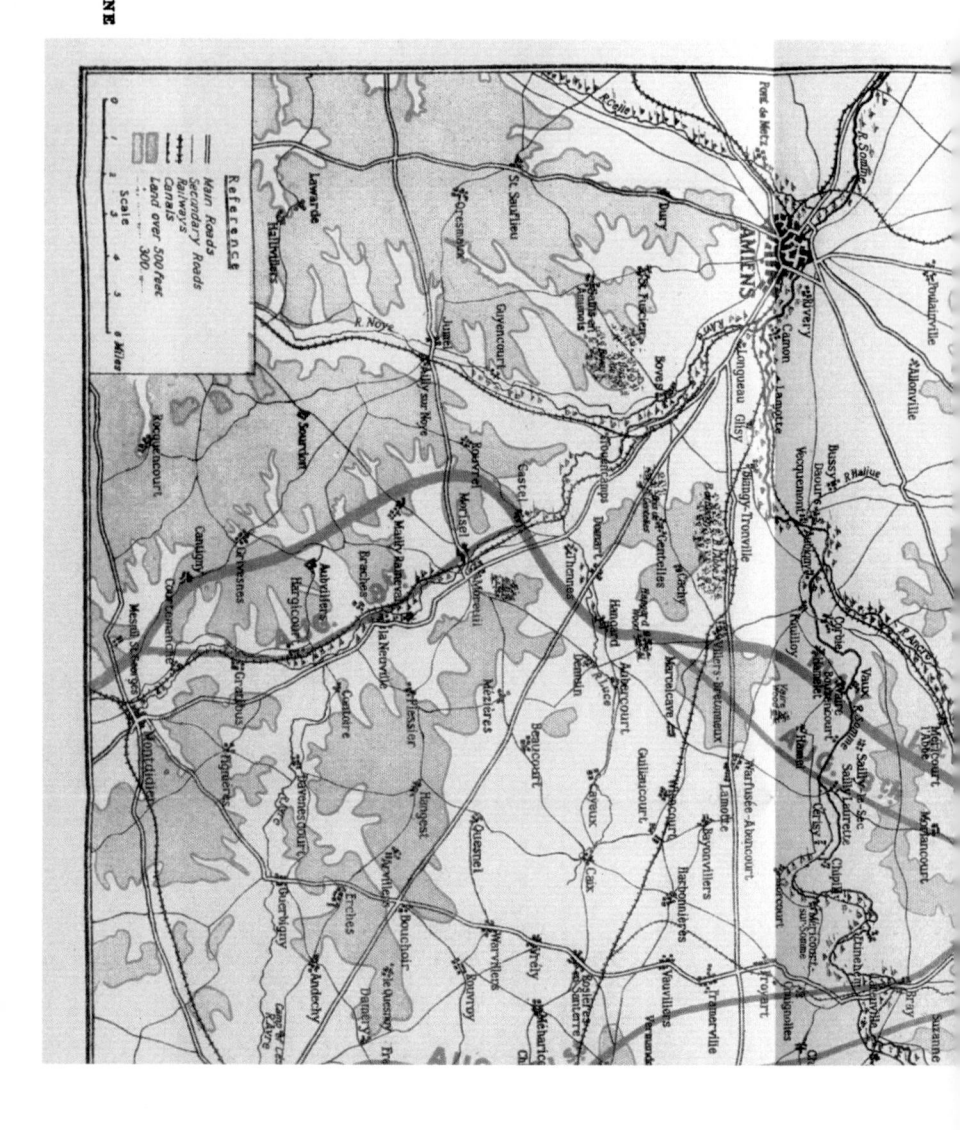

THE ADVANCE ON THE HINDENBURG LINE

Facing page 436

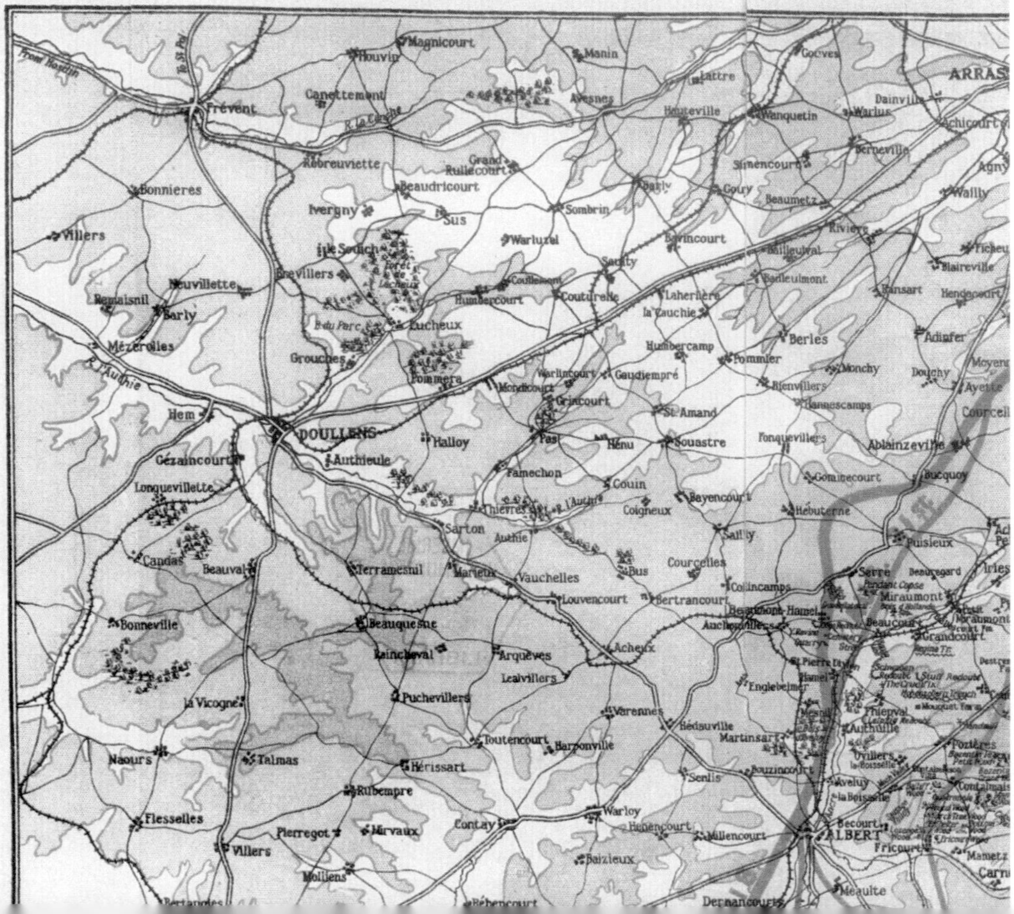
ARRAS
DOULLENS
ALBERT
Frévent
Magnicourt
Houvin
Manin
Lattre
Gouves
Canettemont
R. la Canche
Avesnes
Houteville
Wanquetin
Warlus
Dainville
Achicourt
Rebreuviette
Grand Rullecourt
Simencourt
Berneville
Agny
Bonnieres
Beaudricourt
Sombrin
Barly
Gouy
Beaumetz
Wailly
Ivergny
Sus
Villers
Warluzel
Bavincourt
Rivière
Ficheux
Blaireville
Neuvillette
Remaisnil
Barly
Saulty
Bailleulval
Bailleulmont
Couturelle
Humbercourt
Laherlière
la Cauchie
Ransart
Hendecourt
Lucheux
Mézerolles
R. l'Authie
Grouches
Pommera
Humbercamp
Pommier
Berles
Adinfer
Monchy
Douchy
Ayette
Gaudiempré
Grincourt
Mondicourt
Bienvillers
Hannescamps
Hem
St Amand
Courcelles
Halloy
Pas
Hénu
Souastre
Fonquevillers
Ablainzeville
Gézaincourt
Authieule
Famechon
Gommecourt
Bucquoy
Longuevillette
Couin
Bayencourt
Coigneux
Hébuterne
Thièvres
Sarton
Authie
Sailly
Puisieux
Candas
Beauval
Terramesnil
Marieux
Vauchelles
Bus
Courcelles
Colincamps
Serre
Beauregard
Miraumont
Louvencourt
Bertrancourt
Beaumont-Hamel
Beaucourt
Grandcourt
Auchonvillers
Bonneville
Beauquesne
Raincheval
Arquèves
Acheux
Léalvillers
Englebelmer
St Pierre Divion
Hamel
Mesnil
Thiepval
Authuille
la Vicogne
Puchevillers
Varennes
Hédauville
Martinsart
Ovillers la Boisselle
Pozières
Contalmaison
Naours
Talmas
Toutencourt
Harponville
Hérissart
Senlis
Bouzincourt
Aveluy
la Boisselle
Rubempré
Flesselles
Pierregot
Mirvaux
Contay
Warloy
Henencourt
Millencourt
Bécourt
Fricourt
Mametz
Villers
Molliens
Baizieux
Bertangles
Bécourt
Dernancourt
Méaulte

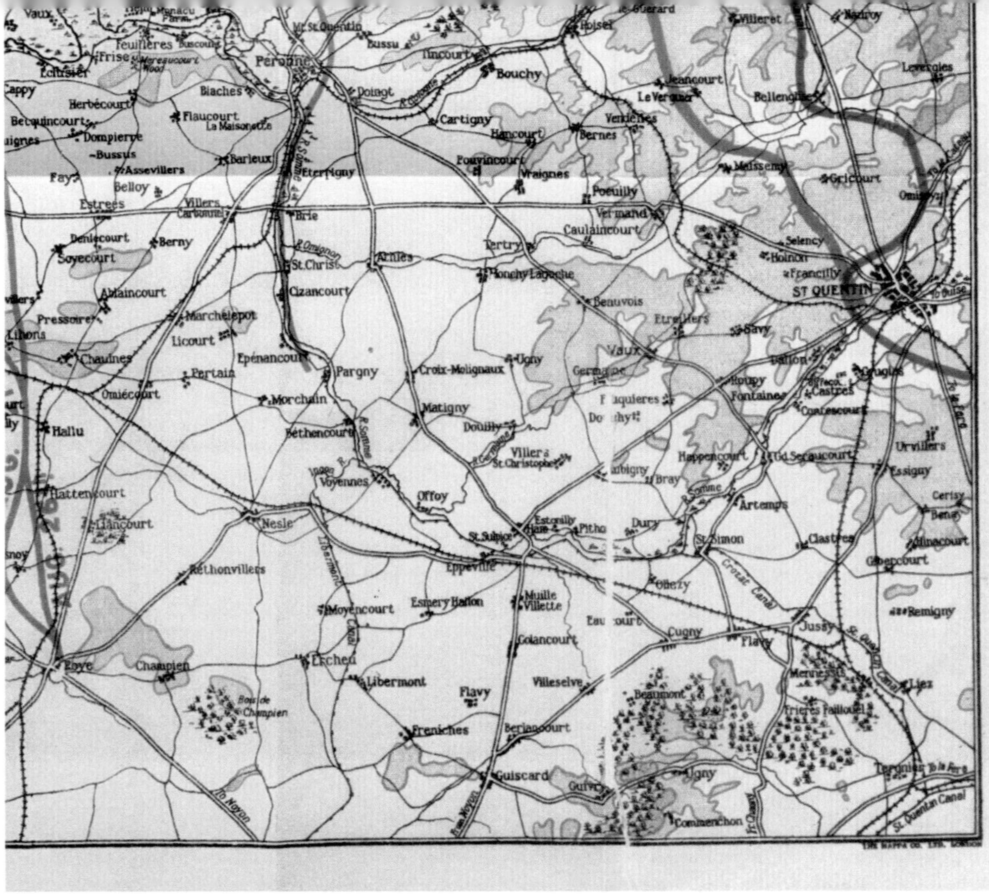

Vaux
Feuillères
Frise
Eclusier
Cappy
Herbécourt
Flaucourt
La Maisonette
Biaches
Péronne
Mt St Quentin
Bussu
Tincourt
Bouchy
Doingt
Cartigny
Hancourt
Bernes
Vendelles
Jeancourt
Le Verguier
Bellenglise
Villeret
Levergies
Dompierre
Bussus
Assevillers
Barleux
Eterpigny
Pouvincourt
Vraignes
Poeuilly
Vermand
Maissemy
Gricourt
Fay
Belloy
Estrées
Villers Carbonnel
Brie
Caulaincourt
Denlécourt
Berny
Soyecourt
St. Christ
Athies
Tertry
Monchy Lagache
Beauvois
Selency
Holnon
Francilly
ST QUENTIN
To Guise
Ablaincourt
Pressoire
Marchelepot
Licourt
Cizancourt
Etreillers
Savy
Lihons
Chaulnes
Pertain
Epénancourt
Pargny
Croix-Moligneaux
Ugny
Vaux
Germaine
Dallon
Roupy
Fontaine
Castres
Contescourt
Omiécourt
Morchain
Matigny
Douilly
Flaquières
Hallu
Béthencourt
R. Somme
Villers St. Christophe
Happencourt
Gd. Seraucourt
Urvillers
Essigny
Hattencourt
Voyennes
Offoy
Aubigny
Bray
Artemps
Cerisy
Nesle
Estouilly
Ham
Pithon
Dury
St. Simon
Clastres
Benay
Hinacourt
St. Sulpice
Eppeville
Ollezy
Gibercourt
Réthonvillers
Muille Villette
Moyencourt
Esmery Hallon
Crozat Canal
Remigny
Cugny
Flavy
Jussy
Golancourt
Roye
Champien
Ercheu
Libermont
Flavy
Villeselve
Beaumont
Mennessis
Liez
Bois de Champien
Frenicles
Berlancourt
Frières Faillouël
Tergnier
To la Fère
To Noyon
Guiscard
Guivry
Ugny
Commenchon
St. Quentin Canal

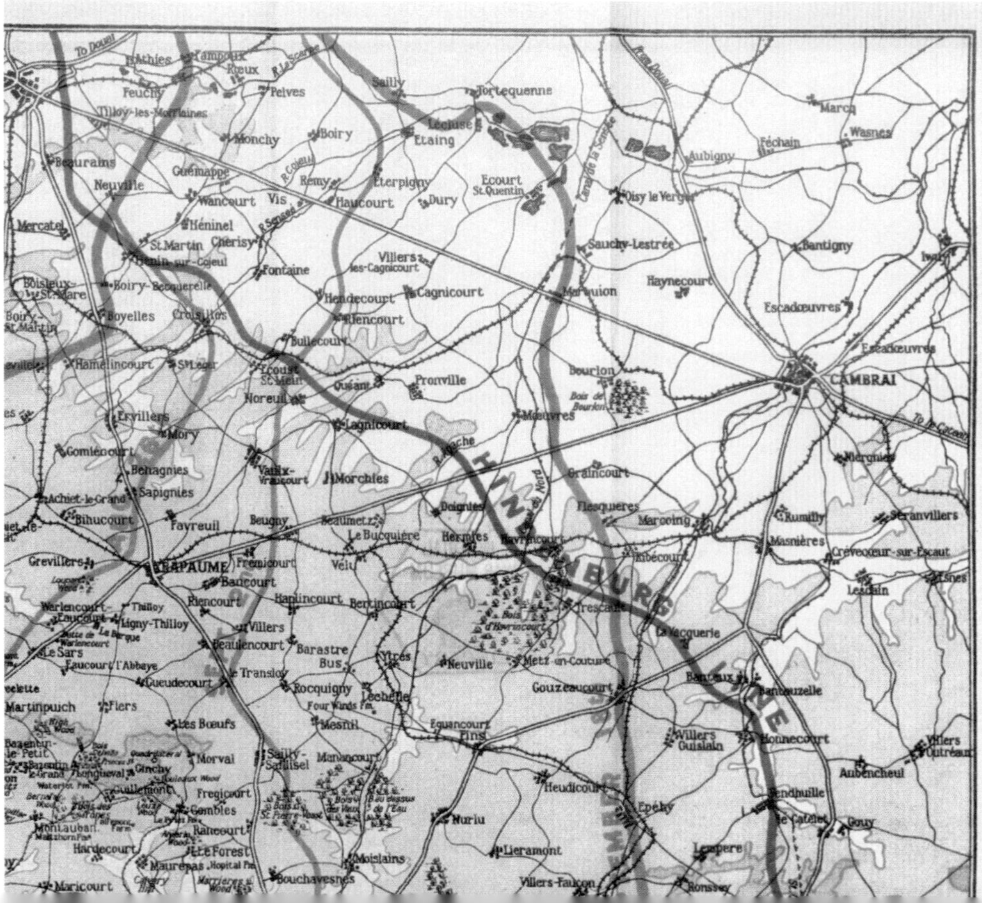

To Douai
Athies
Fampoux
Roeux
R. La Scarpe
Feuchy
Pelves
Tilloy-les-Mofflaines
Sailly
Tortequenne
Lécluse
Etaing
Monchy
Boiry
Beaurains
Guémappe
Remy
Eterpigny
Neuville
Wancourt
Vis
Haucourt
Dury
Ecourt St. Quentin
Canal de la Sensée
Aubigny
Féchain
Wasnes
Marcq
Oisy le Verger
Mercatel
Héninel
St. Martin
Cherisy
R. Sensée
R. Cojeul
Villers les-Cagnicourt
Sauchy-Lestrée
Bantigny
Fontaine
Boisleux-St. Marc
Boiry-Becquerelle
Hendecourt
Cagnicourt
Marquion
Haynecourt
Boyelles
Croisilles
Riencourt
Escadœuvres
Bullecourt
Hamelincourt
St. Léger
Ecoust St. Mein
Quéant
Pronville
Bourlon
Bois de Bourlon
CAMBRAI
Noreuil
Ervillers
Mory
Lagnicourt
Mœuvres
To le Cateau
Gomiecourt
Béhagnies
Vaulx-Vraucourt
Morchies
Graincourt
Achiet-le-Grand
Sapignies
Doignies
Flesquières
Marcoing
Bihucourt
Favreuil
Beugny
Beaumetz
Le Bucquière
Hermies
Havrincourt
Rumilly
Masnières
Séranvillers
Crèvecœur-sur-Escaut
Grévillers
BAPAUME
Frémicourt
Vélu
Ribécourt
Bancourt
Lesdain
Esnes
Warlencourt-Eaucourt
Thilloy
Ligny-Thilloy
Riencourt
Haplincourt
Bertincourt
Bois d'Havrincourt
Trescault
La Vacquerie
Villers
Beaulencourt
Barastre
Bus
Ytres
Neuville
Metz-en-Couture
Le Sars
Eaucourt l'Abbaye
Le Transloy
Gueudecourt
Rocquigny
Gouzeaucourt
Banteux
Bantouzelle
Martinpuich
Flers
Four Winds Fm.
Lechelle
Les Bœufs
Mesnil
Equancourt
Fins
Villers Guislain
Honnecourt
Villers Outréaux
Morval
Sailly-Saillisel
Manancourt
Aubencheul
Ginchy
Guillemont
Frégicourt
Combles
Heudicourt
Epéhy
Vendhuile
Le Catelet
Gouy
Montauban
Rancourt
Nurlu
Hardecourt
Le Forest
Maurepas
Lieramont
Lempire
Moislains
Maricourt
Bouchavesnes
Villers-Faucon
Ronssoy
HINDENBURG

THE DROCOURT-QUÉANT SWITCH

south his troops retired before Horne and Rawlinson behind the Drocourt-Quéant Switch and the main Hindenburg front.

1918
Sept. 2

But he had not reckoned with Haig. For on 2nd September Horne's right wing and Byng's left attacked the Drocourt-Quéant Switch. This was, as the Germans well knew, the key of their position, and on the nine miles between the Sensée and Quéant they had no less than eleven divisions. The attack was delivered by the right wing of the First Army, the Canadian Corps, and the British Fourth Division, and the left wing of the Third Army, the XVIII. Corps, comprising the Sixty-third, Fifty-seventh, and Fifty-second Divisions. The Third Division, on the left of the VI. Corps, was also to move on the right flank. The Fifty-second fought with the Third Division on its right, and thus three battalions of our regiment were engaged side by side in the same action.

The first attack of the Fifty-second Division was delivered by the 155th Brigade from Bullecourt, with the 156th Brigade in support. The 4th K.O.S.B. were on the right and the 4th Royal Scots Fusiliers on the left, and on 1st September Bullecourt was taken as a preliminary, so that the 155th Brigade lay in front of Quéant. The orders for 2nd September were that the Canadian Corps should break through the switch, the Fifty-seventh Division attack Quéant from the north, and the Third Division carry the villages of Noreuil and Lagnicourt; and that, when the flanking operation had sufficiently developed, the Fifty-second Division should attack the Hindenburg Line at Quéant—a line which skirted the south-eastern edge of the town and then ran due east for four miles to the Canal du Nord. The great advance began at five a.m., and by eight o'clock we were through the switch. The move of the Fifty-second Division began at 8.45 a.m., when the 156th Brigade attacked through the 155th. It was at once successful, and by the evening Quéant was in our hands. Only on the south was there a hitch, for the Third Division was in difficulties at Noreuil, with the result

1918
Sept. 3-4

that the Fifty-second Division at the close of the day found its left flank thrust well forward through the Hindenburg Line north of Quéant, while its right was drawn back and facing almost due south. Next day, when the Guards relieved the Third Division, the 155th Brigade, with the 4th Royal Scots Fusiliers leading, cleared the Hindenburg front line as far as the south of Quéant. A single company of the Fusiliers captured five 77 m. and four 10.5 cm. guns. By 4th September the division was close on the Canal du Nord.

The 1st Royal Scots Fusiliers (Lieutenant-Colonel G. Bissett) had no such fortune as their sister battalions farther north. They were on the left of the attack, which was delivered by the 8th Brigade. They were met at the jumping-off place by an intense fire, and in their advance they encountered strong opposition in a sunken road, so that by 5.30 a.m. three company commanders and eight platoon officers had become casualties. The loss of officers meant that the troops missed direction, and soon they were strung out in shell holes from which it was death to move. Lieutenant R. R. Macgregor, cut off from all instructions, with a small party showed remarkable gallantry and resource, but by the evening the battalion was still far from its objectives. That day it had 195 casualties; 6 officers—Lieutenant M. B. Berkeley, Second Lieutenants J. Charlton, N. W. Robertson, J. Atkinson, K. Torrance, and K. C. Crawford—and 34 men were killed; 9 officers and 137 other ranks were wounded; and 9 men were missing. On 4th September the battalion was back in the corps reserve area.

The German front now presented a curious spectacle. The flank of the Hindenburg zone had been turned, but the attack was temporarily checked by the line of water and marsh in the Sensée valley east of Etaing which protected Douai, and which was continued southward from Marquion by the Agache River and the Canal du Nord. For a week the Allied armies were occupied only in pressing the retreat. Their immediate task was to secure the kind of front from which they could launch that final blow for which Foch had been preparing since July. Between March and May 1917 the British had forced the Germans back to the Hindenburg zone, taking in the process 21,000 prisoners and 200 guns. In 1918, starting from a front many miles farther west, they had performed the same feat in one month, and had 70,000 prisoners and 700 guns to their credit.

*1918
Sept. 15-23*

Here we are concerned only with the battle front north of Havrincourt. The next key-point was Mœuvres, which filled the gap in front of Cambrai, and on 15th September it was in the hands of the 155th Brigade of the Fifty-second Division, the 4th K.O.S.B. being in line, the 4th Royal Scots Fusiliers in support, and the 5th Royal Scots Fusiliers in reserve. For eleven days the division was to struggle for the ruins of that village. It was defended by a chain of small posts which ran from north to south along its eastern edge. On the 17th there was a strong German attack, and the 155th Brigade was forced to the western edge of the houses. On the 18th, after an artillery bombardment, an attempt was made to rush our line, but the only Germans who obtained a footing were bombed back by Second Lieutenant D. M'G. Yuille of the 4th Royal Scots Fusiliers with three men. On the 19th the two Scots Fusilier battalions took over the front, and at seven p.m. they attempted to retake Mœuvres, with two companies of the 7th H.L.I. on their left. By 8.45 p.m. some of the 4th Royal Scots Fusiliers had reached the eastern edge, where they were held up, and all night long confused fighting went on in the village. A post of the 5th H.L.I. under Corporal David Hunter (who received the Victoria Cross), which had been holding out for ninety-six hours, was relieved. By the early morning of the 20th Mœuvres was cleared of the enemy. That evening the 155th Brigade was relieved by the 156th, but the 4th Royal Scots Fusiliers remained attached to the latter brigade. There was a severe counter-attack by the Prussian Guard on the 21st, which was beaten off, and on the night of the 23rd the 155th Brigade returned to the line.

1918
Sept. 25–27

One of our posts was captured on the early morning of the 25th, which the 4th Royal Scots Fusiliers promptly retook, and the same thing happened on the morning of the 26th, for the enemy did not surrender Mœuvres without a bitter struggle. But by the 27th the position was finally in our hands. In the fighting Captain A. D. H. Clark-Kennedy, of the 5th Royal Scots Fusiliers, received wounds of which he died.

Meantime the Third Division had been in action farther south, and on 18th September the 1st Royal Scots Fusiliers pushed up to the edge of the Canal du Nord at Havrincourt. The moment had now come for that great advance which the British Commander-in-Chief undertook on his own responsibility, in spite of the doubts of his own Government, and in which, daring greatly, he greatly succeeded. On the 27th Haig struck at the main Hindenburg zone from Cambrai to St. Quentin, though his armies had borne the heaviest share of the summer fighting, and every division had been sorely tried. At 5.20 a.m. on the 27th, just as light was breaking, Byng and Horne attacked on a front of thirty miles between Gouzeaucourt and Sauchy-Lestrée with, from right to left, the IV., VI., XVII., and Canadian Corps. The key of the problem was the debouchment on a narrow front in the Mœuvres area, for the Canal du Nord farther north was too strong to be passed in the face of the enemy. But if it could be crossed there, the northern sector might be turned by an attack fanning out from the bridgehead. This task was entrusted to the Fifty-second and Sixty-third Divisions and the Canadians.

The attack of the Fifty-second Division, delivered by the 157th and 156th Brigades, was southward from Mœuvres on both banks of the Canal du Nord, while the Sixty-third Division on its left, and the Guards on its right, were to work inward towards each other. The task was therefore one of high delicacy and of strictly limited objectives. It was perfectly managed, and early in the day it had overcome a segment of the enemy defence a mile and a quarter long and a mile deep.

THE CANAL DU NORD

Everywhere on the front was the same success. Bourlon and Bourlon Wood, Graincourt and Anneux, fell— places familiar in the old Cambrai battle. Farther south the Third Division took Ribécourt and Flesquières. The 1st Royal Scots Fusiliers were heavily engaged, and had 3 officers—Second Lieutenants L. D. Allan, J. R. Kean, and F. S. Stanton—killed and 96 other casualties. That evening Byng and Horne were everywhere across the Canal du Nord, and close on the Scheldt Canal south of Cambrai.

1918
Sept.27-30

The whole front was now ablaze from the Meuse to the sea, for on that same day, the 28th, the Allies struck at von Armin in the north. A force, commanded by the King of the Belgians, and including the XIX. and II. Corps of the British Second Army, attacked at 5.30 a.m. on a front of twenty miles from south of Dixmude to Ploegsteert Wood. In this attack were the 2nd Royal Scots Fusiliers in the Ninth Division, the 12th Royal Scots Fusiliers in the Thirty-first Division, and the 11th Royal Scots Fusiliers in the Fifty-ninth Division. In the British section, which lay south of the Ypres–Zonnebeke road, there was no warning " preparation." The operation went like clockwork. The Ninth Division had the 28th Brigade (in which were the 2nd Royal Scots Fusiliers) on the right and the 26th Brigade on the left, and by 11.45 a.m. had reached all its objectives in the Broodseinde area. The Scots Fusiliers lost three officers—Lieutenant A. C. B. Freeman and Second Lieutenants J. A. Nisbet and G. A. Low. Next day Plumer cleared Ploegsteert Wood, took Messines, and held all the left bank of the Lys from Comines westward. The 12th Royal Scots Fusiliers (now under Lieutenant-Colonel J. R. Turner), in the Thirty-first Division, advanced to the Lys along the north edge of Ploegsteert Wood and gained all their objectives with few losses. Next day it was the turn of the 11th Royal Scots Fusiliers, who now, for the first time, were engaged in a major action. From the Fauquissart area they advanced six hundred and fifty yards on a frontage of eighteen hundred, suffering fifty-three casualties, including Second Lieutenants F. Isaacs and A. W. McCall killed.

Meantime, farther south, Haig was achieving his purpose. On the 29th came the final blow on the Hindenburg citadel, delivered by Byng's right, Rawlinson's Fourth Army, and the French First Army. The story of the amazing day, of how the Forty-sixth Division crossed the Scheldt Canal and the American II. Corps struggled in the tunnels, does not belong to this narrative. Suffice it to say that that evening saw the end of the real German defence, for Byng and Rawlinson had stormed their way far into the citadel. In days of wind and cloud they enlarged the gap till St. Quentin fell, and Cambrai was utterly outflanked. On 30th September the Australians broke through the northern part of the Beaurevoir–Fonsommes line, the last of the Hindenburg works, and looked into open country. Haig had crossed the two great canals, and destroyed all but the final line of the Hindenburg zone, while that final line in one part had been passed. The time had come for an advance on a broad front which should obliterate the remnants of the Hindenburg works, and with them Germany's last hope of a safe winter position. Her nearest refuge would be the Meuse, and, shepherded by Foch's unrelenting hand, it was very certain that her armies would never reach the banks of that fateful river.

The Fifty-second Division was relieved during the night of 5th October. It had lost heavily in the long battle, and the 155th Brigade had now hardly the strength of a battalion. Both the 4th and the 5th Royal Scots Fusiliers were in action on 1st October, when, after crossing the Scheldt Canal, they attacked the suburbs of Cambrai. The 4th Battalion had 6 officers and 106 other ranks casualties; and the 5th Battalion 11 officers and 164 other ranks. On 2nd October the 4th Battalion had only 2 officers and 90 rifles left. In the 5th Battalion Second Lieutenants R. T. Ross and Robert Montgomery fell; in the 4th Battalion Captain W. F. Templeton and Second Lieutenant F. S. Burleigh. Captain Templeton, who on 1st October had been wounded twice before he received his death-blow, was a fine soldier and much beloved, and he was the laureate of the regiment.[1] He had fought through the war in Sinai, in Palestine, and in France, and it was the irony of fate that one who seemed to bear a charmed life should fall on the eve of victory.

V

Meantime, while the enemy front was crumbling in the West, it had wholly collapsed in the East, for on 26th September Bulgaria had sued for an armistice; and on 1st October Allenby, after scattering the Turkish armies to the winds, had entered Damascus. We must return to the forlorn 8th Battalion of our regiment, which for nearly three years had been suffering the alternate heats and chills and the abiding boredom of Salonika. The Allied front there had been all but stagnant since the futile offensive of May 1917. Sarrail, who as Commander-in-Chief had shown little capacity, gave place in December of that year to Guillaumat, who in turn was succeeded in June 1918 by Franchet d'Esperey. During these summer months it was clear that the Bulgarian *moral* was weakening, and it was resolved, as soon as the great advance in France was under way, to attack vigorously, in the hope of disintegrating her political unity. A striking military success was scarcely hoped for, so formidable seemed her mountain defences.

The main assault was to be delivered by the French and Serbians on the left centre in the space between the Tcherna and the Vardar. It began early on 15th September, when the crest of the enemy position was carried by the Serbians. On the 16th the Allies, on a front of sixteen miles, went five miles forward; and on the 17th they were twenty miles from their starting-point. On the 28th the Serbians had crossed the

[1] *Songs of the Ayrshire Regiment, and other Verses.* (Alexander Gardner, 1917.) See Appendix II.

Tcherna and were pushing towards Prilep, and had all but severed the link between the right and left armies of the enemy. This was the vital part of the action, but it was incumbent on the British and Greek troops on the Allied right, facing the Bulgarian First and Second Armies, to make certain that no enemy reserves were sent westward. Accordingly General Milne attacked east and west of Lake Doiran. West of the lake lay the British Twenty-sixth and Twenty-second Divisions, a Greek division, and a French regiment—the whole under Lieutenant-General Sir H. F. Wilson ; while east of the lake were the British Twenty-eighth Division and another Greek division, under Lieutenant-General Sir C. F. Briggs. The 77th Brigade, in which were the 8th Royal Scots Fusiliers, was temporarily under the G.O.C. of the Twenty-second Division, Major-General John Duncan, who was himself a Scots Fusilier, and had formerly commanded the 78th Brigade. The 77th Brigade was directed against the position called the Grand Couronné, which had baffled our efforts the year before, and was indeed almost impregnable to direct assault. The 8th Royal Scots Fusiliers were in the centre, the 11th Scottish Rifles on the right, and the 12th Argyll and Sutherland Highlanders on the left, the 10th Black Watch having gone to France in the summer. On the brigade left were French troops, and a Greek division on the right.

The attack began at 5.20 a.m. on the 18th, and in face of a heavy artillery and machine-gun fire barrage it carried the point known as the Tongue. But the enemy at once counter-attacked, and the Greeks on the right were driven from the objective they had won, while the French on the left had apparently never moved from their place of assembly. The result was that the brigade had both flanks in the air, and as the enemy was pushing forward enveloping attacks, it was compelled about 10.30 a.m. slowly to withdraw. The commanding officer of the Scots Fusiliers, Lieutenant-Colonel G. G. Lindesay, was wounded, and most of

SURRENDER OF BULGARIA

the officers were already casualties. Accordingly the battalion retired to a ravine, where it was reorganized under two subalterns, Lieutenant Watson and Second Lieutenant Bryce. It was a day of heavy losses—over 400; and among the officers, the adjutant, Captain C. N. Crawshaw, Captain and Quartermaster C. Y. Adamson, Captain R. A. Murray, Lieutenant S. H. Nimmo, and Second Lieutenants W. Lawson and J. R. Templeton were killed.

Major R. W. Geddes took command of the battalion, and during the second fruitless assault on the 19th the Scots Fusiliers were not engaged. But the complete break-through in the west compelled a retreat of the Bulgarian left wing, and on the 22nd the II. Army fell back from the Doiran front, closely pursued by the British and Greeks. The pursuers pressed east of the Vardar across the Belesh Mountains towards Strumnitza. The enemy front had been cut in two, and the halves driven in a divergent retreat. On the morning of the 23rd, when the Serbians were in Ishtip and close on Veles and Uskub, Kosturino, in Bulgarian territory, was taken by the 8th D.C.L.I. of the 79th Brigade. On the 26th came Bulgaria's request for an armistice; on the 28th she accepted the Allied terms; and at noon on the 30th the armistice was signed, and she ceased to be a participant in the war.

Meanwhile the 8th Royal Scots Fusiliers, now organized in two companies, were, after their long inaction, playing the novel part of swift marches and open warfare, though the 77th Brigade, owing to its weakness after the fighting of the 18th, was in reserve. On the 26th they were in Cestova, and on the 27th in Kosturino. They heard at Strumnitza of the armistice with Bulgaria, and they were at Mustapha Pasha when Turkey surrendered—within twelve hours of a projected attack on Adrianople by the Twenty-sixth Division.[1] Then began extensive wanderings, which

1918
Sept. 18-30

---

[1] A number of Scots Fusilier and other officers reconnoitred Adrianople disguised as Bulgarians. One Scot made an excellent Bulgarian, because his Bulgarian boots were too small for him, so he carried them in his hands!

1918
Oct. 8–
Nov. 4
took them successively to Bela and Rustchuk, Varna, Tiflis, and Batoum, till late in 1919 the battalion was disbanded.

VI

The remainder of the tale of the Western front is the tale of the advance to victory. Nothing now lay between Haig and Maubeuge but, in the words of the official dispatch, "the natural obstacles of a wooded and well-watered country." From every side, from Pershing in the south to the Belgians in the north, the Allies were driving the enemy into the bottle-neck of retreat which meant disaster. On 8th October Byng and Rawlinson cleared the last débris of the Hindenburg zone, and next day Cambrai fell to the Canadians. The nerve of Germany was breaking, and she had begun her overtures to President Wilson for peace. But events in the field marched more swiftly than the course of diplomacy. On the 13th Haig had reached the line of the Selle; on the 14th Menin in the north was taken; on the 17th Douai and Ostend were evacuated, and Lille fell. That day, too, saw the forcing of the Selle line, which was completed on the 18th. On the 23rd began the "battle of the rivers" from the Scheldt to the Meuse—the last great contest in the West. On the 26th Ludendorff resigned, and by the last day of October Austria had surrendered to Italy. On 2nd November Haig took Valenciennes, and the line of the Scheldt was wholly turned; by the evening of 4th November he had swept through the Forest of Mormal and taken Landrecies. That day the enemy's resistance was finally broken, and he was no longer in retreat but in flight, for the two wings of his armies were separated for ever. His avenue of withdrawal was now the fifty miles between Avesnes and Mezières, and through this gut the whole remaining German forces in the south must squeeze if they would make good their escape. But that gut was hourly narrowing. Gouraud and Pershing were approaching Mezières; Debeney and Guillaumat were pressing

THE VICTORY IN THE WEST

Facing page 446

NORTH SEA
H O L L A
B E L G I U
Flushing
Bergen-op-Zoom
Zeebrugge
Turnhout
OSTEND
Middelkerke
Westende
Nieuport
Zandvoorde
BRUGES
Nieuworken
St.Nicholas
ANTWERP
Dunkirk
Pervyse
Furnes
Dixmude
Thourout
Pitthem
GHENT
Lokeren
Zele
Schoonaerde
Termonde
Wetteren
Alost
MALINES
Aerschot
Haelen
Cortenaecken
LOUVAIN
CALAIS
R. Yser
ROULERS
Langemarck
Poelcappelle
Passchendaele
Zonnebeke
Gulleghem
Ypres
Cassel
Harlebeke
Deynze
COURTRAI
Oudenarde
Renaix
Grammont
BRUSSELS
Audeghem
Tirlemont
Landen
R. Dendre
R. Scheldt
R. Dyle
R. Nethe
Zandvoorde
Wytschaete
Messines
Menin
Wervicq
Comines
Ploegsteert
Tourcoing
Frelinghien
Houplines
ROUBAIX
Lannoy
Armentieres
Perenchies
Laventie
Aubers
LILLE
TOURNAI
Hainault
Ath
Enghien
Hal
Quatre Bras
Braine l'Alleud
Genappe
Wavre
Ramillies
Nivelles
Enghezee
Gembloux
Soignies
BOULOGNE
St.Omer
Hazebrouck
Aire
Bethune
La Bassée
Cuinchy
Douvrin
Vermelles
Pont-à-Vendin
Lens
Montigny
Peruwelz
St.Ghislain
Obourg
MONS
Harmignies
Binche
Jemappes
Frameries
Audregnies
Malplaquet
Peissant
Condé
Tamines
Auvelais
Arsimont
NAMUR
CHARLEROI
Etaples
Montreuil
R. Canche
St.Pol
Vimy
DOUAI
VALENCIENNES
R. Scarpe
Benain
Rombies
Angre
Bavai
Thuin
Mettet
Dinant
Arras
Avesnes
Arleux
Bouchain
Jenlain
Haspres
Le Quesnoy
MAUBEUGE
Walcourt
Haussy
Solesmes
Viesly
Caudry
Mormal Forest
Solre-le-Chateau
Beaumont
Philippeville
Givet
St.Valery
Abbeville
Doullens
Bapaume
Grancourt
CAMBRAI
Beauvois
Marcoing
Ribecourt
Crèvecœur
Rumilly
Gouzeaucourt
Esnes
Le Cateau
Landrecies
Maroilles
Avesnes
Chimay
R. Ancre
La Boiselle
Albert
Vendhuile
Gouy
Premont
Beaurevoir
Epehy
Bony
Le Catelet
Bohain
Vaux-Andigny
R. Sambre
Péronne
Bellenglise
Bellicourt
Lehaucourt
Verrnand
Holnon
Hirson
Rocroi
R. Bresle
R. Somme
AMIENS
Proyart
Estrées
ST QUENTIN
Bernot
Mesnil
Guise
R. Oise
Villers Bretonneux
Linons
Urvillers
Ribemont
Vervins
Rumigny
Charleville
Mezieres
Cerizy
R. Serre
Signy l'Abbaye
Launois
Omont
SEDAN
Bazeilles
R. Meuse
R. Noye
Montdidier
Roye
Tergnier
La Fère
Oise Forest
Noyon
Marle
OCT. 15th
OCT. 1st
NOV. 1st
OCT. 19th
OCT. 15th
OCT. 10th
OCT. 1st
NOV. 1st
NOV. 5th
LINE ON NOVEMBER 11th
AUG. 8th
SEPT. 6th
AUG. 15th

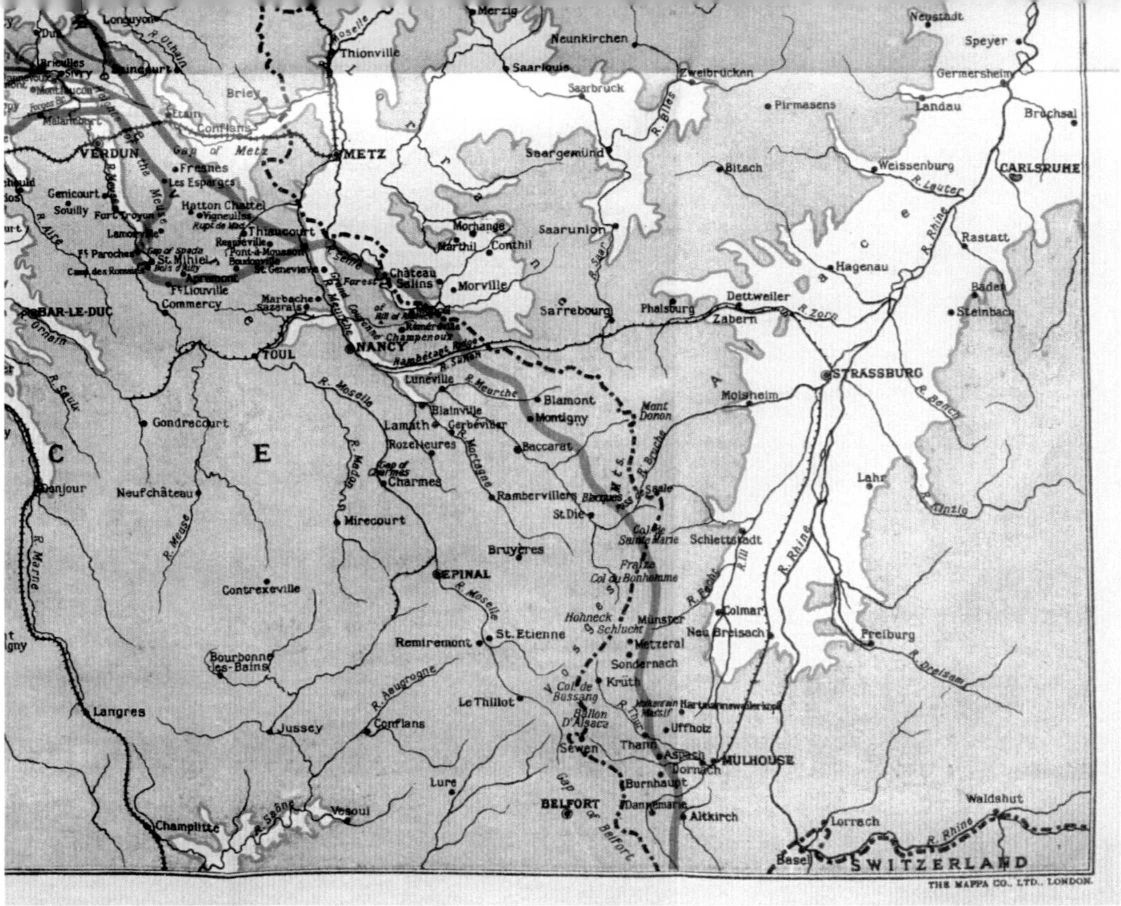

Longuyon
Brieulles
Sivry
Montfaucon
Malancourt
VERDUN
Fresnes
Les Esparges
Genicourt
Souilly
Fort Troyon
Lamorville
Hatton Chattel
Vigneulles
Thiaucourt
Regnéville
Pont-à-Mousson
St. Mihiel
Gap of Spada
Apremont
Camp des Romains
Ft. Liouville
Commercy
BAR-LE-DUC
R. Aire
R. Meuse
Gap of Metz
Briey
Etain
Conflans
Thionville
R. Moselle
METZ
Merzig
Neunkirchen
Saarlouis
Saarbruck
Zweibrücken
R. Blies
Saargemünd
Morhange
Marthil
Conthil
Saarunion
R. Saar
Château Salins
Morville
Sarrebourg
Phalsburg
Dettweiler
Zabern
R. Zorn
Marbache
Sazerais
R. Seille
Forest
NANCY
Champenoux
R. Meurthe
TOUL
Lunéville
R. Vezouse
Blamont
Montigny
Mont Donon
Blainville
Lamath
Gerbéviller
Rozelieures
Baccarat
R. Mortagne
Gap of Charmes
Charmes
Rambervillers
St. Dié
R. Bruche
Saale
Col de Sainte Marie
Schlettstadt
Fraize
Col du Bonhomme
Mirecourt
R. Madon
R. Moselle
Bruyères
EPINAL
Gondrecourt
Neufchâteau
Donjour
R. Meuse
R. Marne
R. Saulx
R. Ornain
C
E
Contrexeville
Bourbonne les-Bains
Langres
Jussey
Conflans
R. Augrogne
Remiremont
St. Etienne
Le Thillot
Lure
Vesoul
R. Saône
Champlitte
Hohneck
Schlucht
Vosges Mts.
Münster
Metzeral
Sondernach
Krüth
Col de Bussang
Ballon D'Alsace
Sewen
Thann
R. Thur
Uffholz
Hartmannsweilerkopf
Aspach
Dornach
MULHOUSE
Burnhaupt
Dannemarie
Altkirch
BELFORT
Gap of Belfort
Colmar
Neu Breisach
R. Fecht
R. Ill
R. Rhine
Molsheim
STRASSBURG
R. Bench
Lahr
R. Kinzig
Freiburg
R. Dreisam
Hagenau
Bitsch
Weissenburg
R. Lauter
Pirmasens
Landau
Neustadt
Speyer
Germersheim
Bruchsal
CARLSRUHE
Rastatt
Baden
Steinbach
Alsace
Lorraine
Waldshut
Lorrach
Basel
SWITZERLAND
THE MAPPA CO. LTD., LONDON.

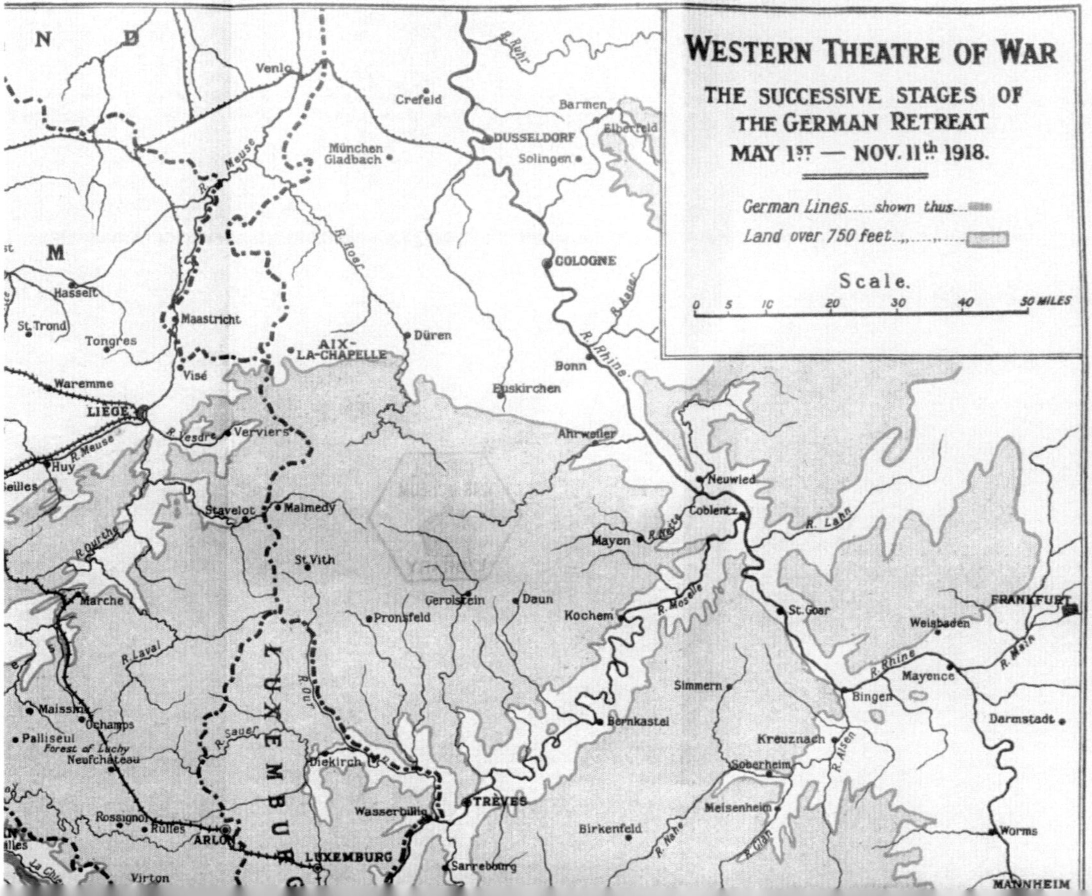

WESTERN THEATRE OF WAR
THE SUCCESSIVE STAGES OF THE GERMAN RETREAT
MAY 1ST — NOV. 11th 1918.
German Lines...... shown thus...
Land over 750 feet...
Scale.
0 5 10 20 30 40 50 MILES
Venlo
Crefeld
Barmen
Elberfeld
DUSSELDORF
Solingen
München Gladbach
R. Meuse
R. Ruhr
R. Roer
COLOGNE
R. Agger
Hasselt
St. Trond
Tongres
Maastricht
AIX-LA-CHAPELLE
Düren
Bonn
R. Rhine
Visé
Waremme
LIEGE
Euskirchen
R. Vesdre
Verviers
Ahrweiler
Huy
Neuwied
Coblentz
R. Lahn
Stavelot
Malmedy
R. Ourthe
Mayen
St. Vith
Marche
Gerolstein
Daun
Kochem
R. Moselle
St. Goar
FRANKFURT
Pronsfeld
Weisbaden
R. Main
R. Laval
R. Our
LUXEMBURG
Mayence
Simmern
Bingen
Maissin
Ochamps
Bernkastel
Darmstadt
Palliseul
Forest of Luchy
Neufchateau
R. Sauer
Diekirch
Kreuznach
R. Alsen
Soberheim
TRÈVES
Wasserbillig
Meisenheim
Rossignol
Rulles
ARLON
Birkenfeld
R. Nahe
R. Glan
Worms
Virton
Sarrebourg
MANNHEIM

THE LAST BATTLES

towards Hirson, with nothing to bar the road; while Haig had the Sambre valley as a highway to Namur. Moreover, Foch had still his trump card to play—the encircling swing of his right by way of Metz to close the last way of retreat. If a negotiated armistice did not come within a week, there would be a *de facto* armistice of complete collapse and universal surrender.

1918 Oct. 11- Nov. 5

Such were the landmarks in the greatest battle in the history of the world. We must glance at the part played by our six battalions. The 1st Royal Scots Fusiliers with the Third Division were not in action in the first half of October. On the 11th Lieutenant-Colonel G. Bissett died of wounds, and was succeeded by Major D. Reitz. On the 22nd the battalion was at Solesmes, and on the 24th was in the action when Byng and Rawlinson attacked in the gap between the Scheldt and the Forest of Mormal. Vertain was to be taken by the 2nd Royal Scots and two companies of the Scots Fusiliers; and then, after an artillery "preparation," Escarmain was to be attacked by the Fusiliers. The operation was completely successful, and 300 prisoners were captured by the battalion at the cost of under 50 casualties. The only officer killed was Second Lieutenant R. Paton. The Scots Fusiliers were at Romeries in reserve on the day of the Armistice. Passing to the extreme British left, the 2nd Royal Scots Fusiliers in the Ninth Division had a month of varied actions. On 5th October the 28th Brigade—the Scots Fusiliers in reserve—attacked and carried the Keiberg Spur. On that day Lieutenant-Colonel Utterson-Kelso was severely wounded. The battalion, now temporarily under Major King, attacked at Rolleghemcapelle on the 14th, and gained its objectives with 130 casualties. Then came the advance from Ledeghem to the Scheldt, the Lys being crossed on the 20th. On the 23rd Lieutenant-Colonel R. Campbell, from the 51st Division, took over the battalion, which was again in action on the 25th. Next day it was relieved, and after a short spell of training was at Gulleghem on 3rd November, and took part in the divisional parade on the 5th for the King and

448 THE ROYAL SCOTS FUSILIERS

1918
Oct. 15–
Nov. 11

Queen of the Belgians. It was in billets at Cuerne when hostilities were suspended.

The 11th Royal Scots Fusiliers in the Fifty-ninth Division, after their heavy fight on 30th September, cleared the Radinghem ridge on 15th October, and on the 17th entered La Madeleine, when they received an enthusiastic welcome from the inhabitants. On the 18th the battalion moved forward as an advanced guard, along with King Edward's Horse, to Ascq, and next day reached Willems, fifteen minutes after the enemy left. On the 20th it was on the west bank of the Scheldt at Pont-à-Chin, and next day attempted a crossing, when Second Lieutenant Paton succeeded, by means of strong telephone wire, in getting the foot-bridge into position. That night the Fusiliers were relieved, and when they returned to the line the war was closing. They were at Velaines on the day of the Armistice.

The 12th Royal Scots Fusiliers in the Thirty-first Division were in reserve for most of October, but on the 20th they moved forward to Lannoy. On the 30th they were in a sharp action in front of Ingoyghem, when they won all their objectives, and lost Lieutenants J. Dunlop and J. Somerville. The following day, in action near Elseghem, Sergeant Thomas Caldwell won the fourth and last of the Victoria Crosses gained by the Royal Scots Fusiliers in the Great War. He was in command of a Lewis-gun section engaged in clearing a farmhouse. "When his section," says the official record, "came under intense fire at close range from another farm, Sergeant Caldwell rushed towards the farm and, in spite of very heavy fire, reached the enemy position, which he captured single-handed, together with 18 prisoners. This gallant and determined exploit removed a serious obstacle from the line of advance, saved many casualties, and led to the capture by his section of about 70 prisoners, eight machine guns, and one trench mortar." The battalion was at Courtrai on 2nd November, and at Revaix when hostilities ceased.

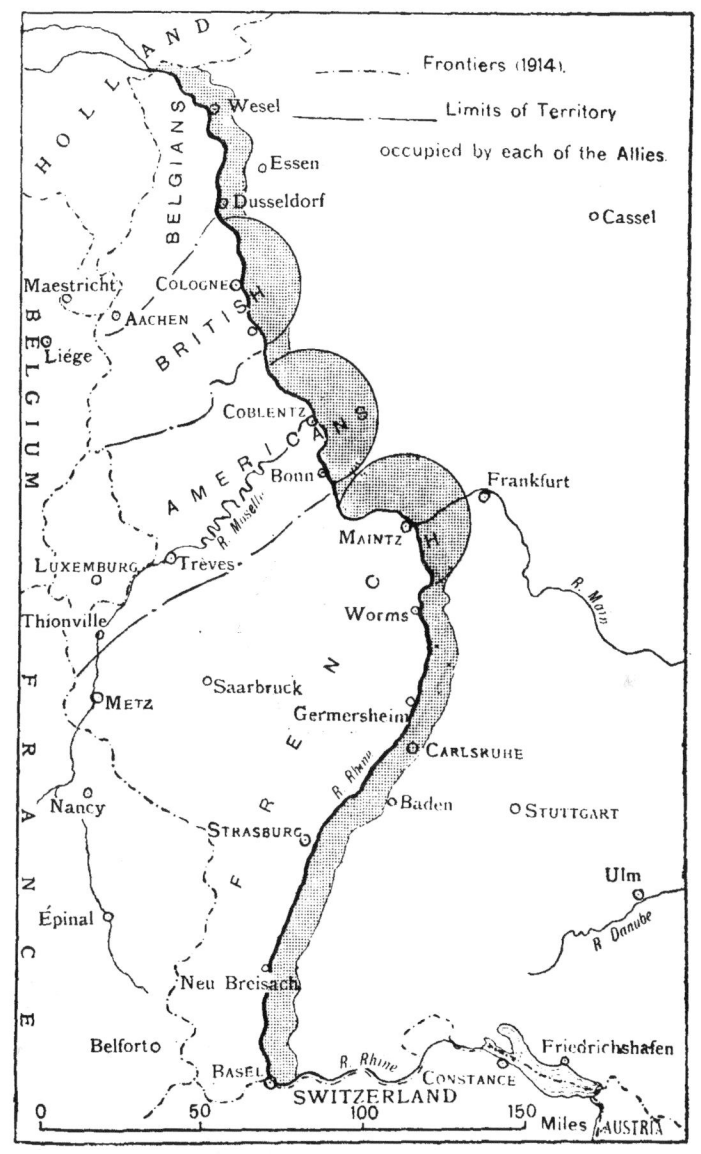

THE ALLIES ON THE RHINE

THE ARMISTICE

But it was for the 4th and 5th Battalions in the Fifty-second Division that the war closed most dramatically. That division set out on 19th October to march from its rest area to the front line. Moving by Lens and Douai, it took over on the 28th the outpost line from the Eighth Division at Hergnies, north of Valenciennes. In front were the German water defences which we were speedily outflanking. On the night of 7th November patrols managed to cross the water on rafts, and next day it was known that the enemy was retiring. On the 10th the 156th and 157th Brigades took Herchies, six miles north-west of Mons; early in the morning of the 11th Jurbise fell, and the 155th Brigade, led by the 4th Royal Scots Fusiliers, continued in pursuit. " Of a sudden," wrote a lieutenant of the 5th H.L.I., " there arose a clatter of hoofs, and an obviously excited transport officer darted up to the commanding officer, brandishing one of the pink forms we had learned to hate. But never before had an army form borne such a message as this. ' Hostilities will cease at 11.00; until further orders troops will not move beyond the position occupied at that time.' " At that hour men of the 4th Royal Scots Fusiliers stood on the very ground where, in August four years before, men of the 1st Battalion had begun the war story of the regiment. On the grey November morning the circle of devotion and service was complete.[1]

1918
Oct. 19–
Nov. 11

Officers who died in 1918

Lieutenant M. ADAM (7th Aug.); Captain and Quartermaster C. Y. ADAMSON (17th Sept.); Second Lieutenant L. D. ALLAN (27th Sept.); Second Lieutenant J. ATKINSON (2nd Sept.); Second Lieutenant T. BELL (26th May); Lieutenant M. B. BERKELEY (2nd Sept.); Lieutenant-Colonel G. BISSETT (18th Oct.); Second Lieutenant J.

---

[1] When, on 15th November, Horne's army officially entered Mons, Major D. Yuille led the party which represented the 155th Brigade. " At an age when most men might reasonably have been expected to watch the war from a comfortable fireside, he had left his schoolmastering and gone to Gallipoli with the R.S.F., serving as its quartermaster. He was never away from his battalion for sickness or any other reason, with the exception of four weeks' leave in Palestine and one in France, and he never once failed his battalion or brigade."—Thompson's *The Fifty-second Division*, pages 572, 573.

BOYD (12th April); Second Lieutenant F. S. BURLEIGH (2nd Oct.); Lieutenant J. J. BROWN (5th Aug.); Second Lieutenant J. CHARLTON (2nd Sept.); Captain A. D. H. CLARK-KENNEDY (18th Sept.); Second Lieutenant K. C. CRAWFORD (2nd Sept.); Captain C. N. CRAWSHAW (19th Sept.); Lieutenant J. DUNLOP (1st Nov.); Lieutenant H. ELSWORTH (21st Aug.); Second Lieutenant W. K. FAIRLEY (12th Aug.); Captain R. G. FERGUSON (11th June); Lieutenant A. C. B. FREEMAN (27th Sept.); Second Lieutenant L. FRY (9th Nov.); Second Lieutenant E. F. GILMOUR (28th March); Second Lieutenant D. R. GLEN (28th March); Second Lieutenant W. T. GOODING (22nd March); Second Lieutenant A. GRANT (3rd Sept.); Lieutenant T. W. GUDGEON (25th Aug.); Captain C. M. HADDEN (28th March); Lieutenant W. B. HODGE (4th Nov.); Second Lieutenant W. A. How (12th April); Second Lieutenant S. B. HURST (26th Aug.); Captain W. R. HUTCHISON (22nd March); Second Lieutenant F. ISAACS (29th Sept.); Second Lieutenant J. R. KEAN (1st Oct.); Lieutenant W. KERR (2nd Sept.); Second Lieutenant E. KNIGHT (20th Sept.); Second Lieutenant H. LAMBROUGHTON (12th April); Second Lieutenant W. LAWSON (19th Sept.); Captain L. H. LINDSAY-YOUNG (25th Dec.); Second Lieutenant J. F. LOGAN (12th April); Second Lieutenant G. A. Low (28th Sept.); Second Lieutenant A. W. McCALL (30th Sept.); Second Lieutenant R. M. M'COWAN (1st Nov.); Lieutenant J. V. MACDONALD (17th April); Captain R. M'HARRIE (9th June); Second Lieutenant R. L. M'MUTRIE (21st Aug.); Second Lieutenant M. M'QUESTIN (28th March); Captain W. C. MAIR (22nd March); Captain G. C. MILLAR (26th Aug.); Second Lieutenant R. MONTGOMERY (1st Oct.); Captain R. A. MURRAY (19th Sept.); Lieutenant E. C. NEPEAN (4th Oct.); Lieutenant S. H. NIMMO (19th Sept.); Second Lieutenant J. A. NISBET (28th Sept.); Lieutenant V. W. NUTKINS (19th Feb.); Lieutenant J. T. PATON (30th May); Second Lieutenant R. PATON (23rd Oct.); Second Lieutenant A. RAMSAY (28th March); Second Lieutenant W. RIDDELL (29th April); Second Lieutenant J. ROBERTSON (21st Aug.); Second Lieutenant N. W. ROBERTSON (2nd Sept.); Second Lieutenant A. J. Ross (30th Jan.); Second Lieutenant R. T. Ross (29th Sept.); Lieutenant A. C. SCOTT (9th June); Second Lieutenant A. SHERRIFF (22nd March); Lieutenant J. SOMERVILLE (31st Oct.); Second Lieutenant F. S. STANTON (27th Sept.); Second Lieutenant T. R. M. TAYLOR (14th Aug.); Second Lieutenant J. R. TEMPLETON (19th Sept.); Captain W. F. TEMPLETON (1st Oct.); Captain R. H. THOMAS (25th March); Second Lieutenant K. TORRANCE (2nd Sept.); Second Lieutenant D. TWEEDIE (5th Aug.); Second Lieutenant J. A. WALKER [attached 1/4th K.O.S.B.] (26th Aug.); Second Lieutenant G. A. WHITE (20th March); Second Lieutenant W. R. B. WOLSTENCROFT (12th April); Captain A. I. WYLLIE (2nd Sept.).

CHAPTER XIX

CONCLUSION

Summary of the work of the Scots Fusiliers in the Great War—Distinguished officers—A typical British regiment—The Scottish Lowland soldier—The Scots qualities in war—The Fusilier type—Regimental tradition.

THE Armistice of November 11, 1918, seems the most fitting date on which to conclude this history. There was indeed much work still before the regiment in the slow months of demobilization and in the varied forms of service which constituted the aftermath of war. The 2nd and the 8th Battalions were for a time with the Army of the Black Sea; the 1st Battalion had to renew the old regimental experience of duty in Ireland under conditions more difficult than the past had ever known; individual Scots Fusiliers, like Lieutenant-Colonel A. P. Skeil (formerly of the 6th/7th Battalion), played a distinguished part in the campaign in North Russia. But with the Armistice the great operations closed. Gradually the new battalions disappeared, the survivors were absorbed into civil life, the regiment returned to its old two-battalion basis, and the even tenor of its regimental history was resumed.

In the Great War it had been less a regiment than one of the training schools through which the manhood of the country passed to the field. Apart from its reserve, home service, and labour units, it had sent nine battalions to the different battle-grounds. Only Mesopotamia and Italy were without contingents of Scots Fusiliers; otherwise they were represented in every main action of the campaign, save Allenby's final drive to Damascus. They had fought from Mons to the Marne, and back by way of the Aisne to First Ypres. They were at Neuve Chapelle and on the fringes of Second Ypres; at Festubert, and Givenchy, and Loos; in every phase of the battle of the Somme; at Arras, and Third Ypres, and Cambrai; in the retreat from St. Quentin, and the battle of the Lys; in all the stages of the advance to victory. They were at Gallipoli, and in the Palestine campaign till Jerusalem fell; they endured the long vigil of Salonika, and shared in the final battle. In the four years' struggle seven of their battalion commanders fell on the field, but there were men like Lieutenant-Colonel E. I. D. Gordon and Lieutenant-Colonel Utterson-Kelso who survived the war after leading their units in a dozen major actions. Between 1914 and 1918 the regiment won 4 Victoria Crosses, 29 D.S.O.'s, 164 M.C.'s, 141 D.C.M.'s, 416 Military Medals, and 74 foreign decorations. But such rewards are apt to be capricious: the more signal proof of its quality was the praise universally given it by the superior command and the fame which it bore among its fellow-soldiers. It had the repute of being wholly trustworthy, of doing its duty to the last iota, of keeping a stout heart in any crisis, and of never withdrawing till it was bidden. For this faithfulness it paid high. The new army battalions were in the forefront of Loos, and Arras, and Third Ypres; the Territorial battalions suffered desperately at Gallipoli and Gaza; the two regular battalions perished in the gate at Ypres when, in October 1914, the enemy's most deadly assault was foiled. On October 25, 1923, the old regimental colours of the 2nd Battalion were deposited in St. Giles' Cathedral in Edinburgh, and the Prince of Wales, as colonel-in-chief, unveiled the memorial tablet. On that tablet were inscribed these words, which in their simplicity are the most fitting comment on the regiment's service: " To the glory of God, and in proud remembrance of 319 officers, 23 warrant officers, 928 non-commissioned officers, and

AIR CHIEF-MARSHAL SIR HUGH TRENCHARD, BART.
(From a photograph by Maull and Fox, 187 Piccadilly, W.1)

SIR HUGH TRENCHARD

4,693 men of the Royal Scots Fusiliers who gave their lives for King and country in the Great War—'But they shall live for ever.'"[1]

The achievement of the regiment cannot be assessed only from the story of its battles, for many Scots Fusilier officers were with other units, or engaged in service apart from the battlefield. Of these the most notable was Air Chief-Marshal Sir Hugh Montague Trenchard, the present colonel. Since the South African War his service had been outside the regiment, mainly in West Africa, and he joined the Royal Flying Corps when it came into being in 1912. At the outbreak of the Great War he was appointed to the command of the Military Wing of the Corps at Farnborough, and entered upon that career which made him one of the foremost agents in the winning of victory. He was not only a great leader in the field, and a great organizer at home, but he created in the new service which he commanded a tradition of efficiency and devotion which was one of the marvels of the campaign. This is not the place to tell that famous story, nor do I dare to write what I would wish about the most modest of men, but some words of Sir Walter Raleigh may be quoted which are the barest truth : " The power which Nature made his own and which attends him like his shadow, is the power given him by his singleness of purpose and his faith in the men whom he commands. He has never called on them to do anything which he would not do himself, if he were not very unfortunately condemned, as he once told the pilots of a squadron, to

[1] The following are the battle honours awarded to the Royal Scots Fusiliers for the Great War :—

"Mons," "Retreat from Mons," "MARNE, 1914," "Aisne, 1914," "La Bassée, 1914," "YPRES, 1914, '17, '18," "Langemarck, 1914," "Gheluvelt," "Nonne Bosschen," "Neuve Chapelle," "Festubert, 1915," "Loos," "SOMME, 1916, '18," "Albert, 1916, '18," "Bazentin," "Flers-Courcelette," "Le Transloy," "Ancre, 1916," "ARRAS, 1917, '18," "Scarpe, 1917, '18," "Menin Road," "Polygon Wood," "St. Quentin," "Bapaume, 1918," "Lys," "Estaires," "Bailleul," "Scherpenberg," "Drocourt-Quéant," "HINDENBURG LINE," "Havrincourt," "Courtrai," "France and Flanders, 1914–18," "DOIRAN, 1917, '18," "Macedonia, 1916–18," "Helles," "GALLIPOLI, 1915–16," "Rumani," "Egypt, 1916," "Gaza," "El Mughar," "Nebi Samwil," "Jerusalem," "PALESTINE, 1917–18."

go about in a Rolls-Royce car and to sit in a comfortable armchair. He has never thought any deed of sacrifice and devotion too much for their powers. His faith in them was justified. Speaking in 1918 to a squadron of the Independent Force, newly brought to the neighbourhood of Nancy for the bombing of the munition factories of Germany, he reminded them that if sending them all at once across the lines, never to return, would shorten the war by a week, it would be his duty to send them. The pilots listened to him with pride. He had their confidence, as they had his. . . . His intuitive understanding of the men who served under him, his quickness in learning the lessons of experience, and his resourcefulness and daring in immediately applying those lessons for the bettering of the Flying Corps, have been worth many brigades to his country." [1]

Other Scots Fusiliers served in high commands. Major-General Sir William Douglas Smith, who went to France in command of the 1st Battalion, received the 9th Brigade in November 1914, and the Twentieth Division in March 1916. Except for a month in 1917, when he had the Thirty-sixth Division, he commanded the Twentieth till April 1918, when he took over the Portsmouth garrison at home. He made the Twentieth Division a most formidable fighting unit, and in the retreat from St. Quentin proved the quality of himself and his men. Major-General Sir Charles Patrick Amyatt Hull, who went out in command of the 4th Middlesex, was presently given the 10th Brigade, which he handled brilliantly at Second Ypres. He proceeded to the command of the Fifty-sixth Division of London Territorials, whom he led at the Somme and Arras, and again in the advance to victory. There was no better brigadier or divisional commander in France, and no wiser mind or more attractive character. Major-General John Duncan we have already seen with the Twenty-second Division at Salonika. Major-General J. H. W. Pollard, after commanding the 2nd Battalion for the first half of 1915, received the 2nd Brigade in August, and was severely

[1] *The War in the Air*, Vol. I., pages 417, 418.

wounded in October. From April 1916 onward he commanded successively the 25th, the 106th, and the 178th Brigades. Brigadier-General W. H. Bowes was in the early months a liaison officer with the French, and subsequently commanded the 8th Brigade in the Third Division till he returned to Staff duties in England. Brigadier-General C. P. Scudamore, who had gained the D.S.O. as far back as the old Burma campaign, was, when the war broke out, secretary of the Surrey Territorial Association. He did admirable work as D.A.A.G. with the Mediterranean Expeditionary Force, and then as A.A.G. of the Egyptian Expeditionary Force, and was six times mentioned in dispatches. Brigadier-General R. B. Gaisford was Inspector of Infantry at home from 1914 to 1916, and in 1917 commanded for five months the XVIII. Corps Reinforcement Camp in France. Brigadier-General R. K. Walsh, who succeeded Pollard in command of the 2nd Battalion, received the 6th Brigade after the battle of the Somme. He commanded his old battalion in 1919 in the Black Sea Force. Brigadier-General Kenneth Lean, who had left the Scots Fusiliers in 1898 to command a battalion of the Warwicks, held an Indian appointment at the beginning of the war, and for some time had a brigade in Mesopotamia. Brigadier-General D. M. Stuart, the son of a previous commanding officer,[1] had the 7th Battalion at home in the beginning of the war, and commanded the 58th Infantry Brigade in France till January 1916, when he returned to training work in England. Brigadier-General A. H. Leggett commanded the 5th Battalion in Gallipoli, and led with great success the 156th Brigade in the Fifty-second Division from the early months of 1917 to the close of hostilities.

The regiment produced, too, many distinguished Staff officers, such as Major R. V. G. Horn, who served successively with the 21st and 46th Brigades and the Forty-ninth and Twentieth Divisions, and Lieutenant-Colonel H. C. Maitland Makgill Crichton, who began the war as A.D.C. to Major-General Hubert Hamilton,

[1] See page 224.

and finished it as G.S.O.I. in the First Army. He was with Geddes's Detachment in their great stand at Second Ypres. Mention may well be made of Major F. E. Thornton of the 1st Battalion, who went to an Indian regiment, the 105th Mahrattas, and fell in Mesopotamia in the advance on Bagdad; of Lieutenant-Colonel E. A. Beck, who in 1914 was brigade-major in the Fifteenth Division, and was subsequently G.S.O.I. to the Forty-first Division in Italy and France; of Lieutenant-Colonel R. Q. Craufurd, who after service with the Fifteenth Division was A.A. and Q.M.G. successively to the Thirty-second, Eighth, and Twenty-ninth Divisions; of Lieutenant-Colonel C. H. I. Jackson, who commanded for a time the G.H.Q. Machine-gun School in France, and in 1918 was Army Machine-gun Officer with the Second Army; of Lieutenant-Colonel H. E. Gogarty, who commanded the 4th Worcesters at the outbreak of war; of Lieutenant-Colonel Quentin Agnew, who carried on the family tradition in the regiment, and besides commanding the 3rd Battalion at home, saw service in Gallipoli as a brigadier, and finally commanded the 9th Labour Group in France; of Lieutenant-Colonel Lord Belhaven,[1] who served in Mesopotamia first as military governor of Basra, then as political officer on the Euphrates, and then as political agent at Koweit, in which capacity he undertook a mission to Nejd in Central Arabia.

The regiment produced other distinguished administrators and diplomatists. Lieutenant-Colonel Sir Donald Robertson, the son of a former commanding officer of the 2nd Battalion, joined the Scots Fusiliers in 1865, and two years later entered the political service, holding posts in Hyderabad and Rewa and Gwalior, until he concluded his career in 1903 as Resident in Mysore. Lieutenant-Colonel David Robertson joined the regiment in 1897, and served with it in South Africa, but the rest of his life was spent in semi-diplomatic posts in the Far East. He was a brilliant linguist, and during the Great

[1] Lord Belhaven is a grand-nephew of Sir Frederick Hamilton, who was colonel of the regiment from 1870 to 1890.

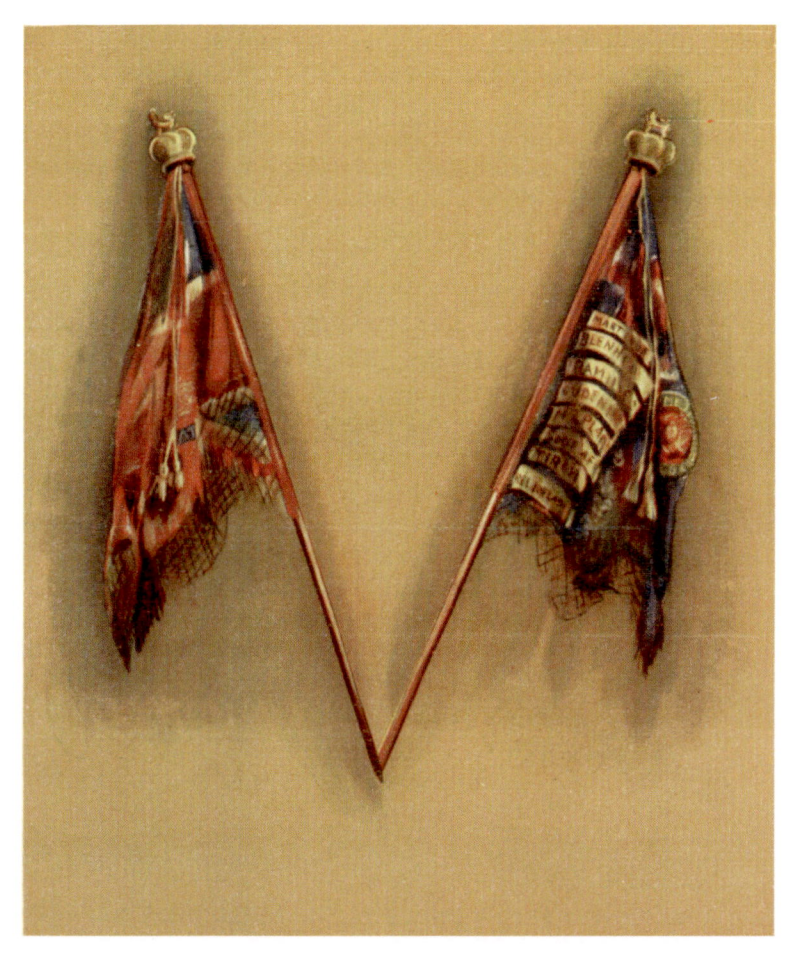

These Colours were presented to the 2nd Battalion at DUBLIN, on 10th August 1878, by the Duchess of Marlborough, and were carried at the Battle of ULUNDI (1st July 1879). They were carried on parade for the last time at BARRACKPORE, India, on 29th December 1921, when the Battalion was inspected by the Colonel-in-Chief, H.R.H. the Prince of Wales. They were subsequently deposited by him in St. Giles' Cathedral, EDINBURGH, on 25th October 1923.

(From a painting by Mrs. Coulson, Ayr)

War, after serving in Russia, he organized a Chinese Labour Corps for France, and was on the staff of the British High Commissioner, Sir Charles Eliot, during the difficult months at Omsk and Vladivostok. Sir George Roos-Keppel, who joined the Royal Scots Fusiliers in 1886, was one of the greatest of Indian frontier administrators. For eleven years he was warden of the north-eastern marches, and handled the border tribes with the patience and sagacity of genius. He pled with Lord Kitchener when war broke out to give him a command in Europe, but Kitchener wisely refused, for there was greater work before him in India. By his dominant personality and his perfect system of intelligence he prevented a frontier outbreak at a time when trouble in that region would have greatly embarrassed us. He retired in 1919 to join the Secretary of State's Council, but thirty years of unceasing toil had worn him out, and he did not long survive to give his wise counsel to the British Government. Few careers have reflected on our regiment greater lustre than his. Lastly, it may be noted that another distinguished Indian soldier had a connection with the Scots Fusiliers. Field Marshal Sir William Birdwood, who had the Australian Corps in Gallipoli and in France, and ultimately commanded the Fifth Army, began his military life in the Scots Fusiliers militia.[1]

The story of the Great War has been told in these pages only in outline, in order that proportion might be kept with the earlier campaigns. For our tale is of nearly two and a half centuries; and the struggle with Germany, though the greatest, was only one of the many wars of Britain in which the Scots Fusiliers had their share. It is a tale of a typical British regiment, sharing in the old days in the popular disesteem of the soldier, ill-paid, ill-fed, little cared for, a shuttlecock

[1] Other names worthy of mention are Lieutenant-Colonel H. S. Ravenhill, who left the regiment for the Army Pay Department; Lieutenant-Colonel Reginald Toogood, who did excellent work in managing the finances of the Regimental Association; and Lieutenant-Colonel Lord Seye and Sele, who organized the Regimental Dinner Club.

too often in the game of politics; fulfilling arduous duty in every corner of the globe, and getting little thanks for it; building up a tradition which grew so potent that it moulded the diverse stuff which entered its ranks to a uniform and splendid pattern. It is the story, too, of the development of the Scottish soldier.[1] Beginning as a force for the policing of the Scottish Lowlands, the regiment came presently to be a kind of microcosm of the Lowland character, a thing as idiomatically Scottish as the Kirk itself. It remained a product of that ancient Scotland which has endured through all the civil and theological strife—the Scotland of the ballads and the folk-songs, which was neither Covenanting nor Cavalier, Whig nor Tory, but preserved, and still preserves, the tenacious loyalties and the toughness of fibre which come from centuries of poverty and hardly-won freedom.

The Scots Fusilier is a typical Lowland soldier, and the soldier, I venture to think, is the typical Lowlander. It is a curious paradox that a race which sees no sense in war has yet a singular aptitude for it, and that a sober and discerning people can adapt itself to the maddest abnormalities. Scotland has always been a mixture of opposites—prudence and quixotry, thrift and generosity, prose and poetry—and her soldiers have had their full share of these noble contraries. So, indeed, has the English soldier; and the truth seems to be that the Scottish fighting qualities are roughly the same as the English, with substantial differences of accent. Both are at once light-hearted and rather serious. Both have an enormous gift for domesticating war, and casting an air of homeliness over the most hideous and unnatural things. Both have also a stock of elemental passion, which can carry them to epic heights, and both are shy of admitting it. Light-heartedness in war is a Scottish tradition. In the old raiding days the Lindsays were " lichtsom " and the

[1] The Scot is the staple of the regiment, but it must not be forgotten that the regular battalions of the Royal Scots Fusiliers have always had a considerable English and Irish contingent, which mixed admirably with the rest.

Gordons were "gay," and the most scandalous Border baron who ever raided Tyne and Teen was reported to be "of a mirthful visage." Much of this equanimity comes from matter-of-fact common sense. The "auld, cauld, dour, deidly courage," with which Alan Breck credited David Balfour, is often the product of tense nerves and the fatalism which is almost despair. Alan's own kind—the more useful kind—he defined as "just great penetration and knowledge of affairs." War is an infernal world; but there our soldier is, in the inscrutable providence of God, so he makes the best of it. He joins it up with his ordinary life, turns the awful into the commonplace, and thereby strips it of most of its awe. He makes jokes about it—not, as he is sometimes represented, in the feverish style of the music-hall comedian—but simply as he makes jokes at home about his work and his play.

It is an astonishing gift, this, of turning the abnormal into the normal, and it is a crowning proof of sanity and good sense. The poet is supposed to be he who finds sublimity in common things, but there is surely a greatness in the converse power which can make homely things out of terror and imminent death. This matter-of-factness is our national form of bravado —our British *panache*. We deliberately rub all the gloss from war, and refuse to make-believe. We deprecate heroism, and a brave man will take a pride in denying his courage and announcing that before the next campaign he intends to go into the Church. Others may talk, quite honestly, like Hotspur, of "plucking bright honour from the pale-faced moon"; the British way is rather that of Sir John Falstaff—"What is honour? A word! A mere 'scutcheon!" Only we labour to practise it. Moreover, the complete saneness of our fighting men means that they are kindly and merciful, for cruelty is generally the consequence of jangled nerves and a fluttering heart.

Sanity, humour, mercifulness—these are great qualities, and they are in a high degree the qualities of the British soldier. If we look for the distinguishing trait of the Scot, we may find it, perhaps, in what our French allies selected for special praise—his peculiar gusto in attack. There is that in the northern blood which can kindle to a whirlwind vigour, so that quiet citizens find themselves for an hour or two berserkers, and a battalion will utterly astonish itself and its commanders. The traditional *perfervidum ingenium* still counts for much. Said a French gunner officer, whose battery was on the British right at Loos, as he watched the advance of the ex-civilians of the Fifteenth Division: " I don't know what effect these fellows have on the enemy, but for me they make my spine cold."

If the Scots soldier is a type by himself, and the Lowland soldier is also subtly different from the Highlander, so too among Lowlanders the Scots Fusilier has his own characteristics. He is a man of the west and the south-west, notably of Ayrshire and Galloway, sprung from the peasantry of whom Burns sang, and whose kin fought at Drumclog and Bothwell Brig, and died on moor and scaffold for a fine point of spiritual independence. The officers have been drawn largely from a countryside where, in the old conflicts, the gentry and the cottars stood for the same cause. It is a land where Saxon and Celtic race-stocks are evenly mingled, and Galloway was till the other day a province by itself, remote from the rest of Scotland. There is a tradition alive of a strenuous past, when men were called to face great issues, and at the same time of a world not too rigidly ordered, for of Galloway at any rate it used to be said that if you pursued a wrong-doer over all Scotland you lost him at the bridge-end of Dumfries. Such a tradition makes for both the civic and the natural virtues, and is a good soil for the production of soldiers. Hence the Fusilier as we know him; conforming largely to one physical type, stocky, muscular, curiously deep in the chest, wearing on his rugged face an air of ferocious geniality; on the moral side pre-eminent in faithfulness and discipline, but with a gift when occasion requires of bold initiative and desperate inspiration. Officers were always in the closest touch with their men, for the class which produced the one had in the old days been the leaders and allies of the class which produced the other. In the Great War new recruits drawn from every corner of Britain speedily conformed to type; and if the shade of some captain of the old Twenty-First had revisited the lines in France he would have joyfully recognized the same stamp of cheerful desperado whom he had led at Fontenoy.

A regiment is like a good school—a fraternity of human beings in which each man sinks certain self-regarding instincts for the sake of a common purpose, and acquires a share in corporate virtues to which as an individual he could not have attained. It develops in time all the idiosyncrasies of a family. In peace, it is a world by itself, with its own gossip and interests, its special loyalties over and above its fidelity to the King. But in war these ties become a thousandfold more intimate. It is so small and forlorn—a little clan islanded amid great seas of pain and death. The regimental tradition becomes a living thing like a personal memory. Old comradeship in sport and work and the easy friendliness of peace time are transformed into something closer even than friendship. Every communal success becomes an individual triumph, every loss an individual sorrow, so that officers come to feel for their regiment an aching affection—the devotion of " a lover or a child." Thomas Gumble, Monk's chaplain who campaigned with the Coldstream Guards, pauses in the midst of his life of the great Duke of Albemarle to speak of his former companions, and the periwigged style of the reverend doctor has of a sudden a true eloquence. " These Coldstreamers were like the nobles of Israel with whom Deborah was so much in love, and of whom she sings in the Book of Judges, because they offered themselves willingly among the people, and jeopardized their lives unto the death in the high places of the field. They were like the sons of Gad, recorded in the Chronicles, that came to David in his great distress at Ziklag, that went over Jordan in the first month, when it had overflown all its banks, and put to flight all those in the valleys. . . . Such were our brave officers, who made their beds upon the ice, and travelled over mountains of snow to redeem their country. Let posterity celebrate their memory, and let the ages to come call them blessed; and I pray God make them happy, even every particular and private soldier that was among them, and keep them in the way of true religion and virtue. . . . That is all I can do for my old friends, to remember and love them."

Some such feeling as that of Monk's honest chaplain must be in the mind of any one who has known a great regiment and studied its history, and a like prayer on his lips. Regimental devotion is a rare and perfect form of human loyalty. A regimental tradition, such as that which for two and a half centuries the Scots Fusiliers have cherished and put to the test, is not only a vital support of the army of which they are a part, but a heritage beyond price of the country which they serve. *Esto perpetua*—till the trumpet is hung in the hall and wars cease upon earth.

APPENDIX I

SUCCESSION OF COLONELS, LIEUTENANT-COLONELS, AND OFFICERS-COMMANDING

Colonels

	Date of Appointment.
CHARLES, fifth EARL OF MAR	Sept. 23, 1678
THOMAS BUCHAN	July 29, 1686
FRANCIS FERGUS O'FARRELL	March 1, 1689
Hon. ROBERT MACKAY	Nov. 13, 1695
ARCHIBALD ROW	Jan. 1, 1697
JOHN, VISCOUNT MORDAUNT	Aug. 25, 1704
SAMPSON DE LALO	June 26, 1706
JOHN, VISCOUNT MORDAUNT	Sept. 4, 1709
THOMAS MEREDITH	May 1, 1710
CHARLES, fourth EARL OF ORRERY	Dec. 8, 1710
GEORGE MACARTNEY	July 12, 1716
Sir JAMES WOOD	March 9, 1727
JOHN CAMPBELL OF MAMORE (later, third DUKE OF ARGYLL)	Nov. 1, 1738
WILLIAM, EARL OF PANMURE	April 29, 1752
Hon. ALEXANDER MACKAY	May 10, 1770
Hon. JAMES MURRAY	June 5, 1789
JAMES HAMILTON	June 20, 1794
Hon. WILLIAM GORDON of Fyvie	Aug. 6, 1803
JAMES, LORD FORBES	June 1, 1816
The Right Hon. Sir FREDERICK ADAM	May 31, 1843
Sir DE LACY EVANS	Aug. 29, 1853
Sir FREDERICK WILLIAM HAMILTON	Jan. 10, 1870
Field-Marshal Sir FREDERICK PAUL HAINES	Oct. 5, 1890
JOHN THOMAS DALYELL	June 12, 1909
Air Chief-Marshal Sir HUGH M. TRENCHARD, Bart.	July 13, 1919

APPENDIX

1ST BATTALION

Lieutenant-Colonels

	Date of Appointment.
WILLIAM, third EARL OF DALHOUSIE	Sept. 23, 1678
THOMAS BUCHAN	1682
Hon. JOHN BALFOUR	1687
THOMAS DOUGLAS	before 1693
WILLIAM ARROT [1]	Sept. 14, 1693
JOHN DALYELL	May 29, 1695
—— LINDSAY [2]	1702
WALTER SHARP	1706
WILLIAM MURRAY	1710
EDWARD WOLFE	May 24, 1718
JOHN, LORD LESLY (later, EARL OF ROTHES)	Jan. 25, 1721
FRANCIS FLEMING	May 29, 1732
Sir ANDREW AGNEW of Lochnaw, Bart.	Nov. 2, 1739
Hon. CHARLES COLVILLE	Aug. 15, 1746
EDWARD MAXWELL	April 27, 1758
JAMES HAMILTON	March 11, 1774
COLIN GRAHAM	Dec. 5, 1792
THOMAS MEYRICK [3]	Sept. 20, 1794
ANDREW ROSS (Junior Lieutenant-Colonel)	Sept. 1, 1795
JOHN DALGLEISH	Dec. 14, 1796
Lord EVELYN JAMES STUART (Junior Lieutenant-Colonel)	Nov. 7, 1797
LYDE BROWN (Junior Lieutenant-Colonel)	June 25, 1802
DONALD ROBERTSON (Second Lieutenant-Colonel)	Aug. 20, 1803
JOHN WILSON (Junior Lieutenant-Colonel)	Aug. 1, 1804
FREDERICK ADAM (Second Lieutenant-Colonel)	Jan. 5, 1805
WILLIAM PATERSON (Junior Lieutenant-Colonel till 1814)	June 20, 1805
CHARLES WILLIAM MAXWELL (Temporary Lieutenant-Colonel)	June 15, 1815
ROBERT HENRY	Dec. 1815
JOHN MERVIN NOOTH	Jan. 1816
JOHN THOMAS LEAHY	Aug. 24, 1821
JOHN CHARLES HOPE	Dec. 4, 1835
GEORGE WARREN WALKER	Nov. 10, 1837
GEORGE DEARE	Dec. 28, 1838

[1] From Groves. Dalton's Lists, 1661–1714, give: "1689. WILLIAM ARROT, Lieutenant-Colonel in 25th. Left 25th September, 1693."
[2] From Groves. Dalton, 1702–1706, gives no mention of Lindsay in 1702, but has: "LINDSAY, Lieutenant-Colonel, October 1704."
[3] In Army List, senior Lieutenant-Colonel, 21st, till 1814.

APPENDIX

RICHARD TYRRELL ROBERT PATTOUN [1] (Junior Lieutenant-Colonel)	Dec. 5, 1843
JOHN THOMAS HILL [2] (Junior Lieutenant-Colonel)	1847
JOHN CROFTON PEDDIE	Oct. 20, 1848
THOMAS GORE BROWN [3]	March 2, 1849
EDWARD THORPE	June 27, 1851
FREDERICK GEORGE AINSLIE	April 23, 1852
JOHN RAMSAY STUART	Nov. 15, 1854
CHARLES RICHARD SACKVILLE, LORD WEST (Junior Lieutenant-Colonel)	March 9, 1855
JOHN THOMAS DALZELL	April 17, 1867
ALFRED TEMPLEMAN	Jan. 23, 1878
RICHARD WILLIAM CHARLES WINSLOE	July 1, 1881
GEORGE FREDERICK GILDEA	Aug. 1883
EDWARD THOMAS BAINBRIDGE	Aug. 25, 1884
WILLIAM ALBERT BRIDGE	July 1, 1887
EDWARD CHARLES BROWNE	July 1, 1891
J. H. SPURGIN	July 1, 1895
A. H. ABERCROMBIE	July 1, 1899
H. H. SMYTHE	July 1, 1903
ARTHUR B. H. NORTHCOTT	July 1, 1907
WILLIAM DOUGLAS SMITH	July 1, 1911

The Great War : Officers-Commanding

Lieut.-Colonel W. DOUGLAS SMITH	To	Nov. 11, 1914
Major D. H. A. DICK	To	March 24, 1915
Major H. P. DE LA BÈRE	To	April 3, 1915
Lieut.-Colonel D. H. A. DICK	To	June 24, 1915
Captain J. C. WHIGHAM	To	July 4, 1915
Lieut.-Colonel M. E. MCCONAGHEY	To	March 28, 1916
Lieut.-Colonel A. M. H. FORBES	To	March 1917
Lieut.-Colonel L. L. WHEATLEY	To	April 17, 1917
Lieut.-Colonel N. McD. TEACHER	To	Sept. 28, 1917
Major J. M. GILLAT	To	Jan. 1918
Lieut.-Colonel E. I. D. GORDON	To	July 22, 1918
Lieut.-Colonel G. BISSET	To	Oct. 5, 1918
Lieut.-Colonel D. REITZ	To	Jan. 1919
Major A. D. MCINNES SHAW	To	May 26, 1919
Lieut.-Colonel F. E. BUCHANAN	To	July 22, 1922
Lieut.-Colonel O. H. DELANO OSBORNE	To	Feb. 16, 1924
Lieut.-Colonel C. H. I. JACKSON		1924

[1] Groves. Army List gives: "PATTOUN, Major, 1843; DEARE and PATTOUN, Lieutenant-Colonels, 1845; DEARE and PATTOUN, 1846; DEARE and PATTOUN, 1847; DEARE and HILL, 1848–49."
[2] Groves.
[3] Army List: BROWNE.

APPENDIX

2ND BATTALION

Lieutenant-Colonels
(1804–1816)

	Date of Appointment.
WILLIAM PATERSON	June 20, 1805
ROBERT HENRY TOWARDS	1812
Brevet-Lieut.-Colonel ROBERT HENRY [1]	1812

(from 1858)

EDWARD LAST	March 26, 1858
EDWARD WILLIAM DE LANCEY LOWE	Oct. 21, 1859
JAMES ELPHINSTONE ROBERTSON	1862
EDWIN ASHLEY TUCKER STEWARD	April 17, 1868
FREDERICK TORRENS LYSTER	Dec. 24, 1870
WILLIAM POLE COLLINGWOOD [2]	May 23, 1874
GEORGE FREDERICK GILDEA	Aug. 25, 1879
RICHARD WILLIAM CHARLES WINSLOE	Jan. 23, 1884
FREDERICK GEORGE JACKSON	Jan. 23, 1887
JAMES WHITTON	Aug. 25, 1890
ARTHUR J. OSBORNE POLLOCK	Aug. 25, 1894
EDWARD ELLIOT CARR	Aug. 25, 1898
W. A. YOUNG	Aug. 25, 1902
W. H. BOWES	Aug. 25, 1906
D. M. STUART	Aug. 25, 1910

The Great War : Officers-Commanding

Lieut.-Colonel A. G. BAIRD SMITH	Oct. 4, 1914
Lieutenant K. C. THOMSON	Oct. 31, 1914
Captain T. B. TRAILL	Nov. 12, 1914

[1] The Army Lists, where no notice is taken of the 2nd Battalion separately, give the following senior officers :—
1804. Lieutenant-Colonel: THOMAS MEYRICK ; DONALD ROBERTSON. Major : W. PATERSON ; CHARLES DARRAH. Captain : ROBERT HENRY (4th in list).
1805. Lieutenant-Colonel : MEYRICK ; ROBERTSON ; JOHN WILSON. Major : W. PATERSON. Captain : ROBERT HENRY.
1806. Lieutenant-Colonel : MEYRICK ; ADAM ; PATERSON. Major : R. HENRY.
1807–1815. No change.
1815. Lieutenant-Colonel : PATERSON. Major : HENRY ; NORMAN PRINGLE.
1816. Lieutenant-Colonel : PATERSON ; CHARLES W. MAXWELL. Major : HENRY.

[2] Major Hazelrigg, Acting Lieutenant-Colonel, 1879, Collingwood having a brigade in the Zulu War.

APPENDIX

Captain R. Q. Craufurd	Dec. 3, 1914
Major A. M. H. Forbes	Dec. 15, 1914
Major J. H. W. Pollard	Jan. 19, 1915
Captain A. H. Connell	Sept. 22, 1915
Captain R. V. G. Horn	Sept. 28, 1915
Major R. K. Walsh	Oct. 9, 1915
Major M. E. McConaghey	Jan. 24, 1917
Lieut.-Colonel W. L. Campbell	April 26, 1917
Major J. C. Whigham	Sept. 31, 1917
Captain J. E. Utterson-Kelso	Oct. 11, 1917
Major A. King	Oct. 6, 1918
Lieut.-Colonel R. Campbell	Oct. 23, 1918
Lieut.-Colonel C. S. Nairne	Nov. 7, 1918
Major A. King	Feb. 1, 1919
Lieut.-Colonel R. K. Walsh	June 3, 1919
Lieut.-Colonel H. E. R. R. Braine	June 3, 1923

4TH BATTALION

Officers-Commanding

	Date of Appointment.
Lieut.-Colonel S. R. Balfour	Aug. 11, 1914
Captain Harold Thompson	Aug. 16, 1915
Captain H. R. Young	Oct. 1, 1915
Captain J. Bruce	Oct. 6, 1915
Lieut.-Colonel K. H. M. Connal	Oct. 21, 1915
Major J. Alexander	Dec. 25, 1915
Major Harold Thompson	Jan. 15, 1916
Major John Alexander	Sept. 1916
Major H. R. Young	Oct. 13, 1916
Lieut.-Colonel Harold Thompson	Nov. 17, 1916
Major R. Dashwood Tandy	May 4, 1917
Major J. Howard Johnstone	Aug. 1917
Major Henry	Sept. 8, 1917
Major J. W. G. Willison	Sept. 15, 1917
Lieut.-Colonel Gibson	Oct. 18, 1917
Lieut.-Colonel R. G. Maclaine	Nov. 4, 1917
Lieut.-Colonel N. G. Stewart-Richardson	Feb. 1918
Lieut.-Colonel B. Cruddas	June 18, 1918
Major R. Bruce	Sept. 29, 1918
Major Barfoot	Oct. 4, 1918
Major C. Gibb	Oct. 5, 1918
Captain G. H. Mills	Nov. 18, 1918
Major C. Gibb	Dec. 1918

5TH BATTALION

Officers-Commanding

	Date of Appointment.
Lieut. Colonel J. B. McCall	1914
Major Russell	Aug. 1915
Captain J. B. Cook	Aug. 26, 1915
Lieut.-Colonel A. H. Leggett	Oct. 1915
Major J. B. Cook	March 1916
Lieut.-Colonel A. H. Leggett	May 27, 1916
Captain R. W. Paton	Sept. 1, 1916
Lieut.-Colonel A. H. Leggett	Nov. 1, 1916
Major R. W. Paton	March 6, 1917
Lieut.-Colonel O. M. Torkington	March 16, 1917
Lieut.-Colonel J. B. Cook	May 1, 1917
Major R. W. Paton	Nov. 8, 1917
Major H. V. Barstow	Jan. 1918
Lieut.-Colonel R. W. Paton	April 5, 1918
Lieut.-Colonel D. M. Murray Lyon	June 24, 1918
Major W. M. Barfoot	Nov. 1, 1918
Lieut.-Colonel D. M. Murray Lyon	Dec. 1, 1918

6TH BATTALION

Officers-Commanding

	Date of Appointment.
Lieut.-Colonel H. H. Northey	1914
Lieut.-Colonel J. H. Dutton	Oct. 1915
Lieut.-Colonel the Right Hon. W. S. Churchill	Dec. 25, 1915
Captain A. D. Gibb	May 7, 1916

7TH BATTALION

Officers-Commanding

	Date of Appointment.
Lieut.-Colonel D. M. Stuart	1914
Lieut.-Colonel A. H. Allenby	July 1915
Lieut.-Colonel C. S. Henning	Aug. 27, 1915

6/7TH BATTALION

Officers-Commanding

	Date of Appointment.
Lieut.-Colonel J. SCOTT	May 13, 1916
Lieut.-Colonel E. I. D. GORDON	June 25, 1916
Major H. P. HART	Jan. 18, 1918
Major D. M. WILKIE	March 23, 1918

8TH BATTALION

Officers-Commanding

	Date of Appointment.
Lieut.-Colonel H. V. BUNBURY	Sept. 20, 1915
Major F. E. BUCHANAN	Oct. 12, 1915
Captain M. R. DICKSON	July 26, 1916
Lieut.-Colonel F. E. BUCHANAN	Aug. 14, 1916
Major M. R. DICKSON	Jan. 1917
Lieut.-Colonel F. E. BUCHANAN	March 1917
Major M. R. DICKSON	Sept. 1917
Lieut.-Colonel F. E. BUCHANAN	Oct. 1917
Major G. W. G. LINDESAY	Jan. 1918
Major R. W. GEDDES	July 1918
Major G. W. G. LINDESAY	Dec. 1918
Lieut.-Colonel R. W. GEDDES	1919

11TH BATTALION

Officers-Commanding

	Date of Appointment.
Captain C. NORBURY (7th Manchesters)	April 1917
Major H. C. MURDOCH (5th Battalion)	Aug. 1917
Lieut.-Colonel R. P. MACLACHLAN	Jan. 1918
Lieut.-Colonel J. N. DE LA PERRELLE	Aug. 11, 1918
Major A. L. MACMILLAN	Sept. 27, 1918

12TH BATTALION

Officers-Commanding

	Date of Appointment.
Lieut.-Colonel J. D. BOSWELL	Jan. 4, 1917
Lieut.-Colonel LORD DUNGLASS	May 1917
Major W. T. R. HOULDSWORTH	July 24, 1917
Major J. C. KENNEDY	March 1, 1918
Major W. T. R. HOULDSWORTH	April 1, 1918
Lieut.-Colonel J. A. MACDONALD	July 1, 1918
Major J. R. TURNER	Aug. 9, 1918
Major H. A. POLLOCK	Sept. 1918
Lieut.-Colonel J. R. TURNER	Oct. 1918

1691. Private.   1685. Field Officer.   1742. Private (full dress).
1790. Private (full dress).   1812. Private (full dress).

1840. Officers (full dress and undress). 1861. Private (full dress), Officer (undress).
1854. Private (full dress). 1902. Officer (full dress).
1916. Private (service dress).

APPENDIX II

REGIMENTAL VERSE

In this Appendix I have collected a small sheaf of verses about the Royal Scots Fusiliers, which the regiment may be glad to have in a compact form.

I

The first is the ballad of Sir Andrew Agnew's doings at Dettingen. I cannot find out anything about the date or the author.

Attention ! all ye soldier lads who love the Twenty-First,
And hear one of its gallant deeds in homely rhyme rehearsed.
On many a hard-fought field, my lads, its laurels have been won,
And always true are those who wear the number " Twenty-one."

It was when, in the olden time, they served in Germanie,
Against the pride and power of France, and all her chivalry ;
Sir Andrew Agnew at their head, they feared no foreign foe,
But sharp and sure the Frenchmen met, and dealt them blow for blow.

The Frenchmen did not care to face old Scotia's Fusiliers ;
So, on the field of Dettingen, they launched their Cuirassiers,
To charge the stubborn phalanx of the sturdy Twenty-First,
And drive for ever from the earth the corps by them accurst.

As, from the Alps, the avalanche comes thundering to the vale,
So charged the Cuirassiers that day, but never could prevail
To shake the stout battalion that stemmed their wild career,
And baffled them, and turned them back with many a ringing cheer.

Three times they charged upon the square ; as often they rode back
Disordered, to form up again, and yet again attack ;
And then Sir Andrew grimly smiled, and from his square withdrew
A section of its bristling front, to let the French ride through.

Amazement took the Frenchmen then, and laughter loud they raised :
"Are Scotia's Fusiliers now led by a commander crazed ?"
And swiftly once again they charge, and ride straight through the gap,
And then Sir Andrew cannily enclosed them in the trap.

The section once more fills the gap, and loud Sir Andrew's call :
"Square ! Inwards face ! your bayonets will do when fails your ball !"
And so it happened on that day ; the fairest troops of France
Were hemmed in by the Fusiliers, and captured horse and lance.

The battle din was over, and all was hushed and still,
When the General met Sir Andrew, and thanked him with good-will :
"The French got in among your men to-day on yonder plain."
"Quite true, your Grace," said Sir Andrew, "but they *didna get oot again !*"

II

The next is the startling portrait of a Scots Fusilier officer in " The Knight and the Lady," in the *Ingoldsby Legends*.

Close by her side, Sat her kinsman, MacBride,
Her cousin, fourteen times removed—as you'll see
If you look at the Ingoldsby family tree,
In Burke's *Commoners*, Vol. XX., page 53.
All the papers I've read agree, Too, with a pedigree,
Where, among the collateral branches, appears
" Captain Dugald MacBride, Royal Scots Fusiliers " ;
And I doubt if you'd find in the whole of his clan
A more highly intelligent, worthy young man ;—
And there he'd be sitting, While she was a-knitting,
Or hemming, or stitching, or darning, or fitting,
Or putting a " gore," or a " gusset," or " bit " in,
Reading aloud, with a very grave look,
Some very " wise saw " from some very wise book,—
Some such pious divine as St. Thomas Aquinas ;
Or, equally charming, The works of Bellarmine ;
Or else he unravels The " voyages and travels "
Of Hackluytz—(how sadly these Dutch names *do* sully verse !)—
Purchas's, Hawkesworth's, or Lemuel Gulliver's,—
Not to name others, 'mongst whom there are few so
Admired as John Bunyan, and Robinson Crusoe.—
No matter who came, It was always the same,
The Captain was reading aloud to the Dame,
Till, from having gone through half the books on the shelf,
They were almost as wise as Sir Thomas himself.

APPENDIX

III

The following pieces are from *Songs of the Ayrshire Regiment and Other Verses* (Paisley: Alexander Gardner, 1917), by Captain W. F. Templeton, of the 4th Battalion, who, after long service in Gallipoli, Palestine, and France, fell on the eve of victory. The first tells of the fight at Dueidar on Easter Sunday, 1916.

The tidings came from Dueidar, the Fifth are hard at bay,
   But fighting, though the odds are ten to one;
Thank God for other Fusiliers not many miles away,
   Who mean to be in time to share the fun.
It's " See your ammunition's right, your water-bottle full,
   You've got your iron rations, haven't you?
It's seven miles to Dueidar, and heavy road to pull,
   But here's the chance to show what we can do."

     So eastward ho! for Dueidar, and buckle to your work,
       Our mates are fighting hard but falling fast;
     We've many a little argument to settle with the Turk,
       And, thank the Lord, we've got the chance at last.

The Fourth are up at Dueidar, and ready for the kill,
   They scarcely stop a minute for a breath;
The first platoon is racing hell-for-leather up the hill,
   And laughing in the very face of death.
There's half a dozen gallant boys already paid the score,
   For Abdul has of sniping made an art;
But now he's far from easy, for he's seen their kind before,
   And knows they're hard to stop when once they start.

     So cheerio! at Dueidar, and keep your minds at rest,
       The lads from Ayr have done their little bit.
     It's up to us to finish, and we'll do it with the best—
       They trust us, for we've never failed them yet.

There's music in the rifle fire and in the Lewis guns,
   There's magic in the tumult of the fray;
And every blow to Abdul is another to the Huns,
   So let them have it in the neck to-day.
We've rushed them in the centre, and we've got them on the flank,
   The lads from overseas attend the chase;
Let loose the wild Australians—and they've got the Lord to thank
   Whose horses are the fastest in the race.

So on, Light Horse, at Dueidar, for we are tired and sore,
    We've finished what we started out to do ;
We've got our dead to bury and to reckon up the score,
    And know we're safe to leave the rest to you.

Now glory to the dauntless Fifth that held their foes at bay,
    And stood as few but Fusiliers can stand ;
And glory to the gallant Fourth that chased the Turks away,
    And lent their mates in need a helping hand :
And glory to the gay Light Horse, and all the rest who showed
    What sterling stuff the sons of Britain are.
The Turk will not forget us should he ever take the road
    That leads across the hills to Dueidar.

So fare-you-well, O Dueidar, with all your gallant men,
    Keep up your heart and calm your little fears,
And tell your stately palm-trees that should Abdul come again,
    You can always reckon on the Fusiliers.

The following two songs, called " Amenities," give the views of officers and men on each other.

I

The Officers speak

We howled at you, and growled at you, and cursed you out and in,
    We danced you round the barracks square a thousand times a day,
We swore to your proficiency in every sort of sin,
    And worse-than-utter-uselessness in every other way.
Your discipline was rotten, and your drill was past a joke,
    We told you to your faces, and you smothered down a laugh,
But had another dared to even hint the things we spoke,
    We reckon we'd have swallowed him—not half !
For, damn it all ! we're proud of you, in spite of all our cant,
The whole hard-bitten crowd of you, what better could we want ?
For when it's dirty weather, boys, it's one and all together, boys,
Hooray, and hell-for-leather, boys, and at them, Fusiliers !

II

The Men speak

We laughed at you, and chaffed at you, and called you bits o' boys,
    We heard you give a wrong command, and chuckled soft and low ;
We soon had got your sizes, spite of all your blooming noise,
    And labelled you with tickets that your mammies wouldn't know ;

We weren't too respectful when we saved you off parade
  (You weren't there to hear us—we made mighty sure of that),
But had another reg'ment said the half of what we said,
  We reckon we'd have eaten them—eh! what?
For, damn it all! we'd follow you with open eyes or blind,
Were Hell itself to swallow you, you'd find us close behind;
For when it's dirty weather, boys, it's one and all together, boys,
Hooray, and hell-for-leather, boys, and at them, Fusiliers!

"Ypres, October 1914," commemorates that great exploit in the regiment's history.

["We came into the field occupied by the Royal Scots Fusiliers. Here they were drawn up, erect and grim as usual, but what a different regiment from the one which had swung out of Lyndhurst Camp less than five weeks before! That magnificently smart regiment of once a thousand men was now reduced to about seventy men, with a junior subaltern in command. The men were mostly without caps, coats, or even putties, war-stained and ragged, but still full of British pluck and pride, with a 'never say die' look upon their faces, which made the heart swell with pride at being connected with such splendid specimens of manhood."—A British Staff Officer in *Blackwood's Magazine*.]

    Seventy men to the roll-call speak,
      Capless and coatless, tired and torn,
    Grim of visage and gaunt of cheek,
      Earth-stained, blood-stained, battle-worn;
    Aye, but their heads are bravely borne,
      Proud their hearts and their eyes aflame,
    All that were left to greet the morn
      Of a band that won to a deathless fame.

    Like a watercourse, when a dam has burst,
      The shock of the Prussian onslaught fell
    On the hapless ranks of the Twenty-First,
      Hiss of bullet and screech of shell;
    Carnage on carnage, hell on hell!
      Others have given—can they stand the strain?
    What men can do, they have done—and well.
      When shall we look on their like again?

    Hopelessly left when the flanks withdrew,
      Knowing the odds they had to face,
    No one questioned the thing to do,
      Death were easy, but not disgrace;
    One proud thought each heart to brace—
      Life is a matter of deeds, not years,
    Ours is the blood of a fighting race,
      We have lived! Let us die like Fusiliers!

Valour of mortal men were vain,
　Slowly the grey-clad masses close ;
　The last few tired, sore-stricken men
　　Sink at length beneath their blows.
And e'en in the hearts of the Huns arose
　Wonder and praise, as their leader said :
" Never had man such matchless foes :
　　God grant peace to the gallant dead."

　.　　.　　.　　.　　.　　.

" Somebody's blunder—good men lost,"
　Says the arm-chair critic, the would-be wise,
" Availing nothing worth the cost ! "
　God ! what he's failed to realize !
What does it mean, this sacrifice ?
　Reckon it not in life or land,
Look at the pride in the tired, strained eyes
　Of the seventy left—and understand !

Seventy men to the roll-call speak,
　Capless and coatless, tired and torn,
Grim of visage and gaunt of cheek,
　Earth-stained, blood-stained, battle-worn ;
Aye, but their heads are bravely borne,
　Proud their hearts and their eyes aflame,
All that were left to greet the morn
　Of a band that won to a deathless fame.

Lastly, there are the memorial verses on Lieutenant-Colonel Harold Thompson, who fell at the Second Battle of Gaza.

Sound let him sleep in the land where he fought so well,
　With some of his own beside him, those that he led
Like an old-time paladin, such as the legends tell
　Of Arthur or knightly Roland. Now he is dead
Indeed, but his spirit invincible lives to inspire
Those who have known him and fought with him still with its fire.

He was ever a fighter, and joyed in the press of the fray,
　Where even the bravest would falter he cheerfully sped,
Like a schoolboy out for a holiday, smiling and gay,
　To fill with the breath of his valour those that he led ;
And often we thought, as he towered at the head of his men,
'Twere a wonder of wonders if ever we saw him again.

Grim Gallipoli, red with the blood of the brave,
  Jewelled with hearts of heroes, knew him well;
Sinai marked him; Syria holds his grave
  Near where the great strong man of Israel fell:
But his unconquerable spirit no land could hold
Goes with the regiment still as it went of old.

So when the struggle is fierce and the foe is strong,
  When courage and hope are low, let his name be passed
With its vision of splendid valour the line along,
  To thrill the hearts of his men like a trumpet blast,
And hurl them straight at the foe, as he would have done,
Till the last tired man has fallen or the field is won.[1]

IV

I add my own "Fragment of an Ode in Praise of the Royal Scots Fusiliers."[2]

Ye'll a' hae heard tell o' the Fusilier Jocks,
  The famous auld Fusilier Jocks!
    They're as stieve as a stane,
    And as teuch as a bane,
  And as gleg as a pack o' muircocks.
They're maistly as braid as they're lang,
And the Gairman's a pump off the fang
    When he faces the fire in their ee.
    They're no verra bonny,
    I question if ony
  Mair terrible sicht ye could see
Than a charge o' the Fusilier Jocks.
    It gars Hindenburg swear
    "*Gott in Himmel*, nae mair
  O' thae sudden and scan'alous shocks!"
    And the cannon o' Krupp
    Ane and a' they shut up
Like a pentit bit jaick-in-the-box,
  At the rush o' the Fusilier Jocks.

---

[1] The Scots Fusiliers in the Great War had another poet, Lieutenant Robert W. Sterling, of Pembroke College, Oxford, who won the Newdigate Prize in 1914 with the poem, "The Burial of Sophocles," and who fell in France with the 1st Battalion on the evening of St. George's Day, 1915. Extracts from his poems will be found in *For Remembrance: Soldier Poets who have fallen in the War*, by St. John Adcock (Hodder and Stoughton).
[2] *Poems Scots and English.* 1917.

APPENDIX

The Kaiser he says to his son
  (The auld ane that looks like a fox)—
    " I went ower far
    When I stertit this war,
  Forgettin' the Fusilier Jocks.
I could manage the French and Italians and Poles,
The Russians and Tartars and yellow Mongols,
The Serbs and the Belgians, the English and Greeks,
And even the lads that gang wantin' the breeks;
  But what o' thae Fusilier Jocks,
  That stopna for duntin' and knocks?
    They'd rin wi' a yell
    Ower the plainstanes o' Hell;
  They're no men ava—they are rocks!
    They'd gang barefit
    Through the Bottomless Pit,
And they'll tak Berlin in their socks,—
Will thae terrible Fusilier Jocks,
Thae terrible Fusilier Jocks!" . . .

APPENDIX III

REGIMENTAL MUSIC

I HAVE to thank cordially Mr. Alexander W. Inglis for permitting me to reprint his appendix on the regimental music of the Royal Scots Fusiliers, which appeared originally in *The Lowland Scots Regiments* (Maclehose, 1918). I have also to thank in this connection the publishers, Messrs. Maclehose; the Association of Lowland Scots; and the editor of the volume, the Right Hon. Sir Herbert Maxwell, Bart., who was formerly Major and honorary Lieutenant-Colonel of the 3rd Battalion.

(1)   THE SHERIFF'S MARCH.

An old quickstep of the 21st Fusiliers, being the tune known as "The rock and the wee pickle tow." It was called "The Sheriff's March" after Sir Andrew Agnew of Lochnaw, who served thirty-one years in the regiment (1718–1746), and commanded for seven years.

[Musical score: Lively. "Now Sandy, the winter's cauld blasts are awa, And Simmer we've seen the beginning o't; I've lang, lang been wearied o' frost and o' snaw, And"]

sair hae I tired o' the spin-nin' o't. For when we were mar-ried our cleed-in was thin, And poor tith.ye ken, made me ei-dent to spin, 'Twa fain luve o' you that first gart me be-gin, And blessings hae followed the spin-nin' o't

The mornin's was cauld and the keen frost and snaw
  Were blawin', I mind the beginnin' o't,
When ye gae'd to wark, be it frost or be it thaw,
  My task was na less at the spinnin' o't.
But now we've a pantry, baith mickle and fu'
O' ilka thing gude for to gang to the mou',
A barrel o' ale, wi' some maut for to brew,
  To make us forget the beginnin o't.

And when winter comes back wi' the snell hail and rain
  Nae mair I sit doun to the spinnin' o't,
Nor you gang to toil in the cauld fields again,
  As little think o' the beginnin' o't.
O' sheep we hae scores, and o' kye twenty-five.
Far less we hae seen wad made us fu' blyth,
But thrift and industry mak puir folk to thrive,
  A clear proof o' that is the spinnin' o't.

APPENDIX

Although at our marriage our stock was but sma',
And heartless and hard the beginnin' o't,
When ye was engaged the owsen to ca',
And first my young skill tried the spinnin' o't;
But noo we can dress in oor plaidies sae sma'
Fu' neat and fu' clean gang to kirk or to ha',
And look aye sae blythe as the best o' them a',
Sic luck has been at the beginnin' o't.

(2) "THE SCOTS FUSILIERS."

I found this tune in the British Museum [Add. MSS. 29371 f. 63—(271)], where it is simply named the "Scots Fusiliers." It apparently belongs to the eighteenth century, and is suitable either for a slow or a quick march, as it sounds quite well played either fast or slow.

A. W. I.

(3) Quickstep of the 21st Regiment of Foot; date about the latter end of the eighteenth century. I have no knowledge of its history or composer.   A. W. I.

(4) MARCH OF THE 21st REGIMENT OF FOOT.

This is a slow march in its first movement, and in the second movement (marked *Allegretto*) is a quickstep formed from an old tune named in the eighteenth century *This is no my ain house*, but is now entitled *This is no my ain lassie*, in consequence of Burns having written a song with that refrain. It was the regimental march of the old Ayrshire Militia, the title of which was altered in 1860 to "The Royal Ayrshire

Regiment of Militia Rifles," and in 1866 to "The Prince Regent's Royal Regim[ent] of Ayr and Wigtown Militia." In 1881, however, when the regiment was reorgani[sed] as the 4th Battalion Royal Scots Fusiliers, it had to adopt the *British Grenadi[er]* which is assigned as the quickstep of all Fusilier regiments. It is interesting to f[ind] *This is no my ain lassie* as the second movement in an old march of the Scots Fusil[iers] published by Stewart & Co., Edinburgh, between the years 1788 and 1792.

I find that the opening bars of the second strain of the allegretto movement di[ffer] from the usual versions of the air of *This is no my ain house.* They have b[een] borrowed from a variation of the melody introduced by James Oswald in Book xi [of] his *Caledonian Pocket Companion*, published about 1759.

The third movement is a tune which I do not know, and it does not seem to b[e of] much interest.

A. W.

APPENDIX

INDEX

ABERCROMBIE, Lieut.-Colonel A. H., vii., 233.
Acton, Lieut., 214.
Adair, Lieut.-Colonel A. C., vii.
Adam, General Sir Frederick, 146, 148, 153, 154, 155, 156, 157, 158, 161, 196.
Adams, General, 199, 208.
Adamson, Captain C. Y., 455.
Afridis, the, 230, 232.
Agnew, Sir Andrew, of Lochnaw, 83, 84, 90, 91, 95, 96, 99, 100, 101, 102, 103, 104, 108, 109, 224, 471, 472, 479.
Agnew, Major Charles, 84 n.
Agnew, Lieut.-Colonel Quentin, 84 n., 456.
Ainslie, Lieut.-Colonel Frederick George, 193, 194, 195, 196, 210, 211, 214.
Aisne, first battle of the, 291-295.
Aix-la-Chapelle, Treaty of, 113.
Alexander, Lieut. A. C. E., 316.
Allan, 2nd Lieut. J. S., 361.
Allan, 2nd Lieut. L. D., 441.
Allan, 2nd Lieut. M. T., 329.
Allenby, Lieut.-Colonel A. H., 320.
Allenby, General Sir Edmund (Viscount Allenby), 299, 322, 323, 375, 398, 399, 401, 405, 407, 408, 443.
Alma, battle of the, 201-203.
Almanza, battle of, 62, 82.
Ambert, General, 162, 164.
American Revolution, the, 120-129.
Amherst, Lord, 119.
Amiens, Peace of, 145.
Anderson, 2nd Lieut. E. L. L., 310.
Anderson, 2nd Lieut. S. S., 337.
Angus, Earl of, 82.
Antigua, 134, 135, 136, 139, 141, 142.
Appleby, 2nd Lieut., 135.
Argyll, John, second Duke of, 60, 64, 75, 77, 79.
Argyll, John, fourth Duke of, 83, 86, 96, 115.
Armin, General Sixt von, 383, 384, 425, 441.
Armstrong, Lieut. A. B., 177.
Arnold, Benedict, 121, 122, 124.

Arras, battle of, 373-382.
Ashton, 2nd Lieut. R. H., 355.
Astley, Lieut., 214.
Athlone, Earl of, 42.
Atholl, second Earl and first Marquis of, 2, 3, 5, 6, 9.
Atholl, James, second Duke of, 100, 104.
Atholl, William, Duke of (Jacobite), 100.
Atkins, 2nd Lieut. H. L., 355.
Atkinson, 2nd Lieut. J., 438.
Auchinleck, Captain, 245, 249.
Auchmacoy, vii., 16.
Austin, 2nd Lieut. J. C., 337.
Australia, service in, 190-191.

BADAJOZ, battle of, 163, 203, 323.
Baden-Powell, Lieut.-General Sir Robert, 272, 273.
Badham, Lieut., 297.
Baillie, Captain, 277, 278.
Bainbridge, Lieut.-Colonel A. T., 2, 28, 29.
Baird Smith, Lieut.-Colonel A. G., vii., 229, 231, 299, 302, 308.
Balaclava, battle of, 205-206, 223.
Balfour, Lieut.-Colonel J. R., 331, 335.
Balfour, John, of Burley, 11.
Balfourier, General, 350.
Baltimore, attack on, 171-173.
Barbados, 133, 134, 135, 185, 222, 223.
Barnett, Lieut. J., 334.
Barney, Commodore, 168, 169, 170.
Barossa, battle of, 162.
Barrett, Captain C. J. C., 310.
Barrett, Lieut. G. M., 229.
Barton, General G., 256, 258, 260, 267, 268, 269, 272, 274, 275, 278.
Barton, 2nd Lieut. H. W. F., 298.
Bathe, Captain, 142.
Battle Honours, 228, 232, 233, 239, 453 n.
Baum, Colonel, 124.
Bavaria, Elector of, 42, 43, 46, 47, 48, 49, 51, 55.
Baxter, Sergeant, 425.
Bazentin-le-Grand, 351, 352.
Beauharnais, Eugène, 159.
Beck, Lieut.-Colonel E. A., 455.

486 INDEX

Beersheba, 393, 394, 398; capture of, 399, 400.
Belhaven, Lieut.-Colonel Lord, 456.
Belleisle, expedition to, 116–117.
Bellenden, Lieut., 96.
Bellenden, Miss, 83.
Bellewaarde, 319, 322.
Below, General Otto von, 412, 422.
Bemis Heights, battle of, 124–125.
Benson, Lieut. T. B., 316.
Bentinck, Lord William, 156, 157, 158, 159, 191.
Bergen-op-Zoom, attack on, 162, 166.
Berkeley, Lieut. M. B., 438.
Bernadotte, 162.
Bernafay Wood, 350.
Berville, camp of, 140, 141.
Berwick, Duke of, 62, 75.
Bir-el-Dueidar, 363, 364, 473, 474.
Birdwood, F.M. Sir William, 337, 457.
Bisset, Lieut.-Colonel G., 432, 447.
Bizanet, General, 165.
Black, 2nd Lieut. E. C., 346 n.
Black Mountain Expedition, the, 251.
Blackman, Lieut. G. H. W., 355.
Blackwood, Lieut. W. L., 388.
Bladensburg, battle of, 168–171, 196.
Blaine, Captain E. E., 271.
Blair, 2nd Lieut. J., 419.
Blair Castle, siege of, 99–104.
Blenheim, battle of, 50–56, 220.
Blood, General Sir Bindon, 230.
Boldero, Captain G. N., 198 n., 215 n.
Bonaparte, Joseph, 148, 149, 152.
Booth, Lieut., 186, 187, 188, 190 n.
Bosquet, General, 202, 203, 207, 209, 213.
Boswell, Lieut.-General J. D., 393.
Botha, General Louis, 256, 263, 264, 265, 268, 271, 274.
Bothwell Brig, battle of, 2, 12, 13, 460.
Boufflers, Marshal, 27, 29, 30, 33, 37, 42, 43, 65, 67, 70.
Boughey, 2nd Lieut. S. H. P., 406, 407.
Bowes, Brig.-General W. H., 280, 298, 454.
Boycott, Captain C. C., 224 n.
Boyd, 2nd Lieut. John, 426.
Boyd, Captain, 160, 161.
Boyd, Lord. See Erroll, Earl of.
Boyle, 2nd Lieut. E. T. O., 307.
Boyle, Captain the Hon. James, 290, 297, 298, 312.
Boyle, 2nd Lieut. T. H., 361.
Brady, Lieut. Felix, 145, 187.
Brady, Lieut. James, 177.
Braxfield, Lord, 109.
Bridge, Lieut.-Colonel W. A., 228.
Brigades, Infantry (in Great War):—
4th Guards, 427.

1st, 309, 326.
2nd, 325, 326, 454.
6th, 455.
7th, 292, 293, 296, 297.
8th, 292, 293, 296, 298, 310, 343, 351, 361, 377, 379, 382, 389, 390, 454.
9th, 285, 286, 289, 292, 293, 294, 296, 297, 299, 322, 342, 454.
10th, 454.
19th, 289, 290.
20th, 302, 315, 429.
21st, 299, 301, 303, 314, 317, 325, 349, 354, 381, 455.
22nd, 301, 317, 325.
25th, 454.
26th, 324, 325.
27th, 325, 344.
28th, 324, 433, 441, 447.
44th, 326, 327, 328, 377, 380, 385, 387, 388.
45th, 326, 327, 328, 376, 379, 380, 385, 386, 387, 388.
46th, 326, 327, 328, 377, 379, 385, 387, 455.
58th, 455.
76th, 385.
77th, 338, 368, 391, 444, 445.
78th, 369, 444.
79th, 445.
89th, 354.
90th, 344, 349, 354, 387, 416.
92nd, 431.
94th, 411.
100th, 427.
106th, 454.
120th, 424, 425.
155th, 331, 332, 333, 335, 337, 363, 365, 395, 396, 397, 402, 403, 405, 406, 407, 413, 435, 437, 438, 439, 442, 449.
156th, 331, 395, 400, 405, 407, 435, 437, 439, 440, 449, 455.
157th, 332, 333, 402, 436, 440, 449.
176th, 427.
177th, 427.
178th, 431, 454.
229th, 393, 407, 431.
1st Australian, 432.
South African, 428, 429.
Briggs, Lieut.-General Sir C. F., 444.
Briggs, Captain G. C., 293.
Briggs, 2nd Lieut., 201.
Brindley, Lieut. C. S., 364.
British Guiana, 185, 186, 187, 222, 223.
Brock, General Isaac, 167.
Brodie, Captain J., 329.
Bronkhorst Spruit, 244, 248.
Brooke, Colonel, 168, 172, 173.

ns of
INDEX

Brown, Corporal David, 149, 151, 154 n., 157, 168, 171, 178 n., 184, 186, 188.
Brown, General Sir George, 199.
Brown, 2nd Lieut. W. R., 390.
Browne, Lieut.-Colonel E. C., 229.
Browne, Captain G., 297.
Browne, Lieut., 245, 251.
Bruce, General, 133, 134.
Bruce, Captain Thomas, 223.
Bruce, 2nd Lieut., 278.
Bryce, 2nd Lieut., 445.
Buchan, Lieut. Alastair, v., 377, 379.
Buchan, Lieut. George, 16 n.
Buchan, Lieut. James, 16 n.
Buchan, Lieut.-Colonel John, 16 n.
Buchan, Major-General Thomas, vii., 16, 17, 20, 21, 22, 40, 285.
Buchanan, Lieut.-Colonel F. E., vii., 338, 369, 391.
Buik, 2nd Lieut. H. D., 378.
Bulfin, Lieut.-General Sir E. S., 399.
Buller, General Sir Redvers, 238, 240, 254, 255, 257, 258, 259, 261, 263, 265, 266, 267, 268, 271, 274.
Bulteel, 2nd Lieut. John, 166.
Bunbury, Lieut.-Colonel H. V., 338.
Bunker's Hill, battle of, 121.
Burgoyne, General John, 122, 123, 124, 125, 126, 285.
Burgoyne, Major R. M., 303, 304, 305, 306, 308, 309 n.
Burgundy, Duke of, 63.
Burke, Edmund, 120.
Burleigh, 2nd Lieut. F. S., 443.
Burma, service in, 233, 236, 250–251.
Burnet, Bishop, 4.
Burr, Captain F. G., 328.
Burr, Captain, 244.
Butler, General Sir William, 224, 225.
Byng, General the Hon. Sir Julian (Lord Byng of Vimy), 304, 375, 411, 412, 414, 415, 416, 418, 419, 421, 422, 434, 435, 436, 440, 442, 446, 447.

CADOGAN, William, first Earl, 64, 66.
Cairnes, Captain Alexander, 15, 19.
Caithness, James, sixteenth Earl of, 16 n.
Caldwell, Sergeant, 448.
Cambrai, 27, 375, 390, 411, 412, 413, 440, 441, 442.
Cambridge, H.R.H. Duke of, 198, 202, 209, 223, 229.
Cameron, clan, 15, 105, 106 n.
Cameron, Lieut. Angus, 153.
Cameron, 2nd Lieut. J. C., 381.
Cameron, Brevet-Major, 185.
Campbell, clan, 3, 18.
Campbell, Major Alexander, 160, 161.

Campbell, Captain Alexander of Fonab, 39.
Campbell, General Sir Colin (Lord Clyde), 188, 189, 202, 203, 16 n.
Campbell, General Sir John, 119.
Campbell, John, of Manore. See Argyll, fourth Duke of.
Campbell, Lieut.-Colonel R., 447.
Campbell, 2nd Lieut. T. S., 381 n.
Campbell, Lieut.-Colonel W. L., 327, 381, 387.
Campbell, Major-General, 155.
Campbell, Major, 53, 56.
Campbell, Lieut., 48, 56, 95.
Campbell of Glenure, 101.
Canada, 117, 121, 122, 130.
Canal du Nord, the, 436, 437, 438, 440, 441.
Canrobert, Marshal, 204, 214, 217.
Capper, Major-General Sir T., 202, 207, 216, 224, 229.
Cardigan, Lord, 199.
Cardwell reforms, the, 227.
Carey, Captain W. N., 226.
Cargill, Donald, 18.
Carleton, Sir Guy. See Dorchester, Lord.
Carleton, Colonel, 162, 163, 164, 165.
Carman, Lieut. J., 380.
Carr, Lieut.-Colonel E. E., 251, 256, 268, 271, 274, 278, 279.
Carr, Lieut. Ralph, 177.
Cartagena, 84, 133.
Castle Menzies, 99.
Cathcart, General Sir George, 199, 209, 212.
Cavaignac, General, 155.
Cetewayo, 237, 238, 239, 401.
Champion, Major, 185, 187.
Charleroi, battle of, 288.
Charles I., 14.
Charles II., 3, 4, 17.
Charles XII. of Sweden, 98.
Charles Edward, Prince, 96, 97, 98, 99, 100, 102, 105, 107, 108.
Charlottesville, 129.
Charlton, 2nd Lieut. J., 438.
Charno, General, 130.
Chatham, Lord, 114, 115, 117, 120.
Chauvel, Lieut.-General Sir Henry, 399.
Chelmsford, General Lord, 237, 238, 239, 240.
Chetwode, Lieut.-General Sir Philip, 393, 397, 399.
Chisholm, 2nd Lieut. A. E., 322.
Christian, Lieut., 261.
Chrystie, 2nd Lieut. J. A., 310.
Churchill, General Charles, 46, 55.
Churchill, Lieut.-Colonel Winston, 344–346, 377 n.

INDEX

Cintra, Convention of, 128.
Clanranald, the Captain of, 79.
Clarendon, Edward, first Earl of, 4.
Clark, 2nd Lieut. A. S. D., 398.
Clark, Corporal David, 215 n.
Clark, Sergeant James, 171 n., 193, 194, 215 n., 221 n., 243.
Clark-Kennedy, Captain A. D. H., 440.
Clarke, Lieut. S. H., 218.
Claverhouse, John Graham of (Viscount Dundee), 9 n., 11, 13, 14, 17, 25, 75, 79.
Clermont, Prince of, 111.
Clery, Major-General Sir C. F., 255, 256, 263.
Clifford, Lieut., 245.
Clifton, skirmish at, 98.
Clinton, General Sir Henry, 125, 126.
Clive, Lord, 114.
Clutterbuck, 2nd Lieut., 307.
Clyde, Lord. See Campbell, Sir Colin.
Cochrane, Admiral Sir Alexander, 168, 172, 174.
Cochrane, 2nd Lieut. William, 390.
Coignies, Comte de, 45.
Colenso, battle of, 257–262.
Colepepper, Lieut., 140.
Collings, Lieut., 241, 244.
Collingwood, Lieut.-Colonel W. P., 227, 236, 237, 239, 241.
Collins, Corporal Henry, 226.
Colville, Lieut.-Colonel the Hon. Charles, 89, 95, 99, 106, 108, 115.
Colville, Lieut., 96.
Condé, 27, 286.
Congreve, Lieut.-General Sir Walter, 261, 349.
Connaught, H.R.H. the Duchess of, 230.
Connell, Captain A. H., 325, 326, 329.
Conran, Captain William, 154, 175.
Cooke, Major-General George, 163, 165.
Cooke, Lieut.-Colonel J. B., 335, 395, 402, 405.
Cornwallis, General Charles, second Earl, 130.
Corps (in Great War):—
I., 287, 292, 293, 300, 301, 303, 304, 306, 313, 324.
II., 286, 289, 291, 292, 293, 296, 299, 302, 309, 312, 313, 351, 385, 441.
III., 321, 349, 357, 416.
IV., 313, 314, 317, 324, 326, 389, 416, 435, 440.
V., 312, 321, 389, 316.
VI., 322, 375, 389, 416, 435, 437, 440.
VII., 375, 416, 420, 421.
IX., 424.
X., 349.
XII., 338.
XIII., 349, 351.
XIV., 385.
XV., 349, 424.
XVII., 375, 416, 440.
XVIII., 385, 389, 416, 420, 421, 437.
XIX., 385, 416, 441.
XX., 399, 400, 407.
XXI., 399, 401, 404.
Canadian, 435, 437, 440.
Indian, 313, 314, 317, 321.
Covenanters, the, 4, 9, 11, 12, 13, 14, 17, 18.
Cozens-Brooke, Lieut. J. G. S., 298.
Craig, 2nd Lieut. J. M., 399.
Craufurd, Captain, 56.
Craufurd, Lieut.-Colonel R. Q., 309, 456.
Crawford, John, twentieth Earl of, 103.
Crawford, 2nd Lieut. K. C., 438.
Crawford, 2nd Lieut. R. S., 318.
Crawshaw, Captain C. N., 445.
Crealock, Major-General, 239.
Crichton, Lieut. H. C. Maitland-Makgill, vii., 455.
Crimean War, the, 197–220.
Cromdale, battle of, 16.
Cromwell, Oliver, 1, 3, 7, 9, 133, 184.
Cronje, Commandant, 247, 257, 266, 268.
Crosby, 2nd Lieut. Sir William, 166.
Cruddas, Lieut.-Colonel B., 431.
Culloden, battle of, 105–108.
Cumberland, H.R.H. Duke of, 90, 91, 95, 98, 99, 104, 105, 106, 108, 110, 111, 112, 113, 114.
Cunningham, Sir John, 6 n.
Cunningham, Captain S. A., 334.
Currer, 2nd Lieut. T. R., 390.
Currie, Lieut.-General Sir Arthur, 435.
Currie, Lieut., 126.
Cutts, Lieut.-General John, Lord, 52–55.

D'AETH, 2nd Lieut., 245.
Dalgleish, Lieut.-Colonel John, 128, 129, 130, 131, 134, 135, 141, 142, 143, 144.
Dalhousie, James, first Marquis of, 192, 193.
Dalhousie, William, third Earl of, 11, 15.
Dalrymple-Hay, 2nd Lieut., 245, 247.
Dalyell, Lieut.-Colonel John, of Binns, 37, 53, 56.
Dalyell, General Thomas, of Binns, 14, 53.
Dalzell, Lieut.-Colonel John Thomas, 226, 227.
Dannenberg, General, 207, 208, 214.
D'Arco, Count, 47.

INDEX

Dardanelles, campaign in the, 330–38.
Darrah, Captain Nicholas, 136, 142, 166.
D'Artagnan, General, 68.
Deare, Lieut.-Colonel George, 191, 193, 194, 195, 196.
De la Bère, Major H. P., 232, 310, 312.
De Lalo, Colonel Sampson, 61, 70.
Delarey, General, 263, 274.
Delville Wood, 351, 353, 428.
Derby, retreat from, 98.
Derby, Major-General John, nineteenth Earl of, 43.
Despard, 2nd Lieut., 245.
Dettingen, battle of, 83, 86–90, 471.
De Wet, General Christian, 255, 263, 274, 275, 276, 277.
D'Humières, Marshal, 28.
Dick, Lieut.-Colonel D. A., 261, 277, 278, 313.
Divisions, Infantry :—

In Crimean War
First, 198.
Second, 199, 203, 207, 208, 210, 212.
Third, 199.
Fourth, 199, 202, 206, 209, 212, 218.
Light, 199, 203, 207.

In South African War
Second, 266.
Third, 263, 266.
Tenth, 272.

In Great War
Guards, 327, 328, 385, 416, 438.
First, 304, 326.
Second, 303, 317, 321, 416.
Third, 287, 289, 292, 296, 298, 312, 322, 342, 343, 353, 361, 373, 376, 377, 379, 381, 389, 416, 418, 419, 421, 422, 426, 432, 435, 437, 438, 440, 441, 417, 454.
Fourth, 416, 437.
Fifth, 289, 290, 296.
Sixth, 416.
Seventh, 299, 301, 303, 307, 313, 314, 315, 317, 325, 344, 349.
Eighth, 303, 313, 314, 317, 349, 385, 386, 449, 456.
Ninth, 319, 324, 325, 326, 344, 377, 416, 417, 424, 425, 428, 430, 432, 433, 441, 447.
Tenth, 399, 400.
Twelfth, 376, 378.
Fourteenth, 322, 376, 416.
Fifteenth, 319, 324, 326, 327, 328, 346 n., 347, 356, 358, 359, 373, 376, 379, 380, 385, 387, 388, 416, 455, 456, 459,
Sixteenth, 416, 428.
Seventeenth, 379, 416.
Eighteenth, 349, 354, 385, 416.
Nineteenth, 416, 424.
Twentieth, 342, 416, 454, 455.
Twenty-first, 327, 349, 416.
Twenty-second, 444, 454.
Twenty-third, 357.
Twenty-fourth, 385, 416.
Twenty-fifth, 424, 429.
Twenty-sixth, 320, 337, 368, 429, 444, 445.
Twenty-seventh, 312, 318.
Twenty-eighth, 312, 318, 444.
Twenty-ninth, 331, 425, 427, 456.
Thirtieth, 344, 349, 351, 354, 356, 361, 373, 376, 378, 381, 385, 387, 389, 416, 418, 419, 420, 421, 425.
Thirty-first, 425, 427, 431, 441, 448.
Thirty-second, 349, 456.
Thirty-fourth, 349, 357, 416, 424.
Thirty-sixth, 349, 416, 454.
Thirty-seventh, 377, 379.
Thirty-eighth, 385.
Thirty-ninth, 385, 416.
Fortieth, 416, 421, 424, 425, 426, 428.
Forty-first, 455.
Forty-second, 331, 367.
Forty-sixth, 442.
Forty-seventh, 324, 416.
Forty-ninth, 429, 455.
Fiftieth, 416.
Fifty-first, 361, 385, 416, 426, 435, 447.
Fifty-second, 319, 331, 334, 337, 362, 365, 366, 368, 393, 394, 395, 397, 399, 400, 402, 403, 404, 405, 431, 435, 436, 437, 438, 439, 440, 442, 449, 455.
Fifty-third, 394, 395, 397, 399, 400, 401, 407, 408.
Fifty-fourth, 393, 394, 395, 397, 399, 400, 401.
Fifty-fifth, 385, 424, 425.
Fifty-sixth, 376, 416, 435, 436, 454.
Fifty-seventh, 437.
Fifty-eighth, 416.
Fifty-ninth, 416, 418, 419, 421, 427, 431, 435, 441, 448.
Sixtieth, 399, 400, 405, 407.
Sixty-first, 416, 426.
Sixty-third, 416, 437, 440.
Sixty-sixth, 416.
Seventy-fourth, 393, 395, 399, 400, 407, 408, 431.
Seventy-fifth, 399, 401, 404, 405.
Royal Naval, 333.
First Australian, 427.
Second Canadian, 343.

490 INDEX

Dobell, Lieut.-General Sir Charles, 393, 397.
Doiran, 338, 390, 391, 444, 445.
Dominica, 134, 136, 142.
Donaldson, 2nd Lieut. W. D., 397.
Dorchester, Guy, first Lord, 121, 122.
Douai, 27, 375, 446, 449.
Douglas, General the Hon. James, 21, 22.
Douglas, Lieut. J., 56.
Douglas, Lieut. J. H. Scott, 239, 240.
Douglas, Sir Robert, of Glenbervie, 32, 33.
Douglas, Lieut. Stuart Home, 145.
Douglas, Major, 174.
Drocourt–Quéant Switch, the, 374, 375, 378, 436, 437, 438.
Drumclog, battle of, 9, 11, 460.
Duckworth, Admiral, 150.
Duggan, Sergeant M. J., 229.
Dumbarton, George, first Earl of, 18, 21.
Dumouriez, General, 286.
Dunbar, Lieut., 56.
Duncan, 2nd Lieut. G. B., 355.
Duncan, Major-General John, 444, 454.
Dundas, General Francis, 139.
Dundas, Henry, 135, 140.
Dundas, General Thomas, 136, 137, 138, 139.
Dundee, Viscount. See Claverhouse, John Graham of.
Dundonald, Lieut.-General Douglas, twelfth Earl of, 256, 258, 261, 264, 266, 267.
Dunglass, Lieut.-Colonel Lord, 393.
Dunlop, 2nd Lieut. A. H., 401.
Dunlop, Lieut. J., 448.
Dunn, Captain, 244.
Dunne, Captain F. T., 353.
Dunne, General Sir John Hart, 198 $n.$, 200.

Eales White, Captain H. H., 329.
Edward VII., H.M. King, 233.
Egerton, Major-General G. G. A., 331.
Egypt, expedition to, 150–151.
Elandslaagte, battle of, 254.
Elles, Major-General, 230.
Elliot, Lieut., 56.
Elliot, 2nd Lieut., 278.
England, General Sir Richard, 199.
Enver Pasha, 404.
Erroll, James, fifteenth Earl of, 108 $n.$
Erskine, Brig.-General J. F., 331.
Eugene, Prince, 43, 45, 46, 47, 49, 50, 55, 58, 62, 63, 64, 65, 68, 69.
Evans, General Sir de Lacy, 196, 199, 203, 207, 227.
Evelyn, John, 10.
Eyre, General, 199.

Fabeck, General von, 301, 302, 309.
Fairlee, Captain, 56.
Fairley, 2nd Lieut. G., 357, 378.
Falkenhayn, General von, 404.
Falkirk, battle of, 99, 106.
Falls, Captain, 245, 246.
Farley, Captain, 70.
Farmer, Major, 135.
Fawcett, Captain L. G., 401.
Fayolle, General, 420.
Ferguson, Adam, 92 $n.$
Ferguson, Lieut. R. F., 334.
Ferguson, Brig.-General, 52, 54, 56.
Fergusson, General Sir Charles, 312.
Festubert, 299 ; battle of, 317, 318.
" Fifteen," rising of the, 75–79, 82.
Finch, Lieut., 278.
Findlay-Hamilton, Lieut. J. E., 318.
Fischer, Colonel, 155.
Fitzclarence, Brig.-General Charles, 306, 307.
Fleetwood, Captain, 303, 305, 306.
Fleming, Colonel Francis, 82.
Fleming, 2nd Lieut. James, 353.
Foch, Marshal, 420, 423, 430, 433, 434, 438, 442, 447.
Fonblanque, Lieut. John de Grenier, 177.
Fontenoy, battle of, 91, 96.
Forbes, Lieut.-Colonel A. M. H., 233, 289, 298, 309, 311 $n.$, 314, 343, 352.
Forbes, Major Ian, 301, 304.
Forbes, James, seventeenth Lord, 184.
Forfar, Archibald, second Earl of, 79.
Forrest, Major W. T., 396.
Fortescue, Hon. J. W. quoted, vii., 9 $n.$, 10 $n.$, 26, 33, 38, 47 $n.$, 51 $n.$, 52 $n.$, 57, 60 $n.$, 61, 66, 74 $n.$, 80, 93, 95, 115 $n.$, 116 $n.$, 117, 125, 126, 141, 143, 153 $n.$, 154, 155 $n.$, 171 $n.$, 174, 180 $n.$, 181.
" Forty-five," rebellion of the, 83, 97–108.
Fox, Lieut.-General the Hon. H. E., 145, 149, 150, 151, 152.
Frameries, 288, 289.
Fraser, Lieut. H. C., 271.
Fraser, General Simon, 123, 124, 125, 126.
Frederick of Hesse, Prince, 99.
Frederick the Great of Prussia, 84.
Frederikstad, battle of, 275–278.
Freeman, Lieut. A. C. B., 441.
French, F.M. Sir John (Earl of Ypres), 254, 255, 263, 286, 288, 289, 294, 295, 296, 300, 313.
French Revolution, the, 132, 166.
Frere, Sir Bartle, 237.
Frezenberg Ridge, capture of, 385–388.

INDEX

Furlong, Captain Charles, 159, 168, 170, 171, 173, 178 n.
Fusiliers, Royal Scots. See under Royal Scots Fusiliers.

GAISFORD, Brig.-General R. B., 455.
Gallipoli, evacuation of, 336–338. See also under Dardanelles.
Garforth, Captain, 135.
Garioch, Captain William, 15.
Garrett, General, 220.
Garth, Major-General, 134.
Gatacre, Major-General Sir W. F., 255, 256, 257.
Gates, General Horace, 124, 125, 126.
Gaza, first battle of, 293–294 ; second battle of, 394–398 ; capture of, 401.
Geddes, 2nd Lieut. Alexander, 177.
Geddes, 2nd Lieut. A. A. F., 318.
Geddes, Lieut.-Colonel R. W., 445.
Genoa, entry into, 159.
George I., 72.
George II., 84, 85, 86, 87, 89, 90, 99.
Germaine, Lord George (Lord George Sackville), 114 n., 122, 126.
Ghent, Treaty of, 178.
Gibb, Major A. D., 345.
Gibbs, Major-General, 175, 176, 177.
Gildea, Lieut.-Colonel G. F., 228, 236 n., 241, 243, 244, 248, 249, 250, 274.
Gillies, 2nd Lieut. H. G., 362.
Givenchy, 318, 424, 425, 427.
Gladstone, Viscount, 280.
Gladstone, W. G., 198 n., 243, 244.
Glencoe, Massacre of, 39 n., 76.
Glendinning, Captain T. H., 396.
Glengarry, 16.
Gogarty, Colonel H. E., 456.
Goldie, General, 212, 213.
Goodeve, Major L., 319.
Gooding, 2nd Lieut. W. T., 419.
Gordon, General Sir C., 136, 137.
Gordon, Lieut.-Colonel E. I. D., 346, 359, 377, 416, 432, 454.
Gordon, Lord Lewis, 105.
Gordon, General the Hon. William, of Fyvie, 145, 166, 184.
Gordon, Captain, 243.
Gordon, Lieut., 56.
Gordon of Achintoul, 78.
Gordon of Glenbucket, 79.
Gore, Brig.-General, 163, 164, 165.
Gore Brown, Lieut.-Colonel Thomas, 195.
Gortschakov, Prince, 207, 208.
Gosseling, Major-General, 168.
Gough, Lieut.-General Sir Hubert, 324, 360, 361, 385, 414, 415, 416, 418, 419, 420.

Gough, F.M. Hugh, Viscount, 192, 194, 195.
Gracie, Lieut. James, 170, 172.
Graham, Brig.-General Colin, 133 n., 140, 141, 142.
Graham, Quartermaster George, 223.
Graham, Lieut. R. M., 316.
Graham, Sir Thomas. See Lynedoch, Lord.
Grammont, Comte de, 87, 89, 94.
Grandby, Lieut., 135.
Grange, Lord, 7.
Grant, Captain William, 39.
Grant, Captain, 143, 144.
Gray, Major Humphrey, 223.
Greer, Dr., 223, 224.
Grenada, 186.
Greville, Charles, 158.
Grey, Henry, third Earl, 182.
Grey, Viscount, of Fallodon (Sir Edward Grey), 282.
Grey, General Sir Charles, 135, 136, 138, 139, 140.
Grierson, 2nd Lieut. J. L. Hamilton, 350.
Grieve, 2nd Lieut. N. H., 362.
Guadeloupe, 135, 138, 139, 140, 141, 142.
Gudgeon, Lieut. T. W., 146.
Guémappe, 376, 380, 435.
Guillemont, 353, 354, 355, 356, 357.
Gumble, Dr. Thomas, 461.
Gustavus Adolphus, 2, 10, 74.

HACKSTOUN of Rathillet, 11, 12.
Haddon, Captain C. M., 422.
Haig, F.M. Sir Douglas (Earl Haig of Bemersyde), 8 n., 287, 300, 313, 337, 339, 341, 348, 351, 356, 359, 371, 372, 373, 374, 380, 382, 383, 413, 414, 423, 427, 434, 437, 440, 442, 446, 447.
Haines, F.M. Sir F. P., 195, 197, 198, 199, 201, 206, 210, 211, 212, 213, 214, 215, 216, 217, 226, 229.
Haldane, Lieut.-General Sir Aylmer, 312, 323, 375.
Haldane, Viscount, 283.
Hamilton, General Sir Bruce, 279.
Hamilton, Lieut.-Colonel Francis William, 250.
Hamilton, General Sir Frederick, 227, 229, 456 n.
Hamilton, General Sir Ian, 330, 331, 333, 335.
Hamilton, Major-General James, 117, 129 n., 130, 133 n., 142, 145.
Hamilton, Captain J., 365 n.
Hamilton, Major-General, 287, 293, 294, 296, 455.
Hamilton of Bangour, 97

INDEX

Hardinge, 2nd Lieut. the Hon. A., 241.
Harris, Lieut. W. L., 355.
Hart, Major-General A. F., 255, 258, 259, 263, 266, 268, 275.
Hart, Major A. P., 416.
Hawley, General, 99, 106.
Hay, Lord Charles, 94.
Hay, Lieut. F. T., 328.
Hay, Lord John, 60, 83.
Hay, 2nd Lieut. W., 343.
Hazelrigg, Lieut.-Colonel Arthur, 237, 239, 241, 243.
Henderson, Lieut. Angus, 382.
Henderson, Lieut. N. W. A., 310.
Henning, Lieut.-Colonel C. S., 326, 346.
Henry, Lieut.-Colonel Robert, 162, 163, 166, 184.
Hesse-Philipstadt, Prince of, 149.
Hessen-Cassel, Prince of, 66.
Higdon, Sergeant, 212, 216.
Highland Host, the, 5, 6.
Hildyard, Major-General Sir H. J. T., 255, 256, 258, 260, 261, 263, 266, 267.
Hill, Lieut.-Colonel John Thomas, 195 n.
Hill, Lieut., 56.
Hill, Corporal J., 364.
Hill 70, 326–328.
Hindenburg Line, the, 372, 374, 380, 384, 435, 436, 437, 438, 439, 440, 442, 446.
Hochstadt, battle of, 43.
Hodgson, Major-General, 116.
Hohenzollern Redoubt, the, 324, 325, 329, 344, 346 n.
Holstein-Beck, Prince of, 54.
Hope, Lieut.-Colonel John Charles, 191.
Horn, Major R. V. G., 306, 329, 455.
Horne, General Sir Henry (Lord Horne), 349, 375, 415, 435, 436, 437, 440.
Horsford, Colonel, 214.
Houldsworth, Lieut.-Colonel W. T. R., 431.
Houston, Captain W. R., 343.
Houston, Lieut., 95.
How, 2nd Lieut. W. A., 426.
Howard of Effingham, General Lord, 184.
Howe, Richard, first Earl, 121, 122.
Hughes, 2nd Lieut., 318.
Hugues, Victor, 139, 141, 142.
Hull, Major-General Sir A., 230, 271, 454.
Hunter, General Sir Archibald, 272, 273, 274, 280.
Hunter, Corporal David, 439.
Hunter, Corporal W., 272.

Hunter, Captain, 154.
Hurst, 2nd Lieut. S. B., 436.
Hurt, Lieut. H. F. E., 211, 212, 215.
Hurt, Captain S. F. A., 297, 298.
Hutcheon, 2nd Lieut. T., 357.
Hutchison, Captain W. R., 419.
Hutier, General von, 412.
Hutt, 2nd Lieut. E. R., 329.

IMAGE, Lieut. J. G., 218.
India, service in, 191–195, 226, 227, 230–232, 235–236, 250, 251.
Ingoldsby, Brig.-General, 92.
Ingoldsby Legends, the, 472.
Ingram, Lieut. W. W., 315.
Inkerman, battle of, 206–216, 223, 307.
Innes, Captain G. V. D'A., 287.
Innis, Lieut., 116.
Inverness Copse, 310.
Ireland, 4, 82, 84, 130, 144–146, 160–161, 188, 195, 196, 224, 280, 451.
Irving, 2nd Lieut. D. P., 355.
Isaacs, 2nd Lieut. F., 442.
Isandhlwana, battle of, 237.
Ischia, 153.

JACKSON, Andrew, 175, 177.
Jackson, Lieut.-Colonel C. H. I., 456.
Jackson, Lieut.-Colonel F. G., vii., 251.
Jackson, 2nd Lieut. T., 334.
Jackson, Lieut. W., 401.
Jacobitism, 16, 75, 97, 98, 108.
James II., 17, 19, 20, 21, 41.
Janssen, Cornelius, 4.
Jape, Captain, 386, 387.
Jemappes, 286, 287, 288.
Jerusalem, capture of, 407–408.
Jervis, Admiral Sir John (Lord St. Vincent), 135, 136, 138, 140.
Joffre, General, 288, 294.
Johannesburg, 233.
Johnson, Dr., 80, 108.
Johnston, 2nd Lieut. T. M., 362.
Johnston, Lieut., 48.
Johnstone, Captain T. Howard, 334.
Joubert, General, 253.
Joyeuse, Marshal, 30.
Junction Station, 399, 402, 403.

KAFFIR WAR, 18, 51–53, 235.
Katia oases, the, 363, 364, 365, 368.
Kean, 2nd Lieut. J. R., 441.
Keane, Major-General Sir John, 173, 174, 176, 177.
Keith, Major, 33.
Kemmel, 427, 428, 432.
Kennedy, Captain C. N. J., 355.
Kennedy, 2nd Lieut. D. H., 387.
Kennedy, 2nd Lieut. Norman, 390.
Kennedy, Lieut. W. D., 396, 398.
Kenneth, Captain A., 334.

INDEX

Kent, H.R.H. Edward, Duke of, 138.
Keppel, Admiral, 116.
Kerr, 2nd Lieut. J. M., 362.
Kidd, Captain Archibald, 156, 177.
Killeen, 2nd Lieut. Roger, 215 n.
Killiecrankie, battle of, 16 n., 25, 32, 37.
Kilmarnock, William, fourth Earl of, 108 n.
Kilwarden, Lord, 145.
Kinburn, bombardment of, 218, 223.
Kincaid, 2nd Lieut. J. B., 382.
King, Major A., 447.
King, Lieut. H., 215 n.
Kinglake quoted, 206, 213, 214, 216.
Kitchener, F.M. Earl, 263, 275, 278, 283, 319, 336, 456, 457.
Kitchener, General Walter, 269, 270.
Kluck, General von, 286, 288.
Knatchbull, Captain, 96.
Knollis, Lieut., 140.
Knox, Lieut., 135.
Kressenstein, General Kress von, 392, 403.
Kruger, President, 241, 253, 271, 273, 275.
Kruseik, 303, 304, 305.
Kygo, Captain, 48.
Kyle, Lieut. H. G., 334.

LA BASSÉE, 66, 295, 296, 297, 313, 323, 423, 424.
Ladysmith, 254, 256, 261, 264, 266, 267, 268, 270, 271, 272, 279.
Laing's Nek, 244, 251.
Lambart, Captain G. E. O. F., 343.
Lambert, Major-General, 175, 176, 177, 178.
Lambroughton, 2nd Lieut. Hugh, 426.
Landen, battle of, 34, 36, 57, 60 n., 61.
Lanyon, Sir Owen, 244.
Last, Lieut.-Colonel Edward, 235.
Latan, Captain, 96.
Lauder, Private D. Ross, 344.
Lauder, Sir John of Fountainhall, 15, 20.
Lauderdale, first Duke of, 3, 4, 5, 14.
Lauffeld, battle of, 111–113.
Law, Major, 250, 251.
Lawrence, General the Hon. Sir H. A., 337.
Lawson, 2nd Lieut. W., 445.
Le Cateau, 72, 289, 290.
Le Gallais, Captain A. G. L'E, 303, 305, 306.
Leahy, Major, 185, 186, 187, 191.
Lean, Brig.-General Kenneth, 245, 455.
Leavach, Lieut., 172, 176, 177, 183.
Lees, Captain John, 398.

Leggett, Brig.-General A. H., 336, 363, 364, 366, 455.
Legh, Captain W. J. (Lord Newton), 198 n.
Leishman, 2nd Lieut. T., 381.
Lermitte, Lieut. H. J., 244 n.
Lesly, John, Lord. See Rothes, Earl of.
Leuse, battle of, 34.
Lewis, Captain B., 135.
Lewis, Captain V., 271.
Lexington, battle of, 121.
Lille, siege of, 65, 423, 446.
Lindesay, Lieut.-Colonel G. G., 444.
Lindsay, Lieut.-Colonel, 62.
Lindsay, Lieut., 185.
Lindsay, 2nd Lieut., 387.
Lindsell, Lieut., 241, 245, 248.
Linlithgow, Earl of, 5, 10 n., 12.
Linsingen, General von, 309.
Liprandi, General, 205, 207.
Livingstone, Adam, 114.
Livingstone, General Sir Thomas, 16.
Livingstone, Lieut., 89.
Lockhart, 2nd Lieut. R. H., 346 n.
Lockhart, General Sir William, 230, 231, 232.
Lockyer, Commander, 174.
Logan, Captain A., 331.
Logan, Lieut. J., 397, 398.
Logan, 2nd Lieut. J. F., 426.
Longueval, 350, 351, 353.
Lonsdale, Lieut. A. C. G., 316.
Loos, battle of, 321–329.
Losses of Regiment in the Great War, 452.
Lottum, Count, 67, 68, 69.
Louis XIV., 26, 27, 30, 31, 34, 41, 42, 46, 48.
Louis, Prince of Baden, 42, 43, 58, 61.
Lovat, Simon, Lord, 76.
Low, 2nd Lieut. G. A., 441.
Lowe, Lieut.-Colonel Edward de Lancey, 235.
Lowe, Sir Hudson, 152.
Lowther, Captain, 70.
Lucan, General Lord, 199, 202.
Ludendorff, General, 362, 430, 434, 446.
Lumley, General, 54.
Luxemburg, Duc de, 27, 29, 30, 31, 33, 34, 35, 36.
Lyde Brown, Lieut.-Colonel, 145.
Lynedoch, first Lord (Sir Thomas Graham), 9 n., 162, 164, 165, 285.
Lyon, Lieut. C. J., 310.
Lyon, Lieut.-Colonel D. M. Murray, 431.
Lys, battle of the, 423–430.
Lyster, Lieut.-Colonel F. T., 188, 189, 190, 236.

INDEX

Lyttelton, General the Hon. Sir Neville, 255, 256, 258, 259, 263, 267, 268.

McArthur, 2nd Lieut. W. B., 343, 378.
Macartney, Lieut.-General George, 81, 82.
McCall, 2nd Lieut. A. W., 442.
McColl, 2nd Lieut. N. B. W., 334.
McConaghey, Lieut.-Colonel M. E., 261, 343, 381.
McCracken, Lieut.-General Sir F. W., 309, 324, 357, 359.
McCracken, 2nd Lieut. J. H., 390.
Macdonald, Lieut. Donald, 156, 177.
Macdonald, 2nd Lieut. J. V., 427.
Macdonald, Captain John, of Kinlochmoidart, 138, 143 n.
Macdonalds of Clanranald, 107.
Macdonalds of Glengarry, 16, 105, 107.
Macdonalds of Keppoch, 19, 105, 107.
Macdonalds of Sleat, 78.
McEwan, Lieut. J. R. D., 361.
Macfarlane, General, 157.
McGachan, Lieut. C., 135.
McGachan, Captain, 96, 108 n.
Macgregor, Captain A. C. H., 274.
Macgregor, Lieut. R. R., 438.
Macgregor-Whitton, Captain P. W. T., 351.
McHaffie, Major James, 156, 177, 183.
McIndoe, 2nd Lieut. W., 379.
Mackay, Lieut. Angus, 154.
Mackay, Captain Donald, 154.
Mackay, General Hugh, 16, 25, 32.
Mackay, Colonel the Hon. Robert, 37, 38.
McKeevor, Captain L. L., 402.
Mackenzie, Lieut. C. E. G., 302.
Mackenzie, Captain Donald, 166.
Mackenzie, Major-General Fraser, 150.
Mackenzie, Captain Kenneth (of Suddie), 19, 21 n.
Mackenzie, 2nd Lieut. R. P., 398.
Mackenzie, Lieut., 126.
Mackintosh of Borlum, 76.
Maclachlan, Lieut.-Colonel R. P., 431.
Maclaine, Lieut.-Colonel R. G., 402
Maclean, Captain Allan, 121.
McLeod, 2nd Lieut. J., 381.
McMutrie, 2nd Lieut. R. L., 435.
McNab, Lieut. James, 154.
McNaughton, Lieut. W. J., 337.
Macphail, Captain, 369.
Macpherson, Cluny, 101.
McQuaker, 2nd Lieut. G. W., 403.
McQueen, Captain R. R., 346.
Madison, President, 167, 171.
Mafeking, 263, 272.
Magdhaba, 368.
Magersfontein, battle of, 257.

Maguire, Private Patrick, 211.
Maida, battle of, 149, 167.
Mair, Captain W. C., 419.
Malcolm, Admiral, 168, 174.
Malplaquet, battle of, 67–70, 83, 286.
Mangin, General, 433, 434.
Mar, John, second Earl of, 6 n.
Mar, Charles, fifth Earl of, 5, 6, 7, 8 n., 9, 10 n., 15 n., 20, 285.
Mar, John, sixth Earl of, 7, 75–79.
Marlborough, John, first Duke of, 26, 27, 30, 41, 42, 43, 44, 45, 46, 47, 48, 49, 50, 51, 52, 54, 55, 56, 57, 58, 59, 60, 61, 62, 63, 64, 65, 66, 67, 68, 69, 70, 71, 72, 73, 74, 75, 76, 85, 285.
Marne, first battle of the, 290–291; second battle of the, 433.
Marrières Wood, 428.
Marsin, General, 47, 48, 49, 51, 55.
Martinique, 133, 134, 135, 136, 138, 140.
Martinpuich, capture of, 358–360.
Maubeuge, 27, 446.
Maxwell, Lieut.-Colonel C. W., 183.
Maxwell, Lieut.-Colonel Edward, 96, 115, 117.
Maxwell, Sir Herbert, 479.
Maxwell, General Sir John, 363.
Maxwell, 2nd Lieut. J., 334.
Maxwell, Captain Walter, 19.
Maxwell, Lieut., 56.
Menshikov, Prince Alexander, 198, 201, 203.
Mercier, 2nd Lieut. Y. W., 322.
Meredith, Colonel Thomas, 71.
Merson, Lieut. M., 382.
Messines, battle of, 383.
Metaxa, Lieut., 271.
Meteren, capture of, 432–433.
Methuen, F.M. Lord, 255, 256, 257, 258, 272, 274, 275, 276.
Meyer, General Lucas, 254, 263, 271.
Meyrick, Lieut.-Colonel Thomas, 141, 143, 144 n.
Middleton, John, first Earl of, 4, 14.
Miguel, Dom, 189, 190.
Mill, 2nd Lieut. W. H., 334.
Millar, Captain G. C., 436.
Milne, General Sir George, 390, 391, 444.
Minden, battle of, 116, 122.
Mitchell, Lieut. A. N., 337.
Mœuvres, 439, 440.
Moffat, Lieut. J. L., 316.
Mohammed Ali, 151.
Monchy-le-Preux, 376, 378, 379, 380, 382, 435, 436.
Monk, George, Duke of Albemarle, 1, 2, 3, 461.
Monmouth, Duke of, 12, 13, 14, 17.

INDEX

Monro, General Sir Charles, 336.
Monroe, Captain, 70.
Mons, 32, 70, 286, 449.
Montagu, Lady Mary Wortley, 7.
Montauban, capture of, 349-350.
Montgomery, 2nd Lieut. Robert, 442.
Montresor, General, 159.
Montressor, Captain, 70.
Montrose, James, first Marquis of, 3, 75.
Montserrat, 136.
Moody, 2nd Lieut. John, 166.
Moore, General Sir John, 131, 144, 149, 151, 152, 156, 167, 182, 188 n.
Mordaunt, John, Viscount, 56, 61, 71.
Morgan, General, 125, 175, 176.
Morland, Lieut.-General Sir T. L. N., 349.
Mormal, Forest of, 289, 446.
Morres, Lieut. the Hon. Francis, 166.
Morrice, Colonel, 163, 164.
Morrison, 2nd Lieut. A. V., 355.
Moyna, Captain E. G. J., 328.
Munro, Sir George, 4.
Murat, 152, 153, 155, 158.
Murphy, Sergeant T., 333.
Murray, Lieut.-General Sir Archibald, 363, 365, 392, 393, 397, 398.
Murray, Lieut. A. H. P., 378.
Murray, Lord George, 98, 100, 101, 102, 103, 105, 106, 107.
Murray, General the Hon. James, 130, 142.
Murray, General Sir John, 157.
Murray, 2nd Lieut. J., 419.
Murray, Captain R. A., 445.
Murray, Lieut.-Colonel William, 71, 82.
Murray, Lieut., 355.

Napier, Lieut. Lord, 128.
Naples, Queen Caroline of, 149, 154, 158.
Napoleon, 128, 132, 146, 148, 149, 150, 151, 157, 159, 167, 183, 198, 309.
Neate, Lieut., 135.
Nelson, Horatio, Lord, 146.
Ness, Lieut., 95, 310.
Neuve Chapelle, battle of, 313-317, 320, 410.
New Orleans, attack on, 174-178.
Newbigging, Lieut. A. T., 382.
Newdigate, Major-General, 239, 240, 241.
Nichol, Captain John, 343.
Nightingale, Florence, 217, 219.
Nimmo, Lieut. S. H., 445.
Nisbet, 2nd Lieut. J. A., 441.
Nivelle, General, 372, 373, 380.
Noailles, Duc de, 86, 87, 94.
Nodding, William, 65.

Nooth, Lieut.-Colonel J. M., 184, 185, 186, 188.
North, Lieut., 231.
Northcott, Lieut.-Colonel A. B. H., 233.
Northey, Lieut.-Colonel H. H., 261, 319, 325, 329.
Nova Scotia, 130, 131.

Oatts, 2nd Lieut. E. P., 382.
O'Farrell, Colonel Francis, 22, 26 n., 28, 33, 37.
Offley, Captain, 135.
Ogilvy, Lord, 105.
Ogilvy, Lieut., 56.
Oliphant, Captain, 96.
Oliver Ellis, by James Grant, 143 n.
Omar Pasha, 198.
O'Neil, Captain, 108 n.
Onraet, Lieut., 271.
Orange, Prince of, 68, 69.
Orkney, General the Earl of, 59, 60, 61, 66, 67, 69, 70.
Ormonde, second Duke of, 71.
Orr, Captain J. B., 387.
Orrery, Charles, fourth Earl of, 71, 81.
Oudenarde, battle of, 63, 64, 111.

Paardekraal, 244.
Pakenham, Major-General Sir Edward, 175, 176 n., 177.
Panmure, William, first Earl of, 115, 117.
Paris, Peace of, 218.
Partonneaux, General, 153, 154.
Paterson, Lieut.-Colonel William, 146, 147, 161, 167, 170, 171, 172, 177.
Paton, 2nd Lieut. R., 447.
Paton, Lieut.-Colonel R. W., 398, 406.
Paton, Captain T. V., 346.
Patterson, Captain, 226.
Pattoun, Lieut.-Colonel R. T. R., 195 n.
Paulet, General Lord William, 223.
Paulov, General, 207, 208.
Peddie, Lieut.-Colonel J. C., 195.
Pedro, Dom, 189, 190.
Pélissier, General, 217.
Peninsular War, the, 143, 155, 157-158, 167, 170, 198.
Penn Symons, General Sir W., 254.
Pennecuik, Alexander, 8 n.
Pennefather, General Sir John, 199, 207, 210, 214, 216, 220, 221, 222.
Péronne, 415.
Pétain, Marshal, 388, 413.
Petter, Lieut. H. R., 382.
Pieter's Hill, battle of, 267-271.
Pigou, Lieut. Henry, 166.
Pirie, Captain W. S., 398.
Pitt, William, 132, 133, 147, 148.

INDEX

Plumer, F.M. Sir Herbert (Lord Plumer), 272, 312, 415, 441.
Poezelhoek, 301.
Pollard, Major-General J. H. W., 308, 309, 314, 325, 454.
Pollock, Lieut.-Colonel A. J. O., 251.
Pollock, Captain M. K., 322.
Pollok-McCall, Lieut.-Colonel J. B., 331, 335.
Polygon Wood, the, 302, 318.
Ponsonby, Major-General John, 426.
Pooley, 2nd Lieut. R. S., 381 n.
Pope, Alexander, 11 n.
Potchefstroom, 244, 245–248, 274.
Prendergast, General Sir H., 250.
Prescott, General, 142.
Preston, battle of, 76.
Prestonpans, battle of, 96, 106, 117.
Pretender, the Old, 62, 75, 97.
Pretoria, 243, 244, 248–249, 274, 275, 280.
Price, Lieut., 140.
Primrose, Lieut., 56.
Pringle, Captain Norman, 151 n., 152, 157, 158, 175, 178.
Proby, General Lord, 163, 164.
Pulteney, Lieut.-General Sir W. P., 349.
Purves, Captain G. G. de B., 329.

QUAAST, General von, 424, 425, 427.
Quin, Major Peter, 177, 183.

RACINE, 30.
Rafa, 368.
Raglan, Lord, 198, 201, 203, 217, 285.
Ramage, Lieut., 116.
Ramillies, battle of, 58–60, 83.
Ramsay, Brig.-General George, 29, 34, 39.
Ramsay, Captain the Hon. Malcolm, 126.
Rand, strike on the, 233–234.
Rankine, 2nd Lieut. David, 166.
Ravenhill, Private C., 262.
Ravenhill, Lieut.-Colonel H. S., 457 n.
Rawlinson, General Sir Henry (Lord Rawlinson), 295, 299, 300, 307, 324, 356, 359, 435, 437, 442, 446, 447.
Regiments—British Cavalry :—
Life Guards, 1, 2, 87.
Royal Horse Guards, 1, 11, 87, 88.
1st Dragoon Guards (King's), 87, 239.
2nd Dragoon Guards, 71.
4th Dragoon Guards, 199.
5th Dragoon Guards, 199.
6th Dragoon Guards, 82.
7th Dragoon Guards, 87.
1st Dragoons (Royals), 2, 87, 88, 199.
2nd Dragoons (Scots Greys), 47, 55, 60, 78, 82, 83, 87, 111, 112, 117, 201.
3rd Dragoons (now Hussars), 78, 87, 88.
4th Dragoons (now Hussars), 78, 87, 111, 199.
6th Dragoons (Inniskillings), 78, 87, 111, 112, 199.
7th Hussars, 87, 88, 111.
8th Hussars, 199.
11th Hussars, 199, 201.
13th Dragoons (now Hussars), 199.
14th Dragoons (now Hussars), 174.
20th Dragoons (now Hussars), 155.
17th Lancers, 199, 240.
Cumberland's Dragoons, 111, 112.
Essex's Dragoons, 71 n.
Regiments—British Infantry :—
Guards 2, 47 n., 48, 52 n., 53, 69, 82, 92–94, 111–115, 163–165, 199, 202–208, 315, 422.
1st (Royal Scots), 2, 18, 20, 29, 31–38, 43, 47 n., 52 n., 69, 82, 92, 162–165, 199, 323, 346, 352–359, 377–379, 380–389, 447.
2nd (Royal West Surrey), 2, 25, 260.
3rd (Buffs), 2, 35, 45, 52 n., 60, 78, 87, 92, 111.
4th (Royal Lancashire), 35, 106, 111, 168, 170–176, 195.
5th (Northumberland Fusiliers), 286, 293–298, 310.
6th (Royal Warwicks), 455.
7th (Royal Fusiliers), 19 n., 62 n., 175–176, 184–185, 199, 209, 286–289, 291–293, 310.
8th (Liverpools), 52 n., 78, 79, 87, 92.
9th (Norfolks), 116 n., 121–124.
10th (Lincolns), 43, 52 n., 53, 291–298.
11th (Devons), 78–79, 87, 92, 261.
12th (Suffolks), 87, 89, 92, 95.
13th (Somerset L. I.), 87, 92, 111.
14th (West Yorks), 78.
15th (East Yorks), 52 n., 133 n., 142, 343, 352, 389.
16th (Bedfords), 38, 43, 52 n., 65 n., 133 n., 299, 420.
17th (Leicesters), 78.
18th (Royal Irish), 65 n., 69.
19th (Yorks), 92, 111, 116 n., 199, 299, 301–303.
20th (Lancaster Fusiliers), 52 n., 87, 92, 121–126, 130, 199.
21st. See under Royal Scots Fusiliers.
22nd (Cheshires), 26 n.

INDEX

23rd (Royal Welch Fusiliers), 45, 47 *n.*, 52 *n.*, 53, 65 *n.*, 78, 87–89, 92–95, 111–112, 199, 275–278, 304.
24th (South Wales Borderers), 45, 52 *n.*, 53, 65 *n.*, 121.
25th (King's Own Scottish Borderers), 34, 78, 82, 92, 111–117, 332–336, 344, 359, 366, 395–396, 403, 431–439.
26th and 90th (Scottish Rifles), 9 *n.*, 29, 32–35, 43, 52 *n.*, 346, 359, 428, 444.
27th (Inniskilling Fusiliers), 151 *n.*
28th and 61st (Gloucesters), 61, 92, 199.
29th and 36th (Worcesters), 111, 168, 306, 434, 456.
30th and 59th (East Lancs), 116 *n.*, 143, 199.
31st and 70th (East Surrey), 87, 92.
32nd and 46th (Duke of Cornwall's L. I.), 87–88, 92, 111, 133–135, 199.
33rd and 76th (West Riding), 92, 111, 163, 199.
34th and 55th (Border), 92, 116 *n.*, 121, 163–165, 199.
35th (Royal Sussex), 152.
37th and 67th (Hampshires), 47 *n.*, 52 *n.*, 87, 111, 116 *n.*, 117, 135, 162.
38th and 80th (South Staffords), 199.
40th and 82nd (South Lancs), 135.
41st and 69th (Welch), 115, 116 *n.*, 163–165, 195, 199.
42nd and 73rd (Black Watch), 3, 92, 199, 444.
43rd and 52nd (Oxford L. I.), 175–176.
44th and 56th (Essex), 162, 168, 170–176, 199.
47th and 81st (North Lancs), 121, 199, 307.
48th and 58th (Northants), 111, 151 *n.*, 240.
49th and 66th (Royal Berks), 199, 213–214.
50th and 97th (Royal West Kent), 199.
53rd and 85th (Shropshire L. I.), 121, 145, 168, 170, 176, 352, 389.
57th and 77th (Middlesex), 199, 212–214, 454.
60th (K.R.R.), 145.
62nd and 99th (Wilts), 121–126, 143 *n.*, 151, 168, 293–299, 302.
63rd and 96th (Manchester), 199, 210–212, 349, 354–355, 387.
(2,625)

65th and 84th (York and Lancaster), 133.
68th (Durham L. I.), 199, 212.
71st and 74th (Highland Light Infantry), 357–359, 424, 439, 449.
75th and 92nd (Gordon Highlanders), 251, 304 *n.*, 323.
79th (Cameron Highlanders), 199, 318, 327, 357–359, 377–379, 385.
83rd and 86th (Royal Irish Rifles), 293.
87th and 89th (Royal Irish Fusiliers), 267–268, 270.
88th and 94th (Connaught Rangers), 199.
91st and 93rd (Argyll and Sutherland Highlanders), 162, 174–176, 199, 346, 359, 377, 380–387, 444.
94th (Highlanders), 240–248.
95th (Rifle Brigade), 174–176, 191, 199, 212–214.
102nd and 103rd (Royal Dublin Fusiliers), 268, 270.
West India Regiment, 176, 235.

Argyll Regiment, 39, 99, 101.
Barrel's Regiment. See 4th Foot.
Ferguson's Regiment, 39.
Grey's Regiment, 116 *n.*
Hamilton's Regiment, 131.
Loudon's Highlanders, 117.
Morgan's Regiment, 116 *n.*
Pulteney's Regiment, 107.
Strathnaver's Regiment, 38 *n.*, 83.
Stuart's Regiment, 116 *n.*
Temple's Regiment, 82.
Tullibardine's Regiment, 39.
Regiments—French :—
Bourbonnois, 32, 68.
Champagne, 68.
Chartres, 32.
Maison du Roi, 58, 59, 64, 68.
Navarre, 68, 69.
Orleans, 32.
Picardie, 60, 68.
Royal Irish, 68, 69.
Reid, Private J., 315.
Reitz, Lieut.-Colonel D., 447.
Renny, Major Robert, 170, 172, 176, 177.
Rhodes, Cecil, 255.
Richard Cœur-de-Lion, 402, 415.
Richardson, Lieut., 126.
Riddell, 2nd Lieut. W., 429.
Riedesel, General, 124.
Rob Roy, 79.
Roberts, F.M. Earl, 263, 266, 272, 274, 275, 285.
Roberts, Captain F., 363, 364.
Roberts, Lieut. the Hon. F. S., 261.
Robertson, Lieut.-Colonel David, 456.

32

498 INDEX

Robertson, Lieut.-Colonel Sir Donald, 456.
Robertson, Major Donald, 145.
Robertson, Captain G., 329.
Robertson, Sergeant Isaac, 154.
Robertson, Lieut.-Colonel J. E., 235, 236.
Robertson, 2nd Lieut. N. W., 438.
Robertson, Major, 152.
Robertson, Lieut., 126.
Rochambeau, 135, 137.
Romani, battle of, 365-367.
Romer, Major-General C. F., 421.
Roos-Keppel, Sir George, 456-457.
Roper, Major, 212.
Rorke's Drift, 237, 239.
Rose, Captain T. A., 287, 288.
Ross, Lord, 12.
Ross, Major Alexander, 173, 177.
Ross, Lieut.-Colonel Andrew, 144 n.
Ross, 2nd Lieut. J. H., 398.
Ross, 2nd Lieut. R. T., 442.
Ross, General Robert (of Bladensburg), 167, 168, 169, 170, 171, 172, 285.
Ross, Major, 156, 157.
Ross-Thomson, Lieut. A., 310.
Rothes, John, ninth Earl of, 82.
Roxburgh, Captain J., 329.
Roxburgh, Lieut. J. W., 397.
Row, Brig.-General Archibald, 38, 42, 45, 52, 53, 56.
Royal Scots Fusiliers, the :—
Formation as Mar's Regiment, 6, 7 ; first equipment, 9, 10 ; strife with the Covenanters, 11-20 ; the Highland companies, 15, 19, 21 n., 39 ; the Revolution of 1688, 21, 22 ; first campaign in Flanders, 23-39 ; battle of Steenkirk, 31-33 ; battle of Landen, 34-36 ; service under Marlborough, 41-72 ; battle of Blenheim, 50-56 ; battle of Ramillies, 58-60 ; battle of Oudenarde, 63-64 ; battle of Malplaquet, 67-70 ; return to Scotland, 72 ; the rising of the "Fifteen," 75 ; battle of Sheriffmuir, 77-79 ; service at home, 79-84 ; battle of Dettingen, 86-90 ; battle of Fontenoy, 92-96 ; the rising of the "Forty-five," 97-109 ; the defence of Blair Castle, 100-104 ; battle of Culloden, 105-108 ; battle of Lauffeld, 111-113 ; Gibraltar, 114-115 ; the siege of Belleisle, 116-117 ; service in America, 121-127 ; surrender at Saratoga, 126 ; service at home, 129-130 ; Nova Scotia, 131 ; service in West Indies, 133-143 ; capture of Martinique, 137 ; capture of Guadeloupe, 139-141 ; service at home, 143-146 ; 1st Battalion in Sicily, Egypt, and the Peninsula, 148-159 ; 2nd Battalion (1804-16)—the Boyd-Campbell duel, 160-161 ; the attack of the 2nd Battalion at Bergen-op-Zoom, 162-166 , the 2nd Battalion disbanded, 166 ; 1st Battalion in America, 166-178 ; battle of Bladensburg, 169-170 ; taking of Washington, 171 ; attack on Baltimore, 173 ; expedition to New Orleans, 174-178 ; the regiment during the long peace, 179-196 ; change in position and equipment of the soldier, 180-183 ; service in France, 183-184 ; service in the West Indies, 185-188 ; the Demerara Rising, 187 ; the "Scots Fusiliers" in Portugal, 188-190 ; service in Australia, 190-191 ; first service in India, 191-195 ; George Deare, 193-194 ; the Crimean War, 197-220 ; the landing in the Crimea, 199 ; battle of the Alma, 201-203 ; battle of Balaclava, 205-206 ; battle of Inkerman, 207-216 ; siege of Sebastopol, 216-220 ; formation of 2nd Battalion (1858), 221 ; 1st Battalion in Malta, 221-222 ; 1st Battalion in the West Indies, 223 ; Ramsay Stuart, 224-225 ; the Caldwell Reforms, 227-228 ; the Tirah Campaign, 230-232 ; the strike on the Rand, 233 ; 2nd Battalion in India, 236 ; the Zulu War, 237-241 ; the war with Sikukuni, 243 ; the first Transvaal War, 244-249 ; defence of Potchefstroom, 245-248 ; defence of Pretoria, 248-249 ; defence of Rustenburg, 249 ; service in Burma, 250-251 ; 2nd Battalion in the South African War, 253-280 ; battle of Colenso, 257-262 ; Spion Kop, 264-265 ; Vaal Kranz, 265 ; the crossing of the Tugela, 266-268 ; Pieter's Hill, 269-270 ; relief of Ladysmith, 271 ; relief of Mafeking, 272 ; entry into the Transvaal, 273-274 ; battle of Frederikstad, 275-278 ; return to England, 280.

The Great War :—

1st Battalion

Retreat from Mons, 286-288 ; battle of Le Cateau, 289 ; first battle of the Marne, 291 ; first battle of the Aisne, 292-295 ; march to the sea, 295-296 ; the fighting at La Bassée, 297-299 ; the attack of the Prussian

INDEX

Guard, 309–310 ; the second battle of Ypres, 318–319 ; in battle of September 25, 1915, 322–323 ; fighting at St. Eloi, 342–343 ; Bazentin-le-Grand, 352–353 ; battle of the Ancre, 361 ; battle of Arras, 377–378, 379–380, 381, 382 ; third Ypres, 389–390 ; retreat from St. Quentin, 422 ; battle of the Lys, 426, 427 ; advance to victory, 435, 438, 440, 447.

2nd Battalion

Retreat from Antwerp, 299 ; first battle of Ypres, 300–309 ; defence of the Kruseik Ridge, 303–307 ; battle of Neuve Chapelle, 314–317 ; battle of Festubert, 317–318 ; battle of Loos, 325, 326, 329 ; battle of the Somme, 349 ; capture of Montauban, 350 ; Guillemont, 354–356 ; battle of Arras, 378–381 ; third Ypres, 387 ; retreat from St. Quentin, 419, 420, 421 ; battle of the Lys, 424, 425 ; fighting at Kemmel, 428, 429 ; capture of Meteren, 432, 433 ; advance to victory, 441, 447.

4th Battalion

In Gallipoli, 331–338 ; Bir el Dueidar, 363–364 ; Romani, 367, 368 ; second battle of Gaza, 394–398 ; advance on Jerusalem, 400–406 ; El Burj, 406 ; arrival in France, 431 , advance to victory, 435, 436, 437, 438, 439, 440, 441, 442, 449.

5th Battalion

In Gallipoli, 331–338 ; Bir el Dueidar, 363–364 ; Romani, 367, 368 ; second battle of Gaza, 394–398 ; advance on Jerusalem, 400–406 ; crossing of the Auja, 407 ; arrival in France, 431 ; advance to victory, 435, 436, 437, 438, 439, 440, 441, 442, 449.

6th Battalion

Battle of Loos, 325–329 ; merged with the 7th Battalion, 346.

7th Battalion

Battle of Loos, 326–329 ; Hohenzollern Redoubt, 346 n.

6/7th Battalion

The taking of Martinpuich, 357–360 ; the autumn on the Somme, 360 ; battle of Arras, 376–377, 379, 380–381 ; third Ypres, 385, 386, 387, 388, 389 ; retreat from St. Quentin, 418, 419 ; battle of the Lys, 427, 428 ; battalion disbanded, 428.

8th Battalion

Lands at Salonika, 338 ; Salonika in 1916, 369 ; Doiran battle, 391 ; battle of September 18, 1918, 445 ; enters Bulgaria, 446.

11th Battalion

Arrives in France, 431 ; advance to victory, 441, 448.

12th Battalion

Formation, 393 ; advance on Jerusalem, 399, 401, 407 ; arrival in France, 431 ; advance to victory, 448.
Royal Scots Fusiliers (Volunteer battalions), 284 n.
Rullion Green, battle of, 2.
Rumbold, Lieut., 261.
Rundle, General Sir Leslie, 247, 248.
Russell, Major J., 335.
Rustenburg, 244 ; defence of, 249.
Rutherford, Sergeant, 212.
Ryswick, Treaty of, 38.

St. Arnaud, Marshal, 198, 201.
St. Domingo, 135.
St. Eloi, 342.
St. Kitts, 136, 139, 141.
St. Leger, Colonel, 123, 124.
St. Lucia, 135, 138.
St. Quentin, 290, 414, 415, 416, 417–423, 425, 440, 442.
St. Vincent, 186, 187, 223.
Salamanca, battle of, 167.
Salonika Campaign, the, 338–339, 368–369, 390–392, 443–446.
Sandby, Lieut., 135.
Sandilands, Captain Andrew, 96.
Saratoga, surrender at, 125–127, 307.
Sarrail, General, 338, 358, 369, 391, 443.
Saxe, Marshal, 90, 91, 92, 94, 110, 111.
Saye and Sele, Lieut.-Colonel Lord, 457 n.
Scandrett, 2nd Lieut., 346.
Scarlett, General, 199.
Scheldt Canal, crossing of the, 442.
Schellenberg, battle of the, 47–48, 53, 55, 56.
Scholefield, Captain, 260.
Schulemberg, 67, 68, 69.
Schuyler, General, 123, 124.
Scilla, 149, 151, 152, 154, 155, 156.

INDEX

Scots Brigade in Holland, 30, 37, 60 n., 69.
Scott, 2nd Lieut. D., 374.
Scott, Captain Francis, 29.
Scott, 2nd Lieut. J. R., 353.
Scott, Sir Walter, 14, 107 n., 109.
Scott Moncrieff, Brig.-General W., 331.
Scudamore, Brig.-General C. P., 251, 272, 454, 455.
Sebastopol, siege of, 203, 219.
Sergeant, Lieut., 95.
Seymour, Sergeant, 219.
Sharp, Lieut.-Colonel Walter, 62.
Shaw, Charles, 189, 190.
Shaw, Sir John, of Greenock, 18.
Shea, Lieut.-General Sir J. S. M., 356.
Shearer, 2nd Lieut. G. S., 328.
Shelley, P. B., 186.
Sherbrooke, Major-General, 151, 152.
Sheriffmuir, battle of, 77–79, 83, 99.
Sherriff, 2nd Lieut., 419.
Shortt, Captain F. de S., 232.
Shutt, Lieut. H. C., 363.
Sicily, service in, 148–159.
Sikukuni, 237, 241, 242.
Sampson, Lieut., 271.
Sinclair, 2nd Lieut. E. A., 381 n.
Skeil, Lieut.-Colonel A. P., 451.
Skerrett, Major-General, 163, 164, 165.
Skipwith, Major, 327 n., 328.
Slezer, John, 10.
Smith, Major A. C. H., 346.
Smith, Lieut. E. H., 419.
Smith, Colonel Haviland, 153, 154.
Smith, 2nd Lieut. H. F., 381.
Smith, Sergeant-Major John, 230.
Smith, 2nd Lieut. J. R. D., 387.
Smith, Admiral Sir Sidney, 149.
Smith, Sydney, 181 n.
Smith, Major T., 359.
Smith, Major-General Sir William Douglas, 85, 93, 96, 233, 310, 342, 454.
Smith, Captain W. S., 373.
Smith, 2nd Lieut., 352.
Smith-Dorrien, General Sir H., 290, 291, 294, 296, 298.
Smylie, Lieut. R. S., 353.
Smythe, Lieut.-Colonel H. H., 233.
Soimonov, General, 207, 208.
Solmes, Count, 33, 35.
Somerville, Lieut. J., 448.
Somme, battle of the, 347–362.
Spears, 2nd Lieut. J., 381.
Spion Kop, battle of, 262–265.
Spurgin, Lieut.-Colonel J. H., 229, 232, 233.
Stair, John, second Earl of, 85, 86, 88, 90, 91, 118, 285.
Stanton, 2nd Lieut. F. S., 441.

Stanuell, Lieut. H. G., 229.
Staples, 2nd Lieut. O. O., 329.
Steele, Lieut.-Colonel J., 271.
Steenkirk, battle of, 26, 31, 32, 33, 60 n.
Stephens, 2nd Lieut. Richard, 215 n.
Sterling, 2nd Lieut. R. W., 318, 477 n.
Stewart, General Sir Herbert, 229.
Stewart, Captain H. W. V., 302, 306.
Stewart, Lieut. James, 177.
Stewart, 2nd Lieut. R. T., 328.
Stewart, Major W., 334.
Stewart, Quartermaster, 96.
Stewart - Richardson, Lieut. - Colonel N. G., 405.
Stirling-Cookson, Captain S. B., 319.
Straiton, Captain Charles, 21 n., 56.
Strang, 2nd Lieut. R., 357.
Strathmore, John, fifth Earl of, 79.
Stuart, Brig.-General D. M., 166 n., 229, 280, 455.
Stuart, Lord Evelyn, 144, 145.
Stuart, General Sir John, 149, 152, 154, 155, 156, 184.
Stuart, General John Ramsay, 194, 198 n., 205, 212, 217, 219, 220, 221, 223, 224, 225.
Stuart, 2nd Lieut. R. N., 318.
Stuart, Captain T. E., 226.
Stuart, Lieut. Viscount, 329.
Stuart, Lieut., 96.
Stuarts of Appin, 105.
Sturrock, Lieut. Andrew, 353.
Sturrock, Lieut. G., 334.
Suchet, General, 158.
Sudan, service in, 229.
Sutherland, Captain H. E., 403.
Sutherland, Quartermaster, 157.
Swales, Lieut. George, 390.
Swan, 2nd Lieut. G. H., 353.
Sweet, 2nd Lieut. J. L. L., 318.
Swyney, Colonel, 210.
Sykes, 2nd Lieut. E. B., 388.
Sykes, Captain H. S., 271.
Symes, Brig.-General, 138, 140.

TALLARD, Marshal, 42, 43, 45, 47, 48, 49, 50, 51, 52, 53, 55, 56, 58.
Tanner, Brig.-General, 429.
Tartan, Scots Fusilier, 228.
Taylor, Major J. C., 331 n.
Taylor, 2nd Lieut. T. R. M., 436.
Taylor, Lieut., 153.
Teacher, Lieut.-Colonel N. McD., 380, 389, 390.
Templeman, Lieut.-Colonel Alfred, 198 n., 215 n., 227, 229.
Templeton, 2nd Lieutenant J. R., 445.
Templeton, Captain W. F., 442, 443, 473–477.
Theebaw, King, 250.

INDEX

Thesiger, Major-General George, 324, 329.
Thiepval, 353, 358, 361.
Thomas, Captain R. H., 421.
Thomson, Captain A. H., 343.
Thomson, Lieut. K. C., 307, 311.
Thompson, Lieut.-Colonel Harold, 335, 364, 366, 395, 396, 397, 476.
Thorneycroft, Major-General A. W., 245, 264, 265.
Thornton, Major F. E., 455.
Thornton, Colonel, 168, 170, 175, 176, 177.
Thorpe, Lieut.-Colonel Edward, 195.
Ticonderoga, 121, 122, 123.
Tinley, 2nd Lieut. James, 352, 353.
Tirah Campaign, the, 230–232.
Tobago, 185.
Todleben, General, 205, 217.
Tolmash, General, 35.
Toogood, Lieut.-Colonel Reginald, 457 n.
Torrance, 2nd Lieut. K., 438.
Tournai, siege of, 66.
Towers-Clarke, Lieut. J. W., 350.
Townsend, Lieut., 96.
Traill, Captain R. T., 309.
Trench, 2nd Lieut. D., 381 n.
Trenchard, Air Chief-Marshal Sir Hugh, vii., 274, 278, 453–454.
Trevallion, Lieut., 56.
Trevelyan, Sir G. O., 127 n., 128.
Tristram Shandy, 33 n., 36, 37.
Trônes Wood, 350, 351, 353, 354, 355.
Tugela, crossing of the, 257–271.
Tullibardine, John, Marquis of, 69.
Tullis, Captain J. D., 287, 310.
Turnbull, Lieut., 126.
Turner, Sir James, 8, 25.
Turner, Lieut.-Colonel J. R., 441.
Tyrawley, Lord, 114.

UTRECHT, Peace of, 72, 73, 82.
Utterson-Kelso, Lieut.-Colonel J. E., vii., 319, 389, 416, 426, 447, 452.

VAAL KRANZ, battle of, 265–266.
Valenciennes, 27, 446.
Valley Forge, 129.
Vandergracht, Lieut., 56.
Vauban, 30.
Vendôme, Duc de, 62, 63, 64.
Victoria, H.M. Queen, 138, 196, 229, 249.
Victoria Cross, awards of the, 262, 334, 399, 407, 439, 448, 454.
Villars, Marshal, 42, 66, 69, 70, 71.
Villeroy, Marshal, 37, 43, 44, 46, 47, 48, 49, 57, 58, 59, 60, 61.
Vimy Ridge, 372, 374, 376.

WADE, Marshal, 81, 82, 85, 90, 91, 98, 118.
Waldeck, Prince of, 28.
Wales, H.R.H. Prince of, v., 452.
Walker, Lieut.-Colonel G. W., 191.
Walker, Colour-Sergeant John, 232.
Walker, 2nd Lieut., 185.
Waller, 2nd Lieut. A. E., 318.
Wallner, 2nd Lieut., 318.
Walpole, Horace, 83, 98, 118.
Walpole, Sir Robert, 82, 84, 118.
Walsh, Lieut.-Colonel R. K., 329, 344, 350, 355, 366, 455.
Ward, Captain, 135.
Warnock, 2nd Lieut. R., 357.
Warren, General Sir Charles, 263, 264, 265, 267, 268.
Washington, capture of, 171.
Washington, George, 126, 129, 255.
Waters, Lieut. John, 177.
Watson, 2nd Lieut. J. E., 328.
Watson, Captain Thomas, 379.
Watson, Lieut., 445.
Watts, General Sir H. E., 307, 308.
Wauchope, Brig.-General Andrew, 255.
Wauchope, Major-General, 150.
Webster, 2nd Lieut. G. W., 319.
Weir, Lieut. H. J., 401.
Wellington, Arthur, first Duke of, 143, 155, 156, 159, 167, 175, 178, 182, 184, 198, 231, 313.
Wemyss, Captain, 70.
Wentworth, Captain, 104.
West, Lord, Charles Richard Sackville, 194, 195, 205, 206, 210, 214, 215, 216, 217, 218, 223.
Wheatley, Lieut.-Colonel L. L., 377.
Whigham, Captain J. C., 303, 305, 306, 319.
Whitaker, Major John, 172, 177.
White, Major Andrew, 11, 13.
White, F.M. Sir George, 253, 254, 261, 270.
White Horse of Hanover, the, 74, 114.
Whitelaw, 2nd Lieut. J. W., 379.
Whitton, Lieut.-Colonel James, 251.
Whyte, General John, 136, 137, 139.
William III., 20, 21, 23, 27, 28, 29, 31, 33, 34, 36, 37, 39, 42, 43.
Williams, Lieut. E. E., 186.
Willoughby, Captain, 238, 243.
Willstrop, Sergeant G. J., 328.
Wilson, Lieut.-General Sir H. F., 444.
Wilson, Lieut.-Colonel John, 145.
Winder, General, 169.
Winsloe, Lieut.-Colonel R. W. C., 218, 228, 241, 245, 247, 250, 251.
Withers, General, 67, 68, 69, 70.
Wodrow, Robert, 4 n., 5, 6 n., 13.
Wolfe, Lieut.-Colonel Edward, 82.

INDEX

Wolfe, General James, 82, 89, 106 n., 107 n., 114, 118, 119, 130.
Wolseley, F.M. Lord, 229, 240, 241, 242.
Wolstencroft, 2nd Lieut. W. R. B., 426.
Wood, F.M. Sir Evelyn, 239, 240, 247.
Wood, 2nd Lieut. E. L., 390.
Wood, Sir James, 82, 83.
Würtemberg, Duke of, 31, 32, 33; in Great War, 300, 304.

YEATMAN-BIGGS, Major-General, 231, 232.

Yonge, Lieut., 89.
York, H.R.H. Duke of, 181, 185.
Young, Major H. R., 333, 396, 397.
Young, Captain John Erskine, 288.
Young, Major W. A., 260, 272, 279, 280.
Yuille, Major D., 406, 449.
Yuille, 2nd Lieut. D. McG., 439.
Ypres, first battle of, 296–310; second battle of, 318–319; third battle of, 385–390.

ZENTA, battle of, 43.
Zulu War, the, 237–241.